LANGUAGE PRODUCTION

LANGUAGE PRODUCTION

Volume 1

Speech and Talk

Edited by

B. Butterworth

The Psychological Laboratory,
Downing Street,
Cambridge CB2 3EB,
England

1980

ACADEMIC PRESS

A Subsidiary of Harcourt Brace Jovanovich, Publishers

London   New York   Toronto   Sydney   San Francisco

ACADEMIC PRESS INC. (LONDON) LTD
24–28 Oval Road
London NW1

U.S. Edition published by
ACADEMIC PRESS INC.
111 Fifth Avenue
New York, New York 10003

British Library Cataloguing in Publication Data

Language production.
Vol. 1
1. Psycholinguistics
I. Butterworth, Brian
418   P37   79–40918

ISBN 0–12–147501–8

Filmset by Willmer Brothers Limited, Birkenhead, Merseyside.
Printed by Fletcher and Son Limited, Norwich.

Contributors

GEOFFREY W. BEATTIE, Department of Psychology, University of Sheffield, Sheffield S10 2TN, England

BRIAN BUTTERWORTH, The Psychological Laboratory, University of Cambridge, Downing Street, Cambridge CB2 3EB, England

BERNARD COMRIE, Department of Linguistics, University of Cambridge, Sidgwick Avenue, Cambridge CB2 3EB, England. *Now at*: Department of Linguistics, University of Southern California, Los Angeles, California 90007, U.S.A.

WILLIAM E. COOPER, Research Laboratory of Electronics, Massachusetts Institute of Technology, Cambridge, Massachusetts 02139, U.S.A. *Now at*: Department of Psychology, Harvard University, Cambridge, Massachusetts 02138, U.S.A.

ANNE CUTLER, Experimental Psychology, University of Sussex, Brighton BN1 9QG, England

CAROL A. FOWLER, Haskins Laboratory, 270 Crown Street, New Haven, Connecticut 06511, U.S.A. *and* Dartmouth College, Hanover, New Hampshire, U.S.A.

MERRILL F. GARRETT, Department of Psychology, Massachusetts Institute of Technology, Cambridge, Massachusetts 02139, U.S.A.

GERALD GAZDAR, School of Social Studies, University of Sussex, Brighton BN1 9QG, England

FRIEDA GOLDMAN-EISLER, Psycholinguistics Research Unit, University College, Gower Street, London WC1, England

STEPHEN D. ISARD, Experimental Psychology, University of Sussex, Brighton BN1 9QG, England

PHILIP N. JOHNSON-LAIRD, Centre for Research on Perception and Cognition, University of Sussex, Brighton BN1 9QG, England

OSCAR S. M. MARIN, Department of Neurology, Baltimore City Hospital, 4940 Eastern Avenue, Baltimore, Maryland 21224, U.S.A. *Now at*: Department of Neurology, Good Samaritan Hospital and Medical Center, 2222 S. W. Lovejoy, Portland, Oregon 97210, U.S.A.

JOSEPH S. PERKELL, Research Laboratory of Electronics, Massachusetts Institute of Technology, Cambridge, Massachusetts 02139, U.S.A.

ROBERT E. REMEZ, Haskins Laboratory, 270 Crown Street, New Haven, Connecticut 06511, U.S.A. *and* University of Indiana, U.S.A.

P. RUBIN, Haskins Laboratory, 270 Crown Street, New Haven, Connecticut 06511, U.S.A.

ELEANOR M. SAFFRAN, Department of Neurology, Baltimore City Hospital, 4940 Eastern Avenue, Baltimore, Maryland 21224, U.S.A.

JAMES SCHENKEIN, Department of Sociology, Queens College, City University of New York, Flushing, New York 11367, U.S.A.

MYRNA F. SCHWARTZ, Johns Hopkins School of Medicine, Baltimore, Maryland 21224, U.S.A. *Now at*: Department of Psychology, University of Pennsylvania, Philadelphia, Pennsylvania 19104, U.S.A.

MARK J. STEEDMAN, Department of Psychology, University of Warwick, Coventry CV4 7AL, England

MICHAEL T. TURVEY, Haskins Laboratory, 270 Crown Street, New Haven, Connecticut 06511, U.S.A. *and* University of Connecticut, Storrs, Connecticut 06268, U.S.A.

Preface

One reason for putting together a book is irritation. It is irritating when a vital reference for a psychologist is not in the psychology but the linguistic library. Students often deal with this problem by not reading the references at all. It is irritating when some crucial idea is nowhere adequately explained for the non-specialist. Students often deal with this problem by remaining ignorant of the idea. It is irritating when everywhere, a topic is dealt with far more narrowly than you think is appropriate. Students deal with this by staying narrow, and so do researchers. The combination of all these irritations and their effects on students was enough to persuade me to undertake the task of putting together a volume on language production.

Originally, I had planned to write the whole volume myself. I had a particular view of language production, and I wanted to expose the public to it. Not only was production susceptible to a variety of investigative approaches, some of which did not fall within psychology, nor even within linguistics, but it was a positive bonus that investigations had not become paradigm-bound as they had in other areas of psychology. People in the production business were interested in phenomena not paradigms, and so methodological pluralism seemed to be the right way to proceed. People not in the business, however, appeared disturbed by the lack of a paradigm, and tended to be rather skeptical of production studies (see my Introduction). However, while I was thinking about how to throw together the various studies, by happy chance I was invited to a symposium organized by Ken Abrams and Madeleine Mathiot at Buffalo. As a result of visiting Buffalo and later, Cambridge, Massachusetts, and Rockefeller, I discovered that there were other people who felt sufficiently in sympathy to be willing to contribute to a book laying out the main ideas and results on production irrespective of their ostensible disciplinary status. With this encouragement, I solicited contributions from people working on production, and I also managed to persuade people working in other areas that their work had a relevance for production. And so, I found myself putting together this volume.

One learns a lot about human nature editing a book. One learns that people don't keep promises—about delivery dates. When you try to write your sections, you find out why they don't keep promises. You also rediscover that people can be helpful without any expectation of reward. Friends, colleagues and students left their own work to discuss mine, and to read what I had written. I am sure other contributors were also recipients of these kindnesses. My own thanks go to Tony Marcel, Howard Pollio, Tim Shallice, Aaron Sloman and to David Good, who also prepared the subject index, as well as to all the contributors. And I cannot help but believe that the publishers have on occasion acted disinterestedly. Academic Press had faith in the project from the start, and, at that time as far as I can judge, for no specially good reason.

Finally, I'd like to thank the person who is in a way ultimately responsible, Frieda Goldman-Eisler, whose work first aroused my interest in speech production. She offered me the opportunity to abandon the study of formal languages for the study of natural language. Even now, eight years or more since I finished the doctorate she supervised, I am just beginning to realise the wisdom of her teachings.

Cambridge, 1979   B. BUTTERWORTH

Contents

1

Introduction:
A Brief Review of Methods of Studying Language Production

B. Butterworth

University of Cambridge

I. Introduction

The properties of human nature that make talk possible have fascinated philosophers since the Enlightenment. For Descartes, animals and machines "could never use speech or other signs as we do when placing our thought on record for others" (1637, p. 116). "Magpies and parrots are able to utter words just like ourselves, and yet they cannot speak as we do, that is, so as to give evidence that they think of what they say" (p. 117); and a machine cannot arrange "its speech in various ways, in order to reply appropriately to everything that may be said in its presence, as even the lowest type of man can do" (p. 116). Thus literally thoughtful talk is incontestable evidence for a fundamental division between human beings and other sublunary creatures, namely, we have a rational soul, they do not.

The role of speech as the medium through which thoughts are conveyed to oneself and to others, and hence a vital component in man's nature as a social, as well as a rational, animal, was recognized by Locke (1700).

> Man, though he have great variety of Thoughts, and such, from which others, as well as himself, might receive Profit and Delight; yet they are all within his own Breast, invisible, and hidden from others, nor can of themselves be made appear. The Comfort, and Advantage of Society, not being to be had without Communication of Thoughts, it was necessary, that Man should find out some external sensible Signs, whereby those invisible *Ideas*, which his thoughts are made of, might be made known to others. For this purpose, nothing was so fit, either for Plenty or Quickness, as those articulate Sounds, which with so much Ease and Variety, he found himself able to make. Thus we may conceive how *Words*, which were by Nature so well adapted to that purpose, come to be made use of by Men, as *the Signs of* their *Ideas*; not by any natural connexion, that there is between particular articulate Sounds and certain *Ideas*, for then there would be but one Language amongst all Men; but by a voluntary Imposition, whereby such a Word is made arbitrarily the Mark of such an Idea. The use then of Words, is to be sensible Marks of *Ideas*. (404–405)

A necessary prolegomenon to his philosophy was thus an analysis of the signification of words, which, for him, meant both an account of how words come to refer to objects in the world and a proto-psychological treatment of words as the expression of mental entities, "Ideas".

More recently, and more scientifically, the problem of the mental apparatus responsible for speech has attracted research and speculation from some of the most profound students of human nature (Hughlings Jackson, 1958; Freud, 1891, 1924; Wundt, 1900; Pick, 1931; Goldstein, 1948; Lashley, 1951; George Miller, 1960). Even so, modern psychologists of language have, by and large, either ignored the problem or treated the research with scepticism or pessimism. Thus, in their introductory psycholinguistic text, Glucksberg and Danks (1975) devote only two pages to production. Johnson-Laird (1974) has written in a general review of psycholinguistics, "the fundamental problem in psycholinguistics is simple to formulate: what happens when we understand sentences" (p. 135). MacNeilage and Ladefoged (1976), reviewing the "production of speech and language" write: "very little is known about the production of language" (p. 75). And even where a text devotes considerable space to production, we find "practically anything that one can say about speech production must be considered speculative even by the standards current in psycholinguistics" (Fodor *et al.*, 1974, p. 434).

Why should the study of production evoke these expressions of skepticism, pessimism and neglect? One reason seems to be that experimental psychologists like to be able to *manipulate* at least some of the relevant variables and to have some *control* over the range of options available to the subject. Usually, this has meant manipulating the input to the subject and restricting the range of responses the subject is allowed to use. In this way, complex phenomena and behaviours can be subdivided into more manageable components, and systematic input-output relations can be established which will lead to confident inferences about the processes intervening between input and output. Now, what we say typically bears little systematic relationship to environmental input (*pace* Skinner, 1957), and thus it would be extraordinarily optimistic to set up manipulations of the input and expect to find systematic outputs, unless the subject is so limited in what he is allowed to say that generalizations to natural spontaneous speech become almost impossible. So psycholinguistics has concentrated on input-end processing—word-recognition, comprehension and the like—where manipulation of stimuli and the limitation of response choices seems a more plausible and fruitful strategy.

A second reason for avoiding production is that speech occurs naturally mainly in conversations, and these are, in many ways, no less than microcosms of the social order. So, in order to get a grip on what is going on in production, not only must the usual set of psychological variables be taken into account, but so must a new range of social variables. The evident complexity of the phenomena and the difficulty of identifying the responsible variable has, no doubt, deterred many potential investigators (for further discussion of this issue, see Butterworth, 1978).

However, there is a price to pay for control in the study of input-end processes. First, the products of word recognition, comprehension or whatever, are not directly observable, but must be inferred from behaviour linked to these processes. Since the experimenter has to limit available responses—or else problems of comprehension combine with the problems of production—the subject is required to generate responses not normally and naturally associated with the stimulus, for example, repeating the word(s) presented, pressing a button on hearing (or seeing) a target, etc., and, of course, one thereby encounters the problem of how to generalize from the experimental task to real-life activity. With production, on the other hand, the natural products or expressions of the underlying processes *are* directly observable, namely, the speech uttered. Indeed, one can use material produced with little or no experimental intervention. So the problem of the generality of the findings is reduced at a stroke.

In addition, it turns out in practice difficult to generalize not only to real-life, but even to other experimental paradigms that are apparently very similar. Hence, it is hard to evaluate the theoretical implications of such equivocal studies.

Let us take an example in which the stimuli are fairly naturalistic, easily manipulable and where the response is as simple as can be. There are large numbers of studies where the subject has to monitor a target while listening to a sentence. As soon as the subject detects the target he must press the button. The idea is that the speed of reaction will indicate how much cognitive work comprehension of the sentence demands at the target location: the greater the current cognitive load, the longer it takes the subject to detect and respond to the target. By manipulating or identifying characteristics of the sentence, it should be possible to tease out which hypothetical processes are engaged in comprehension. For example, if embedded constructions, as compared with right-branching constructions, increase latency to a following target, then syntactic analysis of embedding is cognitively more demanding (Foss and Lynch, 1969). Now, targets have been of two sorts: parts of the sentence (a phoneme, syllable or word) or extraneous noises (tones or "clicks"). Response times to sentence-internal targets are reliably slower near the beginnings of sentences than near the ends (Foss, 1969; Shields *et al.*, 1974; Cutler and Foss, 1977), whereas, response times to extraneous targets are reliably faster at the beginning than at the end (Abrams and Bever, 1969; Green, 1977). And it is not clear why these two very similar versions of the task should yield such radically different estimates of the most general properties of the distribution of current mental load (Cutler and Norris, in press). *A fortiori,* one must treat inferences from these studies about the finer grain characteristics of the comprehension process with extreme skepticism.

In fact, this paradigm has produced other problematic, apparently contradictory, results. Response times to sentence-internal targets appear to depend on the frequency of the preceding word. If that word is common, and presumably easy to access, the RTs are faster than if it is a low-frequency word (Foss, 1969). However, RTs to extraneous signals show exactly the opposite effect: RTs are slowed by the presence of a high-frequency word. The "explanation" of the latter case is that a listener "knows more about the meaning of familiar words, so that when he hears such words in a sentence he retrieves more aspects of their meaning than he does for less familiar words" (Green, 1977). On what evidential basis should inferences be drawn: on the phoneme-monitoring or the noise-monitoring results?

There is an interesting additional complication to all this. Green (1977) found that RTs to extraneous noises were *unaffected* by sentence location (early versus late in the sentence) or by word-frequency when subjects were instructed to memorize the sentence for recall afterwards; only when they were instructed to produce a continuation for the sentence or sentence-fragment they heard did these variables have an effect, and then, as was mentioned, in the opposite direction to their effects on phoneme-monitoring. Thus Green has elegantly demonstrated that in otherwise identical tasks, the strategy a subject adopts can totally alter the pattern of results the experimenter finds. In this case, strategies were deliberately induced by the experimenter, but what is to stop the subject creating a strategy for himself? Manipulating the stimuli and available responses is not the same as manipulating the person; even under tightly-constrained conditions subjects can and will develop a strategy for dealing with the task, and not necessarily the strategy the experimenter intended. There is an obvious theoretical moral: the language-processing system does not automatically operate in the same way under all conditions, or even under apparently the same conditions.

Another nice example of this came from the investigation of a different question using an equally tightly-constrained experimental task. The question is: do readers translate a printed word into a phonological (acoustic or articulatory, according to particular versions of the theory) code in order to understand it? The most widely used investigative tool is the "lexical decision" task. In this task, the subject is presented with a string of letters and has to decide as quickly as possible whether the string is a real word or not. The key stimulus materials are *homophones*, words that sound the same, but are spelt differently, e.g. SALE and SAIL. Now, if real words are translated into a phonological code one might expect homophones to behave differently to non-homophones—exactly what is predicted will depend on additional assumptions. For example, assume the mental lexicon is arranged in terms of frequency of use, and searched starting with the most frequent items; and when a phonological match is made the spelling is checked against the input string. The time taken to reach a decision on SALE, the more common member of the pair, should be the same as for a non-homophone control matched for frequency. However, the time to decide on SAIL should be longer than its matched-frequency control, since entry found coded /sɛɪl| will probably be spelt SALE, so the spelling check will yield a negative and search will have to be continued, both operations costing some additional time. Rubinstein *et al.* (1971) found this pattern of results—it took longer to decide that the lower-frequency member of the pair was indeed a word, as compared to non-homophones of the same frequency. However, Coltheart *et al.* (1977) found no difference between SAIL-type items and their controls. (They also point out that a variety of other tasks, same-different judgments, rhyming tasks, naming latency, used to investigate this question yielded a variety of conflicting answers. One of the main reasons for the conflict, they argue, is that some of these tasks do not *require* subjects to consult their lexicon at all, and so they may adopt a strategy which avoids lexical access. For example, you don't need a dictionary to tell you that BRHND isn't a word.) So what can be concluded about the phonological recoding hypothesis? Very little from the data. But Davelaar *et al.* (1978) did some follow-up studies which revealed interesting aspects of subjects' strategies in this task.

They suggested that the reader may, but need not, use the kind of phonological recoding process described above, but an alternative route that uses graphemic information directly to access lexical items. Now if subjects use the first route only, then low-frequency homophones should be slower than non-homophone controls, whereas if they use the second, then there should be no difference in time since SAIL is at least as graphically distinct from SALE as SOIL. This dual-route explanation was tested in the following way: stimuli in the first condition comprised low-frequency members of homophone pairs, controls matched for frequency and nonwords like SLINT that were orthographically regular but could not be pronounced as a real word. Phonological recoding in this case would always lead to the correct decision. The second condition was the same except that all the nonwords were like GRONE, that would be pronounced like real words, and hence phonological recoding would lead to errors on nonwords. If subjects can strategically adapt by using the appropriate route, then homophones would have an effect only in the first condition; and that is what they found. In fact, with high-frequency homophones response times were the same for the SLINT and GRONE conditions, as one would expect from this model. Again we can see how the pattern of results crucially depends on the strategy adopted by the subject. In this case, the alternative strategies were induced not by instruction, but by carefully selecting the nonword distractors in the task.

The moral of this digression is not that the study of input-end processing is impossible, just that it is much more complicated than it might appear. The opportunity for tight experimental manipulation is no guarantee that results will be straightforwardly interpretable, since the flexibility of the processing system allows subjects an irreducible area of freedom within which to choose how they tackle the task set them.† By forcing subjects to link stimuli to

---

† Even more spectacular examples of this kind of difficulty can be found in other branches of experimental psychology. One of the best-confirmed effects in the whole of psychology is that the time it takes to make choices, depends upon the number of alternatives the subject has to choose among. Merkel (1885, cited by Woodworth, 1938) showed that CRT (Choice Reaction Time) increases by a constant amount when the number of alternatives in the set *doubles*. The effect is now called "Hick's Law", after W. E. Hick (1952), who explained the significance of the doubling manipulation in terms of Information Theory. However, this effect turns out to be crucially dependent on the kind of response the subject has to make. If it is a button-press response, then effect is reliably present, if it is a vocal response then there is no effect of set size at all. This has been demonstrated in a variety of experimental paradigms—memory probing, where the subject has to say "Yes" if a probe item was in a previously presented set, and "No" if it was not; forced choice response, where the subject has to give the name of a numeral drawn from sets of various sizes (both studies by Ogden and Alluisi, unpublished); and probe reaction time (MacLeod, 1978)). Authors talk of "stimulus-response compatibility", but none has a satisfactory explanation of this divergence. Ogden and Alluisi's memory probing experiment is particularly

responses not typically associated with them, normal or habitual strategies will not necessarily be employed. The demonstration of this was, of course, made possible by the alertness and ingenuity of the investigators. Even so, we still do not know why Phoneme-Monitoring and Click-Monitoring yield contradictory results. Nevertheless, we can reasonably expect that the appreciation of strategic adaptability will lead to a greater variety of models tested in more and more accomplished ways.. No less is required of the investigation of production-end processes: alternative hypotheses must be continually evaluated against more and more sophisticated analyses of the speech output. However, since, as I have stated, the natural products of these processes are directly observable, and evidence can be collected without experimental intervention, a solid basis of natural history can be established on which to start erecting theories. Thus in the immediate future, the prospect for results replicable across situations seems brighter in production than in language perception. And it is, perhaps, a trend of some significance, that two of the skeptical authors mentioned above, Garrett and Johnson-Laird, are contributors to this volume.

II. Approaches to Language Production

Until very recently, the study of language production has depended on three investigative tools: the first was the analysis of aphasic speech; at the turn of the century, attention was focussed on the analysis of the speech errors of neurologically intact speakers; and in the 1950s, with the aid of sound reproduction equipment, the analysis of the time course of speech, and particularly hesitations, was pioneered. A more ancient lineage can be attributed to the study of motoric aspects of speech (what is now called "articulatory phonetics"), and which, historically, has made little contact with the study of the *psychology* of language. (History continues into the present: MacNeilage and Ladefoged, (1976), are a current example. See especially their first paragraph.) Lieberman (1977) traces this science back, at least, to Ferrein's investigation of the vocal cords in 1741. In this volume, **Perkell** and **Fowler** demonstrate that psychological models of control can be usefully deployed in the study of articulatory processes, though, interestingly, different control models serve as reference points for the two papers.

A. Studies of Aphasic Speech

It is not surprising that the systematic investigation of the psychology of language, and speaking especially, should have started with the study of

---

mysterious: one might expect that choosing between two relatively "incompatible" button-press responses would be slower by fixed amount than choosing between the "compatible" "Yes" and "No" responses, but why should there be no *increment* in RT for each increase in set size for the compatible response?

aphasic speech. The ease and effortlessness of normal speech disguises the complex psychological history of each of its products. Aphasic speech, on the other hand, is so dramatically different from normal that it calls attention to itself, and immediately sets one wondering what has gone wrong with the machinery. Indeed, neurological damage was thought of as a direct intervention in the psychological mechanism, whose character and the consequences of damage to it can be likened to diagnosing a faulty car mechanism from its performance; faults in different parts of the mechanisms lead to different patterns of performance breakdown, so controlled studies are possible using either lesion site or symptom picutre as independent variables. The Swiss neurologist, Lichtheim (1885), put it succinctly, if rather heartlessly:

> Precisely, the same course is followed in experimental research, with the exception that, in our present subject, the experiments are not instigated at the will of the investigator, but are supplied to him by nature, and that he thus depends for them on happy chance (pp. 433–434).

By "happy chance", the various patterns of speech and comprehension deficit would enable the investigator to infer what hypothesized processes were indissolubly linked, and hence which are, and which processes could be dissociated from one and another, and hence separate. Lichtheim, following Wernicke, constructed a model which looks as if it could have come out of a modern text on human information processing. In it, Lichtheim postulates three processing systems, or "centres": A, auditory word representations ("Wortklangsbilder"); M, motor-word representations ("Wortbewegungsbilder"), and B, a system where "concepts are elaborated", though not a "centre" since it is held to be a function of "the combined action of the whole sensorial sphere". These systems are connected by pathways, including auditory input to A–a, motor output from M–m (see Fig. 1). "Volitional, or intelligent, speech involves centrifugal connections between B and M".

Now "interruptions in M ... give rise to the following association of symptoms: loss of (a) volitional speech, (b) repetition of words", but there will still exist understanding of spoken words. Interruption in A, on the other hand, will lead to loss of understanding of spoken language, but volitional speech will be preserved; repetition will also be impaired since the links from input to output (A–B–M or A–M) will be impaired by the damage at A. Interruptions of the path A–B, would, by parity of argument, lead to loss of understanding and preservation of volitional speech. However, unlike damage to A alone, repetition, via A–M, would be preserved. Additional predictions about the preservation or loss of reading and writing follow from an elaboration of the model, connecting a graphemic input centre to A, and writing centre to M.

The basis for this kind of model lies in the broad pattern of syndromes observed, and in the localization of the lesions associated with these syndromes. Thus, broadly we find patients with lesions in Broca's area (M) who have relatively good comprehension but poor speech; patients with lesions in Wernicke's area (A) show fluent speech but poor comprehension.

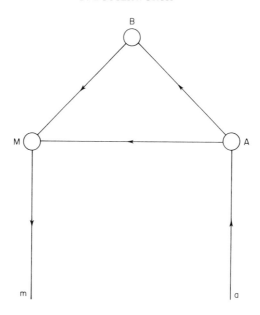

Fig. 1. Connections among language faculties, after Lichtheim. (See text).

The other syndromes predicted are much more difficult to identify and more controversial.

This kind of theory has been opposed on two grounds. First, apparently equivalent neural damage does not always lead to the same symptom picture. Secondly, the model does not explain a finer grained analysis of the syndromes.

Freud (1891), for example, in an incisive critique, attacked the strict neurological localization of centres, but it is his attack on the analysis of speech behaviour that is of interest to us here. He pointed out that aphasic speech is characterized not only by deficiencies, e.g. loss of words, but also by distortions, the "paraphasias"—invented words, deviant pronunciation and scrambled syntax. Now, damage to Centre A (sensory, or Wernicke's aphasia) shows not only loss of understanding, but, characteristically, speech containing paraphasias. "Such a speech disorder could not be explained from [Wernicke's and Lichtheim's] schema [Fig. 1], according to which the kinaesthetic word impressions [at M] are intact, as well as the pathways connecting them with concepts" (pp. 14–15). Wernicke and Lichtheim were well aware of the difficulty these data created and tried to save the theory by supposing that auditory word images at A are also involved in spontaneous speech and serve as an auditory control over production of speech at M. Of course, activation of speech cannot follow the path B–A–M, otherwise the model would have to predict loss of speech output from damage to A as well as to M. The alternative of some kind of convergent control from B and A on M, seems implausible. As Freud (1891) notes, "any controlling influence of A over the production of speech via A–M is entirely useless if it becomes effective only after words have been uttered from M" (16)

Another difficulty Freud drew attention to was the finding that aphasics of all sorts show a loss of words in both comprehension and production. Again, the evidence, broadly, can be construed in favour of the model, but why loss of words in comprehension should have any effect at all on productive capacities remains inexplicable. In the light of these difficulties, Freud, following the great British neurologist, John Hughlings Jackson, advocated a more holistic approach to brain function, an emphasis on careful analysis of the various fractionations of behaviour and the construction of functional (i.e. psychological) models to explain this fractionation.

Freud, like Lichtheim and Wernicke, still operated with a rather primitive notion of language, concentrating on the production and reception of isolated words. Their explanations, as we have seen, are couched almost exclusively in terms of word-images. Hughlings Jackson, on the other hand, stressed the constructional nature of normal, volitional language behaviour. What we can do, and aphasic patients cannot, is put words together, often in new ways, to express an intended proposition. Thus crucial to normal language use is the capacity to organize words into coherent sentences.

Another follower of Jackson, the German neurologist Arnold Pick, incorporated this insight into a detailed psychological model of production. Like Jackson, he believed that aphasic phenomena could only be understood as resulting from disorders of normal function, and thus "full description and analysis of intact functions" (1931, p. 27) is a prerequisite. In addition, he redeploys some of Jackson's most interesting theoretical tools—notably, the idea that through development cortical areas become increasingly tightly organized and damage to these areas causes organization to break down partially with a possible return to an earlier stage of organization (what Freud has called "disinvolution"). This shows itself in failures to differentiate what had previously been distinguishable. This principle of "failure of differentiation"can apply to one or more levels in the functional model thereby causing the various symptom pictures.

Pick traces "the path from thought to speech" through six levels:

(1) Thought formulation. An "undifferentiated" thought is analysed into "a sequence of topics, a sort of *thought pattern*, [which is a] preparation for a predicative arrangement . . . of actions [and] objects". (1931, p. 32). Then follows "a subsequent formulation based upon the various *linguistic means*, unique to that language, such as tone, accentuation, tempo, word-order, and grammatization". This is realized in the following steps:

(2) Accentuation pattern.

(3) Sentence pattern. Both of these depend on the "topical sequence arising from the thought pattern".

(4) Word-finding, of content words.

(5) Grammatization (i.e. morphological adjustments given the syntactic role of the content words, and the insertion of function words).

(6) Conductance to the motor executive apparatus

This sequence of operations is not fixed, but will vary according to the kind of thought to be expressed—"an exclamation, a command or a statement"—and whether a ready-made phrase or sentence is available to do the job.† And Pick suggests that some of these processes may be carried out in parallel, and notes that the accentuation pattern will directly influence how an individual word is pronounced.‡

This model enabled Pick to tackle Freud's key problem—the paraphasias.

> In *verbal paraphasia* [choice of the wrong word], the word determined by thought and by the sentence pattern is inwardly present, or at least there is an intention in this direction, but this normally rigid determination is loosened-up. The coherence is not firm enough to maintain the normal suppression of words evoked by association from the sphere of meaning, from parallel lines of thought, or by other sorts of confusion, and thus it leads to the transmission of one of the inapposite words to the speech mechanism . . . the effect of the *intact* part of the speech process (especially the sentence pattern) on the wrong word is sometimes evidenced as a grammatical modification derived from the correct word. (p. 56)§

Literal paraphasias (phonemic distortions of the correct word) are caused by failure of differentiation at the level of sound structure, and since the motor apparatus is intact, it involves the elicitation of either the wrong sounds, or the sounds in the wrong order. If both the word-finding process and the sound-pattern transmission process are damaged, not only will the patient pick the wrong word, he will also distort it phonemically, thus giving rise to *neologisms*, which are characteristic of the "jargon aphasia" syndrome, a species of Wernicke's aphasia. Notice word order, intonation and grammatization can be intact even if word-finding is distorted. (For a modern examination of Pick's account of the paraphasias, see Butterworth, 1979.)

In this brief and selective survey of the approach to production through aphasia, I have concentrated on Lichtheim because he offered the most detailed model in the classical localizationist tradition, a tradition carried on today by Geschwind among many others. The holistic tradition of Jackson and Pierre Marie, which should perhaps be called the "romantic" tradition, I have illustrated by reference to Freud and Pick; Freud because his brilliant criticisms of Lichtheim received scant recognition when first published, and are underservedly neglected today; Pick because his system of levels in the production system anticipated many recent models, Fromkin's (1971) and Garrett's (1975) for example, though the analysis of the relations between levels is rather different.

---

†See my idea about "leading decisions", Chapter 15 for the same notion expressed in more modern language.

‡ See Chapter 3, for a discussion of direct higher-level influences on phonetic output, and also **Cooper** for syntactic effects on phonetic segments.

§**Garrett** reports the same phenomena in normal speakers. "Morpheme stranding errors" transpose lexical roots which, in their new location, take the morphology of the intended words.

In recent years, the main advances have concerned the introduction of much more detailed and sophisticated linguistic analysis of the speech output. This is very well illustrated by the contribution of **Saffran** *et al*. Pick had noted the close connection between the *satzschema*, or syntactic pattern, and the presence of appropriate morphology and function words, but **Saffran** *et al*. are able to go far beyond this schematic suggestion. They are able to make much more specific the connections between syntactical functioning and the morphological functioning, and they show how, in some cases, word-ordering can be relatively intact, morphological processes and the use of function words impaired.

B. Studies of Speech Errors in Normal Speakers

As with the speech of aphasics, "slips of the tongue" draw attention to themselves and thence to the psychological mechanisms that have to go wrong to produce them. The rationale is similar, of course, to the study of aphasic speech: errors penetrate the fluent disguise of most normal speech. As Meringer and Mayer, the pioneers of this study, put it: "the cover is lifted from the clockwork, and we can look in on the cogs" (1895: VIII. Translated by A. Cutler, from her introduction to the new edition). More specifically, the status of hypothetical units and the functioning of the processes employing them can often be determined. Spoonerisms, for example, where individual phonetic segments are transposed ("Fats and Kodor" for "Katz and Fodor" (Fromkin, 1973; p. 245)), demonstrate that there must exist a stage in production where phonemes are represented as units, and moreover, that the process that sets them up for output must represent phonemes not yet uttered—where else can the "f" in "Fats" come from? The overwhelming conclusion from studies of errors is that slips are not just random deviations in processing, but systematic. Many potential classes of error just do not occur. "Slip of the tongue" is never said as "tlip of the sung", for instance. And it is this sytematicity that makes errors such a fruitful topic to study.

Historically, there have been two main reasons for studying error. First, linguists were interested in the light they shed on linguistic units and linguistic rules. "Tlip of the sung" does not occur because it violates a rule of English phonological sequencing: a word cannot begin with the cluster /tl/. Meringer, whose interests were initially philological, collected data which showed linguistic validity of the phonetic feature, the phoneme and syllable; errors which, for instance, break up consonant clusters demonstrate that these are indeed clusters, not individual phonemes.† Fortunately, Meringer's major work has been recently reprinted with a valuable preface by Culter and Fay, and his contribution can be more readily assessed (Meringer and Mayer, 1895).

---

† Today, the status of the affricates "j", "ch" is controversial, and may be decided by error data: are they really clusters [dʒ, tʃ] or single phonemes? If we can find errors where the hypothesized [d] or [t] moves leaving the [ʒ] or [ʃ] behind, then they are clusters.

Meringer's interest in errors led him to the second main reason for studying them: the evidence they provide for the processes of production, and he offered a number of speculations about these processes. Meringer's contemporary, Freud, as is well-known, also studied errors because they could reveal psychological mechanisms. Morgan (1975), however, was more concerned with the role of unconscious and repressed desires and fears in the aetiology of errors. Although this line of research receives little attention nowadays, a number of important writers have postulated several streams of thought coexisting, such that unintended thoughts interfere with those intended to be expressed. Wundt (1900) talks of "wandering speech" and the "contact effect of sounds", Pick (1931) of "words evoked by association" . . . from "parallel lines of thought" which are normally but not always, suppressed, and Meringer himself has ingenious diagrams showing similar, but not identical, formulations intersecting and leading to errors. Indeed, Freud points out that Meringer and Mayer distinguish errors "arising from the influence of anticipatory or perseverating sounds and words of the same sentence which are intended to be spoken" from "the effects of words outside the intended sentence *whose excitation would not otherwise have been revealed*". Very recently, Baars (1979) has been re-evaluating what he calls "the competing plans hypothesis", and reports studies in which "Freudian" slips were experimentally studied.

> A single list of targets and bias-words was given to three groups of [male] subjects. Half of the spoonerism targets on the list were of the form SHAD BOCK [to elicit BAD SHOCK] (electric shock related outcomes), and half were of like LICE NEGS [to elicit NICE LEGS] (sexually attractive properties of females) . . . One group was told that it might receive electric shock during the experiment while another group had a very attractive female experimenter, provocatively dressed, and a control group received neither treatment . . . Under the Shock-Set, shock-related errors were more than twice as frequent as sex-related errors, while the opposite results obtained in the Sex-Set condition.

Most psychologists' work, however, has tacitly favoured a "Single Plan Hypothesis", and has been concerned with the syntactic, lexical and phonological processes intervening between the thought plan and speech. In this volume, this tradition is ably represented by **Garrett**. An innovation in this line of work is the study of prosodic errors. Although Meringer and Mayer note errors of lexical stress, **Cutler** and **Isard** draw attention to errors of intonation as well, and use both categories of error to draw radical conclusions about the contents of the mental lexicon and about the processes responsible for prosodic decisions.

C. Studies of Temporal Aspects of Speech

Accurate timing of phonations and pauses has depended, of course, on the development of devices for recording speech and for analysing these recordings; hence, this was the last of the main approaches to emerge.

Temporal analysis has taken two courses: first, historically, was the investigation of pausal phenomena; second, the study of segmental lengthening.

Pausal phenomena are discussed in more detail in chapters 4, 5, and 12, and not much can be usefully added here, except some comments on the history of these studies. Apart from some early reports from Bell Telephone Laboratories on speech rate, the first systematic studies of temporal characteristics of speech, and especially pauses, were carried out by Goldman-Eisler. Starting from a clinical interest in what went on in patient-therapist interviews, in successive studies she increasingly focussed on temporal characteristics of the interaction.

> Curiosity about periods of external inactivity was aroused. The technique of measuring on and off periods of speech, however, was no more applied to the totality of exchanges between individuals in interaction, where silence is the period of the interlocutor talking, but to vocal action and silence of one person's output of continuous utterance . . .Pauses interrupting the smooth flow of speech . . . become the main subject of all further investigation . . . If vocal action is a peripheral phenomenon, might not absence of activity indicate the presence of central activity. A technique for studying the relation between speaking and thinking seemed to have been found. (1968, p. 4)

In 1958 she published a key paper experimentally testing one kind of "central activity", word selection. Lounsbury (1954) had offered the hypothesis that pauses "correspond to points of highest statistical uncertainty in the sequencing of units". The background theory was based on Osgood's "habit-family hierarchy" (Osgood, 1953) which stated, roughly speaking, that through experience internalized sequences of stimuli and responses become habitually linked. Where a given internal stimulus is linked to a number of alternative responses the habit strength for each stimulus response link will be weaker than if the stimulus is habitually followed by just one response, *ceteris paribus*. Thus, if a sequence of words is habitually followed by just one word, the linkage will be strong and the transition will be quick and automatic; whereas, if a sequence has been followed by a number of different words, the linkage will be weaker and slower. Another way of putting this would be to say that where a speaker has few choices of continuation then the time to choose will be short, when there are many choices, time to choose will be long and show up in a hesitation pause. Goldman-Eisler (1958) showed that pauses did, indeed, occur at points of high statistical uncertainty, but at the same time demonstrated that the theoretical basis of Lounsbury's hypothesis was unsound. The habit-family scheme requires that dependencies work only in one direction: what is to follow depends *only* on what has already come. Goldman-Eisler found that pauses are determined both by the sequence preceding it and by the sequence following it (see **Butterworth**. Chapter 5 for more details). The implications of this study were far-reaching. It brought speech production into the orbit of the mainstream of experimental psychology by demonstrating it to be tractable to quantitative exploration, and by showing that a variable widely explored in other areas of psychology—probability—applied to speaking. Moreover, it experimentally corroborated what we know from intuition, namely, that speakers plan ahead further than the next word.

Following this study, other researchers began exploring the potential of the investigative tools Goldman-Eisler had pioneered. She, herself, went on to discover other phenomena in the speaker's deployment of pauses, the significance of breath pauses, the selective effect of drugs on certain pausal phenomena, and the significance of these phenomena for our understanding of the speaker's mental processes.

As well as a review of this work, and some extensions of the basic methodology (Butterworth, Chapter 5), this volume contains some interesting new developments. **Goldman-Eisler** reports an application of pause analysis to simultaneous translation. This task is particularly revealing because the content to be expressed is not chosen by the speaker but is determined by the input message, only in the linguistic formulation has he discretion. **Beattie** breaks new ground in his exploration of pauses not only in relation to the speech, but in relation to the nonverbal behaviour of the speaker and the course of the conversational interaction. Interestingly, he shows that the hypotheses about mental processes Goldman-Eisler inferred from pauses can be corroborated by examining patterns of gaze and gesture. It had early been recognized that many pauses may serve a signalling function marking ends of speaking turns (cf. **Beattie**) and end of syntactic units. **Cooper's** paper provides some important new arguments for the precise syntactic motivation for the latter kind of pause.

Cooper also shows that other temporal phenomena can be deployed in the search for underlying mental processes. He has developed methods for analysing the non-phonemic lengthening of syllables and locating the mechanisms responsible for these effects.

D. New Approaches to the Study of Language Production

Language and its setting in conversations has, of course, been studied extensively from non-psychological points of view, but only synchronic syntax has really made any inpact on the way in which psychological processes are conceived and investigated. However, many other kinds of investigation have relevance to production processes, and four examples can be found in this volume.

Comrie shows that diachronic studies can tell us about how words may be represented in the mental lexicon. Change in the way a word is pronounced must reflect an alteration to something psychologically real for the speaker. If this is not the phonetic forms of the word in its various allomorphs, then it must be something more abstract. Detailed analysis of historical instances can reveal what this underlying, more abstract, yet psychologically existent, form must be.

The way in which sentences are interpreted will, of course, depend upon the context in which they are uttered. Perhaps the most important aspect of this context is location in a conversational sequence. **Schenkein** analyses naturally occurring conversations to reveal some of their general properties. It turns out that conversations can be treated as sequences of actions of particular types, and, in the examples he cites, a sequence comprising the action types gets repeated. Sometimes the same speaker will produce a repeat of the action type, sometimes another. In either case, whatever constituted a particular previous action type can be redeployed by the speaker when he designs his current utterance.

It is well-known to linguists that pragmatic factors constrain utterance meaning and utterance form. **Gazdar** lists phenomena which demonstrate the role of pragmatic factors in the syntax, morphology, prosody and phonetic character of utterances, and discusses its implications for models of production.

Fully explicit models of complex psychological processes are only possible in the form of computer programs. As far as language processing goes, programs have been devized primarily to model comprehension. **Steedman** and **Johnson-Laird**, however, draw our attention to attempts to model aspects of production. Their own work is concerned with the problem of designing utterances in the light of what the speaker believes the hearer already knows. They use a computer program to model the speaker's beliefs about the hearer, how they change during a conversation and how they are realized in utterance design. Not only is this a novel approach to production, but it raises a general issue of central importance to our understanding of the psychology of the speaker—of all things that could be said, on what basis does the speaker select what is said?

III. Review and Prospect

In summary, then, a fair amount is already known about language production. Partly this is because production, in fact, is at least no more difficult to study than language perception and comprehension; and even though vastly more labour has been expended on the latter two topics, it is arguable that we have a better understanding of production. The investigation of speech has the advantage that we are dealing with the naturally-occurring products of psychological processes, not an artificial response to a peculiar stimulus. Little or no experimental intervention in the production process is needed for useful results to be obtained, except where the precise character of some specific product is under investigation, as, say, in the study of articulatory mechanisms. Even in these cases, speakers are often required only to repeat what they would normally say just once. The strongest claim I would make is that the results from one approach can be readily collated with the results from other approaches yielding a better and more detailed picture of the underlying processses. I try to make good this claim in my concluding chapter.

References

Abrams, K. and Bever, T. G. (1977). Syntactic structure modifies attention during speech perception and recognition. *Q. J. Exp. Psychol.* **21**, 280–290.

Baars, B. (1979). The competing plans hypothesis: an heuristic viewpoint on the causes of speech errors. *In* "Temporal Aspects of Speech: Studies in Honour of Frieda Goldman-Eisler", (H. Decker ed.) Plenum Press, New York.

Bever, T. G. (1971). The integrated study of language behaviour. *In* "Biological and Social Factors in Psycholinguistics", (J. Morton, ed.) Elek, London.

Butterworth, B. L. (1978). Maxims for studying conversations. *Semiotica* **24**, 317–339.

Butterworth, B. L. (1979) Hesitation and the production of neoligisms in jargon aphasia. *Brain Language* (in press).

Coltheart, M., Davelaar, E., Jonasson, J. and Besner, D. (1978). Access to the internal lexicon. *In* "Attention and Performance", (S. Dornic, ed.) Lawrence Erlbaum, Hillsdale, N.J.

Cutler, A. (1976). Phoneme-monitoring reaction time as a function of preceding intonation contour. *Perception and Psychophysics* **20**, 55–60.

Cutler, A. and Foss, D. (1977). On the role of sentence stress in sentence processing. *Language Speech* **20**, 1–10.

Cutler, A. and Norris, D. (in press). Monitoring sentence comprehension. *In* "Sentence Processing: Studies in Honor of Merrill Garrett" (W. E. Cooper and E. Walker, eds.) Erlbaum, Hillsdale, N.J.

Davelaar, E., Coltheart, M., Besner, D. and Jonasson, J. (1978). Phonological coding and lexical access. *Memory & Cognition* **6**, 391–402.

Fodor, J., Bever, T. and Garrett, M. (1974). "The Psychology of Language", McGraw-Hill, New York.

Foss, D. (1969). Decision processes during sentence comprehension: effects of lexical item difficulty and position on decision times. *Journal of Verbal Learning and Verbal Behaviour* **8**, 457–462.

Foss, D. J. and Lynch, R. H. (1969). Decision processes during sentence comprehension: effects of surface structure on decision times. *Perception & Psychophysics* **5**, 145–148.

Freud, S. (1891). "On Aphasia" Translated by E. Stengel. London: Imago (1953).

Freud, S. (1924). "Slips of the tongue". Pelican Freud Library: Volume 5. Penguin, Harmondsworth.

Fromkin, V. (1971). The nonanomalous nature of anomalous utterances. *Language* **47**, 27–52.

Fromkin, V. (1973). "Speech Errors as Linguistic Evidence," Mouton, The Hague.

Garrett, M. (1975). The analysis of sentence production. *In* "The Psychology of Learning and Motivation", Vol. 9. Academic Press, New York.

Glucksberg, S. and Danks, J. (1975). "Experimental Psycholinguistics: An Introduction", Lawrence Erlbaum, Hillsdale, N.J.

Goldman-Eisler, F. (1958). Speech production and the predictability of words in context. *Quarterly Journal of experimental Psychology* **10**, 96–106.

Goldman-Eisler, F. (1968). Psycholinguistics: Experiments in Spontaneous Speech. Academic Press, London.

Goldstein, K. (1948). "Language and Language Disturbances." Grune and Stratton, New York.

Goodglass, H. and Geschwind, N. (1976). Language disorders (Aphasia). *In* "Handbook of Perception", Vol. VII. Academic Press, New York.

Green, D. W. (1977). The immediate processing of sentences. *Q. J. Exp. Psychol.* **29**, 129–146.

Hick, W. E. (1952). On the rate of gain of information. *Quarterly Journal of experimental Psychology* **4**, 11–26.

Jackson, J. Hughlings (1958). "Selected Writings", Vol. II. Basic Books, New York.

Johnson-Laird, P. N. (1974). Experimental psycholinguistics. *Annual Review of Psychology*, **25**, 135–160.

Lashley, K. S. (1951). "The problem of serial order in behavior". *In* "Cerebral Mechanisms in Behavior". (L. A. Jeffress, ed.) John Wiley and Sons, New York.

Lichtheim, L. (1885). On aphasia. *Brain* **VII**, 433–484.

Lieberman, P. (1977). "Speech Physiology and Acoustic Phonetics", Macmillan, New York.

Locke, J. (1700). "An Essay Concerning Human Understanding", (Ed. P. Nidditch), Oxford University Press, Oxford.

Lounsbury, F. G. (1954). Transitional probability, linguistic structure and systems of habit-family hierarchies. *In* "Psycholinguistics: A Survey of Theory and Research Problems", (C. E. Osgood and T. A. Sebok, eds.) Indiana University Press, Bloomington.

MacLeod, P. (1978). Does probe RT measure central processing demand? *Quarterly Journal of experimental Psychology*, **30**, 83–89.

MacNeilage, P. and Ladefoged, P. (1978). The production of speech and language. *In* "Handbook of Perception", (E. C. Cartrette and H. Friedman, eds.) Vol. VII. Academic Press, New York.

Meringer, R. and Mayer, C. (1895). "Versprechen und Verlesen", A. Cutler and D. Fay, eds.). John Benjamins, Amsterdam (1978).

Miller, G. A., Galanter, E. and Pribram, K. (1960). "Plans and the structure of behaviour."

Ogden, G. D. and Alluisi, E. A. (n.d.) S-R Compatibility Effects in Memory Scanning. Internal memorandum, University of Maryland.

Osgood, C. E. (1953). "Method and Theory in Experimental Psychology", Oxford University Press, New York.

Pick, A. (1931). "Aphasia." (Translated by J. W. Brown.) Springfield, Ill.: Thomas (1973).

Rubinstein, H., Lewis, S. S. and Rubinstein, M. A. (1971). Evidence for phonemic recoding in visual word recognition. *Journal of Verbal Learning and Verbal Behaviour*, **10**, 645–657.

Shields, J. L., McHugh, A. and Martin, J. G. (1974). Reaction time to phoneme targets as a function of rhythmic cues in continuous speech. *Journal of experimental Psychology*, **102**, 250–255.

Skinner, B. F. (1957). "Verbal Behavior". Appleton, New York.

Woodworth, R. S. (1938). "Experimental Psychology". Hole, New York.

Wundt, W. (1900). Völkerpsychologie Vol I: Die sprache Engelmann. Leipzig.

I

The Conversational Setting and Pragmatic Constraints on Production

2
A Taxonomy for Repeating Action Sequences In Natural Conversation

J. Schenkein   *City University of New York*

I. Introduction

Over a September weekend in 1971 a spectacular bank robbery was executed in London. A band of thieves had burrowed through the basements of a handbag shop and fast food outlet into the vaults of a Lloyds Bank. Cutting away at private safe deposit boxes Saturday and Sunday, they eventually collected over £300 000. When the loss was discovered by the bank manager on Monday morning the thieves were long gone.

All this was especially remarkable since police had been notified of the crime while it was in progress. A ham radio operator was dialing through his megacycles just before retiring on Saturday night when he happened to hear a suspicious remark about "sitting on 300 grand". He had intercepted a walkie-talkie communiqué between a man already in the bank vault and another man acting as a lookout on a nearby rooftop. When he reported this suspicious conversation to police he was regarded as a "nut case", and by the time the authenticity of his report had been verified with tape recordings of the intercepted conversations, it was too late. With an excellent sense of good timing, the thieves finished their work before the authorities located the site of their deed.

The tape recordings of the thieves coordinating their robbery were published in all the newspapers, much to the great embarrassment of police officials. Without the tapes of these conversations, the police might well have missed a band of masterminds, but with the tapes, a different story would have to be told. What follows is the transcript of one of these conversations as it appeared in *The Guardian* the day after the robbery was discovered:†

Text for a Bank Break-in

Tape recordings of the conversation heard by Mr. Robert Rowlands, the Wimpole Street radio "ham" who listened to the walkie-talkie conversation of

† The transcript was presented in the newspaper as a backpage appendix to the frontpage story running under the headline "Police inquiry into why they missed the radio raiders". For a detailed analysis of that news account of the bank robbery see Schenkein (1979b).

the Baker Street bank thieves, were broadcast by ITN last night. The substance of
the conversations was as follows:

1st Voice: (presumed to have been a man hidden in the bank vault): "Are you
receiving me?"

2nd Voice: "Loud and clear."

1st Voice: "Right, well listen carefully. We want you to mind for one hour from
now until approximately one o'clock and then go off the air, get some
sleep and come on the air with both radios at six o'clock in the
morning."

2nd Voice   (the lookout, presumed by police to have been on the roof of an eight-
story building overlooking the bank): "This is not a very good pitch
during the day—you know that, don't you? It's all blowing about and
everything."

1st Voice: "Are you sure you will be on the street tomorrow?"

2nd Voice: "I suggest we carry on tonight, mate, and get it done with."

1st Voice: "Look, the place is filled with fumes where we was cutting. And if the
Security come in and smell the fumes, we are all going to take stoppo
and none of us have got nothing. Whereas this way we have all got
300 grand to cut up when we come back in the morning. And if
Security have loused it up for us well at least we have got something."

2nd Voice: "I've heard you. Let me alone and let me have a think for a second."
(tape inaudible).

1st Voice: ". . . What happens if you are sighted?"

2nd Voice: "Sighted. These back stairs are not half as bad as those front. I can
only be booked from one way. I should think I've got a good chance
of not being sighted."

1st Voice: "Well, they join they all say that you should stay there."

2nd Voice: "Well the difference is they don't all feel like . . . My eyes are like
organ stops, mate. I'm not going to be any good tomorrow anyway. I
can hardly see now unless I don't do something."

1st Voice: "But you can go to sleep tonight."

2nd Voice: "How am I going to sleep tonight? For a start off, I won't wake up.
It's a certainty that, and I am not going to sleep away up till 10, am
I?"

1st voice: "You'll have to stay up there. How do you guarantee getting in in the
morning . . . Cor, the noise downstairs, you've got to hear and
witness it to realise how bad it is."

2nd voice: "You have got to experience exactly the same position as me, mate,
to understand how I feel. My eyes are so bad they are blurred and I've
been using (binoculars) all night."

1st voice: "You can have eight hours sleep."

2nd voice: "Where am I going to sleep, mate? Who wakes me up?"

1st voice: "If you don't wake up after eight hours, you are not a normal person,
are you? Listen, it's not a bad rate of pay, is it? It's 30 and probably
another 30 to come, or more."

2nd voice: "What time do you plan to start tomorrow?"

Woman's
voice: "About half eight to nine."

4th voice: "We have done about 90 per cent of the easy ones and we now face

the hard ones. If you are worried about waking up, put the ear plugs in your ear and go to sleep. We will call you up, it will be like an alarm call. We are in a rough state ourselves."
(Reproduced by permission of *The Guardian*, 21 September, 1971).

Apparently, this was a communiqué intended to deliver the latest instructions to the lookout, and things started off in the best tradition of fictional crime sagas:

1st Voice: Are you receiving me?
2nd Voice: Loud and clear.
1st Voice: Right, well listen carefully. We want you to mind for one hour from now until approximately one o'clock and then go off the air, get some sleep and come on the air with both radios at six o'clock in the morning.

Certain considerations of precision in coordinating the robbery-in-progress seem to govern these first three turns at talking. Notice however, that 1st Voice relies on 2nd Voice to adequately perform all of the ancilliary and circumstantial activities out of which the assigned comings and goings on and off the air are to emerge over the next several hours. No hints are offered for satisfying hunger or thirst, responding to a full bladder or a numb leg, dealing with boredom or anxiety, and indeed, the instruction only mentions "get some sleep" without further specification of how that might be accomplished. As it turns out, despite the reliance of 1st Voice on the other's competence with his own mind and body, it is the instruction to "get some sleep" that shortly becomes a major problematic in the negotiation of these instructions. The resulting discussion finds these bank robbers considering the interface between waking up from 8 h of sleep and the proverbial "normal person":

2nd Voice: My eyes are like organ stops mate. I'm not going to be any good tomorrow anyway. I can hardly see now unless I don't do something.
1st Voice: But you can go to sleep tonight.
2nd Voice: How am I going to sleep tonight? For a start off, I won't wake up. It's a certainty that, and I am not going to sleep away up till 10, am I?
1st Voice: You'll have to stay up there. How do you guarantee getting in in the morning ... Cor, the noise downstairs, you've got to hear and witness it to realise how bad it is.
2nd Voice: You have got to experience exactly the same position as me, mate, to understand how I feel. My eyes are so bad they are blurred and I've been using (binoculars) all night.
1st Voice: You can have eight hours sleep.
2nd Voice: Where am I going to sleep, mate? Who wakes me up?
1st Voice: If you don't wake up after eight hours, you are not a normal person, are you? Listen, it's not a bad rate of pay, is it? It's 30 and probably another 30 to come, or more.

While the instructions initially delivered are fashioned into "precise" orders, this discussion arrives at a rather "imprecise" resolution to the sleeping and waking difficulties raised by 2nd Voice. That the coordination of the robbery is entrusted in this instance to a formulation of the waking habits of a "normal person" and the insult such a formulation can carry is especially remarkable. It is true that at least one of the others puts his trust somewhere else:

> 4th Voice: If you are worried about waking up, put the ear plugs in your ear and go to sleep. We will call you up. It will be like an alarm call.

but there are many more instances of practical and tactical imprecision throughout the communiqué. Leaving aside the looseness of such timing markers as "approximately" and "not too late", consider these critical activities that remain contingent or chancy, even as the robbery is well underway:

> This is not a very good pitch during the day—you know that, don't you? It's all blowing about and everything.
> Are you sure you will be on the street tomorrow?
> Look, the place is filled with fumes where we was cutting. And if the Security come in and smell the fumes, we are all going to take stoppo and none of us have got nothing.
> What happens if you are sighted?
> I should think I've got a good chance of not being sighted.
> What time do you plan to start tomorrow?
> And you will have to bluff your way straight down.
> Before we come out we'll arrange a meeting place for you so that we can go where we are going to go. O.K.?

Although there is no sense in abandoning a long and noble tradition of fascination with perfect plans for perfect crimes, it is clear from the instance at hand that a major bank robbery can be conducted under the auspices of rather untidy plans and can succeed while enduring certain foibles of coordination.

But if the plans are somewhat untidy, the interaction is not; if the strategies being negotiated are anxious, the organization of those negotiations is remarkably orderly. For example, following the initial delivery of instructions by 1st Voice, 2nd Voice delivers a complaint that offers grounds for rejecting the plan envisioned by those instructions:

> 1st Voice: Right, well listen carefully. We want you to mind for one hour from now until approximately one o'clock and then go off the air, get some sleep and come on the air with both radios at six o'clock in the morning.
> 2nd Voice: [the lookout, presumed by police to have been on the roof of an eight-story building overlooking the bank]: This is not a very good pitch during the day—you know that, don't you? It's all blowing about and everything.

And just as the initially delivered instructions inherit a complaint that solicits a reconsideration, the suggestion for alternative instructions subsequently delivered by 2nd Voice inherits an analysis that likewise argues for reconsideration:

2nd Voice: I suggest we carry on tonight, mate, and get it done with.
1st Voice: Look, the place is filled with fumes where we was cutting. And if Security come in and smell the fumes, we are all going to take stoppo and none of us have got nothing. Whereas this way we have all got 300 grand to cut up when we come back in the morning. And if Security have loused it up for us, well at least we have got something.

Each of these exchanges consists of an utterance proposing what to do next in the robbery followed by a complaint formulating grounds for rejecting the proposal. In addition to this gross sequential similarity, these two exchanges share a number of orderly features in common. The second utterance of each exchange employs strikingly parallel resources in taking exception to its respective plan. In the first exchange, the complaint of 2nd Voice takes exception to the initial instructions by formulating an experiential domain that is presently unaccessable to 1st Voice; there is simply no way that 1st Voice can see for himself how 2nd Voice is posted in a place that is "all blowing about and everything." Likewise, in the second exchange, the analysis of 1st Voice takes exception to the alternative plan suggested by 2nd Voice by formulating an experiential domain presently unaccessable to 2nd Voice; there is simply no way that 2nd Voice can smell for himself how 1st Voice is working in a place that is "filled with fumes." Each of these second utterances, then, describes a condition currently experienced by its respective utterer and presently unavailable to its respective recipient except by the tendered account of that experience.

Both second utterances find a strategic vulnerability which even a flawless execution of their respective plans would leave undiminished. In the first exchange, the complaint of 2nd Voice addresses a contingency arising only upon successful completion of the initial instructions; even if 2nd Voice perfectly resumes surveillance and radio contact in the morning, the enterprise is jeopardized by his post being "not a very good pitch during the day." In the second exchange, the analysis of 1st Voice addresses a contingency that confronts successful performance of the alternative plan in its course; even if they all continue to work through the night perfectly, the enterprise is continually jeopardized by the possible whiffs of a noseworthy "Security." Each second utterance also locates an "objective" feature, an "impersonal" basis for rejecting the plan at issue. In all that "blowing about", or alternatively, in a vault "filled with fumes", there is surely a hinting at some of the personal difficulties each would have to withstand in executing the plan of the other. But in neither utterance are these difficulties formulated personally at this point. On the contrary, in a particularly selfless contrast to the sleeping and waking trouble that will soon receive explicit formulation by these theives, the observation of 2nd Voice ("This is not a very good pitch during the day.") and the analysis of 1st Voice ("if Security come in and smell the fumes") are both purged of personal considerations.

So here we have two exchanges occurring in very close proximity. Each one begins with an utterance proposing what to do next in the robbery, and each proposal is followed by a complaint that takes exception to the proposal by (a) formulating a strategic vulnerability to the proposal, (b) grounding the complaint in an experiential domain unaviailable to its recipient, and (c) framing the issue in objective apprehensions.

Is all this interactional order possible? Do the similarities of these two exchanges document constraints and resources commanded by ordinary conversationalists designing their utterances with materials found in prior talk? Or, is this some rare interactional event or rank analytic chimera?

II. Repeating Resources in Natural Conversation

As it happens, using materials from prior talk in current talk is enormously common in conversational interaction. Many instances of varied resources repeating will be had from close inspection of any natural conversation.

Repeating features are very often found within a single turn at talking, as in this string of talk:

> 1st Voice: If you don't wake up after eight hours, you are not a normal person, are you? Listen, it's not a bad rate of pay, is it? It's 30 and probably another 30 to come, or more.

In an effort to convince the lookout that he will awaken properly in the morning, 1st Voice invokes the proverbial "normal person"; the thematic metaphor surrounding this use of "normality" is then repeated in the subsequent description of their likely booty as a "rate of pay"—a decidedly "normal" way to describe their take.

Repeated features of prior talk are also very often found in an interactional unit no greater than the current and its just prior utterance, as in these instances from the bank robbers' conversation:

> 1st Voice: What happens if you are sighted?
> 2nd Voice: Sighted. These back stairs are not half as bad as those front. I can only be booked from one way. I should think I've got a good chance of not being sighted.
> 1st Voice: Well, they join, they all say that you should stay there.
> 2nd Voice: Well the difference is they don't all feel like.

The use by 2nd Voice of the word "sighted" draws directly on the occurrence of that word in the just prior utterance, and indeed, many of the repeats in conversation appear to carry topics from one utterance to the next. In initiating his next utterance with a "well", 2nd Voice repeats the "well" used to initiate the just prior utterance; this repeated utterance starter does not appear to carry topical phenomena, but rather, inflectional and structural formats from one utterance to the next, and indeed, many of the repeats in conversation conduct inflectional and structural features through the interaction.

Whether the repeated resources are topical, inflectional, structural, or thematic, those that occur within a single turn at talking or within an exchange of adjacent utterances are readily visible. Consider now the following exchange from a little later in the bank robbers' conversation:

1st Voice: Cor, the noise downstairs, you've got to hear and witness it to realise how bad it is.

2nd Voice: You have got to experience exactly the same position as me, mate, to understand how I feel. My eyes are so bad they are blurred and I've been using [binoculars] all night.

In this exchange the complaint of 2nd Voice is systematically constructed out of materials which occur in the just prior complaint of 1st Voice: the "you have got to" of the second complaint echoes the "you've got to" of the first: the "experience exactly the same position as me" in the second is a version of the "hear and witness it" in the first; the "to understand how" of the second complaint parallels the "to realise how" of the first; in the second complaint it is an issue of how "bad" the eyes are blurred and in the first it is an issue of how "bad" the noise is; and both are complaints about sensory organs that are suffering as a result of using equipment in performance of their respective duties.

The second complaint in this exchange is built as an orderly zag for the zig it locates in the just prior complaint. The exchange has, consequently, all the appearances of a tit-for-tat, and our ordinary sensibilities about one complaint inheriting another can be summoned to ratify that determination. However, the second complaint in this exchange displays a kind of repeated resource that extends well beyond the parameters of the immediately prior utterance: what appears in this exchange of complaints as a zag (viz. "My eyes are so bad") is actually a reinvokation of an earlier complaint by the same speaker (viz. "My eyes are like organ stops"). The utterance is a repeat of an earlier zig, dressed up as a zag, and elaborated somewhat differently as a consequence. In no way does its earlier precedent undermine its current dressing; fitting the repeat of an earlier complaint to features of the just prior complaint of another is one of the ways persons have of sustaining the relevancy, or asserting the supremacy, of the repeated complaint.

What begins to emerge analytically is an appreciation of the simultaneous layering of repeated resources from multiple locales within a single turn at talking. The complaint of 2nd Voice about his eyes that begins with "You have got to experience exactly the same position as me, mate" simultaneously draws its structural format from the just prior complaint of 1st Voice and its thematic issue from the complaint made by 2nd Voice himself four turns earlier.

Now if we compare the sequential environments in which the two complaints about 2nd Voice's eyes occur, a further repeated resource will become evident. Notice now that both of 2nd Voice's complaints occur in a turn at talking that responds to an authoritative pronouncement from 1st Voice in the prior turn:

1st Voice: Well, they join, they all say that you should stay there.
2nd Voice: Well the difference is they don't all feel like. My eyes are like organ stops, mate. I'm not going to be any good tomorrow anyway. I can hardly see now unless I don't do something.

and four turns later:

1st Voice: You'll have to stay up there. How do you guarantee getting in in the morning . . . Cor, the noise downstairs, you've got to hear and witness it to realise how bad it is.
2nd Voice: You have got to experience exactly the same position as me, mate, to understand how I feel. My eyes are so bad they are blurred and I've been using [binoculars] all night.

In both exchanges, the formulation of a dictum by 1st Voice occurs in the turn at talking immediately preceding the complaint about 2nd Voice's eyes:

1st Voice: Dictum
2nd Voice: Complaint

The second complaint about 2nd Voice's eyes not only repeats the structural format of the just prior complaint, and not only repeats an earlier complaint, but constitutes as well a repeat of the action sequence dictum/complaint. The layering of repeated resources within a single turn at talking can be quite extensive.

The action sequence dictum/complaint is an organizing structure found repeated often throughout this particular conversation. Recall the exchange generated upon the initial delivery of instructions to 2nd Voice:

1st Voice: Right, well listen carefully. We want you to mind for one hour from now until approximately one o'clock and then go off the air, get some sleep and come on the air with both radios at six o'clock in the morning.
2nd Voice: This is not a very good pitch during the day—you know that, don't you? It's all blowing about and everything.

Here again, 1st Voice formulates an authoritative pronouncement and 2nd Voice responds with a complaint; and, as we have already seen, features of this first occurrence of the action sequence dictum/complaint reappear in the closely following exchange:

2nd Voice: I suggest we carry on tonight, mate, and get it done with.
1st Voice: Look, the place is filled with fumes where we was cutting. And if the Security come in and smell the fumes, we are all going to take stoppo and none of us have got nothing.

where, for our present interests, we can simply repeat the observations that the proposal of 2nd Voice clearly implies an alternative dictum and the responding analysis of 1st Voice involves a strategic complaint about the alternative plan being suggested.

Not only is the action sequence dictum/complaint repeated four times within this rather brief conversation as we have just seen, but its last two appearance—each one hosting a version of 2nd Voice's complaint about his eyes—exhibit another kind of repeating resource in conversational interaction. After the first complaint about 2nd Voice's eyes, 1st Voice returns with a remedy to the complaint: "But you can go to sleep tonight" And, after the complaint about 2nd Voice's eyes is repeated, 1st Voice likewise returns with a remedy, in fact, a version of the *same* remedy: "You can have eight hours sleep." Both remedies are, of course, officially provided for by the dictum being negotiated in the first sequence and renegotiated in the second; both remedies are subsequently followed by another complaint from 2nd Voice, in fact, both are followed by a version of the *same* complaint:

1st Voice: But you can go to sleep tonight.
2nd Voice: How am I going to sleep tonight? For a start off, I won't wake up. It's
             a certainty that, and I am not going to sleep away up till 10, am I?

and:

1st Voice: You can have eight hours sleep.
2nd Voice: Where am I going to sleep, mate? Who wakes me up?

Each of the last two instances of the action sequence dictum/complaint receive the same kind of subsequent development; in both cases, the complaint about 2nd Voice's eyes receives a remedy consistent with the initial dictum of 1st Voice, and in both cases, the remedy inherits another complaint from 2nd Voice. Both sequences can be schematized as follows:

   I   1st Voice: Dictum
  II   2nd Voice: Complaint
 III   1st Voice: Remedy
  IV   2nd Voice: Complaint

A very substantial chunk of this conversation emerges organized as a pair of tandem action sequences; each consists of four turns at talking; each distributes the same turns to the same speakers; each finds the same action performed in the same turn; and each exhibits the same development:

1st Voice: Well, they join, they all say that   (I)   A: Dictum (stay)
             you should stay there.
2nd Voice: Well the difference is they don't all   (II) B: Complaint (eyes)
             fell like. My eyes are like organ
             stops, mate. I'm not going to be
             any good tomorrow anyway. I can
             hardly see now unless I don't do
             something.

1st Voice:	But you can go to sleep tonight.	(III)	A: Remedy (sleep)
2nd Voice:	How am I going to sleep tonight? For a start off, I won't wake up. It's a certainty that, and I am not going to sleep away up till 10, am I?	(IV)	B: Complaint (sleep? wake up?)
1st Voice:	You'll have to stay up there. How do you guarantee getting in in the morning ... Cor, the noise downstairs, you've got to hear and witness it to realise how bad it is.	(I)	A: Dictum (stay)
2nd Voice:	You have got to experience exactly the same position as me mate to understand how I feel. My eyes are so bad they are blurred and I've been using [binoculars] all night.	(II)	B: Complaint (eyes)
1st Voice:	You can have eight hours sleep.	(III)	A: Remedy (sleep)
2nd Voice:	Where am I going to sleep, mate? Who wakes me up?	(IV)	B: Complaint (sleep? wake up?)

III. Sequential Resources in Natural Conversation

In addition to topical, inflectonal, structural, and thematic resources whose repeats organize features of some current utterance with materials gathered in prior talk, there are *sequential* resources that can and do get repeated. Just as noticing the systematic repeat of single utterance formats in later utterances discloses an order of resources conversationalists command in negotiating their interactions, noticing the repeat of a systematic sequence of utterances discloses an order of resources organizing talk into orderly conversation.

Now the repeat of action sequences consisting of one, two, three, four, five, and six turns is not at all uncommon in the materials I have examined. In the following excerpt from a group therapy session, the sequential format of Roger's turn is repeated for Al's subsequent turn:

> Al: Well we're gonna try it for a while [I wanna] get round it as cheap as possible.
> Roger: Yeh
>   [4 seconds pause]
> Roger: No use buyin a trans til you have to hehh hehh hhh hhh
>   [2 seconds pause]
> Al: Yeah,
>   [4 seconds pause]
> Al: Put Hallibrown's—uh Hallibrans for the rear wheels, Hallibran's six and a half inch, with Goodyear, road-racing tires for traction.
>   (GTS:4:47)

Here Roger's turn begins with a "Yeh," sustains a four second pause, then continues with an elaboration of the "Yeh"; Al's next turn begins with a

"Yeah", sustains a four second pause, and then continues with an elaboration of the "Yeah".

A two turn action sequence very often organizes the telling of a story in two party interactions into an utterance delivering details of the story followed by a brief utterance of appreciation; in the following telephone call between adult sisters, 16 consecutive turns at talking are organized in that fashion:

(I)   Arlene: I took my final, Monday in Anthro/ en I took my, final in hhhh I
              gave—turned in my term paper in uh tch! Pschology on *Thurs*day.
              Yih know, hadtuh get up on the hotseat en I'm jus' *dy*in tuh have
              you read some a' these things the kids wrote.
              hhhh /They were so cute.
(II) Agnes: Really?
(I)   Arlene: Yeah. They rilly—they were just, very, hhh *very* very sweet with
              me, a:nd it was *so* funny, in fac' one of the kids came up tuh me,
              one a' the young, hhh fellas thet—Brad's about twunny two,
(II) Agnes: Mm hm,
(I)   Arlene: A:nd he 'ad been, in, one a' my micro groups right et the very
              be*gin*ning,
(II) Agnes: Mm, hm?
(I)   Arlene: A:nd the kid thet was up there just before I was, jus' completely
              dis-innegrated, before ar *eyes*. He just/uh
(II) Agnes: R:really?
(I)   Arlene: Oh God. He jut' startid telling about what the class meant tuh
              him, en hhh so forth, then 'e startid crying, en Go (hhh) d they—
              ih was jus' *te::*rrible.
(II) Agnes: A/young kid?
(I)   Arlene: *Truh*—hhh Yeah, Richard's about twunny three I think. Tch!
              A:nd uh, he's admitted tuh takin *drugs*. —be*fore* yuh know, en we
              all kinda thought maybe he ed been smokin pot or samp'n thet 'e,
              hhhhhh yih knew, became so intensely emotional over the whole
              thing, but I tell yuh by the time *I* got up there *af*ter 'im, wh (hh)y
              everbuddy was so campletely wrung *out* yuh know, end,
(II) Agnes: /Mm hm,
(I)   Arlene: hhhh —so *qui*et 'n hh so, hu—. hh I just— *yih* know, gave *my*
              short little, dissertation then ev'rehbuddy *writes*. Yih know.
(II) Agnes: Mm/hm.
(I)   Arlene: —About what they, feel towards you, en hhhh en then *af*terwards
              Brad came up en 'e said "*I'd* like—" "Arlene?" he said, I'd like
              t'take you over tuh Shakey's en buy you a beer." Ohh! huh./ hhhh
(II) Agnes: *How* cu:::te.

                                                          (NB:4:2:5)

Not only stories, of course, but a wide variety of interactional enterprises can be organized as tandem two turn action sequences. In the following telephone call to a civil defence headquarters, a brief utterance of attention registers successive details of the caller's place of residence and organizes the identification of her location as a repeating two turn action sequence:

	A:	Civil Defense.
(I)	B:	Uh I live uh on uh two blocks from the lake.
(II)	A:	Yes Ma'am.
(I)	B:	Uh between uh Canal Boulevard 'n puh— and West End.
(II)	A:	Yes Ma'am.

(CD:6:32)

where a two turn action sequence,

(I)	B:	Statement
(II)	A:	Acknowledgement

is found in a tandem repeat with the same "Yes Ma'am" acknowledgement. It is worth pointing out that the caller's subsequent query is likewise treated as an occasion to sustain the sequential format of the prior tandem repeat:

(I)	B:	Is there any danger of being flooded to/night.
(II)	A:	No Ma'am.

where now it is a question, not a statement, that has inherited an answer, not an acknowledgement, and yet the answer is built as an official counterpart to the just prior acknowledgements. Although the sequential format of the initial tandem repeat has been preserved in this question/answer exchange, the exchange does not generate a tandem repeat of itself; instead, the civil defense official now delivers some reassurance to the caller:

(I) A:		In fact uh yer resting a lot easier now than you could've uh rested six hours ago.
(II) B:		Uh huh.
(I) A:		You can have a good night's sleep.
(II) B:		Uh huh.

where the two turn action sequence,

(I) A:		Statement.
(II) B:		Acknowledgement

again organizes four consecutive turns at talking in a tandem repeat with the same "Uh huh" acknowledgement. This time, however, the speakers have reversed positions—it is the official who first proffered consecutive "Yes Ma'am's" to the caller's identification of her residence, but it is the caller who now proffers consecutive "Uh huh's" to the official's reassurance.

Changing speaker positions in a tandem repeat is one of the orderly manipulations of the initial action sequence which conversationalists routinely transact. For the following excerpt from a living room conversation among fiva adults, notice initially how T first repeats J's *"Mishungana crazy"* and then J repeats T's "m:y sugar":

	S:	No I'm not Jewish so I don't know. [low voice]
	T:	Have you ever heard the expression mishugana?
(I)	S:	Mishuga?
	T:	Mishugana mishuga y'know like ah.
(II)	J:	*Mishugana crazy.*
(III)	T:	MISHUGANA CRAZY.

(I)   S: Is that what it is?
(II) T: *Not* m:y sugar uh huh/ uh uh.
(III) J: Yah mah yah mah sugar/yah know-whad I mean?
      T: Goddam *gen*tile I can't believe it uh ha uh uh uh.

(Shiffman: 1–10)

There are a number of repeating resources in this excerpt. The question "Have you ever heard the expression mishugana?" is followed by a question-repeat (in this case, an imperfect repeat of the word in question: "mishuga" instead of "mishugana"); in response to the question "Mishuga?", the original questioner starts building toward some kind of definition with a repeat of both the original word and its imperfect copy (notice that the start of his answer, "Mishugana mishuga" repeats these words in the order they were delivered over the prior two turns); the answer, it turns out, is completed by another participant, J, who repeats the two word format of T's just prior "Mishugana mishuga" replacing the incorrect "mishuga" with "crazy"; T then repeats with gusto the *"Mishugana crazy"* answer. The three part action sequence.

(I)   Question
(II) Answer
(III) Answer-repeat

is then found in a tandem repeat organizing the next three turns at talking: S asks the question "Is that what it is?", T answers with *"Not* m:y sugar uh huh uh uh", and J offers an answer-repeat with "Yah mah yah mah sugar".

In this next instance, a pair of tandem three turn action sequences displays another orderly manipulation which the repeating sequence can host:

(I)   Laurie: an— but since all the uh, security trouble in the building? I've been y'know scared of doing the laundry, down in the basement?
(II) Mary: Whn'cha stablish a buddy system—
(III) Laurie: Well it's alright becuz Ted is going t'be doing it for a couple of weeks til I get my ne:rve ba (h)ch, and/I'm uh,
      Mary: Hnnn
      Laurie: —meeting some of the other tenants but, Y'know, I'm rea:l up, *tight* about it. AND I HATE being afraid of doing the laundry by myself an' things like that.
(II) Mary: You could get tuhgether with somebody on the same floor 'n arrange tuh do the laundry tuh*get*her,
(III) Laurie: Look. *First* of all, *Ted's* gonna be doing it for a couple 'a weeks and t-t'do it with somebody else means y'have tuh, all sorts of problems coordinating your life according to somebody else's schedule, an I can't *sta:nd* that kinde'a thing as you *kn:ow*.

(L&M:5:2)

Here the three turn action sequence.

(I)   Laurie: Complaint.
(II) Mary: Remedy.
(III) Laurie: Rejection of remedy.

occurs in a tandem repeat, but the repeating sequence hosts inflectional animation in each of its parts: the second time around for the complaint is an embellishment of its initial delivery—"I'm rea:l, up, *tight* about it. AND I HATE being afraid of doing the laundry by myself" is considerably more dramatic than "I've been y'know scared of doing the laundry"; Mary responds to the drama of the repeated complaint with a more elaborated version of her initially proposed remedy; and Laurie's second rejection of Mary's proposed remedy is rather more bothered by the proposal than it was the first time around. The three turn action sequence occurs in a tandem repeat, but the repeating sequence has escalated the tension of the issues each part of the sequence addresses. A second time around for a complaint need not be seeking a second time around for a remedy.

Multiparty conversations can distribute speaking positions to a number of participants under the auspices of multiple turn action sequences, and sometimes these are systematically repeated in succeeding turns at talking; in the following excerpt, a four turn action sequence distributes one turn to each of four participants in the encounter, and after a brief pause, the organization of that distribution is systematically repeated:

(I)	Aaron:	It was a *total* disaster for me.
(II)	Betty:	And we'll *never* buy another Chevy.
(III)	Colin:	I would have screamed bloody *murder*.
(IV)	Debra:	And we would have been arrested for disturbing the peace.
		[pause]
(I)	Aaron:	I used to think a new car was free of headaches for a whi(hh)le hheh
(II)	Betty:	But we sure had our share with tha(hh)t one hh
(III)	Colin:	I never considered buying *any*thing but a used car.
(IV)	Debra:	So we've never had *that* kind of tr-trouble.

(ARCD:8:6)

Here Aaron's story ending is formulated as how it was a disaster for *him*, while Betty's continuation of Aaron's utterance makes out a "we" conclusion to the story; Colin then follows with an "I would have" comment, and Debra's continuation of Colin's utterance makes a "we would have" conclusion out of it. In the succeeding four turns at talking. Aaron reports what *he* used to think about new cars, while Betty's continuation of Aaron's utterance reports what "we had" as a consequence of buying that one; Colin then follows with an "I never considered" comment, and Debra's continuation of Colin's utterance makes a "we've never had" conclusion out of it. The repeated and the repeating action sequences are dissected by a pause:

(I)	A:	"I" statement
(II)	B:	"We" (A and B) continuation
(III)	C:	"I" comment (on A's statement)
(IV)	D:	"We" (C and D) continuation
		[pause]
(I)	A:	"I" statement
(II)	B:	"We" (A and B) continuation
(III)	C:	"I" comment (On A's statement)
(IV)	D:	"We" (C and D) continuation

The tandem repeat of mulitple turn action sequences in multiparty conversations can also accommodate changes in speaker positions between the initial and the repeating sequence; in the following instance, a five-part action sequence distributes speaking positions initially to Ken and Roger, while the repeating sequence distributes the same positions to Roger and Al respectively:

(I)	Ken:	Al likes to uh t— to ride sailboats or— or something/
		( )
(II)	Roger:	Not any more hah hehhh
(III)	Ken:	Why. What happened.
(IV-a)	Roger:	She's gone hehhh
(IV-b)	Al:	She is sold. She's gonna be sold.
(V)	Ken:	Oh. Well, he used to/or-he-he still
	Al:	Mm hm
	Ken:	—does in the back of his mind probly.
(I)	Roger:	Now he/likes to drive/fast Austin Healys now.
	Ken:	Or— Or he-he-/he-
(II)	Al:	Not any more.
(III)	Roger:	What happened.
(IV)	Al:	It blew up.
(V)	Roger:	*Did*ju *rea*lly?

(GTS:2:24)

Here the initial action sequence is organized around repairing Ken's statement that "Al likes to uh t— to ride sailboats"; Roger follows Ken's statement with a counter-statement. "Not any more hah hehhh", indicating that more current information about Al undermines Ken's command of Al's latest enthusiasms; Ken then solicits the details merely headlined by Roger's counter-statement with "Why. What happened"; this request for elaboration is followed by Roger's announcement that "She's gone hehhh"—and Al, the subject of the discussion, delivers his own elaboration at this point with "She is sold", suggesting that the subject of the discussion may have rights to speak on details of his own biography even if his speaking intrudes into an action sequence on-going between other participants; and finally, Ken comments on the repair of his initial statement about Al, in this case using his commentary to rescue the original statement with "Oh. Well, he used to or-he-still does in the back of his mind probly." The progress of this initial five part action sequence looks like this:

(I)	Ken:	Statement
(II)	Roger:	Counter-statement
(III)	Ken:	Request for elaboration
(IV-a)	Roger:	Announcement
(IV-b)	Al:	Announcement
(V)	Ken:	Comment

This five part action sequence then occurs again as a tandem repeat, but this time the distribution of speakers is changed:

(I)	Roger:	Statement
(II)	Al:	Counter-statement
(III)	Roger:	Request for elaboration
(IV)	Al:	Announcement
(V)	Roger:	Comment

This time it is Roger who delivers a statement about what Al likes to do with "Now he likes to drive fast Austin Healys now"; and despite his just prior victory over Ken, and despite the appearance of current news in his latest statement about Al, Roger inherits exactly the same counter-statement from Al that he used on Ken—Al repeats "Not any more" at this point; Roger then requests an elaboration with a version of Ken's previous request in the same predicament—Roger says 'What happened?'; Al then makes his announcement with "It blew up"; and finally, Roger comments on the repair to his statement about Al, in this case using his commentary to solicit more details on the news he has not yet heard.

It is important to point out that the analytical categories used to name parts or turns of some action sequence are *names for positions in a sequence of actions* and not explanations, examinations, or exhibitions of the interactional enterprises that can be conducted in those positions. As we have seen, not only can speakers change positions in the initial and repeating action sequence, but the interactional enterprises conducted in some positions can change: In the last excerpt, Ken uses the comment position to retrospectively appreciate his earlier statement about Al "in spite of" the latest information he has heard, while Roger uses the comment position to prospectively appreciate upcoming details about Al "in light of" the latest information he has heard. In the previous excerpt, Betty continues Aaron's "I" Statement with a "We" remark adding emphasis to Aaron's point—when Betty says "We'll *never* buy another Chevy" it underscores Aaron's "It was a *total* disaster for me"; on the other hand, Debra continues Colin's "I Comment" with a "We" remark adding irony to Colin's point—when Debra says "And we would have been arrested" it undermines Colin's "I would have screamed bloody *mu*rder." In the excerpt from the discussion between Laurie and Mary, Laurie first uses the rejection of Mary's remedy to do a "no thank you", but in repeating the rejection Laurie does a "leave me alone". Even though the same interactional enterprise *can* be repeated in the repeat of some position in an action sequence (both T and J use an answer repeat to display an appreciation of the answer) both the Civil Defense official and the caller use an acknowledgement as a version of "yes, go on", and so forth, it should be clear that the name of the sequential position and the interactional enterprises conducted in that position are analytically disengagable.†

† In the conversations of life insurance salesmen and their prospective clients that I have studied, the salesman will routinely use his turn for Comment or Acknowledgement to affiliate with the client and display a point of biographical overlap if at all possible and sometimes even when it is highly unlikely. The client, on the other hand, often seeks no connection with the salesman with his Comments or Acknowledgements. Structurally, both the salesman and the client trade off occupying the same position in an action sequence that repeats several times through the course of the interaction. Interactionally, one time the salesman will Comment and

In the tandem repeat of a six part action sequence contained in the following excerpt, speakers occupy the same positions in the initial and repeating sequences, versions of the same interactional enterprises are performed in all but the sixth position, and there are a number of fine details of the initial sequence that are preserved in the repeating sequence. Karen is winding up an extensive story about how Gregg is cheap, inconsiderate of and embarrassed by his parents, and generally the source of some disappointment to his mother, when she offers the remark "*I've* always liked Gregg," as her general assessment of him; notice initially that this assessment is repeated a few turns later and that each occurrence generates a remarkably parallel development:

		[pause, 7 seconds]
	Karen:	But uh,
		[1.0 second]
(I)		Really, I've— *I've* always liked Gregg.
		[1.0 second]
		—very mu/ch.
(II)	Al:	I wish you'd quit usin that saying.
		[1.7 seconds]
(III)	Karen:	Why:
(IV)	Al:	Because it's terrible.—
(V)	Karen:	—It *is* a terri/ble phrase
	Al:	Mmhm?
(V-b)	Karen:	*Is* it?
(V-c)	John:	Why.
(VI)	Al:	—Mmhm
(I)	Karen:	—I've always—
		I've *al*ways liked Gre/:egg.
(II)	Al:	I wish you'd quit usin it.
		[0.7 second]
(III)	Karen:	Does that sound wro:ng?
(IV)	Al:	It sounds *ter*rible.
(V-a)	John:	In wuh wa:y.
(V-b)	Karen:	In what *wa:y.*
(VI)	Al:	Oh:: f-first of all you-youyer-you go on inna lo:ng lengthy detailed neagative things about this/indivijul-'n then
	Karen:	Hhhhh
	Al:	all'va sudden you say/"Oh I still like him."

(Schenkein:2:36)

After each assessment 'I've always liked Gregg", Al offers the criticism "I wish you'd quit using that saying." Following each of these criticisms, Karen requests an elaboration of the criticism—in the first sequence: "Why:" and in the second with "Does that sound wro:ng?" After each of Karen's queries, Al

---

affiliate, and another time the client will Comment and distance himself from his interlocuter. For a detailed examination of the identity negotations these salesmen and clients transact along with their other business, see Schenkein (1978).

delivers a version of the same elaboration—"Because it's terrible" the first
time, and "It sounds terrible" the second time.

Now in the first action sequence, Karen requests a further elaboration of the
criticism, an elaboration of the elaboration, with "It *is* a terrible phrase", and
thereby provides Al every opportunity to step down his general attack of
Karen's assessment procedures himself. When she has to repeat this latest
request for elaboration, the shift in emphasis from "It *is*" to "*Is* it?" warns of
no surrender by Karen. It is here, during Karen's efforts to solicit another
elaboration, that a third party, John, offers an utterance apparently designed
to make the solicitation of an elaboration all the more vivid—his "Why" ties
directly back to Al's "Because" as an unequivocal request for elaboration of
"Because it's terrible." But none of this generates a second elaboration from
Al, and his "Mmhm" treats Karen's queries as requests for confirmation
rather than as requests for elaboration of the elaboration. It is at this point
that the whole action sequence begins again with Karen's emphasized repeat
of the original assessment "I've *al*ways liked Gregg."

As the repeat of the just prior action sequence unfolds, a number of details
of organization are preserved that are worth noting. Not only does Al follow
the repeat of Karen's assessment with a close version of the same criticism as
we have seen, but he begins both criticisms as an interruption to a candidate
last word for Karen's assessment: in the initial action sequence he begins in the
middle of "much" from "*I've* always liked Gregg. [1.0 second pause]—very
much," and in the repeating sequence he begins in the middle of "Gregg" from
"I've *al*ways liked Gregg." After both criticisms, there is a pause; 1.7 seconds
in the initial action sequence, 0.7 seconds in the repeating sequences. When
Karen delivers her subsequent request for elaboration of the criticism, in both
action sequences she employs inflectional stretches for delivery of a similarly
voiced word; in the initial action sequence 'Why" is stretched into "Why:",
and in the repeating sequence "wrong" is stretched into "wro:ng". In both
action sequences, John offers a collaboration to solicit the second elaboration
from Al, but he participates nowhere else; in the initial action sequence he
offers "Why" and in the repeating sequence he offers "In wuh wa:y".

Whereas the first time through this action sequence generated no second
elaboration from Al, the second time through does at last, get a more extensive
analysis of why Karen's assessment of Gregg "sounds terrible". Putting it all
together, this instance can be schematized as follows:

(I)	Karen:	Assessment
(II)	Al:	Criticism of Assessment
(III)	Karen:	Request for elaboration of Criticism
(IV)	Al:	Elaboration-Assessment of Assessment
(V-a)	Karen:	Request for elaboration of Elaboration
(V-b)	John:	Request for elaboration of Elaboration
(VI)	Al:	Confirmation (no elaboration)
(I)R	Karen:	Assessment
(II)R	Al:	Criticism of Assessment
(III)R	Karen:	Request for elaboration of Criticism
(V-a)R	John:	Request for elaboration of Elaboration

(V-b)R   Karen: Request for elaboration of Elaboration
(VI)R   Al: Elaboration

where the repeating sequence appears poised to elicit an elaboration in the sixth position.

IV. A Taxonomy for Repeating Action Sequences

We have considered a number of repeating action sequences of from one to six parts, with from two to four participants, repeating from one to fifteen times, in a variety of conversational settings among a variety of conversational participants. It is plain enough that the repeating action sequences initially observed in the bank robbers' conversation are no freak of conversational nature and betray no fantasy of analytic imagination. Before I return to the bank robbers' conversation for some last observations, it may be useful to develop here a working taxonomy for repeating action sequences.

We have largely been considering *duplicating tandem repeats*; formally, these can be defined as a sequences of *n* parts, repeating without addition to, or subtraction from, the number of parts in the sequence, and repeating in the turns at talking immediately adjacent to the initial resources sequence. (Cf. the bank robbers' dictum/complaint/remedy/complaint; Arlene and Agnes; the "Yes Ma'am" and "Uh huh" sequences of the Civil Defense call; the "mishugana crazy" and "not my sugar" sequences; the sequences between Laurie and Mary; the discussion about what Al likes to do; and the "I've always liked Gregg" sequences.)

A few of the cases considered have been *duplicating disjunct repeats*; formally, these can be defined as a sequences of *n* parts, repeating without addition, to or subtraction from, the number of parts in the sequence, but *not* repeating in the turns at talking immediately adjacent to the initial resource sequence. Disjunct repeats may exhibit a separation of the initial from the repeating sequence with a brief pause in the talking. (Cf. the turns of Roger and Al which, although duplicating, are separated by a pause; and the "I"/"We" collaborative repeats of the two couples are also separated by a pause.) The separation may be due to an intervening utterance. (Cf. the intervention of "Are you sure you will be on the street tomorrow?" between otherwise duplicating dictum/complaint sequences in the bank robbers' conversation.) The separation may involve an intervening exchange of utterances. (Cf. the question/answer bisecting the "Yes Ma'am" couplet from the "Uh huh" couplet in the Civil Defense call.) The initial resource sequence may be separated from the repeating sequences by the several exchanges of utterances. (Cf. the utterances separating the second dictum/complaint from the third dictum/complaint in the bank robbers' conversation.) There is no reason to suppose that elaborate repeating sequences may not be separated from their initial resource sequence by substantially larger events, conversations, and biographical episodes.

Now in addition to the formal distinction between *tandem* and *disjunct* repeating sequences, it already appears warranted to distinguish technically between *duplicating* and *manipulating* repeating sequences. We can formally define a *duplicating* repeat as a sequence of *n* parts, repeating without addition to or subtraction from the number of parts in the initial resource sequence; virtually *all* the data considered has exhibited this organization to the repeating sequence. We can formally define a *manipulating* repeat as a sequence of *n* parts, repeating *with* some addition (*n* plus one or more) or subtraction (*n* minus one or more) to the number of parts in the initial resource sequence; some other materials will have to be introduced to exhibit the sequential expansions and contractions of manipulating repeats:

(I)	Tina:	What's the name of that liddle shop w— up on Broadway with all the African things?
(II)	Doris:	Ohh that's um, *Li*berty House.
(III)	Tina:	*That's* it.
(I)	Tina:	Anyway have you seen the wonderful baskets, they have, from uh.
(X)	Doris:	Do they carry baskets/I didn't know—
(II)	Tina:	Oh sure. They um, have grea:t backs specially there are these ones now from uh, uh Volta r'— some-place/else in [West Africa].
(III)	Doris:	Gee:: that sounds juss *great*.

(Pollack:4:12)

Here the three part action sequence:

(I)	Tina:	Question
(II)	Doris:	Answer
(III)	Tina:	Acknowledgement

occurs again as a tandem repeat, but the repeating sequence:

(I)	Tina:	Question
(X)	Doris:	Return Question
(II)	Tina:	Answer
(III)	Doris:	Acknowledgement

has been systematically expanded by Doris' Return Question (X). This sort of manipulation of an action sequence has the effect of changing speaker positions in the parts following the expansion; while Tina Acknowledged (III) Doris's Answer (II) in the first run-through, in the manipulated repeat it is Doris who Acknowledges (III) Tina's Answer (III). It makes sense to think of this sort of expansion as an *internal expansion*.†

(I)	Sharon:	Do you wanna take a til nap?
(II)	Jason:	Uh uh.
		[2.0 second pause]
	Sharon:	[coughing] *Achem* chem *chem*.
		[1.0 second pause]

†Other examples of internally expanded action sequences will be found in Jefferson and Schenkein (1977). A related phenomenon, the "nesting" of sequences within sequences is given an early formulation by Schegloff (1972). See also Jefferson (1972) for a discussion of "side sequences" that postpone an ongoing sequence.

(I)	Sharon:	Do you wanna 'nother b/ottle of—
	Jason:	*Uh* uh.
(X)	Tom:	Me neither! Hehhh .hhh heh heh

Here the two part action sequence:

(I) Sharon: Question
(II) Jason: Answer

occurs again as a disjunct repeat, but the repeating sequence:

(I) Sharon: Question
(II) Jason: Answer
(X) Tom: Answer

has been systematically expanded by Tom's addition of a second Answer (X). It makes sense to think of this sort of expansion as an *external expansion*.

When we considered the "I've always liked Gregg" repeating six part action sequence, it was suggested that the second run-through of the sequence appeared poised to elicit an elaboration from Al in the sixth position; recall as well that this was a twice requested elaboration of Al's just prior utterance, "It sounds *te*rrible", and that this prior utterance was an assessment offered to elaborate Al's original criticism "I wish you'd quit usin' that saying." As it happens, a contraction of the action sequence

(I)   Assessment
(II) Request for elaboration
(III) Elaboration

occurs in Al's very next turn at talking:

(I)R	Karen:	—I've always—
		I've *al*ways liked Gre/:gg,
(II)R	Al:	I wish you'd quit usin it.
		[0.7 second pause]
(III)R	Karen:	Does that sound wro:ng?
(IV)R	Al:	It sounds *te*rrible.
(V-b)R	John:	In wuh wa:y.
(V-a)R	Karen:	In what *wa:y*.
(VI)R	Al:	Oh:: f-first of all you-youyer-you go on inna lo:ng lengthy detaild negative things about this/indivijul-'n then
	Karen:	Hhhhh
	Al:	all'va sudden you say/"Oh I still like him."
	Karen:	I *WA*SN'T TALKIN ABOUT ALL IZ NEGA/TIVE QUALITIES/AL,
(IV,V,VI)	Al:	Yeah. And I— I *hate* it.—It's like saying uh, .hh uh::::: uh:::
	Karen:	"I like him in spite of iz faults!"
	Al:	No, that's not saying the same thing.
		[2.0 second pause]
	Al:	It's like "Some'v my best friends'r *Jews*"—is what is sounds like.

After the six part action sequence is completed for the second time, Karen's amplified "I *WA*SN'T TALKING ABOUT ALL IZ NEGATIVE

QUALITIES AL" is followed by a further elaboration of Al's reigning criticism: "I hate it." Notice that this elaboration takes the form of another assessment. This time, however, no request for an elaboration of the assessment is proffered as Al continues his string of talk immediately with a rather famous kind of elaboration: "It's like saying uh,". Al and Karen then negotiate the formulation of an ending to this elaboration beginning, but what I want to point out is that when the prior two action sequences reached the point of an assessment by Al, that assessment inherited double requests for an elaboration from Karen and John, whereas this time, Al delivers an assessment, and without stopping, goes right on to consturct at least the beginning to an elaboration. In the excerpt just considered, the sequence:

(I)	Al:	Assessment
(II-a)	Karen:	Request for elaboration
(II-b)	John:	Request for elaboration
(III)	Al:	Elaboration

has been contracted into:

(C)	Al:	Assessment plus Elaboration

It makes sense to think of this sort of contraction as an *internal contraction*. And finally, consider the following case:

(I)	Mitchell:	Yes, Let's head for that boulder at the top.
(II)	Shepard:	I don't think we'll have time to go up there.
(I)	Mitchell:	Oh let's give it a whirl. Gee whiz. We can't stop without looking into Cone Crater.
(II)	Sheppard:	I think we'll waste an awful lot of time traveling and not much documenting.
(I)	Mitchell:	We'll the information we are going after will be right on top.
(C)	Houston:	O.K. Al and Ed. In view of your assay of where your location is and how long it's going to take to get Cone, the word from the back room is.

(Astronauts: NYT:9:71)

In this excerpt from a conversation between astronauts Alan Shepard and Edgar Mitchell on the moon, and a flight controller in Houston, Texas, a tandem repeat sequence of two parts is manipulated by another kind of contraction. The third time Mitchell repeats his proposal to go to Cone Crater (this time because the information they are after is "right on top"), it is also the third time that the sequence:

(I)	Mitchell:	Proposal
(II)	Shepard:	Objection

begins. Apparently the two prior times was plenty enough of that action for Mission Control, and the third run-through of the sequence is cut off by the flight controller in Texas. One way that a repeating sequence can be contracted then is by an abandonment of some of its parts. Sometimes such abandonment can be imposed from persons neither in the initial resource sequence nor on the same planet. It makes sense to think of this sort of contraction as an *external contraction*.

To summarize: action sequences are regularly repeated in the negotiation of conversational interaction; the relationship between the initial and the repeating sequence can be either *tandem* or *disjunct*, and if it is disjunct, the intervention may be a brief pause, a single utterance an exchange of utterances, several exchanges or utterances, or combinations of these and other events; the repeating sequence can either *duplicate* or *manipulate* the sequential structure of the resource sequence, and if it manipulates, the repeat may be an *expansion* or *contraction* of the resource sequence, and these may be either *internal* or *external*.

		Manipulation			
		Contraction		Expansion	
	Duplication	Internal	External	Internal	External
Tandem					
Disjunct					

This sequentially based paradigm for repeating action sequences provides a descriptive matrix for instances that exhibit still other similarities and differences. But rather than classifying the sorts of interactional enterprises that can be variously conducted in corresponding sequence positions—a notoriously befuddling analytical undertaking, and rather than anticipating the variety of speaker position changes that can occur between the initial and repeating sequences—another structurally incidental variation, this taxonomy formally attends to the sequential organization of conversational interaction.

V. Exiting From Cycles of Repeating Action Sequences

The repeat of action sequences clearly organizes very substantial chunks of interaction, but as we know, not every chunk. Although it was a confrontation with details of the bank robber's conversation that led initially to an analytical preoccupation with repeating sequences, not all the talk captured for us in the newspaper transcript of their conversation is organized into repeating action sequences. The habits of non-repeating sequences deserve more extensive development than I can offer now, but I want to close with a brief consideration of the interface between a repeating and a non-repeating sequence in the bank robber's conversation.

For the action sequence characterized by:

    (I) A: Dictum
  (II) B: Complaint
 (III) A: Remedy
 (IV) B: Complaint,

the turn at talking following position IV appears crucial in the bank robber's conversation. When that position is reached the first time, 1st Voice returns to his earlier Dictum and a duplicating tandem repeat fills the four subsequent turns at talking; when the repeating sequence is completed, 1st Voice delivers an utterance apparently different from the twice invoked Dictum:

> 1st Voice: If you don't wake up after eight hours, you are not a normal person, are you? Listen, it's not a bad rate of pay, is it? It's 30 and probably another 30 to come or more.
> 2nd Voice: What time do you plan to start, tomorrow?

and judging by the response of 2nd Voice, filling that position with a "different" kind of utterance transacts an exit from the cycles of Dictum/Complaint they have just been through. The turn at talking following position IV can, evidently, generate a repeat of the action sequence by returning to position I, or generate a non-repeat by doing something "different."

There are several contrasts which mark the utterance "If you don't wake up after eight hours" as an exit from the twice repeated action sequence. It contrasts with the just prior Complaint of 2nd Voice:

> 2nd Voice: Where am I going to sleep, mate? Who wakes me up?
> 1st Voice: If you don't wake up after eight hours, you are not a normal person, are you? Listen, it's not a bad rate of pay, is it? It's 30 and probably another 30 to come, or more.

The Complaint of 2nd Voice specifically seeks a solution to emphatically *non-rhetorical* questions; where 2nd Voice can sleep and how he can wake up are practical details of the execution of the business at hand. By contrast, the remarks of 1st Voice are fashioned into emphatically *rhetorical* questions; the normality of waking after eight hours of sleep and the bountifulness of "30 and probably another 30 to come, or more" are not issues being raised for open debate. The non-rhetorical utterance of 2nd Voice asserts the continued life of the issues it raises; the rhetorical utterance of 1st Voice asserts the passing of the issues it raises.

The remarks of 1st Voice also contrast to the complaints about executing the plans running throughout the previous sequences. While 2nd Voice's eyes are "so bad", and in spite of "how bad" the noise is for 1st Voice, this latest utterance reminds all the eyes and noses participating that "not a bad" reward awaits them. And as we have already seen, these latest remarks of 1st Voice contrast the theme of "normality" with the "criminal" enterprise being negotiated throughout the previous sequences.

There is also a contrast between this last utterance of 1st Voice and the remarks he offered to occupy this same sequential position four turns earlier:

> 1st Voice: You'll have to stay up there. How do you guarantee getting in in the morning . . . Cor, the noise downstairs, you've got to hear and witness it to realise how bad it is.

While the latest remarks of 1st Voice address *theoretical generalizations* about normal sleeping habits and *optimistic speculations* about some final reward, the corresponding sequential position was filled with *empirical particulars* about the plans and an *anxious account* about some present suffering.

In at least these ways, then, we can observe the "differences" between this latest utterance of 1st Voice and the just prior utterance, the complaints running throughout the preceding action sequence, and the remarks filling the same sequential position earlier. The "differences" we may see, however, are not so strange, are not so unconnected, are not *so* "different", that the utterance presents itself as symptomatic of any kind of inability, ineptitude, or inadvertence. The "differences" are, needless-to-say, orderly manipulations of resources organizing features of the previous talk. The just prior utterance is flush with a pair of questions—"Where am I going to sleep, mate? Who wakes me up?" these latest remarks are initiated with a pair of questions—"If you don't wake up after eight hours you are not a normal person, are you? Listen, it's not a bad rate of pay, is it?". The complaints of 2nd Voice about his eyes, sleeping, and waking are administered to by the "normal person" exhortation that trivializes them, and the complaint of 1st Voice about the noise is not altogether forgotten in the "rate of pay" exhilaration which begins with "Listen . . . " The turn at talking occupying this sequential position previously was filled with a compound utterance, consisting of three sentences, and progressing topically from a reference to "up there" (where 2nd Voice is suffering certain troubles) to a reference to "downstairs" (where 1st Voice is not entirely trouble-free); this latest turn at talking is filled with a compound utterance, consisting of three sentences, and progressing topically from a reference to the "normal person" (who can sleep and wake adequately where 2nd Voice is) to a reference to "rate of pay" (which is being assembled where 1st Voice is). In at least these ways, then, we can document the "similarities" between the latest remarks of 1st Voice and the just prior utterance, the complaints running throughout the preceding action sequence, and the remarks filling the same sequential position earlier.

Obviously, both "similarities" and "differences" are abundant enough that a description of the relationship between any utterance and any other can count on gathering some of each. In attempting to build a formal description of the interface between repeating and non-repeating action sequences we can already move beyond compiling lists of "similarities" and "differences" by attending to the sequential resources organizing talk into conversation. Recall that in the earlier turn following position IV when 1st Voice returned to the Dictum (1), his compound utterance went on to *also* formulate a complaint about the noise downstairs; this time however, *only* versions of a complaint are offered:

> 1st Voice: If you don't wake up after eight hours, you are not a normal person, are you? Listen, it's not a bad rate of pay, is it? It's 30 and probably another 30 to come, or more.

This time, 1st Voice delivers a complaint for 2nd Voice to remedy without also providing a dictum to complain about. The "normal person" remark complains that the worries 2nd Voice has about his sleeping and waking are unnecessary perversions of his ordinary capabilities. The "rate of pay" remarks complain that any inconvenience 2nd Voice is suffering will earn handome compensation. The utterance is a local production of the famous complaint about complaints, "Stop complaining." Rather than now being in the position of responding to a complaint with either a dictum or remedy that has twice failed to exit from the initial and repeating action sequences, 1st Voice is in the position of receiving a response to his complaint. The subsequent utterance from 2nd Voice:

2nd Voice: What time do you plan to start, tomorrow?

performs a remedy to his complaint by, literally, stopping the complaining. Schematically, the initial resource sequence:

(I)   1st Voice: Dictum
(II)   2nd Voice: Complaint
(III)   1st Voice: Remedy
(IV)   2nd Voice: Complaint

is followed by a tandem duplicating repeat; when the repeating sequence is completed and the turn at talking following position IV is reached for the second time, the following occurs:

(II)   1st Voice: Complaint
(III)   2nd Voice: Remedy

Instead of returning to the Dictum (I) as before, 1st Voice returns to the Complaint (II) position formerly occupied by 2nd Voice; his Complaint (II) inherits performance of a Remedy (III) by 2nd Voice. A non-repeating action sequence has emerged from the sequential materials of the prior tandem duplicating repeat. These latest remarks indeed exit from the cycles of Dictum/Complaint by being "different" from the initial and repeating sequences, but the "difference" is a systematic speaker change transacted on the positions in the prior action sequences.

While there are surely other ways 1st Voice might have transacted the interface between repeating and non-repeating action sequences, it is striking that sequential resources provided by the preceding chunks of talk are in fact used. Whether the materials under study exhibit repeating or non-repeating action sequences, the systematic use of resources from prior talk in current talk apparently organizes the conversation. Not only are topical, inflection, structural, and thematic resources provided by the conversation-in-progress, but *sequential resources* are likewise managed systematically by participants negotiating their most ordinary and exotic conversations.†

† The research reported here is greatly indebted to the work of Harvey Sacks. Through his lectures and writings he has had a profound influence on students of natural speech systems and interaction. An interest in the resources consulted and used by speakers fashioning their utterances in conversational interaction will be greatly rewarded by study of his many published and unpublished papers.

References

Jefferson, G. (1972). "Side Sequences" *In* "Studies in Social Interaction," (D. Sudnow, ed.), The Free Press, New York. pp. 294–338.

Jefferson, G. and Schenkein, J. (1977). Some Sequential Negotiations in Conversation: Unexpanded and Expanded Versions of Projected Action Sequences, *Sociology*, **11**, 87–103; reprinted in Schenkein (1979a).

Sacks, H. (1964–1974). Unpublished Lectures, University of California, Berkeley, Los Angeles, and Irvine.

Sacks, H. (1972). "An Initial Investigation of the Usability of Conversational Data for Doing Sociology," (D. Sudnow, ed.), The Free Press, New York. pp. 31–75.

Sacks, H., Schegloff, E. and Jefferson, G. (1972). A Simplest Systematics for the Organization of Turn-Taking in Conversation, *Language*, **50**, 3–68: reprinted in Schenkein (1979a).

Schegloff, E. (1972). "Notes on a Conversational Practice: Formulating Place" *In* "Studies in Social Intersection", (D. Sudnow, ed.), The Free Press, New York. pp. 75–119.

Schenkein, J. (1978). "Identity Negotiations in Conversation," *In* "Studies in the Organization of Conversational Interaction," Academic Press, New York. pp. 64–67.

Schenkein, J. (1979a). "Studies in the Organization of Conversational Interaction," Academic Press, New York.

Schenkein, J. (1979b). "The Radio Raiders Story," *In* "Studies in Language", (G. Psathas, ed.), Irvington Press, Boston. pp. 124–159.

3
Pragmatic Constraints on Linguistic Production[1]

G. Gazdar

University of Sussex

I. Introduction

This Chapter is not a theoretical one. That is, it makes no attempt to develop a general theory to account for the way pragmatic factors affect the process of language production. The body of the paper consists entirely of data: observations concerning particular pragmatic constraints known to exist, organized into a taxonomy that has no particular theoretical status. This data stands as a set of potential counter examples to theories of language production that might be proposed, for example a theory which claimed that the speaker's perceptual experience was irrelevant to the operation of the production counterparts of syntactic movement rules, or a theory which claimed that the phonological component of production functioned independently of the speaker's beliefs and emotions. Almost all the data in this paper has proved, or is proving, extremely problematic for contemporary linguistic theory and I think one has every reason to suppose that it will prove just as discomfiting for substantive (i.e. falsifiable) psychological theories of language production.

The paper proceeds by working its way down the components of a transformational grammar of a traditional type (c. 1965). This is simply to impose some structure on the phenomena under consideration—there is no implicit assumption that a model of language production would need to be organized along these lines. Accordingly we begin with constraints on the choice of expression, proceed to constraints on "movement" rules and clause co-occurrence, then successively to constraints on deletion, morphology and finally phonology. No attempt is made to be comprehensive: each section or subsection contains abbreviated exemplification of representative instances of the type of phenomenon that can be found. Where appropriate I have given references to papers dealing with related phenomena not discussed herein. Almost all the data given has been drawn from the work of others and the reader should seek out the originals if he is to appreciate the full subtleties of the constraints: more often than not I have extracted two or three key

[1] I am grateful to Richard Coates for the French data and the phonetic transcriptions found in Section VII. Also to Brian Butterworth, Richard Coates, Anne Cutler, Georgia Green, Judy Klavans-Rekosh, John Lyons, Geoff Pullum and Aaron Sloman for comments, correction and criticism.

examples from a whole paper devoted to the phenomenon in question. My accompanying text is commensurately brief. The intention throughout is to convey a picture of the *range* and *pervasiveness* of pragmatic constraints—not to explore the baroque elaborations of any particular case in great detail.

Despite the uniquely fragmented state of contemporary linguistic theory at the present time, there is a remarkable consensus with respect to one fundamental issue: the nature of semantic representation. Scholars as disparate as Montague, Chomsky, McCawley, Katz, Sadock and Partee would, I think, now agree that the semantic representation of a sentence is a representation which expresses the logical form of the sentence, or, put differently, a representation which expresses the conditions under which that sentence would be true. Other, non-truth conditional, aspects of the meaning of the sentence are not to be captured in that representation *per se* but are relegated to a separate component of the theory called "the pragmatics", the role and status of which is highly unclear (see Gazdar (1979) for discussion). I shall use "pragmatics" throughout this paper to refer to non-truth conditional aspects of utterance meaning.

The early Generative Semantics attempt (associated most prominently with G. Lakoff (e.g. 1971a)) to capture all pragmatic aspects of meaning, such as implicature, presupposition, topic, speech act type, etc. in the semantic representation itself has now been largely abandoned. Partly this has come about for theory-internal reasons—the failure of the performative hypothesis, the incoherence of semantic treatments of presupposition, etc.—but partly it has come about because linguists have begun to realize that although a finite representation can be made to capture an infinite set of truth-conditions in a theoretically perspicuous manner, there is no obvious way in which a finite representation can be made to encompass all the potentially relevant pragmatic conditions associated with the utterance of a sentence. Worse still, the type of condition appears to vary dramatically from language to language: this has the effect of making "universal semantic representations"—still a goal of many linguists—look uncomfortably cumbersome if pragmatics is included in the representations. For example, the semantic representations of English imperative sentences would have to include a specification of the sex of speaker and addressee since this information is relevant to the formation of imperatives in at least one language (Biloxi, see Section VI below).

If the goal of a language production model is construed to be the construction of an algorithm for converting semantic representations into acoustic or orthographic output then the psycholinguist attempting to achieve that goal has two choices when confronted with the data to be found in this paper. Either he can enlarge semantic representations to incorporate every kind of potentially relevant fact and then apply a context-independent translator to those representations, or he can retain the linguist's currently rather conservative style of semantic representation and apply a translator *that is allowed access at any stage in the translation process to a data-base representing the context*. In computational terms the first disjunct looks to be a very uneconomic way of organizing things.

II. Constraints on Choice of Expression

A. Language Choice

If you speak English and German and you are talking to someone who you know to understand only German then you will speak to that person in German. That observation is so obvious that it hardly merits making were it not for the fact that it represents one extreme of a whole continuum of otherwise subtle pragmatic constraints on one's choice of language. Consider the case of a monolingual English academic visiting a Swedish university: in his company his Swedish colleagues can be heard to address each other in both English and Swedish, English for those parts of the conversation in which he might be expected to participate (e.g. matters of mutual academic interest) and Swedish for those from which he would, in any case, be excluded (e.g. the departmental xeroxing budget). More exotic is the language switching found in certain Australian aboriginal communities:

> Each speaker had at his disposal two separate languages: a Dyalnguy or "mother-in-law language", which was used in the presence of certain "taboo" relatives; and a Guwal, or everyday language which was used in all other circumstances . . . Dyalnguy *had to* be used in the presence of a parent-in-law, child-in-law or cross cousin of the opposite sex. It should also be used—although the necessity was not so strong—with a parent-in-law of the same sex. It could be used more or less optionally with a cross cousin or child-in-law of the same sex. It would not be used in any other circumstances . . . Each Dyalnguy has identical phonology, and almost the same grammar, as its Guwal. However, it has an entirely different vocabulary; there is not a single lexical item common to the Dyalnguy and Guwal of a tribe. (Dixon, 1972, p. 32).

Strange though the facts may be, they do not seem to pose more of a problem for a language production model than does the banality with which this section began. The well documented cases of *intrasentential* language switching by bilinguals are altogether more troublesome for such a model. This switching seems to be invariably constrained by pragmatic factors (rather than, say, exclusively syntactic or phonological ones), speakers and addressees are often quite unaware that it is taking place (cf. the case where one deliberately chooses to speak German because one knows that to be the only language one's addressee can understand), and, most significantly of all, the actual switching itself (to be more precise: the *direction* of switch) can contribute to the meaning of the utterance (Gumperz, 1976).

B. Possible Lexical Items

Unlike the other constraints discussed in this paper, those discussed under the present heading are not constraints on the process of speech production itself but rather pragmatic constraints on one of the resources that the production process employs, namely the lexicon.

Horn (1972) showed that the lexicons of natural languages are prohibited from containing words whose semantic effect is in any case achieved by the use of some other word together with the *conversational implicatures* (see Grice, 1975) to which it gives rise. Thus no languages have words corresponding to *nall (=not all), *nand (=not (... and ...)), *noth (=not both), etc. since the meaning conveyed by these words would not differ from that standardly conveyed by *some, or, either*, etc. respectively. Utterance of (1) typically implies (2) and so we have no need of a word meaning what *nall would mean:

(1) Some of the postgraduates were at the party.
(2) Not all of the postgraduates were at the party.

Gazdar and Pullum (1976) have proposed various constraints to account for the fact that only two or three of the transfinitely many definable truth functions actually show up in the lexicons of natural languages. Their constraints are as follows:

(3) Commutativity: no language may lexicalize a truth-functional connective whose truth conditions are affected by the order of the coordinated clauses.

(4) Compositionality: no language may lexicalize a truth-functional connective whose truth conditions are independent of one or more of the coordinated clauses.

(5) Confessionality: no language may lexicalize a truth-functional connective which allows the compound sentence to be true when all its constituent sentences are false.

(4) is motivated by pragmatic considerations arising out of Grice's (1975) Maxim of Relevance: any connective which violated (4) would be a connective that rendered one of its conjuncts irrelevant. (5) is motivated by pragmatic factors associated with natural language negation (on which see Givon (1975) for full discussion). These three constraints predict that no language will have words or morphemes corresponding to, for example, material implication, the biconditional, Sheffer's stroke, and McCawley's *schmor (1972, p. 540).

C. Choice Between "Synonymous" Expressions

1. Language particular cases

Ferguson (see Gazdar (1976b p. 126)) reports that Moroccan Arabic has two words corresponding in denotation to English *needle*. One of the words can only be used in the morning and the other only in the afternoon. And in Javanese, according to Comrie (1976) the choice between *sega* and *sekul* to refer to rice is determined by how courteous one wishes to be to the person one is talking to.

Many languages have a range of words for motion with respect to an object.

Choice of which word to use is determined by subtle and complex contextual assumptions concerning, for example, the respective locations of speaker and addressee at the time of speaking. In English we have a choice between *come* and *go* in sentences like (6) and (7):

(6) He came to the farm.

(7) He went to the farm.

Fillmore (1975) proposes the following pragmatic constraint on the use of *go*:

(8)   *go* cannot be used unless the motion described is toward a location which is distinct from the speaker's location at the time of utterance.

Hence:

(9)   *He went here.

In Hindi the constraints associated with *ana* (≈ *come*) and *jana* (≈ *go*) apply to normative as well as geographical space, as Sinha (1972, p. 354) shows:

(10) Uskā larkā bewkūf nikal gayā.

      (= His son turned (= went) out a fool.)

(11) Uskā larkā widwān nikal āyā.

      (= His son turned (= came) out a scholar.)

(12) *Uskā larkā bewkūf nika āyā.

      (= His son turned (= came) out a fool.

cf. Clark (1974) for related English data.

2. *Putative universal constraints*

For any individual one might wish to refer to, a natural language provides us with an indefinitely large set of extensionally equivalent expressions. Thus all of the expressions listed in (13) can refer to any one individual:

(13) He
      John
      Smith
      John Smith
      Mr. Smith
      Smithy
      That man
      The man by the bar
      The man I was telling you about
      The person whose name I'd rather not mention

A model of language production which randomly selects from such a set on an occasion of reference will clearly be missing something. Sacks and Schegloff (1977) propose two constraints on the choice of referring expression:

(14) Reference should preferredly employ a "recognitional".

(15) Reference should preferredly be done with a single reference form.

The second of these constraints is a special case of a more general constraint on the choice of expression, a constraint tersely expressed in Grice's (1975) maxim "Be brief!" Grice's maxim can be read as instructing speakers to choose E given two potentially synonymous expressions E and E' such that E' is longer than E. And as instructing addressees on hearing E′ (E and E′ being as above) to assign it a reading distinct from E if that is possible (because if it were intended to mean what E means then E would have been used instead). Something along these lines would provide part of the explanation for R. Lakoff's observation regarding English modal verbs and their respective periphrastics:

> When the speaker agrees with, or takes upon himself, the atomic meaning of the modal, he can use the simple modal form. Otherwise, he must use the periphrastic variant (1972, p. 239).

III. Constraints on "Movement" Rules

Although the discussion below will be phrased in the familiar way in terms of the movement of phrases, nothing substantive hangs on this so far as a model of language production is concerned. Whether or not such a model employs the analogue of the transformationalist's movement rules, the pragmatic constraints noted will have to be captured somehow: the problems they create don't go away if one stops thinking in "movement" terms.

Slifting is the movement rule proposed by Ross (1973) which is responsible for converting sentences like (1a) and (2a) into (1b) and (2b) respectively:

    (1a) Tell me where you were staying.
    (1b) Where were you staying, tell me.
    (2a) I wonder how long he has been floating near me.
    (2b) How long has he been floating near me, I wonder.

Any purely syntactic formulation of this rule will generate anomalous sentences like (3b) and (4b)

    (3a) Never tell Ed where you were staying.
    (3b) *Where were you staying, never tell Ed.
    (4a) They may have wondered how long he has been floating near me.
    (4b) *How long has he been floating near me, they may have wondered.

(All the examples are from Ross (1975, p. 242).) Ross notes that the following pragmatic constraint is operative:

    (5)   Embedded questions can be slifted only if the sentences in which they appear have the (basic or derived) illocutionary force of a request on the part of the speaker for the hearer to provide the relevant information about the *wh*-ed parts of the question that is to be slifted (1975, p. 243)

That most famous of movement rules, the rule of *Raising*, also has pragmatic constraints on its application. Postal (1974, p. 357) notes the following examples (originally due to Cantrall):

    (6)   It struck me that Julius Caesar was honest.
    (7)   Julius Caesar struck me as honest.

Whilst (6) is a perfectly ordinary and utterable sentence, (7), which derives from (6) via Raising, is not really usable by a native speaker of twentieth century English. As Postal points out, (7) could only be used by someone who had had some kind of perceptual experience of Julius Caesar and who had arrived at the judgement expressed in (7) as a result of this experience. Schmerling (1976b) discusses the following examples and their implications for *Raising*:

(8)   I allowed the doctor to examine John

(9)   I allowed John to be examined by the doctor

The pragmatic constraint which applies to *allow* in respect of *Raising* appears to be of the following form: when possible raise the NP which denotes the individual to whom permission was given.

Locative preposing is another movement rule which has a subtle pragmatic constraint on its applicability. Consider the following examples:

(10a)   A mouse scuttled out of the cranny.

(10b)   Out of the cranny scuttled a mouse.

(11a)   A mouse scuttled into the cranny.

(11b)   ?Into the cranny scuttled a mouse.

(12a)   Stuart strode into the pub.

(12b)   Into the pub strode Stuart.

(13a)   Stuart disappeared into the pub.

(13b)   ?Into the pub disappeared Stuart.

As Longuet-Higgins (1976) observes, locative preposing can only apply when the individual denoted by the (underlying) subject of the sentence is assumed to be "coming into view". (11b) is odd because human observers cannot fit into crannies and (13b) is odd because the sentence itself explicitly denies that Stuart came into view (for enlightening discussion of the syntax of the (b) sentences, see Postal (1977)).

The morpheme expressing negation in English can be realized at different points in the sentence thanks to a couple of movement rules known as *Neg-Raising* and *Neg-Attraction*. Sheintuch and Wise (1976) have shown that these two rules are subject to a pragmatic constraint which they formulate thus: "the distance of the neg to the left or right of its neutral position in the surface sentence corresponds to the strength or weakness of the opinion, intent or perception" (Sheintuch and Wise, 1976, p. 552).

(14)   I don't think I saw anyone in the room.

(15)   I think I didn't see anyone in the room.

(16)   I think I saw no one in the room.

(14) derives from (15) via neg-raising and (16) from (15) via neg-attraction. (14), in which the negation morpheme is as far to the left as it can get, expresses most uncertainty as to whether the speaker saw anyone, whereas (16), in which the negation morpheme is as far to the right as it can get, expresses least uncertainty.

Other movement rules known to have pragmatic constraints on their application include *Right Dislocation* (Rodman, 1975), *Emphasis Movement* in Finnish (Karttunen, 1975), *Niching* (Corum, 1975a), *Adjective Preposing* (Green, 1974a), *Dative Movement* (Green, 1974b), *Attribute Preposing* and *Left Dislocation* (Hankamer, 1974).

IV. Constraints on Clause Co-occurrence

A. Conjunction With *AND*

A familiar observation concerning *and* (see Gazdar (1979) for discussion and relevant citations) is that where the sentences conjoined by it
denote events, then the speaker will in general produce those sentences in
an order which reflects the order in which the events denoted took place.
This explains the different interpretations typically assigned to (1) and
(2):

    (1)   Harry stole the money and went to the bank.
    (2)   Harry went to the bank and stole the money.
and the anomaly most people find with (3)—cf. (4):

    (3)   *The Lone Ranger rode into the sunset and jumped onto his horse.
    (4)   The Lone Ranger jumped onto his horse and rode into the sunset.
This ordering constraint is, to some extent, independent of the presence of *and*
(cf. Linde (1976) on ordering in conditionals) thus

    (5)   *The Lone Ranger rode into the sunset. He jumped onto his horse.
However, as Herb Clark (personal communication) has pointed out, there are
other cases where reverse temporal ordering is acceptable with independent
sentences but anomalous when *and* is employed:

    (6)   John broke his leg. He tripped and fell.
    (7)   *John broke his leg and tripped and fell.
    (8)   The car came to a halt. The petrol ran out.
    (9)   *The car came to a halt and the petrol ran out.
    Another widely noted constraint on *and,* though not on other conjunctions,
concerns the permissible order of the conjoined clauses when one clause
presupposes the other. Since whether one clause presupposes the other cannot
in general be decided without reference to the context of utterance (see
Karttunen (1974) and Gazdar, (1979) for demonstrations of this), this
ordering constraint is a pragmatic one.

    (10)   John does have children and his children are bald.
    (11)   *John's children are bald and he does have children.
    (12)   John did fail and he regrets having failed.
    (13)   *John regrets having failed and he did fail.
    (14)   Someone came and it wasn't John who came.
    (15)   *It wasn't John who came and someone came.
The constraint operative in these examples prohibits coordinate sentences of
the form S_0 *and* S_1 when S_0 presupposes S_1. It seems to be specific to *and,* thus
the counterparts of (11), (13) and (15) with *but* substituted are perfectly
acceptable:

    (16)   John's children are bald but he does have children.
    (17)   John regrets having failed but he did fail.
    (18)   It wasn't John who came but someone came.

B. Relevance and Relative Clauses

In Japanese there are two kinds of relative clause, *headed* and *headless*. The headed type can be formed freely whereas the headless type is much more restricted in possibilities of occurrence:

    (19a) Tarô wa sara no ue ni atta ringo o totte, poketto ni ireta
    (19b) Tarô wa ringo ga sara no ue ni atta no o totte, poketto ni ireta
          (= Taro picked up an apple which was on a plate and put it in a
          pocket)
    (20a) Tarô wa Hanako ga kinô katta ringo o totte, poketto ni ireta
    (20b) *Tarô wa Hanako ga kinô ringo o katta no o totte, poketo ni ireta
          (= Taro picked up an apple which Hanako bought yesterday)

(19a) and (20a) employ headed relatives whereas (19b) and (20b) contain headless relatives. The constraint which makes (20b) anomalous is not a syntactic or semantic one: rather it is pragmatic, having to do with the relevance of the relative to the matrix clause. Kuroda (1976, p. 270), to whom these observations are due, formulates it thus:

    (21) The Relevancy Condition: For a headless relative clause to be acceptable, it is necessary that it be interpreted pragmatically in such a way as to be directly relevant to the pragmatic content of its matrix clause.

In English, nonrestrictive relative clauses are subject to a constraint involving relevance. Consider the following putative dialogues:

    (22) A: None of your friends are alcoholic.
         B: John, who was at last night's party, drinks a lot.
    (23) A: None of your friends are alcoholic
         B: *John, who drinks a lot, was at last night's party.

The constraint operative appears to be of the following form: given two clauses S_0 and S_1, if S_0 is more relevant to the topic in hand than S_1 then S_1 may occur as a nonrestrictive relative in S_0, but not conversely (cf. Loetscher (1973), Morgan (1975) for further data and discussion).

V. Constraints on Deletion

A. Due to Illocutionary Force

Consider the following pairs of examples:

    (1a) Why do you paint your nails purple.
    (1b) Why paint your nails purple.
    (2a) Why don't you paint your nails green.
    (2b) Why not paint your nails green.

The (b)-sentences derive from the (a)-sentences via a rule of *you* + TENSE deletion. Notice that this rule is pragmatically conditioned: the (a)-sentences can be interpreted either as genuine questions or as indirect suggestions, the (b)-sentences can only be assigned the suggestion interpretation. A language production model for English will need to include a constraint roughly along the following lines:

(3) To ensure that *why* S is interpreted as *I suggest that not* S: delete *you* + TENSE from S.

In cases where S contains a negation then the two negations cancel out to yield an affirmative interpretation for the sentence: this explains why (2b) is heard as a suggestion that the addressee paint their nails green. (3) has consequences for the acceptability of sentences as the following examples (from Lee 1973, p. 39) show:

(4a) Why don't you resemble your father.
(4b) *Why not resemble your father.

(4b) is anomalous because the deletion forces a suggestion interpretation and yet, since "resembling" is nonvolitional that interpretation is not (readily) available. Note that if you imagine a suitable situation, say a make-up artist talking to an actor, then (4b) becomes acceptable. See Gordon and Lakoff (1971), Lee (1973) and Gazdar (1976a) for further discussion of this curious deletion rule.

You + TENSE deletion may be curious but at least the facts are reasonably well-behaved once one has grasped the principle involved. Altogether more anarchic is the case of a certain "syntactic truncation rule found in colloquial speech" (Morgan, 1975, p. 301):

(5a) Do you have any idea how much this is costing me?
(5b) Any idea how much this is costing me?

(5a) could be produced by a speaker making some kind of rhetorical point ("This is costing me thousands!") or by one genuinely seeking information. (5b) can only be produced by speakers of the latter type. Consider also, in this connection, the following pairs which are due to Brown and Levinson (1979):

(6a) Do you mind if I smoke?
(6b) Mind if I smoke?
(7a) Do you want a drink?
(7b) Wanna drink?
(8a) You ought to pay your bills
(8b) Oughta pay your bills

The contracted (b)-forms have a more restricted range of possible force interpretations than their corresponding uncontracted (a)-forms. Thus (6a) and (7a) can be merely questions, (6b) and (7b) cannot be—they have to carry the force of a *permission-request* and an *offer* respectively. (8a) can be simply a *statement* but (8b) must carry the force of *advice*. This, as Brown and Levinson (1979) show, has consequences for the acceptability of sentences:

(9a) You ought to pay your bills and you do.
(9b) *Oughta pay your bills and you do.
(10a) You ought to pay your bills but you don't.
(10b) Oughta pay your bills but you don't.

(9b) is unacceptable because it involves *advising* the addressee to do something he does anyway. At the present time a general formulation of the pragmatic constraint operative in examples (5)–(10) is not available.

Sadock has noted another curious tie-up between deletion and illocutionary force, one which may be related to the phenomena discussed in the previous paragraph: "the deletion of the second-person subject of imperative-form sentences is obligatory for most of the speech-act types that imperative form encodes. For warnings, however, the deletion is optional. Thus (11b) can be many things, including a warning, but (11a) can only be taken as a warning" (Sadock (1977, p. 70)).

(11a)   Don't you eat too much.
(11b)   Don't eat too much.

B. Not Due to Illocutionary Force

In English, according to Lakoff (1971), the auxiliary verb *will* can sometimes be deleted, but other times it cannot be:

(12a)   The Yankees will play the Red Sox tomorrow.
(12b)   The Yankees play the Red Sox tomorrow.
(13a)   The Yankees will play well tomorrow.
(13b)   *The Yankees play well tomorrow.
(14a)   I will get my paycheck tomorrow.
(14b)   I get my paycheck tomorrow.
(15a)   I will get a cold tomorrow.
(15b)   *I get a cold tomorrow.

Lakoff (1971b, p. 339) from whom this data is taken, credits Kim Burt with discovering the principle which accounts for these examples:

(16)   *Will* can be deleted just in case the event described is one the speaker can be sure of.

Notice that if it is assumed that the quality of the Yankees' performance is wholly determined by a crooked gambling syndicate then (13b) becomes acceptable. Likewise if the speaker of (15b) is known to be a guinea pig in a cold germ experiment.

Morgan (1975, pp. 300–301) has drawn attention to the fact that verb deletion in English comparatives and similes is pragmatically conditioned:

(17a)   Fido is bigger than an alsatian is.
(17b)   Fido is bigger than an alsatian.
(18a)   Fido is as big as an alsatian is.
(18b)   Fido is as big as an alsatian.

All four sentences can be appropriately used if Fido is a large dog (e.g. a St. Bernard). But the (a)-sentences could not be used if Fido is, say, known to be a large chihuahua, whereas the (b)-sentences would be usable in this case, assuming a hyperbolic interpretation. We can formulate the constraint as follows:

(19)   Verb deletion in comparatives and similes is obligatory when it is obvious from the context that the speaker is exaggerating.

Gapping is a well-known deletion rule which allows (20b) to be derived from (20a):

(20a)   John persuaded Bill to examine Jane, and John persuaded Tom to
        examine Martha.
(20b)   John persuaded Bill to examine Jane, and Tom, Martha.

A purely syntactic formulation of *Gapping* would also allow (20b) to be
derived from (21):

(21)   John persuaded Bill to examine Jane, and Tom persuaded Bill to
        examine Martha.

But if (20b) is uttered without emphatic stress on any of the NPs then (21) is
not a possible interpretation of it. Kuno (1976) explains this previously
puzzling observation by invoking the following pragmatic constraint on the
application of *Gapping*:

(22)   Constituents deleted by *Gapping* must be contextually known. On the
        other hand, the two constituents left behind by *Gapping* necessarily
        represent new information and, therefore, must be paired with
        constituents in the first conjunct that represent new information
        (Kuno (1976, p. 310)).

Because of its position in the sentence, the NP *John*, when unstressed, has to
represent old information, thus *Tom* cannot be paired with *John* and (21) is
thereby eliminated as a potential source for (20b) (cf. Jake (1977) on the
pragmatics of *Gapping*).

Other deletion rules known to be subject to pragmatic constraints are *to be*
deletion in English (Borkin, 1973) and *ser + -do* deletion in Portuguese
(Vroman, 1975).

VI. Morphology†

The languages of the world are littered with particles, clitics and affixes whose
only function is to signal the speaker's attitude towards the addressee, persons
referred to, or to the proposition expressed. Most familiar, to layman and
linguist alike, are the deference or politeness markers known as honorifics.
These are found in many languages of which Japanese is perhaps the best
known. Comrie (1976) gives the following examples:

(1)   Tanaka-san ga Mary o matu
(2)   Tanaka-san ga Mary o matimasu
(3)   Tanaka-san ga Mary o omati da
(4)   Tanaka-san ga Mary o omati desu

All four sentences mean that Mr. Tanaka is waiting for Mary but a speaker
who wished to display politeness to his addressee would use (2), if he wished to
display politeness to Mr. Tanaka he would use (3), if he wanted to display
politeness to his addressee *and* Mr. Tanaka then he would use (4). (1) displays
politeness neither to Mr. Tanaka nor to the addressee.

Languages as diverse as Basque, Hidatsa, Finnish and English contain
morphemes which qualify the proposition expressed. Consider Basque:

† The title of this section should not be taken too seriously.

(5a)   Patxi'k lerkai'rekin Franco'ri etorriko da
(5b)   Patxi'k lerkai'rekin Franco'ri etorriko omen da

Corum (1975b, pp. 91–2) observes that, while (5a) and (5b) both mean that Patxi will come with a bomb for Franco, (5b), which contains the morpheme *omen*, would be used in preference to (5a) when the speaker was simply reporting something he had heard and for the veracity of which he was not prepared to take full responsibility.

Hidatsa has a number of sentence-final "mood" morphemes which indicate the degree and the nature of the speaker's commitment to what he is saying (Matthews, 1965, pp. 99–101).

(6a)   wacéo wío i kikúhao ski
(6b)   wacéo wío i kikúhao c
(6c)   wacéo wío i kikúhao toak
(6d)   wacéo wío i kikúhao rahe
(6e)   wacéo wío i kikúhao wareac

What these sentences have in common is the expression of the proposition that the man heard a woman. Examples (6a) to (6c) involve decreasing degrees of speaker commitment to the truth of this proposition: (6a) involves strong commitment, (6b) weaker commitment, and (6c) indicates that the speaker does not know whether the proposition is true or not. Example (6d) would be used by a speaker whose only evidence for the truth of the proposition was that he had heard it from someone else, and (6e) indicates the speaker's belief that the proposition expressed is widely known to be true.

Finnish has a range of clitics which attach to the first word in the utterance and which signal the speaker's attitude to what he is saying. Karttunen (1975, p. 256) offers the following glosses for three of them:

-han :   I am in a position to say this to you
-pa   :   I invite no response
-s   :   I deliver this personally

In English too it turns out, doubtless somewhat to the surprise of native speakers of this "ordinary" language, that morphological choices can be used to convey the speaker's attitude to what he is saying. Consider the following examples:

(7)   A: When is Boris coming?
      B: ⎧ Three o'clock
         ⎪ Why, three o'clock
         ⎨ *Well, three o'clock
         ⎩ Well, his train leaves about now

(8a)   Boris arrives at, ah, three o'clock
(8b)   Boris arrives at, uh, three o'clock
(8c)   Boris arrives at, oh, three o'clock
(8d)   Boris arrives at, well, three o'clock
(8e)   Boris arrives at, why, three o'clock
(8f)   Boris arrives at, say, three o'clock

In (7) B's answer-initial *why* indicates surprise that the question was asked, his answer-initial *well* indicates that the answer is in some sense incomplete: when the answer is apparently complete, as in "well, three o'clock", anomaly results. The examples in (8) illustrate the use of *ah* to indicate that the speaker has only come into possession of the information conveyed at the instant prior to utterance; the use of *uh* to indicate that the information conveyed is approximate; the use of *oh* to indicate that the information conveyed is exact; the use of *well* to indicate that there is more to be said; the use of *why* to indicate that the speaker finds the information conveyed surprising; and the use of *say* to indicate the hypotheticality of the proposition expressed. Much fuller discussion of the properties of these fascinating and neglected English particles can be found in James (1972, 1973) and Lakoff (1973).

English also supplies its speakers with morphemes whose presence and position in a sentence indicate the illocutionary force intended by the speaker, sentence-initial *here* is one such:

(9a)   I want a drink
(9b)   Here, I want a drink
(10a) Can you move your foot
(10b) Here, can you move your foot
(11a) I can do that
(11b) Here, I can do that
(12a) Do you want a drink
(12b) Here, do you want a drink

(9a) can be used as, at least, either a statement or a request, (9b) can only be a request. (10a) can be used as a question or a request, (10b) can only be a request. (11a) can be used as a statement or an offer, (11b) can only be an offer. (12a) can be used as a question or an offer, (12b) can only be an offer. In every case the presence of sentence-initial *here* reduces the range of potential illocutionary forces that the following sentence can be used for.

More familiar, but more puzzling, are the facts concerning the morpheme *please*. This can occur preverbally, sentence-finally and sentence-initially. The preverbal position is the most restricted and the sentence-initial the least restricted (Ross, 1975, p. 238). The exact nature of the restrictions are not at present known, but they appear to be connected with how readily the sentence (without *please*) can be used as a request. This is illustrated by the following data, adapted from Gordon and Lakoff (1971, p. 98) and Ross (1975, p. 238) (cf. Sadock, 1977, p. 71; 1974, pp. 88–90, 104, 107–8, 120–4):

(13a)   Please, I will freeze out here
(13b)   *I will freeze out here, please
(13c)   **I will please freeze out here
(14a)   Please, are you able to call back later
(14b)   Are you able to call back later, please
(14c)   ??Are you able to please call back later
(15a)   Please, can you call back later
(15b)   Can you call back later, please
(15c)   Can you please call back later

Certain South American Indian languages employ particles and affixes whose occurrence in sentences is pragmatically constrained by the relation that sentence, and its parts, bear to the discourse of which it is a part. Thus Cubeo has a particle *cari* which "marks the main event line of a discourse . . . when it tags a noun phrase, it is identifying one of the main characters of the discourse . . . when it tags a verb phrase, it is identifying an action that contributes to the movement of the plot" (Longacre, 1976, p. 469). The language Cayapa has a verb suffix—*ren* whose occurrence on a dependent verb "indicates that the independent verb with which it is associated is on the main event line of the discourse" (Longacre, 1976, p. 469) and whose occurrence on an independent verb "means that while the action of that verb itself is not important to the discourse, the action of the independent verb in the following sentence is important to the structure of the discourse" (Longacre, 1976, p. 470). Longacre goes on to discuss similar devices in Inga, Guajiro and Ica.

Some languages mark the sex of the speaker and/or addressee in their morphology. A classic example of this phenomenon is the oft-cited case of Biloxi imperatives discussed in Haas (1944). The following sentences would all be translated into English as "carry it!":

    (16a)   ki-tkí
    (16b)   ki-taté
    (16c)   ki-kaŋkó

(16a) would have been used (Biloxi is now extinct) when addressing a woman, (16b) would have been used by a woman addressing a man, and (16c) would have been used by a man addressing a man.

VII. Phonology and Phonetics

A. Stress and Intonation

That the stress patterns and intonation contours assigned to English sentences are massively constrained by the context in which the sentences are uttered is a widely recognized but largely mysterious fact. Attempts have been made recently to associate particular intonation contours with particular "meanings" independent of the sentence upon which the contour is imposed (Liberman, 1975; Liberman and Sag, 1974; Sag and Liberman, 1975). These attempts have been criticized by Cutler (1977) who shows that the contour, the context and the sentence uttered are inextricably inter-related.

Much of the work on stress assignment in generative grammar has, to all intents and purposes, ignored the constraints imposed by the context (see for example, Chomsky and Halle, 1968; Bresnan, 1971; G. Lakoff, 1972, for important exemplars). This has been defended by reference to a notion of "normal stress", a notion which Schmerling (1974) shows to be undefinable and lacking a theory-independent characterization. Only Bolinger (e.g. 1972), Ladd (1978) and Schmerling herself (most fully in 1976a) have begun to examine seriously the contextual constraints on English sentence stress. Schmerling proposes, along with certain general syntàctic conditions which also apply, the following two pragmatic conditions on stress assignment:

    (1)   Certain items in an utterance are treated by the speaker as relatively "insignificant" and fail to be assigned stress. (1976a, p. 75)

    (2)   In a topic-comment utterance, stress both the topic and the comment. (1976, p. 94)

There are many examples in the literature which show the effect of contextual assumptions on stress, but we only have space to consider three representative cases here. The first is due to G. Lakoff (1971c, p. 63):

    (3a)   John called Máry a virgin and then she insulted hím.

    (3b)   John called Máry a virgin and then she insulted him.

The speaker of (3a) must be assuming that to call someone a virgin is to insult them, whereas the speaker of (3b) is not making any such assumption.

    Schmerling (1976a, p. 91) gives the following pair of examples:

    (4a)   The statue's head is missing

    (4b)   The statue's head is missing

She observes that (4b) would be an appropriate thing for a museum guide to say to a visitor, whereas (4a) would be the appropriate thing to say if one were reporting an act of vandalism to the relevant authorities.

    The plural quantifier *some* in English is subject to the stress-conditioned phonological contraction process summarized in (5):

    (5)   s$\tilde{\text{A}}$m → [sm̩]

Whether or not the quantifier gets stressed in the first place is subject to a pragmatic condition as the following examples illustrate

    (6a)   [sʌm] graduate students were at the meeting.

    (6b)   [sm̩] graduate students were at the meeting.

The speaker who wishes to imply that some graduate students were *not* at the meeting will produce (6a), whereas the speaker who wishes to remain neutral in that respect will produce (6b) (see Butterworth and Gazdar (1977) for much fuller discussion).

B. Secondary Articulations

Stress and intonation are not the only aspects of phonology to be subject to pragmatic constraints although it is probably widely assumed that they are. In this section I shall draw attention to three cases which I suspect represent the tip of an unexplored iceberg of similar phenomena to be found in the world's languages.

    Corum has observed that speakers of Basque when addressing those with whom they feel some solidarity "will palatalize several consonants which are not otherwise palatalized" (1975b, p. 96). She gives the following examples (1975b, p. 97):

(7) | Nonsolidary | Solidary | English |
|---|---|---|
| polit | pol'it | pretty |
| onon | on'on' | bonbon |
| neska | neška | girl |
| tipi | t'ipi | little |
| tzar | čar | naughty |
| zakur | šakur | dog |
| eder | ejer | beautiful |

Her conclusion is worth quoting:

> Even if the rule of palatalization were able to look back to another level of the derivation, it isn't very clear how such information as to the speaker's feelings would be included in any level of derivation. We are faced with a case of a phonological rule completely dependent on the context of utterance for its environment (1975b, p. 97).

French has a pragmatically conditioned phonological rule that we may refer to as "dismissive labialization". Consider (8a) and 8b):†

(8a) [sɛt etydjã   na pa fɛ d tʀavaj   pãdã tul tʀimɛstʀ]

(8b) [ᵚ[sɛt etydjã: na pa fɛ d tʀavaj   pãdã tul tʀimɛstʀ]]

this student has not done any work during all the term.

(8a) could be used appropriately by someone who was seriously worried about the student's progress, whereas (8b) would be used by someone who had long ago given up being surprised at or caring about the student in question.

Several writers (e.g. Cutler, 1974, p. 117; Zwicky and Sadock, 1973, p. 23) have drawn attention to the ironic or sarcastic use of nasalization in English. This phenomenon is clearly on a par with those just considered.

(9a) [ˆʃʊə dʒ enərət,ɪv sɪmæntɪks ɪz wɛər ɪts rɪəli: æt]

(9b) [~[ˆʃʊə dʒenərətɪv sɪmæntɪks ɪz wɛər ɪts rɪəli: æt]]

Some years ago the present writer could have uttered (9a) but not (9b). The history of linguistics has seen to it that this usability pattern is now reversed.

References

Bolinger, D. L. (1972). Accent is predictable (if you're a mind reader). *Language* **48**, 633–44.

Borkin, A. (1973). To be and not to be. *CLS* **9**, 44–56.

Bresnan, J. W. (1971). Sentence Stress and Syntactic Transformations. *Language* **47**, 257–81.

Brown, P. and Levinson, S. C. (1978). Universals in language Usage: Politeness Phenomena. In "Questions and Politeness: Strategies in Social Interaction" (E. N. Goody, ed.) Cambridge University Press, Cambridge.

Butterworth, B. and Gazdar G. (1977). Quantifier contraction. Paper presented to the Spring Meeting, Linguistics Association of Great Britain, Walsall.

---

† The initial diacritics in (8b) and (9b) indicate that all the bracketed material is labialized or nasalized, respectively.

Chomsky, N. and Halle, M. (1968). "The Sound Pattern of English". Harper and Row, New York.

Clark, E. V. (1974). Normal states and evaluative viewpoints. *Language* **50**, 316–332.

Cole, P. and Morgan, J. L. (1975). "Syntax and Semantics 3: Speech Acts". Academic Press, New York.

Comrie, B. (1976). Linguistic politeness axes: speaker-addressee, speaker-reference, speaker-bystander. *Pragmatics Microfiche* **1.7**, A3–B1.

Corum, C. (1975a). A pragmatic analysis of parenthetic adjuncts, *CLS* **11**, 133–141.

Corum, C. (1975b). Basques, particles, and babytalk: a case for pragmatics. *Proceedings of the 1st Annual Meeting of the Berkeley Linguistics Society*, pp. 90–99.

Cutler, A. (1974). On saying what you mean without meaning what you say. *CLS* **10**, 117–27.

Cutler, A. (1977). The context dependence of "intonational meanings". *CLS* **13**, 104–115.

Davidson, D. and Harman, G. H. (1972). *Semantics of Natural Language*. Reidel, Dordrecht.

Dixon, R. M. W. (1972). *The Dyirbal Language of North Queensland*. Cambridge University Press, Cambridge.

Fillmore, C. J. (1975) Santa Cruz lectures on deixis. Indiana University Linguistics Club mimeo.

Fillmore, C. J. and Langendoen, D. T. (1971). *Studies in Linguistic Semantics*. Holt, Rinehart and Winston, New York.

Gazdar, G. (1976a). Polarity items in interrogatives. *Language Research* **12**, 279–280.

Gazdar, G. (1976b). Quantifying context. *York Papers in Linguistics* **6**, 117–132.

Gazdar, G. (1979). *Pragmatics*. Academic Press, New York.

Gazdar, G. and Pullum, G. K. (1976). Truth-functional connectives in natural language. *CLS* **12**, 220–34.

Givon, T. (1975). Negation in language: pragmatics, function, ontology. *Pragmatics Microfiche* **1.2**, A2–G14.

Goody, E. N. (1978). *Questions and Politeness: Strategies in Social Interaction*. Cambridge University Press, Cambridge.

Gordon, D. and Lakoff, G. (1971). Conversational postulates. *In* "Syntax and Semantics 3: Speech Acts." (P. Cole and J. Morgan eds). Academic Press, New York.

Green, G. M. (1974a). The function of form and the form of function. *CLS* **10**, 186–197.

Green, G. M. (1974b). *Semantics and syntactic regularity*. Indiana University Press, Bloomington.

Grice, H. P. (1975). Logic and conversation. *In* "Syntax and Semantics 3: Speech Acts." (P. Cole and J. Morgan eds). Academic Press, New York.

Gross, M., *et al.* (1973). *The Formal Analysis of Natural Languages*. Mouton, The Hague.

Grossman, R. E. *et al.* (1975). *Papers from the Parasession on Functionalism*. Chicago Linguistic Society, Chicago.

Gumperz, J. (1975). Code-switching in conversation. *Pragmatics Microfiche* **1.4**, A2–D4.

Haas, M. R. (1944). Men's and women's speech in Koasati. *Language* **20**, 142–9.

Hankamer, J. (1974). On the non-cyclic nature of WH-clefting. *CLS* **10**, 221–233.

Horn, L. R. (1972). On the semantic properties of logical operators in English. Indiana University Linguistics Club mimeo.

Jake, J. (1977). Gapping, pragmatics, and factivity. *CLS* **13**, 165–172.

James, D. (1972). Some aspects of the syntax and semantics of interjections. *CLS* **8**, 162–72.

James, D. (1973). Another look at, say, some grammatical constraints, on, oh, interjections and hesitations. *CLS* **9**, 242–51.

Kachru, B. B. *et al.* (1973). *Issues in Linguistics*. University of Illinois Press, Urbana.

Karttunen, F. (1975). Functional constraints in Finnish syntax. *In* "Papers from the Parasession on Functionalism." (R. E. Grossman *et al.*, eds). Chicago Linguistic Society, Chicago.

Karttunen, L. (1974). Presupposition and linguistic context. *Theoretical Linguistics* **1**, 182–194.

Kuno, S. (1976). Gapping: a functional analysis. *Linguistic Inquiry* **7**, 300–318.

Kuroda, S. Y. (1976). Headless relative clauses in modern Japanese and the relevancy condition. *Proceedings of the 2nd Annual Meeting of the Berkeley Linguistics Society*, pp. 269–279.

Ladd, D. R. (1978). The structure of intonational meaning. Ph.D. Dissertation, Cornell University.

Lakoff, G. (1971a). On generative semantics. *In* "Semantics" (D. D. Steinberg and L. A. Jakobovits eds). Cambridge University Press, Cambridge.

Lakoff, G. (1971b). Presupposition and relative well-formedness. *In* "Semantics" (D. D. Steinberg and L. A. Jakobovits eds). Cambridge University Press, Cambridge.

Lakoff, G. (1971c). The role of deduction in grammar. *In* "Studies in Linguistic Semantics". (J. Fillmore and D. T. Langendrem). Holt, Rinehart and Winston, New York.

Lakoff, G. (1972). The global nature of the nuclear stress rule. *Language* **48**, 285–303.

Lakoff, R. (1972). The pragmatics of modality. *CLS* **8**, 229–46.

Lakoff, R. (1973). Questionable answers and answerable questions. *In* "Issues in Linguistics". (B. B. Kachra *et al.*, eds). University of Illinois Press, Urbana.

Lee, C. (1973). The performative analysis of "why not V?" *Language Sciences* **25**, 39–41.

Liberman, M. (1975). The intonational system of English. MIT: PhD dissertation.

Liberman, M. and Sag, I. (1974). Prosodic form and discourse function. *CLS* **10**, 416–27.

Linde, C. (1976). Constraints on the ordering of if-clauses. *Proceedings of the 2nd Annual Meeting of the Berkeley Linguistics Society*, pp. 280–285.

Loetscher, A. (1973). On the role of nonrestrictive relative clauses in discourse. *CLS* **9**, 356–368.

Longacre, R. E. (1976). "Mystery" particles and affixes. *CLS* **12**, 468–475.

Longuet-Higgins, C. (1976). . . . And out walked the cat. *Pragmatics Microfiche* **1.7**, G1–G14.

Matthews, G. H. (1965). *Hidatsa syntax*. Mouton, The Hague.

McCawley, J. D. (1972). A program for logic. *In* "Semantics of Natural Language". (D. Davidson and G. H. Harman eds). Reidel, Dordrecht.

Morgan, J. L. (1975a). Some interactions of syntax and pragmatics. *In* "Syntax and Semantics 3: Speech Acts". (P. Cole and J. Morgan eds). Academic Press, New York.

Morgan, J. L. (1975b). Some remarks on the nature of sentences. *In* "Papers from the Parasession in Functionalism". (R. E. Grossman *et al.*, eds). Chicago Linguistics Society, Chicago.

Postal, P. M. (1974). *On Raising*. MIT Press, Cambridge.

Postal, P. M. (1977). About a "nonargument" for Raising. *Linguistic Inquiry* **8**, 141–154.

Quasthoff, U. (1977). *Sprachstruktur–Socialstruktur*. Kronberg: Scriptor Verlag.

Rodman, R. (1975). The pragmatics of right dislocations. *Pragmatics Microfiche* **1.1** G9–G13.

Rogers, A. *et al.* (1977). *Proceedings of the Texas conference on Performatives, Presuppositions and Implicatures*. Center for Applied Linguistics, Washington.

Ross, J. R. (1973). Slifting. *In* "The Formal Analysis of Natural Language". (M. Gross *et al.*, eds). Mouton, The Hague.

Ross, J. R. (1975). Where to do things with words. *In* "Syntax and Semantics 3: Speech Acts". (P. Cole and J. Morgan eds). Academic Press, New York.

Sacks, H. and Schegloff, E. A. (1977). Two preferences in the organization of reference to persons in conversation and their interaction. *In* "Sprachstrucktur, Socialstruktur" (U. Quasthoff, ed.) Scriptor Verlag, Kronberg.

Sadock, J. M. (1974). *Toward a Linguistic Theory of Speech Acts*. Academic Press, New York.

Sadock, J. M. (1977). Aspects of linguistic pragmatics. *In* "Proceedings of the Texas Conference on Performatives, Presuppositions and Implications". (A. Rogers, *et al.*, eds). Center for Applied Linguistics, Washington.

Sag, I. and Liberman, M. (1975). The intonational disambiguation of indirect speech acts. *CLS* **11**, 487–497.

Schmerling, S. F. (1974). A re-examination of 'normal stress'. *Language* **50**, 66–73.

Schmerling, S. F. (1976a). *Aspects of English sentence stress*. University of Texas Press, Austin.

Schmerling, S. F. (1976b). Synonymy judgements as linguistic evidence. *Texas Linguistic Forum* **4**, 118–131.

Sheintuch, G. and Wise, K. (1976). On the pragmatic unity of the rules of Neg-raising and Neg-attraction. *CLS* **12**, 548–557.

Sinha, A. K. (1972). On the deictic use of 'coming' and 'going' in Hindi. *CLS* **8**, 351–358.

Steinberg, D. D. and Jakobovits, L. A. (1971). *Semantics*. Cambridge University Press, Cambridge.

Vroman, W. V. (1975). Portugese latent passives. *CLS* **11**, 638–48.

Zwicky, A. M. and Sadock, J. M. (1973). Ambiguity tests and how to fail them. *Ohio State University Working Papers in Linguistics* **16**, 1–34.

4

The Role of Language Production Processes in The Organization of Behaviour in Face-to-Face Interaction[1]

G. W. Beattie   *University of Sheffield*

I. Introduction

The main focus of this chapter is the relationship between the cognitive processes underlying spontaneous speech and the organization, and functions, of nonverbal behaviour in conversational interaction. The first aim of the research has been to identify the units of encoding involved in the generation of spontaneous speech using evidence, firstly from hesitations and other paralinguistic phenomena contained in speech (see Goldman-Eisler, 1968), and secondly from nonverbal behaviours (such as speaker-gaze) which accompany speech and appear to reflect cognitive processing in speech (Kendon, 1967). The second aim has been to describe the physical relationship between various forms of nonverbal behaviour and the linguistic, but more especially the psycholinguistic, units comprising spontaneous speech. The third aim has been to consider the implications of speech-based patterns in nonverbal behaviour for the regulation of conversation. The methodology has involved detailed analysis of video-recordings of naturally—occurring (largely dyadic) interactions. The work thus far has concentrated on samples of supervisions and seminars recorded at the Psychological Laboratory, University of Cambridge.

II. Part 1: Encoding Units in Spontaneous Speech

Lounsbury (1954, p. 100) was the first to hypothesize that the distribution of hesitations in speech might reveal something about the nature of encoding units in spontaneous speech. "Hesitation pauses and points of high statistical uncertainty correspond to the beginnings of units of encoding." The earliest experimental studies on this hypothesis focussed on encoding units at the word level, and a significant relationship between hesitations and words of relatively low transitional probability, as measured by the Shannon guessing technique, was reported (Goldman-Eisler, 1958 a, b). However, these studies

[1]This research was carried out at the Psychological Laboratory, the University of Cambridge while the author was a member of Trinity College. It forms part of a Ph.D. dissertation (University of Cambridge, 1978).

have subsequently been criticised both for their use of an unrepresentative sample of speech, and for their dubious statistical analysis (Boomer, 1970).

Other evidence has suggested that the typical encoding unit is somewhat larger than the word. Maclay and Osgood (1959) observed that false starts usually involve not just corrections of the unintended word but also correction of the associated function words. Boomer (1965) analysed the distribution of hesitations with respect to phonemic clauses (which are phonologically marked macrosegments containing one, and only one, primary stress, and ending in one of the terminal junctions/I, II, III/ (Trager and Smith, 1957), and observed that both unfilled pauses (UPs) and filled pauses (FPs: "ah", "er", "um" etc.) tended to occur towards the beginnings of such clauses. He thus concluded that "planning ranges forward to encompass a structured 'chunk' of syntax and meaning" (Boomer, 1965, p. 91), where such chunks were thought to correspond to phonemic clauses. However, the modal position of hesitations was found to be between the first and second word of the clause, and not before the first word, as expected. This result has been given a number of interpretations. Barik (1968) argued that Boomer's decision to regard all UPs at clause junctures (unless accompanied by an FP or word fragment) as "facultative accompaniments of terminal junctures ... essentially linguistic" (1965, p. 89) was too conservative, and he hypothesized that long juncture pauses (i.e. UPs $\geq$ 500 ms) have a cognitive as well as purely linguistic function. By this criterion the modal position of hesitations shifts to before the first word of the clause. An alternative interpretation has suggested that the modal position of hesitations is as observed, because a new syntactic clause is often introduced at this point (Fodor et al., 1974, p. 424). This interpretation suggests that the syntactic clause is the basic unit of encoding. There is evidence from another source to support this hypothesis. Valian (1971), using reaction times as an index of processing load, found that speakers' reaction times to randomly generated tones were significantly faster when the tones occurred on the last, rather than on the first words of syntactic clauses in their speech. However, since syntactic clauses do not invariably begin after the first word of phonemic clauses (Fodor et al., 1974, p. 422), any conclusion from the Boomer (1965) data on syntactic clauses must be tentatively drawn. For stronger support, the analysis of hesitations must be performed with respect to syntactic clauses.

A number of other studies have found that if the duration of individual pause and phonation periods in speech are measured and graphically represented, then, when lines are fitted to represent changes in relative fluency, a cyclic pattern of relatively steep slopes (high pause/phonation ratio) alternating with relatively shallow slopes (low pause/phonation ratio) appears in samples of spontaneous speech, but not in those of prose readings. Moreover, it is typically observed that the fluent phases of these cycles are characterized by fewer filled hesitations (FPs, repetition, and false starts), and by a higher proportion of pauses at grammatical junctures. The amount of pausing in the hesitant phases of these cycles has also been found to be directly related to the amount of phonation in the succeeding fluent phases. It has thus been hypothesized that the fluent phases are planned in the preceding hesitant phases (Henderson et al., 1966; Goldman-Eisler, 1967). Cycle times have been found to range between 10·6 and 39·3 s, with a mean of 18·0 s (Butterworth, 1975) which suggests that such units are substantially larger than individual clauses. These temporal or cognitive cycles have also been found to correspond to intuitively determined "idea" boundaries in the speech text (Butterworth, 1975). This suggests that the main encoding units are semantic and not syntactic in nature.

However, because of a number of lacunae in the research, none of these studies can be considered to allow definitive conclusions about encoding units in speech. The first lacuna in the research is that no study has successfully accounted for all (or nearly all) the hesitation data. In the Boomer (1965) study, only 54·3% of hesitations could be accounted for by holistic planning of the clause, since 45·7% of hesitations occurred later than the second word of the clause. No attempt was made to determine the function of these residual pauses. Similarly, studies of temporal cycles have found that hesitations, whose function could not be semantic planning, occur in the fluent phases of cycles. Henderson et al., (1966) reported that 45·7% of all UPs at non-grammatical junctures occurred in these fluent phases. Butterworth (1976) has suggested that some of these hesitations may be used for lexical selection, and he has in fact shown that approximately 32% of pauses in the fluent phases of cycles precede relatively unpredictable words. The function of the majority of hesitations in fluent phases, however, has still to be elucidated.

The second lacuna in all earlier studies is that inferences about cognitive processes in speech have been made solely on the basis of analyses of hesitations. It is clear, however, that some pauses may have a linguistic or social function, since some (notably UPs at grammatical junctures) occur even in reading (Goldman-Eisler, 1972). Other pauses may have less obvious social functions. For example, it has been hypothesized that filled pauses are used in conversation to prevent interruption by the listener (Maclay and Osgood, 1959; Beattie, 1977). It would clearly be useful to have access to additional information about the nature of cognitive processing in speech. One other potential indicator of cognitive activity is the patterning of gaze of a speaker engaged in conversation. Speaker gaze at the facial region of the listener is mainly used to monitor information from the listener—to ascertain how the message is being received, and to determine if any of the anticipatory movements which precede listener interruption are occurring (Kendon, 1967, 1972). Such monitoring can interfere with the cognitive planning underlying speech and there is evidence to suggest that gaze aversion occurs during planning periods to reduce such interference. Nielsen (1962) observed that subjects averted gaze when preparing arguments in conversation. Kendon (1967) found that gaze aversion was more likely during slow, hesitant speech than during fluent speech. Exline and Winters (1965) found that the overall amount of gaze in conversation was inversely related to the cognitive difficulty of the topic of conversation. Weiner and Ehrlichman (1976), in a re-analysis of the Ehrlichman *et al.*, (1974) data, discovered significantly more instances of eye closing when subjects were answering spatial rather than verbal questions (presumably because more interference is likely between the incoming visual information and the imagery processes required in answering spatial questions). Thus, analysis of speaker gaze does seem to provide information about the occurrence and even the nature of cognitive processing underlying speech, in dialogue.

Thus, the present study analyses the distribution of hesitations in speech, in an attempt to elucidate the main encoding units involved in the generation of spontaneous speech, and, in addition, analyses direction of speaker gaze as further evidence of cognitive processing. Since previous studies have left much of the data unaccounted for, it seems necessary to consider both semantic (temporal cycles) and syntactic units, and to investigate possible interactions between them in the generation of spontaneous speech.

1. *Procedure*

Four interactions were filmed, three were hour-long supervisions involving either a graduate student or a member of staff at the University of Cambridge as supervisor; and an undergraduate. The remaining sample involved two participants of a seminar, engaged in a prolonged interaction. All speakers were male and only one interaction involved a mixed sex pair. The supervisions and seminar took place in a comfortable observation room with Sony video-cameras located behind a one-way mirror. All subjects were informed that filming was to take place.

The present study concentrated on the speech and gaze of five subjects. The speech samples analysed were randomly selected from the speech corpus, with the constraint that the speaker's turn in conversation had to be at least 30 s in length, so that temporal cycles could be identified. The present corpus consists of 202 syntactic clauses, 1433 words and 137 hesitations.

(*a*) *Hesitation Analysis.* Two types of hesitation were examined—unfilled pauses (UPs) and filled pauses (FPs). UPs were defined as periods of silence $\geq$ 200 ms; these were identified and measured using an Ediswan pen oscillograph and pause detector. FPs consist of the following speech sounds /ɑ, ɛ, æ, r, ə, m̩/. The mean duration of FPs were estimated to be approximately 300 ms. The location of each hesitation was marked on the speech transcript. A distributional analysis of UPs and FPs with respect to syntactic (surface structure) clauses was carried out. In the present analyses only the surface structure clauses have been considered (see Fodor *et al.*, 1974). Surface structure clauses longer than ten words were ignored as there were too few of them to allow reliable analysis. Hesitations occurring in the juncture between two clauses were classified as occupying the clause-initial position of the succeeding clause (see Boomer, 1965, p. 84).

A visual analogue of the speech, identifying periods of pausing and phonation, was prepared in the manner described by Henderson *et al.* (1966). Each individual pause and period of phonation was plotted on a graph. Lines were fitted to represent changes in the pause/phonation ratio across time, in such a way as to minimize the deviation of local changes in these two variables from the lines (see Henderson *et al.*, 1966, p. 208). This procedure was checked by two independent judges. Some minor adjustments were necessary before perfect agreement was reached. A transcript of the speech was made, and transition times between cycles and cycle phases were determined from the graphs and mapped into the transcripts, using the timer mixed on the video screen to determine the precise temporal location of any given word in the speech corpus. Thus it was possible to determine which clauses constituted each cycle and each phase of the cycle.

(*b*) *Analysis of Gaze.* Subjects were filmed with Sony cameras, fitted with zoom lenses, and a split-screen video circuit was employed for the judgement of gaze. The occurrence or non-occurrence of speaker gaze at the listener was noted at each word boundary in his speech. In order to avoid a possible distance artefact in gaze judgement (Stephenson and Rutter, 1970), gaze was judged from a videoscreen. The inter-observer reliability for two independent judges in the scoring of gaze was 94·6%.

2. *Results*
(*a*) *Hesitation analysis*
(i) Temporal cycles. When individual pause and phonation periods were graphically represented, and lines fitted to represent changes in relative fluency across time, a cyclic pattern emerged, with hesitant phases (high pause/phonation ratio) alternating with fluent phases (low pause/phonation ratio) see Fig. 1. In all, 20 complete cycles (both phases present) were

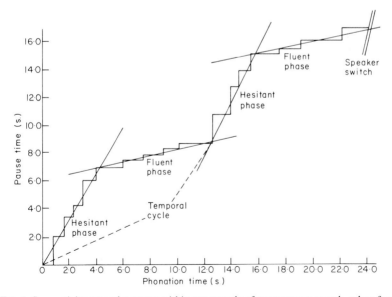

FIG. 1. Sequential temporal patterns within one sample of spontaneous speech, taken from a dyadic conversation. (From Beattie, 1979a.)

TABLE 1

Number and percentage of clauses containing hesitations, whose mean length is also indicated (from Beattie, 1979a).

	Number containing hesitation(s)	Percentage containing hesitation(s)	Number containing hesitation in clause-initial position	Percentage containing hesitation in clause-initial position	Number of hesitations in clause-initial position	Mean length of hesitation in clause-initial position (ms)
All clauses (2–10 words)	73	45·91	51	32·08	62	807
Short clauses (2–5 words)	38	38·38	28	28·28	32	676
Long clauses (6–10 words)	35	58·33	23	38·33	30	966

observed, as well as seven incomplete cycles, bounded by speaker switches. The mean cycle time was found to be 21·88 s (S.D. = 15·68). 47·12% of all single hesitations (UPs or FPs), or combination of UPs and FPs, occurred in the hesitant phases of these temporal cycles, compared with 52·88% in fluent phases.

The cycles contained a mean of 8·80 clauses, hesitant phases a mean of 3·57 clauses, and fluent phases a mean of 5·23 clauses. There was no significant difference in the length of clauses in hesitant and fluent phases ($G = 0·220$, $p > 0·05$; Sokal and Rohlf, 1973). There were 52 short clauses (2–6 words in length) in hesitant phases compared with 66 in fluent phases; there were also 21 long clauses (7–12 words) in hesitant phases and 33 in fluent phases.

(ii) Hesitations and syntactic clauses. The number and percentage of clauses occupied by a hesitation (UP or FP) was noted (See Table I); 45·91% of all clauses contained a hesitation. Long clauses (6–10 words) were significantly more likely to contain a hesitation than short clauses (2–5 words), $G = 5·21$ ($p < 0·05$). This significant effect disappears, however, when the length of clauses, and number of possible positions for hesitations, is taken into consideration ($G = 0·134$, $p < 0·05$).

There was a significant tendency for UPs ($G = 55·13$, $p < 0·001$), FPs ($G = 17·89$, $p < 0·001$), and UPs or FPs ($G = 79·23$, $p < 0·001$) to occur in the clause-initial position. 54·02% of UPs, 57·69% FPs, and 54·87% of hesitations (UPs or FPs) occurred at this point. There was also a significant tendency for hesitations to occur in the first half rather than the second half of clauses, even when hesitations at the clause-initial position are disregarded ($G = 4·26$, $p < 0·05$). 26·55% of hesitations occurred in the first half of clauses (excluding hesitations in the clause-initial position), compared with 15·04% in the second half.† There was also a significant tendency for hesitations to occur in the clause-initial position of long clauses than short clauses ($G = 4·168$, $p < 0·05$). See Table I. The mean length of hesitations preceding long clauses was also greater than the mean length of hesitations preceding short clauses (966 and 676 ms respectively).

This evidence indicates that hesitations do cluster towards the beginnings of syntactic clauses, and this could be taken to suggest that the main encoding unit is the syntactic clause. However, if planning in speech does not transcend clause boundaries, then clauses executed without a hesitation must be examples of "old well-organized speech" (Jackson, 1878; Goldman-Eisler, 1968). In a speech corpus like the one studied, "automatic" speech is rare and thus, if the syntactic clause is the main unit of encoding, the majority of clauses should contain a hesitation (particularly at the clause-initial position). Table I, however, reveals that only 32·08% of clauses had a hesitation in the clause-initial position.

It was also discovered that only 60·0% of the longest clauses studied (ten-word clauses), and 33·33% of eight-word clauses contained a hesitation in the clause-initial position. Furthermore, only 25·81% of three-word clauses and

† 3·54% of hesitations could not be classified in terms of their occurrence in the first or second half of clauses. These occurred in the middle of clauses containing an even number of words.

TABLE II
Number and percentage of clauses, within hesitant or fluent phases of temporal cycles, containing hesitations, whose mean length is indicated (from Beattie, 1979a).

	Hesitant phase of temporal cycle				
	Number containing hesitation(s)	Percentage containing hesitation(s)	Number with hesitation at clause-initial position	Percentage with hesitation at clause-initial position	Mean length of hesitation (ms)
All clauses (2–10 words)	35	53·03	26	38·81	1053
Short clauses (2–5 words)	18	41·86	13	29·55	669
Long clauses (6–10 words)	17	73·91	13	56·52	1205
	Fluent phase of temporal cycle				
All clauses (2–10 words)	38	41·30	25	27·17	672
Short clauses (2–5 words)	20	36·36	15	27·27	682
Long clauses (6–10 words)	18	48·65	10	27·03	657

35·29% of two-word clauses had a hesitation at any point in the clause.

(iii) *Hesitations, syntactic clauses, and temporal cycles.* The number and percentage of clauses, which fell differentially within hesitant or fluent phases of temporal cycles, and which contained a hesitation, were noted. See Table II.

As expected, a higher proportion of clauses in hesitant phases of cycles contained hesitations than did clauses in fluent phases (53·03% and 41·30% respectively). In the case of clauses in hesitant phases of cycles, long clauses were significantly more likely to contain a hesitation than short clauses ($G = 7·836, p < 0·05$), but this was not significant for clauses in fluent phases of cycles ($G = 0·918, p > 0·05$).

There was a significant tendency for hesitations to occur in the clause initial position in both the hesitant ($G = 49·324, p < 0·001$) and fluent phases of cycles ($G = 31·300, p < 0·001$). 60% of hesitations in hesitant phases of cycles occurred at the clause-initial position, compared with 50% of hesitations in fluent phases.

Hesitations were significantly more likely to occur in the clause-initial position of long clauses than short clauses, only in the case of clauses in

TABLE III

Number of hesitations and fluent word transitions accompanied by gaze or gaze aversion (from Beattie, 1979a).

Type of word transition	Gaze	Gaze aversion
Hesitation, clause-initial position (hesitant phase)	12 ⎫ 27	14 ⎫ 24
Hesitation, clause-initial position (fluent phase)	15 ⎭	10 ⎭
Other hesitations (hesitant phase)	8 ⎫ 26	15 ⎫ 27
Other hesitations (fluent phase)	18 ⎭	12 ⎭
Fluent transitions	877	452

hesitant phases of cycles ($G = 4.682$, $p < 0.05$). For clauses in fluent phases, $G = 1.772$ ($p > 0.05$).

The mean length of hesitations in the clause-initial position was also computed (see Table II). The longest of these hesitations (mean 1205 ms) were those preceding long clauses in hesitant phases of cycles. There was no significant difference in the duration of hesitations in the clause-initial position of long and short clauses in fluent phases of cycles (mean durations 657 and 682 ms, respectively).

(b) *Analysis of speaker gaze.* Table III shows the probability of speaker gaze and gaze aversion at hesitations and fluent word transitions.

As predicted from a cognitive hypothesis of nonjuncture hesitations (i.e. hesitations not in the clause-initial position), gaze aversion was significantly more probably at such points than at fluent transitions ($G = 5.596$, $p < 0.05$). 50·94% of all such hesitations were accompanied by gaze aversion, compared with 34·01% of fluent transitions. However, the probability of gaze aversion occurring at hesitations in the clause-initial position and at fluent transitions was not significantly different ($G = 3.446$, $p > 0.05$). 47·05% of hesitations in the clause-initial position were accompanied by gaze aversion. If this class of hesitations is decomposed into those which occurred in hesitant phases of temporal cycles and those which occurred in fluent phases, it becomes apparent that these two categories of hesitation behaved differently. Gaze aversion was significantly more probable during hesitations in the clause-initial position in hesitant phases, than at fluent transitions ($G = 3.950$, $p < 0.05$), but this was not significant in the case of similarly-located hesitations in fluent phases ($G = 0.021$, $p > 0.05$). The percentage of hesitations in the clause-initial position (in hesitant phases of cycles) accompanied by gaze aversion was found to be higher than the percentage of hesitations in other positions, accompanied by gaze aversion (53·85% and 50·94%, respectively).

3. *Discussion*

This study found that the distribution of hesitations in speech is affected both by syntactic units as well as by units considerably larger than individual syntactic clauses. It is interesting to note that the cycles identified in the present study were somewhat longer and more variable than the cycles described by Butterworth (1975). The mean cycle time in the present study was found to be 21·88 s (S.D. = 15·68), compared with 18 s (S.D. = 5·29) in the Butterworth study. These differences may be attributable to variations in the speech content in the two studies. The greater variability of cycles in the present study may be due to the fact that there was some standardization of speech content in the Butterworth study (subjects argued for or against a series of standard propositions).

(*a*) *Hesitations and syntactic clauses.* The distribution of hesitations was found to be related to the syntactic structure of speech. There was a significant tendency for hesitations to occur towards the beginnings of clauses, especially in the clause-initial position (see Table I). However, the apparent functional relationship between hesitations and clause planning was only observed in clauses in the hesitant phases of temporal cycles. In these phases it was observed that long clauses were significantly more likely to contain a hesitation than short clauses, especially in the clause-initial position. Moreover, the mean duration of hesitations in the clause-initial position of long clauses in hesitant phases, was almost double the mean duration of such hesitations in short clauses (1205 and 669 ms, respectively, See Table II). In the case of clauses in fluent phases, there was no significant difference in the relative probability of hesitations occurring in long and short clauses, and little difference in the mean duration of hesitations in the clause-initial position of these clauses (657 and 682 ms). These results suggest that hesitations in the clause-initial position in hesitant phases of cycles may have a proximal clause-planning function, in addition to a distal semantic planning function (Goldman-Eisler, 1967; Butterworth, 1975), whereas those hesitations in the clause-initial position in fluent phases of cycles seem to perform neither function. These conclusions are supported by the analysis of speaker gaze (see Table III), which revealed that gaze aversion (reflecting cognitive load) is significantly more probable at hesitations in the clause-initial position in hesitant phases of cycles, than at fluent transitions, but this was not found to be significant in the case of clauses in fluent phases. This analysis suggests that hesitations in the clause-initial position in hesitant phases of cycles do perform some cognitive function(s), and that similarly positioned hesitations in fluent phases do not. It may be hypothesized that the function of this latter set of hesitations is primarily social—in the case of UPs, to allow time for decoding by the listener (Reich, 1975), and in the case of FPs to prevent listener interruption (Beattie, 1977).

(*b*) *Hesitations, syntactic clauses and lexical predictability.* One question which must be raised is whether the significant relationship observed between hesitations and syntactic clauses could be an artefact of the tendency of unpredictable lexical items to occur towards the beginnings of clauses (and especially in the first position in the clause). Boomer (1965) explicitly dismissed this possibility with the argument that "primary stress typically occurs towards the end of a phonemic clause; almost invariably the last or next to last word in the clause receives the stress". And, as Berry (1953, p. 88) has shown, primary stress is negatively related to word frequency "Thus the high-information lexical words tend to occur towards the end of phonemic clauses." However, such a conclusion is not strictly justified since, as yet, no clear relationship has been demonstrated between the information content of words, operationally defined in terms of unpredictability, and word frequency. Moreover, an example such as "Too many cooks spoil the soup" in which "soup" would certainly have a lower transitional probability than "broth" whilst being of higher frequency, suggests that strict correspondence between word frequency and information content is unlikely. A pilot study of the relationship between lexical unpredictability and clause position was performed on a sample of 30 clauses (15 from hesitant phases of cycles, 15 from fluent phases).† Transitional probability was measured using the Cloze procedure (Taylor, 1953) which consists of deleting words from a text, and employing a number of judges to guess the deleted item. The fewer judges who guess correctly, the more unpredictable the item is held to be. In this application of the procedure, five protocols of each text were prepared, each with every fifth word deleted (each protocol has a different set of words deleted). Each of the five protocols was given to a set of five judges. Thus, each word in the text became associated with a Cloze score of 0, 1, 2, 3, 4, or 5, according to how many judges guessed it correctly.

Table IV shows the relationship between mean Cloze score and clause position.

TABLE IV

Relationship between mean Cloze score and position of word in clauses in hesitant and fluent phases of temporal cycles (from Beattie, 1979a).

Phase of temporal cycle	Clause-initial word	First half of clause	Second half of clause	Mean
Hesitant	4·13	3·16	2·47	3·07
Fluent	3·27	3·31	2·31	2·87

It was discovered that there were significantly more high Cloze score items (4, 5), as opposed to low Cloze score items (0, 1), at the first position in the clause than elsewhere ($G = 4·166$, $p < 0·05$). (In the case of clauses beginning with either an indefinite or definite article, if the Cloze score of the following adjective or noun is considered rather than the Cloze score of the article itself, this is found to have no effect on the result.) 81·48% of clause-initial words were found to be high Cloze score items, compared with 59·02% of all other

† The sample was randomly selected from the Butterworth (1972) corpus. Clauses varied in length from 3 to 14 words, and there were 191 words in the sample.

words in the corpus. There were also significantly more high Cloze score items in the first half than in the second half of clauses, even when clause-initial words are disregarded ($G = 5.748$, $p < 0.05$). 69.45% of words from the first half of clauses were high Cloze score items compared with 45.45% from the second half of clauses. These results are even more striking when it is recalled that measures of transitional probability such as Cloze score, are sensitive to the effects of contextual accumulation (Aborn et al., 1959; Burke and Schiavetti, 1975), and thus, *ceteris paribus*, words occurring later in a clause should be more predictable than words occurring earlier in a clause.

These results thus suggest that the tendency of hesitations to occur towards the beginnings of clauses is not an artefact of lexical unpredictability, since there is a tendency for the more unpredictable words to occur towards the end of clauses.

4. Conclusions (Part 1)

(a) *Encoding units in the production of spontaneous speech.* Despite the fact that hesitations were found to cluster towards the beginnings of syntactic clauses, (and the subsequent demonstration that this was not an artefact of lexical unpredictability), the hypothesis that the clause is the fundamental unit of encoding (Boomer, 1965); Fodor et al., 1974) did not receive support in this study. Three lines of evidence run counter to this hypothesis. The first is the observation that the majority of clauses did not contain a hesitation in the clause-initial position, or at any location in the clause. 81.25% of a four-word clauses did not contain a hesitation in the clause-initial position, and 74.19% of three-word clauses were completely fluent. If it is accepted that hesitations are necessary for cognitive planning in speech (see Beattie and Bradbury, 1979, for some recent evidence), then either it must be assumed that the majority of utterances in the present corpus did not require planning and were therefore "old, well-organized and automatic" (Jackson, 1878), or it must be accepted that planning in speech typically transcends clause boundaries. According to the latter hypothesis, fluent clauses are not "automatic" verbalizations, but new utterances resulting from distal planning. This hypothesis is supported by study of the speech transcripts which reveals little in the way of "automatic" speech. The second line of evidence is the emergence of a macrostructure in the hesitations data which suggests that higher-order units (in the region of 8.80 clauses) are involved in the planning of speech. The third line of evidence derives from two sources—firstly from analysis of the relationship between clause-length and the probability (and duration) of hesitations, and secondly from analysis of speaker gaze. Both analyses suggest that the functional relationship between hesitations and the planning of clauses is context-specific, holding only for clauses in the hesitant phases of temporal cycles. These observations suggest that the hypothesis that planning in speech universally proceeds on a clause-by-clause basis is incorrect.

The evidence obtained in the present study is consonant with the hypothesis that the main encoding units are suprasentential in scope and semantic in nature (Butterworth, 1975, 1976). However, execution of the initial parts of these units does typically commence before the semantic planning of the entire unit is complete. A mean of 3·57 clauses were executed during the semantic planning phases. Moreover, it is interesting to note that this speech seems no more predictable, in terms of Cloze score, than speech in fluent phases (there were 50 high and 25 low Cloze score items in hesitant phases, compared with 44 high and 25 low Cloze score items in fluent phases, $G = 0·450, p < 0·05$; see also Table IV), and it does appear to be planned on a clause-by-clause basis. This evidence thus suggests that both semantic and syntactic encoding units are implicated in the generation of spontaneous speech, with the latter type less extensive than the former. A social hypothesis can perhaps account for the fact that speech does occur in these planning phases; namely that, if output were suspended until a complete semantic plan was formulated, then considerably longer (but fewer) hesitations would be necessary for the generation of speech. One consequence of this would be that listener's attempts to gain control of the conversation would become more frequent and probably more successful (Beattie, 1977). By speaking during semantic planning phases, the speaker can redistribute planning time (using more frequent, but shorter hesitations) whilst keeping the listener interested, and lessening the probability of interruption. This hypothesis does receive some support from a study by Beattie and Bradbury (1979) which demonstrated that subjects can, when necessary, modify their temporal planning structure in monologue, without significantly affecting speech content. This hypothesis of course predicts that the structure of temporal cycles will be sensitive to the social situation. Future research will need to determine if the form of these cycles is affected by the different conversational contexts, and what effect, if any, this has on the speech produced.

III. Part 2: The Organization of Nonverbal Behaviour in Conversational Interaction

A. Speaker Gaze†

Although speaker-gaze has been the subject of much recent research in the area of non-verbal behaviour (see Argyle and Cook, 1976, for a recent review), the precise patterning of gaze and speech has been largely ignored. The small number of studies which have considered gaze patterns, in addition to overall amounts of gaze, have tended to employ rather ubiquitous language concepts, such as "question" or "remark", and have generally ignored the psychological subcomponents of these units which might be relevant to the speaker's visual behaviour e.g. identifiable speech planning phases. As a result, the patterns of gaze which have been reported have displayed considerable variability Libby

†See Beattie (1978b) for an extended description of the study.

(1970) observed that in an interview situation in which the interviewer gazed steadily at subjects who were replying to questions, 84·5% broke gaze during their reply (range 37·1–100%) although only 9·3% broke gaze before the end of the question (range 0–57·4%). Here, embarassing and non-embarassing, personal and nonpersonal questions, demanding long and short answers, were combined in the analysis of gaze patterning. Nielsen (1962), observed that subjects broke gaze at the beginning of a "remark" in conversation in 45·5% of all cases (range 8–84%) and they looked at their interlocutor at the end of a "remark" in 50·5% of all cases (range 25–90%). Undoubtedly the ubiquitous nature of a concept like "remark" is at least partly responsible for this variability, since the precise nature of the verbal exchanges must have varied considerably from dyad to dyad.

The most intensive analysis of the patterning of gaze in conversation, and the only study to focus on possible psychological units within speech, was a study by Kendon (1967). His main observations were that the speaker tended to look at the listener during fluent speech much more than during hesitant speech (50% of the time spent speaking fluently as compared to only 20·3% of the time spent speaking hesitantly). Kendon hypothesized that speaker-gaze had a monitoring function and that such monitoring was incompatible with the planning of speech and therefore gaze aversion occurred during hesitant periods of high cognitive activity.

Kendon also described the patterning of gaze with respect to phrases and phrase boundary pauses,† and found that the speaker tended to look at the listener as he approached the end of a phrase and continued to look during the phrase boundary pause, but averted his gaze as the next phrase began. It was also observed that utterances terminated with prolonged gaze.‡ Kendon hypothesized that gaze had a signalling function at such points, specifically concerned with the transmission of information to the listener about the appropriateness of a listener response, either in the form of a turn-claiming attempt or in the form of an accompaniment signal (an assenting or attention signal).

The aim of the present study is to analyse the distribution of gaze with respect to temporal cycles, units with demonstrable cognitive significance, and possible interactional importance, within low-emotionality dialogues, where gaze behaviour should be largely a function of monitoring and signalling variables. The experimental evidence suggests that cognitive processing load is asymmetrically distributed with respect to the alternating hesitant and fluent phases which constitute each cycle. More cognitive planning seems to occur in the hesitant phase of the cycle than in the fluent phase, since both proximal clausal planning and distal semantic planning occur in the hesitant phase (see Part 1, Section II), whereas the evidence suggests that only proximal lexical decisions are made in the fluent phase (Butterworth and Beattie, 1978). Thus, given the monitoring function of gaze, an approximately inverse relationship

† It is not clear, however what such phrases actually are (see Beattie, 1978b).
‡ "Utterances" were not defined in the original paper but were subsequently defined as "complete in form and content" and were in addition, marked by a change in topic (see Kendon, 1978).

would be predicted between the relative hesitancy of speech and the amount of speaker gaze at the listener.

Evidence also suggests that these cycles constitute semantic units in speech; cycles correspond to "ideas" in the speech text where the "idea" boundaries are determined by a number of judges (Butterworth, 1975). Thus, these cycles may function as important units in interaction and speakers may seek to avoid idea fragmentation, that is within-cycles interruption (understood in the broadest sense to include all listener responses other than attention signals) by inhibiting, where possible, cues which might elicit speaker responses during the cycles, but displaying such cues, including speaker-gaze, at the boundaries of such units.

1. Results

(a) *Gaze and mean hesitancy of phase.* The number of hesitant and fluent phases dominated by gaze or gaze aversion (i.e. with more than or less than 50% gaze, respectively) were noted, as was the slope of each phase (measured in degrees; a 45° slope indicates an equal proportion of pausing and phonation, a 0° slope indicates uninterrupted phonation, a 90° slope indicates extended pausing). The number of changes in gaze state per phase, and the number of words separating each change of gaze state were also recorded (see Table V).

A difference in the relative number of hesitant and fluent phases dominated by gaze did emerge, but this difference failed to reach significance ($G = 2.512$, $p < 0.2$). There was a tendency for both types of phase to be accompanied by more gaze than gaze aversion; however in the case of fluent phases the trend was much more pronounced. The slopes (reflecting the mean percentage of hesitation per phase) of the various hesitant and fluent phases were then compared. In the case of fluent phases, those phases dominated by gaze aversion tended to be significantly more hesitant than the phases dominated by gaze (mean slopes 13·77° and 6·30° respectively, Mann-Whitney U test, $U = 12$, $p < 0.05$, two-tailed test). In the case of hesitant phases there was no significant difference in the slopes of those phases dominated by gaze or gaze aversion (mean slopes 47·07° and 47·55° respectively, Mann-Whitney U test, $U = 38·5$, $p > 0.05$, two-tail).

It should be noted that the dominance of a phase by gaze or gaze aversion is not simply attributable to there being more phonation or hesitation in the phase, since 6 of the 13 hesitant phases dominated by gaze had slopes which were greater than 45° (i.e. there was more pausing than phonation), and none of the fluent phases had slopes greater than 45°, although four of these phases were dominated by gaze aversion. In a number of cases, the distribution of gaze can be clearly seen not to be optimal for cognitive purposes. For example, two hesitant phases had slopes of 90°, i.e. they consisted of prolonged pausing, but these were accompanied by uninterrupted gaze, and not gaze aversion.

Table V also seems to reveal differences in the stability of gaze in hesitant and fluent phases dominated by gaze or gaze aversion, but such differences largely disappear when the number of words is taken into consideration

TABLE V

Patterns of gaze in temporal cycles. (From Beattie, 1978b).

Phase type	Phase dominated by gaze or gaze aversion	No. of H and F phases dominated by gaze or gaze aversion	Mean slope of each phase (in degrees)	Mean no. of changes in gaze state per phase	Mean no. of words separating each change in gaze states
Hesitant	Gaze	13	47·07	2·39	10·04
	Gaze aversion	9	47·55	1·67	11·51
Fluent	Gaze	20	6·30	2·60	12·65
	Gaze aversion	4	13·77	4·25	12·41

(column 4). There was an overall mean of 2·5 changes in gaze state per phase, which suggests that there was a change approximately every 1·76 clauses. There was a non-clausal hesitation every 12·9 words, and a hesitation approximately every eight words, which would suggest that gaze behaviour is more stable than it should be, if it were simply reflecting each fluent-hesitant-fluent transition. There should be 2 n changes in gaze state for every n hesitations, and thus we would predict a mean of approximately six words to separate each gaze state, if gaze were simply reflecting the location of individual hesitations.

(b) *Gaze and syntactic clauses.* Gaze across the first 12 boundary locations of clauses between 2 and 12 words in length was analysed, and the percentage of each boundary location occupied by gaze was calculated (see Table VI).

TABLE VI

Percentage of boundary locations in syntactic clauses accompanied by gaze. (from Beattie, 1978b.)

Phase						Boundary Location						
Type	1	2	3	4	5	6	7	8	9	10	11	12
Hesitant	60·27	50·68	56·76	57·14	57·14	58·33	55·17	57·14	68·75	71·42	80·00	50·00
Fluent	60·61	64·65	59·79	65·85	66·15	69·09	72·73	72·73	75·00	70·00	76·92	85·71
Both	60·47	58·72	58·15	63·55	64·83	68·49	62·96	66·00	73·53	70·70	77·50	75·00

The randomness of these percentages was tested using a one-sample runs test. When all clauses were considered, the distribution of gaze was found to be random ($r = 4$); similarly with clauses falling within hesitant phases ($r = 9$). However in the case of clauses in fluent phases, the distribution was not random ($r = 2$, $p < 0.05$). The percentage of successive boundary locations occupied by gaze tended to increase in a non-random fashion. The mean percentage increase from boundary location 1 to boundary location 12 was 25·10%, in the case of syntactic clauses, within fluent phases. It should also be noted that clauses in fluent phases tended to have significantly more overall gaze than syntactic clauses in hesitant phases, when the percentage of gaze at each boundary location was compared (Wilcoxon matched-pairs signed ranks test, two-tail, $T = 6$, $p < 0.01$).

The second analysis sought to determine if syntactic clauses tended to terminate with gaze. This time, the number of instances of gaze at the first and last position of clauses between 2 and 12 words in length were compared. This was carried out separately for clauses in the hesitant and fluent phases of the cycles. In neither case did a significant effect emerge; in the case of clauses in hesitant phases (Wilcoxon test, $T = 16·5$, $p > 0·05$), in the case of clauses in fluent phases (Wilcoxon test, $T = 15$, $p > 0·05$). The mean percentage of gaze at clause junctures was found to be 60·47%.

The significant results in the first analysis but not in the second indicate that clause length is an important factor. The longer the clause, the more likely it is

TABLE VII

Incidence of gaze at clause junctures nearest termination
of cognitive cycle compared with the incidence at all other
clause junctures (from Beattie, 1979a).

	Gaze	Gaze aversion
Clause junctures nearest termination of cycle	18	4
Other clause junctures	100	71

to terminate with gaze. This is especially the case with clauses in the fluent
phases of cycles.

(c) *Gaze, temporal cycles and clause junctures.* The incidence of gaze at clause
junctures nearest the terminal points of cognitive cycles was compared with
the incidence of gaze at all other clause junctures (see Table VII).

Gaze was found to occur significantly more frequently at clause junctures
nearest the terminal points of cognitive cycles than at other clause junctures
($G = 3.836$, $p < 0.05$). The mean percentage gaze at clause junctures nearest
the terminal points of cognitive cycles was 81.82%.

The gaze which coincided with the ends of temporal cycles was not a
discrete cueing signal. This terminal gaze was initiated a mean of 1.83
syntactic clauses before the end of a cycle (a mean of 12.0 words earlier), and it
continued into the subsequent cycle for a mean of 1.44 clauses (mean of 5.7
words). These figures suggest that such gaze does not function solely as a
signal that an appropriate listener response point has been reached. They
suggest instead that such gaze performs a dual function—firstly, that of
signalling, and conversational regulation, and secondly that of monitoring the
reception of the semantic unit by the listener.

(d) *Filled hesitation and cognitive cycles.* The patterning of gaze and
proportion of gaze within individual hesitant and fluent phases is not simply a
function of a basic cognitive variable plus a compatible reciprocal social
signalling function. There is considerable divergence from the patterns which
would be optimal on cognitive grounds. An analysis was performed to
determine if this divergence had any significant effects on the speech
produced. The amount of filled hesitation, (consisting of FPs, repetitions, all
repetitions of any length judged non-significant semantically, false starts, all
incomplete or self-interrupted utterances, and parenthetic remarks, e.g. "you
know"), occurring in each cycle was analyzed. The measure should prove
sensitive to deficits in forward planning. G_0, G_1 type cycles ($n = 7$) are cycles
in which hesitant phases are dominated by gaze aversion and fluent phases by
gaze. G_1, G_1 type cycles ($n = 11$) are those in which both phases are dominated
by gaze (there were only two instances of G_1, G_0 type cycles, and no examples
of a G_0, G_0 type cycle, in the present corpus). Thus, if speaker gaze during
semantic planning phases does interfere with cognitive processing, there
should be more filled hesitation in both phases of G_1, G_1 cycles than in G_0, G_1

TABLE VIII

Mean filled hesitation rate (measured in words) per phase, and FH rate per unit word spoken, within the hesitant and fluent phases of cycles with the H phase dominated by gaze aversion (G_0, G_1 cycles) or gaze (G_1, G_1 cycles). (from Beattie, 1978b).

		Type of cycle					
	Hesitation type	G_0, G_1 ($n = 7$)			G_1, G_1 ($n = 11$)		
		H	F	Both	H	F	Both
	False starts	1·28	0	1·28	3·64	1·45	5·09
Hesitation rate (in words)	Parenthetic remarks	0·86	1·43	2·29	0·73	1·27	2·00
	Repetition	0·14	0·57	0·71	0·27	0·37	0·64
	Filled pauses	0·86	1·28	2·14	0·55	0·73	1·28
	False starts	0·0689	0	0·0221	0·1558	0·0609	0·1079
Hesitation rate, per unit word spoken	Parenthetic remarks	0·0463	0·0364	0·0396	0·0312	0·0535	0·0424
	Repetition	0·0075	0·0145	0·0123	0·0116	0·0155	0·0136
	Filled pauses	0·0463	0·0326	0·0370	0·0235	0·0306	0·0271

cycles. Table VIII reveals that the false start variable was in fact sensitive to the mismatch between gaze behaviour and cognitive processing.

There were significantly more false starts in G_1, G_1 cycles than in G_0, G_1 cycles (Mann-Whitney U test, $U = 15$, $p < 0.05$, two-tail). False starts were approximately five times as common, per unit word spoken, in G_1, G_1 cycles than G_0, G_1 cycles. There was also an increase in rate of repetition and parenthetic remarks, per unit word, in G_1, G_1 cycles, although these differences failed to reach significance.

2. Discussion

One significant feature of the results obtained in this study was the high proportion of gaze whilst speaking. The mean percentage was 66·8%. (All speakers were male in the present study, and only one of the interactions involved a mixed sex pair.) The comparable figures from Argyle and Ingham (1972) for the percentage of gaze whilst talking was 31% for same sex (male) pairs, and 52% for mixed sex pairs, with the man talking. Nielsen (1962), reported a mean percentage of 52% gaze whilst talking. Furthermore, Exline and Winters' (1965) observation that amount of gaze in conversation is inversely related to the cognitive difficulty of the topic of conversation, would lead one to predict a lower overall level of gaze in the present study, compared with other studies, since the topic under discussion in the present study was certainly more difficult than the conversational topics in many of the studies of gaze and speech. However a number of social considerations can be used to account for the high rate. Firstly, in the present study subjects were acquainted, whereas in most previous studies they were unacquainted. The level of gaze between intimates tends to be higher than between strangers (Argyle and Dean, 1965). Furthermore, the distance between the interactants was fixed, in the present study, at a distance which might have exceeded the distance that acquaintances would normally choose, (some subjects spontaneously commented on this). Thus the intimacy equlibrium model of Argyle and Dean (1965), would suggest that the high rate of gaze whilst talking was to compensate for the increased distance. A compensatory relationship between proximity and gaze, given a certain level of intimacy, has found considerable empirical support (Argyle and Ingham, 1972; Knight, Langmeter and Landgren, 1973; Schulze and Barefoot, 1974; Stephenson, Rutter and Dore, 1973; Patterson, 1973). It may also be hypothesized that the high degree of listener attentiveness produced by supervision-type situations contributed to the high gaze rate, since Cook and Smith (1972), (cited by Argyle and Cook, 1976), found that the amount of gaze whilst speaking increases when a confederate looks continuously. Thus the high rate of gaze observed would seem to be consistent with a number of other observations.

The analysis of the relationship between the temporal cycles of speech and the macropatterns of gaze revealed a loosely coordinated system. The patterning of gaze did seem to reflect the gross temporal structure of the speech. These results appear to conflict with other studies which have found that a Markov chain structure, with a 0·3 s transition state, can account for the distribution of pausing and phonation in speech (Jaffe and Feldstein, 1970), and a Markov chain structure with a 0·6 s transition state, can account for the dyadic gaze states occurring in conversation (Natale, 1976). It should be added that such studies ignore the functional interdependence of speech and gaze by attempting to describe in isolation the pattern of two obviously related phenomena. It remains to be seen to what extent the Markov description of pause/phonation occurrences and of the gaze accompanying speech is compatible with the observations made in this study. It may be possible to reconcile the two sets of observations. For example it can be suggested that the Markov structure of pausing and phonation in speech, reported by Jaffe and Feldstein (1970), may have resulted from gross averaging of samples of speech of different complexity, some of which may not have been sufficiently complex to involve a temporal rhythm (see Goldman-Eisler, 1967). The Natale (1976) study, may have involved speech which did not display a temporal rhythm, given the rather simple topic of conversation (subjects were asked to have a conversation on their impressions of life at university). Alternatively, analyses which have shown that a first order, as opposed to an nth order Markov process, best account for the pattern of dyadic gaze, may even be compatible with the results of the present study, by accounting for the local variation of gaze within the macropatterns observed. One point should be remembered about these macropatterns, namely that variation in the overall length of the cycles was enormous (mean = 21·88 s; S.D. = 15·68). Thus it cannot presently be contended that a higher order Markov structure of any identifiable order would be a better fit for the data, given the enormous degree of temporal uncertainty in the overall length of the cycles. Only careful research in the future will determine which mathematical model best fits the patterning of gaze accompanying complex speech which itself displays a rhythmic strucutre.

The patterning of gaze and proportion of gaze within individual hesitant and fluent phases was shown not to be simply a function of a basic cognitive variable, plus a compatible, reciprocal social signalling function. One possible source of this divergence is the social pressure on interactants in conversations to attempt to create a favourable impression. Research has indicated that various gaze patterns are differentically evaluated e.g. Argyle et al. (1974) found that subjects disliked continuous gaze. Exline and Eldridge (1967) found that subjects thought that speakers were more likely to mean what they said if they looked at them. Kleck and Nuessle (1968) found that confederates who looked only 15% of the time were described as "defensive" or "evasive", whereas those who looked 80% of the time were described as "friendly", "mature" or "sincere". Cook and Smith (1975) found that there was a tendency for confederates who averted gaze to be seen as nervous and lacking in confidence. In fact, positive evaluation was positively related to the amount of gaze. Furthermore, Kendon and Cook (1969) found that subjects preferred individuals who gave long glances, and evaluated less favourably those who gazed frequently and with shorter glances. The tendency for gaze to be more stable than predicted, on cognitive grounds, in the present study, may be attributable to the fact that subjects were attempting to create a favourable impression by using relatively long glances. The high proportion of gaze accompanying certain hesitant periods may also be due to the same basic signal effect. Total gaze aversion would have been the cognitively optimal strategy in a number of cases, but zero gaze is disliked by subjects (Argyle et al., 1974). The fact that social factors may interfere with the cognitively-optimal patterning of gaze, and that this may result in decrements in verbal performance, would indicate that it may be fruitful to look closely at certain delineable populations who show marked abnormalities in both gaze behaviour and speech.

B. Speaker-Movement and Gesture

1. Introduction

An obvious characteristic of conversation is that speakers (and listeners) seldom remain perfectly still during it. There appear to be two fundamentally different kinds of speaker activity: one class of movement, which is not speech-related, involves self-stimulation (e.g. finger-rubbing, scratching etc.) These have been termed body-focussed movements (Freedman and Hoffman, 1967).

The second class of movement is speech-related, and a subset of these movements does seem to reflect the meaning of what is said. These movements can be termed speech-focussed movements (SFMs).

There have been two principle theoretical orientations concerning the significance of speaker movement (it should be noted that most early studies did not differentiate speech-focussed and body-focussed movements). One view based in the psychoanalytic tradition, has held that such movements can reveal speaker's emotional or affective state (Freud, 1905; Deutsch, 1947, 1952; Feldman, 1959). A second view has held that such movements constitute an alternative channel of communication, either augmenting the verbal component (Baxter et al., 1968) or substituting for it (Mahl et al., 1959), although no demonstrable benefit from these nonverbal "signals" has been found to accrue to the listener, except in the case of the communication of shape information, in an experimental situation requiring subjects to describe two-dimensional drawings (Graham and Argyle, 1975). However, Dobrogaev (cited by Schlauch, 1936) found that the elimination of gesture resulted in marked changes in speech performance, with decreased fluency, impaired articulation, and a reduced vocabulary size. Graham and Heywood (1975) also found that the elimination of gesture (subjects were instructed to keep their arms folded) produced some changes in speech content (for example a significant increase in expressions denoting spatial relationships, and a significant reduction in the use of demonstratives), as well as a significant increase in the proportion of time spent pausing. Graham and Heywood concluded that this result suggested that gestures normally facilitate language production, at least on certain topics (i.e. those involving spatial descriptions).

There have been other attempts to relate various types of bodily movement to structural units of language. Birdwhistell (1970) described the relationship between "kinesic markers" and various parts of speech (pronouns, verbs etc). Kendon ((1972) concentrated on larger units of language, but unfortunately used an extremely small sample (1·5 min from one speaker). His conclusion was that "each speech unit is distinguished by a pattern of movement and of body-part involvement in movement. The larger the speech unit, the greater the difference in the form of movement, and the body parts involved." Bull and Brown (1977) using a much larger sample, studied the relationship between posture change and speech, and found that significant changes in trunk and leg postures by the speaker only occurred while new pieces of information were being introduced in the conversation.

The only studies to attempt to relate movement to the psychological processes underlying speech have been by Dittmann (1972) and McNeill (1975). Dittmann (1972) investigated the relationship between an undifferentiated class of "nervous" movements of the head, hands and feet and phonemic clauses (see Part 1 Section II). He discovered that these movements clustered towards the beginnings of hesitant phonemic clauses and thus concluded, following Boomer (1965), that these nervous movements were motor manifestations of the speech encoding process. McNeill (1975) presented a theory of the relationship between gesture and speech (this unfortunately preceded detailed naturalistic description of their inter-relations). This theory was based on the assumption that speech is integrated in terms of the syntagma which is, according to Kozhevnikov and Chistovisch (1965, p. 74), "one meaning unit, which is pronounced as a single output." (Syntagmas have similar dimensions to phonemic clauses, but considerably more emphasis is laid on semantics in their definition.) McNeill argued that throughout development, speech remains directly adapted to the sensory-motor and representational levels of cognitive functioning but with time there occurs a "semiotic extension" of the basic speech mechanism to cover more abstract levels of operational thought. Gestures, according to McNeill, have their origin in this semiotic extension, but they correspond to the sensory-motor schemas underlying speech. The evidence for the theory (based on observations of individuals simultaneously performing tasks, such as mental paper folding, and describing their actions) revealed that iconic gestures were initiated with the onset of speech associated with the basic action schemas, and were prolonged for the duration of these schemas. This theory, however, can be challenged on a number of accounts. First, the assumption that the fundamental unit of encoding is of the same dimension as a clause can be questioned (see Part 1). Second, the relevance of such restricted data for natural movement and speech may be doubted.

The evidence purporting to the existence of higher-order units of semantic planning, described in Part 1, suggested that studies of the relationship between psychological processes in speech and nonverbal behaviour should consider units of language larger than individual phonemic clauses and syntagmas. This is the aim of the present study (reported in more detail in Butterworth and Beattie, 1978). The sample of conversation again consisted of (3) supervisions and a seminar.

2. *Procedure*

The total duration of speech analysed was 849·8 s, chosen in a fairly random fashion. The only constraints on this selection were firstly that the speaker's turn in the conversation had to be least 40 s, so that temporal cycles could be identified, and secondly that some SFMs had to occur. Data was available from seven speakers.

The temporal analysis was carried out as follows: temporal cycles were identified in the manner described in Part 1, and thereby independently of the location of the gestures, since only sound could be detected by the signal detector. (All speakers showed temporal cycles of alternating hesitant and fluent phases; except one, who had a mean pause rate of around 10%.) A timer (to one hundredth of a second) was mixed on to the videorecordings, so the precise timing of words and gestures could be achieved, and the result matched to temporal cycle data.

The present analysis concentrates on three classes of hand and arm movement.

(1) Speech-focussed movements. All movements of the arm or hand except self-touching (e.g. finger-rubbing, scratching). This class

includes gestures, "batonic" movements and other simple movements.
(2) Gestures. More complex movements which appear to bear some semantic relation to the verbal component of the message.
(3) Changes in the basic equilibrium position of the arms and hands, that is, changes in the position where the hands return to after making a SFM.
The classification of each movement into one of the above categories was performed by two independent judges, and disagreements resolved by joint rechecking of the videotape. The exact time of the initiation of each SFM and equilibrium change could be obtained by utilizing the slow motion facility of the VTR. The points were located on the pause /phonation plots, and on transcripts of the verbal output. In the case of gestures, the exact time between the initiation of the gesture and the first phone of the word with which it was associated was noted. The time of each equilibrium change was also noted.

3. *Results*

The number of SFMs, gestures and SFMs-gestures occurring per unit time during pauses or periods of phonation in planning and execution phases were analysed (see Table IX).

The analysis revealed that SFMs occurred most frequently per unit time during fluent phases. The highest incidence of this class of behaviours was in pauses in the fluent phases. SFMs were approximately three times more frequent per unit time during such pauses than during pauses in the hesitant phases.

Gestures yielded an essentially similar distribution but in the case of gestures the trends were much more pronounced. Gestures were approximately five times as frequent per unit time during pauses in the fluent phases than during pauses in the hesitant phases. Gestures were also almost three times as frequent during pauses in the fluent phase as during periods of phonation in the fluent phase.

TABLE IX

The rate of production (per 1000 s) of SFMs, gestures and SFMs-gestures during pauses and phonation in hesitant and fluent phases of temporal cycles. (from Butterworth and Beattie, 1978.)

	Phase of cycle	Pause	Phonation	Mean rate
SFMs	Hesitant	118·4	191·9	153·0
	Fluent	341·0	199·7	226·2
	Mean rate	196·5	197·5	
Gestures	Hesitant	59·2	44·3	52·2
	Fluent	280·1	106·9	139·4
	Mean rate	136·7	89·6	
SFMs-gestures	Hesitant	59·2	147·6	100·9
	Fluent	60·9	92·8	86·8
	Mean rate	59·8	107·9	86·8

The residual class of SFMs-gestures displayed a very different distribution. This time there was no overall difference in the number occurring per unit time during pauses in the hesitant and fluent phases and these behaviours were most common during periods of phonation, particularly in hesitant phases.

An ANOVA revealed that speech-focussed movements were significantly more frequent per unit time in the fluent phases of the cycle than in the hesitant phases ($F = 8.65$, $df = 1$, $p < 0.05$). Furthermore there was a significant phase/activity interaction effect: in the hesitant phase, SFMs are more frequent during periods of phonation, whereas in the fluent phase SFMs are significantly more frequent during periods of hesitation ($F = 7.60$, $df = 1$, $p < 0.05$).

When SFMs were decomposed into gestures and non-gestural SFMs, an ANOVA revealed a significant interaction between movement type and specific location in the cycle. Non-gestural SFMs were most frequent per unit time in periods of phonation in the hesitant phase whereas gestures were most frequent per unit time during pauses in the fluent phases. ($F = 3.15$, $df = 3$, $p < 0.05$). Gestures were least frequent during periods of phonation in the hesitant phase.

This distributional difference between gestures and other SFMs suggests a functional difference. Other SFMs consist mainly of simple batonic movements and their close relation to periods of actual phonation in both hesitant and fluent phases indicates that a common-sense interpretation of them as emphasis markers is well-founded. The asymmetry in the distribution of gestures suggests, on the other hand, that these are not mere emphatic markers, but are functionally related to planning. Since they are relatively infrequent in the hesitant phase itself, they are not connected with the ideational planning process but with the lexical planning process. This hypothesis is supported by their close association with pauses in the fluent phase.

Further evidence of the functional distinction between gestures and SFMs is to be found by comparing their distributions in respect of the form-class of the words they are associated with (see Table X). Gestures are heavily concentrated on nouns (41·3%), verbs (23·8%), and adjectives (15·9%)—classes which contain most of the unpredictable lexical items. Other SFMs, however, are much more evenly spaced over form-classes.

The initiation of gestures usually precedes, and never follows, the words they are associated with. The mean delay being around 0.8 s, with a range of 0·10 s–2·50 s, (Table XI). The length of delay seems unaffected by the position in that clause: again arguing for the connexion of gestures with lexical selection, independent of higher-level plans that determine the syntactic shape of the output.

The relationship between changes in the basic equilibrium position of the arm and hands, phasal transition points and clause junctures was analysed (see Table XII). A significant tendency for changes in the basic equilibrium position to correspond to both the terminal points of hesitant phases ($G = 22.118$, $p < 0.001$), and to the terminal points of fluent phases

TABLE X

Proportion of gestures and SFMs-gestures associated with syntactic classes. (From Butterworth and Beattie, 1978.)

	Noun	Verb	Adj.	Adv.	Pronoun	Prep.	Conj.	Dem. Adj.	Relative Pronoun	Interj.	Etcetera
Percent gestures	41·3	23·8	15·9	1·6	6·3	6·3	3·2	1·6			
Percent SFMs-gestures	28·6	21·4	7·1	4·8	4·8	4·8	7·1	9·6	7·1	2·4	2·4

($G = 39·336, p < 0·001$) was observed. Changes in equilibrium position were also found to coincide with junctures between clauses ($G = 61·448$, $p < 0·001$). These results provide further evidence that the hesitant and fluent phases, identified from changes in the gross temporal patterning of the speech, have some underlying psychological singificance.

4. Conclusions

A number of conclusions may be tentatively advanced. Firstly, there are two fundamentally distinct kinds of SFM—gestures and other SFMs. Secondly, the suggested distinction between the hesitant and the fluent phase discussed in Part 1, receives further support from the distribution of equilibrium changes, and from the relative distribution of gestures observed. Thirdly, gestures appear to be by-products of lexical preplanning processes, and seem to indicate that the speaker knows in advance the semantic specification of the words he will utter; in some cases he has to delay to search for a relatively unavailable item. Some crude semantic specification of lexical items must therefore be part of the ideational planning process. Finally, lexical planning is a necessary, though not a sufficient condition for the occurrence of gestures.

One hypothesis that can be offered to account for the fact that gestures

TABLE XI

Mean duration of the delay between gestures and the associated word, analysed by syntactic class, clause position and clause length. (From Butterworth and Beattie, 1978.)

(a) Syntactic class

	N	V	Adj.	Pron.	Prep.	Dem. Adj.
M_1	0·915	0·736	0·747	1·20	2·33	1·06
M_2	0·770	0·661	0·664	0·905	0·583	1·06

(b) Clause position (in words)

	1–2	3–4	5–6	7–8	8+
M_1	1·29	0·534	0·881	1·82	0·804
M_2	0·737	0·393	0·672	1·22	0·746

(c) Clause length (in words)

	1–4	5–8	9–12	13–16	17+
M_1	0·498	0·868	0·744	0·810	1·26
M_2	0·498	0·706	0·650	0·540	0·990

M_1 = All gestures which show delay.
M_2 = M_1 + gestures which are initiated with or during the word.

TABLE XII

Position in speech of changes in the basic equilibrium position of the arm and hand. (From Butterworth and Beattie, 1978.)

	Number of changes in equilibrium position corresponding to each category	Number of occurrences of each phenomenon not accompanied by change in equilibrium position	G	Prob.
End of hesitant phase	5	20	22·118	$p < 0.001$
End of fluent phase	8	20	39·336	$p < 0.001$
Clause juncture	24	180	61·448	$p < 0.001$
Other	14	1620	—	—

precede lexical items (rather than occur simultaneously with them) is that there is a greater repertoire of lexical items than of gestures to choose from. Lexical items have to be drawn from a large corpus—the mental lexicon probably consists of 20 000–30 000 items. Not all, of course, will be candidates at each choice point, some items will necessarily be excluded by the preceding linguistic context—but in some cases, the number of lexical items which satisfy the semantic and syntactic constraints will be large (these of course will be words of low transitional probability; that is to say, unpredictable in context). On the other hand, the repertoire of gestures typically employed in conversation is relatively small for most people; Neapolitans, with their elaborate and diverse forms of gesture may be an exception. Hick's Law would therefore suggest that in the verbal medium, with a greater number of alternatives to choose from, selection of a lexical item, should take longer than in the nonverbal medium.

IV. Part 3: The regulation of Speaker-turns in Conversation

A number of implications emerge from the studies described so far (on the nature of units involved in the generation of spontaneous speech, and their influence upon the structure of nonverbal behaviour in conversation) for the functions of nonverbal behaviour in conversational interaction, particularly with respect to the regulation of speaker-turns. Some core features of conversation are:

(1) Speaker change recurs or at least occurs.
(2) Overwhelmingly, one party talks at a time.
(3) Transitions from one turn to the next, with no gap and no overlap, are common.
(4) Turn-order is not fixed, but varies.
(5) Turn-size is not fixed, but varies.
(6) Length of conversation is not specified in advance.
(7) What parties say is not specified in advance.
(8) Relative distribution of turns is not specified in advance.
(9) Number of parties can vary.
(10) Talk can be continuous or discontinuous. (From Sacks *et al.*, 1974).

Any analyses of the structure of conversation must attempt to account for features (1)–(3), given features (4)–(10). There have been two main kinds of attempt at a solution to this problem. Ethnomethodologists have attempted to account for the regulation of conversation by focussing their analyses upon linguistic structure. Sacks *et al.* (1974) employed the notion of "unit type" which is a syntactically–based unit ("unit-types for English include sentential, clausal, phrasal and lexical constructions", p. 702). They propose that "the speaker is initially entitled, in having a turn, to one such unit. The first possible completion of a first such unit constitutes an initial transition-relevance place. Transfer of speakership is coordinated by reference to such transition-relevance places, which any unit-type instance will reach" (p. 703). Speaker-switching, it is argued, is effected either by speaker-selection or self-selection rules at such points. The most serious deficiency of this account is the complete omission of paralinguistic and nonverbal cues, despite their demonstrable importance (Duncan, 1972, 1973, 1975; Duncan and Fiske, 1977; Kendon, 1967). Sacks *et al.* (1974, p. 722) do, in fact, admit that their analysis is too restricted, and that it is esential to consider other aspects of speaker behaviour "when it is further realized that any word can be made into a 'one word unit-type' via intonation, then we can appreciate the partial character of the unit-type's description, in syntactic terms."

The alternative approach, favoured by psychologists, has been to concentrate, almost exclusively, on the various nonverbal and paralinguistic behaviours occurring in conversation, with only brief mention of any linguistic entities. Various turn-yielding and turn-requesting functions have been assigned to these nonverbal and paralinguistic behaviours in conversation. For example, Kendon (1967) compared a listener's responses to the speaker when the speaker ended his utterance with or without gaze. When the speaker ended his utterance with gaze, the listener was more likely to take the floor without any perceptible delay. Duncan (1972, 1973, 1975; Duncan and Fiske, 1977) identified six turn-yielding cues in conversation, five being verbal or paralinguistic, and one nonverbal. The five verbal cues were rising or falling pitch at the end of the utterance, drawl on the final syllable, or on the stressed syllable of a phonemic clause, sociocentric sequences (essentially filled pauses or parenthetic remarks), a drop in pitch or loudness in conjunction with the sociocentric sequence and clause completion. The nonverbal turn-yielding cue was the termination of any hand gesticulation, or the relaxation of a tensed fist. One nonverbal cue was also identified which effectively prevented speaker-switching—it consisted of one or both the speaker's hands being engaged in gesticulation, but excluding self and object-adaptors (Ekman and Friesen, 1969). Duncan observed a correlation of 0·96 between the number of cues conjointly displayed, and the probability of a listener turn-taking attempt, in the absence of gesticulation. When gesticulation was occurring, the probability of a turn-taking attempt fell virtually to zero.

There are a number of problems with this kind of approach which omits consideration of linguistic or psycholinguistic structures in speech; these problems should become even more apparent, given the research reviewed thus far, which has elucidated the relationship between verbal and nonverbal behaviours in conversation. Duncan only provides information about the relationship between turn-taking and the conjoint frequency of various turn-yielding cues. He provides no information about the importance of individual cues. Among the cues he has identified, clause completion may be most important, because other paralinguistic cues (rise/fall in pitch, drawl on final syllable) should correlate with it. Other nonverbal cues may bear less obvious relations to linguistic and psycholinguistic structures. For example, in the present corpus, changes in the resting position of the arm and hands tended to occur at clause junctures nearest the ends of phases of temporal cycles. Such phenomena may act as turn-yielding cues, as Duncan suggested. It was also found in the present corpus that listener-responses were significantly more likely at clause-junctures nearest the ends of temporal cycles, than at other clause junctures. Listeners may therefore have been responding either to a nonverbal cue, as Duncan would suggest, or to an imminent change in semantic content heralded by a sudden increase in hesitancy; or more probably, to both, since the listener, through time, would presumably identify the correlation between changes in hand and arm position, and semantic content. We do not know, and the present corpus is too restricted to tell us, how listener responses at the ends of temporal cycles are affected by changes in basic equilibrium position alone. Until such questions are answered, it may be peremptory to conclude that the termination of gesticulations (of whatever order) elicits listener responses independently of linguistic context. Thus far it has not been made clear that confounding variables are not involved.

Apart from suggesting that nonverbal cues may achieve significance as regulatory signals as a result of a coincidence with psycholinguistic boundaries the present studies of encoding units in speech, and the organization of nonverbal behaviours, also suggest that there may be contextual constraints upon the interpersonal functions of such cues. As has already been stated, Kendon (1967) found that gaze at the ends of "utterances" resulted in a higher proportion of immediate speaker-switches than gaze-aversion. Beattie (1978a) considering the actual magnitude of speaker-switches and classifying utterances as either "complete" or "incomplete" (on the basis of being accompanied or unaccompanied by one or more of Duncan's, 1972, turn-yielding cues) failed to corroborate this result. Speaker gaze at the ends of "complete" utterances did not significantly affect the probability of the succeeding switching pause being short in duration. Moreover in contrast to Kendon, significantly more, immediate speaker-switches (≤ 200 ms) were observed to occur when utterances terminated without speaker gaze than with gaze. The situations studied by Kendon and Beattie differed in at least two ways which could potentially affect speaker-gaze. Firstly, the global social contexts were quite different. Kendon studied interactants who were previously unacquainted, and who were asked to "get to know each other", while Beattie studied interactants in supervisions, who were already acquainted. Such differences in intimacy would affect the overall amount of gaze (Argyle and Dean, 1965). Mean percentage whilst speaking was 49·4% in the Kendon study, and 66·8% in the Beattie study. It may be hypothesized that gaze becomes more perceptually salient, and effective as a turn-yielding cue, in a context of general gaze-aversion. The observation by Rutter *et al.* (1978), that speaker-gaze is implicated in a higher proportion of floor-changes between strangers than between friends, would support this hypothesis. The specific linguistic contexts studied by Kendon (1967) and Beattie (1978a) also differed. Kendon studied the effects of gaze at the ends of semantic units ("utterances were complete in form and content" and, in addition, marked by a change in topic, Kendon, 1978). Beattie (1978a) studied utterances which were "complete" (i.e. accompanied by one or more of Duncan's (1972) turn-yielding cues). The main focus of analysis in this study would therefore have been the ends of syntactic clauses (for the most part). Evidence reviewed earlier has suggested that the incidence of speaker-gaze is higher at the ends of semantic units in speech than at the ends of clausal units comprising these larger units. Thus gaze may have played a more significant role in the Kendon study, as a turn-yielding cue, because the particular linguistic contexts studied were probably characterized by a high level of gaze, further highlighted by the fact that the general context was one of gaze-aversion. The hypothesis that the efficacy of gaze as a floor-apportionment signal is affected by psycholinguistic context, which itself determines level of gaze, was tested (see also Beattie, 1979b).

1. Procedure
The interactions described in Part 1. were employed here. 110 speaker-turns and speaker-switches involving five subjects, were considered. Gaze occurrence at the ends of utterances was noted, as was the duration of the succeeding speaker-switching-pauses, measured using an Ediswan pen-oscillograph and pause detector. Inter-observer reliability in categorization of gaze at the ends of utterances was 90·9%.

2. Results
From Table XIII it is apparent that the longest switching-pauses tended to follow "complete" utterances, in hesitant phases of temporal cycles, ending with gaze-aversion ($\bar{t} = 1·918$ s; range 0–5·60 s). The shortest switching pauses tended to follow utterances at the ends of hesitant phases of speech terminating with speaker gaze ($\bar{t} = 378$ ms; range 0–3·20 s) In the former case 23·5% of speaker-switches were immediate (i.e. latency ≤ 200 ms) compared with 50·0% in the latter case.

An ANOVA revealed a non-significant effect for phase type preceding the speaker-switch i.e. hesitant or fluent ($MS = 2·250$, $df = 1$, $F = 1·539$, $p > 0·05$), and a non-significant effect for occurrence/nonoccurrence of gaze at the ends of utterances ($MS = 5·661, df = 1, F = 3·872, p > 0·05$). However,

TABLE XIII
Number and mean duration ($\bar{t}$) of switching pauses (s) following utterances, in hesitant and fluent phases of temporal cycles, terminating with or without gaze. (from Beattie 1979b)

Phase of cycle	Gaze occurrence at end of utterance		Gaze aversion at end of utterance	
	n	$\bar{t}$	n	$\bar{t}$
Hesitant phases	24	0·378	17	1·918
Fluent phases	47	0·808	22	0·533
Both phases	71	0·663	39	1·137

the ANOVA also revealed a significant phase type/gaze occurrence interaction effect ($MS = 19\cdot096$, $df = 1$, $F = 13\cdot062$, $p < 0\cdot001$). In contrast to Beattie (1978a), the mean switching pause was shorter following utterances accompanied by speaker gaze than by gaze aversion (663 ms and $1\cdot137$ s, respectively; mean switching pauses in Beattie (1978a) were 775 ms and 530 ms respectively). One important difference between the studies is the length of utterances—in the earlier study all utterances were considered whereas in the present study a minimum temporal criterion of 30 s was applied.

3. *Discussion*

This study failed to demonstrate, as did Beattie (1978a), that speaker gaze at the ends of "complete" utterances universally facilitates speaker turn-taking in conversation. However, it did demonstrate that gaze at the ends of "complete" utterances can facilitate speaker-switching in specific linguistic contexts—those in which hesitant phases of speech, reflecting a high level of cognitive planning (Henderson *et al.*, 1966), and associated with a lower overall level of speaker gaze (Beattie, 1978b), immediately preceded the speaker-switch. Speaker-gaze at the ends of "complete" utterances (usually clausal junctures, see Duncan, 1972) in hesitant phases was associated with a significant decline in the duration of speaker-switching pauses. This result did not obtain with utterances in fluent phases where background level of gaze tends to be higher (Beattie, 1978b). These results suggest that it is necessary to consider the overall level and distribution of speaker gaze in conversation in order to determine its efficacy in facilitating turn-taking. This study also demonstrated that gaze is not an indispensable cue for turn-taking in conversation, $35\cdot45\%$ of smooth speaker-switches, i.e. those occurring without simultaneous speech, followed utterances terminating with speaker gaze aversion.

The conclusion of this study is that the floor-apportionment function of speaker gaze is context-specific. Moreover, it may be predicted that speaker gaze, will facilitate turn-taking in other social encounters characterized by low levels of gaze (e.g. conversations between strangers (Kendon, 1967); discussion on topics of high cognitive difficulty (Exline and Winters, 1965), and that its effectiveness should vary within any encounter as a function of local variation in its distribution. It should be more effective when cognitive processing load is high (as in the present study) or in discussion of an intimate topic (Exline and Winters, 1965) i.e. in local contexts characterized by low levels of gaze.

Future research into the interpersonal functions of gaze must consider aspects of the social context, which affect the level and distribution of this form of behaviour.

V. Part 4. Conclusions

This research began by investigating the location, and distribution, of hesitations in spontaneous speech in an attempt to reveal, (following

Lounsbury, 1954), the nature of units of speech encoding. However the recognition that some hesitations may possess a number of "social" functions demanded that other types of speaker behaviour, which are potentially informative about cognitive processing in speech, be considered e.g. speaker gaze (Exline and Winters, 1965; Kendon, 1967; Weiner and Ehrlichman, 1976), movement (Dittmann, 1972), and gesture (McNeill, 1975).

The hesitation analysis supported a language production model in which both suprasentential, semantic units (Henderson et al., 1966; Goldman-Eisler, 1967; Butterworth, 1975) and syntactic units (Fodor et al., 1974) were involved, with planning on a clause-by-clause basis only appearing to occur in the semantic planning phases of the larger units ("temporal cycles"). A "social" hypothesis was offered to account for the fact that speech does occur in these planning phases; namely that, if language output were suspended until a complete semantic plan was formulated, then considerably longer (but fewer) hesitations would be necessary for the generation of speech. One consequence of this would be that listeners' attempts to gain control of the conversation would become more frequent and probably more successful (Beattie, 1977). By spaking during semantic planning phases, the speaker can redistribute planning time (using more frequent, but shorter hesitations) whilst maintaining the listener's interest, and reducing the probability of interruption. This hypothesis is consonant with the observations made by Beattie and Bradbury (1979) which were that subjects can, when necessary, modify (to some extent) their temporal planning structure in an artificial verbal conditioning situation without significantly affecting speech content. Again it is suggested that the temporal structure underlying speech is a joint function of the cognitive demands of the speech task, and the social context in which speech occurs. This hypothesis also predicts that in social situations where interruption is unlikely, temporal cycles should be characterized by more hesitant planning phases.

The analyses of the nonverbal behaviour of speakers supported the conclusion concerning the primacy of suprasentential encoding units in speech. Speaker gaze at the listener was found to be organized in a coordinated system with the temporal cycles, with gaze being significantly more common in the more fluent phases of cycles. Subsidiary relationships were also observed between gaze occurrence and syntactic clauses. Speaker movement and gesture also displayed characteristic patterns with respect to temporal cycles. Batonic movements were most common in periods of phonation in the hesitant phases of cycles, whereas iconic gestures were most common accompanying relatively unpredictable content words, and beginning in pauses in the fluent phases of cycles. These results suggested that only in fluent phases of temporal cycles is there some semantic specification of certain content words available in advance of the word actually being uttered. It was also demonstrated that changes in the basic equilibrium position of the arm and hand tended to coincide with the clause juncture nearest the ends of temporal cycles, and speaker gaze at the listener at such junctures was also very high (81·82%). These factors suggested that temporal cycles are important interactional units in conversation-speakers attempt to avoid idea interruption by displaying turn-yielding cues (Duncan, 1972, 1973, 1975) at the terminal points of these units.

This chapter also discussed briefly the rule structure of conversation. In this context it has been shown, that a number of types of paralinguistic and nonverbal behaviour, which are largely governed by the basic cognitive processes underlying speech (e.g. hesitations, speaker gaze, gesture and movement) do acquire significant regulatory functions in conversation (Maclay and Osgood, 1959; Kendon, 1967; Duncan and Fiske, 1977). The present research, however, demonstrated that it is necessary in some cases, to consider the overall distribution of these behaviours, within speaker turns, in order to determine the efficacy of some of the behaviours, as conversational signals, in any given social encounter. Since it has been demonstrated that the overall structure of such behaviour can usefully be described with respect to the basic psychological units of language, it is argued that the fundamental language production processes should be considered in the study of conversation.

One criticism of this research will probably be that the samples of conversation employed were small, and the situations in which they occurred highly specific. In anticipation of this criticism, it must be added that more basic data was considered in the present series of studies than in many other studies of the microanalysis of conversation. Nevertheless, it is recognized that the analyses presented here must subsequently be applied to larger samples of data. The conversations studied were highly specific but it seemed to me that the study of these types of conversation had a number of advantages. Firstly, supervisions and seminars occur naturally in university settings and they can therefore be recorded and analysed with the minimum of experimenter contamination. Secondly, the language occurring in such conversations is not as diverse in form or function as that occurring in other types of context. The ideational and textual components of language (Halliday, 1973) tend to be predominant in such conversations (the beginnings and ends of supervisions are notable exceptions to this, but they tended to be excluded in the present analyses). It can be argued that choice of a sample which does not display excessive variability is essential in exploratory studies of this kind. Nevertheless, future research must attempt to show that the results obtained here are generalizable to other types of conversational context. (It is hard to be over-optimistic about the generalizability of some of the results. Contextual differences in the efficacy of turn-yielding cues have already been hypothesized to exist across social situations, and shown to exist within the same situation.) The third main advantage of studying these types of social situation is that they, in themselves, are important and any knowledge we gain from such research must be useful in aiding our understanding of some of the processes involved in such teaching situations.

Thus to conclude, this work has attempted to draw attention to the complexity and richness of some of the more basic forms of social behaviour and to some of the paralinguistic phenomena which accompany, and partly constitute (see Goldman-Eisler, 1968, Chapter 1), human language. It has attempted to demonstrate that paralingusitic phenomena can tell us a great deal about the psychological processes involved in the generation of speech, and that order can be perceived in the complex array of human nonverbal behaviour, when one considers these basic psychological processes. The approach has been one of attempting to describe human social behaviour with respect to the language which, almost invariably, accompanies, underlies and directs it.

Acknowledgements

I wish to thank Dr B. Butterworth for supervising this research at the University of Cambridge, and also Carol Beattie for her invaluable criticism of earlier drafts of this chapter. I would also like to thank Julie Hodgson for typing the manuscript. This research was financed by a Northern Ireland Research Studentship (1974–1977), for which I am most grateful.

References

Aborn, M., Rubenstein, H. and Sterling, T. D. (1959). Sources of contextual constraint upon words in sentences. *J. exp. Psychol.* **57**, 171–180.

Argyle, M. and Cook, M. (1976). "Gaze and Mutual Gaze", Cambridge University Press, Cambridge.

Argyle, M. and Dean, J. (1965). Eye-contact, distance and affiliation. *Sociometry, 28*, 289–304.

Argyle, M. and Ingham, R. (1972). Gaze, mutual gaze and proximity. *Semiotica, 1*, 32–49.

Argyle, M., Lefebvre, L. and Cook, M. (1974). The meaning of five patterns of gaze. *Eur. J. Soc. Psychol.* **4**, 125–136.

Barik, H. C. (1968). On defining juncture pauses: a note on Boomer's "Hesitation and grammatical encoding". *Lang. Speech, 11*, 156–159.

Baxter, J. C., Winters, E. P. and Hammer, R. E. (1968). Gestural behaviour during a brief interview as a function of cognitive variables. *J. Personal. Soc. Psychol., 8*, 303–7.

Beattie, G. W. (1977). The dynamics of interruption and the filled pause *Br. J. Soc. Clin. Psychol., 16*, 283–284.

Beattie, G. W. (1978a). Floor apportionment and gaze in conversational dyads. *Br. J. Soc. and Clin. Psychol., 17*, 7–16.

Beattie, G. W. (1978b). Sequential temporal patterns of speech and gaze in dialogue. *Semiotica.* **23**, 29–57.

Beattie, G. W. (1979a). Planning units in spontaneous speech: some evidence from hesitation in speech and speaker gaze direction in conversation *Linguistics* **17**, 61–78.

Beattie, G. W. (1979). Contextual constraints on the floor-apportionment function of gaze in dyadic conversation. *Br. J. Soc. Clin. Psychol.* **18**.

Beattie, G. W. and Bradbury, R. J. (1979). An experimental investigation of the modifiability of the temporal structure of spontaneous speech. *J. Psycholing. Res.* **8**, 225–247.

Berry, J. (1953). Some statistical aspects of conversational speech. *In* "Communication Theory" (W. Jackson, ed.). Butterworth, London.

Birdwhistell, R. L. (1970). "Kinetics and Context: Essays on Body-Motion Communication." Penguin, Harmondsworth.

Boomer, D. S. (1965). Hesitation and grammatical encoding. *Lang. Speech,* **8**, 148–158.

Boomer, D. S. (1970). Review of F. Goldman-Eisler. "Psycholingustics: Experiments in Spontaneous Speech". *Lingua,* **25**, 152–164.

Bull, P. E. and Brown, R. (1977). The role of postural change in dyadic conversations. *Br. J. Soc. Clin. Psychol.,* **16**, 29–33.

Burke, J. P. and Schiavetti, N. (1975). Effects of cumulative context and guessing methods on estimates of transitional probability in speech. *Lang. Speech,* **4**, 299–311.

Butterworth, B. L. (1972). Semantic Analysis of the Phasing of Fluency in Spontaneous Speech. Unpublished Ph.D. Dissertation. University College, London.

Butterworth, B. (1975). Hesitation and semantic planning in speech. *J. Psycholinguist. Res.,* **4**, 75–87.

Butterworth, B. L. (1976). Semantic planning, lexical choice and syntactic organization in spontaneous speech. Unpublished paper. University of Cambridge.

Butterworth, B. and Beattie, G. W. (1978). Gesture and silence as indicators of planning in speech. *In* "Recent Advances in the Psychology of Language: Formal and Experimental Approaches" (R. Campbell and P. Smith, eds.). Plenum, New York.

Cook, M. and Smith, J. M. C. (1972). Studies in programmed gaze. Unpublished paper. University College of Swansea.

Cook, M. and Smith, J. M. C. (1975). The role of gaze in impression formation. *Br. J. Soc. Clin. Psychol.,* **14**, 19–25.

Deutsch, F. (1947). Analysis of postural behaviour. *Psychoanalytic Q.,* **16**, 195–213.

Deutsch, F. (1952). Analytic posturology. *Psychoanalytic Q.* **21**, 196–214.

Dittmann, A. T. (1972). The body movement-speech rhythm relationship as a cue to speech encoding. *In* "Studies in Dyadic Communication" (A. Siegman and B. Pope, eds). Pergamon, New York.

Duncan, S. (1972). Some signals and rules for taking speaking turns in conversations. *J. Person. Soc. Psychol.,* **23**, 283–292.

Duncan, S. (1973). Toward a grammar for dyadic conversation. *Semiotica,* **9**, 29–47.

Duncan, S. (1975). Interaction units during speaking turns in dyadic face-to-face conversations. *In* "The Organization of Behaviour in Face-to-Face Interaction" (A. Kendan, R. Harris and M. Key, eds). Mouton, The Hague.

Duncan, S. and Fiske, D. W. (1977). "Face-to-Face Interaction: Research, Methods and Theory." Lawrence Erlbaum, New Jersey.

Ehrlichman, H., Weiner, S. L. and Baker, A. H. (1974). Effects of verbal and spatial questions on initial gaze shifts. *Neuropsychologia,* **12**, 265–277.

Ekman, P. and Friesen, W. V. (1969). The repertoire of nonverbal behaviour: categories, origins, usage and coding. *Semiotica,* **1**, 49–98.

Exline, R. V. and Eldridge, C. (1967). Effects of Two Patterns of a Speaker's Visual Behaviour upon the Authenticity of his Verbal Message. Paper presented to the Eastern Psychological Association, Boston.

Exline, R. V. and Winters, L. C. (1965). Effects of Cognitive Difficulty and Cognitive Style upon Eye Contact in Interviews. Paper read to the Eastern Psychological Association.

Feldman, S. S. (1959). "Mannerisms of Speech and Gestures in Everyday Life",

International Universities Press, New York.

Fodor, J. A., Bever, T. G. and Garrett, M. F. (1974). *The Psychology of Language*. McGraw-Hill, New York.

Freedman, N. and Hoffman, S. P. (1967). Kinetic behaviour in altered clinical states: approach to objective analysis of motor behaviour during clinical interviews. *Perceptual Motor Skills*. **24**, 527–539.

Freud, S. (1905). Fragments of an analysis of a case of hysteria. *In* "The Standard Edition of the Complete Psychological Works of Sigmund Freud", Vol. 7. Hogarth Press, London.

Goldman-Eisler, F. (1958a). Speech production and the predicability of words in context. *Q. J. of exp. Psychol.*, **10**, 96–106.

Goldman-Eisler, F. (1958b). The predicability of words in context and the length of pauses in speech. *Lang. Speech*, **1**, 226–231.

Goldman-Eisler, F. (1967). Sequential temporal patterns and cognitive processes in speech. *Lang. Speech*, **10**, 122–132.

Goldman-Eisler, F. (1969). "Psycholinguistics: Experiments in Spontaneous Speech", Academic Press, London.

Goldman-Eisler, F. (1972). Pauses, clauses, sentences. *Lang. Speech*, **15**, 103–113.

Graham, J. A. and Argyle, M. (1975). A cross-cultural study of the communication of extra-verbal meaning by gestures. *J. Hum. Mov. Stud.*, **1**, 33–39.

Graham, J. A. and Heywood, S. (1975). The effects of elimination of hand gestures and of verbal codability on speech performance. *Eur. J. Soc. Psychol.*, **5**, 189–195.

Halliday, M. A. K. (1973). "Explorations in the Functions of Language", Edward Arnold, London.

Henderson, A., Goldman-Eisler, F. and Skarbek, A. (1966). Sequential temporal patterns in spontaneous speech. *Lang. Speech*, **9**, 207–216.

Jackson, H. J. (1878). On affectations of speech from disease of the brain. Reprinted in "Selected Writings of Hughlings Jackson" (1958), Vol. 2, pp. 155–170. Basic Books, New York.

Jaffe, J. and Feldstein, S. (1970). Rhythms of Dialogue. Academic Press, New York.

Kendon, A. (1967). Some functions of gaze direction in social interaction. *Acta Psychologica*, **26**, 22–63.

Kendon, A. (1972). Some relationships between body motion and speech. An analysis of an example. *In* "Studies in Dyadic Communication" (A. Siegman and B Pope, eds). Pergamon, New York. p. 205.

Kendon, A. (1978). Looking in conversation and the regulation of turns at talk: a comment on the papers of G. Beattie and D. R. Rutter et al. *Br. J. Soc. Clin. Psychol.*, **17**, 23–24.

Kendon, A. and Cook, M. (1969). The consistency of gaze patterns in social interaction. *Br. J. Psychol.*, **69**, 481–494.

Kleck, R. E. and Nuessle, W. (1968). Congruence between the indicative and communicative functions of eye-contact in interpersonal relations. *Br. J. Soc. and Clinical Psychology*, **7**, 241–246.

Knight, D. J. Langmeter, D. L. and Landgren, D. C. (1973). Eye-contact, distance and affiliation: the role of observer bias. *Sociometry*, **36**, 390–401.

Kozhevnikov, V. A. and Chistovich, L. A. (1965). Speech, articulation and perception. U.S. Department of Commerce, Joint Publication Research Service, Washington, D.C.

Libby, W. L. (1970). Eye contact and direction of looking as stable individual differences. *J. Exp. Res. Personal.*, **4**, 303–312.

Lounsbury, F. G. (1954). Transitional probability, linguistic structure and systems of habit-family hierarchies. *In* "Psycholinguistics: A Survey of Theory and Research Problems" (C. Osgood and T. Sebeck, eds). University Press, Indiana.

McNeill, D. (1975). Semiotic Extension. *In* "Information Processing and Cognition: The Loyola Symposium". Lawrence Erlbaum, Hillsdale, New Jersey.

Maclay, H. and Osgood, C. E. (1959). Hesitation phenomena in spontaneous English speech. *Word,* **15**, 19–44.

Mahl, G. F., Danet, B. and Norton, N. (1959). Reflection of major personality characteristics in gestures and body movement. Paper presented at Annual Meeting, American Psychological Association, Cincinnati, Ohio, September, 1959.

Natale, M. (1976). A markovian model of adult gaze behaviour. *J. Psycholinguist. Res.,* **5**, 53–63.

Nielsen, G. (1962). "Studies in Self Confrontation", Monksgaard, Copenhagen.

Patterson, M. L. (1973). Stability of non-verbal immediacy behaviours. *J. Exp. Soc. Psychol.,* **9**, 97–109.

Reich, S. S. (1975). The function of pauses for the decoding of speech. Unpublished Ph.D. Thesis. University College, London.

Sacks, H., Schegloff, E. A. and Jefferson, G. A. (1974). A simplest systematics for the organization of turn-taking for conversation. *Language,* **50**, 697–735.

Schlauch, M. (1936). Recent Soviet studies in lingusitics. *Sc. Soc.,* **1**, 157.

Schulze, R. and Barefoot, J. (1974). Non-verbal responses and affiliative conflict theory. *Br. J. Soc. Clin. Psychol.,* **13**, 237–243.

Sokal, R. R. and Rohlf, F. J. (1973). "Introduction to Biostatics", W. H. Freeman, San Francisco.

Stephenson, G. M. and Rutter, D. R. (1970). Eye-contact, distance and affiliation: a re-evaluation. *Br. J. Psychol.,* **61**, 385–393.

Stephenson, G. M., Rutter, D. R. and Dore, S. R. (1973). Visual interaction and distance. *Br. J. Psychol.* **64**, 251–257.

Taylor, I. (1953). "Cloze" procedure: a new tool for measuring readability. *Journalism Q.,* **30**, 415–433.

Trager, G. L. and Smith, H. L. (1957). "An outline of English structure." American Council of Learned Societies, Washington, D.C.

Valian, V. V. (1971). Talking, listening and linguistic structure. Unpublished Ph.D. Thesis. Northeastern University.

Weiner, S. L. and Ehrlichman, H. (1976). Ocular motility and cognitive processes. *Cognition,* **4**, 31–43.

II
Ways of Investigating Psychological Processes

5

The Production of Sentences, Utterances and Speech Acts: Have Computers Anything to Say?

M. J. Steedman and P. N. Johnson-Laird

University of Warwick, University of Sussex

I. Introduction

One of the major problems for a speaker is to decide what to say. If he merely produces well-formed sentences, or even if he simply recites true statements he will not find his utterances treated seriously as conversation. The speaker has to decide *which* propositions to express, since an utterance has to be relevant to the current discourse and to the particular purposes and intentions that its participants are pursuing.

The speaker's problem is likewise the theorist's problem: if models of sentence production are to be taken seriously, they must account for the fact that speakers only make statements that they have reason to believe their hearers need to hear, that they only ask questions that they consider likely to be answered, and that they only make requests that they assume may be carried out.

In the present paper, we shall address ourselves to the speaker's problem, and argue that the efforts to program computers to produce sentences have led to some understanding of how the speaker decides what to say next.

There are a number of reasons for expressing psychological theories as computer programs. A well-known foible of computers is their literal-mindedness and intolerance of imprecision, and so the existence of a working program provides considerable evidence for the completeness and consistency of the theoretical principles that it embodies. The process of developing so detailed a working model concentrates the mind marvellously, and forces a theorist to make explicit many intuitions that would otherwise be left unformulated. The process is a truly dialectical one, and may lead to extensions or revisions of the original theory. It may even suggest some empirical tests of the theory, provided that the program is kept simple enough for the programmer to discern clearly the distinction between the theoretical principles and the *ad hoc* working assumptions that it embodies. In these respects, a computer program is perhaps no different from any other formal model of a psychological process. There is, however, a special reason for using computer programs to explore theories of linguistic processing: certain features of the semantics of natural language are very naturally captured in terms of procedures (see for example Woods, 1968; Winograd, 1972; Davies and Isard, 1972; Miller and Johnson-Laird, 1976; Johnson-Laird, 1977a; Steedman, 1977). The procedural approach is particularly appropriate for those aspects of significance that depend on the continually changing conversational context—the essence of conversation since a speaker both relies upon the current context and, by his very remarks, changes it.

In order to decide upon something sensible to say, a speaker must in fact possess several distinct sorts of knowledge. One way of classifying this knowledge is into the following categories.

1. *Linguistic knowledge.* A speaker must know how to express a proposition in words, how to form an interrogative sentence, and so on. Hence, he must have a working knowledge of the syntax and semantics of his language.

2. *Factual knowledge.* The speaker must know things about the world. Some of these facts will be simple, such as *John is tall.* Other facts will have more of the character of rules of inference, or recipes for action, such as *to find out what day it is, look at a calandar or ask someone.*

3. *Conversational context.* The speaker must know things about the current conversation, such as that it is about the party that Cuthbert held last night. This information is vital if he is to form referring expressions that will be correctly interpreted.

4. *Conversational principles.* Conversations are not arbitrary: their structure seems to be determined in part by a number of implicit conventions governing discourse. The speaker must know the rules of the game in order to follow them.

5. *Conversational purpose.* Conversations are motivated by the aims or intentions of their participants. At the very least, the speaker must have a purpose, such as *finding out the time* or *telling this person how to get to the station.*

6. *Knowledge of the hearer.* The speaker must have knowledge about the hearer, including the hearer's own knowledge and purposes. The speaker may even have to know what the hearer knows of his own knowledge, and so on. Conversation is often intended to adjust discrepancies between the knowledge of its participants.

7. *Illocutionary knowledge.* The way to achieve a particular communicative intention often depends on constructing an utterance that takes into account the purposes and knowledge of the participants in the conversation. The speaker must decide, for example, whether a remark such as "That cake looks nice" will be more or a less effective way of making a request in a certain context than "Give me the cake".

These distinctions are to some extent arbitrary. Some of the categories may overlap, and some may be very different in character from others. However, it is in terms of these distinctions that we will review the work on language production in Artificial Intelligence. In the final sections of the paper, we will describe some of our own current work on the speaker's knowledge of conversation and his model of the listener's knowledge.

II. The Representation of Linguistic Knowledge

The earliest program to generate an interesting set of English sentences was developed by Yngve (1961). It relied on a context-free phrase-structure grammar based on sentences found in a children's story. Words were selected at random provided they were in accordance with the grammatical categories used by the grammar. The program deliberately avoided the problem of generating sentences to express particular meanings. It produced splendidly anomalous sentences such as:

(1) "When Engineer Small is proud, he has Small under a little and proud smokestack".

The derivation of more sensible sentences can be achieved by establishing classes of words that are semantically similar. A popular exercise in "computational linguistics" is to develop a grammar based on a particular text and then to generate variants of it using such substitution classes of words. Reams of computer poetry have been generated in this way. Here, for example, is such a variation on the stanza from Eliot's Love Song of Alfred Prufock that begins, "The yellow fog that rubs its back upon the window-panes":

The sullen haze that strews her lust upon the hurried streets,
The sullen air that strews her poison on the hurried streets,
Slipped her head into the current of the twilight,
Sauntered beneath the eaves that shade defects,
Let rest against her mouth the grit that rests in streets,
Prowled by the fountain, loosed a mocking cry,
And sensing that it was shrill cicada night,
Squatted low along the walks and paced the sky.

Program by Judith Merriam
(cited in Simmons and Correira, 1978)

A more serious use of computers to explore sets of grammatical rules is exemplified by the work of Friedman (1969, 1971), who has devised a program to help linguists to investigate the interactions between particular transformational rules by using them in the derivation of surface structures from deep structures. The program could be regarded as addressing part of the problem of producing sentences from underlying representations. However, there is suggestive experimental and theoretical evidence (e.g. Fodor *et al.*, 1974; Johnson-Laird, 1974) that the psychological mechanisms of language production and understanding are quite distantly related to transformational rules. In fact, none of the programs that have attempted to model language comprehension and production has made direct use of such rules, whatever the advantages of transformational grammar may be as a formal notation for linguistic descriptions.

A different approach to syntactic analysis relies on the so-called Augmented Transition Network or ATN (Woods, 1970), which was originally developed as a computer program for parsing sentences (Thorne *et al.*, 1968). An ATN in general has the same power as a transformational grammar, but it can recover what amounts to the underlying syntactic relations of a sentence without recourse to a transformational component, and without taking an unreasonable amount of time. It achieves this last feat because its basic operations are predictive and well suited to the analysis of sentences in a left-to-right direction; transformational rules are less well suited for proceeding in this way since they are mappings from one entire syntactic structure onto another. The properties of ATNs are of considerable psychological interest, and such theorists as Kaplan (1972), and Wanner and Maratsos (1975), have described the processes of sentence perception in terms of them. It is important to appreciate that certain linguistic structures such as conjunctions and adverbials are better accommodated by some other sort of procedure, which does not attempt to predict their occurrence—they may pop up almost anywhere in a sentence. Similarly, certain psychological phenomena are better explained by other sorts of theory, e.g. the ability to pick up a speaker's meaning in the middle of a sentence and to use this information to construe an earlier misperceived portion of the sentence. However, one property of an ATN is highly relevant to the purpose of this volume: it is a device that can also be used for producing sentences.

The heart of an ATN is a recursive transition network grammar, which as a class is (weakly) equivalent to a context-free phrase-structure grammar. The transition network grammar can be written as a set of rewrite rules, as in Fig. 1, or (more usefully) as a set of networks, as in Fig. 2.

There is an obvious way of interpreting a context-free grammar as a "top-down" parser, where each rewrite rule of the form:

(2) $A \rightarrow B + C$,

is interpreted as an instruction:

(3)   To parse an A, first parse a B, then parse a C.

Further rewrite rules will in turn define how to parse a B, and so on. Likewise, there is an obvious interpretation of a context-free grammar as a "top-down"

$$S \rightarrow \left\{ \begin{array}{l} NP \\[1em] aux \end{array} \begin{array}{l} \left\{ \begin{array}{l} v \\ aux \\ NP \end{array} \right\} \quad v \end{array} \right\} NP \quad (PP^*)$$

$$NP \rightarrow \left\{ \begin{array}{l} det \quad (adj^*) \quad N \quad (PP^*) \\ npr \end{array} \right.$$

$$PP \rightarrow prep \quad NP$$

FIG. 1. Transition network grammar. (Adapted from Woods, 1970.)

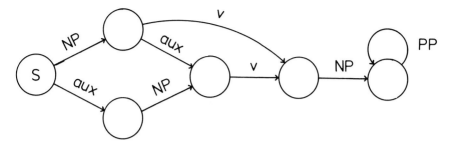

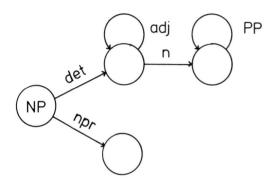

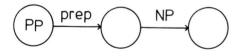

FIG. 2. Transition network. (Adapted from Woods, 1970.)

producer. Each rule in the form of (2) is interpreted as an instruction:

(4)   To produce an A, first produce a B, then produce a C.

In exactly the same way, a recursive transition network grammar can be interpreted either as a parser or as a producer.

In order to cope with natural language, the transition network grammar is augmented in power by associating an action with each arc in the network (see Fig. 2). These actions can be used to build up a syntactic representation of a sentence as it is parsed. Such an *augmented* transition network grammar has the power of a transformational grammar to move constituents around, and thus to capture the relations that hold between, say, a declarative and its corresponding interrogative, an active and its corresponding passive, and so on. Moreover, the ATN grammar retains the property of being readily interpretable both as a parser and as a producer. For example, when a sentence beginning with an auxiliary verb is parsed by the network of Fig. 2, a marker might be put into its underlying structure to identify it as an interrogative. In generating a sentence corresponding to the same underlying structure, the interrogative marker can cause the same arc of the network to be taken and an auxiliary verb to be produced first.

The transition network grammar itself is a surface structure grammar. However, the augmentation of the corresponding parser enables it to build an underlying syntactic structure as it goes. Thus, the surface structure of a sentence is never actually built at all, either in parsing or in generation. Surface structure is rather a description of what the machine *does* in going from sentence to underlying structure or vice versa.

Simmons and Slocum (1972) used an ATN to produce English sentences from an underlying representation that consists of a semantic network similar to the sort proposed by Rumelhart *et al.* (1972). A semantic network represents a whole set of related facts by links between nodes standing for the various entities involved in them, hence it is not so much a tree structure as a "banyan", or tree with many roots (see Isard and Longuet-Higgins, 1971). By directing the ATN to a particular node in the semantic network, Simmons and Slocum's program produces sentences that describe the facts represented in the network. The actual sentences it produces depend on the particular starting point in the network. The program also makes a limited use of pronouns whenever e.g. a proper noun is used, it takes steps to ensure that a subsequent pronominal reference can be made to the same individual. The sentence generator uses verbs as the starting point for generating sentences, and both the semantic network and the ATN rely on the categories of Case grammar: Agent, Object, Location, and so on. The sentences are kept intelligible by breaking them up into separate parts in order to avoid too much embedding:

(5)   John saw Mary wrestling with a bottle at the liquor bar. He went over to help her with it. He drew the cork and they drank champagne together.

A suite of programs devised by Schank (1975) and his collaborators, and known as MARGIE, is capable of paraphrasing sentences and drawing certain types of inference from them. It exploits a rather similar ATN production device. Given a sentence such as:

(6)   John gave Mary a bicycle

MARGIE first sets up a semantic representation of it couched in terms of Schank's (1972) Conceptual Dependency theory: the meanings of verbs are captured by a small set of semantic primitives standing for such actions as propelling something, ingesting it, grasping it, changing its physical location, and so on. The semantic relations between a verb and its various noun phrases are captured by a notation similar to that of Case grammar. The representation of sentence (6) is accordingly:

(7)   ((ACTOR(JOHN)⇔(ATRANS) OBJECT (BIKE REF (INDEF))
       FROM (JOHN) TO (MARY)) TIME (TIME 01) FOCUS ((ACTOR)))

where ATRANS stands for the transfer of an abstract relationship such as possession, the double-headed arrow relates the actor to the act, and the TIME 01 denotes a time prior to the utterance of the sentence. MARGIE contains a second component that uses the conceptual representation of a sentence to produce paraphrases of it or to draw plausible inferences from it. A third component takes a computed conceptual representation of such a paraphrase or inference and produces a sentence from it, selecting both the appropriate words and their syntactic arrangement:

(8)   Mary received a bicycle from John.
        John wanted Mary to have a bicycle.

This component uses an ATN similar to Simmons and Slocum's in order to produce actual sentences; its syntactic repertoire is fairly limited, but the process by which it selects verbs appropriate to the underlying semantics is of some psychological interest and worth considering in more detail.

The program contains a lexicon in which each separate meaning of a verb is defined in terms of a set of characteristics that have to be satisfied by the conceptual representation in order for it to be described by using that verb. In order, for example, to translate the following conceptual representation into words:

(9)   (ACTOR (JOHN)⇔(INGEST) OBJECT (MILK))

it is necessary to retrieve the fact that milk is a fluid, because the appropriateness of a verb often depends upon the nature of objects referred to by its accompanying noun phrases. This sort of information is organized in the form of a "discrimination tree", such as the one for verbs of INGESTING shown in Fig. 3. When the program receives a conceptual representation to be put into words, it first selects a set of one or more relevant discrimination trees on the basis of a rapid matching heuristic. A particular tree is then applied to the conceptual representation, starting with the top-most node. As a result of the comparison between the test associated with a node and the conceptual representation, either the positive or negative path is chosen. Ultimately, the sequence of tests will yield a particular word or, strictly speaking, a lexical entry for a particular sense of a word. Many of the tests on nodes correspond to the semantic markers or selectional restrictions of the semantic theory proposed by Katz and Fodor (1963).

Although discrimination trees were originally developed to account for the results of verbal learning experiments (Feigenbaum, 1963), their use as an organizing principle for the lexicon is psychologically somewhat implausible. As Chomsky (1965) has pointed out, many classificatory distinctions do not yield hierarchies unless one is prepared to impose an arbitrary ordering upon them, e.g. the tree in Fig. 3 could easily be re-arranged so that the test for whether OBJECT is ingested through the mouth comes before the test for whether it is a LIQUID. Moreover, the hierarchical nature of discrimination trees naturally demands serial processing and predicts that the latency to produce a word will depend on the number of nodes that have to be processed. Serial processing would be most inefficient, and what evidence there is from naming experiments fails to support a discrimination tree analysis (Oldfield and Wingfield, 1965; though cf. Levelt et al., 1976). Finally, an entirely

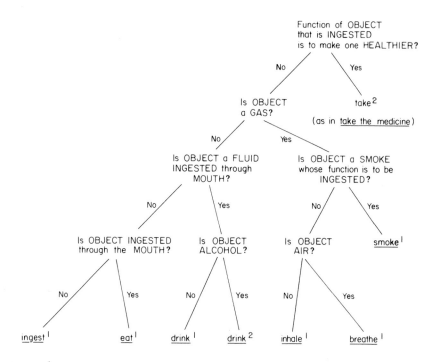

FIG. 3. A decision tree for verbs of ingestion (see Goldman, 1975). Note. The superscripted items denote specific senses of words.

Precondition: x INGESTS y through mouth

Semantic Conditions	Outcomes							
	1	2	3	4	5	6	7	8
SOLID(y)	+	+				−	−	−
LIQUID(y)			+	+	+	−	−	−
GAS(y)						+	+	+
MEDICINE(y)		+		+				−
ALCOHOL(y)					+	−	−	−
AIR(y)							+	
TOBACCO SMOKE(y)								+
Verbs								
x eats y	+	+						
x takes y		+		+	+			
x drinks y			+	+	+			
x drinks					+			
x inhales y						+	+	+
x breathes y							+	+
x smokes								+

FIG. 4. A simplified decision table for verbs of ingestion.

different organizational principle will be required to enable a listener to identify a word and to retrieve its meaning. It is for such reasons that Miller and Johnson-Laird (1976) argued that the mental lexicon is better thought of as organized by "decision tables", such as the simplified one illustrated in Fig. 4, which we have deliberately devised to reflect the same semantic analyses that are used by MARGIE. Such a decision table, which is a familiar device in programming, could be used to select a word by using its conditions as tests to be applied to the semantic representation of propositions to be expressed: as a function of the particular outcome of the tests, the verb(s) with plus signs in the same column are made available. Alternatively, it could be used in comprehension: once a verb has been identified, the plus signs in the same row yield its semantic components as one or more sets of test outcomes. One feature of decision tables is readily apparent from Fig. 4: they permit a many-to-many mapping between verbs and meanings.

Although Kempen (1976, 1977) has argued that certain psychological aspects of sentence production, particularly the nature of hesitations and speech errors, can be explained in terms of Schank's theory and his own related model of production, a major problem in evaluating the MARGIE suite of programs is that the task that they perform is an abstract one, isolated from actual conversation. MARGIE's inferences and paraphrases might, or might not, be plausible if they were made in discourse: it would all depend on the context in which they occurred and the particular individuals to whom reference was made. Let us accordingly turn to the problem of how such knowledge is represented.

III. The Representation of Factual Knowledge and Conversational Context

The simplest way to model a minimal context, and a minimal conversational purpose, is to design a program to answer questions about a model world. In fact, many question-answering programs have had only a primitive capacity to produce sentences, confining themselves to a small set of stock replies, or to filling slots in prepackaged responses. However, Winograd's (1971, 1972, 1973) program, SHRDLU, which handles a wide variety of questions and commands about the arrangements of a number of blocks on a table top (a universe that exists only as a computer simulation), has some interesting skills in production, as well as in comprehension.

Syntactically, SHRDLU has a very limited repertoire of sentences that it can produce. Its productivity in this respect is indeed much more restricted than its ATN-like powers of syntactic analysis, based on Systematic Grammar (Halliday, 1961; Hudson, 1972), and much more restricted than the ATN-driven production programs of Goldman, and Simmons and Slocum. All of SHRDLU's responses are made by using a small number of predetermined sentence patterns: the program fills in slots in the sentence with expressions that are pertinent to the user's original question, command, or statement.

What is interesting is the variety of *functions* of the responses, and the subtle way in which they are adapted to the purposes of the user's original typewritten utterance. For example, if the user asked a question such as:

(10)   What does the box contain?

the program can produce the following appropriate answer, using an indefinite noun phrase:

(11)   A LARGE GREEN CUBE.

On the other hand, the question:

(12)   Which cube is sitting on the table?

can be answered appropriately with a definite noun phrase:

(13)   THE LARGE GREEN ONE WHICH SUPPORTS THE RED PYRAMID.

The program can also substitute pronouns for parts of noun phrases, as in the previous example where the pronoun *one* replaces the word *cube*. The pronouns *it* and *they* are used to refer to entities that have been identified by previous noun phrases in the phrase, as in the following example:

(14)   BY PUTTING A RED PYRAMID ON THE GREEN BLOCK, THEN PUTTING IT IN THE BOX.

The last entity referred to can also be identified by the modifier *that*, as in:

(15)   BY PUTTING A RED PYRAMID ON THE GREEN BLOCK, THEN PUTTING THAT BLOCK IN THE BOX.

SHRDLU is even more skilful in understanding pronouns. This ability depends, of course, on the fact that the program includes a representation of the world to which such expressions can refer: without a world to which reference can be made, any pronominal exercise is crippled before it starts. In fact, SHRDLU's knowledge of the simulated world is considerable and interacts with the process of comprehension in a number of ways. Thus, the program is a major advance towards solving the problem of using *factual* knowledge in conversation, and of representing specific and general facts about the world. Its success in this area is a result of its use of Hewitt's (1969) problem-solving system, PLANNER.

SHRDLU comprehends and uses expressions referring to its own actions in order to answer such questions as:

(16)   When did you pick it up?
       Why did you pick it up?
       How did you pick it up?

It relies on a representation of the actions and utterances that have occurred during the conversation itself. Hence, the program also copes to some extent with knowledge of *conversational context*. Its knowledge of the principles of conversation, however, is rather limited: it treats all interrogatives, except those beginning with the words "Will you . . .", as questions, all declaratives as factual assertions, and all imperatives and "will you . . ." interrogatives as commands; if asked the same question twice, it simply makes the same reply rather than querying the user's intention or pointing out the redundancy.

A program written by Anthony Davey (Davey, 1974; Davey and Longuet-Higgins, 1976) is a direct descendant of certain aspects of Winograd's

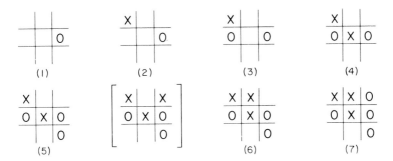

FIG. 5. The moves in a game of noughts-and-crosses.

program. It too, is based on a Systemic grammar, but unlike SHRDLU is almost entirely given over to the production of sentences. The program uses as its universe of discourse a game of noughts-and-crosses, or tic-tac-toe, which it has played with the operator. It produces a paragraph of English describing the progress of the game. An example of a game, in which the program played the noughts and the operator played the crosses, is shown in Fig. 5; a commentary that the program subsequently produced is given in Fig. 6.

The commentary is generated "from scratch", rather than being cobbled together from a predetermined stock of fragments of sentences. The only input is the record of the moves of the game: neither the sentences in the commentary, nor their semantic representations, have any previous existence in the machine. The example should make clear that the program has a superior grasp of pronouns including *one, other, it, they, that* and *those*, and a mastery of the pragmatic role of connectives that allows it to construct a coherent paragraph describing the tactics of the game. The design of the program also reflects one of the characteristic rules of conversation: in building up a referring expression, it treats the user like the tax man—giving him just what he needs, neither too much nor too little—an instance of a conversational principle that Grice (1967) dubbed the Maxim of Quantity.

The first stage in producing a commentary consists in breaking up the sequence of moves into tactically related groups. These groupings are ultimately reflected in the sentence structure of the paragraph, and in the choice of such connectives as *and, but* and *although*. The second sentence in Fig. 6 illustrates this process:

"I started the game by taking the middle of an edge, and you took an end of the opposite one. I threatened you by taking the square opposite the one I had just taken, but you blocked my line and threatened me. However, I blocked your diagonal and threatened you. If you had blocked my edge, you would have forked me, but you took the middle of the one opposite the corner I had just taken and adjacent to mine and so I won by completing my edge."

FIG. 6. A commentary produced by Davey's program. (Adapted from Davey and Longuet-Higgins, 1976.).

(17) I threatened you by taking the square opposite the one I had just taken, but you blocked my line and threatened me.

Moves 3 and 4 are tactically related in that move 3 is a threat, and move 4 is a defence against it. Since this defence successfully frustrates the purpose of move 3, the appropriate connective, *but*, is selected to conjoin the descriptions of the two moves. Move 5 is similarly related to move 4, but merely adding a further clause connected by *but* would fail to make clear with what it was being contrasted. Accordingly, move 5 receives a sentence to itself, prefaced by *however* in order to convey a similar contrastive meaning:

(18) However, I blocked your diagonal and threatened you.

The tactical significance of a bare sequence of moves, which constitutes the input of the program, is interpreted by the machine re-playing both sides of the game. In this way it can understand the purpose of each move, and the reasons for its success or failure. At move 6, for instance, the program recognizes that a better move for its opponent would have been the one shown in brackets in Fig. 5. In order to convey what could have happened, as well as what actually did happen, the program generates a counterfactual conditional:

(19) If you had blocked my edge you would have forked me, but you took the middle of the one opposite the corner I had just taken and so I won by completing my edge.

The connective "so" connects the description of the final move to its predecessor, establishing it as an immediate consequence of the user's error. Decisions about whether to describe a move in a main or subordinate clause are based on the tactical importance of the move in the game. A futile defence, for example, may be relegated to a subordinate clause:

(20) Although you blocked my diagonal, I won by completing my edge.

Subordination also depends on the particular tactical interpretations of a move: example (21) is an appropriate construction, where (22) is not:

(21) I blocked your line and forked you.
(22) I forked you and blocked your line.

The program's ability to pay due attention to such nuances depends on its knowledge of the game, rather than on *ad hoc* rules.

In some respects, the program's use of referring expressions is almost too elegant an embodiment of the Gricean Maxim of Quantity. The distinction between definite and indefinite noun phrases depends, like the various coordination and subordination constructions, upon the nature of the game. The first sentence of the discourse in Fig. 6 provides an example:

(23) I started the game by taking the middle of an edge, and you took an end of the opposite one.

For the purposes of the game, it is immaterial which of the four edges of the board had its middle taken, or which end of the opposite edge was taken in reply. But, since there is only one edge opposite to the first edge (whichever it is), a definite noun phrase is appropriate to describe the second edge. A definite description is also appropriate if the history of the game establishes that only one interpretation of a description corresponds to a legal move. The sentence:

(24)   I took the corner and you took the adjacent square.

is appropriate if there is only one corner, and only one square adjacent to it, that have not yet been taken. Likewise, the actual content of a referring expression reflects the Gricean principle. For example, move 3 involves a square described as:

(25)   the square opposite the one I had just taken . . .

It is not described as "the square opposite", because that would not be sufficiently informative; and it is not described as "the middle of the edge opposite to the one of which I had just taken the middle", because that would be too informative. Many other examples of similar varieties of referring expressions are to be found in Fig. 6. In particular its use of pronominal expressions represents a considerable advance on SHRDLU.

The programs developed by Winograd and Davey are an important step forward in modelling the production of sentences, in that they both utilize factual knowledge and a knowledge of the conversational context in subtle and effective ways, especially in the manipulation of referring expressions. However, neither program has any knowledge of the other participant in the conversation. They simply incorporate fixed assumptions about the listener. Winograd's program, for example, contains the heuristic that the pronoun "it" is most likely to refer to the focus of the preceding sentence, next most likely to refer to its subject, and so on. This purely syntactic procedure works quite well because speakers usually maintain continuity in their remarks, relating them to a single topic that often spans several utterances. But, as Winograd points out, the heuristic, and the semantic procedures that attempt to resolve any difficulties that it creates, are a very weak model of the structure of discourse. The rules for using pronouns in Davey's program similarly depend on keeping a list of potential referents, rather than having a true model of the topic of discourse and the thematic prominence of the various referents.

IV. The Representation of The Thematic Structure of Discourse

The thematic structure of discourse has been investigated by linguists such as Jespersen (1924), members of the Prague school of linguists such as Firbas (1964), the Systemic grammarian, Halliday (1967), and the psychologist, H. H. Clark (1975) and his collaborators. These investigators in their different ways all distinguish between what is assumed in an utterance, the "given" information, and what is asserted or questioned, the "new" information; and Clark has emphasized that there seems to be a general principle of conversation that given information in an utterance should be mentioned before new. Thus, the exchange:

(26)   Did Mary meet John at 2 o'clock?
        No, at 3 o'clock Mary met John.

seems awkward because the reply breaks this rule, whereas the unexceptional exchange:

(27) Did Mary meet John at 2 o'clock?
      No, Mary met John at 3 o'clock.
conforms to the rule. Of course, a non-final tonic stress, or a cleft construction, can be used to signal the fact that the given-new order is not the same as the surface constituent order.

One approach to modelling the given-new contrast is to assume that the underlying representation of the sentence is in some way labelled in order to identify those parts that correspond to given information and those parts that correspond to new information. Martin Kay (1975) has outlined a program that uses such a system, assigning noun phrases to different registers that indicate whether they are given or new, and generating sentences with a device comparable to an ATN. An alternative approach is to abandon this notion of explicit decisions and labels, and instead to assume that the given-new ordering is a direct result of the process of building up the actual message (Johnson-Laird, 1977b). Steedman has devised a simple program that embodies this principle (see Steedman and Johnson-Laird, 1976; Steedman, 1977). The idea exploited by the program can be illustrated by considering how, in principle, a listener would answer a question such as, "Did Mary meet John at 2 o'clock?" The listener first attempts to find those events in memory that involve Mary meeting someone, then he attempts to find among them those that involve meeting John, and finally he asks himself whether there was such a meeting at 2 o'clock. Here, the given information corresponds, not to a single proposition, but to two: the computation outlined above will break down either if Mary did not meet anyone, or if she did not meet John. By representing the given-new ordering as an order of processing, rather than as a static structure, such a failure in the given information is immediately evident. The particular assumption that has failed is likewise readily available to the program.

The order of the steps of the computation in the corresponding passive question is different. In the case of:
(28) Was John met by Mary at 2 o'clock?
the listener's first step is to find those events that involve someone meeting John, then the subset of them in which Mary meets John, and finally to ask himself whether there was such a meeting at 2 o'clock. As long as the answer to the question is "Yes", the difference between it and the corresponding active will not be apparent. But if the question is based on a false assumption, then the point at which the process breaks down will reflect the different ordering of the given information in the passive sentence. This idea is an elaboration of the way in which Winograd's program handles the user's inadequate deployment of referring expressions as in the following exchange:
(29) Pick up the green pyramid.
      I DON'T UNDERSTAND WHICH GREEN PYRAMID YOU
      MEAN.
Referring expressions also involve presuppositions, and Steedman (1977) has argued that a wide variety of thorny linguistic problems concerning presupposition are best tackled by procedural models.

The actual program answers questions about a simple one-dimensional world involving a number of "particles" bumping into each other at various places and times. Questions concerning these events are turned into a series of "goals", or computational steps, much as outlined in the earlier example. Given a question such as:

(30)   Did X hit Y at time 2?

the program responds as a function of the number of goals that are satisfied. If every goal is successful, it responds "Yes". If only the goals corresponding to the given assumptions that X hit something, and that it was Y, are successful, then the program responds with an appropriate reply, such as:

(31)   No. X hit Y at 3.

It produces this "helpful" answer as soon as the final goal corresponding to the new information has failed, and does so by generating a further goal to find out at what time X *did* hit Y. If a goal earlier than the final one fails, then the answer to the question is neither "Yes" nor "No", since a presupposition is false. The program responds by denying the failed presupposition, which it identifies by observing the point at which the computation broke down. For example, if X never did hit Y, it denies the assumption. Furthermore, in order to produce a helpful reply it once again generates a goal, this time to find out what X *did* hit, and responds appropriately:

(32)   X did not hit Y. X hit Z.

The representation of such thematic aspects of discourse by the order in which successive steps of a computation are performed, each one affecting the context in which the next one is evaluated, is at the heart of a series of programs devised to answer questions involving tense and temporal reference (Longuet-Higgins, 1972; Isard, 1974; Steedman, 1978). Although all of these programs, including the one described above, incorporate a simple thematic model of the conversation, none of them embodies any views about our next topic, the purpose of conversation.

V. The Representation of a Conversational Purpose

A program developed by Power (1974, 1977) comes closer than any other to having communicative purposes that change during the course of conversation. It also seems to be the only study in which *two* copies of a program have been used to model *both* parties in a conversation that they conduct entirely by themselves.

The programs, which go by the names of "John" and "Mary", converse about actions in a world consisting only of a door, with a bolt on one side, separating two places called "in" and "out". Although John and Mary are in most respects identical, the programmer can start them off with a different knowledge of their world, such as whether they know the law of their universe: *doors move if you push them provided that the bolt is up.* They can also be given different abilities, such as whether or not they can see, and different goals, such as whether or not they want to get in or out. The point of the program is to investigate the use of conversation to achieve goals; hence, both the world and the syntax of the language for talking about it are kept as simple as possible.

An example of the program's output is given in Fig. 7. The state of affairs at the beginning of the conversation is as follows: John is out, Mary is in, the door is shut, and the bolt, which is on John's side of the door, is up. John can see that the door is shut and the bolt up, but Mary is blind. John can move but is unable to push doors. Mary can do both. John believes, correctly, that *if you push the door, it changes position*, and, incorrectly, that *if you move, nothing happens*. Mary also believes, correctly, that *if you push the door, it changes position*, and that *if you move, you change position, provided that the door is open*. John has the goal of getting in, and Mary has no goal. Since John's deficient knowledge does not allow him to work out a way of getting in for himself, he tries to get Mary to help him, and she agrees to do so because she has nothing better to do. The first part of the ensuing dialogue is shown in Fig. 7.

What is interesting about the twin programs is the way in which they structure their conversation into a number of separate exchanges, each related to achieving the main goal or a subgoal in the plan to achieve it. These exchanges are managed by subroutines called "games", after their antecedents in the work of Wittgenstein (1953). Each game corresponds to a single conversational transaction, such as asking for information (e.g. 12–13), asking for help (5–6), or agreeing on a plan (14 *et seq*). The programs' utterances constitute the moves of the conversational games, and give a direct expression to the idea of a speech act (Austin, 1962; Searle, 1969). (However, there is a one-to-one correspondence between locutionary form and illocutionary force in the programs' utterances. In real life, of course, an interrogative sentence such as "Can you put this bowl on the table?" may have the force of a question, expecting the answer "yes" or "no", or may have that of a request, expecting compliance with it: the particular speech act of a speaker depends on more than the mere words that he uses to expression his intentions. Their intonation, the context in which they occur and general and specific knowledge, may all play a part in helping a listener to grasp the illocutionary force of an utterance. The purpose of the "games" in Power's program is to eliminate any possible misunderstanding of the underlying intention of an utterance, to make plain which particular speech act an utterance is making.)

A game may be played out in a mere two moves, as in the request for help in utterances 5 and 6. It may also lead to the introduction of sub-games and other, non-speech, actions by the players. For example, the utterances from 14 onwards play-out part of the game of agreeing on a plan: there is a brief game to agree to play this game (14–15), followed by Mary's attempt to think of a plan (16–28). She does not have enough information to do so unaided, and hence she and John play out two successive games of obtaining information (16–21) and (22–27). These in turn involve further sub-games.

Power's program contains a component missing from all the programs

*Initial state of world is (JOHN OUT MARY IN BOLT UP DOOR SHUT)

1 JOHN:	Mary.
2 MARY:	Yes.
3 JOHN:	I want to suggest a goal.
4 MARY:	Go ahead.
5 JOHN:	Will you help me get in.
6 MARY:	By all means.

    * The robots have now agreed to co-operate to achieve John's goal.
    * Mary has learned John's goal, and John has learned that she is
    * willing to help. If Mary had been given a goal different from John's,
    * she would have refused to help him.

7 JOHN:	Shall we make a plan.
8 MARY:	John.
9 JOHN:	Yes.
10 MARY:	May I ask you something.
11 JOHN:	Go ahead.
12 MARY:	Are you in.
13 JOHN:	No.

    * Mary interrupted because she did not know whether the goal was
    * already achieved (she is blind, remember); had she been cleverer, she
    * would have inferred John's position from 5. Before selecting a plan to
    * achieve a goal a robot always checks that the goal is not yet obtained
    * and that a plan is thus needed. The interruption at 8, causes both
    * robots to forget 7; John was suggesting a game at 7, but Mary over-
    * ruled him, and it is she who now starts the game to choose a plan.

14 MARY:	Shall we make a plan.
15 JOHN:	OK.
16 MARY:	John.
17 JOHN:	Yes.
18 MARY:	May I ask you something.
19 JOHN:	Go ahead.
20 MARY:	Can you move.
21 JOHN:	Yes.
22 MARY:	John.
23 John:	Yes.
24 MARY:	May I ask you something.
25 JOHN:	Go ahead.
26 MARY:	Is the door open.
27 JOHN:	No.
28 MARY:	I suggest that we get the door open and then you move.

    * After John agreed to help choose a plan at 15, Mary tried to devise
    * one. To do this she needs to know whether the door is open and
    * whether John can move. Since she is blind, she has to ask about the
    * door. At the point we have reached, Mary has learned the following
    * things: that John is out and the door is shut; that John's goal is to get
    * in; that John can see the door and himself; and that John can move.
    * John has learned that Mary cannot see him or the door, and that she
    * is willing to help him.

FIG. 7. Part of a dialogue between Power's twin programs. (Adapted from Power 1977.)

discussed so far. It is a crucial component of utterance that we identified in the introduction to this paper, namely, the conversational purpose that motivates the speaker's speech acts. However, the program still cannot be said to include a model of the other partner in the conversation beyond a few facts concerning their goal and basic abilities. It is the lack of such a model, and of any knowledge about conversation other than that which contained in the rules of the games, that leads to the somewhat pointless exchange of utterances 8 to 13. They could have been readily avoided if Mary had known that people do not seek to achieve goals that are already attained, and had updated her model of John accordingly.

VI. The Speaker's Model of The Listener

A dynamic model of each of one's partners in a conversation, and in particular of their knowledge and aims, is crucial for the natural conduct of discourse. Much ordinary conversation is concerned solely with obtaining such information, and with correcting misapprehensions about it. Human beings, unlike the programs that we have described, will not simply accept remarks that are blatantly inconsistent with their model of the speaker. For example, if the speaker asks a question that they have answered already they will typically respond rather differently from the way they did the first time. Similarly, ordinary discourse is based on very strong assumptions about the nature of conversational transactions and the role of those taking part in them. An example is the use of an indirect speech act, as when a speaker makes a request to someone, say, to pass some cakes by uttering the statement:

(33)   Those cakes look nice.

As in the work on the procedural semantics of the given-new distinction, it is convenient to represent an individual's knowledge, which will involve both simple facts and general rules of inference, as a "database" of assertions and procedures in a PLANNER-like programming language. Such a representation has the advantages of a procedural character, while remaining perspicuous, and clear in its relation to other more directly logically based formalisms. There are certain aspects of PLANNER that are psychologically implausible (see Johnson-Laird, 1977a). Nevertheless, it does provide us with some useful theoretical notions, and in the remainder of this section we will present the outlines of a small-scale computational model of a speaker's developing knowledge of a listener. The model is just comprehensive enough to explain how the speaker can avoid answering a question that he ought to realize cannot be sincerely meant, while still being able to answer sincere questions, whether the questions are expressed directly or indirectly. It is intended to implement the model in a program that is currently being developed (Steedman, 1976) to answer questions and to obey requests about a computer system that allows a number of users to share its resources. The program will have to understand indirect speech acts such as the following request: "Can I use the line-printer?" The proposals that follow are also related to the discussion of speech acts in Power (1977).

A speaker may have a detailed and complex knowledge of his hearer. He may know, for example, that the hearer is a Jehovah's witness, or a linguist with a morbid interest in speech acts, and design his utterances with careful attention to this knowledge. However, let us start with the simple case of one speaker who knows nothing about another speaker other than what has been implicit in the preceding conversation, and let us continue with Power's useful nomenclature and call one speaker, "Mary", and the other, "John". Consider the state of Mary's model when there has been just one utterance in the conversation, addressed to her by John, carrying the illocutionary force of a request to Mary to tell John the time. Such an utterance might be made with one of the following sentences:

(34)   What's the time?
        Tell me the time.
        I want to know what the time is.
        I don't know what time it is.

These utterances differ in politeness, and undoubtedly part of Mary's model of John will depend on which particular one he used. However, a more basic consideration is what John's utterance tells Mary about the state of his knowledge, how this information may cause her to reply, and how, in turn, her reply also affects her model of John's knowledge so that any further request to her to tell him the time will be rejected as breaking the rules of co-operative conversation. We emphasize that *any* further utterance of John's that has the force of such a request will violate the rules of conversation, not just the particular locution that he used the first time.

Mary clearly cannot have much more in the way of a model of John, an individual about whom she knows so little, than can be embodied in a few general assumptions and still fewer specific facts. A plausible first approximation to the most basic assumption that a speaker holds about a hearer is as follows:

(35)   *The speaker assumes that the hearer knows everything that the speaker knows about the world and about the conversation, unless there is some evidence to the contrary.*

Such evidence will frequently be forthcoming, as when the hearer asks a question. Specific facts, such as that *John does not know what time it is* and *John wants me to tell him what time it is* are recorded by the speaker as the conversation proceeds, and naturally take precedence over the general assumption above. Indeed, unlike the general assumption, they may cause the speaker to make a statement.

The principle embodied in assumption (35) must obviously be qualified. If you were always to assume that your listener's knowledge was the same as your own (until proved otherwise), you could never ask anyone the time, because you would assume that they didn't know, either. And, of course, you could never start a conversation with a provocative statement, or utter one in the middle of a discussion, since you would assume that your listener was already aware of its contents. We will have to return to these problems later. The point to be emphasized here is that some such principle seems to be needed to explain why, whatever else Mary knows about the world, she is likely to confine her next remark to a statement on the subject of which John has just revealed his ignorance, namely, the time.

Mary's first task in dealing with John's question is to translate his actual utterance, say, "What's the time?" into a semantic representation suitable for the interpretive component, i.e. the PLANNER problem-solver. The resulting translation will be a call of a procedure for *asserting*, i.e. adding to her database, the PLANNER equivalent of the simple fact that John wants her to tell him the time. This instruction might well take the form of:

(36)   ASSERT [JOHN WANTS MARY TELL JOHN TIME]

The execution of this instruction produces several side effects, brought about by Mary's knowledge of the rules of conversations. One of these rules is the PLANNER representation of the general assumption:

(37)   Demon 1: *If someone wants you to tell them something, then they don't know that something.*

Although this rule is written in English—and we shall continue to present such rules in English—PLANNER is specifically designed to make it easy to represent and use such rules. In particular, it allows them to be represented as "antecedent theorems", or more colloquially, "demons". A demon is a procedure of the form "if ever an attempt is made to assert (add to the database) P, do Q". In fact, P is specified as a pattern which may include variables, as the informal version of demon 1 suggests. Q is any series of PLANNER instructions, which for the purpose in hand will typically consist of attempts to make further assertions. A demon is very like a quantified formula in a formal logic, except that it has built into it the inference rule with which it is to be used—in this case *modus ponens*. It has the character of a rule of inference governing a rather specific set of contents. In fact, the relation of PLANNER to theorem provers based on formal logic is that PLANNER represents general assertions as rules of inference, whereas the formal therorem prover simply adds them to the list of axioms.

Since the assertion in (36) to be added to Mary's database matches the pattern of demon 1, the demon is activated, and its specified actions are carried out, that is, an attempt is made to add the further fact that John doesn't know what time it is, which might be written.

(38)   ASSERT [NOT[JOHN KNOWS TIME]]

Since Mary knows so little about John she presumably has no reason to doubt this assertion, so it takes its place in the database that represents her knowledge of John. The first assertion (36) also sets off another demon, which corresponds to a rule of conversation related to the Principle of Co-operation (see Grice, 1967; Searle, 1969). It says in effect:

(39)   Demon 2: *If you know that someone wants you to do something, then do it if you can.*

When this demon is activated by the first assertion (36), it does not result in a further assertion but rather it sets up a goal for action, to tell John the time:

(40)   GOAL [TELL JOHN TIME]

The goal of telling John the time requires Mary to find out the time, which may be quite simple if she already knows it, or which may require the use of further knowledge, represented as another sort of PLANNER procedure, a "consequent theorem", which lays down a method for achieving a particular consequence:

(41)   *To find out the time, look at your watch.*

Finally, Mary must design a locution that will accomplish the goal of telling John the time, such as:

(42)   The time is 12.35.
         It's 12.35
         12.35.

We will defer the question of which particular one of these alternatives should be used until later. An issue of more immediate importance is how Mary manages not to utter *any* of these replies, if John asks her the same question a second time, using any form of words to do so.

This problem is solved by the existence of a further demon:

(43)   Demon 3: *If you tell someone something, then they no longer don't know that something.*

A consequence of achieving the goal (40) to tell John the time is a further assertion to bring Mary's knowledge of John up to date:

(44)   ASSERT [MARY TELL JOHN TIME]

This assertion matches the pattern of Demon 3, whose execution results in the removal of the earlier fact that John doesn't know the time, and the further assertion of the new fact that John does know the time.

If John now asks the same question:

(45)   What is the time?

then in the changed context of Mary's knowledge about his knowledge, the result is entirely different from the previous case. Once again, the question yields a procedure to make an assertion (cf. (36)):

(46)   ASSERT [JOHN WANT MARY TELL JOHN TIME]

This assertion triggers Demon 1, which attempts to assert that John doesn't know the time (cf. (38)):

(47)   ASSERT [NOT [JOHN KNOW TIME]]

However, this attempted assertion fails, because of a general rule that you do not accept statements that you know to be false:

(48)   Demon 4: *If someone tells you something that contradicts what you know, then do not add it to your knowledge.*

Because this assertion fails, then it follows that the initial attempt to assert (46), that John wants Mary to tell him the time, also fails. And, since *that* is not asserted, Demon 2 that previously resulted in a goal to do what John wanted and tell him the time never gets roused, and so Mary makes no effort either to find out the time or to tell it to John.

However, Mary should do more than maintain an enigmatic silence under these circumstances. As we argued in the case of violations of the given information in a question, a reply should be helpful—that is, it should identify anything that has gone wrong. The production of a helpful reply here could be accomplished by a slightly more complex version of Demon 4, which we will call Demon 4'. When the assertion (47), that John does not know the time, is attempted as a consequence of Demon 1's activation, it activates this demon:

(49)   Demon 4′: *If someone tells you something that contradicts what you know, then:*

(1) *Do not add it to your knowledge*

(2) *Tell them the thing which you know that contradicts their assertion.*

The fact in Mary's database which contradicts assertion (47) is

(50)   [JOHN KNOWS TIME]

(which was put there by Demon 3). Therefore, Demon 4′ causes a goal to tell John this fact to be set up:

(51)   GOAL [TELL JOHN [JOHN KNOWS TIME]]

This goal results in Mary's replying

(52)   You know the time.

Such a remark would in almost any other circumstances be a most unusual thing to say, as it appears to violate the Gricean maxim of Quantity by telling John something that he must by definition know already.

Of course, the above set of demons are not by themselves adequate to represent the full range of real-life knowledge of conversational principles. They are considerably simplified in order to suit an informal presentation. (For example, we have ignored the fact that after a suitable lapse of time, Mary may consider John's repetition of a request to tell him the time as reasonable once more.) More rules of the same kind are needed to explain how Mary may avoid the presumption inherent in response (52) by stating the fact which *led* to her belief that John knew the time, as in

(53)   I have told you the time

Or how she may reply by asking for the reason why this fact didn't have the expected effect

(54)   Didn't you hear me tell you the time?

(55)   Are you deaf?

Moreover, the principles are certainly too strong on their own. Although Demon 4′ implies that one will always attempt to set a speaker right when he contradicts what one knows, one may know things about him that will make one swallow ones pride and say nothing. All that is claimed is that some such set of principles seems to be necessary to guide speakers through the complexities of conversation.

The demons may seem to have been multiplying alarmingly—after the habit of demons—but it turns out that the four that we have proposed seem to be most of those required to deal with a wide variety of locutions all commonly used with the illocutionary force of a question, that is, a request for information. There are numerous ways of indirectly requesting information. There are numerous ways of indirectly requesting information, and any of the following locutions can succeed in asking the time:

(56)   Can you tell me the time?

Do you want to tell me the time?

I don't know if you can tell me the time.

Do you know the time?

Will you tell me the time?

Suppose, in particular, that John's original question is expressed indirectly by:

(57)   Can you tell me the time?

Like all interrogatives, this sentence is initially translated into an instruction corresponding to the literal question, i.e. an assertion that John wants Mary to tell him if she can tell him the time.

(58)   ASSERT [JOHN WANTS MARY TELL JOHN? [MARY CAN
        TELL JOHN TIME]]

where "?" denotes the truth value of the parenthesized proposition. This assertion sets off a chain of events like that which ensued from our very first example of John's question (36), but here the inferences lead to an answer of the form: *Yes I can.* Obviously, this is altogether too simple an interpretation of the question. How is Mary going to be able to recover the real intention of John's question? At this point a further demon must be introduced

(59)   Demon 5: *If someone wants you to tell them if you can do something,
        then they may want you to do it.*

The word *may* is important in this definition: it may *not* be the case that they want you to do it. The computational expression of this modal notion is that, unlike Demon 1, this one does not cause the assertion (e.g. (58)) that sets it off to fail if the assertion (e.g. (60)) that it attempts fails:

(60)   ASSERT [JOHN WANTS MARY TELL JOHN TIME]

In fact, since we have assumed that John's indirect request is the first utterance in a conversation, then the assertion in (60) will presumably not be contradicted by anything that Mary knows. It accordingly succeeds, and the same chain of events as before will lead Mary to tell John the time. Moreover, if John used this utterance after previously making the same request with any appropriate locution, then it would fail because *both* of its illocutionary interpretations would fail: the assertion that John already knows the time causes the indirect request to fail, and the assertion (44) that Mary *did* tell John the time, is sufficient to establish that John already *knows* that Mary can tell him the time, so that the literal question also fails.

Our account of speech acts has yet to be implemented in a program, and the production of working programs is very close to the heart of procedural semanticists, so it is probably not worth elaborating the theory further at this stage, although the remaining indirect requests listed in (56) could be accounted for in the same terms. It is undoubtedly an oversimplified model. Our five major demons are essentially idealizations that underlie speech acts. Like so many aspects of human cognition they are to be taken for granted unless there is explicit information to the contrary, e.g. when someone refers to a dog, you take it to be four-legged; when they mention that they ate lunch in a restaurant, you assume they paid the bill. Likewise, when someone wants you to tell them something, you assume that they do not already know it (Demon 1). All of these inferences can be overruled in certain contexts. A teacher questioning a student in a Socratic vein plainly wants an answer, but *not* because he does not know it. Similar "suspensions" of our other demons are easily envisaged: you do not invariably do things that other people want (contrary to Demon 2); your telling someone something does not unfailingly guarantee that they henceforth know it (contrary to Demon 3), since they may immediately forget it or simply not believe you; and you sometimes add information to memory that contradicts what you already knew (contrary to Demon 4), because the new information may be incontrovertible. Demon 5 is, as we pointed out, a special case of a general principle. We can formulate this principle in a demon:

(61)   Demon 5′: *If someone wants to know whether a preparatory condition on the possibility of your doing something is true, then they may want you to do it.*

This demon explains the illocutionary force of all the indirect requests in (56): *being willing, being able,* and *wanting* to tell someone something, and *knowing* that something, are all preconditions of actually telling them. Provided that this information is included in Mary's knowledge, John's locution will have the desired illocutionary force. However, rather than elaborate the model and its attendant demons, it seems appropriate to turn to a comparison with other accounts of the interpretation of speech acts, and to ask whether there is any advantage to the procedural approach, or whether it merely provides a new notation for old ideas.

VII. Towards an Analysis of Speech Acts

There are a number of similarities between the model presented here and more traditional philosophical and logical accounts of the interpretation of speech acts, in particular those of Grice (1967), Searle (1969, 1975a, b), and Gordon and Lakoff (1971).

Searle's theory in particular is notably "procedural" in character, although not of course expressed in computational terms. We remarked on the similarity of Demon 2 and the "Principle of Co-operation", although the principle itself, unlike the demon, is more a description of what the system does than a rule that it uses. A more specific correspondence is between Demon 5 and a rule (7b) proposed in their logical analysis of speech acts by Gordon and Lakoff, and between its generalization Demon 5′ and part of a generalization (1) proposed by Searle (1975a). It may be helpful to examine the correspondence in some detail.

Gordon and Lakoff's "Conversational Postulate" (7b) is written as follows:

(62)   7b: ASK (a,b,CAN(b,Q))* → REQUEST (a,b,Q)

It means that *if a asks b a question whether he can do an act Q, and that question is "defective", then the question "entails" a request from a to b to do Q.* The term "defective", represented in the rule by the asterisk, means that the context is such that the hearer will assume that the speaker does not intend to convey a question, as for example when the hearer knows that the speaker knows the answer to a question like the following:

(63)   Can you take out the garbage?

In fact, Gordon and Lakoff (1971, p. 87) insist that utterances such as (63) can convey a request *only* when they are defective and when such an assumption is made by the hearer. Searle (1975b) points out that the rule has only a weak explanatory force, since (as Gordon and Lakoff admit) it is merely a specific instance of a generalization (Searle's Generalization 1, Gordon and Lakoff's (6)) to the effect that a speaker can make an indirect request for action by questioning a "preparatory condition", or condition on the possibility of the hearer's performing the action. Moreover, as Searle (1975a) emphasizes, the generalization is *not* a rule of conversation, but a *consequence* of the activity that the speaker and hearer are engaged in, and in particular of the fact that an attempt to perform a request will fail unless its preparatory conditions are fulfilled. An explanation of the illocutionary force of utterances such as *Those cakes look nice* would have to make this point explicit, as there seems to be an unlimited number of indirect ways of making a request.

Searle claims that it is not strictly necessary for the literal meaning of a question to be defective for it to have the force of a request. If someone requests information about the time by saying:

(64)   Can you tell me the time?

they may be in genuine doubt about the hearer's ability, and *at the same time* use the question to make a request. If so, the hearer is quite likely to respond to the literal meaning as well as the indirect request:

(65)   Yes, I can. It's 12 o'clock.

Curiously enough, Searle's own analysis of

(66)   Can you pass the salt?

has more than a suspicion of the idea that indirect speech acts are facilitated when the primary or literal meaning of the utterance is defective, in this case by reason of the obviousness of the answer and its uninteresting character (Searle, 1975a, p. 73, steps 3, 4 and 5). If so, then it should be easier to understand the illocutionary force of *Can you pass the salt*, uttered in such a context, than it is to understand *Can you tell me the time*, uttered in a context where it is unclear whether the hearer is in a position to give the information. This difference seems quite unlikely, and does not seem to be implied by the rest of Searle's analysis.

In the system presented here, the two speech acts, the question and the request, are totally independent since they rely on separate demon processes. Both may succeed, or either one may fail if it is pointless. It is only when *both* fail that the utterance is defective.

Another advantage of the procedural theory is that it makes explicit the distinction between the speaker's knowledge, and the hearer's beliefs concerning that knowledge. It is not enough for a theory merely to reflect the fact that a speaker can make a request by asking a question about whether the hearer can fulfil one of its preparatory conditions, e.g. *Can you tell me the time?* The theory must explain why that is a feasible way to do it, unlike merely making a *statement* about the hearer's wishes:

(67)   You wish to pass the salt.

Likewise, the theory must explain why (68) makes a request, but (69) does not.

(68)   I want you to pass the salt.

(69)   Do I want you to pass the salt?

There is an asymmetry between conditions on the sincerity of the speaker and on the hearer's preparedness. It creates a problem for Searle's account (1975a, p. 77, Problem 2), which seems to indicate that speech act theory itself is not entirely free of the charge of being a redescription, rather than an explanation, of the way that utterances accomplish the purposes of the speaker.

Our Demon 5' explicitly relates the "preparatory conditions" to the actions of the hearer, and Demon 1 relates the "sincerity conditions" to the purposes of the speaker, or rather, to the hearer's representation of these purposes. Hence, utterances such as (67) *You wish to pass the salt* and (69) *Do I want you to pass the salt?* fail to function as indirect requests simply because they fail in their *literal* illocutionary force: the former cannot be a genuine statement since it concerns information that the speaker is most unlikely to have access to, and the latter cannot be a genuine question since, like the infelicitious questions considered earlier, it asks for information that the hearer knows the speaker must already have. This explanation, of course, is equivalent to Searle's (1975a) explanation of the problem, but it is part of the basic behaviour of the procedural account, rather than an extra restriction.

VIII. The Problem of Selecting an Utterance

We have so far said nothing about the seventh and last aspect of a speaker's task, the problems of selecting an utterance appropriate to his conversational purpose and to his model of his hearer. On this subject our remarks will be brief, as befits our lack of knowledge, but also optimistic, since we believe that many of the techniques discussed above apply to this problem, particularly those concerned with understanding speech acts.

When someone wants to know the time, and therefore generates the goal of finding out the time, he may decide to play the conversational game of requesting information, since he knows that it is always likely that someone else knows the time. His problem is that, unlike Power's program, he has many alternative locutions available to him, as first moves in the game. What should he say? Some utterances, such as *I'd like to know the time* will be suggested by the processes that set up the goal in the first place. Others, such as *Will you tell me the time, please?* may arise out of consideration of the possible effect of yet other locutions, such as *Tell me the time,* upon the hearer. On some occasions, the speaker may take his knowledge of the hearer into account as he constructs his utterance. On other occasions, he may well test a candidate locution against his model of the hearer. But how does he exercise such skills expecially when, as often happens, he knows next to nothing about the hearer? It seems likely that the speaker assumes that the hearer has the same rules of conversation that he does himself. Hence, he can test a candidate locution by running it through his own procedures for understanding speech acts. It is only when he has more specific information about the hearer that he will produce such circumlocutions as: *I just can't seem to find out the time, these days.*

Similar considerations apply to more extended discourse. If a speaker is to reply to the indirect request:

(70)   Can you tell me the time?

he may reply by saying, for example, *As a matter of fact, I can. It's twelve noon.* Alternatively, he may simply say, *It's twelve noon.* The speaker must, in Davey's terms, design his discourse in the light of his model of the hearer, and consider whether his sheer ability to give the information is in any doubt.

IX.   Conclusions

In drawing this review to a conclusion, let us return to our starting point, the varieties of knowledge, and ask whether there are any other sorts of information needed for the production of discourse. We have discussed some of the Gricean conventions concerning its substance, but dialogue certainly requires a knowledge of additional conventions that govern its form. As the ethnomethodologists have emphasized, a competent speaker must know the form of words for opening a conversation, and closing it (see for example Schegloff and Sacks, 1973). There may well be other similar "housekeeping moves", as Weiner and Goodenough (1977) have proposed, that signal that a speaker is, for example, giving up his option to contribute further remarks on the current topic of conversation and thus allowing another speaker to introduce a new topic. Since these matters concern form rather than substance, they ought to be relatively easy to codify within a program. A far more difficult problem, once again for speaker and theorist alike, is where the next topic itself comes from. We have considered at least one program with a real conversational purpose, Power's simulation of the use of language in solving a mutual problem, but the robots' goals are largely extrinsic to the conversation, e.g. getting a door opened. In real life, however, one often finds oneself simply having to make conversation.

The art of conversation is closely related to the art of story-telling. Both tax all the resources of a speaker from the ability to think up an idea that will interest an audience through to its expression in coherent and stimulating discourse. There have, in fact, been a number of efforts to develop programs that tell stories. Simmons and Correira (1978) have shown, for example, that the hierarchy of sub-goals generated by a PLANNER-like system that solves a problem can be treated as a structure generated by a "story-grammar" for a description of that problem-solving process. However, perhaps the most relevant exercise for our purposes is Meehan's (1976) program, TALE-SPIN, that generates simple stories and fables. TALE-SPIN sets up an imaginary world, based on a number of choices made by the user, and in simulating the way its individuals interact together creates the events that form the basis of a story. The simulation relies on another PLANNER-like system, the set of planning structures developed by Schank and Abelson (1975, 1977). These workers distinguish between plans for achieving very general goals ("delta goals"), of no particular value in themselves, and plans for achieving more specific goals such as bodily needs ("sigma-states"). Where a particular plan has become a matter of routine through considerable experience with it, it is embodied in a "script". Hence, most of us have scripts for eating in restaurants, shopping in supermarkets, and other similarly stereotyped activities. An important aspect of such knowledge is its consequences for discourse: a speaker can assume that the hearer is in possession of a relevant script. He can accordingly omit large sections of his narrative in the certainty that they can be recovered, if need be, by the hearer resorting to the script.

It is an open empirical question as to whether or not Schank and Abelson's scripts are implemented and utilized in their programs in a way that corresponds to mental processes. What cannot be doubted, however, is that planning is a human propensity, and that frequent experience with a particular plan is likely to crystallize into a prototypical representation of it. Indeed, there may be scripts for certain sorts of discourse or conversation.

There is, perhaps, nothing in the use of computers to study the production of sentences and discourse that could not, in principle, be expressed in ordinary language, or in a formalized language of logic or linguistics. Yet, it is often the case that one notation clarifies problems that seem quite intractable in another. We believe that computer programs, by representing the changing context of conversation quite directly as the changing state of the machine, and by testing theories of mental processes by stringently mimicing them, provide such a useful notation for exploring many aspects of human discourse.

Acknowledgements

We would like to thank our colleagues Stephen Isard and Cathy Urwin for their helpful comments on an earlier draft of this chapter. We also thank the SSRC for grants in support of our research.

References

Austin, J. L. (1962). "How to do Things with Words." Harvard University Press, Cambridge, Mass.

Chomsky, N. (1965). "Aspects of the Theory of Syntax." M.I.T. Press, Cambridge, Mass.

Clark, H. H. (1975). Bridging. *In* "Theoretical Issues in Natural Language Processing" (R. C. Schank and B. L. Nash-Webber, eds.). Preprints of a conference at M.I.T., June, 1975. Reprinted *In* "Thinking: Readings in Cognitive Science (P. N. Johnson-Laird and P. C. Watson, eds). Cambridge University Press, Cambridge.

Davey, A. C. (1974). The formalisation of discourse production. Unpublished Ph.D. dissertation. University of Edinburgh.

Davey, A. C. and Longuet-Higgins, H. C. (1976). A computational model of discourse production. *In* "Advances in the Psychology of Language—Formal and Experimental Approaches" (P. Smith and R. Campbell, eds). Plenum, New York.

Davies, D. J. M. and Isard, S. D. (1972). Utterances as programs. *In* "Machine Intelligence, 7" (D. Michie, ed.). Edinburgh University Press, Edinburgh.

Feigenbaum, E. (1963). The simulation of verbal learning behavior. *In* "Computers and Thought" (E. Feigenbaum and J. Feldman, eds). McGraw-Hill, New York.

Firbas, J. (1964). On defining the theme in Functional Sentence Analysis. *Travaux Linguistiques de Prague*, **1**, 267–280.

Fodor, J. A., Bever, T. G. and Garrett, M. F. (1974). "The Psychology of Language." McGraw-Hill, New York.

Friedman, J. (1969). A computer system for transformational grammar. *Communications of the Association for Computing Machinery*, **12**, 6, 341–348.

Friedman, J. (1971). "A Computer Model of Transformational Grammar." American Elsevier, New York.

Goldman, N. M. (1975). Conceptual Generation. *In* "Conceptual Information Processing" (R. C. Schank, ed.). North Holland, Amsterdam.

Gordon, D. and Lakoff, G. (1971). Conversational Postulates. *In* "Papers from the Seventh Regional Meeting of the Chicago Linguistics Society", pp. 63–84. (D. Adams *et al.*, eds). University of Chicago Linguistics Department, Chicago.

Grice, H. P. (1967). Logic and conversation. *In* "The Logic of Grammar" (D. Davidson and G. Harrison, eds). Dickenson, Encino, Calif.

Halliday, M. A. K. (1961). Categories of the theory of grammar. *Word*, **17**, 241–292.

Halliday, M. A. K. (1967). Notes on transitivity and theme, II. *J. Linguistics*, **3**, 199–244.

Hewitt, C. (1969). PLANNER: a language for proving theorems in robots. *Proceedings of the International Joint Conference on Artificial Intelligence*, pp. 295–301. Mitre Corporation, Bedford, Mass.

Hudson, R. A. (1972). "English Complex Sentences." North Holland, Amsterdam.

Isard, S. D. (1974) What would you have done if . . .? *Theor. Linguistics*, **1**, 233–255.

Isard, S. D. and Longuet-Higgins, H. C. (1971). Question answering in English. *In* "Machine Intelligence" (D. Michie, ed.). Vol. 6, pp. 243–254.

Jespersen, O. (1924). "The Philosophy of Grammar." Allen & Unwin, London.

Johnson-Laird, P. N. (1974). Experimental psycholinguistics. *Annual Review of Psychology*, **25**, 135–160.

Johnson-Laird, P. N. (1977a). Procedural semantics. *Cognition*, **5**, 189–214.

Johnson-Laird, P. N. (1977b). Psycholinguistics without linguistics. *In* "Tutorial Essays in Psychology" (N. S. Sutherland, ed.). Erlbaum, Hillsdale, New Jersey.

Kaplan, R. M. (1972). Augmented Transition Networks as psychological models of sentence comprehension. *Artif. Intell.* **3**, 77–100.

Katz, J. J. and Fodor, J. A. (1963). The structure of a semantic theory. *Language*, **39**, 170–210.

Kay, M. (1975). Syntactic processing and functional sentence perspective. *In* "Theoretical Issues in Natural Language Processing" (R. S. Schank and B. L. Nash-Webber, eds). Preprints of a conference at M.I.T., June, 1975.

Kempen, G. (1976). Sentence construction by a psychologically plausible formulator. *In* "Advances in the Psychology of Language—Formal and Experimental Approaches" (P. Smith and R. Campbell, eds). Plenum, New York.

Kempen, G. (1977). On conceptualising and formulating in sentence production. *In* "Sentence Production" (S. Rosenberg, ed.). Erlbaum, Washington.

Levelt, W. J. M., Schreuder, R. and Hoenkamp, E. C. M. (1976). Structure and use of verbs of motion. *In* "Advances in the Psychology of Language—Formal and Experimental Approaches" (P. Smith and R. Campbell, eds). Plenum, New York.

Longuet-Higgins, H. C. (1972). The algorithmic description of natural language. *Proceedings of the Royal Society of London Ser. B, 182,* 225–276.

Meehan, J. R. (1976). The metanovel: writing stories by computer. Research Report 74. Yale University Department of Computer Science.

Miller, G. A. and Johnson-Laird, P. N. (1976). "Language and Perception." Cambridge University Press, Cambridge and Harvard University Press, Cambridge, Mass.

Oldfield, R. C. and Wingfield, A. (1965). Response latencies in naming objects. *Q. J. Exp. Psychol.* **17,** 273–281.

Power, R. (1974). A computer model of conversation. Unpublished PhD dissertion. University of Edinburgh.

Power, R. (1977). A model of conversation. *Pragmatics Microfiche* 3.

Rumelhart, D., Lindsay, P. and Norman, D. (1972). A process model for long-term memory. *In* "Organization and Memory" (E. Tulving and W. Donaldson, eds). Academic Press, New York.

Schank, R. C. (1972). Conceptual dependency: a theory of natural language understanding. *Cognitive Psychology* **3,** 552–631.

Schank, R. C. (1975). (ed.). "Conceptual Information Processing." North Holland, Amsterdam.

Schank, R. C. and Abelson, R. P. (1975). Scripts, plans, and knowledge. "Proceedings of the Fourth International Joint Conference on Artificial Intelligence." Tbilisi. Reprinted *In* "Thinking: Readings in Cognitive Science" (P. N. Johnson-Laird and P. Watson, eds). Cambridge University Press, 1977, Cambridge.

Schank, R. C. and Abelson, R. P. (1977). "Scripts, Plans, Goals and Understanding: An Inquiry into Human Knowledge Structures." Lawrence Erlbaum, Hillsdale, N.J.

Schegloff, E. A. and Sacks, H. (1973). Opening up closings. *Semiotica,* **8,** 289–327.

Searle, J. R. (1969). "Speech Acts: An Essay in the Philosophy of Language." Cambridge University Press, Cambridge.

Searle, J. R. (1975a). Indirect Speech Acts. *In* "Syntax and Semantics," Vol. 3, Speech Acts. (P. Cole and J. Morgan, eds). Academic Press, New York.

Searle, J. R. (1975b). Speech Acts and Recent Linguistics. *In* "Annals of The New York Academy of Sciences 236, Developmental Psychology and Communication Disorders." (D. Aaonson and R. W. Reiber, eds).

Simmons, R. F. and Correira, A. (1978). Grammar forms for verse, sentences story grammars. Technical Report NL35, Department of Computer Sciences, University of Texas at Austin.

Simmons, R. F. and Slocum, J. (1972). Generating English discourse from semantic networks. *Communications of the Association for Computing Machinery* **15,** 891–905.

Steedman, M. J. (1976). "Answering Questions About Time." mimeo. University of Sussex.

Steedman, M. J. (1977). A procedural model of presupposition. *In* "Speech, Place and Action: Studies of Language in Context." (R. J. Jarvella and W. Klein, eds). J. Wiley, New York.

Steedman, M. J. (1978). Referring to times. "Grammarij 9, Symposium on Semantic Theory." (P. Seuren, ed). Katholieke Universiteit, Nijmegen.

Steedman, M. J. and Johnson-Laird, P. N. (1976). A programmatic theory of linguistic performance. *In* "Advances in the Psychology of Language—Formal and Experimental Approaches" (P. Smith and R. Campbell, eds). Plenum, New York.

Thorne, J. P., Bratley, P. and Dewar, H. (1968). The syntactic analysis of English by machine. *In* "Machine Intelligence", Vol. 3 (D. Michie, ed). Oliver and Boyd, Edinburgh.

Wanner, E. and Maratsos, M. (1975). "An Augmented Transition Network Model of Clause Comprehension." Mimeo. Harvard University, Cambridge Mass.

Weiner, S. L. and Goodenough, D. R. (1977). A move towards a psychology of conversation. *In* "Discourse Processes: Advances in Research and Theory" Vol. I: "Discourse Production and Comprehension" (R. O. Freedle, ed.). Norwood, Ablex, Norwood, N.J.

Winograd, T. (1971). Procedures as a representation for data in a computer program for understanding natural language. AI-TR-84, Massachusetts Institute of Technology.

Winograd, T. (1972) "Understanding Natural Language." Edinburgh University Press, Edinburgh.

Winograd, T. (1973). A procedural model of language understanding. *In* "Computer Models of Thought and Language" (R. C. Schank and K. M. Colby, eds). Freeman, San Francisco.

Wittgenstein, L. (1953). Philosophical Investigations. Translated by G. E. M. Anscombe. Blackwell, Oxford.

Woods, W. A. (1968). Procedural semantics for a question answering machine. Proceedings of the Fall Joint Computer Conference, pp. 457–471. Spartan, New York.

Woods, W. A. (1970). Transition network grammars for natural language analysis. *Communications of the Association for Computing Machinery*, **13**, 591–606.

Yngve, V. (1961). Random generation of English sentences. "Proceedings of the 1961 International Conference on Machine Translation of Languages and Applied Language Analysis, Teddington". HMSO, London.

6
Psychological Mechanisms of Speech Production as Studied Through The Analysis of Simultaneous Translation

F. Goldman-Eisler   *University College, London*

I. Introduction

The importance of simultaneous translation for the study of psychological mechanisms of speech production derives from the fact that it externalizes some of its processes and thus makes them accessible to the use of techniques for locating them. The intermittent silences between chunks of speech, i.e. continuous vocal sequences sandwiched between two pauses, which have been shown to be a characteristic phenomenon in speech production, (Goldman-Eisler, 1968) are for the simultaneous translator a very valuable commodity; for the more of his own output the simultaneous translator can crowd into his source's pauses, the more time he has to listen without interference from his own output. The disturbance such interference creates is very striking when professional bilinguals perform—though the professional has his way of dealing with this situation. The freedom of simultaneous interpreters for adjustment is, however, constrained within the fixed limits of the overall time of the particular input to be translated. The simultaneous interpreter's output cannot last longer or be shorter than that of the input plus, or sometimes minus, a few seconds, which is the duration of the time lag an interpreter can afford without losing the thread. (It was found not to exceed 10 s, with two-thirds being less than 5 s.)

Within the fixed total time the interpreter is free to expand the pause time at the cost of the speech time and vice versa, while at the same time giving a full translation: he then crams more speech into the shorter periods, and the way in which interpreters availed themselves of this freedom was very characteristic of the individuals. With some, the amount of time was redistributed between speech and pausing (the pausing getting longer or shorter) while others follow the original distribution fairly faithfully.

One specific question emerging in this context concerned the length and nature of the segment of the input which the interpreter needs to monitor before he can start encoding the translation. Studies of perceptual segmentation have shown that listeners impose subjective organization on speech output of an even delivery. Fodor and Bever (1965) were able to show by means of clicks that the continuous speech input is segmented according to the constituent structure of the sentence. Garrett *et al.* (1966) considered that in the displacement of clicks in perception the effect of grammar might only be indirect. Perhaps, they asked, speakers tend to pause longer or give some noticeable cue at constituent boundaries which "attracts" the click to these positions rather than the grammatical division itself. By treating sentence recordings acoustically in such a way as to eliminate the possibility of such cues, they were able to show that the segments are not necessarily divided by any markers in the stimulus. They concluded that grammatical structure alone was enough to determine where interruptions were heard and that this depended on a reconstructive process in the listener. The task of their subjects however was a relatively simple one compared with that of the interpreter engaged in simultaneous translation. With the latter, segmentation of the speech perceived is based on comprehension rather than perception, so as to serve the processing of information in the translation act. The situation of simultaneous translation is such that the conference interpreter must continuously monitor, store, retrieve and decode the input of the source language while at the same time re-coding (translating) and encoding the translation of the previous input. It is therefore doubtful whether simultaneous interpreters can start translating as soon as the first word is perceived and maintain a pace elicited by lexical units; whether in other words, the unit of comprehension can be a lexical one. This seems to be the case in shadowing, but while in one sense simultaneous translation is a form of shadowing where straightforward repetition is possible word by word, the translator is concerned with converting the meaning of an incoming message into another code—the target code. Rather than repeating the incoming words, his task is more like transposition or paraphrasing; it involves putting a certain content "into one's own words", and as such is an act of language production at a complex cognitive level.

One important aspect of both shadowing and simultaneous translation is the ear-voice span (EVS). This refers to the time elapsing between the subject's or interpreter's monitoring of the input and his actually repeating or encoding it, respectively. The EVS is as one may expect, longer in simultaneous translation than in shadowing—an average of about four to five words in translation or three words in shadowing according to Treisman (1965). Here we concentrate on the EVS aspect of simultaneous translation. The conference interpreter proceeds in a series of fits and starts following behind the input. One would suppose that he starts as many steps behind as are necessary or sufficient to enable him to begin to translate, i.e. with an EVS of a certain length. As he continues, the EVS increases in length and periodically accummulates until the amount of input to be stored seems to surpass the translator's storing capacity. When this happens, the interpreter must catch up with the input, to bring the distance between target and source down to a manageable proportion. (See Fig. 1.)

The main questions are therefore:

1. What is the length and nature of the segments the interpreter needs to monitor before he can start encoding?
2. How does he segment the input?

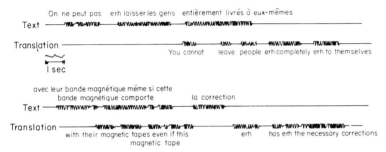

FIG. 1. Visual tracing of recorded source and simultaneous translation.

II. Technique

The technique used was that of transforming double channel recordings of the source language and its simultaneous translation into parallel visual tracings showing vocal speech and hesitation pauses, as I have used in all studies involving speech production, (Goldman-Eisler, 1968).

A. Ear-Voice Span—Linguistic Aspect

While we must assume that semantic comprehension precedes the onset of the translator's vocal production, two questions remain; (1) How much information does he require before he can begin to translate? More specifically, what constitutes the minimum sequence, the smallest unit before which translation cannot be started? (2) What is the maximum unit, i.e. how long an EVS can be tolerated without loss of text in the target?

   Because the smallest possible step a translator can lag behind the source is one word, we can measure the EVS by the number of words, by lexical units. Another possible unit is the predicate phrase, i.e. the syntactical unit, NP + VP. Thus the EVS might be a lexical or a syntactical entity. The parallel traces of speech enable us to examine the linguistic nature of the input preceding its corresponding translation.

B. Results

In only a mean proportion of 7·5% of cases was an EVS unit less than a complete NP + VP. This shows that on the whole interpreters depend on information of a structural nature before they can start translation. The minimum EVS sequence is the NP + VP rather than just a word and, as will be seen later, the VP is a crucial part of the information required. *Thus the unit of meaning upon which translators can act is not lexical but predicative and the segmentation of the input flow follows from propositional principles.*

Hughling Jackson's (1878) dictum: "The unit of speech is the proposition—to speak is to propositionize" is borne out by these data.

C. Language Factor

That the VP is a crucial part of the information required became evident when differential analyses of translations from English, French and German were undertaken. As is known, in German the verb frequently follows the object, so that the sequence in a predicative expression with an object is of the form NP1 (subject) + NP2 (object) + VP: this difference in structure was reflected in the greater lengths of EVS units in translations from German than from English or French. While in the latter cases a bare NP + VP constitutes the essential EVS, a larger chunk has often to be stored before starting translation from German, indicating that the crucial piece of information enabling interpreters to start translation is the predicate. (Any elements interpolated between NP and VP are liable to extend the EVS.) A further finding tying-in with this fact was the greater frequency of a long EVS unit at the end of clauses. This points to a greater ease of storing, comprehension having been facilitated after the verb has been decoded.

D. Ear-Voice Span, Chunking Aspect

Besides the linguistic aspect of the interpreter's segmentation of the source input, there is the aspect of chunking, of concatenation and caesura, of linking and cutting. The process is such that the interpreter first monitors and stores, and then encodes into the target language. During this period, the source may continue his utterance which again must be monitored and stored by the interpreter and subsequently encoded. This encoding proceeds after a certain sequence is monitored, and so on. Simultaneous translators sometimes cut into the source's continuous vocal input; at other times they may continue to monitor two or more vocal sequences of the input separated in the source by pauses, i.e. two or more input chunks, and encode them in one continuous sequence. Thus, while source and target language are uttered, as in all natural speech, in the form of alternate speech and silence periods, there seems to be no systematic or predictable relationship between the two series of alternations.

There are three ways of segmenting this input: (1) Encoding the chunks of speech as uttered in the source. (2) Starting to encode before the chunk in the input has come to a halt. (3) Storing two or more input chunks and then encoding. We shall refer to these three responses in terms of (1) identity, (2) fission and (3) fusion, respectively (in the monitoring and decoding of input material).

Only about 10% of all responses were of the identity class, the rest were about equally divided between the fission and fusion groups. Identity responses seemed to respond to the rate of input, and were also a matter of individual differences, but were otherwise linguistically random and indicating no systematic occurrence.

The segmentation of the source text was then analysed using as criterion the occurrence of fission response as against fusion responses. Comparing chunks in the source with those in translations, we found that the interpreters tended to ignore the input chunkings and imposed their own segmentation on the text. In about 90% of cases they started translating before the input chunk had come to an end, or they delayed translation and stored more than one input chunk before starting, thus exhibiting a marked preference for constructive processes (fission or fusion) over purely receptive ones (identity). It seems that grammatical criteria prevail in the segmentation of input in simultaneous translation. In view of the likely disintegrating effects of the conditions under which this takes place—the linguistic task is highly complex and entails a high degree of stress and pressure of time—it would not be too unreasonable to expect perceptual segmentation to recede from the active principles of grammatical organization towards a more passive, atomistic and disorganized lexical segmentation. However, our data shows that under such conditions simultaneous translation still follows mainly syntactical principles—it is as if, when really put to the test, processing for language production cannot be bothered with less than predicative expressions.

This is also borne out by our data concerning the propositional nature of EVS segments, and in particular those showing that when translating from German, interpreters delay translation longer than when translating from French or English most probably because as mentioned before the predicate in German comes at the end of the proposition and objects or other modifiers precede it. It is only when the interpreter has decoded the predicate that he can start translating.

To test this proposition we analysed one of our texts to see whether the postponement of the verb in the clause had any bearing on the interpreter's choice of fusing input chunks as against intercepting them (fission). The results showed that when the verb was uttered late in the clause the translator preferred to store more input and postpone the translation even if this entailed his not using for translation pause periods of the input. This is further evidence showing the verb to be a main determinant of meaning. To quote Healy and Miller (1970) "The verb defines the plot; the subject merely indicates one of the actors."

E. Simultaneity of the Processes of Reception and Translation

If the input were spread in such a way that its pauses allowed time for the translations of each chunk of speech, so that the translation of Sequence A could be sandwiched between sequences A and B, and the translation of

Sequence B between B and C, translation would in fact be sequential and not simultaneous. As the examination of the visual records shows, the real situation imposes simultaneity between the encoding of the translation of earlier source text, and the monitoring and decoding of the subsequent input. The faster the input, the greater the simultaneity of input and output, of source and target. (A quantitative measure of degree of simultaneity was devised and is reported elsewhere (Goldman-Eisler. 1972).) It is therefore clear that interpreters are capable of performing the complicated operation of monitoring, storing and possibly decoding while engaged in the encoding into the target language of previously received sequences.

The question arose of how these activities, and in particular decoding, are phased, i.e. in what order they are carried through, how decoding relates to storing, which of these is done automatically and which received attention. The question is one of interference between receptive and productive processes studied in the context of simultaneous translation.

Two alternative ways of dealing with the input may be considered: one where the re-coding (the transposition from source into target language) is done on reception of the input and stored in its recoded form, while previously recoded sequences are encoded automatically. Attention in this case would be focussed on the input and the active verbal memory would be involved. Alternatively, storage in active verbal memory is bypassed and the input chunks are stored unprocessed, though decoded, as could be deduced from the kind of segmentation of the input; the input chunks would then be recoded (translated) and vocally encoded into the target language in one go. The argument in favour of the latter alternative was that if previously decoded material needs to be encoded in translation, the most economical procedure seems to be to store the decoded sequence (in the short term memory) as segmented and recode it into the target language only when encoding; making higher level decisions prematurely would strain the system unnecessarily.

We therefore suggest that the acts that are being performed simultaneously are monitoring and segmenting, which implies decoding on the one hand, and recoding and encoding on the other. The proposed supposition is that the latter sequence of processes is the more automatic one, and that decoding the input, involving comprehension, is the one which requires most attention. This had to be demonstrated.

F. Experiment

As mentioned above, we are dealing here with a problem of interference between the receptive and productive processes and the division of attention between them. To answer the question an experiment was designed to allow for the control of the level of interference at the encoding end of the process. Subjects were asked to listen carefully through earphones to a talk, and to perform, at the same time, one of three different tasks. These were:

(a) To count from 1 to 100 and then start again.
(b) To count backwards from 100 to 1 and then start again.
(c) To count from 100 backwards subtracting in this order 1, 2, 3, 4, 5 (e.g. 100, 99, 97, 94, 90, 85) and to start again.

The text heard simultaneously by the subjects lasted approximately 40 min and was divided into three parts, each one matched to one of the test operations. (The order in which subjects performed the three tasks was varied Latin square to eliminate any practice effect.)

We used as input material a talk by Isaiah Berlin (on Alexander Herzen), a talk new to our subjects, of high intellectual level and of absorbing interest. It was delivered at a fast rate, thus demanding concentrated attention. The subjects (academics of various kinds) were told to concentrate on comprehending the input while performing the arithmetical operation, and in the case of the two conflicting, to give priority to comprehension, as there was to be, afterwards, a test of comprehension. (This, in the form of a word completion test, was given after each operation.) This design enabled us to study the interference of cognitive operations at three levels of complexity, standardized at each level.

G. Treatment of Data

Using our technique of double-channel recordings of input and output and the transferring of these to visual records we obtained the following data.

Input
1. The precise time preceding each chunk of speech.
2. The speech time of each chunk of speech.

Output
3. The time between each count (rate of counting).
4. The number or numbers (if several in continuous string) uttered.
5. The speech time of these counts.

All these are synchronized so that the input is marked where the subject uttered the numbers resulting from his counting.

The analyses based on these data showed that F (forward counting) was performed completely automatically, at a fast rate and uttered by some subjects in continuous blocks of tens or even twenties and thirties. B (backward) counting was in most cases somewhat slower and subjects divided in their skill of performing it. (The blocks tended to disappear or become shorter and rarer.) When performing S (subtracting) all subjects slowed down and the block counters of F and B were reduced to generating numbers individually. Subtracting therefore, clearly proved to be an operation making demands on the subject's undivided attention, while F is not. We then correlated the hesitancy (measured by ratio of pause to speech time (P/S)) of the speech uttered in the intervals between the subject's counts or subtractions to the lengths of these intervals (CI).

What we found was that for F hesitancy of the input and length of count intervals (CI) were independent as they were for B. But for the operation of subtracting, hesitancy (P/S) and C/I were significantly and positively related ($r = 0.371$ p $\theta0.01$).

In other words the intervals between counts increase with the difficulty of the counting task, and they increase in proportion to the hesitancy of the input. With two simultaneous tasks, namely decoding the input and encoding the F, B and S operations, one might assume that pauses in the input would relieve the subject of the task of monitoring and be utilized for encoding the numbers. In such a case, one would expect that the more hesitant the input, i.e. the more or longer its pauses, the higher would be the subject's rate of operation and the shorter the interval between numbers produced; this would result in a negative r between P/S and CI. A trend towards such a relationship appeared in the F task—in other words when the operation was completely automatic and free of cognitive complexity. In task B, the two aspects of delay, P/S and CI were independent, but in the difficult task S pauses in the input were generally *not* utilized for the performance of the task, but seemed to have been a factor in impeding the subject from performing his task, in other words occupied his full attention.

These results led to the following conclusions:

(1) The act of vocal utterance, i.e. the peripheral act of speech without processing which F seems to represent, does not interfere with the act of monitoring even highly complex intellectual material. Complex processing, on the other hand, such as subtraction, does interfere, and does so in proportion to the hesitancy of the input. This becomes meaningful if we accept the conclusion based on previous work (Goldman-Eisler, 1968) namely that hesitancy in spontaneous speech indicates that complex cognitive processes are involved in its generation, and that this results in speech of higher information content.

The peripheral act of encoding seems therefore to make no significant demands on attention and does not seem to compete with the monitoring of simultaneous input, *whereas when encoding involves central (complex cognitive) activity* it seems to compete with the monitoring of simultaneous input.

(2) Variations in the degree of this competition depend on the variations of hesitancy in the input. The highest rate of counting, even in the performance of S, was achieved when the input was fluent.

If we accept the hypothesis that hesitancy and fluency in the production of spontaneous speech reflect the rate in the flow of information, the fact that interference increases with the increase of hesitancy in the input text and decreases with the increase of fluency becomes plausible. Interference would be expected to increase and decrease with the increase and decrease in the level of cognitive complexity in the generative processes of speech and as the rate of information increases and decreases.

H. The use of Pauses for Counting Operations F, B and S

The question arose as to the more specific relationship between pausing and the execution of the F, B and S tasks. Did the subjects show any preference for counting during pauses or during the vocal speech of the input? Investigation showed that there is a consistent preference by subjects for performing during the speech of the input. The proportion of counting operations during pauses (around 38%) was remarkably stable for all operations.

However, when the structural location of the pauses was ascertained the picture turned out to be less uniform. In order to have comparable conditions as well as a time interval optimal for the performance of a second task, pauses of 1 or more seconds were selected for observation and their use in counting operations was investigated. Forward counting (F), the clearly automatic task and subtracting (S), the cognitive task, were compared in two linguistic settings, i.e. performed during pauses occurring within sentences and pauses located between sentences. It emerged that in F, the majority of pauses of 1 s or more are used whether located between or within sentences, though a greater proportion are between sentences. In the S operation, the majority of these pauses are used only when located between sentences, while of those occurring within sentences only a minority is used—the majority of sentences of 1 s or more located within sentences are not used for S operations. The difference was highly significant.

This is further evidence showing that in the performance of the encoding task frequency of counting operations is a correlate of the hesitancy of the input. It shows that while spare time of 1 s or more, when occurring after the completion of a sentence, can be turned to use for an independent cognitive task, such spare time is of little use for this purpose when occurring within a sentence of the input. It indicates that for the S operation, this time is not "spare". It seems as if it were reserved and earmarked for the attention being individually focussed on the input until the sentence is finished.

III. Conclusions

How are these conclusions to be translated to apply to the question that stimulated this investigation? It was suggested that of the acts involved in simultaneous translation (namely monitoring, segmenting (involving decoding) re-coding into the target language and encoding the translated sequence) simultaneous performance might reasonably be expected for monitoring and segmenting (decoding) on the one hand and re-coding and encoding on the other. In our experiment the subject was required to give first priority to the comprehension of the input, with the consequence that he was impelled to arrange his arithmetical performance so as not to interfere with the decoding of the input text. By substituting for the act of translation independent operations involving simultaneous encoding at three different and controlled levels of difficulty, differences in the segmentation of the input due to the variations in difficulty of independent encoding could be studied. The following emerged in these terms.

(1) When the encoding operation is easy (F) it is performed automatically. Attention seemed to have been entirely devoted to decoding, with complete simultaneity achieved between the acts of decoding and encoding. In the situation of simultaneous translation one might expect such moments to occur when highly automatic sequences or clichés, matched by ready-made sequences in the target language, are translated. Re-coding in this area requires no selection processes and the more of such sequences the input contains, the more automatic the encoding and the more "simultaneous" translation can be. Simultaneous translation as a realistic performance seems possible because a large part of the content of our usual language consists of highly automatic overlearned sequences and redundancies. In the context of spontaneous production of language it would follow that the uninterrupted flow of vocal utterance is an attribute of unreflected information content generated.

(2) As the input becomes more complex, the situation modelled by the S operation arises. The translator can no longer perform automatically—he becomes involved in complex activity if the input text is such that its re-coding into the target language involves complex cognitive processes over and above those involved in decoding. The segmentation of the input text then becomes geared to the re-coding and encoding in such a way that there is the least interference between decoding and encoding. If hesitant sequences are monitored, without being interrupted by S operations, and if even long pauses of 1 s and more are left unused, as long as they occur in the middle of sentences, while those at the end of sentences are used, we may draw the above inference for the situation of simultaneous translation: that strictly speaking there can be no simultaneous translation when translation requires cognitive action. Thus consecutive translation can alternate with simultaneous translation and the attention which has been tied exclusively to decoding when monitoring a text with pauses within sentences (i.e. whose information content can be presumed to be high) can be liberated for re-coding (and encoding) at the end of sentences.

We may therefore express the original suggestion as to the sequence of processes by saying that while monitoring and segmenting (decoding) may be simultaneous, re-coding and encoding must represent a second phase. This seems to be the case to the extent to which the re-coding is a complex cognitive act, while to the extent that it is part of an automatic action, re-coding and encoding may follow practically at once after monitoring and decoding.

These insights gained from the study of simultaneous translation also throw light on the process of language production generally. The cognitive complexity of the information, of the content to be vocally encoded, i.e. transposed to vocal utterance, whether externally presented as source text or internally conceived as speech intention again appears as the crucial element in the flow of language production and meaningful for the locations of its interruptions.

References

Fodor, J. A. and Bever, T. G. (1965). The psychological reality of linguistic segments, *Journal of Verbal Learning and Verbal Behaviour,* **4,** 414–420.

Garrett, M., Bever, T. and Fodor, J. A. (1966). The active use of grammar in speech perception, *Perception and Psychophysics,* **1,** 30–32.

Goldman-Eisler, F. (1968). "*Psycholinguistics; Experiments in Spontaneous Speech,*" Academic Press, London and New York.

Goldman-Eisler, F., (1972). Segmentation of input in simultaneous translation, *Journal of Psycholinguistic Research,* **1,** 127.

Goldman-Eisler, F. and Cohen, M. (1974). An experimental study of interference between receptive and productive processes relating to simultaneous translation, *Language and Speech,* **17,** 1–10.

Healy, A. F. and Miller, G. A. (1970). The verb as the main determinant of meaning, *Psychonomic Science,* **20,** 6.

Jackson, H. J. (1878). "On Affections of Speech from Disease of the Brain", reprinted in *Selected Writings of Hughlings Jackson,* (1958), Vol. II, pp. 155–170, Basic Books, New York.

Treisman, A. M. (1965). The effects of redundancy and familiarity on translating and repeating back a foreign and a native language, Medical Research Council, unpublished report, PLU/65/12.

7
Evidence from Pauses in Speech

Brian Butterworth   *University of Cambridge*

I. Time

"Time is the measure of all things", not least mental activities; and time when people appear to be doing nothing is the kind of time psychologists most like to measure. After all, *le Penseur*, isn't just sitting on his rock; though for us to discover what he is doing, he must do more than just sit, he must produce some behaviour, for example, speech.

Traditionally, the time between the presentation of a stimulus and the subject's response to it has been used as the index of a wide range of cognitive processes. The logic of this technique is straightforward. The longer the delay between stimulus and response, the more cognitive operations are inferred as being required to produce that response—for a given task. Donders (1868) considered these operations as separable stages in a decision-making process, each stage making its own contribution to response delay. However, it became apparent that experimentally subtracting one stage would not necessarily leave the other stages unaffected. Thus in modern work, the "subtractive" method is not employed. Rather, we consider each stage will be affected by a factor, and we can vary the value of that factor experimentally. To take a very simple early example: in making a choice among a number of alternatives, there will be several stages in the process, but one factor can be altered to affect the overall response time, for instance, we can experimentally vary the number of alternatives from which the choice has to be made. Although it is not claimed that an extra stage is added by increasing the number of alternatives, this factor will determine the time it takes to make a choice (Hick, 1952). Some investigators have even tried to use this technique to probe the cognitive processes required in speech. A stimulus (word or picture) is presented and speakers have to respond as quickly as possible with a phrase or sentence. The delay before the first word of the response is taken as the index of cognitive operations (Taylor, 1969; Lindsley, 1975, 1976; Flores d'Arcais and Joustra, 1976). However, naturally occurring speech is hardly ever so closely tied to an external stimulus, and in this chapter I will consider the silent days present in spontaneous (i.e. unrehearsed) speech.

The basic logic is the same as in the stimulus—response paradigm: the more the delays, the more cognitive operations are required by the output. However, the research strategy must, of course, differ, since the character of the independent variables cannot be manipulated, to any great extent, by the investigator. In the S–R paradigm, if we wish to know whether it takes longer to choose among many alternatives than among few, we can simply manipulate the number of alternatives in the stimulus array and measure the choice time for, say, 2, 4, 8 or 16 item arrays. It turns out, incidentally, that choice response time is directly proportional to the number of alternatives when this is expressed as units of $\log_2$. This relation is now known as "Hick's Law" after its discoverer W. E. Hick (1952).†

The research strategy for investigating speech then, is as follows: the investigator formulates a hypothesis about a process engaged by the speech production system, let us say, choosing a word; in addition, he will hypothesize some factors which will effect this process. So, on the analogy with choice response time, he might suppose that if the speaker is confronted by a wide choice, it will take him longer to choose than if he has a narrow choice. He will then examine samples of spontaneous speech, locate points where, on independent grounds, he thinks the speaker will have a wide choice and points where he will not. According to the hypothesis only the former should be accompanied by a delay, or a longer delay than the latter.

By delay in speech, I mean a period of silence, a pause. These can be located by ear, and some important studies have employed this method (e.g. Maclay and Osgood, 1959; Tannenbaum et al., 1965), but short pauses tend to be missed, and missed more often at clause boundaries than elsewhere (Boomer and Dittman, 1962). Mechanizing pause detection was first introduced by Goldman-Eisler (1956). She used a signal detector linked to a pen-recorder, so that successive periods of articulation and silence could be accurately plotted. Since she was interested in cognitive process, she discounted pauses of less than 0·25 s because the transition between two stop consonants often required a delay of this order for purely articulatory reasons. Her technique and her criterion—or one of 0·20 s—are now generally adopted. In what follows, I shall mean by a "pause", a silence of 0·20 s or greater, determined mechanically.

II. Plans and Planning

This research strategy can examine two related problems. First, what kinds of "Plans" do speakers employ in preparing to speak? That is to say, what levels, or sorts, of representation intervene between the speaker's intention and the manifest phonation? Miller et al. (1960, Chapter 11) argued for a basic unit—the sentence: speakers made a plan for a sentence and then executed that plan. Analogously, Boomer (1965) and Boomer and Laver (1968) argued for the phonemic clauses as the basic unit. (A phonemic clause is an intonational unit consisting of a single intonation contour, one primary stress and a terminal

---

† It is defined that the smallest quantum of information required to decide between two alternatives is the "bit"; hence the number of bits needed to decide among N alternatives is n, where $2^n = N$.

juncture, and is also called a "tone group".) The validity of these claims was to be established by finding pauses occurring mainly between, or near the beginning of, these basic units.

There will be other units, other levels of representation, other "Plans" involved in the transduction from thought to speech (this volume, Chapter 15) some of which can be revealed by a chronometric analysis.

In addition, to Plans, there is "Planning": operations required to formulate a Plan. Often this will be equivalent to the operations in trandsducing one Plan into another. Thus Cooper (this volume) discusses some of the syntactic Planning—transformations of Plans into other Plans—that goes into the organization of the phonological Plan of the speech output.

Insofar as Planning at some level (= for a given kind of Plan) imposes a substantial cognitive load, say, through the availability of many choices, or through the unfamiliarity of the current sequence of Planning operations, then pauses will surface in the speech stream. Generally, then, we still try to infer from the pattern of pauses, the nature of the internal representations, Plans, that the cognitive system employs, and the processes operating on those representations, Planning.

First, a warning about this research strategy.

III. The Communicative Function of Pauses

Unlike studies in the S–R paradigm, the chronometric analyst of real speech is confronted by a set of complications, which, when better understood, should enrich our account of language production rather than confuse it.

Speech is typically, and *par excellence*, a way of communicating with another person, and therefore aspects of speech need to be examined with this communicative function in mind. So pauses may serve not only to make time available for the speaker's cognitive processes, but also to assist the listener in his task of understanding the speaker.

Pauses occurring at sentence boundaries, for example, may give the speaker time to formulate the next sentence (as Miller *et al.* (1960) suggest), but may also help the listener to syntactically segment the input. Moreover, there is recent evidence that listeners do most of their cognitive work at the ends of sentences (Abrams and Bever, 1969; Green, 1977) making sentence boundary pauses doubly helpful to listeners. Goldman-Eisler (this volume, Chapter 6) reports that listeners can make use of clause boundary pauses to carry out cognitive work, but not pauses at other locations: probably because these locations are predictable on the basis of current syntactic and intonational cues, whereas, for the listener, the location of other pauses is unpredictable. Speakers, do to some extent, adapt the distribution (though not the amount) of pauses in response to visual reinforcers (Beattie and Bradbury, 1979), and it would not be implausible to suggest that there is ontogenetic adaptation through interaction, such that successive listeners condition the speaker to pause at these locations.

Of course, pauses may serve both functions (cf. Barik, 1968). This is discussed more fully by Beattie in this volume (Chapter 4). It should be added that some pauses may be communicatively obligatory in that they affect meaning by having a definite structural role, for example, by resolving potential structural ambiguities.

(1) (a) Old men   and women
     (b) Old   men and women
(2) (a) Gentlemen   lift the seat (instruction)
     (b) Gentlemen lift the seat (statement)
(3) (a) Making the green one red (equivalently
     (b) Making the green one   red)
     (c) Making the green   one red

Lady Macbeth: Will all great Neptune's ocean wash this blood
              Clean from my hand? No, this my hand will rather
              The multitudinous seas incarnadine,
              Making the green one red.

Abercrombie (1968) remarks that Garrick initially favoured (3a), but later came to prefer (3c). Even now texts differ in their punctuation of this line.

Both Bloomfield (1933) and Bloch (1946) have noted that pauses marking certain embedded constructions are virtually obligatory, yet need not affect meaning, for example,

(4)   John, the older boy, is away at school.

Bloch attributes pauses partly to "stylistic factors (with more pauses in emphatic or affective speech)" (1946, p. 201). Stylistic pauses, according to Abercrombie (1968) preserve the stress-timing, whereas genuinely tentative pauses break up the timing pattern.

Alas, we cannot, at present, distinguish systematically tentative from pseudo-tentative pauses. Just to measure the time between stresses with the degree of accuracy required is not yet possible, since the crucial measurement is not between word onsets and offsets (which would be simple, usually) but between the "Perceptual Centres" of the stressed syllables (see Morton et al. (1976), for a technique for obtaining the Perceptual Centres of experimental syllables), and there is no way at the moment of determining this for the syllables of spontaneous speech.

A further complication in interpreting pause data arises because some aspects of pausing seem to be conditioned by situational and dispositional anxiety (Goldman-Eisler, 1961a; see Murray, 1971, for a review). In addition, the speaker's perception of the task demands and his own role in it may also influence some features of pause distribution (Good, 1978; Good and Butterworth, 1978).

IV. Working Assumptions

Two working assumptions are needed to get the research strategy off the ground. First, Planning must take up time not used for phonation. Two reasons have been suggested why this might be so. Goldman-Eisler on one hand separates Planning into two sorts, "central" and "peripheral". "Central" processes are voluntary, semantic and original, whereas "peripheral" processes are automatic, syntactic and highly over-learned. The actual execution of a Plan—the articulation of speech itself—is held to be peripheral, and while speech is being articulated, central processes cannot be carried out. Hence, there is a sharp temporal division between the two kinds of process, and pause time will be a direct reflection of the central kind (Goldman-Eisler (1968) see especially pp. 120–129). Alternatively, one can envisage the various processes engaged in production forming a hierarchical "Cascade", such that higher level processes and lower level processes are carried out in parallel, but that some processes just take longer than others. If, for example, articulation itself takes less time than semantic Planning, pause time to accommodate this process will "spill over" either side of a period of articulation. Additionally, Planning may need to be initiated before articulation can begin, but will continue in parallel to it, finishing before articulation has finished. Fry (1969) has advanced a view rather like this. Pauses in this case will represent processes initiated early in the cascade. But it is difficult to derive clearly contrasting predictions about pause distribution from two models in their current degree of specificity.

The second assumption must be, of course, that pause time available equals pause time used. If this were not broadly the case, pauses would signify little about mental processes. This assumption requires the further postulation that speakers cannot or do not stop talking, that they are, in fact, under some time constraints and must keep their output as continuous as possible.

These are only working assumptions, and will need modification. In particular, we will need to make further subdivisions in the kinds of mental operation involved to specify several kinds of Plan and several kinds of Planning. Notably, we will need to divide Planning into "macro" and "micro": the latter is concerned with purely local functions, like marking clause boundaries and selecting words, which can only be implemented locally—clause juncture pauses can only be inserted when the speaker reaches the juncture, and, it turns out, speakers only start to search for a word, when it is needed for the next phrase. Macro-Planning concerns the long range semantic and syntactic organization of a sizeable chunk of speech and therefore cannot be carried out locally. Pauses associated with these functions cannot, therefore, be identified from their local context.

V. Macro-planning, Macro-plans and Macro Pause Patterns

A. Macro-planning

There should, if the working assumptions are broadly correct, be at least a rough and ready relationship between the amount of Planning and the amount of pausing. Reading a prepared text, for example, which requires little Planning compared to unrehearsed speech, should contain, therefore, much less hesitation; and so it turns out (Henderson *et al.*, 1965). Nevertheless, it contains a noticeable amount—10–25% of the total time will be silence. Most of this time probably does not serve the speaker's cognitive processes. Almost all pauses in reading are at clause boundaries, they may serve a communicative purpose, and, of course, some breaks are needed for breathing. And it is striking that whereas less than a third of breathing pauses occur at clause boundaries in spontaneous speech, in readings all occur at these locations (Goldman-Eisler, 1968, p. 97). The reader seems so in control of the production process that he can organize his breathing to coincide with those points where a break will be most helpful to the listener. Moreover, between-sentence pauses in reading tend to be roughly of the same length, 1·0–1·24 s, whereas in spontaneous speech, they vary considerably, with many over 2·50 s, reflecting the varying cognitive demands of speech as compared with reading (Goldman-Eisler, 1972).

Preplanning the content of one will reduce on-line Planning time requirements, and, it turns out, reduces the proportion of pausing in speech (Goldman-Eisler, 1961b, 1968, p. 27). This is, of course, in line with everyday experience: we can be more fluent if we know the topic well. The distribution of pauses in practiced material changes with the amount of practice. On the first occasion of the expression of a particular content, the utterance will have about 59% of the pause time at clause boundaries. With successive (not necessarily verbatim) repetitions, not only does pause time decrease steadily, but it decreases at the expense of non-boundary pauses, so that by the seventh repitition, 85% of the pause time is located at clause boundaries (Butterworth and Caroline Thomas, unpublished data).

Speaking tasks will clearly impose differing demands. Goldman-Eisler (1961b) manipulated task demand in an ingenious experiment. Speakers were presented with a cartoon strip; in one condition, they had to describe the events depicted in frames of the strip. In the second condition they had to interpret the meaning of the cartoon—the point of the joke; once the speaker had seen the point, he said "Got it" and the timing of pausing started. The second condition requires the speaker to abstract from the perceptually present experience, to connect it up with other experiences and to reorder these components into some unified and coherent meaning. Notice, however, that pause data will *not* reflect the time it takes to see the joke, but only the time it takes to Plan the utterance.

As expected, the second condition produced more pausing: the mean pause time per word was three times longer than in the description. In a replication (Butterworth and Thomas, unpublished data), it was found that the change in pause time at clause boundaries, with practice, though striking in the interpretation task (see above), was virtually non-existent in the description task: 65% on the first occasion of utterance, 68% on the seventh repetition.

O'Connell *et al.* (1969) devised a pretty technique for separating the unfamiliarity of the content from the unfamiliarity of individual words in the context (and any concomitant difficulty of lexical selection). Each subject read aloud a five sentence story, then reported it in his own words; and then read a second five sentence story and reported that. Each story had two versions, "normal" and "abnormal". The abnormal version reversed the position of two noun phrases in the third sentence of the normal story, e.g.

(5) Normal: "Der junge Lehrer überlegte einen Moment.
ob er den Schüler bestrafen sollte."

(6) Abnormal: "Der Schüler überlegte einen Moment,
ob der den jungen Lehrer bestrafen sollte."

The idea was that the content of the abnormal versions would be unfamiliar to the subject, since pupils (in Germany, at least) do not normally consider whether they should punish their teacher. It was found that the number of pauses was greater in the report of the abnormal stories, notably in the crucial sentence (and, of course, the number of syllables per second was significantly greater in the reading than in the reports), indicating as expected, that the familiarity of the semantic Planning is reflected in the overall pause time.

In these studies, the formulation of meaning is the major factor affected by the task manipulations. Can we similarly discover an overall effect on pause time of syntactic Planning?

Miller *et al.* (1960) propose two sorts of "Plan", which in my terms would be one sort of Planning and one sort of Plan. The Plan they call a "Motor-Plan", and it consists of a phonological representation of the surface structure of a sentence. This is tranduced into a series of motor commands and executed as a whole. They call the Planning process, the "Grammar Plan" and this consists of the rules of a "Transformational Generative Grammar". When their theory was propounded, it would have been reasonable to expect that the number of transformations required by the Motor Plan would be reflected in pause time, on the analogy of contemporary experiments on input processing (e.g. Miller, 1962; Miller and McKean, 1964). In one subsequent study of spontaneous speech, there is evidence that transformational complexity is relevant. Rochester and Gill (1973) compared the number of disruptions in sentences with two types of subordinate construction. Although pauses are not included in disruptions, which comprise "uhm's", "er's", false starts, repeats etc. it is plausible to suppose that they bear some functional equivalence (Beattie, 1977a; Beattie and Bradbury, 1979). The two types of subordinate constructions were Noun Phrase Complements, like

(7) The fact that (the woman was aggressive) threatened the professors,
and Relative Clauses, like

(8) The book (which was written by Millet) was lauded by all.

According to Rosenbaum (1967), Relative Clause constructions require more transformations. If NPs in the main and subordinate clause are co-referential, the subordinate NP is deleted and replaced by "wh-", an extra transformation. The hypothesis of greater complexity is supported by the finding that Relative Clauses are much less common in the corpus. (Compare Goldman-Eisler and Cohen, 1970; they found that Passive forms constituted less than 10% of any of the corpora they examined.) However, Rochester and Gill's most striking finding was that disruptions were significantly more frequent in Noun Phrase Complements, and they suggest tentatively that the two clause types may differ in their semantics. Moreover, in dialogues there is no effect of subordination generally on disruptions when sentences are equated for length.

Using data from the cartoon experiment, Goldman-Eisler had previously investigated the effects on pause time of syntatic complexity as represented by the proportion of subordinate clauses (the "Subordination Index"—SI). Of course, this measure is not strictly comparable with transformational complexity, and would not, for example, distinguish sentences containing Noun Phrase Complements from those containing Relative Clauses. But, usually, sentences with a subordinate clause will be transformationally more complex than those without.

In the Description Condition, the mean pause time per word was 0·123 s and the SI was 19%. For interpretations, pause time per word was 0·340 s and SI was 49·8%.

> If no other speech samples were available, we might conclude that the structuring of sentences is yet another cognitive act, that as such it is making its own contribution to the increased hesitancy of the cartoon interpretation as compared with the descriptions . . . However, speech in interviews was shown to be of the same complexity with practically the same SI (48·5%) as the cartoon interpretations (and) pausing in interviews is shorter even than in descriptions. (Goldman-Eisler, 1968, p. 71).

To validate these findings within tasks and within speakers, comparisons between arbitrarily segmented passages (about 100 words each) of uninterrupted spontaneous arguments of single speakers, showed no correlation between SI of the passage and the percentage of pausing. Moreover, the distribution of pauses in respect of clause boundaries was unaffected by the SI (Butterworth, 1976). We can see, therefore, that SI can vary independently of the semantic Planning required and the amount of pause time.

Goldman-Eisler carried out two further studies on the status of syntactic Planning. Goldman-Eisler has found in a number of different sorts of experiment over many years evidence which points inescapably to the conclusion that syntactic complexity in itself does not cause output delay in speech production.

Taking simultaneous translations by professional interpreters, and four source texts which the interpreters translated, she found no relation between the proportion of pause time in the text and its SI. Where translators cut loose from the structure of the source text, there was indeed a significant increase in hesitation; but in all but one of these cases, the change was from complex to simple (Goldman-Eisler, 1968, Chapter V).

In another study, she investigated the effect of a tranquilizer (Chlorpromazine) and a sedative (Sodium Amytal) on the structure of sentences produced in interview situations. The rationale for introducing these pharmacological variables was as follows. The sedative would have the effect of depressing the neocortex and hence the highest intellectual functions. The tranquilizer, on the other hand, would affect only vigilance and arousal, since it acts only on the reticular activating system. CPZ had previously been shown to preserve the link between hesitation and cognitive activity, in that only where pausing increased did the intellectual quality of the utterances (cartoon interpretations) also improve.

> How far would the effect of this drug (CPZ) in depressing arousal and reducing vigilance be reflected in the embeddedness of clauses? This question is relevant because embeddedness may be thought to involve the deferment of utterance of linguistic elements held in suspense by virtue of an initial "set" in the sense of Lashley's determination of serial order. The increase of "serial ordering", i.e. of the temporal integration or ordering succession when clauses or phrases are to be embedded in each other, should entail a commensurately increased state of tension between excitatory and inhibitory processes. (1968, p. 74).

Goldman-Eisler found that there is no difference between the SIs of the No drug condition and the sedative condition, but there was a significant drop in the CPZ condition.

Reanalysing the cartoon interpretations made also under the two drug conditions, she again found little difference in SI of interpretations produced under the No drug and sedative conditions. And like the results on the quality of the interpretations, CPZ had very selective effects on the speakers, some subjects exhibiting a dramatic rise from the No drug to CPZ conditions, others an equally dramatic drop. Goldman-Eisler explains this selective action as the ability of the speaker to compensate in the more demanding task, or not, for the relaxing effect of the drug.

> Some individuals when challenged to perform at a higher level, as in the case in cartoon interpretations, are able to mobilize defences [probably tonic] correcting for the relaxing effect of the drug. (loc. cit.)

She concludes:

> As the construction of sentences has so far appeared independent of pause time in contrast to word choice [see next section] and interpretation of meaning, it seems that there are two distinct levels of verbal behaviour. Syntactical operations, which profit from the organism's state of efficiency [presumably a tonic state] seem to be organized at the level of skills. Lexical choices, as well as the semantic complexity of intellectual content on the other hand, are functions of the capacity of organisms for delaying speech action. They profit from the time gained in such delays, and this mechanism indicated that they are organized at the level of acts of cognitive creation. (op. cit. p. 76).

This identification of syntactic Planning with highly-skilled, and thus relatively automatic, performance is not, on reflection, surprising. Although in theory, there are an infinite number of potential sentence types, in practice we use only a tiny subset of these, and we use them very frequently indeed.

Thus the activation of almost any sentence type is likely to be an extremely well-practised piece of behaviour. Unfortunately, we do not have reliable frequency data for sentence types, but the study by Goldman-Eisler and Cohen (1970) mentioned above gives some clue. A simple classification of sentences in Actives and Passives, Affirmatives and Negatives, from a wide variety of speech situations showed that over 90% were Active and Affirmative.

This explanation requires that sentence frames can be organized independently on the lexical items filling slots in the frames. For an independent justification of this view see Garrett's chapter in this volume.

B. Macro-plans

Does the Planning that I have crudely characterized as "semantic" occur continuously through an utterance, or does it occur only at particular points? And what sort of Plan is formulated as a result of this Planning?

To start with the temporal organization of Planning: Henderson et al. (1966) noticed that pause time was not evenly distributed through the utterance, but showed a cyclic pattern. Periods of much pausing (usually more than 50%) alternated with periods of little pausing (usually less than 15%). Moreover, the duration of actual phonation in the fluent periods turned out to be proportional to amount of pause time in the immediately preceding hesitant period. It seemed that in order to get out a given amount of speech, the speaker needed a proportionate amount of prior planning time to prepare it. The location and duration of pauses in hesitant and fluent phases of the temporal cycle is described in more detail below (Section VI).

If a cycle really does consist of one phase primarily for Planning and the other phase for Execution of the Plan, then each cycle should have a textual structure corresponding to a plausible Plan. In 1954 Lounsbury proposed that pauses mark the beginning of "encoding units"; but he believed, before any studies had been carried out, that these pauses would occur mainly within clauses rather than at clause boundaries. For reasons he would have been sympathetic with, and which are discussed in Section VI (Lexical Selection), pauses are highly likely to precede *bilious* and *exquisite* in (9).

> (9) Don't drink, if you're bilious, chicken soup. My mother makes exquisite chicken soup, which is a terrible temptation if your're feeling ill.

Lounsbury would be therefore committed to saying that the word string (10) is encoded as a single unit:

> (10) . . . bilious chicken soup my mother makes . . .

Such strings do not have a textual structure corresponding to a plausible Plan.

The alternative suggestion, mooted originally by Wundt (1912), and revived by Miller et al. (1960), is that a Plan corresponds to a single surface sentence. Even though there is no evidence that a syntactic *process* contributes to pause time, it may still be the case that semantic Planning is organized so as to be expressed in a single sentence. Examination of the textual composition of temporal cycles, however, indicates that this is not the case.

Typically, cycles last about 18 s, but some as long as 30 s, which means that they will contain, on average, five to eight clauses i.e. generally two or more sentences (Butterworth, 1975; Beattie, 1977b). Since, as we have seen, semantic factors were responsible for pause time variations, we should look for semantic rather than syntactic units.

I therefore asked independent judges to divide transcripts of speech like "Ideas". "Idea" being the best instruction I could come up with to direct the judges to look for semantic units without too many preconceptions as to structure. (After all, the single word "justice" may be said to express an idea; a whole text, e.g. Plato's *Republic*, may be said to express an idea, again the idea of justice.) The speech was taken from unrehearsed discussions, where the speaker was trying to argue for a proposition on a moral or political topic. The transcription was in normal orthography, tidied-up to eliminate "um's", "er's", false starts etc. but there was no indication of temporal pattern, apart from normal punctuation points.†

Taking those points in the texts where more than half the judges agreed that one Idea ended and the next began, and comparing these with cycle boundaries, a significant correspondence between Idea and cycle boundaries was found. Although the correspondence was reliable it was not complete. Some cycles did not begin at an Idea boundary, and some Ideas did not coincide with cycles. Why these discrepancies should occur is not clear. Individual differences may account for some of it: in a topic very familiar to the speaker, a single unit may be quite large, but for the unfamiliar judge, this unit consists of several smaller units. The textual structure of Ideas and cycles is being explored in more detail by Beattie (unpublished). One thing is established, however: both Idea and cycle boundaries almost invariably coincide with clause boundaries (Butterworth, 1975) and thus consist of a set of whole clauses. So we can say, at least, that at the semantic level, the speaker formulates a Plan which is supraclausal.

This kind of temporal analysis has been criticized as producing artifactual patterns (Jaffe *et al.*, 1972), but the patterns are validated by the evidence cited here which links them to syntactic and semantic units, and by other recent evidence linking them to patterns of gaze and gesture. (See Butterworth and Goldman-Eisler, 1978, for a review; also Butterworth and Beattie, 1978, for the connexion with gestures, and Beattie, this volume, Chapter 4, for the connexion with gaze.)

One final point concerns the locus for loading Plans for an utterance. Several authors, most notably Morton (1970), have argued for a "Response Buffer" which can hold a string of words for output following lexical

---

† O'Connell (1977), has criticized my use of normal orthography. He says that by punctuating, I have "unwittingly imposed [my] own segmentation of ideas"; but a few lines later admits that "the wide variation in semantic segmentation . . . should give no further pause regarding the psychological reality conceptualised as *sentence*. Butterworth's evidence indicates that a sentence is psychologically *not* synonymous simply with the expression of a 'single idea'." (p. 311)

selection. This buffer is held to operate in both speech production and short-term memory tasks. In the latter, a list of words is presented auditorily for immediate recall, and Morton claims that the words are identified and temporarily stored in the Response Buffer awaiting vocal output as required. Neuropsychologists Warrington and Shallice have identified brain-damaged patients who show selective impairment of auditory-verbal STM (Warrington and Shallice, 1969; Shallice and Warrington, 1970), in which the mean number of words recallable from a list is 2·5 (ignoring order errors; this is more than two standard deviations worse than normal). According to a model of Morton's type, this would mean that the Response Buffer has a severely curtailed capacity—i.e. about 2·5 words *maximum*, since the last item in an auditorily-presented list should be recoverable from another locus. Therefore, phrase length between pauses must be much shorter than normal and there should be more pause time in the speech of such patients. This is generally the case, since this condition is usually accompanied by aphasic symptoms (Saffran, Schwartz and Marin, this volume, Chapter 9), but not invariably so. Shallice and Butterworth (1977) reported one case of severe impairment of auditory-verbal STM, without a concomitant increase in the hesitancy of speech. The most plausible interpretation of these results is that, *contra* Morton, the buffer used in STM tasks is not used in speech.

VI. Micro-patterns of Pausing, Lexical Choice and Syntactic Organization

We turn now to the role of individual pauses. As I hinted in Sections I and II, three functions have been ascribed to individual pauses: they represent delays incurred in choosing words, they represent delays incurred in formulating syntactic Plans and they represent marking of clause endings. In this section I will evaluate these ascriptions, and in the next section I will report a study which draws together macro and micro Planning.

A. Lexical Selection

The earliest cognitive hypothesis of speech chronometry was suggested by Lounsbury (1954): "hesitation pauses correspond to points of highest statistical uncertainty in the sequencing of units" (p. 99). The most likely "order" (level) of units to show this effect, he supposed, would be words. Thus the next word is *statistically* uncertain when, *psychologically*, the speaker has a word range of choices as to what it should be. In line with Hick's Law (see above p. 156) we would expect high uncertainty to correspond to a delay in output. Lounsbury justified his hypothesis by reference to intuition and common experience and by reference to a Markovian version of Stimulus-Response theory, now largely discredited (cf. Chomsky, 1957).

Goldman-Eisler (1958), ever a pioneer, showed that the intuitive grounds were correct but the Markovian grounds, which posits strict left-to-right dependencies, were false. She estimated uncertainty of each word using a variant of Shannon's "Guessing Game" (Shannon, 1948). Transcripts of spontaneous speech were made, the subject would be given a few preceding sentences as context, and then asked to guess the first word of the next sentence. He was told when he had made the correct guess; and, if after a minute, he had not yet got the right word he was told it. And so on until the end of the sentence. Uncertainty was defined as the ratio of correct guesses to all guesses. In a second variant, subjects started at the last word of the sentence and worked towards the first word. Surprisingly the second task proved no more difficult than the first, though there was little correlation between unguessability in the two directions. However, those words which *were* relatively uncertain in both directions, were the best predictors of pause location: almost all of them were preceded by pauses. Thus the inituitive version of Lounsbury's hypothesis was supported—a wide choice requires a delay in output. The Markovian version was disconfirmed, since there are clearly dependencies operating in both directions, enabling backward guessing to succeed. A hierarchical model of language production seems implied, where later nodes influence the determination of current nodes; and this fits common experience. We can anticipate what we will say, not perhaps the exact words, but in outline, and this will constrain current production.

The contribution of lexical selection to the occurrence and location of individual pauses has been confirmed subsequently in a number of studies using different methods for estimating uncertainty. The "Cloze procedure", where words are deleted from the transcript and guessed by subjects, has been employed by Tannenbaum *et al.* (1965) and Butterworth (1972). It turns out as one would expect, that this method is more or less equivalent to the Guessing Game (Burke and Schiavetti, 1975). Indirect support comes from the analysis of an enormous corpus of conference tapes (over 50 000 words) by Maclay and Osgood (1959). They found that pauses were more likely to occur before content words than function words. When the speaker comes to a point where a content word is required he naturally has a much wider choice than where a function word is required: in one corpus examined, function words comprised 59% of all words by token, but only 6·4% by type (Martin and Strange, 1968).

Finally, it should be mentioned that there are a class of aphasics whose ability to find the right word has been severely impaired, though syntax, morphology, phonology and intonation seem more or less intact (cf. Saffran *et al.*, this volume, Chapter 9). The problem appears to be that these patients cannot make the appropriate links between word-meaning and word-sound, for any but the most common words, thus comprehension can be severely impaired, and speech though fluent is circumlocutory or unintelligible. A subclass, called "jargon aphasics", also invent words. In one case that I studied, the patient used neologisms at those points where he should have used a relatively uncommon word. Ninety-five per cent of the neologisms, whose grammatical class could be identified from the surrounding context, stood in place of content words. Most of these were nouns, and whereas pauses only occurred before 22% of real nouns, they occurred before 52% of neologized nouns. Generally, neologisms were far more likely to follow a pause than real words. These data are to be expected, if indeed pauses are used for difficult lexical selections, and moreover show the usefulness of pause analysis in studying aphasics. One piece of additional data indicates the usefulness of aphasia studies for understanding normals. The grammatical morphology of the neologisms—grammatical endings like plurals, tensing etc.—was virtually perfect, thus the morphophonemic process is independent of, and subsequent to, lexical selection. Thus what appears to be selected in lexical selection is not the whole word, but the word-stem ("lexical formative" in Chomsky and Halle, 1968), the endings being added later (Butterworth, 1979). This inference for normal production is supported by data from speech errors from normal speakers, where word stems can be transposed but the endings remain (and accommodate to the new stem where necessary):

(11)   It pays [= /z/] to wait → It waits [= /s/] to pay
(see Garrett, this volume for a discussion).

B. Syntax

As I have mentioned, Wundt (1912) and Miller *et al.* (1960) have suggested that the sentence is a basic Planning unit, and I have argued that pauses at clause boundaries, even though they may constitute nearly half of all pauses, are not good evidence for this, since these pauses may be serving a communicative function. Boomer (1965) has also proposed a syntactic unit as the basic Plan in production and has attempted to use pause data in such a way that the possibility of their communicative role does not arise.

Boomer has proposed that the basic "encoding unit" (= Plan) is the phonemic clause, one intonational unit comprising a single intonation contour with one prominent syllable and one terminal juncture. (Phonemic clauses generally, but not invariably, correspond to syntactic clauses.)

Speech production, he maintains is

> a complex process in which planning ranges forward to encompass a structural chunk of syntax and meaning. As a given clause is being uttered, the next one is taking shape and focus. At the terminal juncture, the next clause may be ready, in which case it will be uttered fluently . . . If, however, the emerging clause has not yet been subjectively formulated, speech is suspended until the entire pattern is clarified. This suspension may be manifested as either a pause or a vocalized hesitation. (Boomer, 1965, p. 157).

The basis for these claims is the non-random distribution of individual pauses *within* phonemic clauses. In about 41% of his sample, pauses occur between the first and second word of the clause.

> The initial word in a phonemic clause sets certain constraints on what is to follow. The selection of the first word has in greater or lesser degree committed the

speaker to a particular construction or at least a set of alternative constructions. According to this view, then, the hesitations in phonemic clauses are most likely to occur after at least a preliminary decision has been made concerning its structure and before the lexical choices have finally been made. (Boomer, 1965, p. 156).

Subsequently (Boomer and Laver, 1968), the theory was amended so that the phonemic clause is fully specified by the time the second word is uttered.

Several problems immediately arise with the data. (1) Only 41% of the *within-clause* pauses are accounted for, i.e. 22% of all pauses. (2) Only half the clauses fit the theory, the other half are uttered fluently, and, it must be supposed, are planned during the preceding clause, but why this should be so of some clauses rather than others is not explained. (3) The probability of occurrence of pauses at the second position should be a function of how much planning the clause requires. Thus long clauses should, *ceteris paribus*, be more likely to show pauses here than short clauses. I reanalysed Boomer's published data (nonfluent clauses only are given, his Table 2), taking as the null hypothesis that each between-word location will be equally likely to manifest a pause. Boomer's hypothesis should be that between the first and second word, the observed frequency of occurrence of pauses will exceed the null hypothesis figure by a larger amount the longer the clause. Using Kendall's tau to correlate the excess-minus null figure for each clause length yielded $\tau = -0.5$, $p = 0.038$: a significant correlation in the wrong direction!

There is also a problem about the replicability of his position effect. In spontaneous discussions, both Beattie (1977b) and I (Butterworth, 1976) found much lower proportions of pauses between first and second words— 14·9 and 8·5% respectively. In my sample, the 8·5% consisted 25 examples, of which 17 could be accounted for by other hypotheses, e.g. ten were located before unpredictable words, two at points of clause embedding and five at phase transitions. Why there should be this discrepancy between Boomer's data and those collected by Beattie and me is uncertain. The speech task Boomer's subjects understood was, as far as we can tell, essentially a monologue. It is *prima facie* plausible that his speakers were less concerned about listener comprehension and were thus more willing to break up clauses. However, both his sample and my sample contained a similar proportion of within-clause pauses—53·4% in his, 50·2% in mine.

One might also query, at a theoretical level, why speakers decided on the first word (whatever it may be) and then the rest of the clause. (cf. Fodor, Bever and Garrett, 1974, p. 424); and there remains the conflict between the original formulation (Boomer, 1965) where the final choice of lexical item is made locally, and the subsequent formulation (Boomer and Laver, 1968), where the phonemic clause "is handled as a unitary behavioural act, and the neural correlates of the separate elements are assembled and partially activated, or 'primed', before the performance of the utterance begins" (p. 9).

To evaluate the alternative models properly, it will be necessary to specify the models more fully, and to analyse the pause data in such a way that the contributions of local and longer-range Planning can be identified.

VII. Partitioning Pause Time into Macro- and Micro-Planning

My purpose in the following study was to identify more precisely the contribution to pause time made by the three Planning functions so far mentioned—semantic Planning, lexical selection and syntactic Planning—and to show how they were related in time.

Samples of speech were taken from three speakers whose task it was to argue for a proposition they agreed with, in an unrehearsed discussion with the experimenter (BB). Pauses were identified mechanically (see Section I), and the unpredictability of each word in the transcript of the speech, was estimated using a Cloze procedures (see Section IV. A). I also divided the transcript into (surface) clauses, and computed the subordination Index (set III) for sub-parts of the whole transcripts.

It was thus possible to assign each word to the following categories:
1. Predictable/Unpredictable (= High or Low Cloze scores).
2. Clause-initial/non-clause-initial.
3. Hesitant/Fluent (= immediately preceded by a pause/not immediately preceded by a pause†).
4. In a Planning phase/in an Execution phase.
and any passages could take the following description
1. Percentage of pausing.
2. Number, duration and percentage of pauses at clause junctures.
3. Number, duration and percentage of clause junctures marked by pauses.
4. Subordination Index.
5. Number, duration and percentage of pauses before Unpredictable words.

In this way, it was possible to discover whether, for example, juncture pauses in Planning phases were used for Planning, and whether lexical selection could be carried out Planning phases as well as locally.

---

† A close examination of the protocols reveals that the speaker not only seems to delay the difficult lexical choice, but, in a number of instances hold up the associated function word, and output it only when the lexical item has been found. This reflects Maclay and Osgood's (1959) observation, that there is a level of organization which comprises "a lexical core with its tightly bound grammatical context", (p. 41). In our data for example, one speaker (S10) said: "get in the way [pause] of future [Cloze = 0] changes." There is support for this interpretation of the speaker's behaviour in that the speaker will sometimes repeat the function word on either side of the pause:
(S10) ". . . those elements with which they [pause] they cannot cope."
The data was recategorized to take account of this feature. If one function word plus a lexical item immediately followed a pause, the hesitant function word was deleted from the data, and the fluent lexical item was "promoted" to the hesitant category, and *its* original datum deleted. This is more conservative than Goldman-Eisler's (1958) procedure, where she counted the first lexical item after a pause, irrespective of the number of intervening function words. Our recategorization resulted in 52 function words being dropped, and the same number of lexical items being promoted. The proportion of hesitant to fluent low Cloze items is about 1:3·5, for high Cloze items about 1:8·5.

TABLE I

Distribution of pause durations, and number of pauses, associated with low Cloze items, clause junctures and other pauses in Planning and Execution phase in four samples of spontaneous speech.

		Pauses				
		1 Preceding low Cloze items	2 At clause junctures	3 At clause junctures which precede low Cloze items	4 Others	5 Total
P- phase	Pause time	13·3	35·4	11·1	58·1	117·9
	N	15	26	9	46	96
	Mean (in s)	0·89	1·36	1·23	1·26	
Ex- phase	Pause time	35·4	35·2	32·6	35·8	139
	N	62	43	38	52	195
	Mean (in s)	0·57	0·82	0·86	0·69	
	Mean P- Mean Ex- (in s)	0·32	0·54	0·37	0·57	
	t-test between P and Ex	2·33 $p < 0.025$	3·47 $p < 0.001$	1·62 $p > 0.10$	3·89 $p < 0.001$	

A. Results

The distribution of pauses corroborated the main findings mentioned above: speech showed the temporal rhythm of Planning and Execution phases, unpredictable words were more likely to be Hesitant, and about 40% of all pauses marked clause boundaries. A detailed analysis of pause categories is given in Table I.

B. Analysis

1. Planning versus Execution Phase Pauses
In Planning phases about half the total pause time could not be assigned either to lexical selection or clause boundary marking; this is about twice the Execution phase figure. Moreover, in each category Planning phase pauses are

longer than in Execution-phases; the clause boundary and "Other" pauses being 0·54 s and 0·57 s longer respectively. Notice also, that whereas in Execution phases 49% of pauses have nothing to do with lexical selection, in Planning phases this figure rises to 75%—I assume that juncture pauses before unpredictable words may be serving lexical selection.

It is plausible to attribute both the increase in duration of clause boundary pauses and the increase in "Other" pause time in Planning phases to the need to carry our non-local functions. The increase in the lexical pauses is more problematic. One possibility is that the speaker is making use of the fact that he has to pause here anyway, and it will not hinder listener comprehension to extend this pause a bit to carry out semantic Planning as well as local lexical selection. A second possibility here is that the speaker is not only searching through his mental lexicon, but also formulating a semantic specification, or *lexical* Plan to guide the search, i.e. he is working out in detail the meaning of the word he needs to fulfil his semantic Plan, and when this is done, searching through his lexicon for a phonological form which best fits that meaning. Thus, by the time he has reached the Execution phase, the lexical Plan for each lexical item will be ready, but the phonological form still needs to be found in the lexicon. The study of speech-related gestures supports the temporal and functional division between formulating a lexical Plan and searching the lexicon. Butterworth and Beattie (1978) noticed a class of gestures that were iconically related to the meanings of individual words. For example, the word *raise* might be accompanied by an upward movement of the hand. Interestingly, the gesture onset usually preceded, but never followed, the associated word: the typical asynchrony being just under 1 s. In Execution phases, where, on this account, one would expect word-meaning to be already specified, gestures usually began in the lexical pause preceding the associated word. This tendency was significantly less marked in Planning phases. We interpreted this as indicating that intended word-meanings were known in advance of finding the right word, with a big temporal lag, in the Execution phase, and that onset asynchronies represented a lowest estimate of time taken to search for the word fitting the lexical Plan.

The evidential grounds are slight for preferring the second possible explanation of the extra pause time before unpredictable lexical items, and a final determination must wait on further data.

2. The Relation Between Lexical Selection and Syntactic Organization

Where a clause starts with an unpredictable lexical item, these two factors combine to increase the probability of a juncture pause, see Table II. But, as can be seen from Table I, column 3, there is no increase in pause *duration* when these factors combine. This suggests that in Execution phases, juncture pauses are "dead time", not serving a speaker function unless a difficult lexical selection had to be carried out and this can generally be accomplished in the time so made available. In Planning phases, juncture pauses appear to consist of some clause marking time in addition to Planning time, and this additional time can be used to do local lexical selection.

TABLE II
Cloze scores for hesitant and fluent clause starts

	Cloze scores		
	0,1	4,5	
Hesitant starts	46	59	105
Fluent starts	17	71	88
	63	130	193

$(\chi^2 = 11 \cdot 97, \text{df.} = 1, p < 0 \cdot 001)$

VI. Conclusions

In unrehearsed speech, speakers engage in time-consuming Planning whereby a general semantic Plan is formulated, in advance, for a chunk of speech output. Periods of Planning alternate with periods in which the Plan is executed. The Plan corresponds to a part of the text that typically comprises several clauses, such that the textual structure of the Plan is evident to readers of the transcript. (Listeners, too, seem sensitive to this textual structure since they orient to ends of the Planning-Execution cycle—see Beattie, this volume.) The Plan appears to comprise lexical Plans, which embody a semantic specification of the lexical items required to express it; and to comprise instructions for the syntactic organization of the several clauses encompassed by it.

Lexical selection can be divided into two component Planning processes: (1) Formulating a semantic specification of the required lexical item—the lexical Plan; (2) Searching through the mental lexicon for an item—a string of phonemes representing the stem morpheme. Both of these processes seem to require a delay in output, as reflected in the pattern of pausing.

Syntactic organization is the result of a syntactic Planning process, which appears to be an automatic consequence of prior semantic Planning, since it causes no output delays, and is integrated into suprasentential semantic units. The syntactic Plan, on these data, appear as a structural frame of slots for lexical items that are often unfilled when speaker begins to articulate the start of the frame. The execution of a syntactic Plan will be interrupted at points where a lexical slot is unfilled. It is possible that several syntactic Plans are fully specified in a Planning phase, along with all or most of the lexical Plans for the current Idea (Semantic Plan); alternatively, the specification of both lexical and syntactic Plans may be developed close to the points at which they are required for immediate output. The gesture data point, if weakly, to the former option. In this volume, other sources of evidence help to provide a more detailed account of Plans and Planning in production. How other evidence ties in with the implications of the pause data will be discussed more fully in the final chapter.

References

Abercrombie, D. (1968). Silent Stress. Department of Phonetics and Linguistics, Edinburgh University. Work in Progress. No. 2, 1–10.

Abrams, K. and Bever, T. G. (1969). Syntactic structure modifies attention during speech perception and recognition. *Quarterly Journal of experimental Psychology*, **21**, 280–290.

Barik, H. C. (1968). On defining juncture pauses: a note on Boomer's Hesitation and grammatical encoding. *Language and Speech*, **11**, 156–159.

Beattie, G. W. (1977a). The dynamics of interruption and the filled pause. *British Journal of Clinical Psychology*, **16**, 283–284.

Beattie, G. W. (1977b). Hesitation and gaze as indicators of cognitive processing in spontaneous speech. Paper to British Psychological Society, London Conference, December, 1977.

Beattie, G. W. and Bradbury, R. J. (1979). An experimental investigation of the modifiability of temporal structure of spontaneous speech. *Journal of Psycholinguistic Research*.

Bloch, B. (1946). Studies in colloquial Japenese. II: Syntax. *Language*, **22**, 200–248.

Bloomfield, L. (1933). "Language". Holt, Rinehart and Winston, New York.

Bloomer, D. (1965). Hesitation and Gramatical Encoding. *Language and Speech*, **8**, 215–220.

Boomer, D. S. and Dittman, A. T. (1962). Hesitation pauses and juncture pauses in speech. *Language and Speech*, **5**, 215–220.

Boomer, D. and Laver, J. D. M. (1968). Slips of the Tongue. *British Journal of Disorders in Communication*, **3**, 2–11 [also in Fromkin (1973)].

Burke, J. P. and Schiavetti, N. (1975). Effects of cumulative context and guessing methods on estimates of transition probability in speech. *Language and Speech*, **18**, 299–311.

Butterworth, B. L. (1972). *Semantic analyses of the phasing of fluency in spontaneous speech*. Unpublished Ph.D. thesis University of London.

Butterworth, B. L. (1975). Hesitation and semantic planning in speech. *Journal of Psycholinguistic Research*, **4**, 75–87.

Butterworth, B. L. (1976). Semantic planning, lexical choice and syntactic organization in spontaneous speech. (Internal report, Psychological Laboratory, Cambridge.)

Butterworth, B. L. (1979). Hesitation and the production of neologisms in jargon aphasia. *Brain and Language*, **8**.

Butterworth, B. L. and Beattie, G. W. (1978). Gesture and silence as indicators of planning in speech. *In* "Advances in the Psychology of Language—Formal and Experimental Approaches" (R. Campbell and P. Smith, eds). Plenum, New York.

Butterworth, B. L. and Goldman-Eisler, F. (1979). Recent studies on cognitive rhythm. *In* "Temporal Aspects of Speech," (A. W. Seigman and S. Feldstein, eds). Erlbaum, New Jersey.

Chomsky, N. (1957). "Syntactic Structures". Mouton, The Hague.

Chomsky, N. and Halle, M. (1968). "The Sound Pattern of English". Harper Row, New York.

Donders, F. C. (1868). [Translated and republished as:] On the speed of mental processes. *Acta Psychologica*, **30**, 412–431. (*Attention and Performance II*, (W. G. Koster, ed.).)

Flores d'Arcais, G. B. and Joustra, J. (1976). "The production of temporal sentences". Progress Report No. 1, Psychologische Functieleer, Rijkuniversiteit Leiden.

Fodor, J. A., Bever, T. G. and Garrett, M. F. (1979). "The Psychology of Language." McGraw-Hill, New York.

Fromkin, V. (1971). The nonanomalous nature of anomalous utterances. *Language*, **47**, 27–52.

Fry, D. B. (1969). The linguistic evidence of speech errors. *Brno Stud. English*, **8**, 69–74.

Goldman-Eisler (1956). Determinants of the rate of speech and their mutual relations. *Journal of Psychonomic Research*, **2**, 137–143.

Goldman-Eisler, F. (1958) Speech production and the predictablity of words in context. *Quarterly Journal of experimental Psychology*, **10**, 96–106.

Goldman-Eisler, F. (1961a). A comparative study of two hesitation phenomena. *Language and Speech*, **4**, 18–26.

Goldman-Eisler, F. (1961b). Hesitation and information in speech. *In* "Information Theory" (C. Cherry, ed.). Butterworth, London.

Goldman-Eisler, F. (1968). "Psycholinguistics: Experiments in Spontaneous Speech." Academic Press, London.

Goldman-Eisler, F. (1972). Pauses, clauses, sentences. *Language and Speech*. **15**, 103–113.

Goldman-Eisler, F. and Cohen, M. (1970). Is NP, P, and PN difficulty a valid criterion of transformational operations? *Journal of Verbal Learning and Verbal Behaviour*, **9**, 161–166.

Good, D. (1978). On (doing) being hesitant. *Pragmatics Microfiche*, 3.2: E1.

Good, D. A. and Butterworth, B. L. (1978). Hesitancy as a conversational resource: some methodological considerations. *In* "Temporal Variables in Speech: Studies in Honour of Frieda Goldman-Eisler," (H. Dechert, ed.), Mouton, The Hague.

Green, D. W. (1977). The immediate processing of sentences. *Quarterly Journal of experimental Psychology*, **29**, 135–146.

Henderson, A., Goldman-Eisler, F. and Skarbek, A. (1965). Temporal patterns of cognitive activity and breath control in speech. *Language and Speech*, **8**, 236–242.

Henderson, A., Goldman-Eisler, F. and Skarbek, A. (1966). Sequential temporal patterns in spontaneous speech. *Language and Speech*, **9**, 207–216.

Hick, W. E. (1952). On the rate of gain of information. *Quarterly Journal of experimental Psychology*, **4**, 11–26.

Jaffe, J., Breskin, S. and Gerstman, L. J. (1972). Random generation of apparent speech rhythms. *Language and Speech*, **15**, 68–71.

Lindsley, J. R. (1975). Producing simple utterances: how far do we plan ahead? *Cognitive Psychology*, **7**, 1–19.

Lindsley, J. R. (1976). Producing simple utterances: details of the planning process. *Journal of Psycholinguistic Research*, **5**, 331–354.

Lounsbury, F. G. (1954). Transitional Probability, Linguistic Structure, and Systems of Habit-family Hierarchies. *In* "Psycholinguistics: A Survey of Theory and Research Problems" (C. E. Osgood and T. Sebeok, eds). Supplement to Journal of Abnormal and Social Psychology, 1954. Reprinted Bloomington, Indiana University Press, Indiana.

Maclay, H. and Osgood, C. E. (1959). Hesitation phenomena in spontaneous English speech. *Word*, **15**, 19–44.

Martin, J. G. and Strange, W. (1968). The perception of hesitation in spontaneous speech. *Perception and Psychophysics*. **3**, 427–432.

Miller, G. A. (1962). Some psychological studies of grammar. *American Psychologist*, **17**, 748–762.

Miller, G. A., Galanter, E. and Pribram, K. H. (1960). "Plans and the Structure of Behavior". Holt, Rinehart and Winston Inc., New York.

Miller, G. A. and McKean, K. E. (1964). A chronometric study of some relations between sentences. *Quarterly Journal of experimental Psychology*, **16**, 297–308.

Morton, J. (1970). A functional model for memory. *In* "Models of Human Memory", (D. A. Norman, ed.). Academic Press, New York.

Morton, J., Marcus, S. and Frankish, C. (1976). Perceptual Centres (P-Centres). *Psychological Review*, **83**, 405–408.

Murray, D. C. (1971). Talk, silence and anxiety. *Psychological Bulletin*, **75**, 244–260.

O'Connell, D. C. (1977). One of many units: the sentence. *In* "Sentence Production", (S. Rosenberg, ed.). Erlbaum, New Jersey.

O'Connell, D. C., Kowal, S. and Hörmann, H. (1969). Semantic determinants of pauses. *Psychologische Forschung*, **33**, 50–67.

Rochester, S. R. and Gill, J. (1973). Production of complex sentences in monologues and dialogue. *Journal of Verbal Learning and Verbal Behaviour*, **12**, 203–210.

Rosenbaum, P. (1967). "The Grammar of the English Predicate Complement Constructions". MIT Press, Cambridge, Mass.

Shallice, T. and Butterworth, B. L. (1977). Short-term memory impairment and spontaneous speech. *Neuropsychologia*, **15**, 729–735.

Shallice, T. and Warrington, E. K. (1970). Independent functioning of verbal memory stores: a neuropsychological study. *Quarterly Journal of experimental Psychology*, **22**, 261–273.

Shannon, C. E. (1948). Prediction and entropy of printed English. *Bell System Technical Journal*, **30**, 50–65.

Tannenbaum, P. H., Williams, F. and Hillier, C. S. (1965). Word predictability in the environments of hesitations. *Journal of Verbal Learning and Verbal Behaviour*. **4**, 134–140.

Taylor, I. (1969). Content and structure in sentence production. *Journal of Verbal Learning and Verbal Behaviour*, **8**, 170–175.

Warrington, E. K. and Shallice, T. (1969). Selective impairment of auditory-verbal short term memory. *Brain*, **92**, 885–896.

Wundt, W. (1912). *In* "Language and Psychology" (A. L. Blumenthal, ed.), pp. 20–33. John Wiley and Sons Inc, New York.

8
Levels of Processing in Sentence Production

M. F. Garrett   *Massachusetts Institute of Technology*

I. Introduction

The study of language production processes is usually considered more
difficult than the study of comprehension processes. Indeed, from time to
time, one encounters the suggestion that it is literally impossible to engage in
such study because we do not have a theory of the proximal, non-linguistic
causes of sentence construction. And, certainly, we do not have such a theory
in the way that we do for comprehension; for that case, we do have some
moderately well-founded suppositions about the excitation of the peripheral
sensory apparatus as a function of the physical (visual or acoustic)
representations of sentences. On reflection, however, there is remarkably little
of what one ordinarily takes to be substantive claims for comprehension
theories which turns on the availability of the physically stipulated
descriptions. Rather, there is much in such theory building which, entirely
within the domain of language specific description, seeks to determine the
computational relations among the several sorts of information available in a
structural analysis of sentences. Thus, one asks, for example, how we may
derive from the information given by a succession of lexical and grammatical
formatives a linguistically defensible syntactic analysis. That is the question
most parsing routines are designed to answer. How does the computational
process in comprehension accommodate itself to the exigencies of a limited
capacity processing memory, assuming as a beginning, any of several possible
linguistic descriptions of input (e.g. phonetic, prosodic, lexical)? That is one of
the questions around which a good deal of comprehension work on perceptual
complexity and segmentation revolves. What are the organizational principles
of the lexical inventory which seem to govern the contact between surface
vocabulary and entries in our "mental dictionary"? That is the lexical access
question. Nowhere in that sample list of problems is the matter of a *known*
non-linguistic form of representation crucial to enquiry. N.B. I do not wish to
assert the irrelevancy of such descriptions for the study of comprehension or,
for that matter, of production†; I wish only to stress the extent to which useful
enquiry may turn on no more than plausible assumptions about the character

---

† For example, work in articulatory and acoustic phonetics is clearly relevant; moreover, work
in those areas is increasingly being tied to "higher order" structures in addition to the sound level
constructs.

of the input representations (e.g., that it is or is not temporally ordered in its "presentation"; that it consists of context free elements or not). By and large, the questions are about the relations among linguistic types. Why should we not raise the same questions about production processes? The stumbling block, if my remarks are correct, is *not* the lack of a non-linguistic theory of first causes of sentence construction, but simply the inconvenience of access to manipulation of those representations. We can, modulo relatively non-controversial neurophysiological assumptions about the relation between distal and proximal stimulus, exercise such control for comprehension study; but the difficulty engendered by our inability to exercise corresponding control in the study of production should not be taken for a *principled* bar to enquiry in that area. No doubt, some questions, perhaps even those taken to be most fundamental, are barred—viz those which concern the constructive processes relating linguistic and non-linguistic representations. But *that* question is also denied for comprehension study at this point. And, many interesting questions of the sort noted above remain in both areas.

How can we study production processes? There are two general modes: direct experimental manipulation and systematic observation of spontaneous speech. In the former domain, one may experiment in the manner of Forster (1974), or Jarvella (1976), or Cooper (this volume), or others some of whom are represented in this volume. Such experimentation inevitably involves the risk of confounding comprehension processes with putative production processes; that problem is, in part, one for experimental design and control, albeit a difficult one—particularly if, as seems likely, some of the constructive processes of production and comprehension "intersect" or are at least responsive to the same structural constraints (see Section VI for some discussion of this point). But, given the inherent difficulty of exercising experimental control in production studies, coupled with the interdependence and possible overlay of production and comprehension systems, the appeal to observational studies of spontaneous language production, both normal and disturbed, provides a naturally complementary strategy to direct experimentation. Systematic study of "failures" of the production process—those engendered by some injury to the central nervous system or those normal nonfluencies and errors (e.g. "hesitation phenomena" and "sponnerisms") that accompany spontaneous speech—may provide the "lever" needed to disambiguate the outcomes of particular experimentation. To this end, production claims of considerable detail may be mustered on the strength of error studies alone; but they, of course, usually have their own peculiar weakness: namely, the reliance on a data base garnered under the rather chaotic conditions of everyday existence.

What seems clear is that production theories will be best assembled against a background of enquiry which quite self-consciously seeks to play experimental and observational studies in counterpoint to each other and to theories of comprehension processes. In this paper, I will discuss some recent research efforts in the study of speech errors, with particular attention to their implications for a characterization of the production as a set of independent processing levels which correspond to levels of linguistic representations†. In so doing, I will try both to bear in mind the implications of experimental production studies, and to consider some possible connections between production and comprehension processes.

II. Speech Error Studies: Background

What are "speech errors", and how have they been studied? Errors like those of (1)–(5) occur in spontaneous, normally fluent speech at a rate frequent enough that casual observation will yield one or more examples of each in a week.‡

(1) Anticipation/perseveration:
    a. You know . . . the song called Yankle Doodle Dandy.
       (intended: Yankee Doodle Dandy)
    b. It's the golly green giant!
       (intended: jolly green giant)

(2) Shifts:
    a. All the home team wons . . . uh . . . home teams won tonight.
    b. What worries me, and what would I want to check, is . . .
       (intended: what I would want)

(3) Exchanges:
    a. We completely forgot to add the list to the roof.
       (intended: roof to the list)
    b. on a sot holdering iron
       (intended: hot soldering iron)

(4) Substitutions:
    a. It doesn't sympathize.
       (intended: synthesize it)
    b. Ask me whether you think it will do the job.
       (intended: Tell me whether)

(5) Blends:
    a. and would like to enlicit your support
       (intended: enlist or elicit)
    b. have you ever flivven at night?
       (intended: flown or driven)

While there is no doubt that errors such as those of (1)–(5) are *relatively* rare, they are not so rare as to suggest a pathological source or a "special" state of mind as their explanation. In short, they are, I believe, properly taken as

---

† See Garrett 1976, for some earlier remarks on this issue.

‡ Estimating the rate of occurrence of speech errors is a more formidable task than it might initially appear. My own approach has been to use "time samples" during which I note all the errors heard from a source in which speech is more or less continuous and at normal speech rates (e.g., a radio talk show or a public lecture). It is certain that error types differ in their rate occurrence (e.g., "exchanges" are less common than "anticipations" or "perseverations"; word substitutions more common than blends), and *individual* speakers vary greatly in their susceptibility to error.

representative of the normal function of language production in the sense that the mechanisms which determine the regularities of error distributions are the mechanisms of normal language production.

In such errors, one finds that the observed utterance either fails to contain intended elements, or contains (specifically linguistic) elements which were not intended or which are mislocated. In many instances, such errors may be spoken fluently, and sometimes without the awareness of the speaker that an error has occurred.

Such errors have been studied from a variety of viewpoints, linguistic and psychological. Whatever the interest, the "methodology" has been, with varying degrees of care, to record in written form† the errors heard in the progress of normal social intercourse, and either to subject those errors to interpretation against the background of an independently espoused linguistic or psychological theory or, more rarely, to seek a sufficiently large corpus of errors as may itself support claims about the processes underlying language production. The former course is that of Freud, who was an interpreter of specific errors rather than a student of the distributional patterns inherent in the errors. The latter course had its first adherent and perhaps best exemplar in Rudolf Meringer (see Celce-Murcia, 1973; Cutler and Fay, 1978, for some discussion of his work). Most contemporary interest has focussed on the sort of enquiry pursued by Meringer, though rarely with his zeal for detail.

The principal problems with this catch-as-catch-can methodology, as well as its practical necessity, have been several times noted in print (viz, Fromkin's remarks in the introduction to her book on speech errors (1973) and references cited therein). They are, broadly drawn, (a) the unknown perceptual and memory contributions to the nature of the error corpora that have been examined (i.e. some errors may be easier to hear and/or recall accurately than others), and (b) the non-systematic sampling of errors (i.e. there are likely to be variations in the incidence and type of errors as a function of situational circumstance and individual speakers). There are several comments that might be made about these problems: first, many of the claims that we will discuss here are based on errors which seem unlikely to have arisen out of perceptual rather than production error (e.g. exchanges of sound or word elements are sufficiently gross distortions as to be little colored by perceptual filtering); second, apparent phonetic adjustments of an error element to its new (error induced) environment, in particular for some features of stress and rule governed phonetic alternation, are plausibly susceptible of a perceptual as well as a production interpretation. This latter problem will only be coped with by detailed acoustic analysis of error productions. Some insight into the locus of the perceptual problem in speech error interpretation may also be

† Boomer and Laver's study (1968) is a notable exception to this generalization. They had recourse to a corpus of 100 tape recorded errors (Boomer's). Their results are moderately reassuring on the issue of perceptual influence on errors, given that the regularities they found in a corpus of 100 errors recorded in writing were borne out in the recorded versions as well.

gained by an examination of regularities in the perception of speech—i.e. "slips of the ear" (see Garnes, 1975; Browman, 1977, for discussions of such errors).†

The arguments in this paper, where not otherwise noted, will be based on the M.I.T. corpus of speech errors,‡ which, though relatively large ($n \Leftrightarrow 4200$), is "classic" in its accumulation and heir to most limitations of that mode. However, an effort to avoid idiosyncratic perceptual biases was made,§ and, where feasible, the conclusions reached have been checked against other published examples, most notably those of Fromkin (1973). Moreover, one should bear in mind that, even given the imponderables of speech error collection, it is the case that most major features of error distributions have been found by a variety of investigators with diverse perspectives; the principal regularities are robust, though they are, of course, susceptible to varying interpretation.

Though interest in speech errors is of relatively long-standing, its focus on linguistic structure, beginning with Meringer, has until recently been more upon structural than upon processing issues. There has been a shift in emphasis to a study of processing mechanisms during the past decade. Though such an interest was certainly not absent from earlier papers (viz. Fromkin, 1971; Fry, 1969), the search for particular semantic, syntactic and phonological process models has become more overt and detailed. In this context, interest in lexical organization and retrieval processes has burgeoned in the past 5 years-this is true of production processes and to an even greater extent in the study of comprehension. This is accountable in part by the development of experimental tools for asking detailed questions about lexical retrieval, and in part because the connection between sentence structure and specific claims about lexical structure has become more elaborate (e.g. Bresnan, 1978; Miller and Johnson-Laird, 1976; Jackendoff, 1975). In what follows, we will first review some of the major features of error distributions that have been noted by a number of investigators, with some comment on

---

† The "slips of the ear" seem rarely to involve elements of nonadjacent words, and to be mostly accounted for by sound substitution and resegmentation, prompted by lexical alternatives—e.g., "harpes zoister" heard as "her peas oyster".

‡ The M.I.T. corpus of errors was compiled by myself and Steffanie Shattuck-Hufnagel (now of Cornell University). The portion of the corpus upon which the observations in this paper are based was that assembled through January 1, 1978. That corpus with addenda will be available as a technical report from our laboratory in June, 1979.

§ Interobserver reliability was checked in two ways: a) Where there was more than a single auditor for an error, it was included in the analysis only if there was agreement on its description; b) the errors of the two principal observers were compared with each other and with those errors contributed by others. In this latter case, there was no significant difference in the corpora other than the greater incidence of vowel and stress errors observed by Shattuck-Hufnagel as compared with Garrett. There is certainly a perceptual contribution to error corpora, and most likely it is greatest for sound and stress errors; for the former case, it also seems likely that the apparent incidence of lexical outcomes (rather than nonsense outcomes) is influenced by their differential ease of recall.

their interpretation. Then, some particular features of exchange errors will be discussed for their bearing on a characterization of the sentence planning process as a set of independent computational levels. In Section IV we will consider an error mechanism which seems to express the major features of contrast in movement errors, and in Section V, we will address the problem of lexical selection and insertion as they may be reflected in word substitution and word blend errors, and consider how they relate to the error mechanism discussed in Section IV. Section VI considers a relation between comprehension and production processes suggested by errors, and Section VII raises some further issues of error interpretation which are difficult of resolution.

III.   Error Types and Sentence Planning Mechanisms

The general question to which basic sentence production studies are addressed is, what are the vocabularies and planning structures in terms of which sentences are constructed? Speech errors bear on that question in several ways.

The most obvious case can be made for movement errors, particularly exchanges of sounds, words or morphemes. Errors like those of (3a) and (3b) provide a prima facie case for the simultaneous presence to the mind of the speaker of temporally distributed portions of the utterance. While no one could doubt the necessity for that general condition to hold at *some* levels (e.g. those sound sequences over which co-articulation effects hold), it is not at all obvious just how much of what is "to be uttered" at any point has been determined prior to utterance, and under what description(s) the to-be-uttered material is available. Exchange errors provide the basis for an argument that some particular pair of elements, that may span one to several words in the intended sentence, are simultaneously present during sentence planning. Notice that this is *not* equivalent to the claim that the full string of elements spanned is also present. One is tempted to make such a move—e.g. to assume that an error like (6) demonstrates the simultaneous representation

(6)   We expect Jom and Terry to be there.
       (intended: Tom and Jerry)

of the substring "Tom and Jerry", and even stronger, that the elements are in construction. That, indeed, is what one would like to be in a position to affirm (or deny), but the mere existence of an error which spans that string does not make even the weaker case for simultaneous representation of all the elements of the substring, let alone that they are in construction. It is clearly possible that the interaction between words which yields an exchange error takes place at a level for which the phrasal membership or grammatical role of a word is irrelevant or simply not yet determined. In order to begin to establish such claims, one needs to find, for any error type, some constraining effects of the environment of the error—in the case of exchange errors, perhaps some influence of the intervening structural elements or of the phrasal environment of which they are a necessary part.

A similar sort of observation may be made for the interpretation of the error elements themselves as being of a certain type (e.g. phone, morpheme, syllable, word). In this case, a straightforward statistical argument may carry weight—e.g. when a *string* of sound elements is involved in an error (as opposed to cases in which only single sound segments seem to be affected), the string rarely has as its *only* analysis that of a string of sound segments; almost invariably there is an analaysis as a syllable, morpheme or word. Whatever the relevant analysis, such consistency as one may discover is important (always assuming, of course, appropriate statistical assurances that such consistency is not a chance occurence—see McKay, 1977, for some discussion of this issue). The case for a particular analysis, however, may be materially strengthened by the discovery that there are constraints on the error type which are statable only at the level of analysis appropriate to description of the error elements.

These observations may be recast in the form of conditions on error analysis such that they will provide evidence for the existence of a processing type—i.e. of a computational system of given vocabulary and processing mechanism. In an earlier paper, these were expressed in terms of two conditions and their interaction:

(1) When elements of a sentence interact in an error (e.g. exchange position), they must be elements of the same hypothesized processing vocabulary.
(2) The structural constraints for a given error type must be of a single processing type.

The strongest outcome is the joint effect of (1) and (2): are the constraints on an error type stateable in terms of descriptions at the level required if one is to describe the interacting elements in the same vocabulary? For example, there will nearly always be a common description available for the elements of an error interaction even if only as phonetic strings, but the important point is that if one is forced to that level of description, the constraints on the error interaction must be only those applicable to phonological description.   (Garrett, 1976, p. 237)

We will first consider some of the regularities that have been observed for speech errors, and then raise the question of what they suggest given the "principles" of error interpretation just outlined.

Some generally accepted features of speech errors. We begin by a consideration of sound errors—those exchanges, shifts, additions, deletions or copying errors which seem to involve only a phonetic segment.

(7) (a) We have a lot of pons and pats to wash.
        (intended: pots and pans)
    (b) A disorder of speech, spictly streaking is.
        (intended: strictly speaking)
    (c) It comes down to a choice of stummer sipends and . . .
        (intended: summer stipends)
    (d) What would the world come to if boys dribbled on their fathers?—
        especially after they reached the rage of eason?
        (intended: age of reason)

   (e) Do you know where I can find a clear pliece
       (intended: a clear piece of glass)
   (f) It happened in the first, second, thirth, and fourth years.
       (intended: third and fourth)

Such errors have been observed to obey the following constraints:

   (a) The interacting elements are metrically and phonetically similar. Sounds which exchange are more likely to be similar in terms of their distinctive feature description than would be expected by chance (McKay, 1970; Fromkin, 1971; Goldstein, 1977; Shattuck Hufnagel and Klatt, 1977). Stressed syllables interact with other stressed syllables; stressed and unstressed do not interact.

   (b) The environments of "moved" elements (shifts, exchanges, anticipation/perserveration) are similar: word initial segments exchange with (copy, or shift to) word initial segments, medial with medial and final with final. When consonants exchange, they are usually both followed by the same or very similar vowels in the intended utterance, and correspondingly (though with somewhat less force) for the consonantal environment of exchanged vowels.

   (c) Phrasal stress and phrasal membership affect the likelihood of any two words contributing to a sound error. In particular, both words in a sound exchange are much more likely than not be be members of the same major phrase (or "phonemic clause" on some accounts), and, perhaps accordingly, the tonic word (marked 1 for phrasal stress) of the phrase is much more likely than not to be one of the two interacting words (Boomer and Laver, 1968).

   (d) Well-formedness at the sound level is preserved in errors. When exchanges or shifts occur, they very rarely create sound sequences which violate the phonological conventions of the language being spoken (Wells, 1951; Fromkin, 1971; Nooteboom, 1967).

   What do these regularities suggest about the nature of the constructive processes for sentences? Transparently, if one accepts the principle that the error descriptions implicate the normally relevant computational descriptions, these error patterns suggest a planning process in which sentence elements are assembled phrase by phrase, and in which the elements themselves are at least partially specified for segmental features—apparently there is some specification at all word positions since sound error interactions occur at initial, medial and final positions—including word and phrase stress. So, a representation like $\mathscr{P}$ might be assumed to govern error interations of the sort we have so far noted.

   ($\mathscr{P}$) ([Bill] [shóvels] [snów])→([Bill] [snóvels] [shów]†.

Note that, in fact, we have as yet no grounds for assigning phrasal or word category labels, since though a phrasal unit is clearly relevant, it is not clear that it need be labeled NP or VP or PP, and that the words included be marked N or V or Adj. Note further that there is no basis in the error regularities so far noted for a claim that the relative degrees of word stress are marked for more than two levels—"some stress" ("salient") versus "no stress" ("weak") is indicated as a contrast for this level.

---

† Brackets indicate that particular lexical identity is assumed to be fixed, but that the form of the item is not fully specified.

We can go beyond the claims warranted by these first observations in two ways: first by a more precise determination of the detail with which the phonetic form and stress facts are represented at the point where sound movement errors occur,† and second, by an examination of the relation which these error types bear to errors (apparently) involving word and morpheme elements.

Consider first the degree of phonetic and metric specification. We have already noted that some considerable detail· of such description must be assumed for the elements which interact; what that degree is and whether the same degree of specification should be assumed for the elements with which they are in immediate construction is as yet unsettled. Point (d) above and some related phenomena are relevant. The preservation of well-formedness at the sound level is an often noted feature of errors—usually this is remarked for the uniformity with which "sequencing constraints" on sounds are honored in errors. Thus, for example, one very rarely finds error outputs in which "illegal" sequences are constructed, as would be the case for an error like (8).

(8) a stop gradient ↦ a _top sgradient.

Though shift errors of this general sort (i.e. "decomposition" of a cluster and construction of a new cluster) are common enough, they are confined to cases in which the error produced cluster is, unlike # sg_ #, a legal sequence, as (9).

    (9) (a) He had a pet spider → . . . spet _pider.
        (b) nasals glides and liquids →
           . . . nasals, lides, and gliquids?
        (c) fewer inflections→
           . . . fluer infections.

Notice that this is not because of some limitation on "practiced articulation" (even setting aside the fact that there are other languages which do not have such a prohibition), for we produce such sequences quite effortlessly (and "thoughtlessly") in casual speech—e.g. "it's going to" is more often than not pronounced /sgənə/.‡

This avoidance of illegal sound sequences could be thought of in two ways: (1) as a prior restraint on the occurrence of error, or (2) as a consequence of sound processing mechanisms which are applied posterior to the occurrence of the error. The first option, though logically possible, seems unrealizable for most cases,§ and the second admits of two interpretations. If errors are "patched up" after the fact, that might be by one of several possible varieties of an error checking and correcting system, or it might arise as the normal

---

† Obviously, the conclusion about grammatical category could be much affected by evidence for a more detailed stress involvement. The interpretation of the fact that, very frequently, the tonic word of a phrase is involved in an error might be that it is the "focus of interest" and/or has priority of lexical realization during sentence planning—or it might be a consequence of some prosodically triggered interaction which would implicate a more detailed phrase structure description for (𝒫).

‡ See Shattuck (1976).

ɣ Prior restraint on the occurrence of sound movement errors requires either clairvoyance or a general prohibition on particular types of movement (e.g., "block all movement from clusters"). The latter won't serve since it will eliminate "legal errors" as well as illegal.

consequence of sound planning for speech. There is something to be said for both possibilities.

It is unquestionably the case that we do monitor our speech and that, depending upon circumstance, we correct a variety of departures from the ideal target, including various mispronunciations. Though I do not wish to discount the importance of such processes for normal language production, nor to *deny* their possible relevance to the cases under discussion, it seems likely that the relevant "editorial" function must be quite subtle and, in particular, applied at an earlier stage than of that which we are consciously aware. It should be remembered that most of the accommodatory phenomena in speech errors, including the honoring of sequencing constraints, occurs in fluent speech, and is often unnoticed by the speaker.

We will accordingly seek some account of the sequencing facts (and related phenomena to be considered shortly) in the organization of the normal sentence planning process.

We may assume that, at the level of processing representation partially exemplified in $\mathscr{P}$, the sound representation for lexical items is abstract, i.e., many details of the final sound description of lexical items will be unspecified. Among others, those features which are responsive to regular sequencing constraints in any given language will be left unspecified, and automatic processes for filling in phonetic detail may apply because they are predictable from their immediate environment.

The problem with this line of explanation is, of course, that the degree of specification of the *intended* site of the moved element will be just suitably underspecified, but the site of new attachment, even though not fully specified, will be, potentially, specified for a feature which is, in fact, incompatible with the error induced environment. Thus, the viability of such an account of the sequencing constraints depends on the degree of abstractness of the representation of word form at the point where such errors take place, and on the flexibility of the routines which "fill in the gaps" in such representations. Note also that the sound representation at $\mathscr{P}$ cannot be *too* abstract, for otherwise it is difficult to see how sound processes involving a specific phonetic segment (i.e. the moved one) could be underway at all.

Though the speech errors' sensitivity to sequencing constraints *may* be accounted for on such a view, they are not the best illustrations of the operation of such processes. There are, however, a broader class of errors which make the case with greater force. These will be referred to here under the general heading of "accommodations"—that is, errors in which the particular phonetic form of elements involved in an error is adjusted to the appropriate form for their new environment.

Among the most compelling aspects of speech error data are those in which the phonetic shape of elements involved in errors accommodates to the error induced environment. Boomer and Laver (1968), Fromkin (1971), Nooteboom (1967), and several others, have all commented on cases like those of (10)–(12) which illustrate various modes of this phenomenon:

(10) (a) It certainly run outs fast
                          /s/
          (intended: runs out fast.)
                          /z/
     (b) Even the best team losts.
                          /s/
          (intended: teams lost.)
                          /z/
     (c) an anguage laquisition problem.
          (intended: a language acquisition.)
(11) (a) easy enoughly
          (intended: easily enough)
     (b) musárpial
          (intended: marsúpial
     (c) Norman Féllarocker
          (intended: Norman Róckefeller)
(12) (a) the wárm breather to air
          (intended: it makes the áir warmer to breathe.)
     (b) Bréakfast is the Wheaties of Champions.
          (intended: Whéaties is the breakfast of champions.)

There are a number of straightforward, but very important, observations to be made given cases like these. The first point, of course, is the demonstration which such errors provide of an ordering among the processes which give rise to utterance. Specifically, they show that the error locus (and presumably the locus for normal processes of comparable type) for cases like example (10) must precede those processes which determine the particular phonetic form of tense and number morphemes or of the indefinite article; and similarly, that the processes of word production which assign stress and vowel quality are posterior to the locus of errors like (11). Finally, the fact that appropriate phrasal stress is preserved for word exchanges has prompted the observation that such stress must be represented independently of the particular lexical content of a phrase at the point where errors like (12) occur. I have argued elsewhere (Garrett, 1975) that these same facts have implications for theories of error mechanism which assign a causal role to relative levels of activation in the motor system. If the activation level of the motor representation for a phonetic element is stress correlated, such variations in level of activation cannot be implicated in error production for those error types which show accommodation of the sort in (11) and (12).

The moral of all the accommodation cases seems to be stateable in terms of representations that are in some measure independent of the particular phonetic shape of the intended utterance. Word and phrase stress is appropriate for error induced forms *because* there is a computationally effective representation of the regularities of stress that is not tied to particular lexical entries, and similarly for the phonetic shape of certain morphemes.

This returns us to the point raised above: the representation in $\mathscr{P}$ has features which represent stress levels, but they are associated with particular phonetic segments in a word. As we have just observed, that will not permit an account of accommodations like those of (11) and (12). That suggests a modification of $\mathscr{P}$ in some way which separates stress levels for both words and phrases from the elements bearing stress.

If $\mathscr{P}$ is thought of as the product of a process, such a separation is straightforward. However, before saying anything further on this point, it will be useful to consider the sound errors from another vantage point: Namely, their contrast with errors which move not sound segments, but morphemes or words. We have, in fact, already noted some such cases in observations about preservation of phrasal stress, e.g. (12). These errors and other similar ones have a number of other features which shed light on the processing which underlies the construction of representations like

A. Word Exchanges versus Sound Exchanges

Given a representation like that of $\mathscr{P}$ and the error processes associated with it (i.e. phrase internal movement of similar elements in similar environments), we may ask whether other error types than sound errors are accountable in terms of such representations. The additional error types to be considered are those movement errors involving words and/or morphemes; these come in several varieties. We will first examine those like (13) and (14) in which a pair of words, both free forms or potentially free forms, exchange position.

(13) Word Exchanges
    (a) You should see the one I kept pinned on the room to my door.
        (intended . . . door to my room.)
    (b) I left the briefcase in my cigar
        (intended: cigar in my briefcase)
    (c) Is there a cigarette building in this machine?
        (intended: cigarette machine in this building?)
    (d) This spring has a seat in it
        (intended: seat has a spring in it)
(14) Stranding exchanges
    (a) I thought the park was trucked.
        (intended: truck was parked.)
    (b) Fancy getting your model renosed
        (intended: getting your nose remodeled.)
    (c) He facilitated what he was doing to remove the barricade.
        (intended: He removed the barricade to facilitate what he was doing.)

Note that at this point we will consider only those cases which have intervening material to serve as "anchor points" for the moved elements as clear cases of exchange. Word movement errors without such intervening material (other free forms, as in (11) or bound forms as in (12)) are ambiguous between a characterization as an exchange and as a "shift"—i.e. a case in which a single element is mislocated relative to an already fixed string (see

TABLE I
Phrasal membership constraints: proportion of errors which
involve elements of same or different phrases

	Within	Between
Word exchanges $n = 200$	0·19	0·81
Stranding exchanges $n = 100$	0·70	0·30
Sound exchanges $n = 200$	0·87	0·13

Within phrase errors are those internal to a "simple" NP
or VP (e.g. an exchange between a main verb and an element
of one of its NP objects is counted as within phrase).

example (20) below. As we will see, a good deal that is of interest turns on
this distinction.

The clear cases of word exchanges show some striking differences from
sound exchange errors. In particular, the strong tendency for the interaction
to be between the members of a single phrase is not found for errors like (11);
quite the contrary, in fact. These errors seem by and large to involve members
of distinct phrases (see Table I).

The behavior of errors like (12) is more complicated: more often than not,
they seem, like sound errors, to involve elements of a single phrase. However,
there are more exceptions to this generalization than for sound exchanges, and
those exceptions share a significant property with the word exchange errors.
That property is *correspondence* of the *grammatical category* of the interacting
elements (see Table II).

Sound exchanges and stranding errors are typically phrase internal and
involve words of differing grammatical category; word exchanges are

TABLE II
(Major) grammatical category constraints. Proportion of
errors which correspond in grammatical category of moved
elements or source of moved elements

	Same	Different
Word exchanges $n = 200$	0·85	0·15
Stranding exchanges $n = 100$	0·43	0·57
Sound exchanges $n = 200$	0·39	0·61

typically between phrases and involve words of the same grammatical category. These two features are clearly related to each other—the likelihood of correspondence of grammatical category is certainly affected by whether the error is phrase internal or not. However, I believe these distributional features, while arising from related causes, are, in fact, distinct. That point will be addressed below in the discussion of anticipation and perseveration errors.

At this point, however, let us consider some implications of the contrast between sound exchanges and word exchanges. These facts, and some others that we will note shortly, seem to indicate a most interesting possibility: namely, that these exchanges arise at different processing levels. In an earlier paper (Garrett, 1975), I characterized the two relevant levels as a *functional* level, in which phrasal membership and grammatical functions of words are determined, and a *positional* level, in which the serial order of words and some aspects of their form are specified. Note that these two terms are studiously neutral with respect to their correspondence to levels of description in a formal grammar. We will consider at a later point (Section VII) some possible formal interpretations of the processing types that error distributions suggest; for the present, the labels "positional" and "functional" should be construed as descriptive of the principal features of the errors which inspire their postulation as computational types.

B. The functional level

If this processing level is focussed on aspects of sentence form which arise from the grammatical roles of lexical items, several positive and negative claims arise: such errors should (always modulo the assumption that errors arise *only* because of similarities of the computationally relevant descriptions at any given point): (a) show similarities of grammatical category and of grammatical relations, (b) be insensitive to similarities of word forms (such as phonetic shape, length, stress location) and to surface adjacency, except where such features are correlated with computationally relevant features. Further, the degree to which meaning relations among words are directly implicated in planning decisions about the phrasal membership and grammatical role of lexical items may be evaluated by looking for an effect of such relations on the probability of word exchanges.

Of the first of these points, Table II is clear: correspondence of grammatical category is the rule. Notice further that the correspondence seems related to the role of the word in a phrase—i.e. the phrasal geometry seems to be parallel for the exchanged elements. See examples (13) and (15) and, in Fromkin's (1973) collection, categories P and X.†

The extent to which similarity of grammatical function is involved is difficult to assess. It is certainly the case that the majority of word exchange

---

†Those categories contain both the types of error I have classified as exchanges and those I have classified as shifts. Of the clear cases of exchange (n = 29) 21 are between phrases and the remaining 8 are in (NP of NP) or (N of N) constructions.

errors are between heads of noun phrases, and of those, the majority (60%) are between NPs in prepositional phrases, although there are a fair number of exchanges between nouns from subject NPs and nouns from prepositional phrases. Beyond these cases, those exchanges which involve verbs and prepositions are persuasive. For example, (15a), (b) and (c) are exchanges between

(15) (a) Older men choose to tend younger wives
        (intended: tend to choose)
     (b) As you reap, Roger, so shall you sow.
        (intended: sow, so shall you reap.)
     (c) No one is taking you into talking . . . (a nap).
        (intended: talking you into taking.)
     (d) How much can I buy it for you from?
        (intended: from you for?)
     (e) Write a request for tickets at two for the box office.
        (intended: for two at the box office.)
     (f) which was parallel, to a certain sense, in an experience of.
        (intended: in a certain sense, to an experience.)

two verbs; the correspondence of their roles at an underlying level is striking.† Examples (15 d), (e) and (f) show exchanges of prepositions. In the MIT corpus, there are no clear examples of an exchange between a preposition and any element of either its own NP argument or any element of any other NP.‡ This is particularly interesting given the fact that for sound exchanges and standing exchanges, verbs *do* interact with an NP head. (N.B. such cases are invariably between the verb and a simple NP argument; that is, such exchanges are internal to a simple VP, usually with a direct or indirect object NP.) What the precise account of this may be is not clear; what is clear is that sound exchanges and word exchanges contrast in the incidence and nature of the involvement of verbs and prepositions, and that correspondence of structural role is the characteristic feature of these elements (as well as nouns) for word exchanges.

On the "negative" points, one can be reasonably assured that similarity of shape is not a strong influence on word exchanges. A glance at the examples in (13) and (15) is convincing if one's standard of comparison is based on errors for which phonetic similarity *does* seem to be effective (i.e. sound exchanges and shifts, and some word substitution errors): there does not seem to be any tendency for correspondence in word initial segments.§ Length and stress are

---

† Note that for 15a and 15d the underlying structures (very roughly: [(older men) (tend) [for-to(older men) (choose) (NP)]]; [Q(I) ((can) (buy) (it) (from you) (for WH-much))]) show the exchanged verbs and prepositions in parallel positions with respect to their arguments, even though this is not at all clear in the surface string.

‡ Note that many of the exchanges of prepositions could be analyzed as exchanges of their NP objects, given the frequently variable order of these adverbial PP's. However, there are several cases, like 15e and f, where that seems unlikely. If problematic cases were eliminated altogether, it would not alter the observation about the contrast between prepositions and their NP arguments vs. verbs and theirs in sound exchange.

§ Note that the most striking cases for a sound similarity argument in word exchanges are also usually possible sound exchanges.

hard to evaluate because of the predominance of one and two syllable words and the constraint of correspondence grammatical category. Even so, there is no strong indication of a requirement of length and stress correspondence. Most telling on this point (and that of phonetic similarity as well) are the cases of phrasal exchange (see Fromkin's category X) as in (16). Though they are

(16) (a) Did you ever go to Bob with the F & T?
          (intended: to the F & T with Bob?)
     (b) I got into this guy with a discussion.
          (intended: . . . into a discussion with this guy.)
     (c) I went to the mechanical mouse for an economy five and dime.
          (intended: . . . to the economy five and dime for a mechanical mouse.)

much less common than word exchanges, they clearly obey the same constraints and there are several cases in which a word and a phrase (usually an idiom or formula phrase) exchange. Given cases like these, an argument for any significant requirement of similarity of form seems quite implausible.

The effects of surface adjacency are also a point of contrast between positional and functional levels precisely because the former level is, by hypothesis, responsible for the serial ordering of elements in the surface string, while the former is concerned with functional relations among sentence elements. And, indeed, if one simply compares the range (in words) over which elements exchange, one finds the probability of a two or more word excursion to be greater for word exchanges than for sound exchanges. Note that this comparison does *not* include movements between immediately adjacent words because, as remarked earlier, such are ambiguous between an exchange and a shift for full word movements although not for sound movement; such immediately adjacent errors make up 41% of the sound exchanges. Hence, if, as seems likely (see below) true exchanges of adjacent words are rare, the contrast in surface distances over which sound error elements and word error elements move is even more striking than the comparison for relative frequencies of the unambiguous exchanges (1 or more words separation) would indicate.

Though the question of meaning relations need not concern us greatly at this point, it is worth noting that there is very little evidence to indicate an effect of meaning relations among words on the likelihood of a word exchange (see Garrett, 1976, for a discussion). This is of interest primarily because such effects would suggest an alternative sort of processing from the one we are considering. In particular, it would indicate that the meaning representations of the words were both available at the functional level and that lexically specific meaning parameters were appealed to, e.g., in the decision about which phrase a word should be assigned to; *a priori* such a view seems entirely reasonable, and the apparent lack of such influences indicates either that the principal features of correspondence between meanings and particular linguistic constructions is established earlier, or, perhaps, that some form of analysis by synthesis is being used, with meaning correspondence established later.

The final, currently relevant, observation about the functional level concerns effects of clausal structure. In past treatments of errors some little attention has been focussed on effects of surface clausal structure, with the general observation being that most movement errors occur within the confines of a single clause. That is true enough; however, it obscures an important distinction among the movement errors. For, most of the effects on sound exchanges (and stranding errors) may be captured by the simple phrasal constraint, but that on word (and phrase) exchanges cannot. Even though word exchanges are predominantly interphrasal, they are also usually intra-clausal (80% are within clauses). Moreover, those exceptions to this constraint are revealing. First of all, in those cases, the parallelism of structure is most striking, and second if there is any case to be made for effects of meaning relations it is here. See examples (15) and (17).

(17) (a) read the newspapers, watch the radio and listen to TV.
          (intended: listen to the radio and watch TV.)
     (b) Once I stop I can't start.)
          (intended: start, I can't stop.)
     (c) that wasn't a tiger, that was a lion.
          (intended: a lion, that was a tiger.)
     (d) Everytime I put one of these buttons off, another one comes on.
          (intended: on, another one comes off.)

In this, the cross-clause errors contrast sharply with the cross-clause errors of sound exchange (though not with cross-clausal stranding exchanges); see examples (18) for which there is little structural parallelism.

(18) (a) Helf, Helf, the wolp is after me!
          (intended: help, help, the wolf.)
     (b) I bess I getter go.
          (intended: guess I better.)
     (c) Did you get yoursev socks, Clease?
          (intended: yourself socks, Cleve?)
     (d) I never know you nuticed.
          (intended: knew you noticed.)

This would suggest that the organization of the structure guiding construction of the functional level representation honors clause structure. That, and the seriousness with which we take evidence of involvement of meaning relations, will affect the formal linguistic interpretation of these planning structures. We also take note of the existence of other experimental and observational evidence bearing on the role of surface and underlying clausal structure, but will defer its consideration to Section VII.

Anticipation and Perseveration Errors: A test of the diagnostic variables. The examination of errors like (19) below will bear on the observations appealed to earlier in order to support the distinction between "functional" and "positional" levels of processing in the analysis of speech errors. The principal features of contrast have been the phrasal membership of error elements and their grammatical role within their intended phrases—I have partly assessed this latter factor by whether grammatical category is or is not honored in the interaction of sentence elements involved in an error. In addition, the correlated variable of degree of separation (in words) of error elements was considered. For exchanges of words (or stems) between phrases, correspondence of grammatical category seems very strongly to be the rule, and this is most particularly marked in those error elements of different clausal membership and/or of several words separation. Exchanges of sounds occur primarily within a phrase, with the interacting elements rarely separated by more than a word, and *perhaps* as a consequence, grammatical category of the error words more often differs than corresponds. On these grounds and a number of others that seemed related, the errors so distinguished are assumed to arise from processing at two distinct levels, both of which are concerned with aspects of the syntactic structure of sentences. Thus, a good deal of the picture of sentence production processes that I have argued for turns in one way or another on the strength of observations about the correspondence of grammatical category for error elements.

One problem with the facts as I have presented them is readily apparent. If errors which exchange sounds (or groups of sounds whether they have a morpheme analysis or not) are constrained to occur (for whatever reason) only between contiguous words, then the chance that such errors will obtain between words of the same grammatical category (or that they will be members of different phrases) will surely be less than for error interactions which may obtain over greater distances. Thus, the genuinely causal factor, one might argue, is simply propinquity, not grammatical role or phrasal membership.

There are a number of drawbacks to such an alternative line, not the least of which is the lack of an account of why propinquity should matter for sound errors more than it does for word errors. Anticipation and perseveration errors are useful in evaluating this and similar concerns.

Errors like those of (19) are compared in Tables III and IV with sound exchanges and word exchanges (see also Fromkin's corpus).

(19) Anticipation and Perseveration errors

    (a) If he says, "here's looking at you babe," take your foot out of the stirrups and wallop him in the chollops.
                            (chops)

    (b) The juice is still on the table. Is that enuice?
                            (enough)

    (c) I dreampt that he droke both arms.
                (broke)

    (d) They first put on a coat of prime, and then a proat of
                            (coat)

    (e) experiences become much more exportant than anything else.
                        (important)

    (f) so that I can start the stape back up.
                (tape)

    (g) I don't understand the order at or.
                (all)

(h) He wants to take the G.O.P. nominowation away from Ford.
                          (nomination)
(i) One bure cures a bad dinner.
         (beer)
(j) The currenth month is.
         (current)
(k) that's forward masking; baskward masking is
                          (backward)
(l) What's your schedule this week?
      I'm frine—I'm fine. I'm free all week.

Tables III and IV permit a comparison of the distribution of anticipatory and perseveratory sound errors (there are a few included that seem to involve morphemes—e.g. (19e)) with exchanges. Table III shows the correspondence of grammatical category for error "source" and "target" as a function of phrasal membership and separation (in words) for the M.I.T. corpus; comparable Fromkin results are bracketed. Table IV presents comparable facts for sound and word exchanges.

The properties of the anticipation/perseveration errors seem to provide a convincing counterweight to the possibility that the correspondence of grammatical category for word exchanges between phrases is a possible result of their greater separation, for here, as often as not, the error elements come from different phrases, at varying separations, and they are of different grammatical category more often than they are of the same category. The contrast in "respect for grammatical category" is particularly clear for the error interactions which span clausal boundaries. For word exchanges, there are virtually no such cases which do not have corresponding categories; for the anticipation/perseveration errors ($n = 336$), there are 44 cases which cross clause boundaries and 21 of these violate grammatical category. One might also note that the anticipation/perseveration errors indicate that the tendency of the sound exchange errors to occur *within* a phrase and to be adjacent is neither accidental nor a necessary feature of sound errors.

One other feature of the anticipation/perseveration errors that is worth mentioning is the occasional involvement of closed class vocabulary items (i.e. function words and inflections) in these errors (42 cases of the 336). In this they contrast sharply with sound exchange errors which do not often involve those classes. Moreover, most of these cases are interactions between an open and closed class vocabulary item, rather than interactions between two closed class items of the same minor category. What seems to be a very powerful constraint on exchange of words (correspondence of category) or exchange of sounds (confined to open class) seems of much lesser importance to the system which gives rise to errors of anticipation and perseveration. We will shortly have occasion to explore more fully the implications of this sort of contrast in the relative involvement in various error types of items from major and minor grammatical categories.

The anticipation and perseveration errors do provide a contrast with exchanges in the apparent influence of grammatical category and phrasal

TABLE III

Anticipation/perseveration errors; M.I.T. Corpus ($n = 220$); Fromkin (1973 Corpus, Categories A, B, D, E, F, G, J, K: $n = 116$)

Interacting elements are:		Grammatical categories of interacting elements are:					
		Same		Different			
		MIT	VF	MIT	VF	MIT	VF
Within the same phrase		39	(19)	78	(43)	117	(62)
Separation in words	0	30	(12)	72	(42)		
	1	9	(7)	6	(1)		
In different phrases		29	(20)	74	(34)	103	(54)
Separation in words	0	2	(2)	26	(6)		
	1	7	(9)	24	(12)		
	2						
	3 or	14	(5)	13	(9)		
	more	6	(4)	11	(7)		
Totals:		68	(39)	152	(77)	220	(116)

TABLE IV

Word and Sound Exchanges; M.I.T. Corpus ($n = 200, 200$)

Interacting elements are:		Grammatical categories of interacting elements are:					
		Same		Different		Totals	
		word	sound	word	sound	word	sound
Within same phrase		28	70	10	104	38	174
Separation in words	0	—	45	—	70		
	1	14	23	7	33		
	2 or						
	more	14	2	3	1		
In different phrases		142	8	20	18	162	26
Separation in words	0	1	0	—	5		
	1	51	4	18	10		
	2	56	4	2	2		
	3 or						
	more	39	0	—	1		
Totals:		170	78	30	122		

membership; nonetheless, it would be too strong to say that these errors are indifferent to such variables. Rather, it seems they are affected more in terms of the rhythmic consequence than their syntactic.

Finally, we should bear in mind in evaluating the anticipation/perseveration analysis that the confidence we can place in the identification of the two error loci is less than for exchanges or shifts. One is, after all, making a bet (and, currently, a statistically unevaluated bet) that the nearby sound elements which are identical to the intruding error elements are, in fact, *the* contaminating influence. Certainly there are sufficiently many of the cases in which correspondence of intruding elements and presumed contaminant is so striking as to surpass coincidence. That subtler cases might exist seems likely; whether such cases would alter the character of the apparent distribution of anticipation/perseveration errors, of course, is an open question.†

C. The Positional level

The features of word exchanges we have remarked on indicate a processing type which contrasts sharply with that of ($\mathscr{P}$), which latter is, in current terms, to be identified with the "positional level". In our discussion of accommodatory errors (e.g., (10–12)), we concluded by noting the need for a separation of the prosodic features of words and phrases from their particular lexical instantiations. Evidently, the functional level itself does not provide for such, but a consideration of the processes which relate functional and positional level representations may do so. In particular, the interpretation we make of stranding exchanges and shift errors converges with the implications of accommodatory errors to suggest a computational device which effects both ends.

The errors we have been calling stranding errors (Fromkin's category S) are rather remarkable in several respects. As the examples in (14) and (20) show, these are errors in which major

(20) (a) I went to get a cash checked.
           (intended: check cashed.)
     (b) You have to square it facely
           (intended: face it squarely.)
     (c) It waits to pay.
           (intended: pays to wait.)
     (d) I've got a load of cooken chicked.
           (intended: chicken cooked.)

"portions" of two words exchange while some "fragment" is left behind. The portions and fragments, by and large, are stem and bound morphemes‡; more

† Note two further possible alternative analysis possibilities: a) I have treated anticipations and perseverations together; they certainly might differ in some ways, although I do not believe in ways that affect the contrasts at issue here; b) I have lumped together single sound (segment) errors and multiple sound errors. The latter are the clearest cases, and, hence, the (possible omission of many of the) former the most likely source of error in the analysis.

‡ In my initial treatment of these errors (Garrett, 1975), I sought a "neutral" characterization of the error process—i.e., one which did not initially assume the existence of errors which move stems and strand morphemes, rather than simply moving syllables or sound fragments while stranding syllables or arbitrary segment strings.

particularly, the bound morphemes are inflectional rather than derivational. Thus, the stranded morphemes are predominantly those in the domain of syntactic processes. This is not to say that derivational morphemes are never stranded; when they are, however, it is most often in conjunction with the stranding of an inflectional affix. In the M.I.T. corpus, 64% of the stranding errors involve only inflectional morphemes, while 23% involve an inflectional morpheme and a derivational morph or a non-morph that is positionally and prosodically appropriate (and often phonetically identical) to an inflection.

To this may be added the observation that the stranding errors appear to be of two varieties: those which, like sound exchanges, are internal to phrases, and those which, like word exchanges, hold between phrases and honor grammatical category. Examples (21) (a) and (b) are particularly interesting in this latter group (the stranded elements are underlined in these two examples).

(21) (a) He facilitated what he was doing to remove the barricade.
         (intended: He removed the barricade to facilitate what he was doing.

    (b) which knows you gotta /m?/
         (intended: which means you gotta know what you're talking about.)

Notice that in each of these errors there are stranded grammatical morphemes (inflexional affixes and complimentizers). In (21) (a), entire phrases move with the verb upon which they are dependent, stranding a framework of grammatical morphemes. In (20) the same stranding of affixal elements appears, but within phrases, and the resulting attachments, in contrast to (21), are sometimes anomolous.

One might describe the apparent operation in terms of the assignment of the major category vocabulary items to an "inflectional frame". There is, of course, no requirement that the description, and the attendant claim about processing operations, be so construed. If we do so, however, it is possible to simultaneously provide a natural reconstruction of the stranding errors and a vehicle for the independent representation of stress which, we noted earlier, seems required.

Thus, the relations among processing types we have discussed so far are assumed to provide for the following: (1) the selection of "planning frames" for elaboration of the positional level representation; (2) such planning frames are to mark specific phrasal geometry, with inflectional and other grammatical morphemes assumed to be features of that frame; (3) stress contours at least, and possibly more general prosodic features as well, are to be represented in the planning frame; (4) assignment of major category vocabulary items to places in the planning frame is accomplished in terms of descriptive constraints marked at the functional level.

IV. An Error Mechanism for Exchanges and Shifts

The observations we have made contrasting the properties of different exchange errors with each other might be reconstructed as a strong hypothesis about the mechanism of exchange errors; from that, there issues a claim about shift errors as well. Exchanges might be argued to arise at two points only: either in the process of assigning an element to a role in the functional level of representation, or in the process of assigning a (partially) phonetically interpreted lexical item to a serially ordered slot in the positional level of representation. In Section III, the vehicle offered for this latter assignment is a "planning frame" marked for grammatical morphemes and prosodic contours. Sound exchanges and most stranding exchanges were hypothesized to occur as a consequence of failures in the assignment of lexical items to slots in such a phrasal planning frame, with word exchange errors, and some stranding errors, arising at a prior stage—i.e. the elaboration of the functional level. Closer consideration of each of these processes suggests features of their organization which allow an evaluation of the hypothesis.

A. Planning Structures and Exchange Errors

Consider first the functional level. If there is a constructive process concerned, among other things, with the assignment of phrasal membership of major category vocabulary items under a relational description—e.g. assuming a predicate-argument form of representation of some sort (of the sort in case grammar, viz. Fillmore (1968) or of the sort in Bresnan (1978), used for the expression of logical structure of lexical items), one might expect errors of assignment of an item to an argument position or predicate position in terms of similarity of the computationally relevant description—if that is grammatical category ([noun]; [verb] . . .], subcategorization features as [± transitive], and possibly grammatical relations ([object], [modifier]), one might well expect the pattern to be one of improper assignment of nouns to the appropriate noun phrases, or verbs to their argument strings, but not verbs substituting for nouns or adjectives for nouns. By the same token, minor grammatical categories ought not interact with major. All these are, of course, features of word exchanges discussed above, and since they prompted the postulation of such a planning level, no more can be claimed than plausible redescription.

There are other features, however, which are, if not logically required, at least strongly indicated by the pattern of argument we have been following. There ought *not* be significant effects of phonetic similarity for errors at this level, if we assume that errors arise because of the computational features of description at any given level. If sound planning is not at issue, sound errors ought not to occur, and sound similarity ought not to be predisposing to error in the planning assignment. This is a strong claim about error mechanisms—i.e. that they are not an "overlay" on the system in which computationally *irrelevant* similarities derail the processing (as would be the case if a very similar sounding noun and adjective were to interact at a point when sound description, though present, is assumed to be *not* involved in decision making). Also, as we noted earlier, if one examines only the error cases in which grammatical category is preserved and the exchange involves distinct phrases (i.e. most of the word exchanges), one finds no clear indication of a phonetic similarity effect.

How then do sound exchanges enter the picture we are constructing? Clearly, similarity of form is at issue in sound exchanges, and given the assumptions we have just laid out, the structures moved in such exchanges *must* be computationally relevant. The most straightforward answer seems to be that assignment to an inflectionally and prosodically specified planning frame will require at least partial specification of the form of the words to be inserted in the frame. Thus, two points of possible effect arise: (1) the correspondence relation between frame features and insertion candidates, and (2) the description which directs retrieval of required forms from the lexical inventory.

If we *exclude* from the functional level processes, information about form of the sort that affects sound exchanges, but at the same time acknowledge, as we must, that specific lexical identity is required at the functional level, we seem constrained to embrace a "double retrieval" hypothesis. That is, those features of lexical description which bear upon meaning relations and upon the syntactic environments in which a word can appear must be available at the functional level (or some higher level) to account for: (1) the word exchanges which do take place at that level, and (2) to provide the sort of information which could guide selection of planning frames for the construction of positional level representations. We will return to this point in Section V.

A second instructive point was mentioned earlier. That is the fact that word exchange errors occur over greater distances than sound exchanges. If surface adjacency is not determined, or if it *is not* at issue at the functional level, surface separation of interacting elements should be inconsequential, except insofar as it might be correlated with the order of construction at the functional level. At this point we note that word exchanges seem more likely to span one or more major grammatical category items as well as being more separated overall. That is, where a sound exchange does span two or three words they are more likely to be closed class ("function words") than is the case for the same error span in a word exchange. To this we add a further observation: the elements which engage in exchanges are themselves almost exclusively major category items, or what we will call "open class vocabulary".

This comports with the suggestion that exchange errors are fundamentally failures of processes which assign open class vocabulary ("content" words) to constructions, whether functional or positional. Obviously, where that assignment is "between phrases" rather than within, the opportunity of an open class element to intervene arises more frequently. And, given the "planning frame" account of sound and combined form exchanges, the restriction to open class vocabulary falls out, since only such vocabulary types will be involved in the processes which are hypothesized to give rise to exchanges. Put in terms of the devices we have postulated: features of the planning frame should not exchange.

B. Bound Morpheme Exchanges and Shifts

The first place to look for evidence bearing on the exchange mechanism hypothesis is clearly derivable from the errors which motivated it: the stranding errors. If stranding errors arise principally from the misassignment of open class vocabulary to planning frames composed in part of the stranded elements, then those stranded elements should not themselves undergo exchange—at least not under the description relevant to their planning frame membership, e.g. inflexional affixes. Note this is not a necessary consequence of the simple existence of stranding errors, but is dependent upon our particular assumption about how exchange errors arise.

The most relevant errors are those in which sound segments occupying word final position exchange, e.g. (22):

(22) End exchanges
    (a) children interfere with your nife lite.
        (intended: night life)
    (b) in the nen text minutes.
        (intended: next ten)
    (c) the singest biggle problem you face?
        (intended: single biggest)
    (d) passage usive.
        (intended: passive usage)
    (e) a monkle's unckey.
        (intended: a monkey's uncle)
    (f) . . . a dutt's buck.
        (intended: a duck's butt)

Such errors are very much less common than exchanges of word initial position segments. Of the 41 cases in the M.I.T. corpus, 4, or 10%, (e.g. (22) c and d) are possibly analyzable as exchanges of bound morphemes.

In Fromkin's published corpus there are eight clear cases of end exchange, listed here as examples (23) a–h, and two problematical ones (i.e. they could be shifts), (24). None are inflectional.

(23) End exchanges from Fromkin (1973).
    (a) taf shelp (intended: top shelf (D1)
    (b) in the argon lexicot (intended: argot lexicon) (D2)
    (c) pat ous (intended: pass out) (D11)
    (d) mirrage immor (intended: mirror image) (D12)
    (e) god to seen (intended: gone to seed) (D14)
    (f) hass or grash (intended: hash or grass) (D15)
    (g) totch nop (intended: top notch) (H2)
    (h) wrink her neg (intended: wring her neck) (15)
(24) (a) official dressting taser (intended: dressing taster) (F25)
     (b) a pess in every clatt (intended: pest . . . class)

There is no absolute way of settling whether the possible exceptions to the generalization are to be taken as word final sound exchanges or as bound morpheme exchanges. Three observations seem relevant. First, given the fact that inflections are extremely frequent as the word final phonetic elements of words, the very fact that clearly *non*-morphemic end segments predominate in these errors would be surprising, given no independent reason for "insulating" them from exchange processes. Second is the occasional occurrence of *sound* exchanges of end segments which actually strand inflections, e.g. (22) e and f.

Such an error pattern fits well with the view that, at the point where sound exchanges occur, inflectional affixes are separately represented from their lexical attachment sites. If these affixes *were* to exchange at all, one might well expect it in instances in which the final sound segment of the word to which they are affixed does itself exchange.

Finally, the nature of sound and morpheme shift errors seems relevant to this evaluation. Though affixal elements are notable by their apparent absence (or, at worst, their rarity) in exchanges, they are equally notable by their prominence in *shift* errors. Most of the shift errors we discussed earlier were clearly sound shifts, and often, though not invariably, involved cluster formations. When one focusses on sound shifts involving word final elements, however, one finds the great majority are morphemic elements, and they seem to be, by and large, the same type of elements that are stranded. Unlike the exchange case, here, their frequency of error matches their ubiquity of use. Examples (25) a-g are typical (see also (2) a).

(25) End shifts.
    (a) That would be the same as add tening.
        (intended: adding ten.)
    (b) I'd forgot abouten that.
        (intended: forgotten about that.)
    (c) It probably get outs a little.
        (intended: gets out.)
    (d) point outed.
        (intended: pointed out.)
    (e) We were in Dallas for the Ram games.
        (intended: . . . for the Rams game)
    (f) It deads end into the . . .
        (intended: dead ends)
    (g) Does your toas past?
        (intended: toast pass?)

Though non-morphemic end shifts occur, e.g. (25) g (see also Fromkin's categories E, No. 28 and I, No. 8 and No. 9), they are very infrequent compared to the apparently morphemic shifts.

Such an error pattern falls naturally out of the mechanism that has been invoked to account for exchanges. Given that there must *be* an appropriate phonetic realization of the inflectional features of the planning frame, the processes of location and attachment which ensue upon assignment of a lexical item to a planning frame site provide the loci of errors like (25).

C. Word Shifts

We have focussed on bound morphemes in the preceding observations. But, of course, the grammatical morphemes include free forms as well as bound. We have already noted that for sound exchanges, stranding exchanges and word exchanges, the error elements are open class vocabulary, mostly nouns, verbs and adjectives, with nouns predominating. Adverbs, (whether simple or derived) and, in general, the minor grammatical categories (excepting prepositions and pronouns) rarely appear in exchanges.

Again, however, this is *not* because these words are not misplaced in sentence construction. They are; but the misplacements are not exchanges; they are, as seems the case for the bound morphemes, shifts; i.e. the improper placement of a single item in an already fixed string. Examples (26) a-h are typical.

(26) Word shifts.

    (a) Did you stay up late very last night?
        (intended: very late last night?)

    (b) unless you got somethin' to beter do?
        (intended: somethin' beter to do?)

    (c) You have to dó learn that.
        (intended: You dó have to learn that.)

    (d) We've just here been once.
        (intended: been here once.)

    (e) They're only the ones that get
        (intended: They're the only ones that get)

    (f) Who did you think else would come?
        (intended: Who else did you think would come?)

    (g) If you can't figure what that out is
        (intended: figure out what that is)

    (h) Hardly this place is well run.
        (intended: This place is hardly well run.)

The argument for treating these errors as shifts rather than exchanges of adjacent words turns on a very general property of the clear cases of word exchanges (i.e. those with intervening material that remains in place): constituents exchange with constituents. If we were to consider the errors classed as shifts to be exchanges, that generalization would be frequently violated (see Garrett (1975) for discussion), as for example in (26) e, f and g.†

The parallel between the bound and free forms in shifts is quite striking. And, if we assume that the forms which shift do so because of processes which

---

† Notice that even if we reject the analysis of these as exchanges, we are still not out of the woods since *either* of two elements might be the shifted one. The specific nomination of, e.g., closed class elements, and especially adverbs, as "moved elements" is thereby rendered less certain. We can have recourse to three observations: (a) again, those cases in which a constituent and a *non*-constituent are involved are unambiguous as to the identity of the moved element; (b) often both possible elements are closed class; (c) the stress "moves with" one of the elements (see text).

map features of planning frames onto strings like ($\mathscr{P}$), and that the closed class vocabulary is represented as such features, we can rationalize the very substantial involvement of "moveable" grammatical elements in shift errors but not in exchanges.

There is one other striking property of the word shift errors which sets them apart from exchanges and which comports with the set of assumptions we have been using. That is their effect on stress (see (26) b, c).

As we noted in the discussion of accommodatory errors, exchanges preserve phrasal stress. That fact forms an important part of the argument for a planning process which separates stress contours from the lexical items which bear them. Word shift errors are the principal source of *exception* to stress preservation. Cutler (1977) points out that in her observations of errors, those in which closed class vocabulary is involved, stress moves with the moved item(s). Though she does not confine this observation to shift errors (rather characterizing it in terms of vocabulary type), her examples and the cases I have observed, indicate that it is not the stress features of minor category items *per se*, but rather their involvement in a shift error that is crucial. These are, however, rather hard to distinguish given the rarity with which closed class vocabulary appears in exchanges.

Assuming the characterization of this stress observation that I have given in terms of error type, it provides an additional source of support for the separation of errors like (26) from those like (15), (16) and (17), and it suggests that features of the prosody, as emphatic stress, are represented in the planning frame.†

Stress features that are algorythmically determinable from the planning frame configuration show accommodation (or, perhaps, just those features that are marked in lexical insertion sites); others do not.‡ It would seem that, in general, "optional" features of sentence construction are specifically borne on the planning frame.

D. Open and closed class vocabulary.

We should at this point take rather explicit notice of the distinction in computational vocabularies that we have been referring to variously as that between open and closed class vocabulary or between major and minor grammatical categories. For the free forms, this distinction corresponds fairly well to the common one between "content" and "function" words. We are well advised, however, to acknowledge that the precise formal character of the distinction is not clear—nor, even, is it clear that there *must* be one. If the relation between computational systems for language processing and formal grammars

---

† Cutler discusses her examples in terms of contrastive stress; my own impresssion, and it is little more than that, suggests the more general, less structurally constrained notion of "emphatic stress" for the cases which violate the accommodatory regularity of errors. It may be that the right thing to say of such stress is that it is associated ab initio with a particular word, and that this accounts for its particular effect in errors.

‡ See in this connection the recent proposals of Liberman and Prince (1977) in which an algorithm based on local phrasal geometry is used to derive stress contours.

is the pragmatically determined compromise that it is sometimes conceived to be, there may very well prove to be no tidy formal resolution. If, however, there is a tightly principled connection between performance theories and theories of competence (i.e. of the knowledge of language structure) derived on distributional grounds, there *will* be a proper resolution of the formal estate of this distinction (see Section VII). On the evidence of the error distributions, at any rate, there is a most important computational distinction. We will consider in Section VI some experimental results which bear on this issue although they do not begin to settle it.

E. The competing plans hypothesis: a "causal agent"

The postulation of competing plans as an explanation for speech errors is a very generally accepted device. Two alternative ways of saying the same thing, or two alternative messages, usually of quite different interpretive burden, both struggling to occupy the same mental and/or articulatory space—that is the essence of the competition hypothesis. Freud and Maringer's views, different though they were in the nature of the source of the competing message forms, both appealed to the competition principle. It has been embraced or acknowledged by most observers of speech errors since. Baars and Motley (1976) have made it the basis for the design of experimental tasks which yield involuntary order errors for sounds, morphemes and words.

The virtue of the competition hypothesis is that it provides a causal force (whether ultimately associated with unconscious motivation or not), as opposed to an account of the mechanisms of error interaction, for example, of the sort we have been considering in Section IV. Two questions suggest themselves: (a) are the mechanisms we have been discussing compatible with a competing plans hypothesis? (b) are there error types which do not readily lend themselves to a competing plans account?

On the first question there seems little problem. The nature of the competing plans view does not suggest any particular mechanism in virtue of which the several parts of competing messages may interact. Hence, the computational devices we have suggested (e.g. functional and positional representations; planning frames; open and closed class vocabularies) may be regarded as a specific claim about the possible types of competition. There is, of course, an added claim embodied in competing plans view, and that is, for example, that the assignment of lexical items to positions in a to-be-uttered string is sensitive to "task irrelevant" inputs (as in the case of two competing distinct messages), or that there is some significant parallelism in the system. This latter claim arises for those cases, like (27), in which the message being communicated is constant but its expression is divergent.

    (27) (a) sudden quicks . . . stops aren't so bad.
            (intended: either "sudden stops" or "quick stops")
        (b) Ed Borkowski's not letting the pressure on here."
            (intended: either "not letting the pressure up" or "is keeping the pressure on")

There is another type of error, a very frequent one, which also has a natural competing plans account, but of a somewhat different character than the two just mentioned. That is the case when ordering of phrases or words is variable, or when the presence of a given element is optional; this is the general case argued by Baars and Motley. For example, (28) a, b. I have observed both these errors on more than one occasion and

(28) how many $\begin{cases} \text{of you are there} \\ \\ \text{are there of you} \end{cases}$ →

     (a) how many are you of there?; and

     (b) how many of there are you?

there are many similar sorts. Confusion of the elements of prepositional phrases very often lends itself well to this view.

There are, however, many errors, perhaps most of the word exchanges and many shifts, for which there are not immediately obvious multiple intended versions. So, for example, (29) a-d are

     (29) (a) I'd go to a teller and they'd tell me to who go see.
                (intended: who to go see.)
         (b) Maybe that has to do something with it.
                (intended: something to do with it.)
         (c) It's a perfect situation for an avid char-caser.
                (intended: car-chaser.)
         (d) I think I deserve an around of plause for that.
                (intended: a round of applause.)

not easy to account for in such a fashion. (See also Fay (1977), for some interesting cases which he reconstructs in terms of transformational operations.)

At this point it does not appear that the competing plans account, barring some general invocation of a "distraction factor", can be extended to all the errors in the same detail as for those like (27) and (28). However, the general principle of competition between planning structures is obviously capable of being thrust into a causal role at many points. The problem is to find a suitably constrained range of such claims. See Baars (1978) for an interesting discussion of the problems and possibilities of the competing plans hypothesis.

V. Word Substitutions and Blends

The discussion thus far has focussed on movement errors of various kinds. However, the mechanisms we have appealed to implicate processes of lexical selection as well as those which assign sentence elements to phrasal or word environments. In the discussion of movement errors, I assumed the accurate functioning of the lexical selection mechanisms which are driven, by hypothesis, on the basis of descriptions at the "message" level of representation. Ideally, there should be a natural way to incorporate word substitution errors of whatever variety into the framework of the sentence construction mechanisms we have been considering. That does, in fact, appear to be possible.

Word substitution errors come in two broad varieties: those like (30) in which one word simply replaces another (intruding word underlined),

(30) (a) Because I've got an apartment now. (appointment)
     (b) No—I'm amphibian. (ambidextrous)
     (c) They haven't been married . . . uh, measured with the precision you're using, and.
     (d) semantic facilitation was at issue in the asterisk experiment. (the italics experiment.)
     (e) He rode his bike to school tomorrow. (yesterday)
     (f) You go wash your hair. (brush)

and those like (31) in which two words have partial representation in the phonetic output. The former are referred to as "substitutions"

(31) (a) S. and P. gone mild. (wild/mad)
     (b) He misfumbled the ball. (mishandled/fumbled)
     (c) That's torrible! (terrible/horrible)
     (d) He's very cable. (calm/stable)
     (e) a slooth move. (smooth/slick)
     (f) a bab of that. (bit/dab)

and the latter as "blends" or "fusions". In an earlier paper (Garrett, 1975), I assigned with little comment both substitutions and blends to the process of selection under message level control. There is something correct about that and something incorrect: semantically driven lexical selection is certainly involved in both types, but not in the same way. It seems likely that these two error types implicate distinct processing stages, although it is unclear precisely how to detail that claim. We will begin by concentrating on word substitutions, and then return to see what their account may suggest for the case of blend errors.

A. Word Substitutions: Subvarieties

Consideration of word substitutions, even briefly, suggests a separation into types: those in which target and intrusion are related by *form*, and those in which they are related by *meaning* (as (30) a, b, c versus d, e, f—see Fay and Cutler (1977) and Garrett (1976) for examples).

The regularities of form that are observed involve: (a) phonetic shape of the initial (and possibly final) segments of the target and intruding word; (b) syllable structure and stress; (c) grammatical category. Fay and Cutler (1977) in their paper on "malapropisms" (their term for the subvariety of word substitutions which show regularities of form) argue for these regularities on the basis of substantial corpus of errors, and the errors ($n = 380$) of that same sort in the M.I.T. corpus are so describable. They argue for a retrieval process which extracts lexical items from an inventory organized according to the parameters of form which relate target and intrusion in malapropisms.

For the contrasting substitution error type, e.g. (30) d, e, f where the relation is in terms of meaning, the situation is rather less clear. Though there are very many cases where a quite straightforward meaning relation holds between target and intrusion, there are also substantial numbers of cases in which the relation is rather vague. If one is simply concerned to affirm a (large) class of meaning determined word substitutions without worrying too much about the precise character of those parameters, there is no problem: such errors are very frequent. If one wished to argue from the error corpus for a particular view of the meaning relations which hold among items in the lexicon, the issue would be a difficult one. For our immediate purposes, the more general conclusion will suffice.

How do these two varieties of word substitution errors fit the model we outlined in Section IV? Consider the following sequence discussed there:

At the functional level there must be selection of lexical items for assignment to argument positions, and for the purpose of guiding selection of specific phrasal planning frames. That selection may be deemed to honor grammatical category, given the behavior of word exchanges. Word substitutions, even where meaning determined, are strongly constrained by grammatical category: target and intrusion correspond. Recall further that we argued for an *insensitivity* of word exchange errors to aspects of word form. Just so for the meaning related word substitutions: if there is a meaning relation, there is rather little evidence for similarity of form.

In short, there seems some reason to assign the meaning related word substitution errors to that aspect of the lexical selection process which is determined by construction of the functional level of representation. There is a problem with this, however, to which we will return momentarily.

At the positional level there must be a selection of words in terms of their suitability to particular planning frames (which include stress and inflectional constraints); this is the first point for which we have some evidence of a need for facts about the form of specific lexical items. Recall that the *sound* exchange errors, which are assumed to occur in the construction of this level, show their greatest similarity at word initial positions; word initial exchanges are by far the most frequent. And, when inflectional morphs are ignored, length of the source words for sound exchanges is usually the same. These are points on which the similarities for malapropisms are marked.

We might, therefore, give some further specification to the "double retrieval" hypothesis which we suggested in Section IV. It is at the stage where retrieval of the particular form of lexical items (specified syntactically at the functional level) is required that malapropisms occur. Indeed, one might suppose that the parameters of similarity among malapropisms are the basis of the retrieval code which is held following lexical specification at the functional level, and prior to the construction of a specific phrasal environment at the positional level.

The general outline of the story seems well enough suited to the facts we have at hand. There are several problems which remain, however. The first is a lack of evidence for effects of meaning relations on word exchanges. We noted in our discussion of those errors that the most plausible candidates for meaning effects arise for the cross-clausal exchanges. But even there the case is weak; there are many cases which have no such account. And in any event, for the major class of such exchanges, there is just no persuasive case for relations analogous to those observed for word substitutions. One is seemingly forced to conclude at this point that the parameters of lexical selection which give rise to word substitutions like (30) d, e, and f are effective at some other point, and the natural assumption is to claim that the point is prior to the lexical elaboration of the functional level.

There is, however, a possible alternative account of the failure of word exchange errors to show significant meaning relations. That is to deny the assumption that such errors *should* appear at all—not because semantic similarity is irrelevant, but because there is rarely an *opportunity* for such errors to occur. If elements in the scope of the planning processes which give rise to word exchanges simply do not ordinarily exhibit significant semantic similarity, then semantically triggered exchanges will be rare; when there is such similarity, possibly in the cross clause errors, effects of meaning relations will be manifest. What this sort of argument assumes is that only very similar items will be candidates for error interaction—a few shared features of meaning are deemed insufficient. Of course, one needs a basis for judging similarity of meaning to pursue this argument. The criterion we have used is that of word substitutions and blends; both these indicate a requirement of strong meaning similarity, the former possibly less than the latter (but see below). We will not pursue this possible argument further, but will simply concede that at present the issue is unclear and requires further examination.

Environmental contaminants. We hinted earlier in our discussion that one might question the propriety of a "semantic" characterization of a class of word substitution errors. After all, it seems a pretty "sloppy" category if one includes cases like "refrigerator" for "fire hydrant" or "flower" for "alarm" (clock), both of which appear in the M.I.T. corpus. Such a move would be ill-advised, however, for a fair amount of the sloppiness (including the two cases listed) may be removed by attending to another rather common feature of word substitution. That feature is the sensitivity to what might be called situational or environmental "contamination". We will discuss that problem and then turn our attention to blend errors before considering again the assignment of word substitution errors to the functional level.

Though the case for it is difficult to certify on the same objective grounds as the form/meaning contrast we have already discussed, there seem nonetheless good grounds for distinguishing another variety of word substitution errors: "environmental contaminants". The best way to provide a feeling for the character of such errors is by example:

(32) Target: Are you trying to send me a message, Dog?
    Situation: Speaker is addressing Dog; Dog is standing by front door looking woebegone. Immediately beside speaker at eye level on a shelf, is a novel with the cover blurb: "A novel of intrigue and menace." Speaker has idly read this while approaching the dog and preparing to speak.
    Output: Are you trying to send me a menace, Dog?
(33) Target: People should take off their old bumper stickers.
    Situation: Speaker is looking at a car bumper with two year old sticker reading, "Dukakis should be governor."
    Output: People should take off their old governor stickers.

These and many other similar examples, all seem to involve the idiosyncratic, situational introduction of a specific word or phrase into the speakers attention while he is speaking or preparing to speak. This suggests a quite different sort of error than those like (30) d, e, f above, in which there is a clear semantic relation between target and intrusion, and for which there is no conscious awareness of the intruding word.

If one pays attention to these sorts of cases where possible, one can "filter" such errors out of the semantic and form related sets. The resultant set of environmental contaminants is a bit of a mixed bag—sometimes one (imagines one) finds a vague meaning connection with the displaced word; more often there is a form relation—not so compelling as the malapropisms, but of the same flavor.

The sets that remain (semantic and form related) after the filtering are presumably "purer". And, indeed, the semantic category seems less chaotic, although not a great change is effected for the malapropisms.

The categories themselves are less interesting, however, (granting their existence) than the implications of the fact that errors arise from the sort of scenarios sketched in (32) and (33). The environmental contaminants suggest an interaction between a processing store used in speech production and the storage systems we use to monitor the passing products of a roving attention.

At this point, one is prompted to think of the "competing plans" proposal. It is possible that the editorial processes used to select from among alternative possible formulations of a message, or to reject materials which are irrelevant to a target message (e.g. from an "unconscious source") may "intersect" the environmental contaminants sort of cases (in the sense that they make use of a common computational resource).

What we should glean from this, barring the suggestion that a careful look at the environmental contaminants type of error† might be worthwhile, is the implication that the semantically motivated errors of (30) d, e, and f probably ought be considered quite apart from these editorial processes, and their

---

† The set of these errors of which I am confident is relatively small. I suspect that a fair number of others lurk in my non-form related set, but are simply not certifiable because of insufficient contextual information about the error.

relegation to a very early stage of processing is probably appropriate, even if we are not sure just what that stage is.

B. Blends

The first thing to note about blends is that the case for a meaning relation is very powerful indeed. The examples in (31) are quite typical (see Fromkin's category U). That relation is not context free, but it is surely true (by inspection or by questioning of the speakers) that either of the two competing words would have suited the communicative intent of the speaker.

Very often a speaker is aware of both of the words which compete for space and yield a blend. Note this is not always a case of being simultaneously aware of both words, although that sensation is often reported; but in those cases where there is not simultaneous awareness during the utterance, there is frequently the *post hoc* observation that one of the forms of the blended output had been contemplated (perhaps even used as part of a false start then reformulated to exclude it) immediately prior to utterance.

What the remarks just made should suggest is that blends seem to have some of the properties of both meaning related word substitutions and environmental contaminants. The most natural suggestion to make is that, because of their equivalent appropriateness to the message being conveyed, the two items of a blend are retrieved at the earliest level and carried down through the processing to the (by hypothesis) late stage of editorial selection in which competing formulations are weeded out. That in turn suggests a much stronger version of what one was inclined to believe on the basis of the existence of blends in the first place: there is significant parallism in the system, and it begins with semantically determined lexical selection.

Blends are something of a puzzle. They do not fit straightforwardly into the outline we have been constructing, for their apparent antecedents are "early" and their apparent error locus late. We must not assume an early point for blending on two grouds: (a) it requires some rather detailed phonetic structure, and that, by current hypothesis, does not occur prior to the assignment of lexical items to the positional level; (b) lexical identity is involved in the constructive processes which map from functional to positional level, and an early blend would, presumably, interfere with that.

One might, given the character of blends, argue for a routine parallism in sentence construction, or reject some features of the analysis we have proposed (e.g. that lexical selection is, by and large, an early feature of sentence planning), or, perhaps, invoke the possibility of an adventitious interaction between the "primary" targets" of speech and the "residue" of abandoned plans via mechanisms similar to those of environmental contaminants. Certainly many blends seem to have the earmarks of such interaction (presence of the intruding word just prior to utterance, or consciousness of the alternatives). In fact, we cannot settle these possibilities, and must leave this case, as with several others, an open one.

C. Substitutions and Exchanges

The possible description of events is as follows: when the initial semantically directed access is executed (meaning related substitutions occur here), the output of that process is held, and used in conjunction with message level features to construct the functional level representation, in the course of which lexical elements are assigned phrasal membership (word exchanges occur here). Detailed phrasal environments are constructed (surface) clause by clause via planning frames, in the course of which (partially) phonetically interpreted forms for open class vocabulary are retrieved on the basis of the lexical representations in the functional level representations ("malapropisms" occur here), and assigned to phrasal positions (sound exchanges and most stranding exchanges occur here). Features of planning frames are interpreted as bound or free forms and mapped onto positions in the lexical string (shifts occur here). Regular sound processes apply to yield a detailed phonetically interpreted string capable of supporting the direction of motor planning systems (accommodatory processes are accomplished here).

The gross character of the production process just outlined does not differ in most respects from several proposals advanced by other observers of speech errors or of other production phenomena. Nor does it differ greatly from a rather straightforward instantiation of grammatical rule system as processing systems. It does, however, associate (by argument) some specific error processes with the putative constructional processes and thereby provides some particular grounds for assessment of error processes against conceptions of production processes.

VI. Relations Between Comprehension and Production

We noted at the outset of our discussion that studies of language production and comprehension must be linked. That, of course, is true not only on pragmatic grounds (e.g. one wishes to know what effect comprehension processes play in determining the outcome of experiments or observations aimed at production), but also on theoretical grounds. Because the two systems are intricately connected, an understanding of language processing will require an explication of that linkage. Some speech error processes have implications for this problem and we will consider them now.

There are two general kinds of connection between production and comprehension systems: first, there is an interdependence of the sort exemplified by "editorial" functions in production. At the grossest level, it is clear that we monitor our speech, and that we do so in order to avert or correct a variety of departures from the ideal target utterance (those of pronunciation, grammar, style, and meaning). But, as we noted in Sections II and V, subtler varieties of editorial functions (at unconscious levels) may well be present. Whatever the nature of the editing processes in production may prove to be, they are loci of possible connection with comprehension processes. We should note, too, the complementary possibility: namely, that comprehension systems may depend on production processes. For example, if there is a significant analysis-by-synthesis component of the comprehension system, that synthesis routine ("top-down analyzer") may be based on the use of parts of the production system.

Neither of these are necessary dependencies, of course. It may prove to be the case that the exigencies of generating candidate structural analyses from the partial cues gleaned in listening to (or reading) language bear little connection to those of constructing a phonetically interpreted syntactic object under the constraints of a meaning representation. The resolution of such possibilities will require a substantially greater elaboration of theory than is currently available to us.

A second sort of connection between the two systems is less a matter of mutual dependency than of mutual exploitation of a common resource. That is the possibility we will consider here, and the "resource", is the inventory of vocabulary element—the mental dictionary—and the associated processes for retrieving entries in it. There are two areas of immediate interest, one stemming from the properties of word substitution errors, and the other from the analysis of exchange errors in which we distinguished open and closed class vocabularies.

A. Word Substitution Errors and Word Recognition

There are two striking things about the errors Fay and Cutler (1977) have labelled "malapropisms"—first that they should occur at all, and second, that their apparent structure should so closely correspond to that which guides word recognition performance in sentence comprehension.

If one were, *a priori*, to predict the sort of word substitution errors to appear in spontaneous speech, those in which a meaning relation holds between target and intrusion would be expected. For, what is at issue in production is, among other things, the selection of words appropriate to a particular meaning. Hence, failures of retrieval like "most" for "least", "fast" for "slow", "aunt" for "uncle", (golf) "club" for (tennis) "racquet", etc. are straightforwardly understandable on the view that words are selected from the mental inventory under (partial) descriptions given as values on semantic parameters. Failures of such a system might well be expected to yield substitutions that are very close in meaning, and, if the selection is at a point where structural roles in a sentence are at issue, the distributional constraints on the substituted items should also correspond closely (as they do). But there is no place in that sort of picture for errors like "sympathy" for "symphony", "colloquial" for "colloquium",? "bodies" for "bottles", "garlic" for "gargle", etc. But, such errors are, it turns out, quite common (at least as speech errors go, they are common).

The similarities of form among target and intrusion are very much those that have been shown experimentally to have particular salience in word recognition. Thus, for example, in detecting mispronunciations while listening to connected discourse, word initial phonetic form seems more significant than does medial or final form (e.g. Marslen-Wilson and Welch, 1978; Cole and Jakimik, 1978). In reading, word initial forms are more significant than medial or final—they apparently control initial lexical access procedures (see for example, Forster, 1976; Taft and Forster, 1976). The effects of length and stress pattern in comprehension are somewhat less clear, but there is certainly a tendency for such variables to influence "mishearings" whether in normal situations or laboratory experiments for listening under adverse conditions.

Fay and Cutler argue that the best accommodation to the fact of malapropisms is to assume that, during production, the forms to be spoken are retrieved from an inventory organized according to similarity of form— the very inventory, in fact, used in listening to determine the lexical identity of heard (or, analogously, read) sentences. In Section IV and V we considered some reasons why such a retrieval process would arise in production and where it might occur in the processing sequence. The point of current interest is that the requirements of production and comprehension seem to be simultaneously served by a single inventory of word forms at least for some aspects of sentence planning.

B. Open and Closed Class Vocabularies

The remaining connection between production and comprehension rests upon a recent series of experiments with word recognition in normal and aphasic speakers. The role of closed class vocabulary that we have argued for in the analysis of exchange and shift errors can be construed as that of providing a principal vehicle for the integration of sentence *form*. The planning frames are composed in major part of the closed class vocabulary and they mediate the translation from a relational sentence representation to one which expresses the detail of phrasal form and apparently carries the seeds of movement transformations as well. The centrality of that structural role in production for this vocabulary distinction is paralleled in comprehension—the closed class vocabulary types provide a primary base for syntactic inference. Demonstrations of this role can be had by recalling the (well known) effects of imposing syntactic structure on nonsense lists (Epstein, 1961). Thus, even without the open class vocabulary, a string like (34) can be assigned rather detailed structure on the basis of inflections and minor grammatical categories. In short, we affirm what few are likely to deny:

(34) Toofs who twink are donkly thieled in the rurlet.

that what we are calling the closed class vocabulary plays a central role in the processing of sentence form whether for production or comprehension. The analysis of speech errors we discussed above makes some specific claims about the role of that vocabulary type in production, and it seems plausible that a similar integrative role for parsing procedures might be claimed (Garrett, 1979).

The specific link we wish to take note of here rests upon the finding that several features of the *recognition* processes for these two vocabulary classes seem distinct for normal speakers but not for patients suffering from an *expressive* language disorder (agrammatism). Bradley *et al.* (in press) report that normal contrasts in recognition of open and closed class forms are absent in the performance of agrammatic aphasics. Thus, for example, only open class vocabulary (nouns, verbs and adjectives) shows a strong effect of frequency ordering for lexical decision tasks in normal speakers (Bradley, 1978), but, for agramatic speakers *both* classes are strongly (indistinguishably) frequency organized. In short, the agrammatic speakers treat the closed class as though it were the same as the open. Bradley (1978) argues on this and several other experimental grounds that the agrammatic speakers lack a specialized retrieval mechanism whose domain is the closed class vocabulary.

It is, of course, a long step from this sort of observation to the view that production processes depend normally on the proper function of some aspects of the comprehension process, and that closed class lexical access is mutually involved. Yet, given the example of the malapropisms for open class retrieval, it does not seem an entirely implausible hypothesis for the closed class, given the performance of agrammatics reported by Bradley *et al.*

The process of lexical retrieval is, of course, only one case of several in which one might look for significant overlap between production and comprehension. It is, at the moment, the only one for which the speech error analysis yields an interesting suggestion. More investigation should yield other cases, particularly in the area of processes exploiting lexically dependent syntactic construction.

VII. Relations,Between Processing Systems and Grammatical Systems

We have eschewed formal interpretations of the processing systems under discussion for one principal reason: it is premature in most cases; the level of detail to be claimed for the *observationally* supportable processing types is not great enough to warrant specific claims. That is not to say, of course, that more detailed analysis may not warrant such interpretation at some time in the future. Accordingly, we will consider some general features of that enterprise and entertain one possible line of interpretation.

A. Production and Comprehension Again

The general question of relations between grammars and processing models may have somewhat different answers for production and comprehension systems. For, while it seems clear that both comprehension and production processes must capture all the interpretively relevant features of linguistic description, it is not necessary that they do so in the same ways. Moreover, it seems very possible that the constraints of form imposed on the two systems differ. The production system must get the details of form "right" in every instance, whether those details are germaine to sentence meaning or not. Just how much latitude that may purchase for comprehension systems is far from clear. However, given that grammars are primarily reconstructions of the distributional regularities of sentence form (albeit in ultimate aid of interpretation), there is an obvious moral: of the two systems, production and comprehension, the *a priori* likelihood of close correspondence between grammatical processes and the computational processes which account for sentence use is greatest for the former.

This question of how grammars constrain theories of processing was discussed in the initial stages of contemporary psycholinguistic enquiry. The consensus was that grammars necessarily constrain the structural "targets" of computational systems, but do not so constrain the manner of calculating those targets (see Fodor and Garrett, 1966; Fodor, Bever and Garrett, 1974). The relation between, for example, specific grammatical transformations and mental operations is an empirical issue, with the expectation being that the connection will be indirect at best. Most experimental outcomes in the study of comprehension comport with that expectation.

It is at least possible that this will prove to have a somewhat different outcome in production studies. For example, many of the word shift errors (e.g. (26) f–h) have the appearance of "failed transformations" (Garrett, 1975). Fay (1977) has argued specifically for this view. It is equally clear, however, that many of the shifts do not have an obvious simple reconstruction as errant transformations. As the theoretical and observational picture becomes clearer that issue may be resolved. At present, it seems very worth a hard try, particularly in light of the linguistic proposals for modifying the transformational apparatus (see Bresnan, 1978; Chomsky, 1970).

Against this background, the issues of Section VI extend beyond the immediate problems of processing theory to the general issue of relations between grammars and processors. For if one finds significant evidence of a correspondence between grammatical rule systems in production, the interpretation of that fact in comprehension theory will be required.

B. Interpretation of the functional and positional levels

In discussing the error distributions, I have treated the functional level of representation as though it were the "first" *specifically linguistic* level of sentence representation (reserving the term "message" to the (possibly) non-linguistic level of organization). Given the more or less traditional organization of transformational grammars, the natural formal correspondent of the functional level would be that of deep structure, and correspondingly for the positional level, that of surface structure. Such an identification is harmless, and possibly of heuristic value, if one does it with a quite selfconscious realization of the range of alternate possibilities. In the text, I have, in fact, talked of the functional level in terms of a predicate-argument form of representation which makes it appear more "abstract" than deep structure—primarily to emphasize the apparent independence of serial organization and error processes at that level. However, one *need* not interpret a deep structure temporarally or spatially, particularly not for those features relevant to error regularities. The point is that there is little about the error pattern to suggest a choice. If the apparent indifference of word exchanges to differences in grammatical relations like that between direct and indirect objects (or perhaps even subjects and objects) is true, and if such features mark argument positions (e.g. in a case grammar) one might even opt for the more "neutral" deep structures (*a la* an "Aspects" model; Chomsky, 1965).

Conversely, one might respond to the observation that surface structures are not "all of a piece", but are rather, motivated by three distinct considerations (phonology, transformations, logical form); in particular, the processes of readjustment rules are a formal device for "abstracting" from syntactic surface structures just those relevant to the phonology—i.e. those relevant to the *pronunciation* of the sentence (see Chomsky and Halle, 1968).

On such a view functional and positional representations might be very similar to each other—as similar as surface structure syntax and the systematic phonemic level (syntax, post-readjustment rules). There is little in the error processes to deny such a move, one which "demotes" the functional level to a seemingly less abstract level. (Given the force of recent suggestions about the character of surface syntax (e.g. Chomsky and Lasnik, 1977), that is perhaps a misleading characterization.) Certainly the parallelism of phrasal geometry in word exchanges is compatible with a more detailed elaboration of syntactic structure than I have appealed to (see Garrett and Kean, forthcoming, for some further discussion of this issue).

Without going any further, I will assume that two points are clear: (a) the error regularities are compatible with a variety of formal interpretations, (b) but there are possible arguments for various assignments, and it awaits ingenuity and the suitable error examples to construct them.

VIII. Conclusion

I have tried to maintain a running summary of the principal issues while proceding through the discussion and will not repeat the obvious here.

There are perhaps two points which deserve final emphasis. The first is that error patterns are a source of data nearly as diverse as that of normally non-errorful structure. Though it need *not* be the case, it appears that the rather transparent stratagem of cataloguing errors in terms of their apparent mechanism yields a processing typology, or comes close enough at least to serve a very useful purpose. Thus, the investment of considerable time and energy into the collection and analysis of such seems warranted on the view that they bear a principled relation to production.

The second point is simply that the current imponderables in analysis are manifold. Many very interesting suggestions have not been considered in the discussion given here. The most interesting observations are yet to be made.

References

Baars, B. (1978). The competing plans hypothesis: An heuristic viewpoint on the causes of speech errors. Paper for Pausological Implications of Speech Production: An Interdisciplinary Workshop, Kassel, Germany.

Baars, B. and Motley, M. (1976). Spoonerisms as sequencer conflicts: Evidence from artifically elicited errors. *American Journal of Psychology*, **89**, 467–484.

Bradley, D. (1978). Computational distinctions of vocabulary type. PhD. thesis, Dept. of Psychology, M.I.T.

Bradley, D., Garrett, M. and Zurif, E. (1979). Syntactic Deficets in Broca's Aphasia. *In* "Biological Studies of Mental Processes (D. Caplan ed.). M.I.T. Press, Cambridge Mass.

Boomer, D. S. and Laver, J. D. (1968). "Slips of the tongue". *British Journal of Disorders of Communication,* **3**, 2–12.

Bresnan, J. (1978). "Toward a realistic theory of grammar". *In* Linguistic Theory and Psychological Reality, (J. Bresnan, G. Milier and M. Halle eds). MIT Press, Cambridge, Mass.

Browman, C. (1977). "Perceptual Processing: Evidence from slips of the Ear". Paper for the Twelfth International Congress of Linguistics, Vienna, Austria.

Celce-Murcia, M. (1973). "Meringer's Corpus Revisited". *In* Speech Errors as Linguistic Evidence, (V. A. Fromkin, ed.). Mouton, The Hague.

Chomsky, N. (1965). "Aspects of the Theory of Syntax." MIT Press, Cambridge, Mass.

Chomsky, N. (1970). "Remarks on Nominalizations". *In* "Readings in Transformational Grammar". (R. Jacobs and P. Rosenbaum, eds). Waltham, Ginn & Co., Mass.

Chomsky, N. and Halle, N. (1968). "The Sound Pattern of English". Harper and Row, London and New York.

Chomsky, N. and Lasnik, H. (1977). "Filters and Control," *Linguist. Inq.* **8**, 425–504.

Cole, R. (1973). "Listening for mispronunciations: A measure of what we hear during speech". *Perception and Psychophysics,* **1**, 153–56.

Cole, R. and Jakimik, J. (1978). Understanding Speech: How words are heard. *In* "Strategies of Information Processing," (G. Underwood, ed). Academic Press, London.

Cutler, A. (1977). "Queering the Pitch". Paper for the Twelfth International Congress of Linguistics. Vienna, Austria.

Cutler, A. and Fay, D. (1978). "Introductory Essay". *In* "Rudolf Merringer and Karl Mayer: Versbrechen and Verlesen". Re-issue, John Benjamins, Amsterdam.

Epstein, W. (1961). "The Influence of Syntactical Structure on Learning". *American Journal of Psychology,* **74**, 80–85.

Fay, D. (1977). "Transformational Errors". Paper for the Twelfth International Congress of Linguistics. Vienna, Austria.

Fay, D. and Cutler, A. (1977). "Malapropisms and the Structure of the Mental Lexicon". *Linguistic Inquiry,* **8**, 505–20.

Fillmore, C. (1968). "The Case for Case". *In* "Universals of Linguistic Theory". (E. Bach and Harmes, eds). Holt, Rinehart and Winston, New York.

Fodor, J. and Garrett, M. F. (1966). "Some reflections on competence and performance". *In* "Psycholinguistic Papers", (J. Lyons and R. Wales, eds). Edinburgh University Press, Edinburgh.

Ford, M. and Holmes, V. M. (1978). "Planning Units and Syntax in Sentence Production". *Cognition*, **6**, 35–53.

Forster, K. I. (1974). "Linguistic Structure and Sentence Production". *In* "Pragmatic Aspects of Human Communication", (C. Cherry, ed.). D. Reidel Publishing Company, Holland.

Forster, K. I. (1976). "Accessing the Mental Lexicon". *In* "New Approaches to Language Mechanisms". (E. Walker and R. Wales, eds). North Holland, Amsterdam.

Fromkin, V. A. (1971). "The Non-anomalous nature of Anomalous Utterances". *Language*, **47**, 27–53.

Fromkin, V. A. (1973). "Speech Errors as Linguistic Evidence". Mouton, The Hague.

Fry, D. B. (1969). "The Linguistic Evidence of Speech Errors". *In* "Speech Errors as Linguistic Evidence", (V. Fromkin. ed). Reprinted in Fromkin (1973).

Garnes, S. and Bond, Z. (1975). "Slips of the Ear: Errors in Perception of Casual Speech". Proceedings of the Eleventh Regional Meeting of the Chicago Linguistics Society, CLS, 214–225.

Garrett, M. (1975). "The Analysis of Sentence Production". *In* "Psychology of Learning and Motivation", Vol. 9. (G. Bower, ed). Academic Press, New York.

Garrett, M. (1976). "Syntactic Processes in Sentence Production". *In* "New Approaches to Language Mechanisms", (E. Walker and R. Wales, eds). North Holland Publishers, Amsterdam.

Garrett, M. (1979). "Word and Sentence Perception." *In* "Handbook of Sensory Physiology", Volume VIII, "Perception", (R. Held, H-L. Teuber and H. Leibowitz, eds). Springer Verlag, New York.

Garrett, M. and Kean, M-L. (1979). Processing structures and the Phonological level of linguistic representation.

Goldstein, L. (1977). "Categorial Features in Speech Perception and Production". Paper presented at the Twelfh International Congress of Linguistics. Vienna, Austria.

Jackendoff, R. (1975). "Morphology and Semantic Regularities in the Lexicon". *Language*, **51**, 639–671.

Jarvella, R. (1976). "From Verbs to Sentences: Some Experimental Studies of Predication". (S. Rosenberg, ed.), "Sentence Production: Developments in Research and Theory". Lawrence Erlbaum Associates.

Liberman, M. and Prince, A. (1977). Stress and Linguistic Rhythm. *Linguistic Inquiry*, **8**, 249–336.

Marslen-Wilson, W. and Welch, A. (1978). "Processing Interactions and Lexical Access". *Cognitive Psychology*.

McKay, D. G. (1976). "Spoonerisms: 'The Structure of Errors in the Serial Order of Speech'." *Neuropsychologia*, **8**, 323–50.

McKay, D. G. (1972). "The Structure of Words and Syllables: Evidence from Errors in Speech". *Cognitive Psychology*, **3**, 210–227.

McKay, D. G. (1977). "Speech Errors: Retrospect and Prospect". Paper for the International Congress of Linguistics. Vienna, Austria.

Miller, G. A. and Johnson-Laird, P. (1976). Language and Perception. Harvard Press, Cambridge, Mass.

Nooteboom, S. (1967). "The Tongue Slips into Patterns". "Nomen, Leyden Studies in Linguisitics and Phonetics". Mouton, The Hague. Reprinted in Fromkin (1973).

Shattuck Hufnagel, S. and Klatt D. (1977). "Single Phoneme Error Date rule out two Dissertation. Department of Psychology, M.I.T.

Shattuck Hufnagel, S. and Klatt, D. (1977). "Single Phoneme Error Date rule out two Models of Error Generation". Paper for the Twelfth International Congress of Linguistics. Vienna, Austria.

Taft, M. and Forster, K. I. (1976). "Lexical Storage and Retrieval of Polymorphemic and Polysyllabic Words". *J. Verbal Learning and Verbal Behavior*. **15**, 607–620.

Wells, R. (1973). "Predicting Slips of the Tongue". *Yale Scientific Magazine*, **XXVI**, 9–30. Reprinted in Fromkin (1973).

9
Evidence from Aphasia: Isolating the Components of a Production Model

E. M. Saffran   *Baltimore City Hospital*
M. F. Schwartz   *Johns Hopkins University*
O. S. M. Marin   *Baltimore City Hospital*

I. Introduction

In the search for clues to the nature of language production, the data from organic pathology have been largely ignored. In part, this reflects a general skepticism about the relevance of aphasiology to normal psycholinguistics—the concern that language function in the brain damaged individual is the product of an aberrant system that does not reflect on the normal state. We have argued that this pessimistic view is not substantiated by the data, and that a different set of operating assumptions can reasonably be adopted (Marin *et al.*, 1976): (1) that the nervous system is organized in terms of functionally meaningful subsystems which are, to some degree at least, anatomically discrete and which can be selectively impaired by neurological disease; and (2) that while brain damage gives rise to symptoms that reflect various mechanisms of inhibition, release, isolation, etc. the resulting behavior patterns do not represent the creation of new subsystems; rather, they reflect a reorganization that emphasizes intact subsystems.

The second point is critical. If instead it can be maintained that pathological language is the product of mechanisms created *de novo* in the injured brain, we will not be justified in generalizing from aphasia to normal language patterns. Observations offered in support of the first assumption will also be invalidated. Fortunately, the evidence suggests otherwise: the adult brain is limited in its plasticity, and the interesting behavior patterns often emerge too soon after brain injury to be considered the product of new language acquisition. To be sure, one implication of a reorganization emphasizing intact subsystems is that capacities may be used "abnormally", in the sense that they are relied upon more heavily, sometimes to perform functions that they do not serve under normal conditions. One cannot generalize, therefore, from a model of aphasic language performance to language performance in the normal state. But it is possible to generalize with respect to the capacities themselves. For example, when an aphasic reads the word "carpenter" as "nails" (Saffran *et al.*, 1976), his performance, however bizarre, need not be attributed to a new, albeit deficient, mechanism for reading. It is more likely that disruption of some aspects of the reading process has allowed mechanisms involving preexisting lexical structures to become more directly manifested in behavior.

If pathological language reflects capacities that existed before the lesion, we should be able to make inferences about the organization of normal language processes from patterns of functional preservation and impairment. Thus, when we find cases where process X is intact and process Y is compromised or absent, and especially if the converse holds for other patients, we are justified in asserting that processes X and Y are subserved by different underlying mechanisms in the normal state. In the case of the reading disturbance mentioned above, it has been possible, using this logic, to isolate two separate mechanisms in reading: one that allows lexical access directly from graphemic information (and that is preserved in patients who make semantic errors in reading aloud), and another that depends on grapheme-to-phoneme conversion (Marshall and Newcombe, 1973; Saffran and Marin, 1977). Furthermore, when the reading process is fractionated in this way, it becomes possible to study the component mechanisms in relative isolation, free of some of the redundancy and complexity that complicate experimental analyses in normal populations (Saffran and Marin, 1977).

If the data from pathology are to be used to contribute to a componential analysis of language function,† subjects must be selected with care; not every aphasic will be a useful subject. There will be many patients with lesions that cut across several functional subsystems who do not show clear dissociations of function. An analysis based on unselected cases can therefore be uninformative, or misleading. A recent example is a study by Jenkins and Shaw (1975), which led to the conclusion that language, functionally as well as anatomically, is the product of an undifferentiated system that operates as a whole.

In the rest of this paper, we will describe some of the pathological phenomena that can help to tease apart the normal language process. We will begin by demonstrating a general dissociation between lexical and syntactic mechanisms in language production, and then go on to a brief description of several forms of lexical impairment. The major portion of this chapter will be concerned with an account of the aphasic disturbance known as "agrammatism."

II. The Dissociation of Syntactic and Lexical Aspects of Language Production

It is by now well recognized that lexical and syntactic processes can be impaired independently in patients with brain lesions (e.g. Jakobson, 1964;

†In fact, this has rarely been the goal of aphasia studies, which have historically focused on neuroanatomical rather than functional questions. We believe it is this historical accident, rather than any inherent limitations in the methodology, which accounts for the irrelevance of so much of aphasiology, both past and present, to normal psycholinguistics (for further discussion along these lines, see Marin *et al.*, 1976).

Luria, 1970; Goodglass and Geschwind, 1976; Marin *et al.*, 1976; Marshall, 1977; Caramazza and Berndt, 1978). The basic dissociation will be evident in these samples of speech production from two of our patients, both of whom are attempting to describe the same picture. In this scene, a man is emerging from a house with a broken window, pointing an accusatory finger at a little girl; a boy, in baseball gear, is crouching behind a fence, out of sight. The first patient says:

   (1)   Patient (P): Like the door . . . crash . . . like, pants . . . shirt . . . shoes . . . the boy . . . the boy . . . the dress . . . I dunno.

Pressed to explain what is going on, he assumes the roles of various characters, as follows:

        P: "Do . . . you do window?" . . . "No I did" (laughs). Like, the boy is hidin' . . . there.
        Examiner (E): Why?
        P: Because, well . . . the man is trying . . . man . . . like, the man . . . because the boy . . . the boy . . . the window . . . like hidin' out, see . . . Okay, like the girl . . . "Was do the window?" and "No, sir" . . . like this . . . "the boy."

The second patient also has a problem, but it is obviously a rather different one:

   (2)   P: The guy did something, right there . . . He ran . . . and she's there like she didn't even know.
        E: Who broke it?
        P: She would never do it. She looks like a really nice kid. He's really getting mad (pointing to the man) . . . *He* did it (pointing to the boy). He broke it.
        E: How?
        P: I can't tell you, but I know what it is. It is just broken. 'Cause this kid did it.
        E: What kind of "kid" is that?
        P: Him.

While both patients clearly understand what is going on in the picture, they are having difficulty communicating this information. The first patient has reasonable command of most of the essential substantives (although nouns are, perhaps, better preserved than verbs), but he is unable to construct complete sentences and has difficulty making use of function words. His problem is primarily syntactic. The second patient seems to have the opposite problem; although she constructs well-formed sentences, they are grossly deficient in specific lexical content. These two excerpts are typical of language production in the aphasic syndromes known as *agrammatism* (the first patient) and *anomia* (the second).

    The basic dissociation in anomic aphasia—syntactic processes well preserved in the face of severe lexical impairment—is also seen in two other pathological states, which are in other respects quite different. In *Wernicke's aphasia*, it is the phonological structure of lexical elements that is most affected;† lexical formatives are riddled with errors, ranging from the substitution of a single phoneme to flagrant neologisms having no apparent relationship to the lexical target. The result is frequently an incomprehensible jargon, as in this example from another patient who is describing the "broken window" picture:

(3) You got the people goin' . . . an' what's more . . . the . . . eh . . . well, you'd have one . . . your beez, your beez. Oh . . . and then . . . come out in a few minutes . . . How many, how many beezes . . . eight many beezes . . . Eera comes a fes an' she an' gone the peesh an' there's the man an' then the young girl, on there she calls an' she's holdin' a koun. Emsin, emshin I guess. A stickit, stickin. Some of those on . . . this seems to be . . . person. He is one, I guess. I dunno. She's tryin' to ping about but I'm not sure. There comes one of 'em, but she reecheenge . . . oh . . . uh . . . uh . . . can't stadik.

A pattern that more closely resembles the production of anomic aphasics is found in some cases of *dementia*, a disorder in which the organic pathology is degenerative and diffuse rather than focal, and the degree of cognitive impairment generally greater than that seen in anomia. This excerpt is from a patient studied in our own laboratory (Schwartz *et al.*, 1979). The patient is describing her two daughters' differing reactions to her communication problem:

(4) Oh yeah, *she's* real nice. She, you know . . . she tells me something and I say "oh, oh, oh" and she says, "Hon, why don't you say that," and I say "Well, ah . . ." Then, when she says it, I say "Oh yeah!" But, oh Lord, my other . . . ah . . . girl, you know, my girl that I have, she says "Mom, now you tell me something!" (feigning anger) and I say "Oh, I can't tell you anything." She says "Ma!" 'cause she's so excited.

There is a notable lack of substantives in this patient's speech. As her illness progressed, the class of content words was in fact reduced to a single item ("shoppin'-center"), which was inflected and substituted for verbs as well as for nouns ("He shoppin' centered it there."). Nevertheless, even at this stage, the patient spontaneously corrected syntactic errors in the course of repeating anomalous sentences spoken by the examiner (see also Whitaker, 1976).

We will not discuss the lexical disturbances further here, except to point out some additional contrasts with the pattern of impairment in agrammatism. In addition to the preservation of the syntactic structure of the utterance, these disorders differ from agrammatic aphasia in the fluency of speech production and the absence of articulatory impairment. Inflectional morphology, which is almost completely absent in agrammatic speech, is also well preserved; this is true even in the jargon of Wernicke's aphasia, where the phonological structure of the lexical formatives is so severely affected (Butterworth,

---

†The status of syntactic operations in these patients is far from understood. While their language output is complexly structured, grammatical morphemes are frequently misused, and selection restrictions on lexical items violated. The resulting pattern is generally referred to as *paragrammatism* to distinguish it from the non-fluent, incomplete phrase structures of the agrammatic aphasics.

1979). Finally, while vocabulary is to some extent compromised in all of these aphasic disorders, the nature of the residual lexical capacity presents a further contrast with agrammatism: nonpicturable words (words like "thing", "one", "place") which predominate in anomic speech, are infrequently used by agrammatic patients (Goodglass et al., 1969); verbs also seem to be better preserved than nouns in the speech of anomics (Fillenbaum et al., 1961; Marin et al., 1976) and Wernicke's aphasics (Butterworth, 1979), while we will see that the converse is true in agrammatism.

Thus while the nature of the lexical problem may differ in these three types of disturbances,† the language patterns that result have certain features in common. There are surely some functional implications in the co-occurrence of these language characteristics, a possibility that we will consider later on in this chapter.

III. Aspects of Language Impairment in Agrammatism

Language output in agrammatism is abnormal in several respects. The characteristic features of the syndrome are the lack of grammatical morphemes, both free and bound, that gives agrammatic speech its "telegraphic" quality; a simplification, and in severe cases, a complete absence of sentence structure; a lexical bias toward referential words; and a problem with articulation. We will look at each of these characteristics in more detail, and then attempt to account for the relationships among them.

A. Syntactic Morphology

The omission of functors and inflectional affixes is the criterial feature of agrammatic speech production. The deficit is not only manifested in spontaneous speech; it is also evident in sentence completion tasks, aimed at eliciting specific syntactic targets (Goodglass et al., 1972; Gleason et al., 1975), and even in repetition tasks, where the patient is provided with a well-formed sentence, and has merely to repeat it verbatim (Goodglass, 1968). Here, for example, are some samples of the repetition performance of one of our own agrammatic patients.

†The mechanisms of the various lexical disorders are not yet well understood, but a number of possibilities have been suggested. According to Luria (1973), the phonemic paraphasias of Wernicke's aphasics, and their frequent failures of lexical comprehension, point toward an instability in the phonemic organization of words—an inability to hold on to phonological information when it comes in, and to organize it for programming output. A different mechanism is proposed for anomia. In such cases, where lexical comprehension, oral reading and word repetition are generally well preserved, the difficulty appears to be at a prior stage of retrieval; Luria postulates a failure to select the output target from a diffusely activated network of related items. Goodglass and Baker (1976) suggest that the integrity of the semantic retrieval itself may be compromised in certain aphasic patients, and we have made a similar argument with regard to the lexical disorder in dementia (Schwartz et al. 1979; see also Warrington, 1975).

(5) Experimenter (E): No, I do not like fish.
     Patient (P): No . . . fish.
     E: One morning, the girl was pulled by the man.
     P: One morning, the . . . the girl is pull . . . pull the boy.
     E: The girl runs to the man.
     P: The girl running the . . . the girl is running on man.

There is a tendency to omit syntactic elements, as in spontaneous speech, or to replace them with other grammatical morphemes; in contrast, the substantive elements are largely retained.

In most agrammatic aphasics, the ability to produce grammatical morphemes is not totally lacking. It is possible, with fair reliability, to order the morphemes in terms of the probability of their appearance in samples of agrammatic speech. The morphemes most likely to be produced are the plural inflection (girl*s*) and the present participle (runn*ing*); among the most difficult are tense markers (future *will*; past *-ed*) and the third person inflection (he run*s*) (Goodglass, 1968; de Villiers, 1974; Gleason *et al.*, 1975).

There exists no parsimonious account of this ordering. It is not highly correlated with transformational complexity or with the pattern of acquisition by young children (de Villiers, 1974). Factors such as informational significance and redundancy are not reliable predictors either; patients may, for example, inflect appropriately for the plural in a context where this information is redundant (e.g. "two cats"), but fail to use tense markers where temporal information is significant and not otherwise indicated in the utterance (Goodglass, 1976). Prosodic factors are clearly important. Many patients have difficulty initiating an utterance with an unstressed morpheme and are more likely to produce an unstressed functor when it occupies a medial position than when it occurs as the first element in the utterance (Goodglass, 1968). Phonological factors are also relevant; the agrammatic patient is more likely to retain the syllabic form of the past tense inflection (want/id/) than the non-syllabic form (smoke/t/); similarly, he is more likely to retain the syllabic (dish/iz/) forms than the non-syllabic allomorphs (/s/ and /z/) of the plural, third person and possessive inflections (Goodglass and Berko, 1960). But still the account is incomplete, for whereas the three constructions just mentioned have the same phonological realizations, they nevertheless differ in degree of difficulty, the plural being the easiest for the agrammatic to produce and the possessive the most difficult (Goodglass and Hunt, 1958).

There is evidence that the agrammatic speaker knows more about the syntactic morphology of the language than his output would indicate. Thus, agrammatics typically try to correct their utterances (Goodglass, 1976), and most of them occasionally succeed in producing even the more difficult targets in structured grammatical tests (Gleason *et al.*, 1975). The patients are also surprisingly sensitive to the anomalous usage of grammatical morphemes (Goodglass, 1976), a phenomenon we have recently replicated in our laboratory. Two agrammatic subjects were asked to judge the grammaticality of sentences, half of which contained errors of the sort that were likely to occur in their own speech (e.g. "Mary is go home today", "Father like his job");

both patients performed considerably better than chance (81% and 96% correct, respectively). Moreover, although it has been shown that agrammatics are impaired in the comprehension of syntactic structures (Caramazza and Zurif, 1976; Scholes, 1978), the comprehension failure largely reflects an inability to deal with the structural aspects of syntax (e.g. word order) rather than with the grammatical morphemes themselves (Schwartz et al., 1978). The difficulty with grammatical morphemes is, then, principally an output problem, the nature of which we will consider later on in this chapter.

B. Sentence Structure

In the most severely agrammatic patients, utterances are almost completely devoid of structure. They consist of a series of words, primarily nouns, separated by pauses and linked, if at all, by conjunctions. The following excerpt, from Goodglass (1976), is illustrative. The patient is attempting to explain his return to the hospital for dental work:

(6) Ah . . . Monday . . . ah Dad and Paul H————— [referring to himself by name] . . . and Dad . . . hospital. Two . . . ah doctors . . . and ah . . . thirty minutes . . . and yes . . . ah . . . hospital. And, er Wednesday . . . nine o-clock. And er Thursday, ten o'clock . . . doctors. Two doctors . . . and ah . . . teeth . . . Yeah . . . fine.

Output of this sort has been referred to as "serial naming" (Luria, 1970).

Patients who are somewhat less impaired are capable of generating simple sentences of the subject–verb (NP–V) or subject-verb-object (NP–V–NP) type, although even these are lacking in obligatory functors and inflections, as in this example from Goodglass (1976):

(7) My uh Mother died . . . uh . . . me . . . uh fifteen. Uh, oh, I guess six month. My mother pass away.

Structural complexity beyond this is minimal. The capacity to expand the noun phrase or the verb phrase is severely limited, and embedded structures of any kind are rarely observed. Thus, constructions involving two adjectives were found to be among the most difficult syntactic targets in the Sentence Completion Test of Goodglass and his co-workers (Goodglass et al., 1972; Gleason et al., 1975); unable to combine the two adjectives in a single noun phrase (as in "a large, white house"), the agrammatic patients would either omit one of the modifiers or relegate each of them to a separate phrase ("a large house, a white house"). The dative construction, which requires an expanded verb phrase (NP + V + NP + NP), was another of the more difficult targets in the Sentence Completion Test. We have found a similar difficulty in our own test of syntactic production, in which pictures are used to probe for specific syntactic forms. In the following examples, four of our agrammatic patients are attempting to describe a picture in which *a girl is giving flowers to her teacher* (we will use italics to designate scenes that are being described):

(8) The young . . . the girl . . . the little girl is . . . the flower.
(9) The girl is flower the woman.
(10) Girl is . . . going to flowers.
(11) The girl is giving . . . giving the teacher . . . giving it teacher.

The inability to produce embedded constructions sets a stringent limit on the kind of information that can be transmitted (imagine the difficulty of expressing an even slightly complex thought without relativization). Some of the peculiarities of agrammatic speech relect the patients' attempts to compensate for this problem. A good example is substitution of direct quotation for indirect discourse, which would entail relative clause formation; unable, for example, to say "She told them to be quiet," the agrammatic patient will typically name the speaker and produce the command (Gleason *et al.*, 1975; Goodglass, 1976). Several instances of direct quotation are evident in (1) above.

There is evidence to suggest that the syntactic ability of the moderately impaired agrammatics may be even more limited than their production of NP–V–NP sequences would seem to indicate. In the course of developing our picture description battery, we noted that the agrammatic patients were having particular difficulty with a set of pictures in which the two objects whose relation was to be described were alike in animacy—both of them animate (as in *the dog chases the cat*), or both inanimate (as in *the pencil is in the sink*). There was a strong tendency to reverse the order of the two noun phrases ("the sink is in the pencil"), an error that rarely occurred when the two objects differed in animacy (as in *the boy pulls the wagon*). To explore this problem further, we constructed a set of 24 drawings depicting animate-animate (*the girl runs to the man*), inanimate-inanimate (*the key is in the suitcase*), and animate-inanimate relationships (*the girl runs to the house; the cat is in the suitcase*) in either action contexts or locative situations. Because some of the more profoundly impaired patients were unable to produce enough utterances that were scorable for word order,† we also used a Sentence Order Test (von Stockert, 1972), which required no verbal output; instead, the subject was given a set of cards containing the constituent elements (e.g. THE WAGON, THE BOY, PULLS) and had to arrange them linearly to form an appropriate sentence.

Figure 1 contains the data from a group of eight agrammatic patients on both the production and sentence order tasks (Saffran *et al.*, 1977). It is

†Since our interest here was exclusively in the ordering of noun phrases, the following scoring procedure was adopted. A scorable response was the first utterance in which there occurred a nominal appropriate to the picture, followed by any segment of a verbal, appropriate or not. A "correct" response was then one in which the appropriate grammatical subject preceded the verbal. The following attempts were scored "correct" for a picture of *a key inside a suitcase*:
The key is.
The key is on . . . in . . . the trunk.
The key . . . on top.
A response was "incorrect" if the object noun phrase preceded the (partial) verbal (e.g. The suitcase is). Trials in which no verbal was attempted were designated "unscorable" (e.g., The key . . . the trunk.).

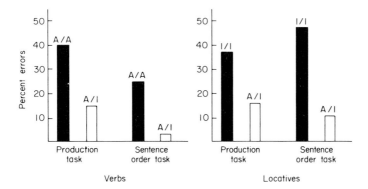

FIG. 1. Word order as a function of animacy in agrammatic performance on production and sentence order tasks. A/A = constructions in which both objects are animate; I/I = constructions in which both objects are inanimate; A/I = constructions in which one object is animate and the other inanimate.

evident that word order is close to random in the animate-animate and inanimate-inanimate conditions, and that performance improves considerably when the objects differ in animacy. These results suggest that the use of correct word order by an agrammatic patient does not necessarily signify that the utterance has been generated by a mechanism that operates in accordance with syntactic rules. Rather, the patients seem to be relying on pragmatic factors for ordering output strings; the most salient object—almost always an animate object—comes first. Only when describing scenes in which animacy is not contrastive does it become apparent that the patients are unable to use syntactic rules for subject selection. Similarly, the use of semantic constraints can mask an underlying syntactic deficit in the language comprehension performance of agrammatic aphasics (Caramazza and Zurif, 1976).

The limitation on structural complexity, along with the effect of semantic saliency, combined to produce some interesting behavior in our agrammatic . subjects. The difficulty arose when we asked them to describe two pictures which reliably elicited passive voice constructions in non-brain damaged controls. Shown a picture of *a boy being hit in the head by a baseball* (the source of the ball not in sight), the patients responded with:

(12)   The boy is catch . . . the boy is . . . out . . . the boy is catching out.
(13)   The boy is in the . . . hits the boy.
(14)   Boy is hurting to it.
(15)   Hit. The man is throwing the ball.
(16)   The boy is catch . . . the boy is hitch . . . the boy is hit the ball.

(This picture elicited passive voice constructions in 46 of 60 normal controls).

And similarly, in the case of *a man being struck by a falling boulder*, we have from the aphasics:

(17)   The little man is fallin' the rocks.
(18)   The man is rock ... the man is falling the rock.
(19)   The boy is clunk ... clunk rock.
(20)   The boy is bump rocks.
(21)   The boy is ... the ... fall, fall on the ground ... the man is falling ...
       falling the rock.

(50% of normal controls used the passive form with this picture).

While the aphasics are clearly unable to construct adequate passive
sentences, it should have been possible for most of them to communicate the
essential information by means of the less-preferred but simpler active
construction ("The ball hit the boy"). Their failure to do so reflects, we
believe, the inability to operate freely with the criteria for selection of
grammatical subject; instead, order is fixed for them by the perceptual salience
of the animate constituent.

Animacy is a factor of considerable importance in normal output as well, a
point forcefully made by the responses of control subjects to the two pictures
just discussed (by resorting to the less frequently used passive voice, they
managed to keep the animate constituent in the role of grammatical subject).
More generally, the special status of agents as grammatical subjects no doubt
derives from their perceptual/conceptual salience as animate entities
(Fillmore, 1968; Osgood and Bock, 1977; for an expanded view of agency, see
Schlesinger, 1977). But normal speakers almost certainly do not respond to
animacy *directly* in their generation of surface structures. If they did, they
would be as baffled as the aphasics by messages involving more than one
animate referent. For normal speakers, these are more than animate entities;
they are agents, patients, beneficiaries and the like, categories which are
subject to ordered rules for the determination of word order and syntactic
structure. These distinctions do not seem to hold in the production of the
agrammatic aphasics.

C. A Bias Toward Reference

The lexical content of agrammatic speech also deserves comment. It is evident
in the brief samples provided thus far that nouns predominate in agrammatic
output (see, for example, (6) above). The few quantitative studies that are
available support this impression. Fillenbaum *et al.* (1961) noted that verb
forms were underrepresented in spontaneous speech samples from patients
with syntactic difficulties; and in a severely agrammatic patient studied by
Myerson and Goodglass (1972), the noun-verb ratio was as high as seven to
one. In analyzing the repetition performance of two of our own patients we
found that 65% of the nouns and only 32% of the verb stems had been
adequately reproduced.

Within the category of nouns, there is a strong bias toward words that are
concrete and referential. In the case reported by Myerson and Goodglass
(1972), two thirds were names of people or places, and almost all of the

remainder were concrete and picturable. A bias toward picturable nouns in the speech of non-fluent aphasics was also found in a quantitative study by Goodglass *et al.* (1969). The use of specific nouns, and certainly of proper names, cannot be explained in terms of word frequency; indefinite nouns ("thing", "way", "time"), which are generally of higher frequency, are not commonly found in the speech of agrammatic aphasics (Goodglass *et al.*, 1969).

Verbs, when they do occur, tend to be either unmarked for person and tense (e.g. "The guy wash the boy", "The girl study", "The boy is climb the fence") or in the form of the present participle (*-ing*), with or without an auxiliary (e.g. "The guy smilin' "). The bias toward the *-ing* form is evident in these attempts to repeat sentences spoken by an examiner (E):

(22) E: The girl reads a book.
P: The girl is reading book.

(23) E: The girl brushes her hair.
P: The girl is brushing hair.

(24) E: The man painted the house.
P: The man painting a house.

(25) E: The truck pulls a car.
P: The truck pulling a car.

The extensive use of the progressive form by agrammatic speakers might possibly reflect the fact that it is one of the most common constructions in everyday speech, and/or that the distinct, syllabic inflection may be easier to articulate than other inflections on the verb stem. But given the general absence of inflectional affixes in agrammatic speech, why inflect the verb at all?

An intriguing answer to this question is that the predominance of the unmarked verb form and the *-ing* inflection in agrammatic speech reflect a tendency to nominalize the verb: that the *-ing* participle really marks the gerundive rather than the progressive aspect, and the unmarked form represents the use of the infinitive, yet another nominalized form of the verb (Goodglass, 1968). This argument is supported by evidence from German-speaking agrammatics, who tend to use the infinitive (e.g. "gehen") in verbal contexts in place of the properly inflected form. Goodglass and Geschwind (1976) point out that "since the German infinitive, unlike the English, has an inflectional ending, this evidence supports the view that the agrammatic . . . is not merely dropping the person and tense markers in English, but rather shifting to a nominalized use of the verb" (p. 409). On this interpretation, the verb is not being used in a predicative sense, but rather to "name" the action.

The relative availability of different types of lexical formatives to the agrammatic speaker is a question that requires further study. It is our strong impression, however, that sentence construction frequently breaks down at the point where a verb must be chosen. Occasionally, the patient solves the problem by substituting a noun, as in the following examples from our picture description corpus.

A picture of a *girl reading a book* elicits:

(26) The girl is bookening.
A girl giving flowers to her teacher:
    (27) The girl is . . . is roses. The girl is rosin.
    The woman and the little girl was rosed.
A baby drinking a bottle:
    (28) The baby bottle-ing.
A woman photographing some flowers:
    (29) The woman is polaroid the flower.
It is also our impression that within the category of verbs there is a range of difficulty along a dimension we might call "inherent" versus "relational". Our observations suggest that the agrammatics find it easier to produce verb forms that describe actions or states that are properties of the actor (e.g. "reading", "running", "smiling") than verbs that encode relationships between objects (e.g. "lifting", "selling", "chasing"). This hypothesis is currently under investigation.

D. Articulation

In addition to the structural and morphological characteristics described in the previous two sections, language output in agrammatism is effortful, poorly articulated, and lacking in prosody. While the telegraphic speech pattern does not seem to occur in the absence of articulatory impairment, there are patients with left hemisphere lesions whose speech is abnormal only in its faulty articulation (Johns and LaPointe, 1976). Unfortunately, there has been no attempt to determine whether there are differences in the articulatory deficits of patients with and without concomitant syntactic impairment; the major studies in this area are based on subjects with expressive disorders ("motoraphasia", "Broca's aphasia") unclassified with respect to grammatical characteristics (e.g. Shankweiler and Harris, 1966; Blumstein, 1973). The articulatory disturbance, which has been termed "phonetic disintegration" (Alajouanine *et al.*, 1939), has the following features: vowels are produced more accurately than consonants; there is particular difficulty with fricatives, affricates and consonant clusters; and there is a tendency to substitute unmarked consonants (e.g. unvoiced stops like /p/ and /t/) for marked consonants (e.g. voiced stops like /b/ and /d/). The pattern of deficit strongly suggests a disturbance in the coordinated sequencing of the various components of an articulatory gesture (Johns and LaPointe, 1976; see also Luria, 1966).

IV. The Nature of The Deficit in Agrammatism

Our goal, in the ensuing discussion, is to rationalize the language deficit in agrammatism in terms of a model of language production. We will look carefully at the components of the deficit and attempt to explain how they fit together. While it is possible that the co-occurrence of symptoms reflects anatomical factors that are fortuitous (damage to anatomical substrates that overlap in space but have no functional relation), we will assume otherwise. Such an account would be psychologically uninteresting and could serve no heurisitic purpose. Instead we will propose a functional explanation for the pattern of deficits in agrammatism. While much of this account is based, thus far, on very little data, it should serve, at the very least, to point to the questions we should be asking of aphasic populations, and to what end.

It will be useful here to spell out two possible formulations of the output deficit in agrammatism as suggested in a recent paper by Marshall (1977). The telegraphic speech pattern could result (1) from failure to elaborate the underlying syntactic representation, so that the surface structure contains only the specifications for the major lexical elements (e.g. $N + V + N$) or (2) from failure in the phonological transcription of grammatical elements that are specified in the underlying representation (e.g. $Det + N + V + ed + Det + N$ is realized as "boy pull wagon").

There have been several attempts to account for the output deficit in agrammatism in terms of an explanation of the second kind. It has frequently been suggested that the omission of grammatical morphemes is a direct consequence of the articulatory impairment: that to maximize the informational content of utterances produced with so great an effort, the patients omit elements that carry relatively little information (articles, auxiliaries and the like), with the result that output is telegraphic (Pick, 1913; Isserlin, 1922; Lenneberg, 1973). More recently, Kean (1977) has proposed that all of the deficits in agrammatism, the comprehension problem as well as the output characteristics, can be accounted for in terms of an underlying phonological deficit. The realization of this deficit, on the output side, is the "reduction of the phonological structure of a sentence" (p. 27); this is accomplished by omitting all elements which are not "phonological words", i.e. which do not function in the assignment of stress patterns. (In English, grammatical morphemes do not figure in the assignment of stress.) It is explicit in Kean's formulation, and implicit in the earlier "economy of effort" hypothesis, that the underlying syntactic representation is well-formed.

Many objections can be raised to both of these explanations, and we will not enumerate all of them here (see Goodglass (1976) and Marshall (1977) for excellent discussions). There is, first of all, the evidence that the articulatory component of the output deficit ("phonetic disintegration") can occur independently of the syntactic impairment. Secondly, while it might be possible to account for the omission of grammatical morphemes in terms of some version of the "economy of effort" hypothesis, or in terms of Kean's (1977) more linguistic conceptualization, neither of these hypotheses can deal with the constructional aspects of agrammatic impairment, and particularly with the word order problem that we have noted above. It is reasonable to assume, rather, that the underlying deficit in agrammatism is at least partly syntactic. The fact that there are difficulties in the comprehension of syntactic structures, as well as in their production, argues compellingly for this view.

The question remains, however, as to the nature of the syntactic deficit and its relationship to other aspects of language impairment in agrammatism.

Can the morphological properties of agrammatic speech be explained, then, in terms of Marshall's (1977) first hypothesis? A failure to elaborate a complete syntactic representation would account both for the limitation to simple syntactic forms, and for the omission of obligatory morphological elements. What it fails to explain is why the occurrence of grammatical morphemes in agrammatic speech is at least partially determined by phonological variables. It may be necessary to propose that there is a problem in the phonological realization of grammatical morphemes, in addition to a basic problem in sentence construction; that is, to accept the second of Marshall's (1977) hypotheses, as well as the first one.

The rejection of a parsimonious explanation for the agrammatic speech pattern is further justified by the existence of aphasic patients who show the *constructional* deficit in sentence production but not the *morphological* one. Recently we had the opportunity to study one such case.† Below are some examples of this patient's responses to our picture description task. Note that while his output is in many ways similar to that of the classical agrammatics, the patient does not omit obligatory grammatical morphemes. He is even able to produce inflectional variants (such as the /s/ allomorph of the third person singular and the non-syllabic /t/ form of the past tense inflection) that are rarely achieved by the agrammatics: A picture of a *girl giving flowers to her teacher* elicits:

(30) Girl . . . wants to . . . flowers . . . flowers and wants to . . . The woman . . . wants to . . . The girl wants to . . . the flowers and the woman.

A truck towing a car:

(31) The . . . man . . . uh automobile and truck . . . the man drives the truck and the automobile.

A woman kissing a man:

(32) The kiss . . . the lady kissed . . . the lady is . . . the lady and the man and the lady . . . kissing.

A boy drying himself with a towel:

(33) Puts . . . the man puts on . . . on his . . . towel.

A woman putting clothes in a washing machine:

(34) The lady . . . the lady launders the . . . the lady puts the washes . . . wash on . . . puts on the wash with the laundry.

Like the classical agrammatics, this patient also has difficulty in the selection of verbs and prepositions‡

†We are grateful to Roger Walters and Patti Linden of the Speech and Hearing Department of the Good Samaritan Hospital, Baltimore, for permission to study this patient.

‡Although spatial prepositions generally are included in the category of function words, they are in many ways more similar to verbs than to other grammatical morphemes. As is often the case with verbs (e.g. "buy" versus "sell"), the choice of prepositions has implications for subject selection (or vice versa; viz., "The star is above the circle" versus "The circle is below the star"). In semantically-based formulations of sentence structure and production, this factor is of considerable importance, and spatial prepositions are often treated as instances of verbs (e.g. Chafe, 1970; Osgood and Bock, 1977). It is significant, therefore, that agrammatic aphasics have

A boy giving a valentine to a girl:
   (35) The boy and a valentine and a girl . . . boy . . . the boy put the valentine into this girl.

A boy being hit by a ball:
   (36) The man . . . the ball flies the man . . . the ball flies and the man is unable to . . .

A woman carrying a tray; on it are a pitcher and a glass:
   (37) The lady is tray . . . the lady is putting the tray and . . . with the jug and glass . . . the lady is placing the tray with the jug and glass.

A cat peeping out from behind an armchair:
   (38) The sofa . . . the . . . cat leans the . . . the cat leans the sofa up . . . the cat and the sofa and the sofa . . . the cat un-under the sofa.

An open suitcase with a key lying inside it:
   (39) The key is behind the trunk.

In further similarity to the classical agrammatic, there is a tendency to use nouns in place of verbs, and to rely heavily on verb forms that derive from nouns:

A man taking a photograph of a girl:
   (40) The man kodaks . . . and the girl . . . kodaks the girl.

A man washing a car with a sponge:
   (41) The man sponges the car.

A man painting a house:
   (42) The . . . paint and the painter . . . the painter washed the paint . . . the painter brushes the paint.

A man washing a baby:
   (43) The man . . . baby . . . the man soaps the baby.

It is also of some interest that, in contrast to the patients with telegraphic speech patterns, articulation was in this case almost normal (there was a slight problem with consonant blends, and a tendency to mispronounce /r/ as /w/).

Thus, while the patient has a great deal of difficulty in putting a sentence together, the simple structures that he does elaborate are well-formed morphologically. It is, of course, possible to conceive of the difference between this patient and the classical agrammatic in terms of degree of impairment—that the isolated occurrence of the constructional deficit represents a milder form of agrammatism rather than a true dissociation of function.† We need to look carefully at the course of recovery in agrammatism to see whether there is support for this position. As our working hypothesis, however, we will adopt the alternative view: that the constructional and morphological aspects of agrammatic production are dissociable, and that the syntactic deficits in agrammatic speech reflect impairments at two separate stages in the production process.

---

comparable difficulties with prepositions as with verbs, and that this type of problem can be dissociated from the failure to realize other grammatical morphemes.

   † We do not know how frequently this condition appears in the aphasic population. Patients like this one have probably not been differentiated from classical agrammatics. It is only when one begins to think in terms of a production model that such distinctions become important.

The conjecture that there are separable constructional and morphological deficits can be justified in terms of a model for normal language production. On *a priori* grounds, it is reasonable to suppose that the phonological specification (of at least many) of the grammatical morphemes must occur rather late in the development of the utterance. Although the requirement for a syntactic morph may be specified in the syntactic frame for the utterance (e.g. Det + N + V + ed + Det + N), the phonological realization of the grammatical morpheme will depend on the phonological properties of the lexical formative that precedes it (e.g. "*a* fruit" versus "*an* apple") or to which it is appended (e.g. "eat/s/" versus "consume/z/"). The implication for a production model is that phonological specification of the grammatical morpheme cannot precede lexical insertion. Good evidence that this is so comes from normal speech errors, as in these examples from Fromkin (1971); "*a* current argument" → "*an* arrent curgument"; "plant the seed/z/" → "plan the seat/s/". It is generally assumed that segmental errors of this sort arise at the point of insertion of phonologically specified lexical formatives into the syntactic frame. Since the syntactic allomorph is appropriate to the achieved rather than the intended lexical content (*an* rather than *a* "arrent curgument"), its phonological specification must occur subsequent to lexical insertion (Fromkin, 1971; Garrett, 1975; see also Butterworth, 1979, for relevant data from jargon aphasia).

We can therefore account for what we have hitherto called the morphological aspects of agrammatic production by hypothesizing an impairment at a stage in the production process where the phonological form of the utterance is finalized.† The functions that are compromised include the phonological specification of grammatical morphemes, and possibly other "morphophonemic" operations as well (Fromkin, 1971). It is presumably after this stage that "automatic phonetic and phonological rules take over, converting the sequences of segments into actual neuro-motor commands" for the articulation of the utterance (Fromkin, 1971, p. 51). Where there exists a disorder at the prior "morphophonemic" stage (as we have hypothesized is the case for agrammatic aphasics), consider now the status of the automatic phonetic processes: the input that is received for "conversion to motor commands" is likely to be deficient, and this deficiency will be reflected in the articulatory output, possibly in the form of "phonetic disintegration." Accordingly, we predict that deficits in syntactic morphology, of the sort characteristic of agrammatism, will not occur in the absence of accompanying disorders of "articulation" (i.e. phonetic realization). As far as we know, this co-occurrence restriction holds throughout the literature on aphasia.

---

†We are attributing at least part of the problem with grammatical morphemes to an impairment at a "phonological" stage of the language process. Kean's (1977) account of agrammatism, on which we have commented earlier, also proposes a phonological "impairment". However, Kean's conceptualization of a phonological disturbance, coming as it does out of formal linguistic theory, is very different from our own process-oriented view. What is more important is that the phonological deficit provides the *complete* account of agrammatism for Kean, who denies any impairment at a syntactic level.

The converse restriction does not hold, however, and there is nothing in our model which suggests that it should. In cases of "pure" disorders of articulation, the production machinery will be compromised only at its latest stages—at the level of conversion to motor commands, or perhaps in the dispatch of the commands themselves. In any case, the prediction from our model is that the characteristics of the articulatory impairment should differ in patients with and without accompanying syntactic problems. Unfortunately, but not surprisingly, the relevant studies have not yet been done. These distinctions are of interest only when one views the pathological phenomena from the perspective of a model for production.

V. Residual Language in Agrammatism

We have not yet addressed the problem of the lexical content of agrammatic speech—the bias toward concrete, referential words and the apparent inaccessibility of verb forms that is the converse of the pattern we see in patients with lexical disturbances. The use of concrete nouns and nominalized verb forms, holophrastically and in limited combination, accounts for most of the residual language in agrammatism. In a way, this is the most fascinating problem that is posed by agrammatic speech, the one that brings us to the very heart of the capacity to encode cognitive structures in linguistic form.

The view that is emerging from our work is that agrammatic language production reflects a rather direct mapping from a conceptual representation, without mediation by a system of syntactic rules. We would further characterize the mapping as one-to-one: each symbol corresponds to a single primitive in an underlying cognitive representation. In conceptualizing the problem in this way, it is possible to account for both the structural and morphemic properties of agrammatic speech, and by inverting the model, to explain the comprehension deficit as well.

The problem may be most clearly exemplified in the data for language comprehension. In a study that is preliminary to a large scale investigation of comprehension processes in aphasic patients, we have tested the ability of eight agrammatic subjects to comprehend a wide range of syntactic structures (Schwartz et al., 1978); these include grammatical morphemes (e.g. pronouns, plurals, spatial prepositions, morphemes of negation) as well as word order contrasts around a verbal element, either an action verb (e.g. "the girl touches the boy") or a spatial preposition ("the square is above the circle"). The patient listened to the sentence twice, and responded by pointing to a picture that most closely represented its meaning. In addition to the correct picture, there were usually two distractors, one offering a minimal syntactic contrast (*the room is tidy* versus *the room is not tidy*) and another that differed along some lexical dimension (*a broken sidewalk*). The agrammatics had relatively little difficulty with all but one category of the grammatical morphemes, a class we have designated, following semantically inclined linguists like Fillmore (1968) and Chafe (1970), as "case marking prepositions"; these are exemplified in structures like "a phone call *to* a boy" versus "a phone call *from* the boy." The error rate for the case-marking prepositions was 38%, while the error rate for the other grammatical morphemes hovered around 10%.

The principal difference between the case marking morphemes and the other morphemes that we tested is that these prepositions are semantically empty; they serve only to mark the relation which the noun phrase bears to the verbal element (in the previous example, whether the boy is the initiator of the phone call—the agent of the implicit verb—or the recipient). The significance of the failure with the case-marking prepositions is underscored by the fact that the patients also performed poorly on the word order contrasts, where again the problem was to determine the underlying case relationships, in this instance, as marked by the order of noun phrases around a verbal element. The error rate was 23% on the verb contrasts and 41% on the spatial prepositions.† The agrammatics' performance with spatial prepositions provides a particularly strong demonstration of the underlying deficit: the patients were clearly able to understand the semantics of the prepositions themselves, as indicated by the 7% error rate when the contrast was with another locative morpheme (e.g. *the shoe is in the box* versus *the shoe is on the box*); but they were unable to use the word order to map the nouns into the locative relationship—to decide whether the circle was on the square or the square on the circle. The word order problem has also been noted in other studies of syntactic comprehension in aphasics (Parisi and Pizzamiglio, 1970; Lesser, 1974). ‡

The comprehension data suggest, then, that while the patients can comprehend the semantic implications of individual lexical elements, they do not appreciate the implications of morphemes in combination (except as the combinations are semantically restrictive—that is, they can understand that "the dog eat the bone", but not that the dog must be the pursuer in "the dog chases the cat" (Caramazza and Zurif, 1976)). In other words, the mapping from surface structure to the underlying semantics is one-to-one.

On the production side, direct, one-to-one mapping is epitomized in the virtually holophrastic utterances of the most severely impaired patients (as in example (6) above). In cases that are less severe, the directness of mapping is evident in the order in which elements emerge in agrammatic utterances—the

---

†The difference in performance on these two types of word order contrasts can be explained in terms of semantic factors that compensate, in part, for the word order problem. Most of the verbs that we used describe actions that "inhere" in the agent (as, for example, in "the dancer applauds the clown" or "the mother smiles at the baby"). There is less polarity in the locative relationship; the preposition describes a relationship between two objects, and is in no sense a property of one of them. This analysis is supported by the fact that the patients made more than twice as many errors to sentences in which the verbs were "relational" (e.g. verbs like "chase" and "follow") than they did when the verbs were "actor-inherent" ("smile" and "applaud").

‡Given the difficulty that the agrammatic patients have with these semantically reversible sentences, it was remarkable to find that the demented patient whose production (4) is sampled earlier in the chapter was able to determine agent and object on the basis of word order alone. She was, for example, completely unable to distinguish between a horse and cow; but if we gave her a picture and said to her, "The cow is kicking the horse; point to the cow", she would point to the agent—the cow if the picture happened to be the appropriate one, the horse if the picture was of *a horse kicking a cow* (Schwartz *et al.*, 1979).

effect of animacy in determining word order, and the inability to switch to the active voice when the recipient of the action is salient. One-to-one mapping is evident in the difficulty with verb forms that is found, in some degree, in all of the agrammatic patients: the tendency to nominalize the verb (to name actions rather then express functional relationships among elements of the sentence), and the particular difficulty in accessing verbs which are relational rather than actor-inherent. In general, it can be said that the patients have difficulty producing linguistic structures that encode relations, whether these structures are morphemes—verbs or prepositions—or sentences. Thus they are unable to "propositionize", to use Jackson's (1878) early characterization of the deficit; or as Jakobson (1964) has said of agrammatism, "dependent" words, together with "the fundamental syntactic relationship . . . of dependence", are lost. What remains is the capacity to make reference.

Our feeling is that the difficulty with verb forms is at the root of the problem, but at this point we are unable to spell it out any further. It is unlikely that the linguistic deficit reflects a basic cognitive disorder. Clearly, the agrammatic patients represent these dependencies at some level of cognitive function; otherwise they should be more impaired in their nonverbal interactions with the world than they are. We have shown, furthermore, that they are able to abstract relational information from the pictures that we show them; after the picture is removed, the patients can easily demonstrate the action using dolls and other objects (e.g. *the dog chases the cat, the girl runs to the man*), although they are unable to express the directionality of the action linguistically. One possible explanation for the linguistic deficit is that the agrammatic is unable to encode relationships in a form ("mentalese", in the terminology of Fodor *et al.* (1974)) that would allow access to the appropriate linguistic structures. Another is that agrammatism entails a loss of particular kinds of lexical items, in addition to the loss of syntactic forms (see Marin *et al.*, (1976), for some suggestions along these lines); the fact that we see the opposite pattern of lexical breakdown in other brain-damaged patients provides some support for the notion that referential words are represented differently than other kinds of lexical elements. Whatever the answer turns out to be, the analysis should bring us closer to the well-obscured interface between language and the underlying cognitive structures than we have come thus far in the study of normal production.

References

Alajouanine, T., Ombredane, A. and Durand, M. (1939). "Le Syndrome de Desintegration Phonetique dans l'Aphasie." Masson, Paris.

Blumstein, S. (1973). "A Phonological Investigation of Aphasic Speech." Mouton, The Hague.

Butterworth, B. (1979). Hesitation and the production of verbal paraphasias and neologisms in jargon aphasia. *Brain and Language* (in press).

Caramazza, A. and Berndt, R. S. (1978). Semantic and syntactic processes in aphasia: a review of the literature. *Psychological Bulletin.*

Caramazza, A. and Zurif, E. B. (1976). Dissociation of algorithmic and heuristic processes in language comprehension: evidence from aphasia. *Brain and Language* 3, 572–582.

Chafe, W. L. (1970). "Meaning and the Structure of Language." University of Chicago Press, Chicago.

de Villiers, J. G. (1974). Quantitative aspects of agrammatism in aphasia. *Cortex*, **10**, 36–54.

Fillenbaum, S., Jones, L. V. and Wepman, J. M. (1961). Some linguistic features of speech from aphasic patients. *Language and Speech*, **4**, 91–108.

Fillmore, C. J. (1968). The case for case. *In* "Universals in Linguistic Theory". (E. Bach and R. T. Harms, eds). Holt, Rinehart and Winston.

Fodor, J. A., Bever, T. G. and Garrett, M. F. (1974). "The Psychology of Language." McGraw Hill, New York.

Fromkin, V. (1971). The non-anomalous nature of anomalous utterances. *Language*, **47**, 27–52.

Garrett, M. F. (1975). The analysis of sentence production. *In* "The Psychology of Learning and Motivation". (G. H. Bower, ed.). Academic Press, New York.

Gleason, J. B., Goodglass, H., Green, E., Ackerman, N. and Hyde, M. (1975). The retrieval of syntax in Broca's aphasia. *Brain and Language*, **2**, 451–471.

Goodglass, H. (1968). Studies on the grammar of aphascis. *In* "Developments in Applied Psycholinguistic Research". (S. Rosenberg and J. Koplin, eds). MacMillan, New York.

Goodglass, H. (1976). Agrammatism. *In* "Studies in Neurolinguistics". (H. Whitaker and H. A. Whitaker eds). Academic Press, New York.

Goodglass, H. and Baker, E. (1976). Semantic field, naming and auditory comprehension in aphasia. *Brain and Language*, **3**, 359–374.

Goodglass, H. and Berko, J. (1960) Aphasia and inflectional morphology in English. *Journal of Speech and Hearing Research*, **3**, 257–267.

Goodglass, H. and Geschwind, N. (1976). Language disorders (aphasia). *In* "Handbook of Perception". Vol. 7. (E. C. Carterette and M. Friedman, eds). Academic Press, New York.

Goodglass, H., Gleason, J. B., Bernholtz, N. A. and Hyde, M. R. (1972). Some linguistic structures in the speech of a Broca's aphasic. *Cortex*, **8**, 191–212.

Goodglass, H. and Hunt, J. (1958). Grammatical complexity and aphasic speech. *Word*, **14**, 197–207.

Goodglass, H., Hyde, M. R. and Blumstein, S. (1969). Frequency, picturability, and availability of nouns in aphasia. *Cortex*, **2**, 74–89.

Isserlin, M. (1922). Über Agrammatismus. *Zeitschrift fur die Gesamte Neurologie und Psychiatrie*, **75**, 332–410.

Jackson, J. H. (1878). On affections of speech from disease of the brain. *Brain*, **1**, 304–330.

Jakobson, R. (1964). Towards a linguistic typology of aphasic impairments. *In* "CIBA Foundation Symposium on Disorders of Language". (A. V. S. de Reuck and M. O'Connor. eds). Churchill, London.

Jenkins, J. J. and Shaw, R. E. (1975). On the interrelatedness of speech and language. *In* "The Role of Speech in Language". (J. F. Kavanaugh and J. E. Cutting, eds). M.I.T. Press, Cambridge, Mass.

Johns, D. F. and LaPointe, L. L. (1976). Neurogenic disorders of output processing: apraxia of speech. *In* "Studies in Neurolinguistics", vol. 1. (H. Whitaker and H. A. Whitaker, eds). Academic Press, New York.

Kean, M. L. (1977). The linguistic interpretation of aphasic syndromes: agrammatism in Broca's aphasia, an example. *Cognition*, **5**, 9–46.

Lenneberg, E. (1973). The neurology of language. *Daedalus*, **102**, 115–133.

Lesser, R. (1974). Verbal comprehension in aphasia: an English version of three Italian tests. *Cortex*, **10**, 247–263.

Luria, A. R. (1966). "Higher Cortical Functions in Man." Basic Books, New York.

Luria, A. R. (1970). "Traumatic Aphasia." Mouton, The Hague.

Luria, A. R. (1973). Towards the mechanisms of naming disturbance. *Neuropsychologia*, **4**, 417–422.

Marin, O. S. M., Saffran, E. M. and Schwartz, M. F. (1976). Dissociations of language in aphasia: Implications for normal function. *Annals of the New York Academy of Sciences*, **280**, 868–884.

Marshall, J. C. (1977). Disorders in the expression of language. *In* "Psycholinguistics Series 1: Developmental and Pathological". (J. Morton and J. C. Marshall, eds). Elek Science, London.

Marshall, J. C. and Newcombe, F. (1973). Patterns of paralexia: a psycholinguistic approach. *Journal of Psycholinguistic Research*, **2**, 175–199.

Myerson, R. and Goodglass, H. (1972). Transformational grammars of three agrammatic patients. *Language and Speech*, **15**, 40–50.

Osgood, C. E. and Bock, J. K. (1977). Salience and sentencing: some production principles. *In* "Sentence Production: Developments in Research and Theory". (S. Rosenberg, ed.). Erlbaum, Hillsdale, N.J.

Parisi, D. and Pizzamiglio, L. (1970). Syntactic comprehension in aphasia. *Cortex*, **6**, 204–215.

Pick, A. (1913). "Die agrammatischen Sprach Storungen." Berlin: Springer-Verlag.

Saffran, E. M. and Marin, O. S. M. (1977). Reading without phonology: Evidence from aphasia. *Quarterly Journal of experimental Psychology*, **29**, 515–525.

Saffran, E. M., Schwartz, M. F. and Marin, O. S. M. (1976). Semantic mechanisms in paralexia. *Brain and Language*, **3**, 255–265.

Saffran, E. M., Schwartz, M. F. and Marin, O. S. M. (1977). Semantic factors in agrammatic speech production. Paper presented to the International Neuropsychology Society European Conference, Oxford, England, August, 1977.

Schlesinger, I. M. (1977). "Production and Comprehension of Utterances." Erlbaum, Hillsdale, N.J.

Scholes, R. (1978). Syntactic and lexical components of sentence comprehension. *In* "The Acquisition and Breakdown of Language: Parallels and Divergencies". (A. Caramazza and E. Zurif, eds). Johns Hopkins Press, Baltimore.

Schwartz, M. F., Marin, O. S. M. and Saffran, E. M. (1979). Dissociations of language function in dementia: A case study. *Brain and Language*, **7**, 277–306.

Schwartz, M. F., Saffran, E. M. and Marin, O. S. M. (1978). The nature of the comprehension deficit in agrammatic aphasia. Paper presented to the Sixth Annual Meeting of the International Neuropsychology Society, Minneapolis, February, 1978.

Shankweiler, D. and Harris, K. S. (1966). An experimental approach to the problem of articulation in aphasia. *Cortex*, **2**, 277–292.

von Stockert, T. (1972). Recognition of syntactic structure in aphasic patients. *Cortex*, **8**, 323–334.

Warrington, E. K. (1975). The selective impairment of semantic memory. *Quarterly Journal of experimental Psychology*, **27**, 635–657.

Whitaker, H. (1976). A case of isolation of the language function. *In* "Studies in Neurolinguistics", vol. 2. (H. Whitaker and H. A. Whitaker, eds). Academic Press, New York.

III

Prosody, Phonology and Phonetics

10

The Production of Prosody[1]

A. Cutler and S. D. Isard *University of Sussex*

I. Introduction

Prosody is the sauce of the sentence—it adds to, enhances or subtly changes the flavour of the original. And like a good sauce, the realization of a sentence's prosodic structure is a blend of different ingredients none of which can be separately identified in the final product. Thus it is rarely possible to say: syllable A is longer than syllable B simply and solely because syllable A bears lexical stress and syllable B does not; or: this particular fall in pitch is due exclusively to the presence of a clause boundary.

Accordingly, we will not attempt in this paper to describe separately the determinants of each component of the suprasegmental pattern i.e. the specific factors which lead to durational variation, pitch changes and variations in amplitude. Rather, we will concentrate on what we hold to be the major sources of prosodic effects, which can be grouped into four main categories: lexical stress patterns of individual words; the placement of sentence accent; syntactic structure; and a variety of pragmatic factors such as choice of speech act and attitudinal indicators, which influence the overall shape of the intonation contour.

We shall not attempt to relate the influence of these sources directly to numbers of milliseconds or precise changes in pitch. Instead we will try to describe their effect at an abstract prosodic level, whose units can then be realized as specific pitches and durations, rather in the way that the abstract phonological level is realized in surface phonetic form.

To describe the units of the abstract prosodic level, we shall draw on terminology that is more or less common among British writers on the subject. In particular we shall speak of "tone groups", intonational units realized as a major pitch movement, possibly preceded by a preparatory run-up and followed by a subsequent tailing off. Halliday (1967), Crystal (1975), and O'Connor and Arnold (1961) give classifications of the major pitch movements and of the run-ups and aftermaths that can go with each.

There are three main decisions that must be taken with respect to the tone-group structure of a sentence:

---

[1] We are very grateful for discussions with our colleagues Tony Ades, Chris Darwin, Phil Johnson-Laird and Christopher Longuet-Higgins. Anne Cutler acknowledges the support of a grant from the Science Research Council.

(i) Where the tone group boundaries will fall,

(ii) Which syllable within a tone group will have the major pitch movement associated with it,

(iii) What the major pitch movement will be.

(i) is determined largely by the syntactic structure of the sentence. One tone group per clause seems to be a sort of neutral, default case (see Halliday (1967) and Crystal (1975)).

(ii) is primarily influenced by placement of accent, while

(iii) is largely the product of pragmatic factors. It is possible, however, for the three sorts of influence to poach on one another's territory, as when the decision to emphasize two words in a single clause forces the clause to take two tone groups, or when the syntactic structure of a compound noun phrase dictates which syllable to accent in order to emphasize the noun phrase as a whole.

Consider, by way of illustration, the "that one sank" clause of (1)–(3) below.

(1)   (My first boat blew up, and so I bought another and) that one *sank*.

(2)   (I had a boat, but it sank, and so I bought another and) *that* one sank.

(3)   (A: You mean your old boat sank? B: No, I bought another boat and) *that* one *sank*.

In (1) and (2) the clauses are covered by a single tone group. Placement of emphasis dictates that the major pitch movements occur on "sank" and "that" respectively. The type of pitch movement in both cases is a fall, appropriate to a simple contrast between the accented item and the corresponding item in the previous clause.

In (3) the choice to emphasize both "that" and "sank" leads to a two tone group clause. Again the contrasted item "that" is given a fall in pitch, but "sank", which is carried over from the question, and in a sense provides the setting within which "that" is contrasted, is given a pitch contour which first falls and then rises.

A fourth decision which we want to place at the abstract prosodic level is one which ultimately determines the lengths of the phonetic components which make up the utterance. Some writers, e.g. Klatt (1975) and Cooper (this volume), take the position that segmental durations such as vowel lengths are determined directly on the basis of syntax and the intrinsic nature of the phoneme concerned. Others, notably Abercrombie (1965), Halliday (1967) and Lehiste (1977) prefer to divide the utterance into "feet", stretching from one stressed syllable to the next. According to this scheme, the feet are assigned target lengths, which are shared out among the syllables composing the feet and then among the phonemes composing the syllables. Witten (1977) suggests one algorithm for achieving the sorts of feet discussed by Abercrombie (1965).

We shall take this second approach, and in particular we shall discuss the influence of syntactic structure on the placing of foot boundaries, rather than directly upon phoneme lengths.

It would, of course, be desirable to display a detailed model of the way in which all of these decisions are taken. Unfortunately, if not surprisingly, we are not in a position to attempt such a feat. We do, however, have certain remarks to make about the role of each of the factors mentioned above and we shall devote one of the four following sections to each.

II. Lexical Stress

At some point during the sentence production process the words which will be uttered are looked up in the mental lexicon—that is to say, the appropriate phonological realization of each semantically specified unit is located. In each polysyllabic word one syllable is marked for heavier stress than the other(s), and the eventual phonological instantiation of the word will include this stress marking. There are several acoustic consequences of lexical stress: the stressed syllable can be longer in relative duration than the unstressed syllables, and may also be spoken with greater physical intensity. If sentence accent falls on a polysyllabic word, it is on the stressed syllable that the pitch movement associated with accent will be realized. The vowels in unstressed syllables may reduce to /ə/. Lehiste (1970) describes these effects in detail.

There is evidence that words are listed in the mental lexicon in a phonological form more abstract than the surface phonetic form. This evidence comes largely from the study of speech errors, particularly the classic work of Fromkin (1971, 1973). She observes, for instance, that consonant clusters involving the nasal [ŋ] and a stop may split into [n] plus stop, as in (4):

(4)   The ban will pake 5·6% interest
      (Target: The bank will pay . . .)

This suggests that underlying the surface form of bank [bæŋk] is a more abstract form with the final cluster /nk/. Fromkin also observes that velar nasals may themselves split into two segments, [n] and [g]:

(5)   swin and swaig
      (Target: swing and sway)

which again suggests the psychological reality in speech production of an abstract /ng/ underlying [ŋ]. Many phonologists, notably Chomsky and Halle (1968), have argued that [ŋ] is in fact derived from such an underlying form.

Further support comes from a study of semantically unrelated word substitution errors, or malapropisms, by Fay and Cutler (1977). In this study the target (word which was intended) and error (word which was uttered) pairs were found to be very similar in sound, particularly in their initial segments. It was hypothesized that malapropisms arise when the speech production device picks from the mental lexicon, instead of the word it is seeking, one of that word's near neighbours; close neighbours in the lexicon are very similar in sound because the lexicon is primarily arranged by phonological similarity. At the point (counting from left to right) at which a particular target and error departed from identity, the two words were in general very similar in distinctive feature marking, which Fay and Cutler took as a suggestion that "phonological similarity" in the mental lexicon is defined in terms of distinctive features.

There were however some exceptions to this generalization, and among these was a group of errors in which at the point of departure from identity one of the two words contained a vowel whereas the other contained the glide [y], e.g. *movie* (Target: *music*), *genuine* (Target: *general*), *musicians* (Target: *magicians*). Chomsky and Halle (1968) argue that such words as *music* do not contain the segment /y/ in their underlying representation, but that it is inserted by rule into the surface form. Fay and Cutler pointed out that a comparison between the underlying representations of such pairs would involve the distinctive feature difference between two vowels rather than between a vowel and a glide and hence would result in more similar feature marking which in turn would reduce the discrepancy between this small group of errors and the major body of the malapropism corpus.

If we assume a mental lexicon in which the phonological representations of the listed words are in a form more abstract than the surface form, then a question arises as to the representation of lexical stress patterns. Chomsky and Halle (1968) have formulated rules which derive the surface stress patterns of English words. The analogous rules which derive the surface phonetic form of a word from an underlying abstract form appear to be actively involved in the speech production process; is lexical stress also determined mechanically by rule in production?

The alternative to application of the stress rules in production is a listing, in the mental lexicon, of the appropriate stress marking as a part of the phonological representation of each word.

Evidence from speech errors involving erroneous placement of lexical stress appears to support the latter proposal. Typical lexical stress errors include (6)–(9):

(6) Now the paradigm involves présenting—presénting . . .
(7) I've got my book so we don't have any conflícts.
     (Target: cónflicts)
(8) Everyone knows that economists—that ecónomists . . .
(9) I need the number of the Psychól—Psychológical Corporation.

In (6), the verb *present* has mistakenly been stressed on the first syllable, i.e. has the stress pattern of the noun *present*; in (7) the reverse is the case: *conflict* (N) has been stressed as if it were *conflict* (V); in (8) *economists* bears stress on the third syllable, suggesting the adjective *economic(al)*; in (9) the stress has moved from the third to the second syllable, which is where it falls in *psychologist* and *psychology*.

These correspondences are not atypical; all lexical stress errors exhibit them. The erroneously produced stress pattern is always that of another word (thus no such errors as *administrative* are observed); and this word is always morphologically related to the intended word. As a consequence of this, lexical stress errors only ever occur in morphologically complex, or derived, words (thus an error such as *window* does not occur). A more extensive analysis of this type of error may be found in Cutler (1979); see also Fromkin (1977).

It will be argued that these errors arise as a result of confusion between two differently stressed forms in the mental lexicon and that they provide evidence for the inclusion of stress marking in the lexical entry. Alternative explanations are unable to account for the regularities which these errors exhibit. Thus the suggestion that they are blends between two alternative candidates for utterance founders on the observation that all known types of blends involve two words of the same grammatical category (or two equivalent constituents) whereas lexical stress errors always involve two words of different grammatical categories. The possibility that they might result from simple exchange or shift of stress features cannot in any way account for the failure of non-derived words to show such errors or for the constraint that the errors always give the stress pattern of a morphological relative of the intended word. The same is true of the proposal that misplaced lexical stress is a consequence of confusion between words at the articulatory program level. And, importantly, it is also the case that misapplication of stress rules could not account for these regularities; the stress rules apply to derived and nonderived words alike, and it is unclear why errors should occur in one instance but not in the other, and unclear why misapplied rules should always assign stress to a syllable which does bear it in some related word.

An explanation which accounts for all the features shown by lexical stress errors is the following: words derived from a common base are stored together in a single lexical entry, with, inter alia, each word's stress pattern being specified as part of its representation. Lexical stress errors arise as a result of confusion within the lexical entry—the stress pattern selected is not that of the intended word but of some other member of the entry. Thus the pattern is always that of a related word since the error occurs within the common lexical entry; and stress errors only ever appear in derived words because only derived words share a lexical entry with other words—non-derived words have private lexical entries.

Thus the characteristics of lexical stress errors argue against the mechanical application of stress assignment rules as part of the speech production process. A question which is not however resolved by the available data is whether the specification of stress internal to the lexical entry is in terms of stress features marked for each syllable, or whether the appropriate rule for each word is appended to its phonological representation. These two proposals may in fact be indistinguishable with respect to their realization in the type of lexical stress error which occurs. However, it is not clear that application of the stress rule appropriate for, say, an adjective to a noun derived from the same base might actually lead to the stress falling on that syllable which bears it in the adjective. The Chomsky-Halle stress rules invoke as a major determinant of lexical stress the number of syllables in the word as well as such factors as the phonemes which terminate the word, i.e. whether the word ends with a vowel, a consonant or a consonant cluster. Related nouns and verbs and adjectives very often differ on exactly these characteristics, the exception being such noun-verb pairs as *object, conflict* etc. If only pairs of this latter type were involved in lexical stress errors, we might have no basis for feeling that the specification of the appropriate stress *rule* as part of the lexical entry was a less satisfactory description than the specification of the stress *features*. However, most of the lexical stress errors involve word pairs with different endings and different number of syllables (e.g. examples (8) and (9) above). In these cases it is at least a reasonable supposition that the rules would not, when applied to, for example, the shorter form, result in stress falling on that syllable which bears it in the longer word. These considerations are by no means conclusive, but they suffice to render preferable to us an account of stress specification in the lexical entry which includes the actual listing of the stress marking, or stress features, for each syllable.

It may be felt that our conclusion that stress is listed in the lexicon and *not* determined by mechanical application of stress assignment rules is in conflict with recent linguistic evidence concerning the psychological reality of these rules. Nessly (1974), for example, has shown that English speakers can, with great reliability, decide upon the appropriate pronunciation (including stress pattern) of invented "words" which they have never seen before, and that the stress patterns they choose are in accord with English stress assignment rules. This, not in itself surprising, finding indicates that native speakers at some level know the principles upon which lexical stress assignment in their language functions. But "psychological reality" of stress assignment rules does not imply at all that the rules are applied every time a polysyllabic word is uttered. Nor is it necessarily "inefficient" or "uneconomical" to postulate a system which includes both knowledge of the rules and stress marking of individual words. Computational efficiency, to which end the system is presumably designed, involves a trade-off between the speed with which operations can be performed on the one hand, and the size of the system, i.e. the storage space it takes up, on the other. Thus it is not unreasonable to suppose that the gain in speed of operation resulting from stress specification within the lexical entry is sufficient to justify any increase in storage demands which result from it. The internalized stress rules are as a consequence made redundant in normal production, but cannot be jettisoned since they are needed to cope with new words, names, or nonsense, i.e. with any item which does not already have an entry in the mental lexicon.

III. Accent

Just as within a polysyllabic word one syllable has greater prominence than the others, so within an utterance of more than one word greater prominence is given to one word than to others. The syllable on which sentence accent falls is the syllable which bears the lexical stress of the accented word, so there is a sense in which we can think of lexical stress as embodying the potential for sentence accent. In this section we will consider the way in which the placement of sentence accent is determined during the production of a sentence.

Perhaps the simplest proposal (for implementation in a production model) is that accent placement is a function of syntactic structure. This, in skeleton form, is the claim made by Chomsky and Halle (1968), and by others, for example Bresnan (1971). It is not important for the present discussion to describe in detail the rules which they propose for accent placement. Two facts about such systems, however, are very important. The first is that accent placement by rule is determined with reference to syntactic structure alone, i.e. without reference to semantic or pragmatic considerations. The second point follows from the first; it is clear that syntactically driven rules will apply only one accent pattern to a particular syntactic structure, but it is immediately obvious that for any sentence there are many options for accent placement. Any of the seven words in (10) for instance, *could* bear the primary sentence accent:

(10)   They don't grow bananas in Northern England.

Thus it is a necessary characteristic of systems such as that of Chomsky and Halle that they claim that each sentence has a "normal" or "neutral" accent placement, i.e. the placement which is determined by the syntactically driven rules. Alternative placements are all special cases—in the Chomsky/Halle system non-neutral accent placement is described as expressing *contrast* on the accented word with another word, or constituent, in the sentence, in another sentence, or implied by the context.

Appealingly simple as the syntactic proposal is, it does not appear appropriate to incorporate it in a speech production model. Rules such as Chomsky and Halle's constitute a procedure taking only syntactic information as input to produce an accent pattern. It is not clear how, or whether, the rules can be integrated into a larger system that takes semantic and pragmatic factors into account.

Furthermore, considerable linguistic effort has recently been devoted to demonstrating that a syntactic model does not correctly describe the placement of sentence accent in neutral cases. In the vanguard of the attack have been Bolinger (e.g. 1972) and Schmerling (1974, 1976). Criticism has been directed at both of the above-mentioned aspects of the Chomsky-Halle position, namely that accent placement can be determined by syntax alone, and that each sentence has one "neutral" accent pattern.

Schmerling (1976) provides a compelling illustration that for even a very simple two-word sentence the accent placement is determined by contextual factors. In the year in which two ex-presidents of the United States died, Schmerling reports, she was informed of their respective deaths in an interestingly different manner. Harry S. Truman died after a long illness which was extensively reported in the media, and Schmerling was informed of his death in the following words:

(11)   Truman diéd.

Lyndon Johnson, on the other hand, died of a sudden heart attack; Schmerling heard of this as follows:

(12)   Jóhnson died.

Schmerling is undoubtedly correct in her claim that the differing accent placement in these two sentence resulted from the differing contexts. Truman was known to be sick; the new information in (11) concerns his death, so the verb is accented. In (12) the new information is that something happened to Johnson, to whom nothing in particular was expected to happen.

Another telling counter-example to the syntactic determination of accent was provided by Ladd (1978). It was first pointed out by Newman (1946) that the class of sentences of the type of (13)

(13)   I have plans to write

customarily takes sentence accent on the noun when the noun is the direct object of the verb ("I must write plans"), but on the final verb when that verb is a complement to the noun ("I plan to write"). Ladd (1978)†, however, devised contexts for a version of this construction in which the syntactic factors determining accent placement were completely over-ridden by contextual factors. These examples are worth quoting in full. In (14) the verb-as-complement reading is appropriate despite accent on the noun:

(14)   a. George had no idea he was supposed to follow Helen.
        b. Whaddya mean—Helen left diréctions for George to follow!

and in (15) the noun-as-direct-object reading is appropriate even though accent falls on the verb:

(15)   a. George feels pretty bad about ruining dinner, but the package had no directions.
        b. Gee—didn't you look over on the counter by the toaster? Helen left directions for George to fóllow!
        (Ladd, 1978: pp. 138–139)

Likewise, many counter-examples have been offered to the normal/contrastive distinction. It has been observed that certain sentences appear to have only a "contrastive" accent pattern and no "normal" pattern:

(16)   Even a chíld can build it!

Speakers unanimously place the accent in (16) on "child", although the Chomsky-Halle sentence accent rules would deem that a contrastive rather than the normal placement for this sentence.

Similarly, many emphatic accent placements do not appear to contrast with anything; it seems far-fetched to claim that (17) expresses a contrast with, for example, (18):

(17)   There's nó way I'm going to go along with that!
(18)   *There's sóme way I'm going to go along with that!

Furthermore, it is often the case that accent is assigned to a word for no other reason than to avoid placing it on some other word. Consider the (b) sentences in (19) and (20) below:

(19)   a. John's gone to North Dakota to study the mating habits of the native linguist.
        b. But there aren't any linguists ín North Dakota!
(20)   a. I'd hate to be a dentist.
        b. Me too—I'm sure glad there are people who want to bé dentists.
        (from Ladd, 1978)

†Counter-examples were also provided by Bolinger (1958, 1972) and by Berman and Szamosi (1972).

It is clear that the accenting of *in* and *be* respectively does not arise from a contrast with another preposition or another verb, but from the fact that the words which might otherwise have been accented have been used in the previous utterance. Accenting them might therefore give an impression of redundancy. Thus the accent has been moved away from the repeated words, and has ended up on words which do not themselves in this instance have any reason for claiming prominence. In other words, the accent pattern results not from *accenting* of the emphasized word but from *de-accenting* of others. An excellent discussion of the phenomenon of deaccenting is given by Ladd (1978). Some recent examples from the authors' own experience are (21) and (22):

(21) I didn't read any newspapers all the time I was writing my Ph.D.—but that was because I was in Austin, Texas, where there aren't any newspapers tó read.

(22) If you'd like to gather tó the little bath we'll look at that next.

(22) was spoken by a tour-guide giving a commentary on a series of Roman baths. The "little bath" itself had not been previously mentioned; many other baths had been. In fact it is not necessary for a de-accented word to have actually occurred in the preceding context; it can be implied by it:

(23) a. Where'll we have dinner—the Dim Symptom?
      b. Shirley won't eát Chinese food.

Conversely, de-accenting can be precipitated by preceding use of the de-accented word in a different sense:

(24) He's so sharp he's even cálled Sharp.†

Sometimes de-accenting can lead to an accent pattern which could in a different context have resulted from accenting, or emphasis;‡ compare, for example, the indignant utterance (26) as spoken by an adult in reply to (27) or by a child in reply to (28):

(26) I was reáding the book!

(27) I put away that book and the other stuff on the table.

(28) Did oo have fun playing with the bookie-wookie?

In the former instance the accent on *reading* results from de-accenting of *book*, in the latter it results from focus on new information, since the act of reading has not, in (28), been taken for granted as what one does with books.

We will not attempt to develop here an original and detailed case in favour of the determination of sentence accent by semantic and pragmatic (contextual) factors rather than by syntax; for the complete arguments we refer the reader to the authors we have cited. We would however like to utter a cautionary word or two. The arguments against the syntactic position have often amounted to outright rejection of its concepts. Thus Schmerling (1974) claims that the notion of "neutral" accent is quite useless; any accent placement embodies presuppositions about the discourse context. Ladd (1978) argues that there is no such thing as contrastive accent—only

---

† Note that there are limits to the indirectness:

(25) * She's so sharp she's even cálled Cutler.

‡ A nice example of this is given by Ladd (1978; p. 117).

differences in focus as a result of reference to various aspects of the context. We believe that both of these rejections are a little too sweeping. Let us take first the case of contrastive accent. It should be obvious from the above discussion that we agree with Ladd and other critics of the syntactic position that "contrastive" is not an appropriate catchall term for any semantically placed accent. Nevertheless, that contrast exists apart from focus can be demonstrated by manoeuvering it into a sentence along with focus. Thus in (29b), several words are focussed; some of them are contrastively accented, some not.

(29) a. London's the capital of Scotland, isn't it?
      b. No, Edinburgh's the capital of Scotland, London's the capital of England.†

The *kind* of accent which falls on those words which occurred in (29a) (London, Scotland) differs from the kind of accent falling on the words expressing new information (Edinburgh, England). The former bear a fall-rise accent, the latter a simple falling accent (see our discussion of examples (1)–(3) in the introduction to this paper). All four words are accented, or, in Ladd's terms, focussed; but those which also express a contrast have a falling accent, those which don't express contrast bear a fall-rise. (The types of accent are of course reversed if (29b) serves as an answer to:

(30) Edinburgh's the capital of England, isn't it?)

That is to say, when several items in a sentence are focussed, those which are contrasted can be distinguished intonationally from those which are not; the accentual system is richer than would appear from a description, for example Ladd's, which seeks to subsume contrast under the general rubric of focus.

Now let us consider the possibility of a role for "neutral" accent placement. In some sentences semantic and pragmatic reasons do not pick out a particular word for sentence accent. In (31), for example, a contrast is drawn between two constituents as wholes:

(31) I was not surprised to hear Susan was mad about old móvies, but that she didn't like Chinese foód surprised me.

Movies and *food* are accented not because they are contrasted with other particular items (e.g. *clothes*, *men*), but simply because they are in each case the rightmost items in the constituent; they bear accent on behalf of their constituents, so to speak.

This kind of default accent is, we believe, the one sense in which the notion of neutral accent can be justified. The way in which accent is placed in the default case was formulated in detail by Newman (1946); as re-stated by Schmerling (1976) the principle is:

(32) Given a sequence of stresses which are equal and greater than other stresses within the intonational unit, the last such stress will be more prominent than the others.

(By "intonational unit" Newman referred to what we have called "tone group".)

---

†We are grateful to Christopher Longuet-Higgins for this example. More detailed remarks on contrast can be found in Isard (1978).

The principle can be seen in operation in a sentence such as (33), from Chomsky (1971) and Jackendoff (1972):

(33)   Was he warned to look out for an ex-convict in a red shirt?

The accent on *shirt* might represent contrast with some other word, in which case (34) might be a good reply, or simply accent on the constituent as a whole, in which case any of (35)–(37) would be acceptable:

(34)   No, an ex-convict in a red hát.
(35)   No, an automobíle salesman.
(36)   No, an ex-convict in a dínner suit.
(37)   No, the FBÍ.

Shifting the accent in (33) to, for example, "red" or to "convict", renders it no longer neutral, and (35)–(37) no longer appropriate replies.

Ladd (1978) gives a comprehensive account of default accent, which he describes as focus on the entire constituent. We would prefer to shift the emphasis slightly and call it focus on *what* the constituent *denotes*, rather than, for instance, on *how* it denotes it. In (31), for example, although *movies* and *food* are not contrasted with other comparable words, there *is* a contrast which is being drawn, namely between that attribute of Susan's which did not surprise the speaker and the other attribute which did. The hearer is intended to appreciate this contrast without paying particular attention to any of the individual words in each embedded sentence. So the speaker accents the embedded sentences, using however the neutral or default accent.

A complete account of sentence accent placement, therefore, includes neutral accent (in a minority of cases rather than the majority which syntactically motivated accent rules would claim to account for). It also includes contrast, and focus, as well as accentuation of a particular word achieved by de-accenting some other word. We will shortly discuss the order in which these various factors exercise their effects in sentence production. First, however, we will round out the picture we have given of above-word-level stress with a few remarks on compound stress.

"Bláckbird" expresses a meaning different from "blàck bírd" and "Énglish professor" from "Ènglish proféssor". The former of each pair, more heavily stressed on the initial element, is a compound noun. Others, for example Chomsky and Halle (1968), have given thorough accounts of compound stress patterns. What is important for our present discussion is that compounds act as a unit in the competition for accent. However complex a compound, whether the initial element is for instance itself a compound, as in (38), or is an Adj-N sequence, as in (39), the compound as a whole has one and only one most prominent syllable:

(38)   Chémistry research laboratory.
(39)   Indo-European sýntax text.

When the neutral or default accent falls on a compound as the rightmost element of a constituent, then, it accents that syllable which is the most prominent in the compound (just as accent falling on a word is realized in that syllable which bears lexical stress). Thus the (a) sentences of (40) and (41) bear a possible neutral accent; the (b) sentences are acceptable replies.

(40) a. Was he working at a chémistry research laboratory?
      b. No, at a garbage dump.
(41) a. Did you buy an Indo-European sýntax text?
      b. No, a flowerpot.

Compound stress is determined at an early level in the production process, prior to the placement of sentence accent. Some compounds (e.g. *blackbird*) are presumably lexicalized, and their stress patterns would accordingly be retrieved along with their phonemic specification from the mental lexicon. Others would be constructed when the search for a lexical unit to express a complex meaning (e.g. "Indo-European syntax text") failed to come up with an entry (e.g. "Lehmann"), and various components of the complex meaning had to be separately retrieved and combined to form it. By the time accent placement operates, in any event, compound nouns enter into the calculation essentially as single words.

Thus the sentence production operation which determines which of all the syllables in a sentence will be the most prominent is carried out on a string of words which (a) if polysyllabic have their stressed syllable marked, and (b) are grouped if appropriate into compounds with the most prominent syllable in the compound marked. Semantic and pragmatic factors then determine accent placement to express focus, contrast or deaccentuation (we know of no evidence that these are separate, ordered operations).

It is interesting to note that the semantic/pragmatic factors can over-ride the earlier assignments of syllable prominence. For instance it is quite possible to pick out a single component of a compound for contrast:

(42) No, of course I didn't say Indo-Germánic syntax text, I said Indo-Európean syntax text.

This is hardly surprising, since contrast can even over-ride lexical stress, as in the well-known example:

(43) This whisky wasn't éxported, it was déported.

Similarly, de-accenting can also result in accent falling on some other syllable in a compound than the usually stressed one; the stress shifts (possibly by the operation of some form of the default principle) to the rightmost nearest word, i.e. to the next word to the right, e.g. (44), or to the next to the left if nothing not de-accented remains on the right, e.g. (45):

(44) I thought you said you knew nothing at all about syntax—so how come you've got an Indo-European syntax téxt?
(45) I thought you said you owned no syntax texts at all—that there's an Indo-Európean syntax text.

The only remaining component of the accent assignment operations is the neutral or default accent which applies last of all, and indeed only applies if the semantically motivated accent placement has left something for it to apply to—a string of words marked for focus or contrast as a whole but containing within it several equally prominent lexical (or compound) stresses. The default principle makes the rightmost of these most prominent and the operation of accent placement is therewith complete.

Correct description of the determination of sentence accent, we have seen, is not a simple matter; it incorporates reference not only to the semantics of the message, but also to the structure of the sentence and the discourse context. The language production model, therefore, must also allow for these differing inputs when accounting for accent placement.

IV. Isochrony and syntactic boundaries

Pike (1945) makes a distinction between what he calls syllable-timed languages, in which each syllable is of roughly equal length, and stress-timed languages, in which stressed syllables occur at roughly equal intervals. French is supposed to be an example of the former sort of language, and English of the latter. It is important to note that the stressed syllables in question here are not necessarily accented, but are generally just the syllables marked for stress in the lexicon. Syllables not so marked are also stressed for these purposes if they do receive accent (e.g. "no linguists iń North Dakota"). The intervals from one stressed syllable to the next are termed feet.

Attempts to find isochronous (equally timed) feet by measuring wave forms of English speech have generally failed. A "tendency toward isochrony" is sometimes detected in studies where an extra unstressed syllable is inserted between two stressed syllables, and although the duration between the stressed syllables does go up, it goes up by less than the length of the extra syllable, the other syllables having been compressed to make up for its presence (Huggins, 1975; Fowler, 1977). As Fowler notes, this phenomenon may indicate that the speaker is trying to make the next beat occur as close as possible to "the right time", but it is not in itself evidence that the "right times" are evenly spaced.

Abercrombie (1965) explains some of the wider deviations from isochrony by positing "silent stresses", which are essentially skipped beats. He points out, among other things, that such silent stresses also occur in verse, where the existence of the regular beats themselves is less controversial. He cites

My / sire / ˆ is of a / noble / line /

from Coleridge's "Christabel", as well as

To / be or / not to be / ˆ / that is the / question.

Some may find even more compelling the extra, silent, beats that he postulates at the ends of the first two lines of the limerick form, as in

There / was a young / man from Cape / Horn / ˆ

Who / wished that he'd / never been / born / ˆ

Lehiste (1977) reviews the isochrony literature and comes to the conclusion that isochrony is at least in part a perceptual phenomenon. That is, we hear the times between stressed syllables as being more nearly equal than they really are. This conclusion is supported by recent work of Donovan and Darwin (1979).

Donovan and Darwin present subjects with sentences all of whose stressed syllables begin with the same phoneme, say /t/, as in

(46)   He turned up by ten talking of terrorism.

The subjects are then asked to adjust a series of clicks so as to make them occur with the same timing as the /t/s in the sentence. The subjects can hear the sentence and the clicks as often as they like, but they cannot hear them simultaneously. The subjects tend to space the clicks more evenly than the /t/s are spaced in the sentence, suggesting that they hear the /t/s to be spaced more evenly than they really are.

At this point we are faced with the possibility that hearers might simply impose an isochronous interpretation on anything that they take to be spoken English, and that even if there is a tendency toward isochrony in the physical signal, it is not necessary to the perception of isochrony. Lehiste (1977) rejects this idea on the grounds that differences in the length of interstress intervals can not only be perceived, but they can be used to convey linguistic distinctions. In particular, she claims that speakers use lengthened interstress intervals to mark syntactic boundaries, and that in order for this to be possible, speaker and hearer must both have some notion of an unlengthened interval to use as a standard.

Lehiste asked subjects to read aloud sentences in which ambiguous phrases like "old men and women" were embedded. The subjects were asked to read the sentence in two different ways, one in which the phrase was supposed to be grouped as "(old men) and women" and the other in which it was supposed to be grouped as "old (men and women)". Further groups of subjects listened to the sentences to make certain that they were perceived as intended.

When the length of the segment "men and women" was measured, it was found to be dramatically longer in the case where "(old men) and women" was the intended reading. Lehiste makes the proposal that this lengthened segment constitutes a deliberate disruption of isochrony, and that such disruptions are used to signal the presence of syntactic boundaries. "It is in this sense," she writes, "that isochrony is integrated into the grammar of English at the syntactic level" (Lehiste, 1977, p. 262).

Lehiste's theory still leaves us with a number of questions to consider. Perhaps the most immediate is whether it is possible to say anything further about the amount by which speakers will lengthen interstress intervals in order to achieve their purpose of marking syntactic boundaries. Will the amount of extra length be related to the length of a notional unlengthened interval in some systematic way, or will it perhaps increase in an otherwise unpredictable fashion with the "amount of emphasis" that the speaker wants to achieve? And if the relation is systematic, is it possible that the increased duration results not from a complete disruption of isochrony, but rather from "skipping a beat", so that the duration of longer intervals is twice that of shorter ones, but an underlying rhythm is maintained?

Such a possibility is at least consistent with data presented in Lehiste (1973), where subjects were asked to disambiguate sentences of the form "Steve or Sam and Bob will come". The distance between "Steve" and "Sam" was roughly twice as great in the case where the intended reading was "Steve or (Sam and Bob)", and similarly the distance between "Sam" and "Bob" was approximately twice as great when "(Steve or Sam) and Bob" was intended.

In her report of the study involving the "old men and women" examples, Lehiste gives only the comparative lengths for the entire segment "men and women", and not the lengths of individual feet. We have run a small study on a set of similar sentences and measured the lengths of the feet. The sentences used were

(47) I'm allergic to ripe marrows, melons and cucumbers.
(48) We bought expensive brandy, port and cigars.
(49) He sells used cars, bikes and trailers.

In Lehiste's sentences, the ambiguity to be resolved was whether the adjective, "old", applied to just one item, "men", or two, "men and women". We chose sentences where the adjective could apply to three items instead of just two, because we thought that in these cases we might detect a tendency to restore isochrony by lengthening all three items, and not just the first.

We asked each of five subjects to read each sentence in both possible ways, e.g. in the case of the first sentence to give one reading corresponding to "ripe (marrows, melons and cucumbers)" and another corresponding to "(ripe marrows), melons and cucumbers". We then measured two interstress intervals for each sentence: one from the vowel onset of the stressed syllable of the first listed item to the corresponding point in the second item, and then from there to the third listed item. In the case of the first sentence this means taking the time from the beginning of the first vowel of "marrows" to the beginning of the first vowel of "melons", and similarly from "melons" to "cucumbers". There are other proposals for the way in which interstress intervals should be measured (see, for example, Morton et al., 1976), but they would not give very different results for our purposes, and these measurements are relatively straightforward to make.

Measurements were made on digitized wave forms sampled at a rate of 8000 Hz on a PDP-12 computer. We used a wave form editing program written by C. J. Darwin which displays a wave form on a screen and allows one to insert pointers into the wave form. The distance between pointers can be measured to within 0·1 ms. Each measurement was performed twice, and discrepancies were well within 5 ms, so we feel reasonably confident in claiming accuracy to within 20 ms.

Our measurements showed that in the sentences where the adjective was meant to apply to all three nouns, e.g. "used (cars, bikes and trailers)", the subjects made the two feet we measured nearly equal. The average ratios of the first foot to the second foot in these sentences are shown in Table I.

When the subjects read the sentences with the other meaning intended, the first foot was considerably lengthened, as Lehiste's theory would predict. The average ratios of the lengthened first feet to the original first feet (e.g. "cars" in "(used cars), etc." to "cars" in "used (cars, etc.)") are given in Table II. The increase very nearly amounts to a doubling of the original length.

If we consider the ratios of first feet to second feet in the sentences where first feet are lengthened, the averages are again in the neighbourhood of 2 (see Table III). However these averages conceal what appear to be systematic differences among the individual subjects. For instance, one of the subjects

TABLE I

Mean ratio across subjects of first measured foot to second
measured foot when adjective was meant to apply to all nouns

Sentence 1	("ripe marrows, etc.")	0·885
Sentence 2	("expensive brandy, etc.")	1·004
Sentence 3	("used cars, etc.")	1·071

TABLE II

Mean ratio across subjects of first measured foot when adjective
was meant to apply to first noun only to same foot when
adjective was meant to apply to all nouns.

Sentence 1	("ripe marrows, etc.")	2·021
Sentence 2	("expensive brandy, etc.")	2·010
Sentence 3	("used cars, etc.")	1·974

TABLE III

Mean ratio across subjects of first measured foot to second
measured foot when adjective was meant to apply to first noun
only.

Sentence 1	("ripe marrows, etc.")	1·857
Sentence 2	("expensive brandy, etc.")	1·812
Sentence 3	("used cars, etc.")	1·724

Mel, had ratios of 2·126, 2·246, and 2·629, consistently above 2, while another, Derek, had ratios of 1·087, 1·355 and 0·856, much nearer to 1.

Our intuitive impression from listening to the tapes of the subjects' utterances is that there is a tradeoff between the use of comparatively longer first feet, and the use of intonation. That is, Derek's pitch changes were much more marked than Mel's.

If speakers of English do in fact make such a trade-off, it provides further justification for an abstract level of prosodic groupings, where different speakers would have in common the intention of marking off a syntactic unit by assigning it a grouping of its own, and would then diverge as to the way in which the presence of this grouping would be signalled, in one case by pitch movement and in another by adjusting the timing.

We can note in this connection that while Lehiste wants to use disruption of isochrony as a way of setting off syntactic units, Crystal (1975: pp. 16–21) suggests rules for doing the same job with intonation, adjusting the domains of pitch movements in order to show which words should be grouped together. Neither set of rules takes account of the phenomena on which the other is based. However, Halliday (1967) proposes that the tone group should be viewed both as an intonational unit, and as a rhythmic unit consisting of a number of feet. If we adopt this proposal, we can postulate that the syntactic units in question are given different tone groups, and then that the tone groups may be distinguished by pronounced intonation contours, or by a change of timing.

In Section III we rejected the notion that the syntactic component of sentence production generally determines accent placement. The syntactic component nevertheless exercises a considerable effect on the prosodic structure of the sentence by specifying the tone group divisions. This information may then be realized either as durational or as pitch variations.

V. Holistic Contours

At the Chicago Linguistic Society meeting in 1974 Mark Liberman and Ivan Sag produced an amusing demonstration that an intonation (fundamental frequency) contour could by itself convey a certain amount of meaning. The contour in question was the one borne, for example, by the incredulous reply (50b):

    (50)   a. I've got elephantiasis, I'm gonna die.

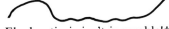

          b. Elephantiasis isn't incurable!†

In reply to the question:

    (51)   Ivan, would you mind dropping my pet whale off at the aquarium on your way to school today?

the contour alone was performed on the kazoo; it was clear to the audience that the reply was an indignant objection to the request. Liberman and Sag called this intonational pattern the "contradiction contour". In a subsequent paper (Sag and Liberman, 1975) they isolated other holistic contours which they also associated with particular meanings.

The notion that intonation contours have intrinsic meaning has been espoused by a number of linguists, and, indeed, has been postulated in a much stronger version than that claimed by Liberman and Sag. Pike (1945; p. 20), for instance, stated: "Many intonation contours are explicit in meaning. Whenever a certain sequence of relative pitches is heard, one concludes that the speaker means certain things over and above the specific meanings of the words themselves. A change of pitch contour will change the meaning of the sentence."

In this strong version, the contours-have-meaning claim poses some interesting possibilities for a language production model. It would be relatively simple to incorporate into such a model an intonational lexicon in which contours were paired with their fixed meanings, and to divide the meaning of an utterance into that part to be conveyed by the words and

†The drawn contour represents the variation of fundamental frequency against time (allowing for some inaccuracy due to the mismatch between acoustic duration and orthography) on a Kay SonaGraph spectrogram of the utterance.

another part to be conveyed by the intonation contour. This latter part could then be looked up in the intonational lexicon and the appropriate contour retrieved in the same way that looking up meanings in the word lexicon results in the phonetic forms of words being retrieved.

Once again, however, we find that an apparently simple and appealing model which seems to be suitable for incorporation into a production model turns out not to account for the prosodic facts. The problem is that for such a proposal to work the meanings assigned to the contours must be, to a certain extent at least, supra-contextual; for each contour there must be an element of common meaning (or, if the contour is ambiguous, a finite set of meanings) which can be observed in every instance of the contour in use. It can be demonstrated that this is not the case.

Liberman and Sag's "contradiction contour", for example, seems to express above all impatience in the following context:

(52)   Father (to son who has been ignoring a friend's attempt to attract attention from outside the window):

Go and see what the fellow wants!

To say that what is common to the contexts of (50), (51) and (52) is, for instance, that the speaker disapproves of his audience's attitude, is to fail to do justice to the richness of the effects of the contour in each context.

Even in Liberman and Sag's own contexts the effects are richer than can be captured by the general term "contradiction". Liberman and Sag point out that Ivan's answer to Mark's request in (51) could be a wide range of quite different utterances, e.g.:

(53)   a. I'm not having that smelly beast in my car.
       b. You don't have a pet whale.
       c. You know it wouldn't fit in my VW.
          and so on.

They also point out that certain other utterances don't work so well—"require some fairly unnatural assumptions in order to be construed as contradictions", in their words (p. 422)—for example:

(54)   a. I'm not very fond of that animal.
       b. I'm more than happy to take him along.

But there are also whole classes of contradictions which couldn't take their contour; for instance, it only "fits" on declaratives and some imperatives, not on questions so that (55 a and b) would sound very odd if intoned in that manner:

(55)   a. Why on earth should I do that?
       b. How could I ever fit it into the VW?

Moreover, it is possible to make minor changes to those sentences which will fit, e.g. (53 a–c), which render them unsuitable for the contradiction contour without in the least altering their contradictory import:

(56)   a. I'm just not having that smelly beast in my car.
       b. You don't even have a pet whale.

        c. You know it just wouldn't fit in my VW.
Similarly, replacing (53c) with (57) does not change the speaker's message but
does make the "contradiction contour" inappropriate:
        (57)   It wouldn't fit in my VW as you very well know.
A more complicated objection seems to be that the semantics of the utterance
are more closely constrained than Liberman and Sag realized; not only does
the speaker have to object strongly to the request, but he has to state the
reason for his objection (as in 53 a–c). (58 a and b), objections without a reason
given, do not work:
        (58)   a. That's the most outrageous thing I've ever been asked.
               b. I wouldn't do that for anything.
Oddly enough, there is an alternative contour which seems to express
contradiction in this context and which is appropriate for all of (53), (55), (56)
and (58) as well as (54) and (57):
        (59)

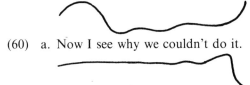

        You know I never give lifts to whales.
The acoutic characteristics of this contour are a high initial section followed
by a slight rise and rapid fall to a low, flat terminal section. The positioning of
the fall depends on the positioning of sentence accent in the utterance (on
"have" in 53, on "fond" in 54a, on "any" in 58b, for example). We do not by
any means wish to claim, however, that this contour is a synonym of Liberman
and Sag's contradiction contour; it is too easy to think up contexts in which
only the contour of (59) is appropriate (e.g. 55–58) or in which the two have
markedly different effects.

        (60)   a. Now I see why we couldn't do it.

        b. Now I see why we couldn't do it.
(60a), for example, expresses sudden enlightenment—Aha!—and,
importantly, suggests that the speaker is about to amplify, to reveal the reason
he has just discovered; (60) on the other hand suggests irritation, perhaps
because the speaker has had to repeat the utterance.
        The point of this extended set of examples is simply that intonational
meaning is contextually constrained. The effect of a particular contour differs
with the context in which it occurs, and different contours can, depending on
context, have similar or radically different effects. Not even the simplest of
intonational effects is free from contextual variation. Take, for example, a
pair of contours described by Sag and Liberman (1975). They point out that
(61) can be either a suggestion or a genuine question, whereas (62) can only be
a genuine question:

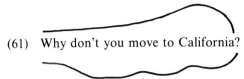

(61)   Why don't you move to California?

(62)   Why don't you move to California?

One of the functions of the contour of (62), they claim, is to "freeze" the utterance into a literal interpretation and rule out the indirect speech act of suggestion which can be carried by many questions (e.g. just about any question beginning "Why don't you . . ."). This effect again turns out to be dependent on the utterance itself and its context. For instance, (63) is a suggestion with either contour:

(63)   Why don't you go away?

With the contour of (62) it is a more direct suggestion, in fact, and certainly a more offensive one, than with the contour of (61).

A more detailed treatment of the context–dependence of the intonational effects described by Liberman and Sag is given by Cutler (1977).

It is, unfortunately, a negative kind of argument that we have made in this section; we have been concerned to show only that the claim that intonation contours have fixed meanings, or even constant pragmatic effects (e.g. on the literalness of a question), does not hold up. The effect of a particular contour is strongly constrained by the utterance which carries it and by the context in which this utterance is spoken. Accordingly, the choice of contour must be made with reference to contextual factors. We now turn our attention to the incorporation of contour selection into a language production model.

Gazdar (this volume) has demonstrated that the number of language production decisions which are affected by pragmatic, or contextual, factors is very large indeed. Selection of an appropriate intonation contour is, indeed, one of the phenomena he has cited. We believe that the choice of contour can be compared in complexity to the choice of a particular syntactic structure; both are pragmatically determined decisions between a restricted number of alternative ways of expressing the intended message. In other words, the speaker chooses between, say, the contours of (50) and (59) with reference to a particular message-in-context in much the same way that he chooses between the active and the passive voice. It is superfluous to point out that very little is known so far of the way in which such decisions are carried out. The implication for a production model, however, is that the output of the contour selection component is not uniquely determined by the output of other components (syntactic, semantic) but, like the syntactic and the semantic components, makes reference to the discourse context of the utterance.

Among the tasks of the contour selector we have discussed so far only one, choice of a holistic pitch contour; but it is likely that certain other effects have their origin at essentially the same point in sentence production. One of these is ironic tone of voice (Cutler, 1974), the sneering way of saying a sentence so as to give it a conveyed meaning which is the reverse of the literal meaning. A speaker's decision to say, e.g. (64) in an ironic manner, rather than saying (65), is determined by pragmatic factors.

(64)   Looks like it's going to be a really groovy party.

(65)   I'm afraid this party is going to be rather boring.

Another such phenomenon is sentence tempo; to give just one instance, an effect of imminent threat can be achieved by slowing down the utterance in an exaggerated manner:

(66)   Were—you—thinking—of—hitting—that—child?

Finally, we should point out the obvious fact that the output of the contour selector is presumably in an abstract form; its eventual realization in speech may be modified by other aspects of the prosodic structure. Contrastive accent may, for example, result in a pitch peak falling on the accented word without altering the effect of the contour, for example:

(67)   a. Everyone's moving to California, I'll be all alone.

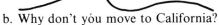

      b. Why don't yóu move to California?

In the "pure" form of this contour the fall would occur on the final syllable, as in (61), but (67b), as (61), is a suggestion rather than a genuine question. Liberman and Sag (1974) also point out that their "contradiction" contour coexists with shifts in sentence accent. Similarly, tempo is independent of accent placement (accent could plausibly fall in (66) on *were, you, hitting, child,* for example), as is ironic tone of voice:

(68)   Looks like thát's going to be a really groovy party.

Syntactic boundary placement, of course, determines the length of the constituent over which the contour is extended, and the lexical stress patterns of the chosen lexical items determine the syllables upon which the pitch movements demanded by a contour will be carried out. Selection of a holistic contour is, however, independent of these factors; interaction occurs at the point at which the output of the many components of the language production process are phonetically realized.

VI. Conclusion

We cannot claim to have given a complete description of the production of prosody. We have, for instance, not considered the phonetic realization of prosodic effects, but have confined our discussion to a more abstract level. Moreover, we have treated our four sources of prosodic variance as independent, although it is clear that at the level at which they are realized in the utterance they must interact.

Nevertheless, we feel that the four main divisions of this paper reflect the major decisions affecting the prosodic shape of a sentence. It will be apparent that we do not believe that all prosodic effects simply "fall out" of decisions taken, during the course of sentence production, about, for example, lexical items and syntactic structure. We feel that at certain stages during the production of an utterance specifically prosodic decisions are taken. This conclusion has obvious consequences for the formulation of a model of language production. While on the one hand lexical stress patterns are determined by the output of the lexical component, and tone group boundaries are at least in part set by the choice of syntactic structure, accent placement and selection of intonation contour are decisions which have exclusively prosodic results. The production model should incorporate both an accent determination and a contour selection component.

All parts of the production process can make errors, including those parts which have major prosodic effects; many different types of prosodic error are described by Cutler (in press). Consideration of prosodic errors can materially influence the way we model language production; an example of this is the argument in Section II of this Chapter. Furthermore, the manner in which prosody interacts with errors of all types can prove highly instructive, as many speech error researchers have noted. For example, it has often been remarked (e.g. Meringer and Mayer, 1895; Boomer and Laver, 1968; Garrett, 1975) that exchanges of elements below the level of the word preserve lexical stress: stressed vowels and syllables exchange with each other, unstressed vowels and syllables likewise, but stressed do not exchange with unstressed. This regularity forces the assumption that such exchanges take place at a level at which the utterance is divided into feet. Prosodic characteristics, in other words, assist in identifying the level at which a particular error arises. They can also assist in classifying particular errors. Cutler (in press) cites the error:

(69)   Do you talk on the telephone with which ear?

which, as the drawn contour indicates, was spoken with the intonation appropriate for a yes-no question rather than for a wh-question, suggesting that it may have arisen as a result of a blend with an alternative yes-no question rather than simply as a wh-question which got its word order mixed up. Similarly, inferences about detection of one's own errors can be drawn from prosodic characteristics; the speaker of (69), for example, can be assumed not to have detected the anticipation error *words* as it occurred:

(70)   Notice that these are the only two words that apply above the wórd level.

      (Target: the only two rules . . .)

This conclusion arises from the fact that the second, intended, occurrence of the word *words* bears sentence accent, whereas, as the discussion in Section III made clear, the second occurrence of a given lexical item in a sentence is normally deaccented. We can assume that the erroneous earlier occurrence of *words* was not available to the accent placement system.

Sentence accent in fact interacts in a very interesting way with word shift and exchange errors. When two lexical items exchange places, the accent structure of the sentence customarily remains unchanged, e.g.:

(71)   We have a láboratory in our computer.
       (Target: we have a compúter in our laboratory)
       from Fromkin, 1973.
(72)   Something funny smélls!
       (Target: something smells fúnny)

Fromkin (1971) drew on this regularity in constructing an early model of language production based on speech error data—a model which, unusually among such models, attempted to account specifically for prosody as well as the rest of the sentence. She suggested on the basis of the exchange error findings that accent placement might be determined by the syntactic and semantic structure of the utterance prior to the retrieval of words from the lexicon. The rationale for this ordering was that it would allow words to be inserted from the lexicon into the wrong slot in a syntactic frame, i.e. into a slot marked for accent rather than into a slot which was not so marked, or vice versa.

There are several reasons for preferring, instead of this early model of Fromkin's, an account in which lexical look-up precedes accent placement. For one thing, the de-accenting process can make reference to prior occurrence of particular words rather than meanings. For another, the word on which accent falls is sometimes determined by the particular lexical item chosen, as when a choice is made between a simple verb and a synonymous verb–particle combination:†

(75)   a. John promised to hoúse the visitors, but not to feéd them.
       b. John promised to put the visitors úp, but not to feéd them.

We would therefore not agree that errors such as (71) and (72) necessarily imply that sentence accent must be placed before lexical lookup. The regularity which Fromkin noted about such errors is, however, particularly interesting, since it allows us to draw a contrast with errors such as (76–78), in which the words which have exchanged places are not lexical words but members of the vocabulary's closed class (e.g. prepositions, pronouns, etc.):‡

(76)   Can I turn óff this?
       (Target: Can I turn this óff?)
(77)   Well I múch would have preferred the owl.
       (Target: I would have múch . . .)
(78)   It's useful so that they don't know how far they ín are.
       (Target: . . . how far ín they are)

As may be seen, the accent in such errors falls on the particular word, not on the slot, which should have borne it in the intended utterance. (Further examples are given by Cutler (1979).) The prosodic characteristics of exchange

---

† Evidence that choices of this nature are made at the lexical level is provided by lexical blends (assumed to occur when two synonyms are available in the lexicon) between simple verbs and verb-particle combinations, e.g.:

(73)   I just snabbed it! (From Garrett, 1975; explained as a blend of *snap up* and *nab*—the reference is to finding a bargain while shopping.)
(74)   Aren't you going to telephone her up? (*telephone* and *call up*; from Fromkin, 1973).

‡ See Bradley (1978) for evidence that closed class words do not form part of the main lexicon.

errors therefore provide strong support for the contention of Garrett (1975) that lexical words and closed class words are involved in fundamentally different types of error at different levels of the production process.

The moral we wish to draw is this: not only is the production of sentence prosody intrinsically interesting, but attention to prosodic phenomena can prove of great value with many differing aspects of the design of a language production model. Although we have not attempted in this paper so rash a project as the construction of such a model, we hope that our remarks have shed some light on how it should be done.

References

Abercrombie, D. (1965). Syllable quantity and enclitics in English. *In* "Studies in Phonetics and Linguistics," Oxford University Press, London.

Berman, A. and Szamosi, M. (1972). Observations on sentential stress. *Language*, **48**, 304–325.

Bolinger, D. (1958). Stress and information. *American Speech*, **33**, 5–20.

Bolinger, D. (1972). Accent is predictable (if you're a mind-reader). *Language*, **48**, 633–644.

Boomer, D. S. and Laver, J. D. M. (1968). Slips of the tongue. *British Journal of Disorders of Communication*, **3**, 1–12.

Bradley, D. C. (1978). *Computational Analysis of Vocabulary Type*. Ph.D. dissertation, M.I.T.

Bresnan, J. (1971). Sentence stress and syntactic transformations. *Language*, **47**, 257–280.

Chomsky, N. (1971). Deep structure, surface structure and semantic interpretation. *In* "Semantics" (D. D. Steinberg and L. A. Jakobovits, eds). Cambridge University Press, London.

Chomsky, N. and Halle, M. (1968). "The Sound Pattern of English". Harper and Row, New York.

Crystal, D. (1975). "The English Tone of Voice." Edward Arnold, London.

Cutler, A. (1974). On saying what you mean without meaning what you say. *Papers from the Tenth Regional Meeting, Chicago Linguistic Society*, pp. 117–127.

Cutler, A. (1977). The context-dependence of "intonational meanings". *Papers from the Thirteenth Regional Meeting, Chicago Linguistic Society*, pp. 104–115.

Cutler, A. (1979). Errors of stress and intonation. *In* "Errors of Linguistic Performance: Slips of the Tongue, Ear, Pen and Hands" (V. A. Fromkin, ed.). Academic Press, New York.

Donovan, A. and Darwin, C. J. (1979). The perceived rhythm of speech. Ninth International Congress of Phonetic Sciences, Copenhagen, 1979.

Fay, D. A. and Cutler, A. (1977). Malapropisms and the structure of the mental lexicon. *Linguistic Inquiry*, **8**, 505–520.

Fowler, C. A. (1977). *Timing Control in Speech Production*. Ph.D. dissertation, University of Connecticut.

Fromkin, V. A. (1971). The non-anomalous nature of anomalous utterances. *Language* **47**, 27–52.

Fromkin, V. A. (ed.) (1973). "Speech Errors as Linguistic Evidence." Mouton, The Hague.

Fromkin, V. A. (1977). Putting the emPHAsis on the wrong syLABle. *In* "Studies in Stress and Accent" (L. M. Hyman, ed.). University of Southern California, Los Angeles.

Garrett, M. F. (1975). The analysis of sentence production. *In* "Psychology of Learning and Motivation", vol. 9 (G. Bower, ed.). Academic Press, New York.

Halliday, M. S. (1967). "Intonation and Grammar in British English". Mouton, The Hague.

Huggins, A. W. F. (1975). On isochrony and syntax. *In* "Auditory Analysis and Perception of Speech" (G. Fant and M. A. A. Tatham, eds). Academic Press, London.

Isard, S. D. (1978). A note on contrastive stress. *Pragmatics Microfiche*, **3**, 2-G1.

Jackendoff, R. S. (1972). "Semantic Interpretation in Generative Grammar". MIT Press, Cambridge, Mass.

Klatt, D. (1975). Vowel lengthening is syntactically determined in connected discourse. *Journal of Phonetics* **3**, 129–140.

Ladd, D. R. (1978). *The Structure of Intonational Meaning*. Ph.D. dissertation, Cornell University.

Lehiste, I. (1970). "Suprasegmentals". MIT Press, Cambridge, Mass.

Lehiste, I. (1973). Rhythmic units and syntactic units in production and perception. *Journal of the Acoustical Society of America* **54**, 1228–1234.

Lehiste, I. (1977). Isochrony reconsidered. *Journal of Phonetics,* **5**, 253–263.

Lehmann, W. P. (1974). "Proto-Indo-European Syntax". University of Texas Press, Austin, Texas.

Liberman, M. and Sag, I. (1974). Prosodic form and discourse function. *Papers from the Tenth Regional Meeting, Chicago Linguistic Society*, pp. 416–427.

Meringer, R. and Mayer, K. (1895). "Versprechen und Verlesen: eine psychologisch—linguistische Studie". Göschen, Stuttgart. Re-issue, (A. Cutler and D. A. Fay, eds). John Benjamins, Amsterdam, 1978.

Morton, J., Marcus, S. and Frankish, C. (1976). Perceptual centers (P-centers). *Psychological Review*, **83**, 405–408.

Nessly, L. (1974). *English Stress and Synchronic Descriptions*. Ph.D. dissertation, University of Michigan.

Newman, S. S. (1946). On the stress system of English. *Word*, **2**, 171–187.

O'Connor, J. D. and Arnold, G. F. (1961). "Intonation of Colloquial English", Longmans, London,

Pike, K. L. (1945). "The Intonation of American English". University of Michigan Press, Ann Arbor.

Sag, I. and Liberman, M. (1975). The intonational disambiguation of indirect speech acts. *Papers from the Eleventh Regional Meeting, Chicago Linguistic Society*, pp. 487–497.

Schmerling, S. F. (1976). "Aspects of English Sentence Stress." University of Texas Press, Austin, Texas.

Schmerling, S. F. (1974). A re-examination of "normal stress". *Language*, **50**, 66–73.

Witten, I. H. (1977). A flexible scheme for assigning timing and pitch to synthetic speech. *Language and Speech*, **20**, 240–260.

11

Diachronic Arguments for the Psychological Reality of Abstract Phonology: A Critical Review

B. Comrie   *University of Cambridge*

I. Introduction

Diachronic linguistics, the study of how languages change through time, has not traditionally been the branch of linguistics that has most inspired collaboration with psychologists interested in language. Yet data from diachronic linguistics can often provide important evidence for or against the attribution of psychological reality to abstract linguistic analyses. If native speakers of a language introduce some change into their language, then clearly this change must be statable in terms that are real to the native speakers; and if these terms are neither phonetically real nor directly correlatable with features of the real world surrounding the native speakers, then they must be psychologically real. In the body of this paper I examine in detail a number of examples of sound changes that are not statable without reference to abstract phonological representations, which latter therefore seem to be psychologically real. However, the particular proposals for abstract phonological representations advanced by proponents of orthodox generative phonology in some cases run counter to such diachronic evidence for the psychological reality of abstract representations.

II. Abstract Representations

One of the main characteristics of the development of linguistics within the past 20 years, especially within the various schools of transformational-generative linguistics, has been the positing of abstract levels of linguistic representation, related by means of rules to more superficial levels correlating more directly with observables in the data. Another characteristic, which holds for many (though by no means all) proponents of transformational-generative grammar, is that these abstract representations are claimed to have psychological reality, in that native speakers of the language concerned are held to have internalized either these abstract representations (in the case of representations of lexical items) or a set of rules capable of specifying the (infinite) set of abstract representations (in the case of representations of combinations of lexical items into larger units, including sentences). The combination of these two characteristics holds, for instance, of the work of Noam Chomsky and his closest associates.

In attempting to assess the claims of transformational-generative grammar, in particular taking this theory as psychologically real, one of the main problems has been the attempt to justify (or, equally, refute) the claims about psychological reality. The degree of abstractedness posited within transformational-generative grammar is sufficient to preclude direct introspection or any immediate experimental validation, and for this reason more refined techniques are required in order to test whether a given proposed abstract representation does or does not have psychological reality. In the present paper, I shall argue that one possible kind of evidence bearing on this problem is evidence from the historical development of languages. It is not, of course, the only kind of evidence, but in Section IV, I shall try to justify the claim that it is one kind of such evidence, and to assess some of the attempts that have been made in the literature to justify assigning psychological reality to various such abstract linguistic descriptions.

The data is restricted to evidence from phonology. Although phonology does not, perhaps, possess the same initial attractiveness, especially to the non-professional linguist, as do syntax and, especially, semantics, yet still I feel that the argument developed in the following pages should prove of interest and relevance to psychologists interested in the general problem of the possible psychological reality of abstract representations. Although generative phonology is abstract, in the sense of not being directly derivable from or convertible into raw data, yet it is considerably less abstract than are the kinds of representations proposed in, for instance, syntax: phonology is much more closely tied to the phonetic nature of speech than is syntax. Although different linguists have disagreed over whether semantics should be considered very abstract (because so far removed from physical sound) or rather concrete (because of its relation to properties of the real world described by speakers of a language), it remains true in either case that descriptive techniques in semantics have not progressed to the extent that they have in phonetics, so that in practice semantics is much less easy to come to terms with than phonetics or phonology. For these reasons, phonology provides one with a useful laboratory within which to test claims about psychological reality.

In preparing the present paper, I have had very much in mind an audience of psychologists who are interested in language, but who have not necessarily acquired any technical competence in following and evaluating linguistics argumentation *per se*. Phonological argumentation almost inevitably requires the presentation of a reasonable amount of material, often from unfamiliar languages, and requires from the reader a certain amount of effort in order, first, to assimilate the data and, secondly, to appreciate the relevance of the data to the theoretical discussion at hand. For non-linguist readers, I would therefore emphasize that the data in Section IV is an essential part of the argumentation which cannot be skipped over without missing the basis of the argument. Equally, the data are presented solely because of their relevance to the general argument, as they do contribute significantly to the general conclusions I wish to draw. Linguists, on the other hand, may find that this paper has relatively little new to tell them. The data are all sets of data that have been reasonably fully discussed in the earlier literature, where they have been given generative phonological analyses; moreover, the kinds of critiques against these analyses, at least as psychologically real analyses, have often also been at least outlined in the literature. However, what seems not to have happened to date is a coming together of psychologists and linguists on the basis of discussions of the kind that form the body of this paper. If this paper serves to bring about a dialogue of this kind, it will have fulfilled its primary purpose. †

III. Methodology of Generative Phonology

The model of generative phonology which we shall be discussing is essentially that of "orthodox" generative phonology, as instantiated, for example, in Chomsky and Halle (1968). This model represents a high degree of consensus among a number of linguists working on phonological theory and the phonological description of a wide range of languages. Although perhaps no two of these linguists would agree on every single aspect of generative phonology, there is still sufficient overlap among those working within this framework for one to be able to speak of a coherent overall framework. As already indicated, generative phonology is part of a wider approach to linguistic analysis (transformational-generative grammar) which works with abstract levels of representation. In phonology, one can think of at least two levels of representation: (a) a phonetic representation, close to the physical speech signal, but abstracting away from those variables over which speakers have no possible systematic articulatory control or which hearers cannot systematically discriminate; this is thus a relatively concrete level of representation; (b) a phonological representation, which is an abstract representation. Given a division into two representations of this kind, an obvious question to ask is what the motivation for the abstract level is. I shall return to this question in a moment, though before doing so it is necessary to clarify some terminological points that may otherwise engender confusion.

The levels labelled (a) and (b) above are called by Chomsky and Halle the "systematic phonetic" and "systematic phonological" representations respectively. The designation "systematic phonetic", rather than just

†An earlier version of this paper was presented to the Psycholinguistics Seminar, Psychological Laboratory, University of Cambridge. I am grateful to all those who attended this seminar and participated in the ensuing discussion, which first opened my eyes to the possibility of initiating a dialogue of this kind. For discussion of many of the phonological points included in this paper I am grateful to two of my linguist colleagues, Richard Coates and Roger Lass.

"phonetic", is intended to indicate that this is not simply raw phonetic data, but rather phonetic data that has been systematized to some extent, in particular to the extent that discriminations below the human being's articulatory and perceptual threshold are excluded. The designation "systematic phonological", rather than just "phonological", serves a useful purpose in that, in most earlier discussions of phonology, the term "phonological" (or, interchangeably, "phonemic") had a rather narrower signification. In pre-generative phonology, this term refers primarily to the ability of sound distinctions to distinguish different (lexical or grammatical) forms. If a sound distinction differentiates forms in this way, as does the distinction between initial *p* and *b* in English *pin* and *bin*, then the distinction is phonemic, and *p* and *b* are held to be distinct phonemes, with different representations on the phonological (phonemic) level. If a sound distinction cannot be used to differentiate forms in this way, then the distinction is allophonic, the two sounds are allophones of the same phoneme, and are represented in the same way in the phonological representation; thus, in many dialects of English, the *l* of *leaf* is phonetically distinct from the *l* of *feel* (the latter having a "darker" quality, technically velerization, caused by raising the back of the tongue towards the soft palate), but this phonetic distinction cannot be used in English to discriminate forms. The distinction between 'clear' and 'dark' *l* is, however, one which speakers can in principle control and hearers can perceive, and in some other languages the difference between these two sounds can serve to distinguish forms, e.g. Polish *laska* "stick" (with clear *l*) versus *łaska* "love, favour" (with dark *l*). Within generative phonology, it has been argued, most comprehensively by Chomsky (1974: pp. 85–112), that this level of pre-generative (taxonomic, autonomous) phonemics is not required in a linguistic description, indeed that the assumption of such a level can lead to unmotivated complicating of the description. The level in pre-generative linguistics that corresponds most closely to the generativists' systematic phonological level is the morphophonemic level, as indicated below.

Within the transformational-generative approach, the most general kind of justification that can be given for a specific proposal concerning the level of abstract, systematic phonology, is the ability of this level to integrate into an overall description of the language under investigation in such a way that this overall description both provides a characterization of the native speaker's tacit knowledge of his language and relates this knowledge to the general capacities, independent of any particular language, of humans as linguistic animals. In practice, this general characterization does little to delimit the range of possible theories (in particular, given the difficulty of direct psychological testing), so that generative phonologists have tried to devise more specific procedures to aid them in working out abstract underlying representation and, more particularly, in evaluating rival proposals as to the systematic phonological level. It would be misleading to think of generative phonology as a set of techniques for producing systematic phonological representations, in the way that taxonomic phonemics can, with some justification, be seen as a set of techniques for producing taxonomic phonemic representations—indeed, many of the proponents of taxonomic phonemics (Bloomfield, Harris, Bloch) saw themselves quite explicitly as doing just this. Generative phonologists have been very critical of this "discovery procedure" approach to phonology and linguistics in general, preferring rather to view their theoretical constructs (such as systematic phonological representations) as hypotheses subject to instantiation or refutation by empirical testing of their predications. However, the need to delimit the class of possible solutions to phonological problems, and to be able to evaluate competing solutions, has meant that in practice certain techniques have come to serve the function of quasi-discovery procedures. The qualification "quasi-" is because these are not seen as blind procedures that must be followed, in the taxonomic phonemicist's sense, but rather as procedures that guide the phonologist towards an abstract representation, and impose certain constraints on such abstract representations by specifying certain tasks that such a representation must be capable of performing. One of these tasks is that, wherever possible, a given morpheme should be given a single underlying representation (at the systematic phonological level), even where at more superficial levels (in particular, the systematic phonetic level) it may require different representations in different environments. I shall now illustrate this piece of methodology in further detail.

The general import of the methodology can perhaps be seen more clearly in some of the early work on transformational-generative syntax. One of the original motivations for setting up deep structures (abstract representations) in syntax was to account for the notion of sentence-relatedness. The two English sentences *John likes cheese* and *does John like cheese?* are clearly related, in that the second is the question corresponding to the first. However, in terms of their surface syntactic representations, this notion of sentence relatedness is very diffuse, since the distinction between the two sentences is not represented by any single feature of statement versus question, but rather by a combination of features: the insertion of the auxiliary verb *do*, the shifting of the finite verb (the one that shows agreement with the subject) to sentence-initial position, and a change in the intonation of the sentence, represented orthographically (in a very unsatisfactory manner) by the use of the question mark. Within transformational-generative syntax, however, these two sentences can be assigned, in deep structure, either the same representation (as in Chomsky (1957)) or nearly identical representations (as in Katz and Postal (1963)), in which latter case they might differ by the presence of a node Q in the interrogative but not in the declarative; the greater difference in surface structure would be the result of the application of transformational rules to these deep structures, in particular the deep structure of the question, to bring about such changes as the insertion of the auxiliary, the shift of the finite verb, the change in intonation, and the deletion of the Q node.

In phonology, a similar phenomenon can be observed. Quite often the same item has different pronunciations in different environments. For instance, English has the two words *divine*, pronounced [divain], and *divinity*, pronounced [diviniti]; common to both words is the element *divin(e)*, with the meaning "godly, heavenly", but its pronunciation is in the one case [divain], in the other [divin]. Somewhat more technically, the single morpheme *divin-* has two allomorphs, [divain] and [divin]. Another example concerns the endings of regular plurals in English, i.e. plurals of the type *cats, ducks, dogs, thrushes*, as opposed to irregular plurals like *oxen, teeth, people*. The pronunciation of this regular plural ending varies according to the final segment of the stem to which it is attached: if this final consonant is a sibilant, then the ending has the pronunciation [iz], as in [θrʌʃiz]; if the final segment is a voiceless consonant (other than a sibilant), then the pronunciation is [s], as in [kæts]; if the final segment is any other (i.e. a vowel, or a voiced consonant other than a sibilant), then the plural ending is pronounced [z], as in [dogz]. In pre-generative terminology, one would say that the alternation between the various allomorphs of a single morpheme is the sphere of morphophonemics (also called morphophonology and, especially in Continental Europe, morphonology), i.e. that component of the overall linguistic description that relates morphemes and phonemes. In generative phonology, which lacks the taxonomic phonemic level, both pre-generative morphophonemics and phonemics are subsumed under the one phonological component (phonology) of the grammar, which relates the systematic phonological (approximately, the earlier morphophonemic) level to the systematic phonetic level. One of the aims of generative phonology is thus to provide a single systematic phonological representation for such morphemes as *divin-*, plural *-s*, even where they differ at the systematic phonetic level.

So far I have kept to English examples, for the sake of familiarity, but from the viewpoint of detailed presentation it is somewhat easier if one takes an example from German, since this illustrates the relevant points particularly clearly. German has two words, spelled *bunt* "multicoloured" and *Bund* "federation", but both pronounced [bunt].† Quite generally, German does not have words ending in a voiced obstruent (plosive, such as [d], [b], or fricative, such as [v], [z]). However, in other forms of these words, we may find the stem-final consonant pronounced differently. For instance, the neuter singular indefinite of the adjective *bunt* is *buntes*, pronounced [buntəs], whereas the genitive singular of the noun *Bund* is *Bundes*, pronounced [bundəs]. Wherever these morphemes occur before a vowel (within the same word), they are pronounced differently from one another, *bunt* having a stem-final [t], and *Bund* a stem-final [d]. Since the morpheme *bunt* does not participate in any morphophonemic alternation, we may assume that its systematic phonological representation is essentially the same as its systematic phonetic representation (apart from the omission of a number of phonetic parameters that are never distinctive in German, and which we are tacitly omitting throughout this discussion), i.e. /bunt/. For *Bund*, however, with the allomorphs [bunt] and [bund], we want to find a single systematic phonological representation covering all the allomorphs. The question

---

† In German, nouns are always spelled with an upper case initial letter.

TABLE I
Systematic phonological and systematic phonetic levels

	bunt	buntes	Bund	Bundes
Systematic phonological	/bunt/	/buntəs/	/bund/	/bundəs/
Systematic phonetic	[bunt]	[buntəs]	[bunt]	[bundəs]

therefore arises as to whether this should be /bunt/ or /bund/, or possibly some third representation distinct from either of the allomorphs. The main criterion that comes into play in deciding which of these possibilities to prefer is that the phonetic representation should be derivable from the systematic phonological representation, as far as possible, by the application of regular rules; moreover, there should not be more rules than are required to handle the morphophonemic alteration. Postulation of a third form as the underlying representation would be redundant, in this case.† Postulation of /bunt/ as the underlying representation would mean that a rule would be required to voice stem-final /t/ to [d] before a vowel. However, such a rule would apply equally to underlying /bunt/ meaning "multicoloured", predicting incorrectly that the neuter singular indefinite of this adjective should be [bundəs]. Thus if we were to take /bunt/ as the underlying form of *Bund*, then for every morpheme in German ending in an obstruent we should have to state, as an arbitrary lexical specification, whether or not it undergoes this voicing rule. If, however, we take /bund/ as the systematic phonological representation, then we require a rule of final obstruent devoicing, which will devoice the final /d/ or *Bund* /bund/ to give [bunt], but will not affect the non-final *d* of *Bundes* /bundəs/, which will remain as [bundəs]. Moreover, if we look at other words in German ending in obstruents, we find that this rule of devoicing applies without exception right across the language: individual morphemes in systematic phonological representation have either a voiceless obstruent (which always appears phonetically as a voiceless obstruent) or a voiced obstruent (which appears phonetically as a voiced obstruent before a vowel, as a voiceless obstruent otherwise).

Diagrammatically, the German situation can be represented as in Table I. In examining Table I, we can also make explicit the notation that we have adopted tacitly in the preceding discussion. Systematic phonological representations are enclosed in slants, e.g. /bund/; occasionally, we need to refer to (non-systematic) representations between the systematic phonological and systematic phonetic levels, for instance where a number of rules apply in sequence, the output of one being the input to the next, and we may use the same notation with slants for such intermediate representations. Indications of the pronunciation of items are enclosed within square brackets, e.g. [bunt];

† In the case of the English *divine–divinity* alternation, Chomsky and Halle (1968) suggest that the underlying form should have neither /ai/ (cp. [divain] (nor /i/ (cp. [diviniti]), but rather a segment combining features of both, namely /i:/, i.e. /divi:n/.

TABLE II
Alternations between diphthongs/long vowels and short vowels in English

(a)	divine	[di'vain]	divinity	[di'viniti]
(b)	profound	[prə'faund]	profundity	[prə'fʌnditi]
(c)	obscene	[ob'si:n]	obscenity	[ob'seniti]
(d)	profane	[prə'fein]	profanity	[prə'fæniti]

strictly, such systematic phonetic representations should contain a full specification of all phonetic parameters to the extent that these are under the systematic control of speaker-hearers, but needless to say my sample representations omit a host of details that are not relevant to the problems to hand. Citations in conventional orthography are in italics.

The kind of data just discussed are, in a sense, the best possible for the application of the methodology outlined above: one can set up a single underlying representation, which is convertible into the various allomorphs by means of perfectly regularly operating rules. Many of the examples with which phonologists work are less neat than this, for instance in that they require a certain degree of lexical or morphological specification of applicability of rules. This can be illustrated with the English vowel alternations in such pairs as *divine–divinity*, as shown in Table II. These alternations are discussed in detail, within the framework of orthodox generative phonology, by Chomsky and Halle (1968), and here I shall limit myself to certain observations concerning such alternations. First, the alternations are to a certain extent lexically conditioned, in that certain lexical items undergo the alternation, while others do not, with no generalization specifying which do and which do not. For instance, the adjective *obese* [ou'bi:s] has a corresponding noun *obesity*, just as *obscene* has *obscenity*, but the noun is pronounced [ou'bi:siti], with long [i:], and not *[ou'besiti], i.e. this lexical item, exceptionally, does not undergo the alternation. Secondly, the rule is to a certain extent morphologically conditioned, in that certain suffixes require the alternation (apart from with exceptional lexical items like *obese*), whereas other suffixes, with essentially similar phonetic shape, do not allow the alternation. Thus the suffix *-ic* requires the alternation, e.g. *metre* [mi:tə] (or [mi:tr] in dialects that retain post-vocalic r), but *metric* [metrik]; whereas the suffix *-ive* does not have this alternation, e.g. *plaint* [pleint], *plaintive* [pleintiv].† But despite the necessity of introducing lexical or morphological conditioning in certain instances, it still remains true that generative phonology tries, wherever possible, to set up single underlying forms from which all allomorphs can be derived by the regular application of rules; lexical

† Examples where there is also change in the position of stress are subject to a rather different set of rules, so that over all such pairs as *demonstrate* ['demənstreit] and *demonstrative* [də'monstrətiv], with a long vowel in the former but a short vowel in the latter, turn out not to be exceptions to the generalization that the rule discussed in the text does not apply before *-ive*. Full details of this and other rules are given in Chomsky and Halle (1968).

and morphological conditioning are only introduced where it would otherwise be impossible to set up a single underlying form for the various allomorphs.

Although the methodology of devising a single underlying form for all allomorphs is not the sole criterion used in generative phonology for establishing or justifying systematic phonological representations, it is generally acknowledged to be the least controversial of the various criteria that have been suggested; see, for instance, Schane (1974) for a more detailed examination of the various criteria, including morphophonemic alternation, that have been proposed. In an attempt to restrict the abstractness of systematic phonological representations, i.e. to place constraints on the extent to which the systematic phonological representation may differ from the systematic phonetic representation (other than in the omission of redundancy), Kiparsky (1973) argues that morphophonemic alternation should be the sole criterion used in justifying a systematic phonological representation that differs from a systematic phonetic representation. Thus this criterion represents the strongest point of orthodox generative phonology, and any criticisms that can be levelled against it cannot be dismissed as peripheral attacks on a minor weakness or on a strawman.

On the basis of the examples so far, it might seem that the application of the principle of a single systematic phonological representation for all allomorphs should be a relatively straightforward matter, one which could almost be raised to the level of a discovery procedure. In practice, however, a number of complications arise. First, problems are created by alternations of limited productivity, i.e. alternations that are limited to a small number of lexical items or morphological environments, and which cannot be extended to new items entering the language. An obvious example of this is suppletion, where allomorphs of a morpheme have no phonetic similarity, such as the English pair *go–went*: although there is minimal phonetic similarity between the two words, they behave functionally just like regular stem and past tense forms such as *love–loved* with little or no morphophonemic alternation. Since generative phonological rules have the possibility of changing one segment into another (as in the shift of /d/ to [t] in the derivation of *Bund*), and indeed also of deleting and inserting segments, it would be possible, from a formal viewpoint, to derive both *go* and *went* from a single underlying representation, but this would involve a number of rules that are highly conditioned lexically. With such an example as *go–went*, probably no generative phonologist would be seriously tempted to set up a single systematic phonological representation with phonological rules accounting for the alternation, rather than just either having distinct systematic phonological representations or having the systematic phonological representation appropriate to *go* and replacing it completely for the past tense *went*, much as if one lexical item were to replace another. However, there are other examples where the distinction is more difficult to draw: an alternation may characterize only a handful of examples (as with English plurals formed by internal vowel change, e.g. *tooth–teeth*, *foot–feet*, *mouse–mice*, *man–men*, and a few others; or the pairs *father–paternal*, *mother–maternal*, *brother–fraternal*), or it may be unclear whether a small degree of phonetic similarity between allomorphs is to be attributed to chance rather than to a single underlying form (see, for instance, Foley's analysis (1967) of the Latin verb "to be" where he succeeds in establishing a single underlying representation of the stem as /s/ for such forms as *sum* "I am", *est* "he is", whereas most linguists would probably treat this as suppletion).

A second problem is that it is not always easy to decide unequivocally the precise range of words that should be included as instances of "the same morpheme". For instance, probably no-one would doubt that in the following pairs each member contains the same morpheme: *long–length, wide–width, broad–breadth*, since the semantic relation is transparent, the second member being the abstract noun corresponding to the first. However, this is less clear when we come to *foul–filth*, where the second cannot be characterized as simply the abstract noun corresponding to the first; although diachronically *filth* was the abstract noun from *foul*, their meanings have since diverged, so that many native speakers of Modern English probably do not feel any particular connection between these two words. In English, where many words with the same Indo-European origin have come into the language both via the native Germanic vocabulary and as loans from Latin and the Romance languages, and where moreover the Romance loans tend to be more learned, it is often the case that certain related words are known only to a small percentage of the speakers of the language, and are therefore not available to most speakers in establishing systematic phonological representations. Few English speakers would be able to follow Lightner (1975: p. 618) in constructing a systematic phonological representation for *fart* that relies crucially on the alternation found with *petard*.

In the data discussed in detail below, I shall be relying primarily on morphophonemic alternations that are regular and that apply to a wide range of lexical items, alternations moreover that involve forms of morphemes that are part of the basic stock of the language concerned, so that they can be presumed to be available to all native speakers of the language. This applies in particular to the crucial Maori examples in Section IV.A. Thus I am restricting myself to what is the best evidence for the orthodox generative phonological position, i.e. again attacking it, where attacks are made, at its strongest point, rather than restricting myself to peripheral critiques of weak spots that could, perhaps, be abandoned without destroying the over all edifice of orthodox generative phonology.

Finally in this section, one should note that in current work on phonology there is a marked movement against the very abstract kinds of systematic phonological representation as given in, for instance, Chomsky and Halle (1968). This movement was initiated in large measure by Kiparsky (1973), in his attempt to restrict the criteria for establishing systematic phonological representations to morphophonemic alternations. Other phonologists have departed more radically from the orthodox generative paradigm, in the direction of more concrete phonological representation; see, for instance, Hooper (1976) for a fully developed theory of this kind. However, orthodox generative phonology, at least of the degree of abstractness permitted by

Kiparsky, does still live on, so that this critical discussion of it is not of purely historical interest.

To summarize this section, one should note the following key points. First, systematic phonological representations are set up in order to have, as far as possible, a single representation for all allomorphs of a given morpheme. Secondly, it is claimed that systematic phonological representations, like other levels of abstract representation, have psychological reality. These two points are, of course, quite independent of one another logically, so that their conjunction involves a very strong empirical claim, namely that the (or at least: one of the) underlying phonological representations that provides a single representation for all allomorphs of a morpheme will have psychological reality. So far, and indeed in much of the literature on generative phonology, the assumption of psychological reality is gratuitous, given that the connection between the methodology of generative phonology and the psychological reality of its analyses is contingent. In the next section, we shall examine the possible relevance of diachronic considerations in testing the psychological reality of systematic phonological representations.

IV. Diachronic Considerations

It is well known that languages change through time, and that these changes can affect various levels of analysis: lexically, old lexical items go out of use or are replaced by new ones, new lexical items enter the language; morphologically, old forms are lost, new forms are created, old forms can be replaced by new forms with the same function; and in the sound system, it is possible for the sounds of a language to change, most typically with a very high degree of regularity, in that the same sound in the same environment tends always to change in the same way. Until quite recently, it was widely held that sound change was primarily a change in phonetic representation: changes in phonetic representation might have implications for the taxonomic phonemic system (in that formerly distinct phonemes might coalesce phonetically into a single phoneme by merger), and in many cases it would be more economical to state a sound change as a change in taxonomic phonemic representation, thus omitting a number of irrelevant minor phonetic distinctions, but the basic view, inherited from the nineteenth-century Neo-Grammarian school, was that sound change involves speakers of a language adopting some change in the phonetics of their language. With the advent of generative phonology, given its emphasis on abstract systematic phonological representations, linguists began looking for evidence that sound change could be predicated not of phonetic representations, but rather of the abstract underlying representations they were setting up in their model, primarily on the basis of morphophonemic evidence. If one were to find good evidence of this, namely examples where a sound change could only be stated by making crucial reference to an abstract underlying representation, then this would be good evidence for the psychological reality of this abstract underlying representation. The argument, in more detail, would be in the following terms: speakers of a language can only carry out changes on the basis of entities (items, categories, representations) that are somehow available to them as speakers of the given language. If an observed change cannot be described directly in terms of the phonetic representation (or even its tidied up version, the systematic phonetic representation), then this must mean that native speakers have available to them some more abstract level of representation, in terms of which the observed change can be described. Essentially, the only way in which they can have access to such an abstract level of representation (given that the majority of speakers of a language have no explicit knowledge of the techniques of generative phonology) is if that level of abstract representation is psychologically real. The speakers who introduce and propagate the change would thus have a psychologically real abstract representation differing from the (systematic) phonetic representation. We shall make this clearer by means of an example.

The example is taken from the historical development of German. As noted in Section III, on a generative phonological analysis, German has a rule which devoices word-final obstruents, so that corresponding to the systematic phonological representation /bund/ we have a systematic phonetic representation [bunt], pronounced exactly the same as systematic phonetic [bunt] from systematic phonological /bunt/. Now, in fact this synchronic rule is the reflex of a diachronic rule (sound change). In Old High German, such words as *Bund* were actually pronounced with a final voiced obstruent, and were therefore phonetically distinct from such words as *bunt*. By the Middle High German period, however, word-final obstruents had, as a result of a sound change, become devoiced, so that from then on *Bund* and *bunt* were homophonous. Another word where this devoicing took place is *Weg* "way", which was originally pronounced with a final [g], subsequently with a final [k]. Oblique forms of *Weg*, such as genitive *Weges*, where the *g* is followed by a vowel, retained the pronunciation with [g], since the consonant is not here in word-final position. Thus just as underlying /d/ can be posited in *Bund* on the basis of morphophonemic alternation, so can underlying /g/ be posited for *Weg*. In the Middle High German period, *Weg* was pronounced [wek], and *Weges* was pronounced [wegəs].†

Subsequent to the devoicing of word-final obstruents, a further sound change took place in German whereby vowels were lengthened before voiced obstruents. Prior to this change, one pronounced [vek] and [vegəs]; subsequent to the change, one pronounced [vek] (no lengthening, because the following obstruent is voiceless), but [ve:gəs] (lengthening, because of the following voiced obstruent). The historical development is as set out in Table III. In this series of changes, each change can be stated in terms of the phonetic representation, and there is no need to appeal to abstract underlying

† To avoid introducing irrelevent complications, I have retained Modern German orthography throughout. Note that orthographic *w* is pronounced [v] in Modern German, but was probably pronounced [w] in Old and Middle High German; as this change is not relevant to the discussion, I shall from here on write [v] throughout.

TABLE III
Final obstruent devoicing and vowel lengthening as sound changes
in German

	Weg	Weges	
Stage I	[veg]	[vegəs]	Final devoicing
Stage II	[vek]	[vegəs]	Lengthening
Stage III	[vek]	[ve:gəs]	

representations in the changes discussed so far. Stage III is, incidentally, still current in a number of German dialects, and is a common regional feature among North Germans who otherwise speak standard German.

Let us now forget for a moment, the diachronic dimension, and carry out a synchronic generative phonological analysis of the phonetic forms and morphophonemic alternations at Stage III. On the basis of the consonantal alternation, just as with *Bund*, we can set up /g/ as the systematic phonological representation of the final consonant. We also have the alternation between short [e] and long [e:]; there are some words that have a long vowel before a voiced consonant in all forms (these words had long vowels even in Old High German), so that it is not possible to predict a short vowel in the endingless form from a long vowel in the form with an ending. If one follows the inverse derivation, deriving the long vowel in the genitive singular from a short vowel, then one does not require lexical specification of a large number of exceptions, so that this direction of derivation is to be preferred, establishing the short vowel as part of the systematic phonological representation. Two synchronic phonological rules are required, the one to devoice word-final obstruents (as we have already seen with [bunt] from /bund/), and another to lengthen vowels before voiced consonants. The ordering of these two rules is crucial: if vowel lengthening preceded, or were simultaneous with, final obstruent devoicing, then the vowel of /veg/ would be lengthened to give, ultimately, [ve:k], which is not correct for Stage III. Therefore devoicing must precede lengthening, as in Table IV. In Table IV, where a given rule has no effect on a given form (e.g. word-final obstruent devoicing on /vegəs/), a blank is used to mean "no change". It will be noted that the generative phonological analysis of Stage III effectively recapitulates the historical development from Stage I through Stage III (compare Tables III and IV), although we did not use data

TABLE IV
Generative phonological analysis of stage III (Table III) in German

	Weg	Weges
Systematic phonological representation	/veg/	/vegəs/
Final devoicing	vek	
Vowel lengthening		ve:gəs
Systematic phonetic representation	[vek]	[ve:gəs]

from earlier stages of the language in working out this generative phonological analysis.

In Modern Standard German, *Weg* is pronounced [ve:k], and *Weges* is pronounced [ve:gəs], i.e. in contrast to Stage III both forms of this lexical item have a long vowel. This stage, Stage IV, represents a further inovation *vis-à-vis* Stage III. We must now ask whether this innovation, like those that led up to Stage III, can be described in purely phonetic terms, i.e. is it possible to stage a general rule that will change phonetic [vek] at Stage III into [ve:k] at Stage IV? The answer is that it is not possible. At Stage III, in addition to words like *Weg* with vowel and consonant alternation, there are also words like *Dreck* "dirt" that have neither alternation. i.e. nominative singular *Dreck* [drek], genitive singular *Dreckes* [drekəs]. Since such words have no alternation, their systematic phonological representation is essentially the same as their systematic phonetic representation (apart from detailed specification of redundant features in the latter). In terms of phonetic representation, however, [vek] and [drek] fit into exactly the same class: vowel lengthening in German, whether as a sound change or as a synchronic rule, is conditioned by the following consonant, never by the preceding consonant, so that in terms of phonetic representation there would be no way, other than idiosyncratic lexical specification, of describing the change from Stage III [vek] to Stage IV [ve:k], but with retention of [drek] from Stage III to Stage IV. Yet it is precisely this differentiation that is made, with near perfect regularity, in the change from Stage III to Stage IV in the historical development of Modern Standard German. Now, if one imagines that at Stage III speakers of this form of German had access to the generative phonologists' systematic phonological level, i.e. if this abstract representation were psychologically real, then it is easy to describe the shift from Stage III to Stage IV: speakers of Stage III carried out a sound change of lengthening vowels before underlying (systematic phonological) voiced consonants, irrespective of whether they remained voiced in phonetic representation or not. The vowel of [ve:gəs] (/ve:gəs/) was already long phonetically, so no change is detectable here; the vowel of [vek] (/veg/) was lengthened to give [ve:k], an innovation *vis-à-vis* Stage III, because the following consonant is voiced at the systematic phonological level, although it is phonetically voiceless; the vowel of [drek] (/drek/) remains unchanged, since the following consonant is voiceless at the systematic phonological level.

There are two further points one should note before moving on to a more critical appraisal of this example. First, there are some words that underwent final obstruent devoicing as a diachronic rule between Stages I and II (Table III), but which did not have any morphophonemic alternation with other forms retaining the voiced consonant because of a following vowel. One such item is the adverb *weg* "away".† At Stage I this was pronounced [veg]; at Stages II and III it was pronounced [vek]. Since it does not participate in any morphophonemic alternations, there is no reason to give it a systematic

---

†Etymologically, *weg* "away" is relatable to *Weg* "way", just as *away* and *way* are relatable etymologically in English, but synchronically it seems that they have to be treated as distinct items.

TABLE V
Generative phonological analysis of stage IV (Modern Standard German)

	Weg	*Weges*
Systematic phonological representation	/ve:g/	/ve:gəs/
Final devoicing	ve:k	
Systematic phonetic representation	[ve:k]	[ve:gəs]

phonological representation other than /vek/, therefore one would expect that, between Stages III and IV, it would not be subject to the innovation of lengthening vowels before underlying voiced consonants. And, indeed, this expectation is borne out: the Modern Standard German pronunciation of *weg* is [vek], differing therefore from *Weg* [ve:k]. Secondly, since Modern Standard German *Weg* has long [e:] in all its forms, there is, synchronically, no vowel alternation, and therefore no morphophonemic evidence for setting up an underlying form with short /e/. A synchronic analysis of Modern Standard German (Stage IV) might well be as in Table V, with the synchronic (morphophonemically based) analysis no longer recapitulating the diachronic development.

The account which I have just given of the historical development of word-final obstruent devoicing the vowel lengthening in German may be taken as an orthodox account within orthodox generative phonology as applied to synchronic and diachronic linguistics; further examples of the same type are discussed, for instance, by King (1969).† But before accepting that we have an argument, from diachronic evidence, for the psychological reality of systematic phonological representations, we must make explicit just what has in fact been argued for. I have argued that a certain observed diachronic change in German cannot be described in terms of the systematic phonetic representation immediately preceding the change. This is prima facie evidence for the psychological reality of systematic phonological representations, but cannot be accepted as definitive evidence until all other possibilities have been eliminated. In other words, it is conceivable that there might be explanations other than psychological reality of systematic phonological representations to account for a diachronic change that is not describable in terms of a modification directly applicable to the phonetic level. We shall now examine some such alternative explanations, arguing that while they may involve a certain dilution of the generative phonological position, they do not materially affect the appeal to abstract representations, although the degree of

---

†Although King (1973) modifies his earlier position, at times substantially, on a number of points, these do not affect the attribution of psychological reality to underlying representations. In particular, whether one assumes that sound changes entering the language can apply directly to abstract phonological representations (as in King (1969)), or whether one assumes that such innovations are always applied initially to phonetic representations, but can then be reordered with respect to other phonological rules so that they apply to underlying representations (the position of King (1973)), in either case the underlying representations must be available to speakers of the language.

dilution may well mean that the generative position is not a particularly radical innovation *vis-à-vis* traditional historical phonology.

Since the basic evidence for setting up systematic phonological representations distinct from systematic phonetic representations is morphophonemic alternation, and since morphophonemic alternations can be stated as alternations between items on the systematic phonetic level, one could reformulate the appeal to systematic phonological representations in terms of a more directly phonetic appeal to phonetic alternants. If we take our German example as an illustration, then the change from Stage III to Stage IV would be stated somewhat as follows: vowel lengthening, which previously applied only before voiced obstruents, is now extended so that it also applies before those voiceless obstruents that alternate with voiced obstruents (but not before those that do not). The phonetic representation [vek] (*Weg*) would be changed to [ve:k] by this rule because of the alternation [k]–[g] as seen in [ve:gəs]. On the other hand, [drek] (*Dreck*) would be unaffected, because it has no alternation with *[dreg], and likewise [vek] (*weg*) would remain unaffected. This is a somewhat more refined version of the traditional Neo-Grammarian approach to such examples, which would say that [vek] changes to [ve:k] by analogy with other forms in the same paradigm (i.e. other forms of the same lexical item), such as [ve:gəs]. Apparently, then, it is possible after all to describe the change between Stage III and Stage IV without appealing to systematic phonological representations, since in the discussion of this paragraph all the representations are phonetic. However, it still remains true that there is an appeal to something abstract, namely the fact that there exists a relation of morphophonemic alternation between [vek] and [ve:gəs] at Stage III. The innovation of Stage IV has not really been stated in purely phonetic terms, because these would not be able to distinguish cases like [vek] (*Weg*) from those like [drek]; the representation of [vek] with which I am working is still implicitly abstract, since in addition to the phonetic representation [vek] there is the added proviso that this form alternates morphophonemically with [ve:g]-, in, for instance, [ve:gəs]. More accurately and explicitly, the representation at Stage III would be something like: [vek] ~ ([ve:g]-). The part of the representation in parentheses, stating that there is a morphophonemic alternation, makes the representation at least in part abstract, since the fact of morphophonemic alternation is not a phonetic property of [vek]; the representation of [drek] would not contain any such parenthesized sub-representation, indicating that there is no morphophonemic alternation. Thus, although this modified analysis does not refer directly to systematic phonological representations, it does refer to an abstraction, so that the general problem of the psychological reality of abstract representations is not removed thereby. The reformulation does, however, serve to show that the implicit attribution of psychological reality to abstract representations is perhaps not quite so much of an innovation as generative phonologists have sometimes led one to believe, although those earlier phonologists in whose analyses the appeal to the reality of abstract representations is implicit might well have been horrified if the appeal had been made explicit to them.

I shall now turn for a moment to some data from the history of the English language, which have been analysed by generative phonologists in a way similar to the German data above, although here there is a slightly different kind of alternative analysis that does not appeal directly to systematic phonological analyses, although it does involve a different kind of abstract representation. The data concern the pronunciation of the Middle English (MiE) long vowels in sixteenth-century English (C16) and in the seventeenth century (C17) and later. The historical changes are set out in Table VI, and the generative phonological analysis follows Halle (1974). Examination of Table VI shows that, in general, it is possible to account for the changes separating C16 from MiE and C17 from C16 in terms of changes applying to phonetic representations, with one exception: the reflexes of Middle English [æː] and [aː]. In the sixteenth century these are identical, as [eː], whereas by the seventeenth century they have diverged again, giving [iː] and [ei] respectively, as in Modern English. In other words, in Middle English none of *feet*, *beat*, or *late* rhymes with any of the others; in the sixteenth century *feet* and *beat* do not rhyme, whereas *beat* and *late* do; since the seventeenth century, *beat* and *late* no longer rhyme, but *feet* and *beat* do. An even clearer example is provided by *meet* and *meat*, which are homophones ([miːt]) in Modern English, but were distinguished as [miːt] versus [meːt] in sixteenth-century English (and indeed still in some contemporary regional dialects of English); in the sixteenth century, conversely, *meat* and *mate* were homophones. Halle argues that although reflexes of Middle English [æː] and [aː] were phonetically identical in sixteenth-century English, yet on the basis of morphophonemic alternations they were distinct in systematic phonological representation, the latter being similar to the Middle English phonetic representation. By a later change, underlying /æː/ and /aː/ were differentiated, despite their phonetic identity as [eː], the former giving [iː], the latter [ei].

Unfortunately, Halle does not document in detail the morphophonemic alternations that justify the dichotomization of sixteenth-century English phonetic [eː] into phonological /æː/ versus /eː/, especially in the native (non-Romance) vocabulary, where alternations of the type illustrated in Table II are rare. An alternative analysis is provided by Weinreich *et al.* (1968: pp. 147–148). They argue that in the sixteenth century, both the "sixteenth-century" and the "seventeenth-century" systems co-existed, although they were socially differentiated, the system identifying *meat* with *mate* rather than with *meet* being considered prestigious. Inhabitants of London would,

TABLE VI
Sixteenth and seventeenth century reflexes of middle English long vowels

MiE	[iː]	[eː]	[æː]	[aː]	[ɔː]	[oː]	[uː]
C16	[ai]	[iː]	[eː]	[eː]	[oː]	[uː]	[au]
C17	[ai]	[iː]	[iː]	[eː]	[oː]	[uː]	[au]
Example:	*ride*	*feet*	*beat*	*late*	*road*	*food*	*house*

however, have been familiar, at least passively, with both systems, and the change which subsequently occurred was a shift in the social evaluation of the two systems, the system identifying *meat* with *meet* rather than with *mate* acquiring the greater prestige. For speakers of the prestige norm, there was indeed a sound change, in that [mi:t] replaced [me:t] as the pronunciation of *meat*, but this can be accounted for solely in terms of phonetic representations and relations between variant pronunciations, without any necessary appeal to systematic phonological representations. Thus the prestige speakers concerned would be able to distinguish, at the earlier period, between items where everyone pronounces [i:] (e.g. *meet*), items where everyone pronounces [e:] (e.g. *mate*), and items where they themselves pronounce [e:] but other social groups pronounce [i:] (e.g. *meat*). The last category could be represented as [me:t] ∼ ([mi:t]), the parenthesized part here representing socially conditioned (rather than morphophonemic) alternation. This representation, though abstract, does not refer to systematic phonology, and can serve as a basis for the change in pronunciation of *meat* from [me:t] to [mi:t]: only those items with phonetic [e:] and the socially conditioned alternation with [i:] were affected, and not items that had phonetic [e:] but no such alternation (e.g. *mate*).†

A. A Critical Example

Thus far, the reader may feel that no really crucial evidence has been advanced for or against the psychological reality of systematic phonological representations. Although we have shown that certain sound changes presuppose reality going beyond the simple phonetic representation of the item that changed, we have seen that the abstractness in question can be seen just as easily in terms of a relation to other phonetic representations as in terms of systematic phonological representations differing from the systematic phonetic representation. We want now to turn to a set of data which illustrates that the appeal to systematic phonological representations is either incorrect or, even if correct in a modified form, would involve so much lexical and morphological specification to the rule involved that one would no longer be concerned with a regularly applicable phonological rule, i.e. of the type that provides the strongest evidence for the generative phonological position with respect to systematic phonological representations and their psychological reality. The data are from Maori, the native Polynesian language of New Zealand, and are taken primarily from Hale (1973: pp. 413–420).

In Maori, each verb has a number of forms, of which we shall here be concerned with two: the basic form (lacking any affix), and the passive (with a passive suffix). Table VII gives the basic and passive forms of a representative

---

†Note, moreover, that a few items escaped this reevaluation of prestige norms: thus the current pronunciation of *great* as [greit], like *grate* rather than *greet*, is the same as the sixteenth-century prestige pronunciation.

TABLE VII
Basic and passive verb forms in Maori

Basic	Passive	English
patu	*patua*	strike
kite	*kitea*	see
awhi	*awhitia*	embrace
koorero	*koorerotia*	say
hopu	*hopukia*	catch
moto	*motokia*	strike with fist
kino	*kinongia*	dislike
aru	*arumia*	follow
inu	*inumia*	drink
mau	*mauria*	carry
maatau	*maatauria*	know
mero	*merohia*	stab
kimi	*kimihia*	seek

selection of verbs, together with their English glosses.† The data in Table VII could serve as a textbook exercise in generative phonology (and readers might care to treat it as such before reading the analysis given below), given the criteria that one should set up a single underlying form for all allomorphs of a given morpheme, and as far as possible have regular operation of phonological rules with no lexical or morphological conditioning.

Looking at the data in Table VII, one notes that, in all but the first two items, the passive is marked by the addition of a consonant and -*ia*. However, which consonant is added is not predictable from the basic form, since the consonant may be *t*, *k*, *ng*, *m*, *r*, or *h*, and the choice of consonant is not conditioned phonologically. This suggests that the consonant should be treated, at the systematic phonological level, as part of the verb stem. The passive ending will then be -*ia*, and a rule will be needed to delete word-final consonants.‡ In the first two items in the lefthand column, there is no consonant before the passive ending, which suggests that these stems end in a vowel at the systematic phonological level as well as at the systematic phonetic level. The passive ending here is -*a* rather than -*ia*, so that we can set up a rule deleting the *i* of *ia* after a vowel. The systematic phonological representations of the words in Table VII will thus be as in Table VIII, with the plus sign indicating the boundary between the morphemes in the passive.

†There are a few further types not illustrated in Table VII and requiring, on any analysis, some further phonological rules, but they do not affect the argument developed here, and I therefore feel justified in omitting them for present purposes. Since Maori orthography is essentially a taxonomic phonemic transcription, i.e. a systematic phonetic transcription minus redundancies, I have used Maori orthography rather than adding a transcription in square brackets, which would simply repeat the orthographic representation. Note that *wh* is orthographic for [f], and *ng* for [ŋ].

‡ In fact, Maori has no word-final consonants at all phonetically, except in recent unassimilated loans from English. The syllable structure in native words is invariably (C)V(V).

Within orthodox generative phonology, one can say that this is *the* correct analysis to the data given so far. Historically, there is some comparative evidence from the other Polynesian languages that this analysis also recapitulates the historical development, the loss of final consonants having originally been a sound change, which then continued as a synchronic phonological rule because of the morphophonemic alternations to which it gave rise. However, in his generative analysis of Maori, Hohepa (1967) does not use this analysis, but rather one that makes widespread use of idiosyncratic lexical features. He assumes that the systematic phonological representation of each of the verb stems is the same as its basic form, i.e. /patu/, /awhi/, /hopu/, /kino/, /aru/, /mau/, /mero/, etc. and moreover that the systematic phonological representation of the passive suffix is /tia/. This means that, with the exception of *awhi(tia)* and *koorero(tia)* of the verbs listed, each verb will have to be assigned an idiosyncratic feature, saying either that the initial /ti/ is to be deleted (to give *patua*, *kitea*) or that the initial /t/ is to be changed to some other consonant, with specification of whether this consonant is *k*, *ng*, *m*, *r*, or *h*. In terms of economy of description, and of course from the viewpoint of orthodox generative phonology, Hohepa's analysis is clearly less preferred than that embodied in Table VIII. However, there is good evidence that Hohepa's analysis is synchronically correct for Maori and that the analysis of Table VIII is incorrect, so that even if at an earlier stage in the development of Maori the analysis of Table VIII was psychologically real, this system was reanalysed along the lines suggested in Hohepa, with /tia/ as the systematic phonological, and basic systematic phonetic, representation of the passive morpheme.†

Evidence for the correctness of Hophepa's analysis is of several types, but can be divided into (a) phenomena which, though not incompatible with the generative phonological analysis, are less readily explicable on the basis of this analysis than on the basis of Hohepa's analysis, and (b) phenomena that are

TABLE VIII

Systematic phonological representations of Maori forms in Table VII

Basic	Passive	Basic	Passive
/patu/	/patu + ia/	/arum/	/arum + ia/
/kite/	/kite + ia/	/inum/	/inum + ia/
/awhit/	/awhit + ia/	/maur/	/maur + ia/
/koorerot/	/koorerot + ia/	/maataur/	/maataur + ia/
/hopuk/	/hopuk + ia/	/meroh/	/meroh + ia/
/motok/	/motok + ia/	/kimih/	/kimih + ia/
/kinong/	/kinong + ia/		

†Hale (1968: pp. 87–88) notes that it seems quite general in the Polynesian languages for this kind of reanalysis to take place, although different languages have different preferred consonants. Thus Hawaiian forms all passives by adding ʕia to the basic form (with a final vowel); Hawaiian ʔ corresponds to Maori *k*.

incompatible with the generative phonological analysis, at least in so far as they require the introduction of arbitrary lexical or morphological conditioning in phonological rules—the avoidance of such conditioning was the main advantage claimed for the generative phonological analysis.

One point is that the consonant in the passive used with an individual verb can vary quite considerably from region to region in Maori, and even individual speakers will use now one consonant, now another, with the same verb. Within the generative phonological analysis, especially when dealing with variation internal to a single speaker, this would mean either that the speaker has two distinct underlying representations for the same verb, say one with final /t/ and one with final /k/, which is hard to reconcile with the notion of a single systematic phonological representation for all allomorphs; or that individual lexical items are subject idiosyncratically to rules that change their final consonant. Within Hohepa's analysis, where the assignment of a given consonant to a given verb is lexically arbitrary in any case, it is less surprising that speakers should vary somewhat in their choice of consonant, or that different dialects should have settled on different consonants in the same verb. Moreover, there is a general tendency for -*tia* to replace the other consonant possibilities, suggesting that /tia/ is the basic variant which is resorted to except when the speaker in question knows to apply a rule shifting /t/ to one of the other consonants.

Addition of the passive suffix in Maori is productive, in the sense that it can be applied to lexical items other than those verbs (and certain other parts of speech) that traditionally allowed it. And whenever a new passive form is created in this way, it is invariably with the suffix -*tia* added to the citation form of the lexical item concerned (which, of course, will end in a vowel, like all native and assimilated foreign words in Maori). Some nouns (or at least, what from an English viewpoint would be considered nouns) seem always to have been able to occur as passive verbs in Maori, and these have traditional passive forms that may have some suffix other than -*tia*, e.g. *poo* "night", *poongia* "be overtaken by nightfall", so that here the generative phonological analysis would suggest systematic phonological representations /poong/, /poong + ia/. In general, however, such formations have -*tia*, e.g. *wahine* "woman", *wahinetia* "become (be transformed into) a woman". Another class of words that takes the passive suffix is the class of adverbials, since Maori has a rule whereby adverbials have to agree in voice with their verb, thus giving collocations of passive verb and passive adverbial as in: *i patu-a rawa-tia te hoariri* "the enemy was killed outright", literally "Past strike-Passive completely-Passive the enemy" (Biggs 1969: p. 115). All such adverbials have the suffix -*tia*, quite irrespective of the suffix found on the verb (thus *patu* takes -*a*, but we still find *rawa-tia*). Loanwords from English, of which at least the earlier loans are adapted into Maori so that they end in a vowel in their citation form, all take the suffix -*tia* in the passive, e.g. *whakahoonore* "to honour" (from *hoonore* "honour" with the causative prefix *whaka-*), passive *whakahoonoretia*. If one were to insist on the generative phonological analysis, where the passive suffix has the systematic phonological representation /ia/

(which becomes, it will be recalled, -a after a vowel), then one would have to assume that the systematic phonological representations of all the lexical items we have been discussing in this paragraph—indeed, of all Maori lexical items that do not otherwise receive a systematic phonological representation ending in a segment other than /t/—would have to end in /t/, i.e. /wahinet/ "woman", /rawat/ "completely", /whakahoonoret/ "to honour". While not impossible, this analysis would make Maori a remarkably unbalanced language statistically. If we assume that the systematic phonological representation of the passive suffix is /tia/, all the forms discussed in this paragraph are exactly as expected.

In fact, loanwords present an even greater problem, because some more recent loans from English are adopted into Maori more or less in their English form, in particular with retention of final consonants. The generative phonological analysis would predict that these should add -ia to form the passive; Hohepa's analysis would suggest that they should add -tia, even though this would result in a consonant cluster, absolutely forbidden in native words. And again, the prediction made by Hohepa's analysis is correct: such loans do take the passive suffix -tia. The only way of reconciling this with the generative phonological analysis would be to claim that, where an English word ends in a consonant, it is adopted into Maori by giving it a systematic phonological representation ending in two consonants, the English final consonant plus /t/; the /t/ remains when the passive suffix /ia/ is added, but is dropped word-finally. This serves only to increase yet further the strangeness of Maori systematic phonological representations on this analysis.

The final piece of evidence, which gives the main problem for the generative phonological analysis, is that derivatives of a verb do not necessarily take the same consonant in the passive as does the simplex verb. The precise facts here seem to be subject to considerable dialectal, if not idiolectal, variation, but examples of this kind seem to occur in all varieties of Maori. For instance, Hale (1973: p. 417) describes a variety of Maori where all causative verbs, with the prefix whaka-, have passives in -tia, irrespective of the passive of the simplex verb, e.g. mau "carry", passive mauria, but whakamau "cause to carry", passive whakamautia.† Krupa (1966) notes a compound verb tarahono "to pile up", derived from hono "to join"; the passive of hono is honoa, whereas the passive of tarahono is tarahonotia. In fact, in all such cases known to me where the derived verb has a passive suffix different from that of the simplex verb, the derived verb has in fact the allomorph -tia. The only way of incorporating such data into the generative phonological analysis, with the passive suffix /ia/, would be by postulating a rule that changes a stem-final consonant to t (or inserts t if the stem ends in a vowel, as with /hono/ "join"). This rule would, however, have to be lexically or morphologically

---

†This is not, incidentally, the variety of Maori usually described in grammars (especially pedagogical grammars) of the language. Examination of the Maori-English vocabulary in Biggs (1969), for instance, shows that in the variety of Maori described by Biggs a whaka- derivative regularly takes the same passive ending as the simplex verb.

TABLE IX
Alternative generative phonological analysis of Maori data

Systematic phonological	Systematic phonetic	
/hono + tia/	honoa	by loss of /ti/ of passive
	honotia	no change
/tara + hono + tia/	tarahonotia	no change
/maur + tia/	mauria	by loss of /t/ of passive
	mautia	by loss of stem-final /r/
/whaka + maur + tia/	whakamautia	by loss of stem-final /r/

conditioned, since with some items it is obligatory (e.g. *tarahono*, in some varieties of Maori all causatives in *whaka-*), whereas with other items it is optional (all items that have a passive form not ending in *-tia*, even where there is a parallel form in *-tia*); there may even be varieties of Maori where some items will not be able to undergo this rule at all, i.e. in varieties that eschew the generalization of *-tia* beyond forms where it is accepted traditionally and neologisms.

My argument on the basis of Maori data has been directed primarily against the assumption, crucial to the orthodox generative analysis, that the passive suffix is underlyingly /ia/ rather than /tia/, and careful examination of the preceding argument will show that I have not actually argued against the part of this orthodox analysis which claims that the verb stems should have a final consonant, as in Table VIII.† Suppose one now concedes that the systematic phonological representation of the passive suffix is /tia/—a major concession from orthodox generative phonology, since it presumes that at some stage in the history of the Maori language a reanalysis took place such that the psychologically real analysis did not correspond to the optimal generative phonological analysis—and ask whether it is still possible to maintain systematic phonological representations where the stem has the form as in Table VIII. As illustrative material, we shall look at the systematic phonological representations, on this analysis, of the passives *honoa* (alternative, at least for some speakers, *honotia*), *tarahonotia*, *mauria* (alternative, at least for some speakers, *mautia*), *whakamautia* (for those speakers for whom this is the only form). These are set out in Table IX. This analysis requires two rules: (a) a rule deleting the /t/ of the passive morpheme after a stem-final consonant and the /ti/ of the passive morpheme after a stem-final vowel; (b) a rule deleting the stem-final consonant before another consonant (and also word-finally). To a given form, either (a) or (b) must apply (except that with vowel-final stems, the application of (b) is vacuous, since there is no stem-final consonant), and the problem is to specify which one of them should apply to a given form. Whatever solution is adopted within this framework, some morphological conditioning will be required. First,

†This point was brought to my attention by J. L. M. Trim.

non-verbs and loans from English must be excluded from the application of rule (a), otherwise the passive of *rawa* and *whakahoonore* would come out as **rawaa* and **whakahoonorea*, which are not even possible alternatives to the correct forms *rawatia* and *whakahoonoretia*. (This is unless one makes the unreasonable assumption that all such forms end in /t/ in systematic phonological representation.) Secondly, for certain derived verbs (e.g. *tarahono*, and in the relevant dialect causatives in *whaka-*), one must specify that rule (b) (stem-final consonant deletion) applies to the exclusion of rule (a) (deletion of the initial /t/ of the passive suffix), i.e. even for native forms some morphological specification is required. Other native verbs may undergo either (a) or (b), giving doublets of the type *honoa/honotia, mauria/mautia*. (The output of either (a) or (b) to systematic phonological/ awhit + ia/ will be *awhitia*).

In discussing the Maori data, I have contrasted an orthodox generative phonological analysis, one of whose motivations was to avoid idiosyncratic morphological or lexical conditioning, with an analysis that relies crucially on idiosyncratic conditioning of this kind (Hohepa's analysis). I have tried to show that Hohepa's analysis is indeed preferable, when one takes into account a wider range of data, and that attempts to modify the orthodox generative analysis necessarily introduce precisely the kind of idiosyncratic non-phonetic conditioning that it was designed to avoid, in addition to introducing various other complications. The historical background to this situation seems to be the following. The generative phonological analysis, as set out in Table VII, does seem to recapitulate the early diachronic development of these verbal forms in Maori (or rather, in some ancestor of Maori, since this much is common to the Polynesian languages). Presumably to the speakers of this ancester of Modern Maori, at some stage, the analysis of Table VII was synchronically psychologically real—at the very least, this would have been true for those speakers who introduced the sound change of dropping word-final consonants. Subsequently, however, speakers of pre-Maori reanalysed the verb form data, along the lines of Hohepa's analysis, with vowel-final verb stems and a passive suffix /tia/ (systematic phonological representation), corresponding usually to phonetic *tia* except for certain lexical exceptions. From now on, *tia* was the only productive allomorph of the passive suffix, it was applied to all new words entering the language and to all parts of speech other than verbs entering the verb morphology system; moreover, it was extended by some speakers to causative verbs in *whaka-*, and optionally even to those verbs which can, by way of lexical exception, have one of the other allomorphs. Ultimately, this is working towards a system where the systematic phonological representation /tia/ has only the one allomorph *tia*. In terms of Hohepa's analysis, all of this development finds a perfectly natural account. In terms of the orthodox generative analysis, one could only say that the Maori have gone and "messed up" what must once have been a textbook set of data for generative phonological analysis—and their having done so flies in the face of claims that the orthodox generative phonological analysis has psychological reality.

V. Conclusions

The body of this paper has attempted to show that analyses preferred by orthodox generative phonology cannot be characterized as psychologically real. This poses something of a dilemma but, as always, there are two ways out of the dilemma. First, one could maintain that orthodox generative phonology is in some sense "correct", but abandon the claim that the analyses to which it leads are psychologically real. Perhaps it would be misleading to use the adjective "correct" to qualify such an analysis, one might rather say that such an analysis is "valid", either as an intellectual achievement in its own right (somewhat like pure mathematics), or in the solution of some particular practical problem (e.g. in a data-processing system where there is strong preference for minimizing the amount of storage-space used, this militating against specification of lexical idiosyncrasies and in favour of simple underlying representations and rules of great generality, i.e. in favour of economy of description). Secondly, and inevitably for the psycholinguist, one could insist on psychological reality, and try to work out criteria for linguistic analysis that do correlate with what little we know about the psychological reality of phonological analyses (for instance, the evidence from diachronic linguistics). This paper has been essentially negative, in pointing out the deficiencies in an accepted paradigm, but without proposing an alternative to take its place. However, the realization that there is something wrong with what we have at present is an important first step on the road to devising some more suitable kind of analysis in the future.

References

Biggs, B. (1969). "Let's Learn Maori." A. H. and A. W. Reed, Wellington.

Chomsky, N. (1957). "Syntactic Structures," Mouton, The Hague.

Chomsky, N. (1974). Current Issues in Linguistic Theory. *In* "The Structure of Language: Readings in the Philosophy of Language", (J. A. Fodor and J. J. Katz, eds), pp. 50–118. Prentice-Hall, Englewood Cliffs, New Jersey.

Chomsky, N. and Halle, M. (1968). "The Sound Pattern of English." Harper and Row, New York.

Foley, J. (1967). La Prothèse dans le Verbe Latin *Sum. Languages* **8**, 60–66.

Hale, K. (1968). Review of Patrick W. Hohepa, *A Profile Generative Grammar of Maori* (1967). Journal of the Polynesian Society **77**, 83–99.

Hale, K. (1973). Deep-Surface Canonical Disparities in Relation to Analysis and Change: An Australian Example. *In* "Current Trends in Linguistics", (T. Sebeok, ed.) vol. 11, pp. 401–458. "Diachronic, Areal, and Typological Linguistics," Mouton, The Hague.

Halle, M. (1964). Phonology in Generative Grammar. *In* "The Structure of Language: Readings in the Philosophy of Language," (J. A. Fodor and J. J. Katz, eds.). Prentice-Hall, Englewood Cliffs, N.J.

Hohepa, P. W. (1967). "A Profile Generative Grammar of Maori," (*International Journal of American Linguistics*, Memoir 20), Indiana University Press, Bloomington, Indiana.

Hooper, J. (1976). "An Introduction to Natural Generative Phonology." Academic Press, New York.

Katz, J. J. and Postal, P. M. (1963). "An Integrated Theory of Linguistic Descriptions". (= Research Monograph No. 26), M.I.T. Press, Cambridge, Mass.

King, D. (1969). "Historical Linguistics and Generative Grammar," Prentice-Hall, Englewood Cliffs, N.J.

King, D. (1973). Rule Insertion, *Language* **49**, 551–578.

Kiparsky, P. (1973). "Phonological Representations." *In* "Three Dimensions of Linguistic Theory," TEC, Tokyo, pp. 1–136.

Krupa, V. (1966). "Morpheme and Word in Maori", Mouton, The Hague.

Lightner, T. M. (1975). The Role of Derivational Morphology in Generative Grammar, *Language* **51**, 617–638.

Schane, S. A. (1974). How Abstract is Abstract? *In* "Papers from the Parasession on Natural Phonology", (A. Bruck, R. A. Fox, and M. W. La Galy, eds) pp. 297–317. Chicago Linguistic Society, Chicago.

Weinrich, U., Labov, W. and Herzog, M. (1968). Empirical Foundations for a Theory of Language Change. *In* "Directions for Historical Linguistics: A Symposium", (W. P. Lehmann and Y. Malkiel, eds.), pp. 95–188. University of Texas Press, Austin, Texas.

12
Syntactic-to-Phonetic Coding

W. E. Cooper *Massachusetts Institute of Technology*

I. Introduction

Speech is characterized by a number of properties that appear to be governed, in part, by the speaker's syntactic code. These properties include pauses, the durations of speech segments, the operation of phonological rules across word boundaries, and contours of fundamental frequency. By studying these properties as a function of syntactic structures, it is possible to make a number of inferences about the nature of the speaker's code. To see why this is so, we consider a general model of information-flow for speech production.

As a complex mental activity, speech production may be assumed to involve a number of levels of information-flow whose operations are distributed in time. One possible model of this process, shown in Fig. 1, will serve as a basis for introducing the central topic of this chapter—how a speaker's syntactic code influences the phonetic representation of an utterance.

At the first stage of coding, the speaker formulates an idea or set of ideas about which he intends to speak.† The speaker's idea is then translated into linguistic form as a semantic representation.‡ At the next level, a partial grammatical representation of the utterance is formulated. This partial representation may be assumed to include a decision about whether the utterance is a declarative, imperative, or question, as well as a decision about the identity and ordering of some high-level phrase structure nodes.

The speaker then chooses a few of the major lexical items, including, for example, the head noun of the subject NP and the verb. Following these selections, a further elaboration of the grammatical representation is computed to include modifiers of the subject and predicate. In turn, lexical items are chosen to represent these newly elaborated categories, and the grammar-lexical processing recycles until a full terminal string is computed.

The internal computation of the grammatical structure itself is assumed to proceed from top-down, and, within each hierarchical level, from left-to-right.

---

† This coding may be abandoned for speech not intended to convey meaning, but we restrict our concern here to meaningful conversation.

‡ It is conceivable that the coding of ideas and their translation into a semantic representation do not exist as separate levels of processing, but we will not pursue this possibility since it has no critical bearing on the discussion to follow.

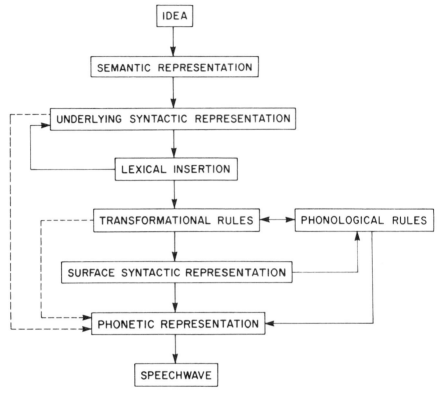

FIG. 1. A possible information-flow model of speech production. Dotted lines represent controversial routes of information-flow to which some of this paper is addressed. Note that the information carried by these dotted lines could, alternatively, be transmitted via the solid lines. In addition, the placement of Semantic Representation is not meant to imply that *all* semantic processing is conducted at this level. In fact, there is linguistic rationale for the notion that some semantic interpretation is applied after the computation of a surface structure.

The general approach taken here is similar to that of Yngve (1960),† with the exception that the present model includes grammar-lexical recycling.

When a fully elaborated underlying structure has been formulated, it is assumed that the structure may undergo certain transformations which move, add, or delete constituents, analogous to transformational rules in a generative grammar (Chomsky, 1965). The existence of such a level of speech coding is controversial at present, chiefly because there is little empirical evidence which can be brought to bear on this issue (for a review, see Fodor *et al.* (1974).

†Whereas Yngve's model is primarily concerned with constraints on short-term memory during the output phase of a planned utterance, our model is primarily concerned with the stages of planning that largely occur before the onset of speech itself. In a fully elaborated model, of course, the planning operations would overlap the output of speech to a great extent.

The output of the transformational level is a surface structure representation. Phonological rules of stress assignment may apply to the output of the surface computation and possibly earlier, during the transformational stage (Bresnan, 1971). Phonetic segments are selected based on the output of the surface structure.

In addition to phonological rules and the selection of phonetic segments, there appears to be a need for a set of *syntactic-to-phonetic* rules, including rules for pausing, segmental lengthening, and fundamental frequency inflections. I will elaborate on these rules in the remainder of this chapter.

For present purposes, the important feature of the model in Fig. 1 is the direction of information flow between the syntactic and phonetic representations. If, as assumed here, the speaker formulates at least a partial syntactic representation prior to a phonetic representation, then it is entirely possible that the precise nature of the syntactic code influences the phonetic form of the utterance.

The study of syntactic-to-phonetic coding appears to offer a unique opportunity to make inferences about the nature of the speaker's grammatical code on the basis of observable speech properties. Accordingly, work has been undertaken to specify (a) the types of grammatical domains that can exert an influence on phonetic coding, and (b) the precise form of the grammatical representation in cases where a syntactic-to-phonetic influence has been observed. The latter effort arises particularly for syntactic structures for which competing alternatives can be defended on independent linguistic grounds.

Experimentally, the task of studying syntactic-to-phonetic influences can be defined as one of examining acoustic details of speech as dependent variables, while manipulating grammatical structures as independent variables. In the work reviewed here, the dependent variables included both prosodic and segmental features.

The observations and experiments to be reviewed have been directed at providing a basis for a theory of syntactic-to-phonetic coding, but it should be pointed out that such studies also offer benefits as guides to research on speech synthesis and perception. For example, it is currently believed that the quality of synthetic speech would be improved by the implementation of a more elaborate set of prosodic rules. These rules may rely heavily on grammatical control. Ultimately, such an implementation should remove the halting, arhythmic quality of synthetic speech, a drawback that currently impedes intelligibility to such an extent that extensive listening is impractical.

In research on speech perception, we do not know enough about the nature of grammatical influences on phonetic coding to make intelligent guesses about the degree to which such influences would be detectable by listeners, and, more importantly, whether such influences would be utilized by listeners in recovering aspects of grammatical structure. On the basis of recent work with speech production, it is becoming possible to design and test hypotheses in this area.

The rest of this chapter is organized as follows. In Section II studies on speech timing are reviewed which permit inferences about the influence of grammatical coding. In Section III, related studies of fundamental frequency contours are discussed. Aspects of a theory of syntactic-to-phonetic coding are formulated in Section IV. Finally, in Section V, I outline the theory's implications for further work in speech production, synthesis, and perception.

II. Influence of Grammatical Coding on Temporal Properties of Speech

A. Pauses

One of the first places to search for the influence of grammar on speech timing involves pauses, since pauses can often be ascertained by informal listening (but see Martin (1970)). Pauses may be produced for a variety of reasons in speech, and it is important to distinguish their underlying determinants at the outset. We will not be concerned here with pauses that reflect word-finding difficulty, general hesitation, or drastic changes in the planning of the semantic content of an utterance (cf. Boomer, 1965; Goldman-Eisler, 1968; Martin, 1971). Instead, our concern will lie with pauses that appear to be syntactically determined. Typically, such pauses appear at the ends of major syntactic constituents (Goldman-Eisler, 1968, 1972; Martin, 1970; Grosjean and Deschamps, 1975). By contrast, hesitation pauses often occur within major constituents (Boomer, 1965). Another distinguishing property of syntactic pauses is their probability of occurrence at precise locations in an utterance, the probability being greater for syntactic pauses than for hesitations.

As in the case of most phonetic variables studied here, syntactic pauses occur optionally rather than obligatorily in most sentences (cf. Downing, 1970), and the duration and location of such pauses depend on extra-grammatical factors such as overall speaking rate and the length of the constituent, in terms of its number of syllables (Bierwisch, 1966; Grosjean et al., 1977). But despite this optionality and partial control by extra-grammatical factors, pauses can provide useful clues about the form of a speaker's syntactic code.

A well-known example involves the location of pauses in multiply right-branching sentence structures, as in (1):

    (1)   This is the cat that caught the rat that stole the cheese.

In general, it has been assumed that syntactic pauses occur at the ends of major constituents. Chomsky (1965, p. 13) has, however, pointed out that the locations of pauses in (1) occur typically after *cat* and *rat*, and that these locations do not correspond with the ends of major constituents. The bracketing for (1), given in (1′), would predict, according to the constituent-final assumption, that no pauses should occur until after the sentence-final word *cheese*.

(1') [$_S$this is[$_{NP}$the cat[$_S$that caught[$_{NP}$the rat[$_S$that stole the cheese]$_S$]$_{NP}$]$_S$]$_{NP}$]$_S$

Either the assumption regarding constituent-final pausing is incorrect, or the grammatical coding of (1) differs from (1') at the stage of the speaker's processing at which pauses are determined. The latter alternative has been advocated by Chomsky and Halle (1968), Lieberman (1967), and Langendoen (1976), who suggest that a readjustment rule applies to (1') to derive (1''), such that the embedded clauses become sister-adjoined to the main clause, as shown in Fig. 2.

(1'') [[$_S$this is[$_{NP}$the cat]$_{NP}$]$_S$[$_S$that caught[$_{NP}$the rat]$_{NP}$]$_S$[$_S$that stole the cheese]$_S$]$_S$

The readjustment rule serves to "flatten" the tree structure, so that, instead of containing multiple right-branching, the sentence contains multiple conjoined clauses of equal hierarchical status. Given this structure, pauses are inserted appropriately after *cat* and *rat*.

This example illustrates a common problem confronting those who wish to make use of temporal phenomena in arriving at the form of a speaker's grammatical code. First, a general assumption is made—syntactic pauses occur at the ends of major constituents. Then, we find an apparent exception—(1). To account for the apparent exception, we must either alter the presumed structure of the exception or abandon the general assumption. In this particular case, the former course has been adopted. However, it is worthwhile to examine where we would be led by considering the latter alternative.

To review the evidence on which the assumption regarding constituent-final pausing is based, consider the following sentences.

(2)   Although John went to the movies with Sue, I decided not to go along.

(3)   I am leaving tomorrow, but John is leaving Friday.

In both (2) and (3), pauses may optionally be inserted at the location of the comma, corresponding to the end of the clause. However, in these sentences, the pause location may alternatively be specified as occurring just before the *beginning* of the second clause. On the basis of these sentences alone then, it is not clear whether pauses are determined by a right bracket, terminating one clause, by a left bracket, starting another, or by both. Significantly, if the rule for pausing were determined at the *beginnings* of clauses rather than at their ends, then the pause locations in (1) would be automatically accounted for by (1'), without the need to postulate the readjustment rule yielding (1'').

To select between the left- and right-bracket hypotheses, we must consider sentences like (4) and (5).

(4)   I know a man who lives in the house next door.

(5)   Everyone in the garden believes that petunias are pretty.

In these sentences, the second clause is structurally embedded within the main clause, so that the beginning of the embedded clause does not coincide with the end of the main clause. In such cases, the end of the main clause occurs at the end of the entire sentence string. In (4), the embedded relative clause begins with the relative pronoun *who*, and, in (5), the embedded complement clause begins with the complementizer *that*. In both cases, no pause typically occurs at the beginning of the embedded clause, suggesting that pausing is in fact primarily determined by the endings of clauses rather than by their beginnings. If so, then the approach taken by Langendoen (1976) and others is well-founded.

However, problems remain, and their resolution leads to a more general rule

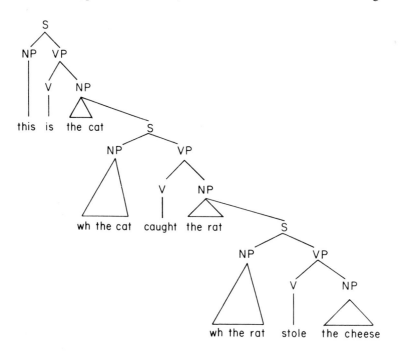

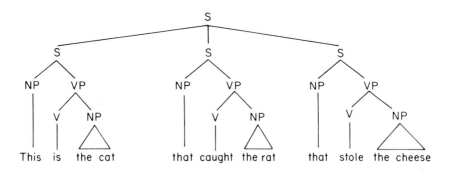

FIG. 2. Underlying (top) and readjusted (bottom) tree structures for Sentence (1).

of pausing. If the principle of constituent-final pausing is to be retained, we must provide an account for pausing in nonrestrictive relative clauses, like (6).

(6) John, who is believed to be sick, was seen outdoors yesterday.

In this sentence, pauses typically accompany both the beginning and the end of the relative clause. The pause at the end of the relative clause can be accounted for by constituent-final pausing. A problem arises, however, in accounting for the pause at the *beginning* of the nonrestrictive relative. This problem extends to parenthetical expressions, as in (7), where a pause may occur just prior to the beginning of the parenthetical.

(7) a. John, I think, is sick.

b. John, by the way, should not leave Chicago before dawn.

c. John should, I guess, take out the garbage.

It appears that an account of the pauses in (6) and (7) may be based on the notion (receiving some motivation from linguistic studies) that nonrestrictive relatives and parentheticals are conjoined with the main clause at the level of coding at which pauses are inserted (see Thompson (1968), for discussion of a conjoined source for nonrestrictive relatives). Given this assumption, the pauses for (6) and (7), as well as the data in (1)–(5), can be accounted for by a single principle, given in (8).

(8) *Pause rule for conjoined clauses.* Insert pauses at the beginning and end of a clause that is immediately dominated by the highest S node in the phrase structure.

With (8), all the pause data reviewed thus far can be accounted for (assuming the structure (1″) for (1)), including the pauses that occur at the beginning and end of each string. Further support for a rule like (8) has been provided by Downing (1970, 1973) and Emonds (1976). As Downing notes, (8) must be slightly amended, however, to rule out pausing at the beginning of extraposed clauses (see also Stockwell, 1972).

This principle also handles pausing that accompanies sentences in which the canonical word order has been violated by root transformations— transformations that move a constituent and attach it to the highest S in the tree (Emonds, 1976). Examples of sentences in which a root transformation has moved a constituent to the front appear in (9b–d).

Experiments by Cooper and Paccia (1977) have shown that

(9) a. The owner of the park shows gold to the children. (SVO-canonical order)

b. The owner of the park she scolded the children. (Left Dislocation)

c. The statue in the park Cher showed to the children. (Topicalization)

d. At Brockton's city park Cher scolded the children. (PP Preposing)

speakers typically pause at the end of the preposed constituent, just after *park* in (9b–d) compared with (9a).[†] If it is assumed, with Emonds (1976), that the

---

[†] Emonds (1976) advances the intuition that pauses (included in his term "comma intonation") accompany left and right dislocation but not topicalization and PP preposing. The experimental data (Cooper and Paccia, 1977), however, indicate that pausing accompanies topicalization and PP preposing as well, when other factors are controlled. The experimental data provide the basis for the generalization of (8) discussed in the text.

preposed constituents are attached to the highest S in the tree, and that, furthermore, the rule for pausing applies after preposing transformation, then the pausing in (9b–d) can be accounted for as a case of constituent-initial pausing under (8). On this view, the pause is determined not at the end of the preposed constituent but at the *beginning* of the main clause. In a converse manner, (8) (or a similar rule like Downing's) also provides an account of pausing just before a constituent that has been moved to the end of a string by a root transformation like Right Dislocation (Ross, 1967), as in (10).

(10)   I like it, this hammer.

Any other attempt to provide a unified account for pausing in the variety of cases reviewed thus far becomes very unwieldy. The pause rule (8) thus represents an improvement over the earlier constituent-final rule.

But the story for pausing is still not complete. Consider another class of syntactic pause, illustrated in (11).

(11)   The tall, handsome man left without saying a word.

Here, a pause may be inserted between two adjectives which both modify the head noun *man*. Clearly, this pause cannot be handled by (8). It is not at the boundary between conjoined clauses nor at the boundary of any major grammatical constituent. Note that pausing does not occur between the two adjectives if they are separated by a conjunction, as in (12).

(12)   The tall and handsome man left without saying a word.

Since the presence of a conjunction typically eliminates the pause, it may be speculated that the conjunction and pause each serve the same purpose, namely to separate the two conjoined constituents in the processing of both the speaker and listener. The pause in (11) may be viewed as a replacement for the missing conjunction. More specifically, it is possible that the speaker programs time intervals at an underlying level of syntactic coding for the uttering of each constituent, and, when a constituent is deleted during a subsequent stage of coding, a pause is inserted in its place so as not to disrupt the overall temporal program already established for the utterance. The pauses described for sentences (1)–(10), however, cannot be accounted for in this manner, so (11) still stands as a demonstrably different kind of syntactic pause from that subsumed under (8).

Now consider sentence (13).

(13)   John ate the rice, and Harry, the beans.

In this sentence, the verb of the second clause has been deleted under identity with the first verb by Gapping (Ross, 1970; Jackendoff, 1971; Stillings, 1975). The pause optionally inserted after *Harry* in (13) may be viewed like the pause in (11). Here, the pause replaces the deleted verb. We may propose that, in addition to (8), a second general rule of syntactic pausing exists to account for examples like (11) and (13). This additional rule permits pausing as a replacement for a deleted constituent.

As just stated, the rule may be too general, since pauses do not typically occur just before the parenthesized words in (14)–(16), when these words are deleted.

(14)   I know the man (that) Harry shot.
(15)   Bob finished his homework and (he) went outside.
(16)   Bob (finished work) and Harry finished work.

It appears, rather, that the rule for pausing accounting for (11) and (13) is restricted to deletions that do not involve daughters of S (that is, categories NP and VP immediately dominated by S). An alternative formulation would retain an unrestricted pause rule for all deletion sites but eliminate (14)–(16) on the basis that these sentences do not contain true deletions but have virtually identical underlying and surface structures. Currently, this possibility is likely for (15) and (16) on linguistic grounds (Dougherty, 1970; Hudson, 1976).

Finally, consider (17), in which the parenthesized words may undergo deletion.

(17)   John cooked (the beans) and Harry ate the beans.

It is controversial whether or not a true deletion occurs here (Ross, 1967; Koutsoudas, 1971; Hudson, 1976). Chomsky (1957) originally noted that sentences like (17) are typically accompanied by contrastive stress on the two verbs, as well as by a pause at the deletion site. The optional pause here can be handled by the rule for pausing at deletions noted above, or, alternatively, by the pause rule for conjoined clauses in (8), under the assumption that (8) operates on surface rather than underlying structures.

A rule for pausing at deletion sites carried the implication that a level of coding analogous to tranformations exists in speech coding, and hence, that a distinction between underlying and surface structure exists (see Fig. 1). By accounting for pauses in terms of the notion *deletion*, we are forced to postulate an underlying structure from which deletion could have occurred. While it is conceivable that the rules covering (11) and (13) could be reformulated in terms of surface structure variables only, attempts to do so have produced rules that lack the generality of the deletion rule.

In conclusion, it appears that the study of pausing can provide some valuable information about the form of the speaker's syntactic code. Further discussions on this point are provided by Stockwell (1972), Downing (1973), Goldman-Eisler (1972), and Grosjean (1976). A particularly well-developed treatment is provided in Downing's (1970) doctoral thesis. This thesis is concerned with perceptually-defined pauses that appear to occur obligatorily. As mentioned above, Downing's main rule covering such pausing is similar to (8) (see also Stockwell, 1972, for a critique of Downing's position).

B. Segment Durations

Like pauses, the durations of phonetic segments may be syntactically determined. Constituents are often accompanied by lengthening of the duration of the last syllable, or of the last few syllables (Martin, 1970; Lindblom and Rapp, 1973; Klatt, 1975; Kloker, 1975; Cooper, 1976a). Although this lengthening is not as noticeable to a listener as pausing, segmental lengthening is typically a more consistent indicator of major constituent boundaries in speech production (see Cooper and Paccia, 1977 for numerous examples).

Studies of grammatically-determined lengthening have focused on two issues: (1) whether constituent-final lengthening is controlled by a level of grammatical coding that corresponds more nearly to an underlying or surface structure representation, and (2) whether the locations of lengthening favor one or another analysis in cases where the locations of boundaries are in dispute on purely linguistic grounds. To date, the work on each of these two issues has provided answers for a few structural distinctions. Before delving into a discussion of the results, some general remarks on experimental method are in order.

1. Experimental methods

In order to study a speaker's computational processes, it would be most desirable to study a corpus of spontaneous speech. While certain general effects can be studied in this manner (e.g. Kloker, 1975), work on specific hypotheses cannot be conducted with proper control or efficiency using such a data base. A number of syntactic and extra-syntactic factors combine to influence phonetic attributes in normal speaking (Klatt, 1976), and an experimental method is needed to study each of these factors in isolation, providing a basis for subsequent study of interaction.

Accordingly, a sentence-reading procedure (Cooper, 1976a) was devised in which the phonetic form of the utterances could be tightly controlled. In each test, a short list of sentences (or paragraphs) is read by a speaker after a period of practice during which he is familiarized with a task and the particular materials. Each sentence contains one or more key words, placed at the location(s) of syntactic boundaries or other locations of interest. The choice of key words is influenced by the degree to which their phonetic representation facilitates acoustic analysis. In studies of speech timing, for example, key words must be readily segmentable from a digitized oscillographic trace of the speech waveform.

The sentences of each group typically contain the same number of syllables and share as many words as possible, compatible with signalling the structural distinction under study. The stress pattern of the sentences is matched as closely as possible so that any effects may be attributed to a direct syntactic influence rather than to an intermediary influence of stress.

By using normal English sentences in our studies, we can build a data base that will be useful in guiding the study of interactions between syntactic effects and other influences on speech timing. The construction of appropriate natural sentences is often difficult but offers an advantage over procedures that involve nonsense mimicry of natural speech (Lindblom and Rapp, 1973; Liberman and Streeter, 1976). The latter procedures may provide an adequate means of studying stress effects, but the use of real sentences is needed to study the effects of syntax and its interaction with other variables (e.g. cross-word phonetic conditioning, Section II.C.) in a setting that approximates natural speaking. The results of these experiments can also be applied directly to practical problems of speech synthesis.

Each of a group of 10–20 speakers is tested individually in a large sound-insulated chamber for approximately 40–50 min per session. During this time, each speaker is presented from about seven to ten sentence lists, each list representing a separate experiment. At the beginning of a session, the speaker is told that the general purpose of the experiments is to study the syntactic control of speech sound properties. The speaker is then told that he will be given practice in reading lists of sentences in order to train him to utter each sentence "as a unitary whole, as if it were spoken spontaneously," rather than "word-by-word," as in unpracticed reading. The speaker is encouraged to speak as naturally as possible but to avoid placing contrastive or emphatic stress on any word or syllable in a sentence, unless specifically instructed otherwise for the purpose of experiments designed to test stress effects.

Following these preliminary instructions, the speaker is given the first of a series of lists of sentences. The speaker is told to consider each sentence in the list independently of the others (the order in which sentences and lists are presented to speakers is pseudo-randomized). During practice, the speaker is asked to utter a given sentence aloud once, providing the experimenter with a final opportunity to check for contrastive or emphatic stress and to check recording levels. The speaker then utters the given sentence for recording.

The speaker is told to expect to produce a few mispronunciations during the test. For mispronunciations, or for any changes from the normal intonation or timing which the speaker chooses to adopt, the speaker is instructed to pause, utter the word "repeat," and then say the sentence token again. After reading a given list, the speaker is provided a short rest period, encouraged to take a drink of water, and then asked to begin the practice procedure with a new list.

Acoustic analysis of segment durations is performed using an oscillographic display of speech, digitized at a sampling rate of 10 kHz on a PDP-9 computer. The segment durations are measured from this display with the aid of a computer-controlled cursor (Huggins, 1969). The cursor is maneuvered by velocity and position dials to mark the onset and offset of each key segment. The time difference between the segment onset and offset is displayed on the oscilloscope screen to the nearest 100 μs. For key word segments beginning with a word-initial voiceless stop consonant and ending with a vowel preceding a voiceless stop (e.g. /je/ of "Jake"), the reliability of each measurement has been determined to be within 3 ms, based on a duplicate set of measurements made without the experimenter's remembrance of, or reference to, the original measurements for the same utterances.

By using a practiced reading procedure, it is likely that speakers will exhibit a greater amount of preplanning than in most spontaneous speaking situations. Our results will thus be more indicative of the preplanning *capabilities* of the speaker than of the preplanning typically applied in spontaneous speech. However, as shown by Kloker (1975), one of the main phenomena on which our studies are based, namely clause-final lengthening, occurs in spontaneous speech as well as in practiced reading. It is therefore likely that many of our results generalize to spontaneous speech.

2. *The role of surface versus underlying structure*

The fundamental property of a transformational grammar is its specification of more than a single level of grammatical description. Regarding a model of speech production, we would like to know whether more than a single level of syntactic coding also exists in speech production, and, if so, whether segmental lengthening at constituent boundaries is determined by a level of coding that corresponds more nearly to surface or underlying structure.

Thus far, most of the work on this problem has focused on sentence structures that are derived via transformations that delete a constituent (Cooper and Paccia, 1977). The results suggest that both surface and underlying levels of coding may be involved in the control of segmental lengthening. The work on deletions will not be reviewed in detail because this study is not yet complete.

3. *Clause-conditioned lengthening and competing surface structures*

Our study on this issue stems from the debate on the existence of a rule of Raising. This rule purportedly moves an NP underlying subject of a subordinate clause into surface position as an NP direct object of the main clause, as shown in Fig. 3. Postal (1974), among others, has defended the existence of such a Raising transformation, whereas Chomsky (1973) and Bresnan (1976), among others, oppose it. This particular rule has generated much attention in linguistics because solutions to issues about the general form of the transformational component appear to hinge on the analysis. In studying a speaker's performance, we are not concerned with the purely linguistic considerations that surround the arguments for and against this putative transformation, although these are interesting in their own right. What we wish to determine is whether the level of grammatical coding used by the speaker in controlling clause-conditioned lengthening corresponds more nearly to a structure derived via one of these alternative analyses.

The main experiment in this study (Cooper, 1976b) involved the following five sentences.

(18)   a. The host expected Kate to be at breakfast. (EXPECT-INF = *expect* infinitival complement)
       b. The host expected Kate would be at breakfast. (EXPECT-THAT = *expect that* complement)
       c. The host expected Kate at the big breakfast. (EXPECT-SIMPLE = *expect* single surface clause)
       d. The host persuaded Kate to be at breakfast. (PERSUADE-INF = *persuade* infinitival complement)
       e. The host persuaded Kate at the big breakfast. (PERSUADE-SIMPLE = *persuade* single surface clause)

Sentences (18a, b, and d) involve two-clause structures containing a main clause and an embedded complement clause. Sentences (18b) and (18d) represent a well-known distinction, first pointed out by Chomsky (1965), in which the complement of a verb *expect*, as in *expect Kate X*, does not entail *expect Kate*, whereas the complement of a verb *persuade*, as in *persuade Kate X*, does entail *persuade Kate*. The logical distinction between the complements of *expect* and *persuade* can be drawn out by considering passive sentences like (19).

(19)   a. The host expected Kate to be brought by an escort.
       b. The host persuaded Kate to be brought by an escort.

Sentence (19a) is synonymous with the active string *The host expected an escort to bring Kate*, whereas (19b) is non-synonymous with the corresponding string *The host persuaded an escort to bring Kate*. Structurally, the difference between the complements of *expect* and *persuade* has been captured by an

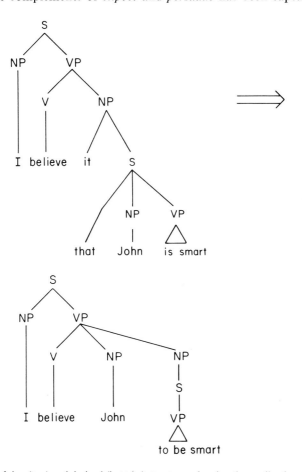

FIG. 3. Underlying (top) and derived (bottom) structures showing the application of Raising.

underlying syntactic representation proposed by Rosenbaum (1967), who postulated the structures shown in Fig. 4.

For our purposes, the key feature of these structures is that the main verb *expect* occurs just prior to the beginning of the subordinate clause in underlying structure, whereas the verb *persuade* does not. Thus, to the extent that these structural relations are maintained in surface structure, lengthening should occur for a segment of the verb *expect* but not for a segment of the verb *persuade*, when these verbs are followed by a complement clause, as opposed to the rest of the main clause in a single-clause string (the latter is represented by (18c) and (18e)). This prediction is based on the assumption that lengthening occurs for a segment located just prior to the beginning of an embedded clause.

The three complement-containing sentences of (18a, b, and d) can be derived from the underlying structures of Fig. 4. To derive (18d), one can delete the second occurrence of the NP *Kate* under identity with the first occurrence of *Kate* by the rule of Equi NP Deletion (alternative derivations exist, but do not bear on the present arguments). This derivation preserves the relevant clause-structure relations of the underlying structure, with *persuade* occurring two words before the beginning of the subordinate clause. Sentence (18b) also preserves the structural relations shown for *expect* complements in Fig. 4, with *expect* occurring just prior to the beginning of the subordinate clause. The complementizer *that* has been deleted from (18b), in order to render the stress contour of this sentence more similar to the other complement-containing sentences of (18).

The controversial derivation involves (18a), which contains the *expect* infinitival complement. Here, Chomsky maintains that the derivation is similar to that for (18b), with expect occurring just before the subordinate clause. Postal (1974) contends, however, that a transformation of Raising lifts the subordinate occurrence of the NP *Kate* into the object position of the main clause during the derivation of (18a), such that, in surface structure, *expect* appears two words before the beginning of the subordinate clause, as does *persuade* in (18d).

The aim of the experiment was to measure the duration of a segment of the main verbs in (18a, b, and d) to determine whether segmental lengthening reflects grammatical coding that is akin to one or the other of these two linguistic analyses. As control sentences, (18c) and (18e) were chosen, in which the verbs *expect* and *persuade* appeared in surface strings containing only single-clause structures. Based on the assumptions that (a) surface-clause relations determine clause-conditioned lengthening to some extent, as suggested from data reviewed in the previous subsection, and (b) clause-conditioned lengthening occurs for a segment located just prior to the beginning of a subordinate clause, also supported by data of the previous subsection, it was predicted that lengthening should be observed for the key segment /spɛkt/ of *expected* in (18b) relative to (18c) but not for the segment /swed/ of *persuade* in (18d) relative to (18e). For (18a), the controversial case, a lengthening effect similar to that predicted for (18b) was predicted on the basis of syntactic coding

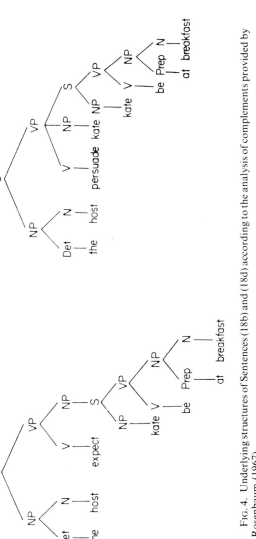

FIG. 4. Underlying structures of Sentences (18b) and (18d) according to the analysis of complements provided by Rosenbaum (1967).

analogous to that proposed by Chomsky, while no lengthening was predicted on the basis of coding represented by Postal's analysis.

Fifteen speakers read the sentences of (18), and the results for the verb segments showed a statistically significant lengthening effect for the segment of *expected* in both (18a) and (18b) relative to the duration of this segment in (18d), as predicted on the basis of Chomsky's analysis. In comparison to other effects to be reviewed, the lengthening was small in magnitude, averaging about 15 ms. Statistical significance was attained because the effect was systematic across speakers, as in the case of most of the effects of segmental duration to be reviewed. No lengthening was observed for (18d) over (18e), as predicted on the basis of the uncontroversial analysis of *persuade* complement structures.

In addition to measuring the segment durations of the main verbs, measurements were also computed for the duration of the NP *Kate*, which, according to a Raising analysis, should trigger clause-conditioned lengthening in (18a), since *Kate* is located just prior to the beginning of the subordinate clause after the purported Raising transformation has applied. However, only a slight, statistically nonsignificant effect was noted, when phonetically-conditioned effects imposed by differences in the phonetic segments following *Kate* were taken into account (Cooper, 1976b, Experiment II). The lack of any significant difference in the durations of a segment of *Kate* for (18a) and (18b) is consistent with Chomsky's linguistic analysis, in which *Kate* occurred in the same structural position for both sentences. Thus, the results of this study for both verbs and NP segments provide a measure of support for clause-conditioned lengthening at a level of grammatical coding that corresponds to the non-Raising linguistic analysis proposed by Chomsky. An attempt was made to test the generality of the results with sentences containing other complement-taking verbs (Cooper, 1976b, Experiment III). The results provided some support for the claim that the results observed for *expect* and *persuade* generalize to other verbs exhibiting this structural distinction, although this support was not unanimous.†

4. Phrase boundaries

In addition to the lengthening effects observed at clause boundaries, lengthening has also been observed at major *phrase* boundaries (Klatt, 1975; Sorensen *et al.*, 1977). In the study of Sorensen *et al.*, it was shown that the longer duration of nouns than verbs in typical contexts can be ascribed to the fact that nouns usually occur in phrase-final position, unlike verbs.

C. Syntactic Boundaries and the Application of Phonetic Rules

In addition to segmental lengthening and pausing, syntactic boundaries influence the application of phonetic rules which normally operate across

---

†Data for *believe* provided the best support for the *expect*-type structure. As noted by Bresnan (1972), *believe* is actually a better trigger of NP complementation than *expect*, since the latter is ambiguously representative of *expect* or *expect* (*for*).

word boundaries. It is assumed that, at some processing level, a speaker applies phonetic rules over some specified syntactic domain, such that phonetic information lying outside this domain cannot be taken into consideration in the application of the rules. Thus, for a given syntactic domain X including phonetic segments $[s_1, s_2 \ldots s_n]_X$, phonetic rules applied to any segment s_i can utilize information contained only in segments (typically adjacent to s_i) contained within X. Unlike the concept of the transformational cycle, syntactic coding domains in speech production are assumed to operate on successively narrow domains of material and consistent with left-to-right constraints on speech production, as discussed in Section I.

By determining which cross-word phonetic rules apply across a range of different syntactic boundaries, it is possible to obtain information about the scope of syntactic domains in speech coding. Recent experimental studies on this topic will be reviewed, along with a discussion of related linguistic observations.

1. *Experiments*

One phonetic rule studied for the effects of syntactic blocking involves the influence of an unstressed syllable on the duration of a preceding stressed syllable. The unstressed syllable serves to shorten the duration of the preceding stressed syllable compared to the latter's duration in a stressed-stressed sequence (Lindblom, 1964; Barnwell, 1971). Whether this rule, referred to here as the Trochaic Shortening Rule (TSR), is actually a shortening effect in the environment of a following unstressed syllable or a lengthening effect in the environment of a following stressed syllable is a question of interest in its own right which need not concern us here (see, however, Bolinger (1976)). Huggins (1974, 1975) showed that TSR operates across word boundaries but that the cross-word effect may be blocked by an intervening syntactic boundary, in particular, the boundary between the subject NP and predicate VP of a single-clause sentence. Unfortunately, the blocking effect was not observed with much consistency across different sentences, a failure that may be traced to a lack of control for the immediate phonetic environment of the measured segment.

The basic idea put forth by Huggins—that a major syntactic boundary could block a cross-word phonetic rule—offered an opportunity to study the domains of syntactic coding and their effect on phonetic rules. Accordingly, experiments were conducted to establish whether the potential effects of syntactic blocking would be observed for TSR in a more controlled phonetic setting, and, if so, whether a variety of so-called "strong" and "weak" syntactic boundaries would serve to block TSR (Cooper *et al.*, 1977b).

Test sentences were designed in pairs, testing within-word and across-word effects of TSR. Example sentence pairs appear in (20)–(22).

(20) a. The police kept *Clint* until nine o'clock that night.
    b. The police kept *Clint*on till nine o'clock that night.
(21) a. Horace bought *Clint* an enormous turtle.
    b. Horace bought *Clint*on enormous turtles.

(22) a. The longshoreman must *li*ght an inflammable carton.
    b. The longshoreman must *li*ghten inflammable cartons.

In each sentence, the italicized portion refers to the measured segment. The measurements revealed that TSR was blocked across a variety of syntactic boundaries, including the boundaries between a NP or PP and a separate clause as well as between two PPs. On the other hand, the rule was not blocked across boundaries between an NP direct object and NP indirect object (21) or between a verb and NP direct object (22). Unlike some other effects of segmental lengthening, the blocking effects, when they occurred, were represented by large differences in the duration of segments, often averaging 20% or more. The difference in blocking was accounted for in terms of a theory of boundary strengths which relied on the notion of Branching Depth. This term refers to the extent to which a given phrase node branches hierarchically (see Fig. 5 for examples). The relevant index is the depth of branching, not the number of particular branches from a given node. The property of Branching Depth may assume any integer value, and, on this account, very strong syntactic boundaries include those which separate phrase nodes having large integer values of branching depth. A collapsing convention may be introduced to retain the larger integer of branching depth for two phrase nodes of differing depth at a given boundary. The boundary between two main clauses is thus marked as a strong boundary, as is the boundary between an NP and VP of a main clause. Very weak boundaries include those between an adjective or determiner and a head noun, in accordance with intuition.

Of the various syntactic boundaries tested in the experiments with TSR, two of them failed to show a blocking effect. As can be seen in Fig. 5, these two boundaries are structurally weaker, according to the metric of Branching Depth, than the boundaries which did show a significant blocking effect. It appears that, for TSR, a blocking effect is produced whenever the syntactic boundary borders a phrase node having a Branching Depth of ≥ 2.

The results of the experiments on TSR could, however, be accounted for in a manner that would not rely on the notion of blocking. This alternative account relies on differences in phrase-final lengthening. According to this account, phrase-final lengthening occurs exclusively or primarily for the very last syllable of a phrase. Coupled with the assumption that different phrase types produce different magnitudes of phrase-final lengthening, this account represented a reasonable alternative to the blocking account.

To test for the presence of blocking in cases where differences in phrase-final lengthening do not occur, two additional rules were studied. One involved the effect of a following voiced versus voiceless consonant, the other involved palatalization. The first rule failed to show sizable cross-word effects regardless of the syntactic boundary type, rendering it useless for our purposes. The second rule, palatalization, provided a satisfactory cross-word test of the blocking hypothesis. Palatalization (of the type studied here) is a phonological rule whereby a dental stop consonant is palatalized in the environment of a palatal (e.g. *did you* becomes /dɪj(y)u/ (Hyman, 1975)). In a

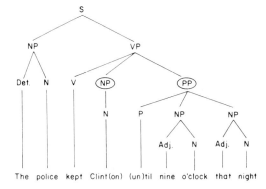

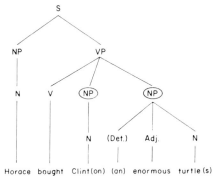

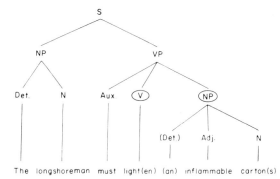

Fig. 5. Approximate surface structure trees for a sentence (top) in which blocking of TSR was obtained and for two sentences in which no blocking occurred. The circled nodes represent the most inclusive phrases that border the boundary under consideration, but which do not dominate any nodes across the border. These tree diagrams illustrate differences of relative boundary strength according to the Branching Depth metric. In the top tree diagram, the circled PP branches twice. The total phrase branching of the circled nodes in the middle and bottom tree structures is only one branching. In an elaboration of these tree structures, in terms of Chomsky's $\bar{X}$ notation, the same approximate strength relations would hold for the boundary types studied here.

variety of sentences, we found that palatalization was blocked across word boundaries to a greater extent when the intervening syntactic boundary represented a major boundary. The results thus indicate that blocking of the type proposed earlier does occur at strong syntactic boundaries.

Currently, work on palatalization is directed at selecting between theoretical accounts of blocking in terms of Branching Depth and alternative metrics of boundary strength. Among the alternative metrics, two involve the notions of Node Height, defined in terms of the number of nodes to reach the highest S node, and Daughter-of-S, defined in terms of nodes immediately dominated by S. According to the Node Height alternative, blocking occurs for constituents that are sufficiently high in the tree structure (note that this metric, unlike Branching Depth, fails to predict the results for TSR for the three structures shown in Fig. 5). According to the Daughter-of-S hypothesis, blocking occurs for constituents immediately dominated by S. By testing the relative merits of these competing accounts, as well as accounts based on linguistic studies of word boundary markers (Chomsky and Halle, 1968; Stanley, 1973), it should be possible to provide an answer to the question "What constitutes a strong syntactic boundary?" as this question applies to the blocking of cross-word phonological effects. Ideally, the answer to this question will also predict effects of lengthening and pausing, under the assumption that these phenomena are under the control of a single syntactic code (see Cooper and Paccia, 1977).

2. *Linguistic observations*

The concept of syntactic blocking has also been studied in linguistic research on phonological rules. Selkirk (1974), for example, has proposed that French liaison contexts are sensitive to syntactic categories in a manner that provides support for the $\bar{X}$ theory of categories (Chomsky, 1970).

In French, a word-final obstruent is typically deleted in the environment of a following consonant, as in *dans la salle*, in which the /s/ of *dans* is deleted. Liaison contexts are those contexts in which the deletion rule fails to operate, as in *dans une salle*, where the /s/ of *dans* is pronounced. If liaison contexts were determined on a purely phonological basis, one would expect liaison to occur *whenever* a word-final obstruent is followed by a vowel. Yet Selkirk observed that liaison is blocked in the environment of many syntactic boundaries. Unlike palatalization in English, liaison in modern French appears to be blocked for all but the most minor boundaries, as between a determiner and head noun. In elevated speech, Selkirk notes that liaison contexts are extended somewhat, including boundaries between an inflected member of grammatical category X and its complement, both of which are dominated by $\bar{X}$ (Chomsky, 1970). The term *complement* as used here refers to a constituent generated as a sister to the X categories noun, verb, or adjective. Rotenberg (1975), however, questions the validity of the elevated style assumed by Selkirk, and it is possible that the blocking of liaison is determined more by stress pattern than by syntactic boundaries *per se*.

D. Phonetic Blocking Effects on Constituency

In the previous subsection, we considered the possibility that syntactic coding domains constrain the operation of cross-word phonetic rules. But speakers may also attempt to block a syntactic relation of constituency by lengthening a word segment and inserting a pause. A case in point involves the well-known phrase *the old men and women*. Syntactically, the phrase is ambiguous between the bracketings (a) [*old men women*] and (b) [*old men*] [*women*]. A speaker who intends to convey the second of these two structures may lengthen *men* and insert a following pause, thereby indicating to the listener that the adjective *old* modifies *men* only. This effect has been documented by Lehiste (1973). It appears that the speaker may utilize an optional late rule to insert a pause at a right bracket of a constituent where the presence of the structural bracket is assumed not to be easily detected by the listener.

E. Node Height and Structural Disambiguation

Another class of structural ambiguities may provide special information about the way in which the hierarchical properties of a speaker's syntactic representation influence speech timing. These ambiguities have been discussed in previous literature simply to demonstrate the existence of a syntactic influence on speech timing and/or fundamental frequency, but only recently has the common generality been discovered tying these ambiguities to a single structural account.

Consider the following sentences.

(23) I left *Chuck* with a better understanding of his problem.

(24) My Uncle Abraham presented his *talk* naturally.

(25) Here is the famous *Duke* James.

It appears that a single rule can account for the lengthening and pause which speakers use in attempting to disambiguate each of these sentences (Cooper *et al.*, 1978). According to this rule, lengthening and a pause occur just prior to a word in case it modifies the higher of two possible constituents in the syntactic tree structure. In (23), for example, pausing and lengthening favor a reading in which the prepositional phrase modifies the verb phrase of the main clause rather than the object of the main clause. In (24), lengthening and pausing favor a reading in which *naturally* modifies the entire sentence rather than the verb phrase. In (25), lengthening and pausing favor a reading in which *James* is a vocative rather than an appositive with the N *Duke*. The various structural relations covered by these cases are shown diagrammatically in Fig. 6. In each case, pausing and lengthening favor the reading in which the material which follows the pause and lengthening modifies the higher of two constituents preceding the pause. This rule suggests that Node Height relations play a role in speech timing. If correct, the rule provides one of the strongest cases in favor of hierarchical coding in speech production. In addition, it offers a chance at testing the psychological validity of particular phrase structure nodes (e.g. VP).

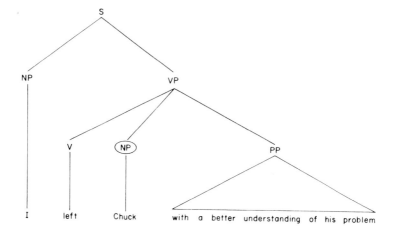

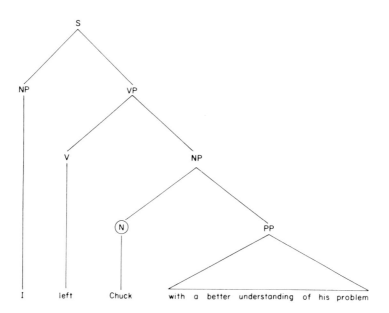

Fig. 6. Surface structures of Sentences (23)–(25). The upper structure for each sentence represents the structure in which the material to the right of the italicized segment in the text modifies the higher of the two possible modifiees in the tree structure (see Cooper *et al.*, 1978. for further discussion).

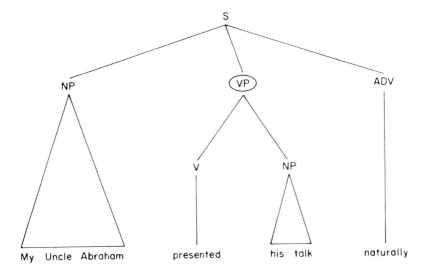

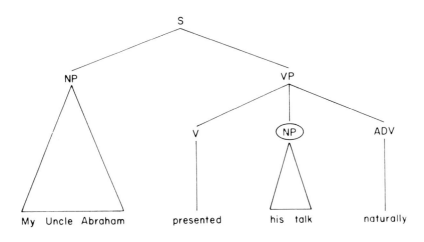

FIG. 6.—*Continued.*

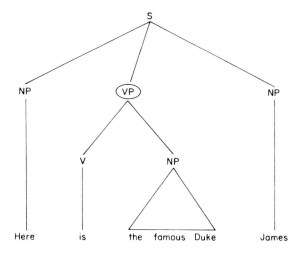

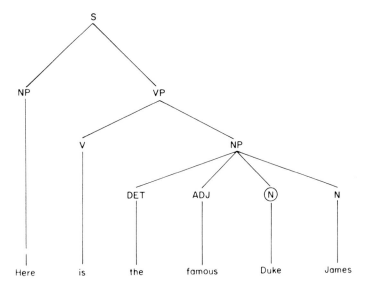

FIG. 6.—*Continued.*

But before we conclude that the Node Height rule is correct, two linear alternatives must be considered. According to one of these, disambiguation favors a reading in which the material to the right of the pause modifies the material whose last segment is farther away from it in the linear string. This rule could account for examples such as (23) and (25) but not for (24), since, in the latter sentence, both possible modified constituents end just before the pause, as shown in Fig. 6.

Another linear alternative account predicts that pausing favors a reading in which the material to the right of the pause modifies a constituent whose *first* segment is farther away from it. This account could include (24) as well as (23) and (25).

However, the Node Height principle can be shown to be superior to this linear alternative when additional sentences are considered (see Cooper *et al.*, 1978; Cooper and Paccia, 1977 for details).

F. Disambiguation and Deletion Sites

According to one recent formulation in generative grammar, certain sites of movement transformations may serve as phonetically null traces that act as bound variables in the structural descriptions of subsequently applicable syntactic rules (Chomsky, 1976; Fiengo, 1974). Experiments with preposing rules (Cooper, 1976a; see also Chapter 4 this Volume) failed to show any significant timing effects under the control of such traces. However, a type of structural ambiguity has revealed a segmental lengthening effect that, while not providing evidence for a trace in the sense described by Chomsky,† indicates that lengthening may be observed at the site of a deletion. Consider the following sentence.

(26)   Monique likes Claudette more than Kate.

This sentence is ambiguous, containing the two readings represented in (27).

(27)   a. Monique likes Claudette more than Monique likes Kate.
       b. Monique likes Claudette more than Kate likes Claudette.

In each reading of (27), the utterance-final word *Kate* may act as an underlying subject or object. Some ambiguities of this type fail to show systematic effects on speech timing (Lehiste, 1973; Cooper, 1976a; see also Chapter 7 this Volume). This particular case, however, involves another variable that appears to be responsible for an effect. This variable is the location of material deleted from the underlying structure of the sentence. For the reading in which *Kate* serves as subject (27b), the deleted material of (26) occurred immediately after *Kate*. For the reading in which *Kate* serves as object (27a), the deleted material occurred immediately before *Kate*.

In an experiment (Cooper and Paccia, 1977), it was shown that the duration of *Kate* was longer for the reading of (27) in which this word preceded the deletion site. Note that this result runs counter to the possibility

---

†Chomsky (1976) invokes the trace notion for movement rules but not for deletions.

that clause-final lengthening is determined at the level of underlying structure (Section II.A.1). Such an account would predict lengthening for the case in which *Kate* followed the deletion site, since, in this instance, the utterance-final word appeared in clause-final position in underlying structure. The lengthening effect rather appears to be produced by the deletion site. This result provides another piece of evidence that the transformational derivation of a sentence is part of the speaker's grammatical code.

A second case in support of this notion involves the deletion rule of Gapping. Gapping deletes the second occurrence of a verb under identity with the first occurrence of the same verb, as in (28b).

(28)   a. The lecture began before lunch and the test began before three.

b. The lecture began before lunch and the test before three o'clock.

In this sentence, the second occurrence of *began* has been deleted. As noted earlier, it was shown in an experiment (Cooper and Paccia, 1977) that the duration of a segment of *test* was lengthened in the Gapped version (28b) relative to the full version in (28a). Other sentence pairs also showed this effect. The results for Gapping, similar to those for the structural ambiguity noted in (27), suggest that deletion sites trigger segment lengthening, provided, of course, that the deletions do not also radically alter the clause structure of the sentence (see Cooper and Paccia, 1977).

Linguistic observations suggest that deletion sites may also serve to block certain reduction rules. King (1970) observed, for example, that auxiliary reduction is blocked at the site of certain deletions, as in (29b).

(29)   a. John has taken more from you than Bill has from me.

b. *John has taken more from you than Bill's from me.

Auxiliary reduction may also be blocked at the site of certain movement transformations, as in (30b).

(30)   a. I can't get over how gentle they are with. you.

b. *I can't get over how gentle they're with you.

A more elaborate discussion of such cases is provided by Baker (1971) and Zwicky (1970), who discuss the problem of whether these cases are to be accounted for by reference to deletion and movement sites *per se*, or, alternatively, by differences in stress pattern which such transformations produce. In general, a stress-conditioned account (Baker, 1971) appears favorable, although this proposal must also contend with counterevidence.

More recently, it has been shown that the deletion site produced by Gapping serves to reduce the frequency of palatalization, a phonological rule already discussed in Section II.A (Cooper *et al.*, 1977a). This blocking could not be attributed to the presence of an accompanying pause at the word boundary.

G. Cross-clausal Effects on Speech Timing

Both the phenomena of clause-final lengthening and the blocking of phonetic rules at clause boundaries suggest that, at some level of the speaker's coding, the clause is a relevant domain of syntactic representation which influences speech timing. However, there also exist certain influences on speech timing that operate across clause boundaries. Such effects can be reconciled with the clause-conditioned effects on timing if the cross-clausal effects are determined at a prior stage of coding, before any clause-by-clause analysis is performed.

An example of cross-clausal effect has been revealed for sentences below.

(31). a. Dick will take the jeep and Clark will take the truck.
      b. Dick will take the jeep but Clark will take the truck.
      c. Dick will take the jeep since Clark will take the truck.
      d. Dick will take the jeep if Clark will take the truck.

In a large-scale study of two speakers (Cooper *et al.*, 1977c), durations were measured for segments of six different words in each of these four sentences. The measured words included *Dick*, *take$_1$*, *jeep*, *Clark*, *take$_2$*, and *truck*. Each speaker read each of the sentences 40 times in succession to enable a test for the presence of significant correlations among the nonadjacent word segments. The results showed significant correlations, both within and across clauses (see Cooper, *et al.*, 1977c for details). Positive correlations were generally observed for words of the same grammatical relation (e.g. subject, object) across clause boundaries. The possibility of unitary processing of words bearing the same grammatical relation is in agreement with evidence from exchange errors in spontaneous speech (Shattuck-Hufnagel, 1979).

A second example of cross-clausal timing effects has been revealed for the semantic property of coreference (Cooper, 1976c). Consider the following sentence.

(32). Kate told Jane that she didn't need to pass French.

In this sentence, the pronoun *she* is coreferential with either *Kate* or *Jane*. In an experiment involving 12 speakers, it was observed that the duration of the antecedent was lengthened in (32) with respect to the duration of the same word segment in the nonantecedent reading. Thus, *Kate* was longer in the version in which *she* referred to *Kate*, while *Jane* was longer in the version in which *she* referred to *Jane*. For about half of the speakers, the duration of *she* was also lengthened considerably when it referred back to *Kate*, the antecedent located on a higher constituent in the structural tree than *Jane*. This result may be predicted by the Node Height principle discussed for structural ambiguities in Section II.E.

The results for *Kate* and *Jane*, conditioned by the coreferent *she*, indicates that the influence of coreference on speech timing is not blocked by the presence of the boundary between a main clause and an embedded complement (in this case, the complement introduced by *that* in (32)). We thus have here another case in which a timing interdependency exists between segments that lie on opposite sides of a clause boundary. For the semantic relation of coreference, it is plausible to assume that this interdependency is computed at a level of semantic coding (see Fig. 1) before a syntactic representation (and hence, before a clause structure) is applied.

H. Conclusion

We have seen that the speaker's syntactic representation exerts an influence on three temporal properties of speech—pausing, segmental lengthening, and the blocking of temporal relations that normally occur across word boundaries. In each case, it can be shown that these properties are influenced directly by the syntactic code (Cooper and Paccia, 1977).

III. Influence of Grammatical Coding on Fundamental Frequency Contours

Grammatical coding appears to influence a speaker's fundamental frequency (F_0) in many cases where timing is also affected. Although experimentation with F_0 as a dependent variable has in general not been as tightly controlled as related work on speech timing, some results with F_0 seem sufficiently well established to review here.

A. Clause Boundary Effects

Clause boundaries are typically accompanied by a fall-rise pattern in F_0 (Lea, 1972; Atkinson, 1973; Maeda, 1976; O'Shaughnessy, 1976). The F_0 fall occurs prior to the syntactic boundary. The F_0 rise may begin either just before the boundary (in which case it is termed a *continuation rise*) or just after the boundary. A peak in F_0 is typically observed on the first stressed syllable of the post-boundary constituent (Lea, 1975). In experiments using sentence materials matched for phonetic environment in the region of the clause boundary, Cooper and Sorensen (1977) obtained significant and large-magnitude fall-rise patterns at the boundaries between conjoined main clauses and at the boundaries between main and embedded clauses, the pattern being somewhat more pronounced for the conjoined clause boundaries.

B. Phrase Boundary Effects

As with speech timing, the effects of phrase boundaries on F_0 are similar to those produced at clause boundaries (Maeda, 1976; O'Shaughnessy, 1976). Cooper and Sorensen (1977) obtained fall-rise patterns at the boundaries between a main NP and VP and between preposed constituents and the remainder of a sentence. More pronounced post-boundary rises in F_0 occurred after preposed constituents than in normal SVO order strings.

C. Ambiguities

A number of authors, including Lieberman (1967), Atkinson (1973), Liberman (1975), and O'Shaughnessy (1976), have pointed out that structural ambiguities of the type discussed in Section II.E may be disambiguated by F_0 contours. An example appears in (23), repeated here for convenience. The two alternative structures for this sentence were shown in Fig. 6.

(23). I left Chuck with a better understanding of his problem.

In this sentence, the prepositional phrase *with a better understanding of his problem* modifies either the direct object *Chuck* or the verb phrase *left Chuck*. When the latter reading is intended, speakers typically produce a fall in F_0 during *Chuck*, accompanied by a following continuation rise and pause. Similar effects may be observed for (24)–(25). It thus appears that the Node Height relation of the modified constituent not only produces a pause but also a terminal F_0 contour when the modified constituent represents the higher of two possible modified constituents.

D. Declination Resetting

It is generally believed that local F_0 inflections are superimposed on a gradually falling F_0 baseline contour (Bolinger, 1964), termed the *declination line* (Cohen and t'Hart, 1967). Recent work on the attributes of declination lines has been conducted by Maeda (1976) and O'Shaughnessy (1976).

The declination contour is of interest from the standpoint of syntactic-to-phonetic coding because we suspect that the syntactic code regulates the domain over which the contour is computed. In particular, it is expected that the declination contour is reset to a new high starting value at major clause boundaries, but only under certain specified conditions. Cooper and Sorensen (1977) have conducted experiments to test this form of declination resetting. The outcome of this work suggested that the fall-rise pattern observed at the boundary between two relatively short main clauses represented a local inflection rather than complete resetting of the declination contour.

IV. Theory of Syntactic-to-Phonetic Coding

In the previous sections, we have reviewed some of the major effects of a speaker's grammatical code on duration and F_0 contours. We have also considered grammatical effects on segmental properties, including palatalization and auxiliary reduction. A theory of syntactic-to-phonetic coding must be constructed to account for these effects and provide a basis for further hypothesis-testing. Thus far, no such theory is available. Previous theoretical work on speech timing (Martin, 1972) and fundamental frequency (Liberman, 1975) have been concerned with the effects of stress for the most part. In addition to stress effects, however, it appears that the speaker's grammatical code exerts a direct influence on phonetic properties, and it is this aspect of the theory of speech production that concerns us here.

At the first level of phonetic coding constrained by syntax, rules are applied over the broadest possible syntactic domain, typically corresponding to a domain beginning and ending with an S bracket.† At this level, many of the syntactic-to-phonetic features that we have reviewed are programmed, including clause-final lengthening, optional pausing, and an F_0 inflection consisting of a fall in F_0, all of which occur at the end of the domain. These three features may be viewed as domain-final effects that stem from a relaxation response. This response slows down the speaker's timing, thereby producing lengthening and an optional pause, as well as slowing down laryngeal activity, producing a lowering of F_0. The relaxation of the speech system appears to provide a unified account of the direction of these domain-final effects. On the other hand, this account leaves domain-initial pausing and lengthening‡ unexplained. Conceivably, these effects are produced in order to permit the speaker a fraction of extra processing time to plan the next constituent.

Some phonetic rules that operate across word boundaries may also apply at the largest syntactic domain; including, for some speakers, the rule of palatalization. Following this level, phonetic rules are applied at successively narrow domains, including major phrases and embedded clauses and then minor phrases. It is expected that for different phonetic rules, different speakers, different rates of speech, and so on, the coding domain at which the rule applies will differ (Bierwisch, 1966).

The notion of successively narrow coding provides a first-order account of why, for example, clause-final lengthening is typically larger than phrase-final lengthening. Lengthening is applied to the clause-final segment on the most inclusive domain of coding. But, lengthening is applied again at phrase-domain cycles, since the clause-final segment is also the final segment of the VP and typically the direct object NP as well. A general empirical claim embodied in the theory is that the amount of lengthening for a given segment should be proportional to the number of distinct domains of coding that end at that segment. In linguistic terminology, the amount of lengthening should thus be proportional to the number of right brackets immediately following the segment, under the assumption that each bracket corresponds to a distinct domain of successively-narrow coding in speech production.

A multitude of details remain to be specified for the model, particularly the time course of computational operations. It is expected that the operations of some distinct levels overlap slightly in time, and it is almost certain that such

---

†Cross-clausal effects such as those reviewed in Section II.G are assumed to apply before this syntactically-constrained level. If this assumption is correct, the cross-clausal effects should apply with the same force regardless of the clause types involved. In addition, it should be noted that certain phonological rules, possibly including glottalization in the presence of a juncture (Kahn, 1976), may apply across word boundaries regardless of the presence of a clause boundary.

‡ Domain-initial lengthening has not been studied systematically in English, but does appear in Swedish (Lindblom and Rapp, 1973) and Italian (Nespor and Allen, 1977).

overlap will alter the predictions of the model regarding effects of blocking in particular. In addition, nongrammatical influences, particularly the length of a given constituent and speaking rate, influence decisions for inserting pauses, etc. (Bierwisch, 1966; Grosjean and Deschamps, 1975). The framework suggested here nonetheless appears to handle the data presented thus far to a first approximation, and it is sufficiently explicit to make some testable predictions regarding the outcome of future experiments.

V. Hypotheses

A. Speech Production

In this concluding section, the implications of the preceding discussion will be presented for further work on speech production, speech synthesis, and speech perception. Regarding production work, the model outlined in the previous section makes a number of testable predictions. For one, the model predicts that the amount of domain-final lengthening for a given segment should be proportional to the number of right brackets immediately following the segment. This prediction is based on the notion of top-down, left-to-right processing of domain-final lengthening effects. To test the prediction adequately, it would be appropriate to measure the amount of lengthening for a given segment in clause-final position, varying the number of distinct phrase right-brackets that co-occur at the boundary without simultaneously varying the length of the sentence as a whole. Although the outcome of this experiment will help to determine the adequacy of the model, it will not bear on the critical top-down assumption, since cumulative lengthenings at more than one phrase right-bracket could, in principle, be applied simultaneously.

In addition, the model of syntactic-to-phonetic coding makes predictions about the nature of errors in spontaneous speech. Garrett (1975), among others, has remarked that speech errors involving the exchange of two lexical items typically occur within the confines of a single clause. On the present view, it might be expected that many exchange errors are further constrained to occur within phrase boundaries, under the assumption that errors may be located at any of a number of successively narrow coding domains. The difficulty, of course, is to be able to distinguish this prediction from one which simply states that exchanges occur between items that are relatively close to one another in the linear string, as measured by the number of intervening words or syllables.

B. Speech Synthesis

Currently, programs to synthesize speech by rule incorporate few if any syntactically-conditioned effects on speech prosody, and, as noted earlier, it appears that a large portion of the halting, arhythmic quality of such speech can be traced to this drawback. From this discussion, it should be clear that one of the main features of coding that may improve the quality of synthesis is the marking of left and right clause brackets for the purpose of segment lengthening, pause insertion, and F_0 fall-rise. A rule could be implemented to lengthen, for example, the last stressed syllable before a double S bracket, by about 30% of its inherent duration. A double S bracket would, in addition, serve to block cross-word phonetic rules operating at later stages in the synthesis program. On the basis of the results reviewed here, other specific effects could also be implemented.

C. Speech Perception

This work raises the question of whether listeners can detect and utilize such effects in recovering structural information during ongoing sentence perception. Thus far, we know almost nothing about the listeners' possible utilization of these cues, although we know a little about the listener's ability to simply detect their presence. Klatt and Cooper (1975) conducted experiments in which judgments of segment duration were required of listeners for a given word in different sentence contexts. In one experiment, the sentences were constructed by electronically deleting or reduplicating individual glottal cycles of the central portion of the vowel. Listeners could detect differences in the vowel duration that were on the order of one or two glottal cycles. This result suggests that lengthening effects, such as those that occur at the boundary between two conjoined clauses, may be readily detected. However, work has yet to be directed at the more important question of whether listeners might *use* this information in decoding constituent structure.

In addition to the possible cue value of segmental lengthening and pausing, it would be of interest to test whether the presence of major syntactic boundaries blocks perceptual computation of speech rate and other prosodic variables. In tests assessing the influence of speech rate on the perception of phoneme distinctions carried by voice onset time, Summerfield and Haggard (1972) observed that rate effects were obtained within about seven words of the key segment. But if speakers' computation of speech rate is reset on a clause-by-clause basis, the presence of a clause boundary might block the perceptual effect of rate. Similarly, syntactic blocking effects might be observed in cases reported by Meltzer *et al.* (1976) concerning the disruption of rhythmic expectancies in a phoneme-monitoring task.

Finally, studies of perception can be directed at the question of whether a unitary perceptuo-motor system, serving both speech perception and production, plays a role in the processing of syntactically relevant speech cues. In the study of Klatt and Cooper (1975), some preliminary evidence in favor of such a unitary system was provided by the finding of a highly positive correlation between listeners' threshold for detecting differences in vowel duration and their average *production* of vowel durations in the same sentence contexts. This result suggests that a unitary adjustment factor operates in both speech perception and production as a fine-tuning device for the processing of timing information in speech. Further correlational testing may determine whether other speech cues (e.g. fundamental frequency) are controlled by a unitary system.

VI. Concluding Remarks

Taken together, the studies reviewed here indicate that a speaker's syntactic code exerts a highly systematic influence on the acoustic properties of speech, including duration and fundamental frequency. Systematic testing of these effects promises to provide a more precise description of the speaker's grammatical code than has heretofore been possible. In addition, the pinpointing of large-magnitude effects in speech production continues to serve as a guide for related work on speech synthesis and perception.

At a theoretical level, primary emphasis can be placed on the development of a theory of processing at syntactic boundaries. This theory should provide a unified account of a number of phenomena, including lengthening of segments and pauses, blocking of cross-word phonetic conditioning, and fall-rise patterns of fundamental frequency. The search for a unified account of the locations of these effects proceeds on the assumption that these superficially diverse phenoma are under the joint control of a single syntactic code.

With its focus on the speaker's syntactic computations, this theory is designed to account for the location and relative magnitude of various phonetic effects. A separate theory is required to provide an account of the direction of these effects. Why, for example, do speakers lengthen rather than shorten speech segments at major syntactic boundaries? Is lengthening a reflection of a general relaxation response, or is it a reflection of the need to "buy time" to plan an upcoming constituent (Lindblom and Rapp, 1973; Cooper, 1976a)? Why do speakers produce fall-rise patterns of F_0 at major boundaries rather than rise-fall patterns, and are the directions of the timing and F_0 effects accounted for by the same principle (Cooper and Sorensen, 1977)? We are currently working to answer these questions. For present purposes, it is important to note that our primary goal here has been to examine properties of the speaker's syntactic code, and progress on this issue has been made in the absence of a detailed account of the direction of phonetic effects that are under syntactic control.

Acknowledgements

This work was supported by NIH Grant NS-13028 and an NIH Post-doctoral Fellowship. I thank Jonathan Allen, François Grosjean, Steven Lapointe, and Jeanne Paccia for discussions. A revised and expanded treatment of this topic appears in Cooper and Paccia (1977).

References

Atkinson, J. E. (1973). *Aspects of Intonation in Speech: Implications from an Experimental Study of Fundamental Frequency.* Ph.D. Thesis, University of Connecticut, Storrs, Conn.

Baker, C. L. (1971). Stress level and auxiliary behavior in English. *Linguistic Inquiry* 2, 167–181.

Barnwell, T. P. (1971). *An Algorithm for Segment Durations in a Reading Machine Context.* Technical Report No. 479, Research Laboratory of Electronics, M.I.T.

Bierwisch, M. (1966). Regeln für die Intonation deutscher Sätze. *Studia Grammatica* 7, 99–201.

Bolinger, D. (1964). Intonation as a universal. *In* "Proceedings of Linguistics IX", pp. 833–844. The Hague: Mouton.

Bolinger, D. L. (1976). Length, vowel, and juncture. *Bilingual Review* 3, 43–61.

Boomer, D. S. (1965). Hesitation and grammatical encoding. *Language and Speech* 8, 148–158.

Bresnan, J. W. (1971). Sentence stress and syntactic transformations. *Language* 47, 257–281.

Bresnan, J. W. (1972). *The Theory of Complementation in English Syntax.* Ph.D. Thesis, M.I.T., Cambridge, Mass.

Bresnan, J. W. (1976). Nonarguments for Raising. *Linguistic Inquiry* 7, 485–501.

Chomsky, N. (1957). "Syntactic Structures". The Hague, Mouton.

Chomsky, N. (1965). "Aspects of the Theory of Syntax". MIT Press, Cambridge, Mass.

Chomsky, N. (1970). Remarks on nominalizations. *In* "Readings in English Transformational Grammar." (R. Jacobs and P. S. Rosenbaum, eds). Ginn, Waltham, Mass.

Chomsky, N. (1973). Conditions on transformations. *In* S. R. Anderson and P. Kiparsky (eds), "A Festschrift for Morris Halle", pp. 232–285. New York: Holt, Rinehart, and Winston.

Chomsky, N. (1976). Conditions on rules of grammar. *Linguistic Analysis* 2, 303–350.

Chomsky, N. and Halle, M. (1968). "The Sound Pattern of English". New York: Harper and Row.

Cohen, A. and t'Hart, J. (1967). On the anatomy of intonation. *Lingua* 19, 177–192.

Cooper, W. E. (1976a). "Syntactic Control of Timing in Speech Production". Ph.D. Thesis, M.I.T., Cambridge, Mass.

Cooper, W. E. (1976b). Syntactic control of timing in speech production: a study of complement clauses. *Journal of Phonetics* 4, 151–171.

Cooper, W. E. (1976c). Speech timing of coreference. "Proceedings of the First International Conference on Speech, Acoustics, and Signal Processing", p. 548. Philadelphia: IEEE.

Cooper, W. E. and Paccia, J. M. (1977). "Syntax and Speech Coding". Book in preparation.

Cooper, W. E. and Sorensen, J. M. (1977). Fundamental frequency contours at syntactic boundaries. *Journal of the Acoustical Society of America,* 62, 683-692.

Cooper, W. E., Egido, C. and Paccia, J. M. (1977a). Grammatical control of a phonological rule: palatalization. *Journal of Experimental Psychology. Human Perception and Performance*, in press.

Cooper, W. E., Lapointe, S. G. and Paccia, J. M. (1977b). Syntactic blocking of phonological rules in speech production. *Journal of the Acoustical Society of America,* 61, 1314–1320.

Cooper, W. E., Sorensen, J. M. and Paccia, J. M. (1977c). Correlations of duration for non-adjacent segments in speech production: aspects of grammatical coding. *Journal of the Acoustical Society of America*, **61**, 1046–1050.

Cooper, W. E., Egido, C. and Paccia, J. M. (1978). Grammatical control of a phonological rule: palatization. *J. Exp. Psychol. Human Perception and Performance* **4**, 264–272.

Dougherty, R. (1970). A grammar of coordinate conjoined structures. *Foundations of Language* **46**, 850–898.

Downing, B. T. (1970). *Syntactic Structure and Phonological Phrasing in English*. Ph.D. Thesis, University of Texas, Austin, TX.

Downing, B. T. (1973). Parenthesization rules and obligatory phrasing. *Papers in Linguistics* **6**, 108–128.

Emonds, J. E. (1976). "A Transformational Approach to English Syntax". Academic Press, New York.

Fiengo, R. W. (1974). *Semantic Conditions on Surface Structure*. Ph.D. Thesis, M.I.T., Cambridge, MA.

Fodor, J. A., Bever, T. G. and Garrett, M. F. (1974). "The Psychology of Language: An Introduction to Psycholinguistics and Generative Grammar". McGraw Hill, New York.

Garrett, M. F. (1975). The analysis of sentence production. *In* "Advances in Learning Theory and Motivation", (G. Bower, ed.) Vol. 9. 133–177. Academic Press. New York.

Goldman-Eisler, F. (1968). "Psycholinguistics: Experiments in Spontaneous Speech". Academic Press, New York.

Goldman-Eisler, F. (1972). Pauses, clauses, sentences. *Language and Speech* **15**, 103–113.

Grosjean, L. (1976). La structure syntazique et les temps de pause en lecture. Working paper, University of Paris III.

Grosjean, F. and Deschamps, A. (1975). Analyse contrastive des variables temporelles de l'anglais et du francais: Vitesse de parole et variables composantes, phènomenes d'hèsitation. *Phonetica* **31**, 144–184.

Grosjean, F., Grosjean, L. and Lane, H. (1977). The structure of silence: Pausing in reading at slow rate. Unpublished working paper, Northeastern University, Boston, MA.

Hankamer, J. (1971). *Constraints on Deletion in Syntax*. Ph.D. Thesis, Yale University, New Haven, CT.

Hudson, R. A. (1976). Conjunction reduction, gapping, and right-node raising. *Language* **52**, 535–562.

Huggins, A. W. F. (1969). A facility for studying perception of timing in natural speech. *Quarterly Progress Report of the M.I.T. Research Laboratory of Electronics* **95**, 81–83.

Huggins, A. W. F. (1974). An effect of syntax on syllable timing. *Quarterly Progress Report of the M.I.T. Research Laboratory of Electronics* **114**, 179–185.

Huggins, A. W. F. (1975). On isochrony and syntax. *In* G. Fant and M. A. A. Tatham (eds.), "Auditory Analysis and Perception of Speech". Academic Press, New York.

Hyman, L. M. (1975). "Phonology: Theory and Analysis". Holt, Rinehart, and Winston, New York.

Jackendoff, R. S. (1971). Gapping and related rules. *Linguistic Inquiry* **2**, 21–35.

Kahn, D. (1976). *Syllable-based Generalization in English Phonology*. Ph.D. Thesis, M.I.T., Cambridge, MA.

King, H. V. (1970). On blocking the rules for contraction in English. *Linguistic Inquiry* **1**, 134–136.

Klatt, D. H. (1975). Vowel lengthening is syntactically determined in a connected discourse. *Journal of Phonetics* **3**, 129–140.

Klatt, D. H. (1976). Linguistic uses of segmental duration in English: Acoustic and perceptual evidence. *Journal of the Acoustical Society of America* **59**, 1208–1221.

Klatt, D. H. and Cooper, W. E. (1975). Perception of segment duration in sentence contexts. *In* "Structure and Process in Speech Perception". (A. Cohen and S. G. Nooteboom, eds), pp. 69–89. Springer-Verlag, Heidelberg.

Kloker, D. (1975). Vowel and sonorant lengthening as cues to phonological phrase boundaries. Paper presented at the 89th Meeting of the Acoustical Society of America, April.

Koutsoudas, A. (1971). Gapping, conjunction reduction, and coordinate deletion. *Foundation of Language* **7**, 337–386.

Langacker, R. W. (1974). Movement rules in functional perspective. *Language* **50**, 630–664.

Langendoen, D. T. (1976). Finite-state parsing of phrase-structure languages and the status of readjustment rules in grammar. *Linguistic Inquiry* **6**, 533–554.

Lasnik, H. (1972). *Analyses of Negation in English*. Ph.D. Thesis, M.I.T., Cambridge, Mass.

Lea, W. A. (1972). *Intonational Cues to the Constituent Structure and Phonemics of Spoken English*. Ph.D. Thesis, Purdue University, Lafayette, Ind.

Lea, W. A. (1975). Prosodic aids to speech recognition. vii. experiments on detecting and locating phrase boundaries. Sperry Univac Report No. PX 11534.

Lehiste, I. (1973). Phonetic disambiguation of syntactic ambiguity. *Glossa* **7**, 107–121.

Liberman, M. Y. (1975). *The Intonational System of English*. Ph.D. Thesis, M.I.T., Cambridge, Mass.

Liberman, M. Y. and Streeter, L. (1976). Use of nonsense-syllable mimicry in the study of prosodic phenomena. *Journal of the Acoustical Society of America* **60**, S27 (Abstract).

Lieberman, P. (1967). *Intonation, Perception, and Language*. MIT Press, Cambridge, Mass.

Lindblom, B. (1964). A note on segment duration in Swedish polysyllables. *Quarterly Progess and Status Report*, Speech Transmission Laboratory, K.T.H. Stockholm, 1.

Lindblom, B. and Rapp, K. (1973). Some temporal regularities of spoken Swedish. *Papers from the Institute of Linguistics*, University of Stockholm, Publication 21.

Maeda, S. (1976). *A Characterization of American English Intonation*. Ph.D. Thesis, M.I.T., Cambridge, Mass.

Martin, J. G. (1970). Judging pauses in spontaneous speech. *Journal of Verbal Learning and Verbal Behavior* **9**, 75–78.

Martin, J. G. (1971). Some acoustic and grammatical features of spontaneous speech. *In* "The Perception of Language". (D. J. Horton and J. J. Jenkins, eds). C. E. Merrill, Columbus, Ohio.

Martin, J. G. (1972). Rhythmic (hierarchical) versus serial structure in speech and other behaviors. *Psychological Review* **79**, 487–509.

Meltzer, R. H., Martin, J. G., Mills, C. B., Imhoff, D. L. and Zohar, D. (1976). Reaction time to temporally-displaced phoneme targets in continuous speech. *Journal of Experimental Psychology: Human Perception and Performance* **2**, 277–290.

Nespor, M. A. and Allen, G. D. (1977). Segment and word durational correlates of syntactic boundaries in Italian. *Journal of the Acoustical Society of America* **61**, S91 (Abstract).

Nash, R. (1970). John likes Mary more than Bill. *Phonetica* **22**, 170–188.

O'Shaughnessy, D. (1976). *Modelling Fundamental Frequency, and Its Relationship to Syntax, Semantics, and Phonetics.* Ph.D. Thesis, M.I.T., Cambridge, Mass.

Postal, P. M. (1974). "On Raising: One Rule of English Grammar and Its Theoretical Implications". MIT Press, Cambridge, Mass.

Rosenbaum, P. S. (1967). The Grammar of English Predicate Complement Constructions. MIT Press, Cambridge, Mass.

Ross, J. R. (1967). *Constraints on Variables in Syntax.* Ph.D. Thesis, M.I.T., Cambridge, Mass.

Ross, J. R. (1969). A proposed rule of tree-pruning. *In* "Modern Studies in English: Readings in Transformational Grammar", (D. A. Reibel and S. A. Schane, eds.), pp. 288–299. Prentice-Hall, Englewood Cliffs, N.J.

Ross, J. R. (1970). Gapping and the order of constituents. *In* "Progress in Linguistics". (M. Bierwisch and K. E. Heidolph, eds). Mouton, The Hague.

Rotenberg, J. (1975). French liaison, phrase structure, and semi-cyclical rules. Unpublished paper, M.I.T. Cambridge, Mass.

Selkirk, E. (1974). French liaison and the $\bar{X}$ notation. *Linguistic Inquiry* **5**, 573–590.

Shattuck-Hufnagel, S. (1979). Speech errors as evidence for a serial-ordering mechanism in sentence production. *In* "Sentence Processing". W. E. Cooper and E. C. T. Walker, eds). Lawerence Erlbaum Associates, Hillsdale, N.J.

Sorensen, J. M., Cooper, W. E. and Paccia, J. M. (1977). Speech timing of grammatical categories. *Cognition*, in press.

Stanley, R. (1973). Boundaries in phonology. *In* "A Festschrift for Morris Halle". S. R. Anderson and P. Kiparsky, eds.). Holt, Rinehart and Winston, New York.

Stillings, J. T. (1975). The formulation of Gapping in English as evidence for variable types in syntactic transformations. *Linguistic Analysis* **1**, 247–273.

Stockwell, R. P. (1972). The role of intonation: reconsiderations and other considerations. *In* "Intonation". (D. Bolinger, ed.), pp. 87–109. Penguin Books, London.

Summerfield, A. Q. and Haggard, M. P. (1972). Speech rate effects in the perception of voicing. *Speech Synthesis and Perception* (Research on speech synthesis and speech perception in the Psychology Laboratory, Cambridge University) **6**, 1–12.

Thomson, S. A. (1968). Relative clauses and conjunctions. The Ohio State University *Working Papers in Linguistics* **1**, 80–99.

Williams, E. S., III (1974). *Rule Ordering in Syntax.* Ph.D. Thesis, M.I.T., Cambridge, Mass.

Yngve, V. H. (1960). A model and an hypothesis for language structure. *Proceedings of the American Philosophical Society* **104**, 444–466.

Zwicky, A. M. (1970). Auxiliary reduction in English. *Linguistic Inquiry* **1**, 323–336.

IV
Articulatory Process

13

Phonetic Features and the Physiology of Speech Production

J. S. Perkell   *Massachusetts Institute of Technology*

I. Introduction

As we learn more about the physiology of speech production, it is becoming increasingly difficult to reconcile physiological data with linguistic models. There appears to be a great disparity between discrete representations that lack temporal specifications and articulatory movements which are precisely-timed, spatially variable, asynchronous and quasi-continuous. This apparent disparity has led to suggestions that: (1) discrete representations may actually be misleading in the search to understand the nature of speech production, and (2) it might be more fruitful to study articulatory movements and basic physiological mechanisms without being constrained by the limitations inherent in "static" linguistic models (cf. MacNeilage, 1972; Moll *et al.*, 1977; Netsell and Abbs, 1977; Fowler *et al.*, in this volume).

This chapter presents a theoretical overview of the segmental aspects of speech production. The overview incorporates static, more phonetically oriented elements and dynamic, more physiologically oriented elements. The static and dynamic elements are interrelated, so it is not necessary to exclude consideration of one while trying to understand the other. In fact, one main point of the overview is that phonetic models and speech physiology may be related to one another in a natural way. It is suggested that the physiological properties and capabilities of the speech production mechanism exert strong influences on the form of phonetic models; and many of the concepts embodied in phonetic models capture important aspects of the unique nature of speech as in internally-generated, natural and creative form of sequential motor behavior. The overview is outlined in the following paragraphs and discussed in more detail in the remainder of the chapter.

Speech production consists of a series of asynchronous movements of the respiratory and vocal tract mechanisms which produce an acoustic signal. At the segmental level, these movements seem to be the result of a control process which has an underlying input in the form of a discrete sequence of events or phonetic segments. A given sequence of phonetic segments can be represented by a matrix in which the columns correspond to the segments and the rows correspond to distinctive features. The features reflect, in part, the phonetic capabilities of the production mechanism for producing sounds with different acoustic properties. It is hypothesized that matrix-like specifications of utterances underly the segmental component of the input to the production process, and that the production mechanism utilizes a complex set of strategies to transform a discrete input into the continuous movements that characterize speech.

One basis for a description of the features is suggested by the quantal nature of speech production and perception (Stevens, 1972). Particular configurations and modes of operation of the production mechanism seem to generate acoustic signals with certain stable or quantal properties. In addition, the perception mechanism seems to possess capabilities to select out or detect particular attributes of the acoustic signal. In general, the inventory of features is determined on the basis of relations between capabilities of the vocal tract to generate signals with distinctive and acoustically stable characteristics and capabilities of the perception mechanism to detect those characteristics.

The properties of the sound generated by the vocal mechanism are determined, of course, by the configuration of the air passages between the glottis and lips, the static pressure below and above the glottis, and the configuration and state of the vocal-fold surfaces. From the point of view of sound production, then, the articulatory description is best specified in terms of positions, configurations and states of the surfaces of certain structures in relation to others and of forces on these surfaces.

It is proposed that an inventory of features is manifested as a matching of auditory patterns corresponding to the detection of distinctive acoustic cues with *orosensory* patterns corresponding to distinctive sound producing states. These "orosensory" patterns consist of proprioceptive, tactile and more complicated air-pressure and airflow information from the entire vocal tract (Stevens and Perkell, 1977). Patterns of this information would define physiological, orosensory "goals" for the production mechanism—goals from which the acoustic properties of the sound output can be predicted. As examples, the orosensory goals for the features† "high" or "back" might consist of specific patterns of contact of the sides of the tongue body with the teeth and pharyngeal wall. The orosensory goal for the feature "coronal" might be contact of the sides of the tongue blade with the teeth or alveolar ridge, and the goal for "obstruent" might be attainment of a certain level of intra-oral air pressure, as sensed by receptors on the upper airway surfaces. Achieving any of the orosensory goals produces the quantal acoustic characteristic associated with the corresponding feature.

Feature definitions like these are basically static in nature. In actual speech production, sequences of phonetic segments in the form of feature-defined "sensory-goal matrices" are converted into a single set of "motor goals" which changes with time. This continuously-changing set of motor goals would serve as the basis for the production of articulatory movements.

While the orosensory goals relating to the surfaces of the various

---

† For the purpose of discussion, the feature names are those used by Chomsky and Halle (1968).

articulatory structures may be largely independent of context, the motor activity that is required to achieve these goals is likely to depend strongly on other goals that are to be achieved within the phonetic segment, in adjacent segments, and on suprasegmental influences. In addition, in order to achieve the appropriate acoustic properties, the actualization of the goals by various components of the articulatory mechanism must be properly timed in relation to one another. Thus the transformation between a discrete input and articulatory movements must be a complex one. Observations in speech physiology which are interpreted with respect to a discrete framework have led to the description of anticipatory and perseveratory coarticulation, rate and stress dependent undershoot of articulatory targets, "intrasegmental" motor command reorganization, apparent physiologically-related influences on sound segment durations, cross-speaker variability for the same articulatory gestures, and intratoken variability for the same speaker.

These observations imply that in the course of learning how to utilize feature-specified goals in connected speech, the speaker develops a number of complicated strategies for converting goal sequences into motor commands. Presumably the development and utilization of these strategies must incorporate: the capability to preplan complexes of asynchronous movements, the fluctuating use of various forms of feedback and components of "motor programs" in executing movement sequences, and apparently the application of some kind of principle of economy of effort. In order to develop these control strategies, the speaker must internalize a "knowledge" of a number of vocal tract properties, including constraints imposed by the individual mechanical response properties of different articulators and the functional limitations of the speech motor control system. These system properties also contribute to determining intrinsic durational information which may serve as one basis for determining timing.

In summary, speaker-hearers have anatomical and neurological characteristics which help determine the inventory of distinctive features. The feature correlates are manifested in each individual as propensities for making feedback-mediated matches between acoustic property-generating characteristics of the production mechanism and property-detecting characteristics of the perception mechanism. The speaker also develops a complicated set of strategies for converting sequences of feature-specified goals and suprasegmental influences into articulatory movements. In acquiring and then utilizing these strategies, the speaker is constrained in part by the physical properties and physiological capabilities of the production and perception mechanisms.

A number of the ideas contained in this overview have been discussed by Lindblom (1971a; 1975), Lieberman (1970, 1976), MacNeilage (1970, 1972), Kent, (1976) and other authors. In the following two sections, the overview will be discussed in more detail, with reference to findings and concepts from phonology, speech physiology, and the control of movement. In the fourth section of the chapter, the overview is summarized again, as an outline of a "conceptual model" of speech production. It should be stressed that the overview is theoretical and general. It represents one of many possible ways of looking at the speech production process, and it is advanced with the intention of furthering discussion and stimulating experimentation.

II. Distinctive Features: The Static Framework

A comprehensive set of distinctive features was first formulated by Jakobson *et al.* (1951). In this formulation, the features were defined as binary "choices" between "opposites", such as polar qualities of a category (i.e. grave versus acute or compact versus diffuse) or the presence or absence of a quality (i.e. voiced versus unvoiced or nasalized versus non-nasalized). The distinctive features were said to be the ultimate (non divisible) entities of language which combine in concurrent bundles to form or specify phonemes. Although these features were defined primarily in acoustic terms, the names were meant to denote linguistic contrasts. It was recognized that there were redundancies conditioned by simultaneous feature superposition, and that the features did not capture contextually-determined allophonic variations.

In a later reformulation Chomsky and Halle (1968) expanded the number of features and described them primarily in articulatory terms. For example, the features "high", "low" and "back" were defined in terms of tongue body position; the features "sonorant", "vocalic" and "consonantal" were defined in terms of degrees of vocal-tract constriction; and the features "coronal", "nasal" and "rounded" were defined in terms of configurations or shapes of the tongue tip, the velum and the lips. The importance of acoustic and perceptual correlates of the features was also recognized, and several strong claims were elaborated about their nature.

(1) The features are universal, identical with the set of phonetic properties that can be controlled in speech, and they represent the phonetic capabilities of man (see also, Jakobson, 1968).

(2) They have phonological and phonetic functions. The phonological features are binary, classificatory, abstract in nature, and they carry the names of the phonetic features. The phonetic features can be characterized on physical scales which describe aspects of the speech event that are under (partially) independent control.

(3) The values assigned to the phonetic (feature) representation (and presumably the relationships between this *n*-ary representation and the binary phonological representation) are determined by the "phonetic component" of the grammar.

(4) Utterances can be represented in terms of phonetic feature matrices which are mentally constructed by the speaker-hearer in actual performance.

Some of these ideas are controversial, and alternative arguments about the nature of distinctive features have been presented (cf. Ladefoged, 1971; Lisker and Abramson, 1971). We are currently incapable of resolving these arguments, but for the purposes of discussion, it can be useful to examine issues such as the reality of feature representations, feature definitions, the binary nature and the orthogonality of features, and the form of "rules of the phonetic component" of the grammar.

A. On The Nature of Distinctive Features

In the introduction, it was suggested that distinctive features are determined in part by the quantal nature of speech production and perception. According to our hypothesis, the speech production correlates of the features are "orosensory goals" for the articulators. Each goal corresponds to a state of some aspect of articulation (such as a localized pattern of contact of two articulators, a pattern of forces due to an air pressure level, or a configuration) which results in a stable and distinctive acoustic output, regardless of the states of other aspects of articulation. For example, raising the tongue tip so its sides contact the hard palate and teeth produces an acoustic pattern with certain distinctive properties, independent of the configuration of the tongue body, the lips or the larynx. Creating an increase in intraoral air pressure produces a characteristic noise burst or transient, regardless of the place of constriction. Thus there is a set of states of the articulators that is "preferred" or "determined" by quantal (discontinuous) relations between articulation and sound. These states correspond to orosensory goals which are *quantally-preferred* or *quantally-determined* feature correlates. While there is some evidence that supports the quantal hypothesis (Stevens, 1972; Stevens and Blumstein, 1975) a great deal of research needs to be done in this area.

1. *Findings on goal-oriented behavior*

Several lines of evidence from speech physiology tend to support the idea that the production mechanism functions on a feedback-mediated, goal oriented basis. The fact that speech deteriorates following "post-lingual" deafness indicates that auditory feedback is in some way important for the attainment of articulatory goals. However, since the deterioration is only gradual, auditory feedback seems to be necessary for the establishment and maintenance of these goals and not for the moment-to-moment control of articulatory movements.

Relatively long-lasting alterations in the state of the production mechanism from natural causes (such as loss of teeth), clinical procedures (surgery), or experimental manipulation (injections of local anaesthesia or insertion of bite blocks or artificial palates) produce changes in articulatory behavior which are referred to as "compensatory articulation" or "compensatory reorganization".† Observations on compensatory articulation also suggest that articulatory goals can be monitored and adjusted by using auditory and orosensory feedback patterns. Measurements of mandible motion following the insertion of an artificial palate have shown evidence of compensatory patterns beginning 15 min from the time of insertion and taking up to several

---

† The term "reorganization" is used in a general sense to refer to a restructuring or reprogramming of commands or control signals.

days for completion (Hamlet and Stone, 1974). It has also been found (Lindblom, 1971b; Lindblom et al., 1977) that a subject is apparently able to produce an acoustically acceptable vowel on the first glottal pulse even while the mandible is being held at abnormally large openings. However, several attempts are required if oral tactile sensation is reduced in conjunction with the abnormally-large opening (Lindblom et al., 1977). These results seem to be fairly convincing evidence for the use of some kind of spatial-tactile reference in computing steady-state compensatory articulations. In an experiment in which mandibular excursions were diminished following injections of a local anesthetic, Abbs (1973) found that lip movements had increased in order to overcome the reduced mandibular displacements.

Experiments which produce compensatory reorganization can be difficult to interpret with respect to normal speech patterns (cf. Leanderson and Persson, 1972), but goal-oriented function has also been demonstrated with paradigms which presumably do not allow time for "reorganization" to occur or do not interfere with speech production. Folkins and Abbs (1975) applied sudden resistive loading to the mandible during bilabial stop closure for randomly selected tokens. They found that the vertical movement of the lips increased in order to complete the closure, even on the first trial. In a later analysis (Folkins and Abbs, 1976), increases in integrated EMG activity were found to accompany the increased lip movements. These results seem to show that the overall gesture is programmed to achieve the goal of lip closure and that "motor control signals to the lips are adjusted on the basis of on-line information concerning the relative positions of the lips and jaws . . ." (Folkins and Abbs, 1975). Similar conclusions can be drawn from an experiment by Hughes and Abbs (1976) which involved no interference with articulatory movements. In this experiment measurements were made of lip and mandible displacement corresponding to vowel production for numbers of repetitions of the same utterance. The results showed variable, but reciprocal amounts of movement of the lower lip and mandible in achieving the relatively stable acoustically-important lip opening "goal". Variability of lip and mandible movements across repetitions was found to be significantly greater than variability of the interlip measurement. These results were interpreted as evidence for operation of the principle of "motor equivalance", or motor programming on a goal-oriented rather than movement oriented basis. The finding of greater variability in the prespeech "ready" position than the initial speech "target" position of the mandible (MacNeilage et al., 1970) is also consistent with the idea of goal-oriented motor programming.

Goal-oriented behavior would also account for the variability which has been observed in the way different individuals control tongue height and vowel configuration (Ladefoged et al., 1972; Dowla and Perkell, 1977), pharyngeal expansion (Bell-Berti, 1975), movements of the lips (Gay and Hirose, 1973) and lingual configuration (Harris and Raphael, 1973). Different individuals may have differently-shaped vocal tracts and tendencies for somewhat different modes of neuromuscular behavior. For example, differently-shaped palatal vaults might require somewhat different patterns of tongue displacement (as seen in midsagittal cineradiographic tracings) to achieve similar, quantally-preferred area functions (Dowla and Perkell, 1977). The manner in which goals are realized may vary from one individual to the next, and variation would be more evident in measurements that are less directly related to acoustically-important parameters. However, the underlying quantal principles which determine the goals should be the same for all speakers.

2. Constraints on the nature of feature correlates

It is possible that humans are endowed with propensities to produce sounds containing quantal and distinctive acoustic patterns. Lieberman et al. (1972) have suggested that the unique configuration of the human vocal tract allows for the production of a much wider range of "speech sounds" than the vocal tracts of other homonids. It seems reasonable to suggest that humans must possess the arrangement of muscles which makes possible the production of quantally-preferred articulations, and it is probably also the case that certain frequently-used articulatory gestures are preferred on an anatomical basis. For example, the behavior of an anatomically-based tongue model (Perkell, 1974) suggests that the maximum degree of vocal-tract narrowing produced by contraction of the styloglossus muscles does not occur along the direct axis of contraction of the muscles, but further forward in the vocal tract. This effect is due to an upward bulging of the tongue which seems to accompany styloglossus contraction. The more anterior location of the narrowing might coincide with the place of articulation which is preferred on an acoustic basis for velar consonants (Stevens, 1972). On the basis of an examination of vocal-tract area functions, Wood (1977) has suggested that there are four constriction locations for vowels which may be preferred by both acoustic and anatomical factors. More obviously, the tongue tip is naturally in a position opposite the alveolar ridge, where articulation produces distinct acoustic cues. In other words, the particular anatomical arrangement of vocal-tract structures may make quantally-preferred configurations easier to produce than intermediate configurations.

In addition to geometric or anatomical factors there may also be sensory and low-level neuromotor predispositions to produce certain configurations. There is some limited evidence for differential sensitivities to contact on different areas of the tongue, palate and lips (Dubner et al., 1978; Ringel and Ewanowski, 1965; Grossman et al., 1965). It is also known that the laryngeal structures contain mechanoreceptors and that the teeth are sensitive to touch by virtue of receptors in the periodontal ligaments. Future investigations may show that some acoustically-preferred patterns of articulatory contact correspond in some way to the production of distinct, and quantally-definable patterns of tactile feedback (Stevens and Perkell, 1977).

Low-level neuromotor predispositions to produce certain types of articulatory gestures could exist in the form of "prewired" motor programs such as those involved in swallowing (Doty, 1968; Sumi, 1973), sucking

and possibly respiration, crying and chewing (Dubner *et al.*, 1978).
In the cases of swallowing and sucking, complex, stereotyped sequences of
motor gestures can be elicited in newborn animals by simple stimulation of the
perioral or oropharyngeal mucosa. The swallowing sequence appears to be
composed of separate movement subcomponents which have been
hypothesized to be used in speech (Doty, 1968). Although ideas like this are
highly speculative, it may be hypothesized that humans learn to exert adaptive
control over components of pre-existing motor program "circuitry" for the
execution of certain speech gestures.

3. *Hypotheses on the nature of "Fundamental Control Elements"*

The concept of acoustically-mediated goal-oriented articulatory behavior has
been discussed in a general way by several investigators, primarily in terms of
articulatory or acoustic "targets". Lindblom (1963) has suggested that vowel
targets are defined acoustically as asymptotic values (of formant frequencies)
which can be looked at as invariant attributes. MacNeilage (1970) has
proposed that a language learner builds up an internalized spatial
representation of the oral area. Invariant (phonemic) targets would be
specified with respect to the spatial representation, and these targets would be
the basis for the generation of context-dependent movement patterns with the
aid of "closed loop" control. Nooteboom (1970, 1972) has claimed that
"perceptual" targets should be the basis for computing appropriate spatial
targets for the individual articulators. Kent (1976) has suggested that quantal
acoustic principles may help to explain the establishment of goals which can
be used to compute muscle forcing functions.

Our overview agrees in general with several of these ideas. In particular, we
hypothesize that orosensory goals are the production-related correlates of
distinctive features. The goals are determined by anatomical, sensory,
neurological and quantal-acoustic constraints. The goals may include
patterns and forces of contact between articulators that oppose one another,
levels of intraoral air pressure and air flow, and amounts of tension that
muscles may develop. Phonetic segments are specified as combinations of
goals (goal complexes), and utterances are specified as sequences of goal
complexes. Specifications of utterances in the form of sequences of goal
complexes serve as a basic for articulatory movements in a way which is
outlined in Sections III and IV.

B. Implications of a Quantally-determined Goal-oriented Feature Framework

Distinctive features have been viewed as being not orthogonal or completely
independent of one another, either on the phonemic (classificatory) or
phonetic (articulatory) level (cf. Fant, 1973). These constraints are reflected in
the fact that some feature combinations are not possible, and in any given
language certain combinations of feature specifications may include many

redundancies. Chomsky and Halle (1968) discuss the "intrinsic content" of features which influences the occurrence of expected or natural classes of rules and (feature-specified) symbol configurations. At the phonetic level, there are interdependencies of feature manifestations in the acoustic and certain articulatory domains (Fant, 1973). For example, interdependence of feature manifestations at one articulatory level is reflected in "reorganization" of motor commands (cf. Lubker, 1975; Harris, 1970), which must be made in part to compensate for mechanical interactions among the articulators (as will be discussed further in Section III.B.). Fant (1973) suggests that feature "invariance" is generally relative rather than absolute.

As we have mentioned, features could have invariant correlates in the domain in which they are defined, but expression of the features may produce lack of invariance in other domains. The lack of motor command invariance as reflected in EMG patterns has served as one of the major stimuli to defining "invariant" units in spatial terms (MacNeilage, 1970, 1972) or in terms of states, as noted above. In general, positions or movements of individual articulatory structures also are probably not good feature correlates or "primary control parameters" because more than one feature may influence the behavior of any articulatory structure. For example, the use of the mandible position as an important "control parameter" in a vowel production model (Lindblom and Sundberg, 1971) must take into account the fact that the mandible is influenced by goals which require movements of the tongue, lips and larynx for both vowels and consonants (cf. Kent, 1970; Ladefoged et al., 1972; Mermelstein, 1973; Gay and Hirose, 1973). Quantally-determined sensory goals which relate most directly to distinctive sound producing vocal-tract states may come as close as possible to being invariant speech production correlates of features as noted above, but a considerable amount of research needs to be done on this question.

Ladefoged (1971) has suggested that some features are acoustically-based and others are based on articulatory constraints. This notion has been elaborated by Lieberman (1970): there may be variation in the relative importance of articulatory and perceptual bases for features. In terms of the quantal nature of speech production, this idea leads to the suggestion that some features have better defined quantally-determined auditory-perceptual correlates than orosensory correlates. The features "syllabic" and "consonantal" might fall into this category. Other features, such as those corresponding to place of articulation, may have better defined orosensory than perceptual correlates. In the case of features with better-defined auditory correlates, the orosensory correlates would tend to be more variable and vice versa.

Variability in the degree of definition or "sharpness" of quantal effects (Lieberman, 1976) implies that some (possibly less frequently occurring) linguistic distinctions may correspond to features which have weak quantal bases. For example, this might be the case for features differentiating intermediate vowels which have been postulated to be delineated in some kind of continuous, multi-dimensional perceptual space (cf. Fant, 1973; Lindblom and Sundberg, 1971; Lieberman, 1976; Labov *et al.*, 1972).

A number of factors should influence whether or not feature-related goals are reached in any given utterance. Many of these influences revolve around a trading relationship between the need to transmit information at the phonetic level and the capability to do so at higher levels of the message. Children may have to rely more on information in the acoustic signal to clarify the perception of sentences than adults (who rely heavily on syntactic and semantic information) (Menyuk, 1972). It is generally believed that with mature speech, the amount of background noise, bandwidth of communications devices, different speaking situations (conversation, formal speaking, various experimental situations), familiarity of the listener with the subject matter, dialects, habits and many other factors all influence the precision of articulation and the degree to which goals are achieved. As an example, in casual speech, an utterance "did you want to" may be realized as /jəwánə/. A related factor may be the importance of the acoustic correlates of different goals as critical cues for the listener. For instance, the inability of the cleft palate speaker to achieve the goal associated with the feature "obstruent" seems to have a particularly disturbing effect on the listener, while speakers' failure to produce clear distinctions between some intermediate vowels or to devoice intervocalic stop consonants is largely ignored.

In line with the idea of variable precision in expression of different features, Mermelstein (1973) discusses the concept of "target regions" and different degrees of "pertinence" for target attainment by different articulators. Gay (1974) and Gay *et al.* (1974) suggest that vowel targets should be expressed in terms of spatial fields which are defined by the acoustic limits of the vowel in order to account for observed acoustic and spatial variability.

In summary, several possible implications of the hypothesized nature of distinctive features correlates have been discussed:

(1) The degree of feature independence or orthogonality depends on the domain in which feature correlates are defined. In terms of production, the orosensory domain may be the one in which feature correlates are most independent and invariant.

(2) There could be variability in the relative importance of auditory-sensory and orosensory bases for different features.

(3) There may also be variability in the degree to which features are defined on quantal bases, and it is possible that some (less frequently employed) features may be defined along continuous scales.

(4) The precision or reliability with which feature correlates are actually expressed may vary according to a number of factors including stage of language maturation, speaking situation and the inherent nature of individual features.

Considering the extremely limited state of current linguistic and physiological knowledge, no theory can be proposed which will account faithfully for all of our observations. On the other hand, evidence from acoustics (cf. Stevens, 1972; Stevens and Blumstein, 1975), perception (cf.

Studdert-Kennedy, 1976a), speech errors (cf. Fromkin, 1970; Shattuck-Hufnagel and Klatt, 1975), production, and linguistics suggests in general that the notion of a discrete, feature-specified, goal-oriented underlying framework makes a useful working hypothesis. From this point of view, one important part of trying to understand speech physiology is to continue to look for distinctions which are motivated on linguistic, acoustic and physiological bases while also trying to account for complicating factors such as those discussed above.

III. Speech Production Strategies: The Dynamic Framework

With an "input" in the form of a feature-specified underlying representation, our hypothetical overview must account for the transformation into articulatory movements. The transformation between binary (phonological) and "multi-valued" (phonetic or articulatory) representations has been thought of as being mediated by a set of "rules of the phonetic component" of the grammar (Chomsky and Halle, 1968; Fant, 1973), or "implementation rules" (Lieberman, 1970; see also Liberman, 1970). Our overview, hypothesizes that: (1) in the general case phonetic features have actual physiological correlates in the form of orosensory goals, and (2) there is a set of "rules" that describe the transformation between feature (goal) matrices and articulatory movements.

According to Fant (1973) rules of the phonetic component would describe the production, acoustic, and perceptual correlates of each feature, given the intrasegmental co-occurrence of features and the intersegmental context. The rules for production are hypothesized to produce "neural reorganization of control signals" which would involve or account for a number of factors including a principle of least effort, co-articulation, stress, tempo, speaker, etc. These rules are viewed as being essential to justifying the validity of any set of phonetic features. Implementation rules (Lieberman, 1970) "determine what articulatory maneuvers will follow from a phonetic feature in a given context as well as the extent of the maneuver." Such rules may be language-specific, universal and individual.

From our point of view rules of this general nature should describe the "strategies" that a speaker may actually use in transforming a discrete underlying framework into articulatory movements. A strategy is thought of as a mechanism for accomplishing the transformation between the input and output of a hypothetical stage in the production process. We do not know enough about motor control to describe strategies in any more than the most superficial and general terms, and they are not proposed as hypotheses for actual motor control functions. However, the strategies must be subserved by functions of the speech motor control system, and they should account for the complexities of the dynamic behavior of the articulatory mechanism (see Kent and Moll, 1975).

It is generally believed that a considerable amount of the control of many simpler types of movement is due to interactions between "central patterning" and peripheral feedback (cf. Evarts *et al.*, 1971; Bizzi, 1975). In speech production, discussion has revolved around the relative uses of preplanning and feedback mechanisms in strategies for speech motor control (cf. Kent, 1976; Ohala, 1972; Kozhevnikov and Chistovich, 1965; Leanderson and Lindblom, 1972). The use of feedback has a number of advantages which center around reducing the computational load on preplanning mechanisms. On the other hand, the existence of speech errors and suprasegmental effects on respiration and fundamental frequency is strongly suggestive of some kind of preplanning. Preplanning should allow for very brief inter-event intervals, but it requires a powerful and flexible set of rules for motor organization, as well as a knowledge of the properties of the production mechanism (Kent and Moll, 1975).

Preplanning may operate over different domains at different stages in the production process. For example, preplanning for syntactic influences on duration and fundamental frequency probably operates over the domain of relatively large syntactically-defined units (see Cooper, this volume; Cutler and Isard, this volume). On the other hand, co-articulation might be thought of as a preplanning mechanism which operates in a relatively short temporally-defined domain with little regard for phonetic boundaries. These ideas will be discussed further in the following four subsections on strategies for determination of timing, reorganization, co-articulation and computation of motor commands. In Section IV, the strategies are illustrated schematically.

A. Segment Durations and Control of Timing

One apparently necessary component of a set of speech production strategies is a system for determination and use of "intrinsic" segment durations (cf. Klatt, 1976; Lehiste, 1970). Intrinsic durations are hypothesized to represent weighted average durations of segments as they occur in various contexts. Presumably a speaker internalizes a "knowledge" of these durations as a part of the acquisition and use of speech production strategies. Alternatively, durational information for segments could be stored as the segments occur in larger units such as morphs or words, as part of lexical representations. This issue is discussed further below. In either case, intrinsic durations should be constrained by factors such as articulatory displacement, dynamic response properties of articulators, capabilities of the motor control system, and capabilities of the auditory mechanism to process time-varying properties of the signal. Higher level factors such as phonologically-determined durational distinctions also exert influences.

With preprogramming, it should be possible for bidirectional dependencies (forward and backward interactions) to be expressed in the timing of articulatory movements (cf. Kent and Moll, 1975). MacNeillage (1972) and Lehiste (1970) have discussed several observations on segment durations which appear to follow this pattern to a certain extent. That is, there are durational effects which can be interpreted as being due to physiological properties of the articulation of "preceding" or "following" segments.

The greater durations of phonemically nondistinct vowels preceding voiced (as opposed to voiceless) consonants may be related to a need for more rapid and forceful closure movements to contain the higher intraoral air pressure associated with the voiceless stops. The longer vowel durations preceding fricatives (as opposed to stops) may be related to the need for a more precise articulatory configuration for the fricative. And the increasing vowel durations with movement of the place of articulation of the following consonant from labial to alveolar to palatal may be caused by the increasing degree of involvement of the consonant articulator in producing the vowel and/or different maximum possible rates of articulator movement.

With respect to consonant durations, the apparent greater length of bilabial stops could be due to the relative freedom of the lips and mandible from involvement in adjacent segments. The greater length of voiceless stops and fricatives (as opposed to their voiced cognates) could be related to the need for enough time to perform the glottal abduction and adduction maneuver associated with voiceless consonants. As a final example, there is an interesting interaction between place of articulation, closure duration and the following VOT duration for voiceless stops (Stevens and Klatt, 1974; Zue, 1976; Williams, 1977). The duration of closure plus VOT is apparently constant, but closure duration decreases and VOT increases as the place of consonant articulation moves from bilabial to dental to velar. The total duration (closure plus VOT) may be determined by the glottal abduction-adduction maneuver. The increasingly longer VOT following dental and velar stops may be necessary to prevent voicing while the tongue body is still moving towards the following vowel configuration.

Studies of articulatory movements and the timing of electromyographic activity have tended to corroborate acoustically-based findings and hypotheses. The velocity and extent of movement of different articulatory structures seem to be related to a number of factors including: the distance to be traveled (Kent, 1970), intra-oral pressure during stop consonants (Putnam and Ringel, 1972), interactions between articulators (Sussman et al., 1973), stress (cf. MacNeilage et al., 1970a; Harris, 1971), and speaking rate (cf. Gay et al., 1974; Amerman et al., 1970; Kent and Moll, 1972; Gay, 1974; Lindblom, 1963; Kent et al., 1974). The timing of the onset of lip-closing muscle activity for bilabial stops following Swedish vowels and has been shown to be related to articulatory distance, that is, the less rounded the vowel, the earlier the muscle activity begins with respect to lip contact (Leanderson and Lindblom, 1972). For the tongue muscles, the greater vowel duration before voiced (versus voiceless) consonants has been shown to correlate with longer vowel-related muscle activity (Raphael, 1975).

The data on segment durations and articulatory movements suggest that there are several physical and physiologically-related constraints which influence intrinsic durations and segmental-level context-dependent timing effects:

(1) Trading relationships among speed of movement, precision of movement termination, amount of displacement and required forces.

(2) Mechanical or anatomical interactions as they influence the functions of "independent" articulators in adjacent segments, and

(3) Maximum possible rates of articulator movement (see MacNeilage, 1972).†

A pre-planning strategy which makes adjustments in timing on the basis of segmental must incorporate or have access to a "knowledge" of these constraints.

There are numerous suprasegmental influences on segment duration and timing including semantic, syntactic, word level, stress-related, positional and syllabic factors (cf. Klatt, 1976; Lindblom and Rapp, 1973; Nooteboom, 1972; Cooper, 1976), and rules have been proposed to account for many of these higher level influences as well as for segmental-level effects (cf. Laferriere and Zue, 1977). A detailed treatment of timing effects is beyond the scope of this discussion, but it is proposed that the application of such rules should be considered as somewhat independent preplanning mechanisms for the determination of timing. The extent to which lower level (i.e. within morph or word) rules operate each time an utterance is generated will depend on how much low-level timing information is stored as part of the lexical representation.

The strategy for determination of timing would convert a feature (sensory goal) matrix-like specification of an utterance along with suprasegmental information into a temporal sequence of sensory goal invocations. This strategy is illustrated schematically in Section IV.

B. Reorganization and Determination of "Motor Goals"

In Section II.B, it was suggested that positions or movements of individual articulatory structures probably are not good feature correlates, because sensory goals corresponding to more than one feature may influence the behavior of any articulatory structure. Raising and lowering of the velum is probably the gesture which correlates most clearly with the occurrence of a single feature. But even movement of the velum shows evidence of peripheral motor command reorganization (Harris, 1970; Lubker, 1975), presumably because of the influence of other features. In other words, motor commands to the velum seem to be reorganized, depending on the nature of concurrent commands to other articulators. The tongue tip also seems to be more or less capable of independent function, but it must be raised to a different degree depending on the position of the tongue body. The tongue body is clearly influenced by several features (cf. Perkell, 1971; Lieberman, 1975), and it has

† Other findings (Keuhn, 1973; Muller et al., 1977) suggest that biomechanical properties of some articulatory structures (i.e. the lips) are not necessarily rate limiting in a direct physical sense. However, these properties may have indirect effects on the timing and magnitude of movements by influencing motor programming strategies.

already been mentioned that the mandible must be influenced by goals which are achieved by functions of the lips, tongue and even the larynx.

The requirements of suprasegmental factors such as stress, emphasis and intonation also influence segmental articulations. For example, the overlapping influences of intonation and segmental articulations on the larynx are evidenced by the well-known differences in fundamental frequency contours following voiced versus voiceless stop consonants. Stress has been found to produce a "reorganization" of motor commands to the tongue (Harris, 1971) and the lips (Harris et al., 1968).

Reorganization can be thought of as a preplanning strategy which transposes a temporal specification of relatively independent sensory goal invocations (the output of the timing strategy) into a temporal specification of "motor goals" or goals for individual articulators. The main purpose of this transposition is to reconcile overlapping (possibly conflicting) requirements of different co-occurring orosensory goals on each articulatory structure. For example, the mandible and its controlling musculature might have conflicting spatial targets imposed by the co-occurrence of the feature specifications "-high" (requiring a lowered tongue body and mandible) and "+round" (requiring rounded lips and a raised mandible). The levator palatini muscles (which raise the velum) would be required by the feature specification "-nasal" to contract more when it coincides with the feature specification "+high" than "-high" (possibly because contraction of the palatoglossus muscle to help raise the tongue also might tend to pull down on the velum through an anatomical interconnection, and/or because of acoustic factors).

The reorganization mechanism would "sum" such overlapping, co-occurring requirements of different orosensory goals on each articulator to produce a single configurational and muscle tension target (called a "motor goal") for that articulator. The function of the reorganization strategy is influenced by anatomical relationships and certain low level aspects of neuromuscular function such as the length-tension characteristics of the muscles. This strategy might be thought of as incorporating knowledge of the relationships between sensory goals and the structural positions or muscle tensions required to achieve the goals. Compensations such as those produced in response to the insertion of bite blocks or pseudopalates (cf. Lindblom et al., 1977; Hamlet and Stone, 1974; Nooteboom and Slis, 1970) might be thought of as being due to minor adjustments in the strategy. Speakers presumably use auditory and/or orosensory feedback to make these adjustments.

C. Co-articulation

Co-articulation is the simultaneous expression of non-competing aspects of articulation of more than one phonetic segment in a sequence. "Anticipatory co-articulation" describes the occurrence of aspects of articulation of "future" segments during a particular segment and "perseveratory" co-articulation describes the perseverance of aspects of articulation of "preceding" segments. For example, in the pronunciation of the word "snoop", lip rounding for /u/ anticipates the vowel by beginning during the /s/, and nasalization perseveres from the /n/ into the /u/. The results of anticipatory and perseveratory co-articulation can be thought of as intermixing of aspects of articulation of several adjacent segments (see reviews by Daniloff and Hammarberg, 1973 and Kent and Minifie, 1977).

Different combinations of measurements of movement, EMG activity and acoustics have been used to study the co-articulatory behavior of the velum (Dixit and MacNeilage, 1972; Moll and Daniloff, 1971; Kent, *et al.*, 1974; Ushijima and Hirose, 1975, the lips (Amerman *et al.*, 1970; Leanderson and Lindblom, 1972; Daniloff and Moll, 1968; Benguerel and Cowan, 1974) the tongue (Ohman, 1966; MacNeilage and DeClerk, 1969; Bell-Berti and Harris, 1974; Gay, 1975) and the mandible (cf. Sussman *et al.*, 1973).

Results vary somewhat depending on the particular articulator, the type of speech and the language, but several general principles emerge from these studies and others like them. Both anticipatory and perseveratory co-articulation occur, up to six segments in advance of and two or three segments following the "target" segment. With some limited exceptions (cf. Ushijima and Hirose, 1975; Gay, 1975) it has been found to occur whenever possible, that is, unless it is inhibited by over-ruling preceding or following gestures. It usually spans syllable, word and phrase boundaries.

Anticipatory articulation can be thought of as being produced by a look-ahead procedure which covers a "time window" corresponding to approximately four to six segments at any one moment (Henke, 1967). The look-ahead procedure assigns a priority or urgency to each motor goal (which is subsequently transformed into a motor command). The urgency for each goal depends on how early the first specification of the goal appears in the look-ahead window. In other words, the sooner a goal has to be achieved, the higher a priority rating it would receive. The development of this strategy seems to involve a principle of economy of effort (Lindblom, 1971a; Fant, 1973). That is, the speaker appears to learn not to move any more abruptly toward a goal than is absolutely necessary. In developing this strategy, the speaker must account for the different mechanical response properties of individual articulators. So in a sense, anticipatory co-articulation could be a means of preplanning sequences of movements in a manner that most efficiently compensates for the heterogeneous structure of the production mechanism. It has also been suggested that anticipatory co-articulation might provide perceptual cues (cf. MacNeilage, 1972; Daniloff and Hammarburg, 1973).

As mentioned previously, it might be more appropriate to think of the span of anticipatory co-articulation in terms of a "time window" as opposed to numbers of phonetic segments. This idea is consistent with its hypothesized biomechanical motivation and the recent findings of Bell-Berti and Harris (1977) that lip rounding before an /u/ begins a "fixed time" before voicing onset of the vowel, independent of the number of preceding segments. It is also significant to note that the co-articulation strategy is hypothesized to operate following reorganization, on a structure-determined rather than purely feature-determined basis. In this case, different structures might evidence different characteristic look-ahead time windows, depending on their individual biomechanical response properties.

In the studies of Gay (1975) and Ushijima and Hirose (1975) some effects of syllable-boundaries on co-articulatory behavior have been observed. (Possible "syllabic" effects on motor programming are discussed below.) When contrasted with other studies, these results suggest that co-articulation, like many other aspects of speech production, may show variation depending on the speaker, utterance type, speaking situations, etc. The differences between these and most other results should be explored further.

Perseveratory co-articulation seems to operate differently from anticipatory co-articulation (cf. Ushijima and Hirose, 1975; Daniloff and Hammarberg, 1973), and it is generally thought to be due at least in part to "sluggish" gesture relaxation.†

Up to this point, the existence of preplanning strategies has been posited for determining timing, reorganization, and co-articulation. Each one of these mechanisms could operate over a different domain with respect to the input string of phonetic segments. As a result of the application of these strategies, a feature matrix-like specification of an utterance would be converted into a continuously-changing set of "motor goals" accompanied by timing and magnitude information. Various forms of feedback about vocal tract properties and behavior should play relatively long-term roles in the establishment and maintenance of orosensory goals and preplanning mechanisms, but in general, it is suggested that there is little effect of feedback on the moment-to-moment function of these mechanisms. The next section reviews work on the moment-to-moment use of feedback for determining motor commands. These mechanisms, along with the preplanning strategies described above are discussed with respect to findings and hypotheses on motor control.

D. Determination of Motor Commands and the Control of Movement

If there is a stage in the programming of speech movements in which preplanning mechanisms have established temporally ordered sequences of articulatory goals, there must be mechanisms for the translation of goal sequences into contraction pattern for the muscles (or activity of α motorneurons).

There are several ways in which the hypothesized motor goals may be translated into motor commands on a moment-to-moment basis. The conversion may be direct, and in this case, goals would have to contain complete timing and magnitude information for contractions of individual muscles. This mechanism is least "economical" in that it places the largest computational load on preplanning mechanisms. Indirect conversion of motor goals to motor commands could utilize peripheral feedback loops which include the muscles and mechanoreceptors as well as internal loops

† See footnote, p. 350.

which have only indirect interaction with the periphery. Both forms of feedback may be more "economical" in reducing the amount of required preprogramming.

1. On the moment-to-moment use of feedback mechanisms

Several peripheral reflex mechanisms are available for use in controlling vocal tract musculature in speech. These include mandibular stretch reflexes and facial (Kugelberg, 1952; Ekborn et al., 1952) and laryngeal (c.f. Sawashima, 1970) reflexes as well as projections of muscle spindle afferents from the trigeminal mesencephalic nucleus to hypoglossal and trigeminal motor nuclei (Doty, 1968). As has been hypothesized for other reflex mechanisms (Henneman, 1968; Bizzi, 1975) these vocal-tract peripheral reflex pathways might be used to some extent in elaborating details of motor commands on the basis of simpler "goal-like" inputs. In fact, the use of the word "reflex" to describe any of these mechanisms could be misleading, because it refers only to a response to an external stimulus. Such responses could make up small proportion of the uses of these mechanisms (cf. Oscarsson, 1971).

There have been very few convincing demonstrations of the participation of peripheral reflex mechanisms in the control of articulation, perhaps because of the richness and redundancy of feedback modalities in the vocal tract and the difficulty of designing experiments to isolate any single effect. However, several interesting attempts have been made to look for evidence of the participation of reflexes in speech movements. These effects would be short-latency because they involve fast-acting (about 40 ms or less) mechanisms. Since there is not enough time for a conscious reaction or "compensatory reorganization" to enter into the expression of short-latency effects, any that could be demonstrated might function in the control of normal articulatory movements.

Smith and Lee (1971) attempted to elicit a stretch reflex in the orbicularis oris by mechanically interrupting lip closure at randomly selected times. They did not find the short latency increase in muscular activity which would characterize the stretch reflex. However, in 60% of the trials, there was a short-latency (about 5 ms) decrease in muscle activity which they suggested was related to the facial reflex in some unspecified fashion. In a more recent related experiment Netsell and Abbs (1975) have found that orbicularis oris reflex (EMG) responses to electrical stimulation of the infraorbital nerve (which carries facial reflex afferents) were greatest in amplitude during closure for a /p/, at an intermediate level when the lips were passive and lowest during the labial opening. They suggested that one interpretation of this result might be that during lip movement, the excitatory influence of afferents on bulbar motorneurons are modulated by suprabulbar mechanisms. In other words, this result might be interpreted as evidence that a motor goal (lip closure) is being elaborated in part by a facial reflex pathway. On the other hand, the possibility cannot be excluded that the increased EMG reflected a preprogrammed command which was facilitated by the artificially induced afferent inflow.

Two experiments on the possible role of intra-oral air pressure as a feedback parameter (suggested, for example, by Malecot, 1966; Hutchinson and Putnam, 1974) have produced tentative, possibly conflicting results. Putnam and Shipp (1975) have reported no measurable change in the duration of laryngeal (PCA) EMG activity in response to an unexpected, partial venting of intraoral air pressure during the production of prestressed /p/. This result appears to indicate that intra-oral pressure is not sensed and used in the short-latency control over the timing of cessation of laryngeal abduction during the stop. In a similar experiment (Perkell, 1976) a vacuum system was used to produce an unexpected intraoral pressure decrease during intervocalic /p/ under conditions of normal labial sensation and labial anaesthesia. During the combined anaesthesia and negative pressure condition, there was a significant increase (20 ms) in the duration of labial closure plus VOT for one subject. This result suggest that in the absence of the sensation of lip closure and pressure build-up during the stop, the command for glottal adduction at stop release was delayed by 20 ms. However, an extension of this paradigm (Perkell and Gay, unpublished) laryngeal EMG measurements were made and showed tentatively that there were no feedback-related effects of intraoral pressure reductions.

These results, along with the previously-mentioned jaw-movement interruption results (Folkins and Abbs, 1975, 1976) provide only very fragmentary and conflicting evidence on the moment-to-moment role of peripheral feedback mechanisms.

One main argument against the moment-to-moment use of peripheral feedback is that the inter-event intervals in speech may be too brief in comparison with reflex loop delay time (cf. Kent and Moll, 1972). However, an examination of vocal-tract peripheral reflex loop capabilities suggests that these mechanisms might be useful. Stretching a muscle (by tapping on overlying tissue) characteristically produces a biphasic reflex response. In segmental (limb) reflexes, the earlier (myotatic) component of the response is monosynaptic. The later component is polysynaptic, and it may reflect not only signals from proprioceptive afferents, but also exteroceptive and joint afferents (cf. Marsden, et al., 1977; Nashner, 1976). The late component of the segmental stretch reflex has been called the "functional stretch reflex" (FSR). It can be useful in compensating for externally imposed disturbances, and it is variable in appearance, depending on the subject and the task. The FSR, and possibly other reflex mechanisms can be "preset" when the nature of the disturbance is predictable.

Facial reflexes are similar in having two components (Ekborn et al., 1952; Kugelberg, 1952), but both components are presumed to be polysynaptic (McClean et al., in press; Dubner et al., 1978). There is also evidence of neuronal elements which can integrate cortical and peripheral inputs and which act on vocal-tract α motorneurons (Porter, 1967). Such neurons could be components of pathways which mediate both components of facial reflexes. A great deal of descending control information is thought to impinge on interneurons, and it has been hypothesized that the same descending signal might at different times encounter different [feedback dependent] states in segmental interneurons (Burke, 1971), allowing the on-line [goal-oriented] elaboration of motor commands by peripheral reflex pathways. Even with loop delays up to 40 ms and muscle contraction delays in the range of 40 ms (cf. Atkinson, 1973), it is conceivable that peripheral reflex pathway could be "recruited" to help control the completion phases of vocal-tract movements, especially with the time gained by anticipatory co-articulation. It would be unlikely for movements to be initiated under reflex pathway mediation.

While it may be possible for peripheral feedback mechanisms to be used in speech, the emerging view from work on other forms of movement is that such reflexes serve mainly to provide relatively modest load compensation when a load disturbance is applied (cf. Bizzi et al., 1978).† With respect to the FSR, if disturbances cannot be predicted, the motor control system seems to rely less on segmental reflexes and rely more heavily on centrally initiated, delayed responses to disturbances (Nashner, 1976). From this point of view, the normal absence of disturbances in speech suggests a reliance on central mechanisms, including "internal feedback".

In addition to feedback loops which include peripheral structures, there are numerous feedback pathways completely within the central nervous system (cf. Evarts et al., 1971, Arshavsky et al., 1972; Grillner, 1975; Taub and Berman,1968, Allen and Tsukahara, 1974). For example, some of the same polysynaptic peripheral reflex pathways which may be used for the elaboration of motor commands contain interneurons that project information about the activity of these "lower motor centers" to higher level structures (Oscarsson, 1971). Such an "internal feedback" mechanism could monitor the state of spinal centers before and during movements to permit assessment of descending commands before they take effect. Thus, programming errors could be detected and corrected with minimal delays (Burke, 1971).

Theories on the function of the cerebellum and its interconnections to other parts of the motor control system (cf. Bell and Dow, 1967) have suggested that the cerebellum is involved in learning motor skills (Marr, 1969; Evarts and Thach, 1969) and that it acts as a "computer" to provide "feedforward" control without the need for peripheral feedback (Ito, 1972). Allen and Tsukahara (1974) suggest that different parts of the cerebellum take part in (a) learning and preprogramming movements and in (b) updating or modifying motor commands. The latter function uses collateral efferent information about the intended movement along with afferent information about the results of previous motor commands. Although speculative, those ideas suggest a role for internal feedback mechanisms in elaborating and executing motor programs. Peripheral feedback about ongoing movements could be used to compare actual with expected results of motor programs to aid in fine adjustment of subsequent movements.

2. Feedback and "Central Patterning" in the control of movement

Regardless of the precise nature of feedback mechanisms, the ideas mentioned

† Except mandibular reflexes in which a large proportion of the stiffness appears to be a response to muscle stretch (Goodwin et al., 1978).

above suggest that the use of these mechanisms must be viewed in relation to preplanning mechanisms which must play a major role in speech production. Preplanning of complexes of skilled movements is probably similar in some ways to "central patterning" of simpler types of movements.

In a review of a number of studies of locomotion in animals, Grillner (1975) has suggested that a stereotyped pattern, particularly for timing of the activity of individual muscles is controlled by a separate spinal level central pattern generator for each limb. Peripheral reflex mechanisms are hypothesized to adapt movements to the environment and compensate for external disturbances, but segmental reflex signals don't actually interact with the central generators. Interlimb coordination seems to be accomplished by interneuronal circuits within the spinal cord and brainstem. Descending control signals apparently act not only on the spinal generator itself, but also on different spinal pathways so as to adjust the entire spinal circuitry (including reflex pathways) to the intended movement (Grillner, 1975).

In the coordination of head turning and rapid (saccadic) eye movements in monkeys, two different patterns are observed depending on whether visual stimuli are presented to the animal at random intervals or in a paradigm which allows the animal to anticipate the timing of the stimulus. With random presentation, approximately simultaneous, initial bursts of EMG activity are observed in neck and eye agonists, accompanied by silence in antagonists. In this mode, a central program apparently initiates the movements which are subsequently coordinated and elaborated by peripheral reflex mechanisms (including the vestibular apparatus). With the non-random stimulus presentation, the animal is able to make a predictive head movement which anticipates the stimulus and begins well before the eye movement. Under these conditions, the head movement is achieved with a gradual increase in the activity of the agonists which is mirrored by a decrease in the activity of the antagonists (Bizzi et al., 1971, 1972; Bizzi, 1975).

Swallowing involves the coordiation of about 20 different muscles with motorneurons belonging to several brainstem motor nuclei. The coordinating neurons of a brainstem-level "swallowing center" are capable of generating a complex excitatory and inhibitory pattern in the appropriate motor neurons, even with the brainstem transected above the trigeminal motor nucleus, with elimination of proprioceptive and tactile feedback, or with portions of the motorneuron pool deleted. There are, however, some slight variations in the swallowing pattern which occur with differences in the size and consistency of the bolus, or as a consequence of stretching certain muscles. In humans, vastly greater flexibility of papatopharyngeal and laryngeal mechanisms is hypothesized to reside, in part, in refinement of the medullary interneuronal network (Doty, 1968).

In simpler voluntary movements (Maton and Bouisset, 1975; Garland and Angel, 1971; Vallbo, 1971), experimental evidence suggests that movements are initiated under supraspinal (preplanned) control, but that peripheral feedback mechanisms could play a role in regulating later components, including termination. Preplanning for these voluntary movements must take into account a number of biomechanical factors such as the current state of the system, dynamic characteristics of the desired movements and the length-tension properties of the muscles.

For complex sequences of voluntary movements, it may be that sequencing occurs too rapidly to allow for nerve conduction and muscle contraction delays associated with peripheral feedback loops. In fact, it may be neccessary for feedback mechanisms to be suppressed in skilled movement sequences (Van der Gor and Wieneke, 1969).

A recent series of studies on typewriting (Terzuolo and Viviani, unpublished) has shown that time-normalized patterns of interstroke intervals in skilled typing are very reproducible for individual subjects. The patterning unit appears to be the word, as opposed to smaller subunits such as letter pairs, and the patterns are different across subjects. Attempts to disrupt feedback in various ways led to the suggestion that there is some limited interaction of the "pattern" or "template" with peripheral inputs, but the precise nature of the interaction is not clear.

Although a number of details vary with the type of movement and central and peripheral structures involved, almost all of these findings suggest interactions between "central patterning" (or preplanning) mechanisms which provide a "framework" for the movement and feedback mechanisms which play different roles in elaborating movement details. The findings on typewriting suggest that part of the preplanning function for complexes of skilled movements may involve the utilization of "templates" or "patterns" which have been stored as part of the learning process.

3. *Hypotheses on the control of articulatory movements*

Although the evidence on the use of peripheral orosensory feedback in speech is incomplete, it is hard to avoid the conclusion that non-auditory feedback is used on a moment-to-moment basis. As numerous authors have suggested, various forms of feedback may be used in a fluctuating and redundant fashion (cf. Kent, 1976; Sussman, 1972; Bowman, 1971; Scott and Ringel, 1971; Ringel, 1971; Borden *et al.*, 1973). Probably the most persuasive argument for the use of feedback on a moment-to-moment basis rests on the many findings of variability and particularly those of motor equivalence (Hughes and Abbs, 1976); however, much more work is needed along these lines. The suggestion that inter-event intervals may be too short for the use of peripheral feedback (cf. Kent and Moll, 1975) needs to be examined more carefully. The segment durations in consonant clusters such as /spl/ may be very brief, but movements of separate articulators that produce such rapid sequences may last long enough to allow for feedback pathways to participate in some aspects of their control. A careful examination of movement durations, muscle contraction times and loop delays may help determine whether or not peripheral feedback may truly be excluded from consideration.

On the other hand, the existence of precisely and rapidly sequenced movements suggests strongly that the timing of the onsets of these movements is preplanned (Kent and Moll, 1975). Additional indirect evidence for preplanning, possibly over differently-defined domains, comes from many other results on timing, reorganization and co-articulation. In terms of the findings on other forms of movement, we can think of higher level preplanning mechanisms functioning as a "creative" pattern generator which elaborates unique sequences of central commands or "motor goals" depending on the configuration of the input phonetic string and suprasegmental constraints on stress, timing, and intonation.

It is not inconceivable that patterns of temporal (and possibly spatial) information for goal sequences corresponding to larger units such as morphs or words are stored as part of lexical representations during learning. To some extent these patterns would be incomplete, to allow for the superposition of the effects of context when utterances are actually generated. Storage of patterns in this manner might have the advantage of reducing the computational load at utterance generation time. Such a storage mechanism could account for the reproducibility of patterns of articulation which has been discussed by some authors (cf. Fowler *et al.*, in this volume).

The mechanism for anticipatory co-articulation is somewhat similar to the predictive mode of head and eye coordination (Bizzi *et al.*, 1972) in that both mechanisms appear to take advantage of a "knowledge" of "future" timing and magnitude information to program movements in a smoother, possibly more efficient manner. Thus, anticipatory co-articulation might be a short-range preplanning strategy which is motivated by a need for biomechanical efficiency, or "economy of effort".

To the extent that preplanning mechanisms cannot or do not elaborate fine details of motor commands, "lower level" motor mechanisms compute motor commands by comparing "motor goals" (expressed in terms of muscle tensions and lengths, contact of surfaces, etc.) with the "current" state of the system. These mechanisms include various feedback pathways (internal and peripheral) as well as "circuitry" for motor programs such as swallowing. A strategy to perform this function is outlined in Section IV.

4. *Interactions of spatial and temporal aspects of speech motor*
   programming
Numerous authors have hypothesized that "syllables" are coherent motor programming units (cf. Lehiste, 1970; Kozhevnikov and Chistovich, 1965; Studdert-Kennedy, 1976b; Gay, 1975). Even though there has been only a small amount of direct evidence to support such hypotheses, it is tempting to speculate that the temporal acoustic intensity fluctuation which correlates with the feature "syllabic" (Fant, 1973) plays some role in governing speech rhythm or intersyllable intervals (Kent, 1976). The idea that some controlling elements (such as the feature "syllabic") may have a temporal (as opposed to static or timeless) basis suggests that there may be somewhat separate underlying influences on temporal and spatial aspects of articulation.

The notion of separate controls of temporal and spatial aspects of articulation is supported indirectly by results of "feedback" experiments which have utilized injections of a local anesthetic to block sensory branches of the trigeminal nerve. It is difficult to interpret the feedback-related aspects of nerve block experiments because the blocks seem to produce several confusing effects, including some apparent motor paralysis (Borden *et al.*, 1973; Putnam and Ringel, 1972; Smith and Lee, 1971) and changes in the activity of muscles which should not be directly affected by the sensory block (Borden *et al.*, 1973; Leanderson and Persson, 1972). However, these and other (Hutchinson and Putnam, 1974; Prosek and House, 1975) experimenters have noticed in general that the resulting speech is characterized by alterations in place and manner of articulation as well as segment durations, but *not* in the overall temporal pattern. These very general impressions should be explored in more detail.

The non-linguistic factor of speaking rate also has an influence on the timing and magnitude of articulatory commands, and this influence seems to depend on several factors. Studies of the effects of speaking rate have shown that at increased rates, there can be undershoot of tongue movements toward vowel targets (Lindblom, 1963; Kent and Moll, 1972; Gay, 1974) which is accompanied by lower EMG levels (Gay *et al.*, 1974). The lips show speaking-rate effects which are different for vowels and consonants. Rate increases seem to produce undershoot of vowel targets (Amerman *et al.*, 1970), and increases in EMG activity and speed of movement for bilabial consonants including /w/ (Gay and Hirose, 1973; Gay *et al.*, 1974). Both increases and decreases in mandibular velocities as well as undershoot have been found with higher speaking rates (Abbs, 1973; Amerman, *et al.*, 1970; Kent and Moll, 1972), and rate effects have been found to be a function of required amount of displacement (Gay *et al.*, 1974). Rate increases have caused the velum to produce undershoot and no velocity increases (Kent *et al.*, 1974), and the dynamic behavior of the laryngeal structures is apparently rate dependent (Sawashima, 1970).

It has been hypothesized that undershoot is due to the limiting response properties of the articulators (Lindblom, 1963) and that articulatory rate is dependent on the speed with which neural commands can be translated into articulatory movements (Lehiste, 1970). These factors may indeed be involved in rate effects; however, it has been found that different speakers use different strategies for controlling rate. Some speakers increase movement velocities at higher rates with less resultant undershoot, and others reduce movement displacement, producing undershoot (Keuhn, 1973). It is possible that in the development of strategies to control articulatory movements, some speakers tend more than others to sacrifice precision in the acoustic signal for the sake of expending less effort. †

These findings and hypotheses tend to support the idea that the complicated strategies which control articulatory movements are influenced not only by "low-level" properties of the system, but also by interactions between movement and perceptual factors and individual differences in the development of perceptual and neuromuscular behavior.

† See footnote, p. 350.

IV. Summary: Outline of a Conceptual Model of The Physiology of Speech Production

In this section, the preceding discussion is summarized as an outline of a conceptual model of speech production. The model is presented in block diagram form, and it attempts to provide a somewhat coherent account of the physiological transformation between a feature-specified input and articulatory movements. The block diagrams serve mainly as schematic representations of the mechanisms discussed above, and no claims are made for the reality or unique status of these representations. Models like this one must be highly speculative, very general† and continuously subject to revision, and it is recognized that many alternative models are possible. The model is useful primarily as a means of drawing observations on physiological mechanisms into a single comprehensive framework. This framework suggests that production strategies are highly interdependent and that they have overlapping influences on the few physiological parameters which are available for measurement.

Figure 1 shows a block diagram of the three major components of the model. The input to the model is in the form of a sensory goal (distinctive feature) matrix in which the columns represent phonetic segments (Ss) and the rows represent the sensory goal (SG) correlates of the distinctive features. These correlates may be in the form of patterns of articulator contact (for the features "high, "back", "coronal"), levels of intraoral air pressure ("obstruent"). force of contact ("tense") or configurations ("rounded"). The bottom row of the input matrix, labeled "SUP" symbolizes all accompanying suprasegmental information. The output of the model is in the form of articulatory movements.

The top block of Fig. 1 represents preplanning strategies for the determination of timing, reorganization and co-articulation. The second block represents the strategy for the "on line" determination of motor commands, and the bottom block represents the peripheral vocal tract, including the muscles, the structures to which the muscles are attached and feedback receptors. Internal and peripheral feedback pathways are represented by the "upward flowing" arrows on the left side of Figs 1–3. In general, feedback on a long-term basis is used more by strategies represented toward the upper end of the figures, and moment-to-moment feedback is used more by strategies represented toward the lower ends.

Figure 2 is a block diagram representing the preplanning subcomponents for determining timing, reorganization and anticipatory co-articulation (look ahead). The strategy for determining timing is represented by the top block. The details of timing mechanisms are not treated here, and it is assumed that the operation of a timing strategy produces a temporal specification of sensory goal invocations which is symbolized as a sensory goal "score" at level 2 in Fig. 2. In the score, the horizontal "axis" represents time, and the width of

† For example, the model does not account for the almost universal occurrence of reduction (see p. 346) in natural speech.

each darkened cell represents the duration of the sensory goal invocation. As examples, darkened cells might represent information of the form, "maintain a certain level of intraoral pressure for a specific time interval" or "maintain a particular pattern of contact between sides of the tongue and the upper teeth for a specific time interval." At level 2 segment distinctions are preserved, but there is some temporal "jitter" at segment boundaries to account for intrasegmental asynchrony of goal manifestations (such as timing differences between glottal and supraglottal events in stop consonants).

The second block in Fig. 2 represents the strategy for reorganization. It has been mentioned that every articulator is influenced by sensory goals corresponding to more than one feature and also by suprasegmental factors. The overlapping effects of different influences on each articulator are reconciled by a mechanism which "sums" these effects to produce a temporal

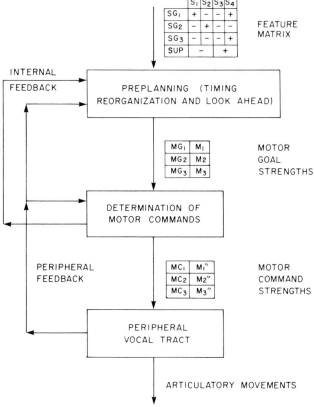

FIG. 1. A block diagram of the three major components of the conceptual model of speech production. The input to each component is represented above its block and to the right of the downward flowing arrow, and the output is represented below. The upward flowing arrows to the left of the blocks represent feedback information. The functions of the components are outlined in the text.

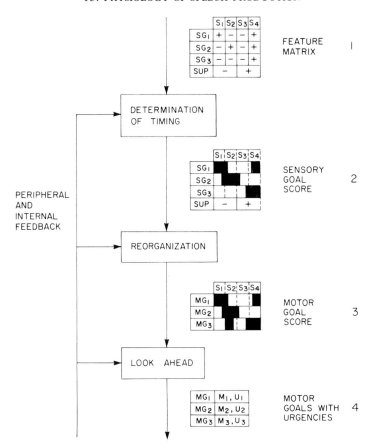

FIG. 2. A block diagram of the three preplanning subcomponents of the conceptual model. The functions of the subcomponents are outlined in the text.

sequence of motor goal invocations, symbolized at level 3 in Fig. 2 by the "motor goal score". In this score, the horizontal axis corresponds to time and each row corresponds to a different relatively independent articulatory structure and its controlling musculature (such as the mandible, the lips, the framework of the larynx, the body of the tongue, the tongue tip, etc.). For each articulator, each darkened cell represents a different spatial (muscle length and/or tension) "target" which is to be reached and maintained for a specific time interval. As examples, the darkened cells in the row corresponding to the mandible could represent different "target" openings, and the cells in the row for the tongue body could represent different spatial locations in the oropharyngeal cavity. At this level, both timing and magnitude effects of suprasegmental influences have been taken into account. Note that the motor goal score is structure specific and not feature specific.

The third block in Fig. 2 represents the strategy for anticipatory co-articulation. This function is preformed by a "look-ahead" mechanism which covers a time window corresponding to about six segments. The span of the window (as reflected in the location of its "leading" or "right" edge) may vary according to the mechanical response properties of each articulator and other less mechanical factors. The window scans left-to-right through the input motor goal score along the time axis at a constant rate. The segment "currently" being produced occupies the left end of the window, and the mechanisms assigns an "urgency" to each motor goal depending on how early (near the left end) the next (darkened cell) specification of the goal appears in the window. In other words, the sooner the next motor goal has to be achieved, the stronger an urgency it is assigned. At any one time, the output of the look-ahead mechanism is a single, structure-specific set of motor goals (MGs) which includes the spatial (and possibly muscle tension) specification of each goal (Ms) along with its urgency (Us). Since the output at this level represents the operation of the reorganization strategy as well as a structure-specific look-ahead mechanism, the co-articulatory behavior we observe does not represent feature independence directly.

It has been mentioned that partial programming information for larger units such as words may be stored in the form of "templates" and used as a basis for utterance generation. Depending on the degree to which such a hypothetical storage mechanisms is used, preplanning mechanisms would function less during utterance generation and more during learning of the "templates". Of course, on-line mechanisms would always have to function to a certain extent to account for context-dependent effects in domains which are more global than those of the stored units. Internal and peripheral feedback (about the properties of the production mechanism and its behavior) are used by preplanning mechanisms, almost exclusively on a long term basis for refinement and maintenance of their function, as well as for learning.

The component for determining motor commands from motor goals is diagrammed in Fig. 3. It consists of two subcomponents, the "upper motor center" and the "lower motor center". This mechanism must involve many more central nervous system structures than is implied by the block diagram, and the use of a two stage process is motivated by functional rather than anatomical or physiological considerations (as is the case with the other components of the model).

The primary function in converting motor goals into motor commands consists of a procedure for making "on line" or moment-to-moment adjustments based on the current state of the system. The many findings of variability and in particular the phenomenon of motor equivalence are accounted for by the use of feedback mechanisms. It is hypothesized that most adjustments for variation are accomplished by internal feedback mechanisms which elaborate motor commands from goals.

The two blocks and the internal feedback pathway connecting them in Fig. 3 represents the mechanism for producing premotor commands (PMCs) and then motor commands (MCs) from motor goals (MGs). The procedure requires an ability to predict the consequences of motor commands as they are

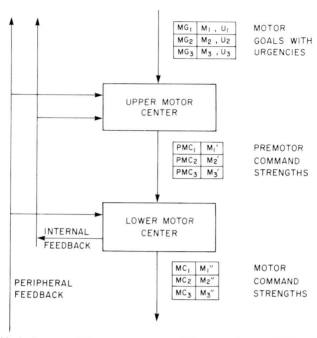

FIG. 3. A block diagram of the subcomponents of the conceptual model for the "on-line" determination of motor commands. The functions of these subcomponents are outlined in the text.

represented in "lower motor center". It is hypothesized that this ability is acquired or refined as speech motor control becomes habituated by comparing predictions about movements (the state of the lower motor center) with the results of those predictions (as monitored by peripheral feedback) (Lindblom *et al.*, 1978). Using the predictive ability, premotor commands (PMCs) are computed (in the "upper motor center"), moment-by-moment, on the basis of an "error signal" which represents differences between input motor goals and the state of the lower motor center (as reflected in internal feedback). It is possible that peripheral feedback is used to monitor and perhaps contribute to details of this process (cf. Kent, 1976), but for the most part, premotor commands are translated directly into motor commands (MCs) for individual muscles by the lower motor center. The motor commands are output to the final component of the model, the peripheral vocal tract. Peripheral feedback about the physical and physiological properties of the vocal tract is hypothesized to influence the nature of the sensory goal correlates of the phonetic features as well as speech production strategies.

From the block diagrams, the model appears to be oversimplified, but each strategy presumably has a level of complexity which is not reflected in the rather general and incomplete description that has been presented. As additional evidence is considered, future descriptions will undoubtedly be different, and more complicated. In spite of the difficulties with descriptions of this nature, they are useful in helping maintain some perspective on the complicated and indirect nature of the relationship between phonetic formulations and physiological data. We hope that future versions of this theory and any that may develop from alternative points of view (cf. MacNeilage, 1972; Moll *et al.*, 1976; Netsell and Abbs, 1976; Fowler *et al.*, in this volume) will contribute to an understanding of the special nature of speech production as a process which is influenced by auditory-perceptual, acoustic, physiological and linguistic constraints.

Acknowledgements

I am very grateful to Professor Kenneth N. Stevens and my other colleagues in the Speech Communication Group for the helpful discussions we have had as well as Professor Emilio Bizzi of M.I.T., Professor Sheila Blumstein of Brown University, Professor Bjorn Lindbolm of Stockholm University and Doctor Charles Larson of the University of Washington for their very useful comments. This work was supported by the National Institutes of Health Grant NS04332.

References

Abbs, J. H. (1973). The influence of the gamma motor system on jaw movements during speech: A theoretical framework and some preliminary observations, *Speech Hearing Res* **16**, 175–200.

Allen, G. I. and Tsukahara, N. (1974). Cerebrocerebellar communications systems, *Physiological Reviews,* **54**, 957–1006.

Amerman, J. D., Daniloff, R. and Moll, K. L. (1970). Lip and jaw coarticulation for the phoneme /æ/, *Journal of Speech and Hearing Research*, **13**, 147.

Arshavsky, Y. I., Berkinblit, M. B., Fukson, O. I., Gelfand, I. M. and Orlovsky, G. N. (1972). Orgin of modulation in neurones of the ventral spinocerebellar tract during locomotion, *Brain Research*, **43**, 276–279.

Atkinson, J. E. (1973). Response time in laryngeal muscles in controlling F_0: Results of a correlational analysis, *Journal of the Acoustical Society of America*, **54**, 310(A).

Bell, C. C. and Dow, R. S. (1967). Cerebellar Circuitry, *Neurosciences Research Program Bulletin*, **5**, 2.

Bell-Berti, F. (1975). Control of pharyngeal cavity size for English voiced and voiceless stops, *Journal of the Acoustical Society of America*, **57**, 455–461

Bell-Berti, F. and Harris, K. S. (1974). The motor organization of some speech gestures, *Journal of the Acoustical Society of America*, **55**, S79(A).

Bell-Berti, F. and Harris, K. S. (1977). Anticipatory coarticulation: Some implications from a study of lip rounding, *Journal of the Acoustical Society of America*, **62**, Supplement No. 1, S16.

Benguerel, A.-P. and Cowan, H. A. (1974). Coarticulation of upper lip protrusion in French, *Phonetica*, **30**, 41–55.

Bizzi, E. (1975). Motor coordination: Central and peripheral control during eye-head movement. *In* "Handbook of Psychobiology", (M. S. Gazzaniga and C. Blakemore, eds). Academic Press, New York.

Bizzi, E., Kalil, R. E. and Morasso, P. (1972). Two modes of active eye-head coarticulation in monkeys, *Brain Research*, **40**, 45–48.

Bizzi, E., Kalil, R. and Tagliasco, R. (1971). Eye-head coordination in monkeys: Evidence for centrally patterned organization, *Science, N.Y.*, **173**, 452–454.

Bizzi, E., Dev, P., Morasso, P. and Polit, A. (1978). Effect of load disturbances during centrally initiated movements, *Journal of Neurophysiology*, **41**, 542–556.

Borden, G. J., Harris, K. S. and Catena, L. (1973). Oral feedback II. An electromyographic study of speech under nerve block anaesthesia, *Journal of Phonetics*, **1**, 297–308.

Bowman, J. P. (1971). "The Muscle Spindle and Neural Control of the Tongue: Implications for Speech". C. C. Thomas, Springfield, IL.

Burke, R. E. (1971). Control systems operating on sinal reflex mechanisms. *In* "Central Control of Movement", (E. V. Evarts, E. Bizzi, R. E. Burke, M. DeLong, and W. T. Thach, eds), *Neuroscience Research Program Bulletin*, **9**, 1.

Chomsky, N. and Halle, M. (1968). "The Sound Pattern of English", Harper and Row, New York.

Cooper, W. E. (1976). Syntactic Control of Timing in Speech, Ph.D. thesis, Department of Psychology, M.I.T.

Daniloff, R. G. and Hammarberg, R. E. (1973). On defining coarticulation, *Journal of Phonetics*, **1**, 239–248.

Daniloff, R. G. and Moll, K. (1968). Coarticulation of lip rounding, *Journal of Speech and Hearing Research*, **11**, 707–721.

Dixit, P. and MacNeilage, P. F. (1972). Coarticulation of nasality: Evidence from Hindi. Abstract of a paper presented at the 83rd meeting of the Acoustical Society of America.

Doty, R. W. (1968). Neural organization of deglutition. Chapter 92, in "Handbook of Physiology IV", 1861–1902.

Dowla, F. and Perkell, J. S. (1977). Quantal nature of speech for vowels: Implications of cineradiographic and palatographic observations, *Journal of the Acoustical Society of America*, **62**, Supplement No. 1, S15(A).

Dubner, R., Sessle, B. J. and Storey, A. T. (1978). "The Neural Basis of Oral and Facial Function", Plenum Press, New York.

Ekborn, K., Jernelius, B. and Kugelberg, E. (1952). Perioral reflexes, *Neurology, (Minneap.)*, **2**, 103.

Evarts, E. V., Bizzi, E., Burke, R. E., DeLong, M. and Thach, W. T. (eds.) (1971). Central Control of Movement, *Neurosciences Research Program Bulletin*, **9**, 1.

Evarts, E. V. and Thach, W. T. (1969). Motor mechanisms of the CNS: Cerebrocerebellar interrelations. *In* "Annual Review of Physiology", (V. E. Hall, A. C. Geise and R. R. Sonnenschein, eds) pp. 451–498. Palo Alto, Annual Reviews, Inc., Palo Alto.

Fant, G. (1973). "Speech Sounds and Features, M.I.T. Press, Cambridge, Mass.

Folkins, J. W. and Abbs, J. H. (1975). Lip and jaw motor control during speech: Responses to resistive loading of the jaw, *Journal of Speech and Hearing Research*, **18**, 1, 207.

Folkins, J. W. and Abbs, J. H. (1976). Additional observations on responses to resistive loading of the jaw, *Journal of Speech and Hearing Research*, **19**, 820–821.

Fromkin, V. A. (1970). The non-anomalons nature of anomalons utterances, *Language*, **47**, 27–52.

Garland, H. and Angel, R. W. (1971). Spinal and supraspinal factors in voluntary movements, *Experimental Neurology*, **33**, 343–350.

Gay, T. (1974). A cinefluorographic study of vowel production, *Journal of Phonetics*, **2**, 255–266.

Gay, T. (1975). Some electromyographic measures of coarticulation in VCV utterances. Status Report on Speech Research, SR-44, Haskins Laboratories, New Haven, 137–145.

Gay, T. and Hirose, H. (1973). Effect of speaking rate on labial consonant production, *Phonetics*, **27**, 44–56.

Gay, T., Ushijima, T., Hirose, H. and Cooper, F. S. (1974). Effect of speaking rate on labial consonant-vowel articulation, *Journal of Phonetics*, **2**, 1, 47–63.

Goodwin, G. M., Hoffman, D. S. and Luschei, E. S. (1978). The strength of the reflex response to sinusoidal stretch of monkey jaw closing muscles during voluntary contraction, *Journal of Physiology*, **279**, 81–111.

Grillner, S. (1975). Locomotion in vertebrates: Central mechanisms and reflex interaction, *Physiological Reviews*, **55**, 247–304.

Grossman, R. C., Hattis, B. F. and Ringel, R. L. (1965). Oral tactile experience, *Archives of Oral Biology*, **10**, 691–705.

Hamlet, S. and Stone, M. (1974). Reorganization of speech motor patterns following prosthodontic changes in oral morphology. Proceedings of the Speech Communication Seminar, Stockholm, Aug. 1–3, 79–86.

Harris, K. S. (1970). Physiological aspects of articulatory behavior. Status Report on Speech Research SR-23, pp. 49–67, Haskins Laboratories, New Haven.

Harris, K. S. (1971). Vowel stress and articulatory reorganization. Status Report on Speech Research, SR-28, pp. 167–178, Haskins Laboratories, New Haven.

Harris, K. S. and Raphael, L. J. (1973). Activity of some extrinsic and intrinsic tongue muscles in the articulation of American vowels, *Journal of the Acoustical Society of America*, **53**, 1, 295(A).

Harris, K. S., Gay, T., Scholes, G. N. and Lieberman, P. (1968). Some stress effects on electromyographic measures of consonant articulations, Status Report on Speech Research, SR-13/14, pp. 137–152. Haskins Laboratories, New York.

Henke, W. L. (1967). Preliminaries to speech synthesis based on an articulatory model. Proceedings of the 1967 IEEE Boston Speech Conference, pp. 170–177.

Henneman, E. (1968). Spinal reflexes and the control of movement. Chapter 75. *In* "Medical Physiology", (V. B. Mountcastle, ed.). C. V. Mosby, St. Louis.

Hughes, O. M. and Abbs, J. H. (1976). Labial-mandibular coordination in the production of speech: Implications for the operation of motor equivalence, *Phonetica*, **33**, 199–201.

Hutchinson, J. M. and Putnam, A. H. B. (1974). Aerodynamic aspect of sensory deprived speech, *Journal of the Acoustical Society of America*, **56**, 5, 1612.

Ito, M. (1972). Neural design of the cerebellar motor control system, *Brain Research*, **40**, 81–84.

Jakobson, R. (1968). Child Language, Aphasia and Phonological Universals, A. R. Keiler (translation), Mouton, The Hague.

Jakobson, R., Fant, C. G. M. and Halle, M. (1951). "Preliminaries to Speech Analysis", MIT Press, Cambridge, Mass.

Kent, R. D. (1970). Lingual mechanics in speech production. Paper presented at the 1970 meeting of the American Academy of Arts and Sciences.

Kent, R. D. (1976). Models of speech production. *In* "Contemporary Issues of Experimental Phonetics, (N. J. Lass, ed.) pp. 79–104. Academic Press, New York.

Kent, R. D. and Minifie, F. D. (1977). Coarticulation in recent speech production models, *Journal of Phonetics*, **5**, 155–133.

Kent, R. D. and Moll, K. L. (1972). Cinefluorographic analyses of selected lingual consonants, *Journal of Speech and Hearing Research*, **15**, 3, 453–473.

Kent, R. and Moll, K. L. (1975). Articulatory timing in selected consonant sequences, *Brain and Language*, **2**, 304–323.

Kent, R. D., Carney, P. J. and Severeid, L. R. (1974). Velar movement and timing: Evaluation of a model for binary control, *Journal of Speech and Hearing Research*, **17**, 3, 470.

Keuhn, D. P. (1973). A Cinefluorographic Investigation of Articulatory Velocities. Ph.D. thesis, University of Iowa.

Klatt, D. H. (1976). Linguistic uses of segmental duration in English: Acoustic and perceptual evidence, *Journal of the Acoustical Society of America*, **59**, 5, 1208–1221.

Kozhevnikov, V. A. and Chistovich, L. A. (1965). "Speech: Articulation and Perception", U.S. Department of Commerce translation J. PRS. 30: 543.

Kugelberg, E. (1952). Facial reflexes, *Brain*, **75**, 385–396.

Labov, W., Yaeger, M. and Steiner, R. (1972). "A Quantitative Study of Sound Change in Progress", U.S. Regional Survey, Philadelphia.

Ladefoged, P. (1971). "Preliminaries to Linguistic Phonetics", University of Chicago Press, Chicago.

Ladefoged, P., DeClerk, J., Lindau, M. and Papsun, G. (1972). An auditory-motor theory of speech production. Working Papers in Phonetics, **22**, pp. 48–75. U.C.L.A.

Laferriere, M. and Zue, V. W. (1977). Flapping rule in American English: An acoustic study, *Journal of the Acoustical Society of America*, **61**, Supplement 1, S31(A).

Leanderson, R. and Lindblom, B. E. F. (1972). Muscle activation for labial speech gestures, *Acta-Oto-Laryngologica*, **73**, 4, 362–373.

Leanderson, R. and Persson, A. (1972). The effect of trigeminal nerve block on the articulatory EMG activity of facial muscles, *Acta-Oto-Laryngologica*, **74**, 271–278.

Lehiste, I. (1970). *Suprasegmentals*, MIT Press, Cambridge, Mass.

Liberman, A. M. (1970). The grammars of speech and language, *Cognitive Psychology*, **1**, 301–323.

Lieberman, P. (1970). Toward a unified phonetic theory, *Linguistic Inquiry*, **1**, 3, 307–322.

Lieberman, P. (1976). Phonetic features and physiology: A reappraisal, *Journal of Phonetics*, **4**, 2 91–112.

Lieberman, P., Crelin, E. S. and Klatt, D. H. (1972). Phonetic ability and related anatomy of the newborn, adult human, Neanderthal man, and chimpanzee, *American Anthropologist*, **74**, 287–307.

Lindblom, B. E. F. (1963). Spectrographic study of vowel reduction, *Journal of the Acoustical Society of America*, **35**, 1773–1781.

Lindblom, B. E. F. (1971a). Numerical models in the study of speech production and speech perception. Some phonological implications. Paper presented to the VIIth International Congress of Phonetic Sciences, Montreal. (Also a report, Dept. of Speech Communication, Royal Institute of Technology, Stockholm, Sweden.)

Lindblom, B. E. F. (1971b). Neurophysiological representation of speech sounds, Publication 7. Paper from the Institute of Linguistics, University of Stockholm.

Lindblom, B. E. F. (1975). Experiments in sound structure, Plenary address, Eighth International Congress of Phonetic Sciences, Leeds, England.

Lindblom, B. F. and Rapp, K. (1973). Some temporal regularities of spoken Swedish, Publication 21. Papers from the Institute of Linguistics of University of Stockholm.

Lindblom, B. E. F. and Sundberg, J. (1971). Acoustical consequences of lip, tongue and jaw movements, *Journal of the Acoustical Society of America*, **50**, 4, 1166–1179.

Lindblom, B., McAllister, R. and Lubker, J. (1977). Compensatory articulation and the modeling of normal speech production behavior. Paper presented at the

Symposium on Articulatory Modeling, Grenoble, France, July 11–12.

Lindblom, B. E. F., Lubker, J. and Gay, T. (1978). Formant frequencies of some fixed-mandible vowels and a model of speech motor programming by predictive simulation, *Journal of Phonetics*, **7**, 147–162.

Lisker, L. and Abramson, A. S. (1971). Distinctive features and laryngeal control, *Language*, **47**, 767–785.

Lubker, J. (1975). Normal velopharyngeal functions in speech, *Clinics in Plastic Surgery*, **2**, 249–259.

MacNeilage, P. F. (1970). The motor control of serial ordering in speech, *Psychological Review*, **77**, 182–196.

MacNeilage, P. F. (1972). Speech physiology, chapter 1 in "Speech and Cortical Functioning", (J. H. Gilbert, ed.), Academic Press, New York.

MacNeilage, P. F. and DeClerk, J. L. (1969). On the motor control of coarticulation in CVC monosyllables, *Journal of the Acoustical Society of America*, **45**, 1217–1233.

MacNeilage, P. F., Hanson, R. and Krones, R. (1970). Control of the jaw in relation to stress in English, *Journal of the Acoustical Society of America*, **48**, 119(A).

MacNeilage, P. F., Krones, R. and Hanson, R. (1970). Closed-loop control of the initiation of jaw movements for speech, *Journal of the Acoustical Society of America*, **47**, 104(A).

Malecot, A. (1966). The effectiveness of intraoal air-pressure pulse parameters in distinguishing between stop cognates, *Phonetica*, **14**, 65–81.

Marr, D. (1969). A theory of the cerebellar cortex, *Journal of Physiology*, **202**, 437–470.

Marsden, C. D., Merton, P. A. and Morton, H. B. (1977). The sensory mechanism of servo action, *Journal of Physiology*, **265**, 521–535.

Maton, B. and Bouisset, S. (1975). Motor unit activity and preprogramming of movement in man, *Electroencephalography and Clinical Neurophysiology*, **38**, 658–660.

McClean, M. D., Folkins, J. W. and Larson (in press). The role of the perioral reflex in lip motor control for speech, *Brain and Language*.

Menyuk, P. (1972). "The Development of Speech", The Bobbs-Merrill Studies in Communicative Disorders, Bob-Merrill, Indianapolis.

Mermelstein, P. (1973). Articulatory model for the study of speech production, *Journal of the Acoustical Society of America*, **53**, 1070–1082.

Moll, K. L. and Daniloff, R. G. (1971). Investigation of the timing of velar movements during speech, *Journal of the Acoustical Society of America*, **50**, 678–684.

Moll, K. L., Zimmerman, G. N. and Smith, A. (1977). The study of speech production as a human neuromotor system. *In* "Dynamic Aspects of Speech Production", (M. Sawashima and F. S. Cooper, eds), pp. 107–127. University of Tokyo Press.

Muller, E., Abbs, J., Kennedy, J. and Larson, C. (1977). Significance of perioral biomechanics to lip movements during speech. Paper presented to the American Speech and Hearing Associaton, Chicago.

Nashner, L. M. (1976). Adapting reflexes in controlling the human posture, *Experimental Brain Research*, **26**, 59–72.

Netsell, R. and Abbs, J. H. (1975). Modulation of perioral reflex sensitivity during speech movements, *Journal of the Acoustical Society of America*, **58**, Supplement 1, S41(A).

Netsell, R. and Abbs, J. H. (1977). Some possible uses of neuromotor speech disturbances in understanding the normal mechanism. *In* "Dynamic Aspects of Speech Production", (M. Sawashima and F. S. Cooper, eds), pp. 369–392. University of Tokyo Press.

Nooteboom, S. G. (1970). The target theory of speech production. IPO Annual Progress Report No. 5, Institute for Perception Research, Eindhoven, Holland, 51–53.

Nooteboom, S. G. (1972). A survey of some investigations into the temporal organization of speech, IPO Annual Progress Report No. 7, pp. 17–29. Institute for Perception Research, Eindhoven, Holland.

Nooteboom, S. G. and Slis, I. (1970). A note on the degree of opening and the duration of vowels in normal and "pipe" speech, IPO Annual Progress Report, No. 5, pp. 55–58. Institute for Perception Research, Eindhoven, Holland.

Ohala, J. J. (1972). The regulation of timing in speech. Record of the 1972 Conference on Speech Communication and Processing, AFCRL-72-0129, IEEE Cat. No. CHO 596–7 AE, 144–147.

Ohman, S. E. G. (1966). Coarticulation in VCV utterances: Spectrographic measurements. *Journal of the Acoustical Society of America*, **39**, 151–168.

Oscarsson, O. (1971). Communication. *In* "Central Control of Movement", (E. V. Evarts, E. Bizzi, R. E. Burke, M. DeLong and W. T. Thach, eds), *Neurosciences Research Program Bulletin*, **9**, 98–103.

Perkell, J. S. (1971). Physiology of speech production: A preliminary study of two suggested revisions of the features specifying vowels. Quarterly Progress Report No. 102, pp. 123–139. Research Laboratory of Electronics, M.I.T.

Perkell, J. S. (1974). A Physiologically-Oriented Model of Tongue Activity During Speech Production, Ph.D. thesis, M.I.T.

Perkell, J. S. (1976). Responses to an unexpected suddenly induced change in the state of the vocal tract. Progress Report No. 117, pp. 273–281. Research Laboratory of Electronics, M.I.T.

Porter, R. (1967). Cortical actions on hypoglossal motorneurons in cats: A proposed role for a common internuncial cell, *Journal of Physiology*, **193**, 295–308.

Prosek, R. A. and House, A. S. (1975). Intraoral air pressure as a feedback cue in consonant production, *Journal of Speech and Hearing Research*, **18**, 133.

Putnam, A. H. B. and Ringel, R. L. (1972). Some observations of articulation during labial sensory deprivation, *Journal of Speech and Hearing Research*, **15**, 529.

Putnam, A. H. B. and Shipp, T. (1975). EMG-aerodynamic measures for intervocalic /p/ production, *Journal of the Acoustical Society of America*, **57**, Supplement No. 1, S70(A).

Raphael, L. J. (1975). The physiological control of durational differences between vowels preceding voiced and voiceless consonants in English, *Journal of Phonetics*, **3**, 25–33.

Ringel, R. L. (1970). Oral sensation and perception: A selective review. *In* "Speech and the Dentofacial Complex: the State of the Art", *American Speech and Hearing Association Reports*, **5**, ASHA, Washington, 188–206.

Ringel, R. L. and Ewanowski, S. J. (1965). Oral perception: 1. Two point discrimination, *Journal of Speech and Hearing Research*, **8**, 389–398.

Sawashima, M. (1970). Laryngeal research in experimental phonetics. Status Report on Speech Research SR-23, pp. 69–116. Haskins Laboratories, New Haven.

Scott, C. M. and Ringel, R. L. (1971). Articulation without oral sensory control, *Journal of Speech and Hearing Research*, **14**, 804–818.

Shattuck-Hufnagel, S. R. and Klatt, D. H. (1975). Analysis of 1500 phonetic errors in spontaneous speech, *Journal of the Acoustical Society of America*, **58**, Supplement 1, S62(A).

Smith, T. and Lee, C. Y. (1971). Peripheral feedback mechanisms is speech production. Paper presented at the VIIth International Congress of Phonetic Sciences, Montreal.

Stevens, K. N. (1972). The quantal nature of speech: Evidence from articulatory-acoustic data, *In* "Human Communication, A Unified View", (P. B. Denes and E. E. David, eds), pp. 51–66. McGraw-Hill, New York.

Stevens, K. N. and Blumstein, S. E. (1975). Quantal aspects of consonant production and perception: A study of retroflex stop consonants, *Journal of Phonetics*, **3**, 215–233.

Stevens, K. N. and Klatt, D. H. (1974). Role of formant transitions in the voiced-voiceless distinction for stops, *Journal of the Acoustical Society of America*, **55**, 653–659.

Stevens, K. N. and Perkell, J. S. (1977). Speech physiology and phonetic features. *In* "Dynamic Aspects of Speech Production", (M. Sawashima and F. S. Cooper, eds), pp. 323–341. University of Tokyo Press, Tokyo.

Studdert-Kennedy, M. (1976a). Speech perception. *In* "Contemporary Issues in Experimental Phonetics", (N. J. Lass, ed.), pp. 243–293. Academic Press, New York.

Studdert-Kennedy, M. (1976b). Universals in phonetic structure and their role in linguistic communication. Status Report on Speech Research SR-48, pp. 43–50. Haskins Laboratories, New Haven.

Sumi, T. (1973). Importance of pharyngeal feedback on the integration of reflex deglutition in newborn animals. *In* "Oral Sensation and Perception", (J. F. Bosma, ed.). DHEW Publication No. (NIH) 73–546, pp. 174–184. U.S. Dept. of Health Education and Welfare, Betheseda, MD.

Sussman, H. (1972). What the tongue tells the brain, *Pyschological Bulletin*, **77**, 262–272.

Sussman, H., MacNeilage, P. F. and Hanson, R. J. (1973). Labial and mandibular dynamics during the production of bilabial consonants: Preliminary observations, *Journal of Speech and Hearing Research*, **16**, 397–420.

Taub, E. and Berman, A. J. (1968). Movement and learning in the absence of sensory feedback. *In* "The Neurophysiology of Spatially Oriented Behavior", (S. J. Freedman, ed.), pp. 173–192. Dorsey Press, Homewood, Ill.

Vallbo, A. B. (1971). Spindle response at the onset of isometric voluntary contractions in man, time difference between fusimotor and skeletomotor effects, *Journal of Physiology*, **318**, 405–431.

Van der Gon, J. J. D. and Wieneke, G. H. (1969). The concept of feedback in motorics against that of preprogramming. *In* "Biocybernetics of the Central Nervous System", (L. D. Proctor, ed.), pp. 287–304. Little Brown, Boston.

Williams, L. (1977). The voicing contrast in Spanish, *Journal of Phonetics*, **5**, 2, 169–184.

Wood, S. (1977). A radiographic analysis of constriction locations for vowels. Working Papers 15, pp. 101–132. Phonetic Laboratory, Department of General Linguistics, Lund University.

Zue, V. W. (1976). Acoustic Characteristics of Stop Consonants: A Controlled Study. Ph.D. thesis, Dept. of Electrical Engineering and Computer Science, M.I.T.

14

Implications for Speech Production of A General Theory of Action

C. A. Fowler   *Dartmouth College and Haskins Laboratories*
P. Rubin   *Haskins Laboratories*
R. E. Remez   *Indiana University*
M. T. Turvey   *University of Connecticut and Haskins Laboratories*

I. Introduction

Phonetic and phonological segments have substantial linguistic/theoretical support as real and universal units of language systems. Quite naturally, investigators of speech production have taken these units to be constituents of a speaker/hearer's linguistic competence and have focused investigation on discovering their correlates in the articulatory and acoustic records of utterances. These searches have met with little success, however, and the recent literature betrays some disenchantment with this as an investigatory strategy. Several investigators have proposed as an alternative that production theory develop its own units and concepts (e.g. MacNeilage and Ladefoged, 1976; Moll *et al.*, 1976). These categories would be based on production records as interpreted from the perspective of theories of coordinated movement perhaps, but would be unbiased by *a priori* notions borrowed from linguistic theory as to what the units ought to be like.

Our theoretical approach is related to this, but is somewhat less radical. We agree that concepts general to the control of coordinated movement are relevant to understanding the control of the articulators and need incorporation into production theory (cf. Abbs and Eilenberg, 1976; Moll *et al.*, 1976). In addition, we agree that correlates of linguistic segmental units, as production theorists have described them, are absent in articulation. But we are not yet ready to agree, therefore, that investigations of speech production ought to be conducted without reference to linguistic segmental units.

This strategy is likely to exacerbate the difficulty of reconciling the units that a speaker/hearer is assumed to know with those that he uses. Furthermore, speech *perception* theorists are faced with the same kind of disparity (cf. Studdert-Kennedy, 1978; Pisoni, 1978). If they were to take an analogous tack to that proposed by the production theorists cited above, doubtless they would discover a third set of units irreconcilably distinct both from those of linguistic theory and those of production theory.

The strategy that we have adopted involves a reassessment of some of the properties of linguistic units, based in part on concepts general to the control of coordinated movement. Our aim is to discover some way to characterize these units that preserves their essential linguistic properties, but also allows them to be actualized *unaltered* in a vocal tract and in an acoustic signal.

As the production literature describes them, abstract linguistic units have three properties that lack articulatory correlates: they are discrete, static, and context-free. In contrast, units of production, whatever they may be, are essentially dynamic and continuous. Furthermore, to the extent that articulatory approximations of linguistic units are discovered, they appear to be context-adjusted.

We suspect, perhaps naively, that these incompatibilities are only apparent and derive from a misunderstanding of abstract linguistic units on the part of production theorists. Linguistic theory expresses what is systematic in language. In that sense, and only in that sense, it captures what a language-user knows about his language. It does not claim to specify what a language-user knows, *as he knows it*; thus it does not necessarily concern itself at all with dimensions of description of its constituents that can be realized either in a vocal tract or even a mind. (Whether or not this is a sensible strategy is not at issue here.)

For example, in reference to phonetic segments, linguistic theory characterizes each one in terms of its locus in a system of phonetic relationships. Thus, a given segment is assigned values (features) along all and only the dimensions of description that are relevant to specifying its relationship to other segments. (These dimensions are given articulation-or acoustic-based names, but it would not change the *abstract* system to relabel them, "north-south", "X_1-X_2", and so on.)

"Discrete/continuous" is not a phonetic dimension of description, and one can imagine two alternative reasons why it is not. One is that *all* phonetic segments are discrete, and featural descriptions only specify distinctive features. But we favor the other possibility that "discrete" is unspecified because it is an irrelevant dimension of description of an *abstract* linguistic segment.

In speech production, "discreteness" has to do with the spatiotemporal overlap of production units. Due to coarticulation, articulatory approximations to linguistic units are not discrete in this sense; rather they overlap considerably. However, this has nothing to do with the linguistic description of a segment. The latter does not concern itself with sequences of segments, but only with locating a vocalic segment in a vowel space and a consonantal segment in a consonant space. Nor is discreteness of segments relevant to a phonetic or phonological representation of a word or sentence. The essential *linguistic* property here is "sequence" or "serial order" (so that, for example, /æ k t/, /t æ k/ and /k æ t/ are distinct). Discreteness is the way in which *orthographic* or *phonological-symbolic* representations of these sequences preserve their serial order, but it is not the way that articulation preserves it. Nonetheless, serial order is preserved in *some* way in articulation since /æ k t/, /t æ k/ and /k æ t/ are differently produced.

Consider also the property "static". This, too, is a value along an irrelevant dimension as far as abstract linguistic units are concerned. Although the essential properties of linguistic segments can perhaps be realized in a static medium, as when language is written down, a dynamic realization need not be considered necessarily destructive to those properties.

We will consider the dimension context-free versus context-adjusted in some detail later. Here we simply suggest that linguistic segments as known and as uttered must have context-free or invariant properties. In order for a phonological category to *be* a category for a language-user, its essential properties must be context-free. Theories of coordinated movement offer a way of understanding how the superficial variability of articulation may have underlying invariance.

It has been our suggestion that the mismatch between abstract linguistic units and articulatory categories may only be an apparent one. Such a mismatch may arise when an immutable assignment of values (e.g. discrete, static) to linguistic units is assumed by production theorists. Designations such as these, however, are along dimensions (discrete/continuous, static/dynamic) to which these values as abstract linguistic units are, in fact, indifferent.

We do not believe that a theory of speech production can afford to disregard the systematicities among linguistic units as described by linguistic theory. Nor can it ignore, as linguistic theory may allege to, the fact that these systematicities are known in a particular way and are used in particular ways by speaker/hearers. The obligations of a production theory with respect to these units is to give them values on those dimensions of description that may be irrelevant to abstract linguistic theory, but that are central to the realization of the units as they are embodied in the knowledge and vocal tract of a talker.

Our suggestion is that linguistic units, as they are known to a language-user and as they are spoken and perceived by him, are: *qualitatively separate and serially ordered* (but not discrete), *dynamic*, and *context-free*. These dimensions and their values seem to us to do no violence to the essential *linguistic* properties of segments. Yet they permit the claim that there is no essential difference between the segments that a language-user knows and those that he speaks and hears.

Support for these proposals is derived from a particular perspective on coordinated movement (e.g. Bernstein, 1967; Greene, 1972; Turvey, 1977a). Shortly we will review the relevant information from that source, but first we would like to provide some negative support for our view that linguistic segments as known and uttered are compatible through a critique of the conventional view which says that they are not. We call proposals in the spirit of the conventional view "translation theories", and suggest that this label covers all, or virtually all, extant theories of speech production.

II. Translation Theories: an Evaluation

In contrast to the view that we have put forward, it is generally agreed that the distinction between abstract and actual segments cannot be avoided—that neither the linguistic nor the articulatory descriptions of speech segments is inaccurate and that the two are irreconcilably distinct. Each is said to characterize a different *level* of abstraction in the speech system and to be invoked at different *stages* in the production of speech (Daniloff and Hammarberg, 1973; Hammarberg, 1976; MacNeilage and Ladefoged, 1976). In particular, abstract phonological segments are pre-motor cognitive entities that thereby can serve both as outputs of perceptual processing and as inputs to an articulatory mechanism. Dynamic articulation is the final product of the articulatory mechanism which alters the properties of abstract segments to fit the demands of vocal tract production and of the ear (see below).

The translation process between a sequence of discrete, static, context-free segments that a talker has in mind to say and the continuous, dynamic, context-adjusted ones that he in fact utters is not a simple one. According to Liberman and Studdert-Kennedy (1978) (see also Liberman *et al.*, 1967) the translation involves a "drastic restructuring" of planned phonetic segments. They believe the restructuring to be necessary in order to match the cognitive requirements of communication with properties of the vocal tract and ear. In their view, were abstract segments reproduced literally in an utterance, listeners would be unable to comprehend the spoken message of a talker. One cognitive requirement of communication is that a spoken message be produced rapidly. This requirement has to do with the fact that the semantic information jointly provided by phonological segments is spread over long stretches of speech. Thus, in order for a hearer to extract a talker's semantic message, a meaningful chunk must be produced rapidly enough that its initial part is still available in the hearer's memory when the final part is produced. A second cognitive requirement is that the order of the segments is extractable from the acoustic signal so that, for example, such words as "tack", "cat" and "act" may be distinguished.

Vocal tracts, however, cannot produce discrete segments rapidly enough to satisfy the first cognitive requirement; nor can auditory systems extract the temporal order of rapidly produced isolated sounds (e.g. Warren, 1976). For these reasons, according to Liberman and Studdert-Kennedy, abstract linguistic segments are complexly restructured in articulation. The result is coarticulated speech. In a spoken utterance, information about each abstract segment is spread over several acoustic segments and each acoustic segment provides information about more than one abstract segment. In this way, more linguistic segments can be signaled in a given amount of time than could be possible were each segment temporally distinct from its neighbors.

Current theories of speech production differ from this account in detail, but are like this account in that they tend to be translation theories; that is, they acknowledge the incommensurability of abstract and actual segments and thereby are obligated to describe how the one transforms into the other in the processing surrounding speech production. What follows is a brief evaluation of the logic and adequacy of translation theories.

A. The Logical Status of Translation Theories

A decision that the differences between abstract and actual segments are irreducible invites complicated theories both of speech production and of speech perception where simpler ones might otherwise have sufficed. The translation theory's main explananda arise solely from the irreducibility claim. Were it the case that talkers had only one kind of sound segment to work with instead of two, then the aspects of speech production currently held to surround the translation process would no longer require explanation.

In addition, we should point out that the implications of the irreducibility claim extend also to theories of speech perception. Any transformation that takes discrete, static, context-free segments into continuous, dynamic, context-adjusted gestures of the vocal tract must be considered destructive of essential properties of the abstract segments. Therefore, a perceiver has to reconstruct the talker's phonological intent from an impoverished acoustic signal. (For a well-known and graphic description of the destructive effects of coarticulation on the acoustic signal, see Hockett's easter egg analogy (1955).)

In contrast, if one were to adopt a non-translation view of speech production, which supposed that the essential properties of phonological segments are preserved in an utterance, the possibility would remain that the acoustic products of vocal-tract gestures fully specify the speaker's phonological intent. That is, a theory of "direct" speech production leaves open the possibility of a theory of direct speech perception as well.

The particular point we wish to make with regard to theories of speech production and speech perception is an instance of a larger point concerning the construction of general theories of acting and perceiving. To illustrate this larger point we will focus our arguments on visual perception. For it is not unreasonable to claim that the problem of perception as defined and the proposed solutions to that problem both originate in, and receive continued impetus from, the attempts of past and present philosophers and psychologists to understand visual experience and its physical support. Moreover, it will be apparent that the received orientation to coordinated movement is conceptually consistent with the received orientation to visual perception.

It has become a matter of doctrine that the light to an eye is equivocal about properties of the environment (see Turvey and Shaw, 1979). More precisely, it is assumed that the laws which map environmental properties into the light as an energy medium are "destructive" in the sense that the light lawfully reflected from (and presumably patterned by) environmental properties is not specific to those properties. Very often this doctrine has reduced to a comparison of two very different sets of descriptors: On the one hand there are the descriptors of the environment as it relates to the animal (for example, surfaces of support for locomotion, places to hide, courting behavior of a conspecific) and on the other hand the descriptors of the light as identified by the physicist, namely, photons or individual rays varying in intensity and wavelength. When stated in this inequitable-descriptors form, the doctrine of an intractably nonspecific relationship between environment and light (cf. Turvey and Shaw, 1979) lays the ground rules for identifying the problem of perception. If the descriptors of the proximal stimulus (the light at the eye) are as they are defined, then they are clearly incommensurate with the descriptors of perceptual experience, for the latter are in reference to such things as surfaces of support for locomotion, places to hide, etc. It follows, therefore, that the problem of perception is the problem of identifying the sequence of internal cause and effect relationships or the sequence of internal transformations that *translate* the impoverished and fine-grained descriptors of the proximal stimulus into the rich and coarse-grained descriptors of perceptual experience.

If the mapping from environment to light is *destructive*, then the mapping from light to perceptual experience must be *reconstructive*; and to achieve this reconstruction perceptual theorists have been compelled to postulate a large variety of epistemic mediators (cf. Turvey, 1977b), among which may be numbered hypothesis testing, matching to memory and innate principles of organization. The gist of the conventional orientation to visual perception (and to perception in general) can be stated briefly: given two mismatched vocabularies or descriptor sets that putatively define the starting point and end point of perception, that is, the proximal stimulation and the perceptual experience, how is the former translated into the latter? The gist of an alternative orientation, and one that we endorse, can be given an equally brief statement: Can a *single* vocabulary or descriptor set be found in which can be defined both the proximal stimulation and the perceptual experience, so that no translation is needed? At the heart of this alternative orientation is the assumption that the mapping from environment to energy medium (say, the light) is not destructive, as time-honored doctrine would have it; rather, the light to an eye is lawfully structured in ways that are specific to the properties of the environment. On this alternative view, when the light is structured by environmental properties, there are descriptors of the light to be found that correspond unequivocally to those properties, and that some of these descriptors can be intercepted by any given animal. But since there is no longer an assumed mismatch between the descriptors of the environment and those of the proximal stimulation, there is no longer reason for assuming a mismatch between descriptors of the proximal stimulation and those of perceptual experience (see Mace, 1977; Shaw *et al.*, in press; Turvey and Shaw, 1979).

This alternative orientation to perception that we have espoused was first proposed by Gibson (1950, 1966). As the logician Hintikka (1975) has observed in reference to Gibson's theory: "the conceptual moral is that the *perceptions* that can surface in our consciousness *must be dealt with in terms of the same concepts as what we perceive.* The appropriate way of speaking of our spontaneous perceptions is to use the same vocabulary and the same syntax as we apply to the objects of perception" (see p. 60). It is this "conceptual moral" which we believe ought to be similarly pursued in the theory of action. The orientation to coordinated movement, as intimated above, has been consistent with the familiar orientation to perception; the vocabulary of intentions, like the vocabulary of perceptions, has been conventionally construed as distinct and largely separate from the vocabulary of activity. If there is a mismatch between the descriptors of intention and the descriptors of muscle-joint activity, then "translation" identifies the problem of action. However, in an alternative orientation to action, which echoes the alternative orientation to perception, the problem of action is to find a single vocabulary or descriptor set in terms of which intentions and muscle-joint activity conflate.

Returning to the instance of action theory that is of present concern, namely, speech production, we might enquire as to the *a priori* plausibility of the translation-type theory. In our view, the concept of abstract forms that cannot be realized nondestructively in any medium is implausible for several reasons. One is the absence of any obvious way in which they could be acquired. It is one thing for an adult perceiver to bring these concepts to bear *a priori* on an acoustic signal (cf. Hammarberg, 1976). But if the signal can only be interpreted by an individual who *has* these concepts, how does a child learn them? Evidently, we have to suppose that they are innate. But this is to invoke "innate knowledge" not *as* an explanation, but instead of one. It is inappropriate to pawn the acquisition problem off on the biologist if it is as unclear how the concepts could be acquired by a species in evolution as it is how they could be acquired by an individual (Turvey and Shaw, 1979).

Second, it is not evident *why* these concepts should have arisen in evolution. If evolution, like ontogeny, is considered a process whereby an organism maintains or enhances its compatibility with selected aspects of the world (cf. Shaw *et al.*, 1974), it must be disadvantageous for an organism to seek to impose fictitious categories on a spoken utterance as a translation theory demands. ("Fictitious" here refers to categories that are not "in the world", but only "in the mind"; see Hammarberg, 1976, for an expression of this view.)

The above identify reasons why translation theories of speech production are logically insecure. Let us now proceed to a brief overview of their adequacy as accounts of speech production.

B. The Adequacy of Translation Theories

A common thread (perhaps *the* common thread) through all psycholinguistic accounts is the appreciation for Lashley's (1951) identification of the issues in, and potential solutions to, the control problems posed by language. His particular rendition was so convincing that many individual theories of production which followed it appear to stand in its review, especially on the issues of priming and integration. In the original, these issues respectively involved: (1) the selection and ordering of abstract entities (themselves possessing no temporal valence) and, (2) the expression of these ordered entities in a hierarchically controlled manner by the response mechanism. These two aspects of production have been variously termed (higher level) activation, facilitation, patterning, preplanning and sequencing for the first, as opposed to (lower level) expression, execution, articulation and motor control for the second.

The argument for separating the act of speaking into largely distinct stages recognizes a simple fact about language; ignoring the ineffable shadings of meaning, a single idea can have infinitely many equivalent realizations from the standpoint of both the actual linguistic entities employed and the alternative progressions of peripheral events which immediately create the speech sounds. Because of this lack of straightforward isomorphism among thought, word and muscle, some intermediary agency must obviously determine the ideally appropriate constellation of linguistic elements and response parameters to convert idea to utterance.

The underlying unanimity in the various elaborations of the problem of serial order should not dissuade us from noting several essential failures in the program. These are not inconsequential to the choice of hypothesis of control, as would be a deletion or refinement of a rule of syntax. Rather, they urge the reconsideration of the idea of two distinct levels of description. The goal of higher level functions (in theories which have this specialty) is assumed to be a sequence of linguistic elements, usually phonemic, in which the derived order is prospective of the intended utterance as well as faithful to the semantic content. While this output is a description, more or less, of the abstract structure of the message, it is not really a plan for action; it would be such only if language were a commerce involving the exchange of though-phrases expressed in IPA notation. Articulation, the vehicle by which the message is actually delivered, requires that a lower level neuromuscular process fulfill the plan of the higher level "mental" process through vocal tract efforts. One way to view this relationship of higher level to lower is that the tailoring of the plan to fit the peculiarities of the motor system, is essentially a detail of physiology; while interesting to consider, the facts of the motor system largely agree with the production concept of a higher level plan transferred to a lower level system for routine completion.

The inadequacy of this approach to the serial ordering problem is brought out by a brief consideration of the aforementioned job of tailoring (or translating). Attempts to discover segments in the speech stream—for example in muscle events, articulatory movements, vocal tract area functions, or in the acoustic signal—that correspond to the segments listed in the higher level representation, have met with little success. Given this predicament, it appears that, as the problem is conventionally conceived, the adaptation of linguistic plans for the requirements of articulation involves a great deal of creativity on the part of the tailoring function.

An example of the creativity of a tailoring function occurs in vowel production. Producing vowels seems to involve approaching a relatively invariant shape of the vocal tract, but from various directions depending on the vowel's articulatory context (MacNeilage, 1970). A second example is provided by the compensation findings of Folkins and Abbs (1975) and of Lindblom and Sundberg (1973) (see also Lindblom *et al.*, 1979). Both studies show that talkers can compensate immediately, or almost immediately, for imposed disruptions of normal articulation (unexpected resistive loading in the experiment of Folkins and Abbs, and a bite block in that of Lindblom and Sundberg). These capacities are not handled in the typical higher level plan, but neither can they be dismissed as details of the physiology.

The foregoing considerations suggest that any putative tailoring functions cannot be simple. More than this, however, Fowler (1977) argues that the hypothetical distinction which necessitates a tailoring function—namely, that between the higher order plan and its executor—is a false distinction. Among other things, it has fostered a view that plans represent timeless (static) segments of speech, even though the view is falsified by quantities of data. (See for example, Lisker (1974, 1976) for reviews and discussions of this point.) In addition, many models of speech production that have adopted the distinction are unable to account either in the plan or in the tailoring function for many of the characteristics of running speech. In particular, they do not adequately handle coarticulatory phenomena (Kent and Minifie, 1977), adjustments for speaking rate and stress, and speech rhythms (Fowler, 1977).

One conclusion inspired by the dynamic aspect of speech is that solutions to the serial ordering problem that have proposed higher level plans written in a static vocabulary may be inadequate by design. In order to deflect, rather than to confront, the important constancy problems in production, as well as the remainder of the serial ordering problem, the tailoring assumption was invoked. We believe that this will not do if what is desired is a description of language *production*. Instead of viewing the peripheral machinery as a necessary evil, as linguistically oriented dualistic models are prone to do, a more appropriate description might consider production to be the acts, not merely the thoughts, of the speaker. A *plan* in this sense would be a physiologically considerate description of the act, and not only an abstract summary of its significance. This kind of plan would be sensitive to what can actually be said, rather than to that which can only be cogitated.

Now, one of the fundamental points we wish to argue from a general perspective on action is that the style of control of any activity must reflect the contingencies of execution while complying with the aim of the activity. In a similar vein, the objective of natural phonology (Donegan and Stampe, 1977) in some cases is to remove the distinction between competence and performance, the mediate and the immediate. In that view, the traditional operating principles of modern phonology, formal simplicity and abstract distinctiveness, represent the needs of the professional linguist more than they characterize the structure of language. In an analysis kindred to ours, natural phonologists claim that the solutions for many of the conundra in linguistics are to be sought in the dynamics of talking, rather than in the bloodless domain of formal grammars. But what possibilities for understanding organization during speech become available through scrutiny of the putatively lower, more basic properties of speech acts? The remainder of the paper may be viewed as a response to this question.

III. Principles of a General Theory of Coordinated Movement

We have argued that a critical assumption tends to characterize current accounts of speech production: it is of an irreducible difference between the properties of linguistic segments as they are *known* to a language-user and those of speech sounds as they are uttered and realized acoustically. The assumption bears major responsibility for the character of theories of speech production and perception. For their part, speech production theories are compelled to characterize a translation process from mental plan to vocal performance. The translation process is supposed to destroy crucial information about segment identity. Perception theories are obliged, thereby, to explain how abstract segments are reconstructed on the basis of acoustic stimulation that is impoverished in respect to specifying abstract segment identity.

We have given reasons for trying to avoid translation type theories; it becomes appropriate, therefore, to consider the possibility of a theory of direct (non-translational) speech production. A reconciliation was proposed above between the characters of abstract and actual segments to the effect that segments, both abstract and actual, are essentially dynamic; their defining properties are context-free, and in relation to other segments in an utterance they are qualitatively separate, one from the other, and they are serially ordered. The considerations that lend plausibility to this characterization have two sources. The primary source is a theoretical perspective on coordinated movement owing to Bernstein (1967), Greene (1972) and Turvey (1977a). This perspective offers a way to understand how the essential properties of abstract classes of acts may be preserved unaltered in various instantiations of them. The second source is the literature on speech production itself. First we will discuss some of the key concepts encountered in studies of coordinated movement, then we will examine such concepts in light of the relevant speech production data.

A. Some Relevant Properties of the Control of Coordinated Movement

It is commonplace for speech production accounts to characterize a talker's control over his articulators in the following way. Planned phonological segments are given a distinctive featural representation. Some of the members of the feature bundles characterizing each segment are spread or shared among neighboring segments in the plan. The effect is to increase the similarity of adjacent feature bundles and, thus, to avoid abrupt changes in articulatory specification at segment edges (Daniloff and Hammarberg, 1973). Feature bundles are executed in sequence as their component features are translated into commands to muscles. The accounts of Daniloff and Hammarberg (1973), MacKay (1969, 1970) and Liberman and Studdert-Kennedy (1978) are proposals of this sort.

A number of considerations render the last (and perhaps least controversial-seeming) stage of this proposed sequence at best implausible. These considerations, detailed below, are the context-conditioned relationship between innervation of muscle and its outcome in movement, the "degrees of freedom problem", and the inherent organization of the musculature into systems. By reformulating this stage of articulatory control, we believe that we can obviate its being considered separate from its predecessors. The result in principle could be a non-translational, or direct, theory of speech production.

1. *Context-conditioned variability*

Bernstein (1967) observed, and after him many others (Hubbard, 1960; Grillner, 1975; Turvey, 1977a; Turvey *et al.*, 1979), that the relation between a central "command" to a muscle and its consequences in movement is equivocal. One source of this equivocality is the context of extant forces, muscular and otherwise, with which a commanded muscular contraction interacts. A simple example makes this clear. Intuitively, if an actor wishes to raise his forearm by rotating it about the elbow joint, he has only to send down a command to contract the flexion agonist. But, in fact, contraction of the brachioradialis or the biceps only leads to flexion at the elbow under restricted conditions—namely, conditions in which none of the extant forces on the arm when combined with the new forces alter the intended character of the movement. If the forearm had been extending at the elbow when the command arrived, the result might only have been a deceleration of extension. If the forearm were fixed, the command's consequence might be a rotation of the body at the elbow joint. In short, a given command will have different consequences for movement depending on the nature of the force field into which it was inserted.

Thus, an alternative is evidently required to the proposal that plans for movement include commands coded in the vocabulary of muscles which completely specify an intended movement. Somehow the control over movement must be realized by *bending* the current field of forces in an intended direction (cf. Bernstein, 1967; Hubbard, 1960; Fowler and Turvey, 1978). In addition, the nature of this bending must be contingent on the character of the field to be bent. An implication for speech production must be that there is no simple relationship between the distinctive features of a phonological segment and contractions of particular muscles.

An example, in speech production, of the context-conditioned variability in the relationship between a muscle and its role concerns the muscles of articulation (see, also, below). According to Zemlin (1968), the palatoglossus muscle may either lower the soft palate or raise the back of the tongue, depending on which is the freer to move. The mylohyoid may raise the hyoid or depress the jaw, and the geniohyoid may raise the hyoid and protrude the tongue or depress the mandible. Which of the alternatively possible roles are made manifest will depend on whatever other forces are operative on the different articulatory structures. Presumably, this kind of context-conditioned variability underlies the observed absence of invariant electromyographic (EMG) correlates of phonetic segments.

There is another source of context-conditioned variability that is physiological, rather than mechanical or anatomical, in nature; it is due to descending neural fibers synapsing on interneurons primarily, rather than directly on motoneurons. This indirect innervational pathway allows other influences than hypothetical muscle commands on the activities of motoneurons.

Muscles of the vocal tract are innervated by the cranial nerves whose cell bodies are in the brain stem. In primates some limited proportion of fibers from the motor, premotor and somesthetic cortical areas synapse directly on these cranial nerves. However, the system of direct fibers is only supplemental to the more substantial system of cortical fibers that innervate interneurons of the brain stem (Kuypers, 1958; Carpenter, 1972). Interneuronal networks typically receive input from many descending and afferent neural fibers. Thus, the state of an interneuronal network depends on inputs from several sources. Indeed, Evarts *et al.* (1971) speak of interneurons as nodal points of integration of information. Apparently they are not passive recipients of supraspinal inputs. Rather, supraspinal influence constitutes one among many influences on the state of interneuronal networks.

A system of the kind just described seems to preclude movement control via cortical *commands* to muscles. Apparently any commands would be changed when they reached the system of interneurons. None of this precludes a role for messages of central origin in movement control. But it does exclude a role of supplying commands to muscles. What is needed, we would argue, is a set of muscular forces that relates to the set of nonmuscular forces in such a way as to yield the needed movement. In this view the role of supraspinal influences looks to be organizational rather than executive.

2. *The degrees of freedom problem*

A description of any arbitrary time-slice of an act of speaking would be very lengthy and complicated if it were to catalogue all of the muscles being regulated in the service of the speech act, and the manner of their interregulation. Not only are the muscles of the vocal tract controlled and intercoordinated, but they in turn are coupled, at the very least, to the muscles of the respiratory system. And the muscles of respiration themselves are subject to a special speech-mode of regulation (e.g. Ladefoged, 1968). Described in this detail, and recognizing the very rapid rate at which articulatory events are perpetrated, talking seems to constitute an extraordinary feat of motor control.

In fact, virtually all naturally occurring activities are feats of this sort. Bernstein characterizes the "degrees of freedom problem" as the theorist's problem of explaining how the many degrees of freedom of the body (however they are counted: in terms of muscles, joints, trajectories of limb segments, etc.) are regulated in the course of an act. Precluded is a proposal that each degree of freedom is individually controlled at every point in time during an act. There are too many degrees of freedom (Greene, 1972, estimates dozens in the head-neck system alone), and there are too many points in time in an act, for a like manner of control to be workable. Clearly, there must be some way in which many degrees of freedom can be automatically regulated through the individual control of very few. The next section will describe how this seems to be done in the case of some activities. It will be instructive first, however, to look at the implicit solution to the problem of degrees of freedom in models of speech production.

Although writers in the speech literature often remark on the extraordinary complexity of articulatory events, extant models of speech production rarely confront more than a small part of the degrees of freedom problem. For example, the prototypical speech model given earlier is both remarkable and intriguing in regard to the aspects of the production act that its articulatory plan leaves out. All that the plan *does* represent, in fact, are the values along just those dimensions of description (of a talker) that distinguish a particular speech segment from any other. Unspecified are dimensions of description of a talker's activities not directly relevant to the speech act; dimensions (if any) whose values are invariant to all speech segments, and most importantly, dimensions that *are* relevant to speaking and whose values are controlled, but at a slower rate than segmental controls—for example, speech breathing and the suprasegmental aspects of an utterance.

We recognize that not all proposals or models conform to this prototype (for example, the hierarchical model of Kent, 1976). But many do, and they are particularly interesting in respect to their implicit solution to the problem of degrees of freedom. The contents of their articulatory plans conform to a general strategy in the theory of language for the systematic description of languages. That strategy is to simplify the description of a language, and to express its orderliness by separating its regular, invariant properties from properties that are idiosyncratic to particular components. Thus, abstracted from a listing of the rules of a particular language are universal rules of grammar. Similarly, removed from the lexical entry of a word in a particular language are any of its properties that are predictable by the general rules of the language (e.g. Chomsky, 1965). Likewise, in the case of the articulatory plan, according to production theory, the strategy is to exclude from the moment-to-moment description of the planned utterance everything except its aspects that are idiosyncratic to each moment.

By itself, of course, a plan of this sort is inadequate because it fails to explain how the slower, systematic motor events surrounding segmental articulation are regulated, or how they are integrated with segmental events. But they do express a strategy that may be as useful to a talker as its grammatical counterpart is to a linguist and presumably to a child learning a language.

One can think of the relationship between a grammatical rule, say, and a particular instantiation of it in a sentence as like that between the equation for a circle $((x-h)^2+(y-k)^2=r^2)$ and its realization as a particular circle $((x-5)^2+(y-2)^2=45)$. The regularity that the general rule expresses provides a *frame* which sets out what is essentially invariant across all of its instantiations. Equally important, it establishes slots or parameters (h, k, r) which constrain the particular ways in which instances are allowed to be idiosyncratic. The parameters h, k and r are not *substantial* properties of a circle, but are *attributes* or adjectival properties of them. *And it makes no sense to speak of the parametric values without expressing what they are parameters of.* We suggest that speech production may be similarly characterized. There are regularities to which all utterances and all parts of all utterances conform. These include the special mode of breathing, the phonation mode of laryngeal adjustment (Wyke, 1967, 1974), suprasegmental timing constraints, the near alternation of consonants and vowels and, in English, the near alternation of stressed and unstressed syllables. These regularities provide an organizational frame (of the musculature, as we will suggest below) for an utterance that both establishes the *possibility* of producing segments, and constrains the ways in which particular segments can be idiosyncratic. Viewed in this way, the idiosyncratic aspects of an utterance—that is, the distinctive features of its successive segments—are parametric values *of* an extant organization; they are not substantives in themselves.

In summary, what seems to us attractive about the articulatory plans of translation theories is their reasonable (if tacit) solution to the degrees of freedom problem. That solution recognizes that some aspects of an act of talking need not be regulated from moment-to-moment because their time-scale of execution is longer than a segment. And, by virtue of that, their moment-to-moment manifestations are determinate. All that is specified from moment-to-moment in a plan are those aspects of talking that are idiosyncratic to each moment. What is unattractive about the proposals, however, is that they mistakenly impute substantive properties to attributes. Evidently the idiosyncratic features of particular segments in a plan are not things in themselves, but rather are attributes of things. Hence, they make no sense described apart from a characterization of their frame (cf. Garner, 1974, for a general discussion of features as attributes of a system). What is required in a specification of a plan for an utterance is a way to preserve this kind of solution to the degrees of freedom problem, while capturing the necessary support provided features by coarser-grained regularities of talking.

3. *The inherent organization of the musculature into systems*
All of the acts that animals perform intentionally are coordinated. This implies that they are products of organized relationships among muscles, since

in the absence of those relationships, different muscles would tend to compete and oppose each other's effects (cf. Weiss, 1941). A "commands to muscles" view of motor control proposes, in effect, that an actor's plan fails to recognize or to exploit those necessary organizations (cf. Easton, 1972).

However, there is substantial evidence that muscle systems are marshalled in the service of various aims. This is one important way in which the "degrees of freedom problem" is minimized. The muscle systems, called "coordinative structures" (Easton, 1972; Turvey, 1977a; Turvey *et al.*, 1979), are functional groupings among muscles. A system like a coordinative structure that performs a function incorporates an optimal balance between its freedom to undergo change and limitations on its freedom (cf. Pattee, 1973). A rigid object, a table for instance, does not function because all of its degrees of freedom are tightly constrained. At the other extreme, an aggregate, say of grains of sand, is hardly constrained at all, but it does not function either. Systems that perform a function are somewhere in between. They are specialized by virtue of the limitations they place selectively on their degrees of freedom, but they are not so tightly constrained as to effect rigidity. Rather, their freedom is to perform a coherent activity of some particular type.

Coordinative structures are "built" via physiologically mediated biasings of the musculature called tunings (see Turvey, 1977a for a review of this evidence). The biasings facilitate or inhibit the excitability of certain muscles and thereby both alter the relationships among muscles and determine the *kind* of activity they will promote.

Some properties of the coordinative structure are modulable. Because of that, these muscle systems are said (e.g. Greene, 1972) to promote an equivalence class of acts, much as the general equation for a circle delimits an equivalence class of instances. The modulable properties of the coordinative structure are the properties along which the class members differ and are like the *parameters* of the equation for a circle. This property of a coordinative structure gives it its versatility and adaptiveness, because it enables a single organization of the muscles to govern activities with different superficial properties. (For example, as we will see, a single organization of the muscles may govern locomotion at different rates and with different gaits over rough or smooth terrains.)

An act is believed to be governed by functionally embedding (as opposed to temporally concatenating) coordinative structures. Each nesting level delimits a broader equivalence class of movements than the finer-grained level nested within. That is, the definition of "equivalence" broadens in that the essential properties defining the class weaken and reduce in number. The more coarse-grained nesting levels are established by altering the relationships among smaller coordinative structures, and at the same time they act as constraints on the lower ones.

Once a nesting of coordinative structures has been marshalled, the control task is minimal, because each coordinative structure performs its function autonomously (see below). Thus, at most, the actor addresses these muscle-systems as units (rather than addressing their constituent muscles individually) when he assigns values to parameters of the mappings that describe the muscles' interorganization.

Locomotion provides a supreme example of an act that conforms to this mode of description. The neuromuscular organization of a locomoting quadruped is one in which small systems of muscles are nested within larger systems whose role is to coordinate the activities of two limbs. These systems, in turn, are parts of a superordinate system whose domain of governance is the whole step (Easton, 1972; Grillner, 1975).

Shik and Orlovskii (1965), among others, have monitored the stepping cycle of a single limb of an animal who is suspended over a treadmill so that only the single limb touches the treadmill belt. This procedure allows the investigators to examine the muscular organization of a single limb when it is stepping. The relative onset times of flexion and extension of the hip, knee and ankle joints are patterned invariantly over cycles. The same patterning is observed in a spinal animal (Grillner, 1975). These observations suggest quite strongly that stepping by a limb is the product of systemic relationships among muscles that are established at the spinal cord. The organization is one that generates a stereotypic pattern of muscular activation and movement. It can do so relatively independently of supraspinal influences (see Shik and Orlovskii, 1976) and absolutely independently of commands to muscles. The role of supraspinal influences, in part, seems to be to establish the locomotor "mode" of organization of the spinal cord and musculature (Shik *et al.*, 1966) and not to trigger components of the step.

The participation of the intra-limb coordinative structures in a larger system of muscles is observed by allowing two limbs, or all four limbs, to touch the treadmill. Under conditions of undisturbed stepping, the relative onset times of flexion and extension in the two or four limbs are also patterned in a stereotypic way in time. Thus, not only does each limb evidence a relatively fixed pattern of activity, but also the stepping cycles of pairs of limbs are intercoordinated.

The intercoordination among the limbs is made more apparent when one limb is disturbed while the animal is walking on the treadmill (Shik and Orlovskii, 1965). If a limb is prevented temporarily from initiating its transfer stage (the stage during which the limb is off the surface of support), so that its stepping cycle is out of its usual phase relation to the other limbs, it is gradually brought back into phase over several cycles. This is effected by the muscles in a way that alters the stepping cycles of the *unperturbed* limbs, as well as the perturbed limb itself. These findings confirm that *intra*-limb coordinative structures are organized into larger systems that regulate *inter*-limb stepping.

The nestings of muscles govern not just one sequence of movements, but rather an equivalence class of acts. Locomotion at different rates and with different gaits can be described as the products of a single nested system of muscles with one or two modulable parameters (Arshavskii *et al.*, 1965; Easton, 1972). Likewise, Shik and Orlovskii's (1965) mathematical model of interlimb coordination incorporates the animal's ability to accommodate its stepping cycle to the inhomogeneities of environments. These investigations of locomotion provide a particularly well-understood example of an equivalence class of acts that is governed by relatively autonomous and adaptive nested systems of muscles.

In summary, one way in which the coordinative-structural mode of organization minimizes the degrees-of-freedom problem for an actor is by allowing him to address several muscles as a unit. Thereby he controls the many degrees of freedom that a nesting of coordinative structures regulates by deliberately providing values for just a few.

There is a second way as well. In an act of walking, coordinative structures provide only some of the forces necessary to control locomotion. The remainder are provided by gravity, friction and the reactive forces created by the actor's contacts with the surface of support. Moreover, in walking, some movements require no muscular control at all—most of the transfer phase, for example (Grillner, 1975)—because the actor's momentum brings them about. Muscular control is only required, and is only used by a skilled actor, to change inertial states (Hubbard, 1960).

IV. An Action Theoretic View of Speech Production

A. Taking Advantage of Nonmuscular Forces

As pointed out above, the kinds of considerations that are relevant to a general description of the control of coordinated movement are paralleled in the more local domain of speech production. A brief examination of some recent literature in this area should serve to illustrate these concerns. An excellent review of the role played by the context of nonmuscular forces in the overall speech production process is presented by Abbs and Eilenberg (1976). Let us identify some of their key observations as they relate to the kind of story of motor organization that we have been discussing.

Abbs and Eilenberg present a ·hypothetical example of the sort of phenomenon that we have labelled as "context-conditioned variability". Consider the problem of opening the jaw, a movement that is due in large part to the effective muscle force generated by the anterior belly of the digastric muscle (ABD). A schematized model of this system (see Fig. 1) assumes simple mandibular rotation about the axis at the condyle. With fixed skull and hyoid bone position, a specification of the effective muscle force as a function of jaw position is possible. Mandibular rotation can be accounted for in terms of the component of the total ABD muscle force that is tangent to the arc of rotation (Ft), with magnitude of the Ft vector being proportional to the angle between the ABD force vector and the tangent vector. Put simply, this model illustrates a case where a descending constant motor influence would yield a variable output, that is, variable jaw opening movement, depending upon the position of the jaw. Abbs and Eilenberg point out that observations of EMG activity undertaken while studying a movement such as this must be considered in

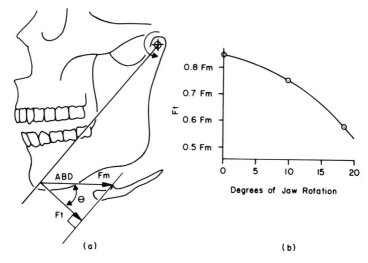

(a)   (b)

FIG. 1. [From Abbs and Eilenberg, 1976, Figure 5.6, p. 150.]

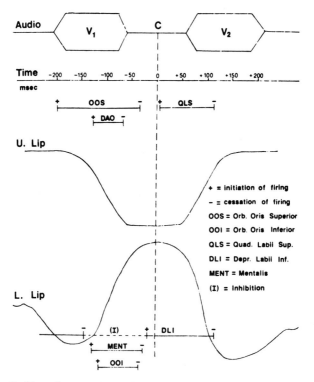

FIG. 2. [From Sussman, MacNeilage and Hanson, 1973, Figure 2, p. 403.]

conjunction with the effective jaw lowering force of the particular muscle in question—a force, then, that is varying.

Let us consider a further example, one that expresses the exploitative use of nonmuscular forces, in this case the inherent elasticity of the muscles. EMG activity in the orbicularis oris muscle (see Fig. 2) is seen to cease just prior to release in the production of bilabial closure with a vowel-consonant-vowel frame (Sussman *et al.*, 1973: Abbs, 1973a; Abbs and Netsell, 1973). It may be claimed that the release of a bilabial stop in a case such as this takes advantage of the inherent change in the elasticity of the lips, which covaries with changes in the level of orbicularis oris contraction. Bilabial stop release seems to result from an apparent cessation of this muscular activity—a cessation that results in a decrease in the stiffness of the lips that is necessary for closure, with the concomitant result of lip opening.

Abbs and Eilenberg extend this kind of description even further by attempting to separate the influences of passive components and active muscle properties in just such an articulatory system. An indication of the organization among such subsystems can be found in a series of experiments (Abbs and Netsell, 1973; Abbs, 1973a) which examines the contributions of muscle forces and passive elasticity in lower lip movements. Subjects were required to alternately move and relax their lower lip. Recordings of EMG signals during these activities from the orbicularis oris and the depressor labii inferior muscles indicate that the passive elastic component of lower lip movement can be separated from those components that represent active muscle forces. An examination of Fig. 3 reveals that, with passive elasticity considered as a "springmass" system, lower lip displacement is to be

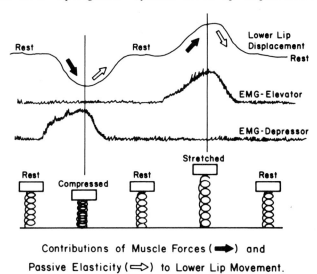

Contributions of Muscle Forces (➡) and
Passive Elasticity (⇨) to Lower Lip Movement.

FIG. 3. [From Abbs and Eilenberg, 1976, Figure 5.7, p. 152.]

accounted for in terms of the conjoint influences of muscular and nonmuscular forces.

These illustrations speak to the same concerns as those which must be confronted in *any* consideration of the organization of movement. Descriptions solely in terms of command signals to muscles must give way to a more structured understanding of the complementary relation between forces supplied muscularly and the forces supplied reactively and otherwise (cf. Fowler and Turvey, 1978).

The principle of control that is being discussed can, as a first approximation, be conceptualized as *exploitative* rather than compensatory. The different nonmuscular forces that are manifest in speech—namely, those arising from the mass and elasticity properties of articulatory structures, those arising from air pressures and flows, that due to gravity and, in general, those that are biomechanical in nature, both passive and active—should not, in our view, be considered negatively as sources of variability to be overcome by deftly timed and weighted commands to muscles. On the contrary, they should be construed positively as usable aspects of a highly flexible organization. A quote from Ashby (1956) pinpoints this theme: "when a constraint exists advantage can usually be taken of it" (p. 130). And the issue in narrower perspective is given due expression by Abbs and Eilenberg (1976):

> Just as the back swing in ball throwing is an attempt to add momentum, it may be that some of the bizarre patterns of movement observed during speech production result from system utilization of inertial or elastic properties. Further, it is possible that some of the movements and muscle activity patterns that have been implicated as evidence of *higher level control* in abstract models (such as *coarticulation*) may represent system activity utilization of mechanical properties. In any case, it is clear that one cannot observe movements and/or EMG patterns and make inferences to underlying neuromuscular mechanisms without an appreciation of these passive principles. (p. 152)

B. The Equation-of-Constraint Perspective on The Concept of Coordinative Structure

There is an especially useful perspective that we might take on the concept of coordinative structure in order to advance our understanding of the concept and to highlight what it entails, particularly for speech. We consider this perspective in this section and we do so prefatory to a literature review which provides tentative evidence for coordinative structures in speech production.

Here, we review Saltzman's (1977) discussion of degrees of freedom and equations of constraint. The degrees of freedom for a given system are the least number of independent coordinates required to specify the position of the system elements without violating any geometrical constraints (Groesberg, 1968; Timoshenko and Young, 1948). Consider two elements in a two-dimensional space as depicted in Fig. 4(a).

A total of four independent coordinates are needed to specify the respective positions of A and B, namely, $x_1 y_1$ (for A) and $x_2 y_2$ (for B). The system

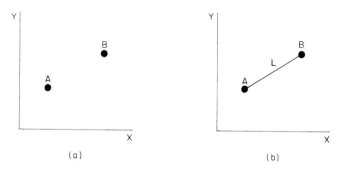

FIG. 4 (a). A two-element system with no equations of constraint.
(b) A two-element system with one equation of constraint.

depicted in Fig. 4 has four degrees of freedom, since a change in one coordinate will not limit the possible values of any of the others. Consider now the two elements in Fig. 4(b). These elements are connected by a line of fixed length L and their respective coordinates are not independent, since they must satisfy the following *equation of constraint*:

$$(x_2 - x_1)^2 + (y_2 - y_1)^2 = L^2$$

In this case, given the specification of three of the coordinates, the fourth is not free to vary. The system depicted in Fig. 4(b) has three degrees of freedom. As a general rule, the number of degrees of freedom of a system is given by $(Dn - c)$, where D is the dimensionality of the space, n is the number of elements in the system and c is the number of equations of constraint. For Fig. 4(a) the space is two-dimensional, the number of elements is two, and the number of equations of constraint is zero; hence there are four degrees of freedom in this system. For the system depicted by Fig. 4(b) the dimensionality and number of elements are both two, but there is one equation of constraint, hence this system, by the general rule, has three degrees of freedom.

With these preliminary remarks at hand, let us proceed to develop what might be called an *equation-of-constraint* perspective on the concept of coordinative structure. We do so through an example used elsewhere (Turvey *et al.*, in press), but one which will receive, in these pages, a slightly different and, we believe, more useful interpretation.

Imagine a rather simple airplane with five hinged parts: the ailerons on the rear edge of the wings which can be moved up or down regulating roll; two elevators on the horizontal portion of the tail section which can likewise be moved up or down regulating pitch; and a rudder on the vertical tail fin that can be moved right or left regulating yaw. Let each of the five hinged parts be free to adopt one of nine positions; the ailerons and elevators can go into four different positions above and four different positions below the zero position (zero being defined as flush with the wing for the ailerons and flush with the horizontal tail portion for the elevators); and the rudder can go into four positions to the right and four positions to the left of its zero position (defined as flush with the vertical tail fin). If the five hinged parts are independent of each other then, in the pilot's perspective, the airplane has five degrees of freedom, since for each of the five hinged parts ($n = 5$) only one coordinate is needed to define its position ($D = 1$) and there are no equations of constraint ($c = 0$).

Let us reduce the degrees of freedom by introducing the following three equations of constraint, given the convention that movements up from and to the right of zero are positive positions and movements down from and to the left of zero are negative positions. One equation of constraint is given by yoking the left aileron (LA) to the rudder (R) so that as the left aileron moves up, the rudder moves to the left by the same number of positions; that is, $LA = -R$. A second equation of constraint is given by the yoking of the right aileron (RA) to the rudder so that when the right aileron moves up, the rudder moves to the right by the same number of positions; that is, $RA = R$. And the third equation of constraint is given by yoking the right elevator (RE) and the left elevator (LE) so that they move in unison up and down by the same number of positions; that is, $RE = LE$.

The five hinged parts have now been reduced to two subsystems, namely, the ailerons-rudder subsystem (since the ailerons are linked via the rudder according to $RA = -LA$), and the elevators subsystem, each subsystem having one degree of freedom. In short, a system of five degrees of freedom with a possible 54 049 states (9^5) has been reduced to a system of two degrees of freedom with a more manageable set of 81 possible states (9^2). But a further reduction is possible, albeit through a constraint of a coarser grain. Preserving the airplane theme, the two subsystems themselves can be linked through the joystick according to an equation of constraint such as ($P = kQ$), where P is the ailerons-rudder subsystem responsible for banking and turning. Q is the elevators subsystem responsible for rising and falling and k is a constant. We now have a system of one degree of freedom; the dimensionality is one (as before), the elements are two in number and there is one equation of constraint.

The airplane example nicely captures what we take to be a prominent feature of coordinated movement: *When a group of muscles, or at coarser grain, a group of muscle collectives, functions as a unit (that is, as a coordinative structure), indices of the individual muscles, or individual collectives, appear to covary in terms of a relatively fixed relationship that is indifferent to overall magnitude changes in the indices.* (Elsewhere (Turvey *et al.*, in press), following Boylls (1975), the invariant relationship has been referred to as a structural prescription and the magnitude of the indices as a metrical prescription.) More generally, the airplane expresses the view, noted above, that coordinated movement is engendered by functionally embedded (as opposed to temporally successive) equations of constraint defined over elements of different grains. On this view, and in keeping with the gist of the preceding sections, coordination is to be understood not in terms of the "issuing of commands", but rather in terms of the "arising or specification of constraints" (Remez and Rubin, 1975; Fitch and Turvey, 1978).

What kind of indices upon muscles or muscle collectives might "covary" owing to an equation of constraint? The index for a muscle might be its level of innervation or the time, relative to the group's behavior, at which a muscle is innervated. Where the focus is the organization over a number of links in a biokinematic chain—such as an individual limb in running, or the cervix, thorax and pelvic girdle in breathing (Gurfinkel *et al.*, 1971—the index might be coarser, such as joint angle (e.g. Arutyunyan *et al.*, 1968, 1969) or the torque generated at a joint. And where the focus is the relation among the limbs, say during locomotion, the index might be even more coarse-grained, such as cycle time. Thus, in the alternate step gaits, limbs of the same girdle are 0·5 of a cycle out of phase with each other and obstinately preserve this relation in the face of manipulations that alter disproportionately the cycle times of the individual limbs (Kulagin and Shik, 1970).

A set of elements together with a set of equations of constraint identifies a control system in this sense: the degrees of freedom of the set of elements so constrained is less than the degrees of freedom of the set in free-variation. Given the *equation of constraint* perspective on coordinative structures that we have just developed, we now ask what kind of system is it that equations of constraint (written, as it were, on the neuromuscular apparatus) give rise to? Our tentative answer is that the kind of system so created is analogous to a self-regulating and biasable vibratory system (Fitch and Turvey, 1978; Turvey, 1977a). The motivation for this answer derives from the work of Asatryan and Fel'dman (1965) and Fel'dman (1966a, 1966b) which receives a brief description in the paragraphs that follow.

Under some conditions a neuro-muscular system can be established by an actor (to govern forearm movement relative to the elbow joint) that is similar in its properties to a spring system. A linear spring system can be described by the equation: $F = -s(l - l_0)$, where l_0 is the length of the spring when there are no forces operating on it; l is the current length of the spring; s is a stiffness parameter; and F is the force developed by the spring. The behavior of an actual spring is governed completely by the external forces $(-F)$ exerted on it. In contrast to a real spring, the elbow system, which is shown to behave like a spring, incorporates some internal controls. It is not governed solely by the value of $-F$. Significantly, it can alter l_0, the zero-state of the system. (l_0 is the joint angle at the elbow that the system will assume in the absence of any forces on it. It is an abstract variable whose value is established by the collaborative activities of several muscles.)

Asatryan and Fel'dman (1965) demonstrated the spring-like properties of the joint-muscle system in the following way. A subject attains and holds some joint angle. His forearm is resting on a mobile horizontal platform whose axis of rotation allows elbow flexion and extension. Suspended from the platform are a set of weights (at the subject's wrist) that promote extension. To hold steady the specified joint angle, the subject has to counteract exactly the moments of the forces of the weights exerted on his arm. In terms of the equations above, he must establish some l_0 such that the difference between l_0 and l (the joint angle specified by the experimenter) multiplied by s just counteracts the $-F$ due to the weights. If the spring analogy is appropriate, then:

(1) If the investigator releases some of the weights, thereby changing $-F$, and if the subject allows his angle to change passively, it should move to a new l such that the difference between the new l and the established l_0 counteracts the new $-F$. A graph plotting F by l should be linear if the elbow behaves like a linear spring. But, in any event, if it is analogous to a spring system, the curve should be simple and lawful.

(2) A family of *parallel* curves should characterize a family of experiments across which the subject is asked to hold different steady-state joint angles. (To counteract the same weights, a different l_0 must be set by the subject when the experiment prescribes that he holds different ls. l_0 is the x-intercept in an F by l plot, and s is the slope. Hence, $F \times l$ plots of experiments evoking different l_0s should yield parallel curves with one curve intersecting the x-axis to the right of the other.)

These predictions were borne out in the experiments. The curves for all experiments were nonlinear, but lawful. Across experiments (that is, across different prescribed ls) the curves were parallel indicating that the subject altered l_0 to perform the task. The experimenters concluded from these results that for the purpose of the experiment the subjects established a joint-muscle system with spring-like properties. When asked to hold a particular joint angle at the elbow, the subjects did so by resetting the "zero-state" of the joint-muscle system (i.e. l_0).

There are several features of the coordinative structure as a vibratory system metaphor that we find attractive and which we believe to be of special relevance to issues in speech production. First, a vibratory system is intrinsically cyclic or rhythmic *but it need not behave cyclically or rhythmically.* Suppose we modeled a mass-spring system by the following equation:

$$mX''(t) + kX'(t) + sX(t) = 0$$

where $X(t)$ is the displacement of the system from the equilibrium at time t, $X'(t)$ and $X''(t)$ are the first and second derivatives respectively, and where m, k, s stand, in that order, for the mass, the damping (or frictional) parameter and the stiffness parameter. Where these parameters are related as $0 < k^2 < 4$ ms) the system oscillates with the amplitude of oscillations decreasing with time. But if the parameters are related as ($k^2 \geq 4$ ms) the system does not oscillate; to the contrary it rapidly achieves the equilibrium position in less than a cycle. The point is that it is often tempting to conceive of rhythmic and nonrhythmic behavior as distinct cases requiring possibly separate mechanisms. In a mass-spring system we have a concrete example of a single mechanism that can do both; whether its behavior is rhythmic or not depends simply on the current parameterization of the system. (As an aside, in pursuing the vibratory system metaphor we take note that the intuitive object that we are trying to understand might be more judiciously labeled coordinative *cycle* rather than coordinative *structure*.)

A second significant feature of a vibratory system follows from the first, namely, that the steady-state or equilibrium position is indifferent to the initial conditions and is determined only by the system parameters. Within limits, a mass-spring system can be stretched or compressed to any degree yet it will, on free-vibration, equilibrate at the same length. And we may note that the kinematic details of its equilibrating behavior will differ from one set of initial conditions to the next. We are reminded that kinematics refers to the descriptions of motions in contrast to dynamics which refers to the explanation of motions. Included in the vocabulary of kinematics are such terms as distance, direction, velocity, etc. while the vocabulary of dynamics includes terms such as force, viscosity, stiffness, momentum, etc. Which brings us to the third notable feature of a vibratory system: the kinematic details of a vibratory system's behavior are determined by its dynamic properties—the system parameters—in conjunction with the initial conditions (e.g. degree of initial stretch or compression); and it would be incorrect to claim that the kinematic details are determined by an *internal representation* of these details, for nowhere within a vibratory system is there a representation, symbolic or otherwise, of the kinematic details of the behavior consequent to disequilibration (Fitch and Turvey, 1978).

There is one further feature of a mass-spring system that we would do well to note: a mass-spring system *is not a servo-mechanism*. The goal of a servo-mechanism's activity is set by an external command that provides the reference signal from which, subsequent to feedback, error signals are derived and on the basis of which corrections are determined. While we could easily speak about a mass-spring *as if* it were a servo-mechanism complete with reference signal, feedback and error signals, we would be guilty of unduly stretching these servo-mechanism concepts; indeed, we would be guilty of introducing fictitious quantities. The "goal" of a mass-spring system in *intrinsic* to the system; it is a necessary *consequence* of the configuration of dynamic properties, rather than something imposed from outside as a causal *antecedent* of the system's behavior. In a mass-spring system there is neither feedback to be monitored nor errors to be computed and corrected and, patently, no special devices for performing these operations.

C. On Explaining "Immediate Readjustments"

We turn now to a curious phenomenon of speech production in order to compare the kind of explanation afforded by the vibratory system metaphor with that afforded by a more conventional view. Lindblom and Sundberg (1971) reported that speakers can produce natural vowels with a bite block between their teeth, without the need for extensive relearning. More recent and complete evidence is to the effect that speakers fitted with bite blocks and instructed to produce isolated vowels do so within the range of variability for normal vowel production. And, most significantly, they do so without the need for acoustic feedback; acoustic measures reveal satisfactory vowel production in the first pitch pulse of speech (Lindblom *et al.*, 1979). A similar outcome is obtained when lip protrusion is impeded during the production of rounded and unrounded vowels. Compensation for impedance of lip protrusion is achieved for each vowel by differentially lowering the larynx to a degree that preserves the vocal tract length characteristic of each vowel. Even on the first trial, under these conditions, vowels are acoustically normal (Riordan, 1977).

How might the phenomenon of "immediate readjustment" be accounted for? Substantial reasons have already been given elsewhere (e.g. MacNeilage, 1970) for dismissing open-loop explanations of phenomena of the kind under analysis, and we will not pursue these reasons here. The issue of interest to us is how well a *closed*-loop explanation fares in this regard. All such explanations lie, of course, within the purview of the servo-mechanism metaphor. Thus, in closed-loop explanations a sensory referent is proposed, tied either to the environmental goal of the movement such as, say, a spatial target or an acoustic pattern, or to the commands to produce the movement (compare Adams, 1971; MacNeilage, 1970; Pew, 1974; Powers, 1973; Schmidt, 1975). The comparison of sensory feedback, a perceptual signal (p), with the referent signal (r) defines an error signal (E) which provides a basis for correcting the lower-level mechanism(s) responsible for controlling the referent (see Fig. 5).

In the phenomenon under analysis, feedback related to the acoustic

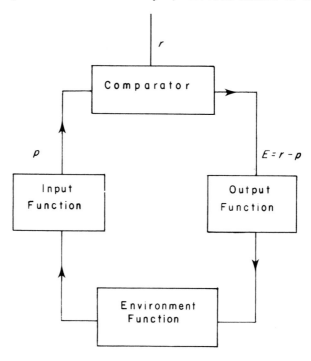

FIG. 5. An individual control system.

consequence of the movement may be absent—we are reminded that in the Lindblom *et al.* (in press) demonstration vocalization is normal in the first pitch pulse. This fact would seem to rule out a closed-loop explanation in which the referent is tied to the acoustics. But it does not rule out a closed-loop explanation in which the referent is felt vocal tract shape. Nor does it rule out the following special version of a closed-loop explanation. The manifest plasticity and context-appropriateness of movement has invited some students of coordinated movement to invoke a more cognitive style of control than that embodied by a bare-bones servo-mechanism. The claim is that more central mechanisms use the techniques of model-referenced (or schema-referenced) control (e.g. Arbib, 1972; Ito, 1970) in order to *predict* the commands needed for goal-directed movement given variation in initial conditions (see also Schmidt, 1975). Let the model be of the actual servo-mechanism (Eccles, 1969) in which the motor commands and sensory consequences are simulated. We can then see how the requisite commands for the actual servo-mechanism problem are arrived at through a process of error-correcting, precisely, that set of simulated commands is selected which produces simulated sensory consequences matching the reference signal. All of this, of course, is assumed to precede the actual commands to the musculature; and so it must if the model-referenced control notion is to account for the "immediate readjustment" phenomenon. But let us examine closely the error-correcting process, whether it be in an actual or simulated closed-loop, and whatever the referent signal, for we have serious doubts about its tractability.

Suppose that three (relatively) independent muscles, when acting together, bring about a change in some notable vocal tract parameter. And suppose, not unreasonably, that of all possible combinations of the states of these muscles only a subset will yield a given value of the aforementioned parameter. The problem is this: When the actual value (the perceptual signal, p) and the desired value (the reference signal, r) do not match, how are the states of the individual muscles adjusted (that is, how is a more apt combination of their states found) so as to reduce this mismatch? How is the means of adjusting informed about the adjustments to be made? The magnitude of error indicates how near the collective action of the three muscles is to the desired values, but it fails to indicate how their individual states are to be adjusted to reduce the perceptual signal—reference signal mismatch.

The problem can be illustrated briefly (see Fowler and Turvey, 1978, for a more complete discussion). Consider Fig. 6 which depicts a two-tiered control system composed of three lower level or first-order control systems (CS_{11}, CS_{12}, CS_{13}) and one higher level or second-order control system (CS_{21}). Each first-order system supplies CS_{21} with a perceptual signal. In keeping with the general servo-mechanism strategy of unidimensional feedback, the perceptual signal of the second order system, p_{21}, is a linear transformation of the three, first-order perceptual signals, p_{11}, p_{12}, p_{13}. Thus, $p_{21} = a_1 p_{11} + a_2 p_{12} + a_3 p_{13}$ (cf. Powers, 1973). That signal is subtracted from the reference signal, r_{21}, of the second-order system. The result, $E = r_{21} - a_1 p_{11} -$

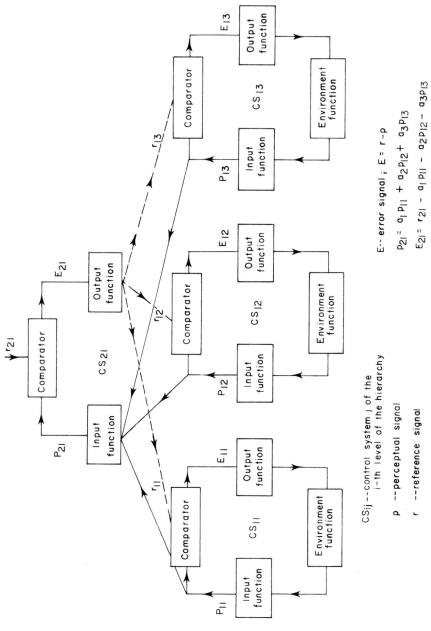

E -- error signal; E = r - p

$$P_{21} = a_1 P_{11} + a_2 P_{12} + a_3 P_{13}$$

$$E_{21} = r_{21} - a_1 P_{11} - a_2 P_{12} - a_3 P_{13}$$

CS_{ij} -- control system j of the i-th level of the hierarchy

p -- perceptual signal

r -- reference signal

FIG. 6. A hierarchy of control systems: Three first-order systems nested under one second-order system.

$a_2p_{12} - a_3p_{13}$, is the error signal of the second-order system. This error signal is the basis for selecting the reference signals, r_{11}, r_{12} and r_{13}, of the first-order systems.

Unfortunately, for any given error signal there are very many possible combinations of values for r_{21}, p_{11}, p_{12} and p_{13} that might yield that error, even if some boundaries are set on the possible ranges of values that each might take on. The error signal might be entirely due to an error of one of the first-order systems; or it could be one of many combinations of errors on the part of all three first-order systems. In summary, unidimensional feedback must rarely be informative in a hierarchical closed-loop system because, typically, there is a one-to-many mapping between an error signal and the conditions that may have provoked it.

The servo-mechanism conception is attractive when the entity commanded to produce a reference-matching perceptual signal has but one degree of freedom (such as the commonly described servo-mechanism—the thermostatically controlled home-heating system). The attractiveness of this mechanism, in its unqualified form, decreases, however, as we increase the number of degrees of freedom in the commanded entity. In the absence of any well-defined, and possibly special-purpose (Gel'fand and Tsetlin, 1962, 1971), search procedure, the error-correcting process on n degrees of freedom would be essentially random and temporally indefinite.

Let us now consider an interpretation of the "immediate readjustment" phenomenon in the equation of constraint perspective. Given a set of variables related by an equation of constraint, if one of the variables is fixed, the others are not free to vary but must assume those values that preserve the equation. In the airplane example above, if the equation of constraint linking the ailerons-rudder subsystem and the elevators subsystem identifies an invariant ratio, for example, $P = kQ$, then if P's value is frozen Q *must* assume whatever value is necessary to keep invariant the ratio k.

The ability of speakers to generate acceptable vowel qualities in the face of a fixed position of the mandible or of the lips, can be accounted for in very much the same way. Like the ailerons, elevators and rudder of the airplane, the components of the vocal tract, including the mandible, tongue, lips and larynx, can be described as linked by equations of constraint. More simply, the components are represented as variables in an equation that defines the relationships among them. The constrained relationships among components of the vocal tract "create" a vibratory system—that is, a system with an intrinsic goal which it attains from any starting point by virtue of its dynamic configuration. When a bite block is introduced in the system, it fixes the values of the variable for jaw position. As we have indicated, under conditions in which the value of a variable is fixed, the remaining variables assume values that preserve the equation of constraint. So long as the requisite values are attainable by the components of the vocal tract, the effect of a bite block should be negligible.

The assumption here is that an invariant vibratory-like organization of the muscles underlies vowel production. In very large part the aim of the final part of this paper is to substantiate this claim. At this point, we proceed to consider evidence that coordinative structures are involved in speech.

D. Fine-grained and Coarse-grained Coordinative Structures in Speech

An emphasis on volitional aspects of motor behavior has resulted in a viewpoint that would be conducive to coordinative structures as we speak of them, but only in terms of handling nonvolitional, or automatic, functions. We prefer, instead, to emphasize that this form of analysis of motor behavior extends across all domains, both volitional and nonvolitional. Some brief examples should serve to show how such concerns manifest themselves in aspects of speech production not generally included in various theories, for example respiration, and those more commonly discussed, as in the cooperation between articulators and structures in the supralaryngeal system. (See Fowler, 1977, for a more detailed examination of the role of coordinative structures in speech production.)

An examination of the respiratory system reveals that basic reflexes operate both in vegetative breathing and in speech, with the apparent purpose of regulation of the initiation and termination of inspiratory activity (see, for reviews, Kaplan, 1971; Lambertsen, 1974). Briefly, the medullary respiratory center receives several kinds of vagal and hypoglosseal influence, supplementary to its own intrinsic activity; among these are afferents originating in (1) alveolar stretch receptors (which signal pulmonary distention); (2) aortic chemoreceptors (which monitor blood CO_2 level); and (3) aortic and carotid baroreceptors (which monitor blood pressure). These receptors signal the various changes due to the respiratory cycle, and can be used in a control system for inspiratory and expiratory oscillation independent of higher cortical influence.

At a more macroscopic level vegetative respiration and speech respiration are seen to be quite different. During vegetative breathing, the activity of the inspiratory muscles and the inspiratory portion of the respiratory cycle are in phase (Lenneberg, 1967). Furthermore, except during forced expiration, that phase is typically accomplished passively—that is, by relaxing the muscles of inspiration and by allowing the elastic recoil forces of the lungs to work unaided and unopposed. The expiratory phase occupies about 60% of the cycle. During speech, however, the sequence of events is somewhat different (Draper *et al.*, 1959; Lenneberg, 1967). In speech, the activity of the inspiratory muscles is out of phase with the act of inspiration. Their activity extends into the early part of expiration where they act to check the descent of the ribcage that characterizes passive expiration. Immediately following the decline and offset of activity in the inspiratory muscles, the internal intercostals, that are muscles of active expiration, come into play. If phonation is prolonged, two other muscles that may contribute to expiration, the rectus abdominis and the latissimus dorsi, are also marshalled (Draper *et al.*, 1959).

As a result of this coordinated activity, the proportion of the respiratory cycle occupied by the expiratory phase is about 0.87 (Lenneberg, 1967) and the subglottal pressure is maintained at a nearly constant level, despite the continual decrease in the volume of the air in the lungs (Draper *et al.*, 1959; Lieberman, 1967). Lenneberg (1967) refers to these coordinated activities of the muscles of inspiration and expiration as "synergisms", a term that others have used in a sense that relates to, but is not identical with, the sense in which we use coordinative structures. This particular macroscopic coordinative structure can be conceptualized as a device whose task is to control subglottal pressure, much as the microscopic reflexes regulate stretch and CO_2 levels in the blood. The macroscopic coordinative structure is superimposed on the smaller ones when an individual chooses to speak. Notably, in the experiment of Draper *et al.* (1959), similar sequences of muscular events occurred over a range of controlled subglottal pressures. That is, the same coordinative structure may govern an utterance over all amplitudes of production, the different subglottal pressures or amplitudes of production being *metrical* variations of the governed act, rather than an invariant property.

An examination of the literature provides further evidence for macroscopic coordinative structures in speech at the level of supralaryngeal control. The interpretation of this body of data by speech theorists has been that clusters of articulatory commands to muscles tend to be released simultaneously (Daniloff and Hammarberg, 1973; Kent *et al.*, 1974; Kent and Moll, 1975). But we have seen that, in view of the physiological, mechanical and anatomical indeterminacies of the relationship between a central signal and its peripheral effect, control centers cannot send *commands* to individual muscles. In our view, a more likely interpretation of these data may be that coordinated gestures in speech are evidence of coordinative structures. The coordinative structures are marshalled via biasing operations, but they generate the coordinated gestures autonomously.

Synchrony between articulators is evident in a study by Kent and Netsell (1971), which shows that the gestures of the tongue body and the lips are coordinated during the production of the word *we* in *We saw you*. A figure relating the displacement of the tongue body to that of the lips over different stress patterns of the phrase (*we* saw you; we *saw* you; we saw *you*) shows that the relationship between the two variables is invariant over differences in stress. Kent and Netsell obtain a similar result for the dipthong /oɪ/ in the noun-verb opposition of *CONvoy* and *conVOY*, and tentatively conclude that, "for sounds like /wi/ and /oɪ/, which are characterized by coordinated movements of two articulators, the stress contrast must alter both gestures or neither gesture" (see p. 40).

Additional evidence for the cooperation between articulators can be seen in experiments by Kent *et al.* (1974) and Ushijima and Hirose (1974) on velar control and movement. For example, Kent *et al.* (1974), using as a basis for analysis cinefluorographic films of tongue and velum movements, conclude that their data indicates that in many cases "articulatory movements seem to be programmed as coordinative structures so that movements of the tongue, lip, velum and jaw often occur in highly synchronous patterns" (see p. 487). Such patterning can be seen in the articulation of a word like *contract*, where the initiation of velum lowering coincides with the release of oral closure for /k/, and velum elevation starts as the tongue-tip movement begins for the consonant /n/. As the authors point out, the goal of velum opening in such a case has been achieved and reversed *prior* to the time of attainment of the concomitant goal of oral constriction.

Of further interest are cases in which articulatory gestures are not synchronized at a particular moment, but rather occur in a constrained pattern over time. Notice that evidence of this can only be obtained by comparing similar utterances or by comparing the utterance produced at different rates. That is, a nonsynchronized pattern can be detected only if it remains invariant in different contexts. Recent data of Bell-Berti and Harris (1979) appear to show that the onset of lip-rounding precedes the measured acoustic onset of the rounded vowel /u/ by a relatively fixed interval, regardless of the preceding consonantal context. Some of the data of Kent and Moll (1975) may be given a similar reading.

There is some limited evidence that the relative timing of gestures of the tongue body, velum and lips tend to be ivariant over a change in rate of speaking (Kent *et al.*, 1974). For each articulator and for each of two speakers, figures are provided which superimpose the movement tracings at two different rates during the production of "soon the snow began to melt". The rates of speaking were in the ratio 2:1. To facilitate a comparison of the movements' relative timing at the different rates, the investigators compressed the time-scale of the slower movement relative to that of the fast movement. For both speakers, and for all three articulators, the tracings at the two rates of production were nearly identical. Thus, the relative timings of the movements of a particular articulator and the timing relationships among articulators remained nearly invariant over a two-fold increase in rate. These findings are commensurate with the coordinative structure conception, but there is reason for caution. For instance, Gay and Ushijima (1974) show that the muscle activity for consonants is of greater amplitude, and that of vowels of lesser amplitude, during rapid as opposed to slow speech. We should remark, however, that only EMG data were provided and making inferences from muscle contraction to movement is difficult at best and illegitimate at worst (Hubbard, 1960). In addition to the data of Gay and Ushijima, we may note the evidence provided elsewhere (for example, see Klatt, 1976) for articulatory undershoot for vowels, but not for consonants, at a fast rate of speech. The figures of Kent *et al.* (1974), however, do not show any tendency for the movements of the tongue body to be any less extreme in fast speech than they are during slow speech.

E. Techniques For Examining Speech Motor Organization

A final mention should be made of some techniques that might prove useful as tools for isolating and examining the proposed coordinative-structure underpinnings of speech. These techniques all involve procedures that are, in one form or another, disruptive to normal activity. Such approaches have been used with success in more general examinations of action systems (Asatryan and Fel'dman, 1965; Fel'dman, 1966a, 1966b; Shik and Orlovskii, 1965), and their application in the study of speech production could prove valuable. An example of this methodology can be found in a study by Sears and Newsom Davis (1968) in which sudden alterations in mechanical load during breathing were applied. The occurrence of such disruptions during voluntary activation of the respiratory muscles resulted in concomitant changes in EMG activity of the intercostal muscles. Disruptive loading and unloading were accomplished by introducing transient changes in the pressure in an obstructive airway, which yielded small, but rapid, changes in lung volume, and by admitting timed pressure pulses of air into the breathing circuit. Loading, which effectively increased lung volume, resulted in immediate increases in EMG activity, while unloading produced a brief plateau, or period of inactivity, in this signal. The brief latencies of the EMG responses indicated their reflex nature. Further, the results of this study indicated that this reflex structure was sensitive to both changes and rates of changes in lung volume. The authors, then, concluded that their experiments provided, "positive evidence in conscious man of a reflex system that automatically tends to stabilize the voluntary demands for respiratory movement" (p. 190).

In a similar vein, Folkins and Abbs (1975) examined the effect of disruptive jaw loading on lip movements. In their experiment subjects were asked to repeatedly produce the phrase, "a /haepaep/ again". On about 25% of the test utterances, jaw loading was applied randomly by introducing a clamping force to a prosthodentic splint, which effectively provided a transient resistance to upward jaw movement. Simultaneous recordings were made of the EMG activity of the medial ptyerygoid, temporalis, masseter and orbicularis oris superior muscles, and of inferior-superior movements of the upper lip, lower lip and jaw, through the use of a strain gauge. The loading force was applied during the bilabial closure movement that corresponded to the initial /p/ in the test utterance, preventing the jaw from reaching its usual degree of elevation during this activity. Even though this resistance was applied, subjects attained lip closure in all cases. An examination of the data from the physiological monitoring indicated that the compensatory gestures that permitted lip closure were exaggerated upper and lower lip displacements, and slightly exaggerated velocities of lip closing gestures. In a follow-up study (Folkins and Abbs, 1976), the authors provided additional evidence that the compensatory gestures were not merely of a passive nature, as would be the case, for example, if the momentum of the lips had moved them further than normal. The results of this replication study indicated increases in the EMG activity from the depressor anguli oris and the buccinator muscles. Folkins and Abb's interpretation was that the activity of these muscles, which contribute to upper lip depression, provides evidence for *active* compensatory adjustments in the labial muscles. The results of both of these studies are explained most simply in terms of a low-level jaw-lip control system that is responsible for lip closure. Folkins and Abbs suggest that its mode of operation is such that it *adapts* its strategy to current conditions, rather than programming a particular gesture in advance.

Techniques that interfere with normal speech production activities are not restricted to the application of such impedances. Examples of other procedures include the adaptation by subjects to bite blocks—we took note of these above—and dental prostheses. Fairly extensive reorganization is needed when subjects are fitted with dental prostheses that alter the configurations of their vocal tracts. Amerman and Daniloff (1971), relying on listener judgments, found normalization of vowel production within 5 min of the insertion of a prosthesis in a subject's mouth. In a similar procedure Hamlet and Stone (1976) fitted subjects with three different types of prostheses. The effects on the production of vowels were striking. Compensation for vowel changes was variable among the subject pool and was not always successfully accomplished, even after a week of adaptation. In addition, a period of readjustment was required by subjects subsequent to the removal of these prostheses. In the case of the bite block studies, we might be viewing the ability of the articulators to attain, simply, a functional reorganization within an equivalence class of permissible, potential organizations. It is possible that when experimental prostheses are used, the subjects have been moved beyond this "ballpark" of permissible organizations and fundamentally restructure their articulatory approach to the new task at hand—an endeavor that they, apparently, find very difficult to undertake.

A final class of disruptive techniques involves the use of differential nerve blocks and selective anesthetization to examine the role played by oral sensory and other forms of feedback and the contribution of lower-level systems to the productive act (cf. Ringel and Steer, 1963; Scott and Ringel, 1971; Borden *et al.*, 1973a, b; Abbs, 1973b; Putnam and Ringel, 1976; Abbs *et al.*, 1976). At present, an integrated understanding of the implications of these studies seems to be hindered, in part, by methodological and interpretive disagreements. However, the application of such procedures in coordination with other forms of physiological monitoring may prove to be valuable as a method for probing aspects of organization in the action system.

One technique for examining *tuning* in action systems involves a form of probing of spinal nervous activity (see Turvey, 1977a, for a review). Examples of this approach can be found in the work of Gottlieb and his associates (Gottlieb *et al.*, 1970; Gottlieb and Agarwarl, 1972, 1973), in which reflex activity was elicited prior to a voluntary movement. In the work of Gottlieb *et al.*, for example, subjects were required to continuously track target levels of force by step effort of either plantar flexion or dorsiflexion. Hoffman reflexes (H-reflex) were elicited by electrical stimulation of the popliteal fossa at various points during the voluntary force-generating activity. Simultaneous measurements were made of the monosynaptic H-reflex and the EMG activity in the gastrocnemius-soleus muscle group (agonist in plantar flexion) and the anterior tibial muscle (agonist in dorsiflexion). If the H-reflex was elicited in the 60 ms period that preceded any EMG indication of voluntary motor unit activation, a marked increase in its amplitude was observed when the voluntary activity was plantar flexion. During dorsiflexion, in which the gastrocnemius-soleus group functions as the antagonist, the amplitude of the H-reflex reflected inhibition. A biasing is thus apparent in which the control structure takes advantage of modulation in the agonist-antagonist opposition.

This technique provides an elegant way of tapping into different neuroanatomic levels, with particular emphasis towards examining the state of the segmental apparatus and its relationship to movement; as in the case considered above, experimental results indicate a pre-movement segmental tuning. Recently, a similar technique has been applied in a speech production context. Netsell and Abbs (1975) have developed an approach similar to that of Gottlieb and his associates that demonstrates a way in which an aspect of the control structure of the facial musculature can be continuously modulated, or tuned. This procedure involves the elicitation of the perioral reflex during static muscle contraction and the production of the syllable /pa/, with concomitant recordings of EMG activity from the orbicularis oris superior muscle. The results show a facilitation of the afferent-efferent pathway during muscle contraction in both the static case and during bilabial closure. The amplitude of the perioral reflex during orbicularis oris shutdown was smaller than that recorded during the resting state, indicating a complementary inhibition. This systemic behavior, a "continuous modulation" in the terms of Netsell and Abbs, represents a further demonstration of the physiological biasing we have referred to as tuning.

In summary, in this portion of the paper we have briefly reviewed some of the relevant literature in the field of speech production with the intention of directing our attention toward the need to view such data from the broader perspective afforded by concepts that have had application in the general study of coordinated movement. This sort of attempt has, of late, begun to be seen as an attractive and necessary alternative to traditional approaches employed in examining speech physiology (Fowler, 1977; Harris, 1976; Moll et al., 1976).

V. Toward a Theory of The Direct Perception and Production of The Sounds of Speech

A. Linguistic Segments as Invariants

We have reviewed the experimental literature suggesting that control over articulation is fundamentally similar to control over other kinds of acts. At this point, it is worthwhile to reconsider the insights that these properties of motor control may provide in reference to two issues raised above; namely, those having to do with the essential properties of linguistic segments as they are perceived and uttered.

1. *Can segments that are dynamic and coarticulated nonetheless have invariant (context-free) properties?*

A coordinative structure is a functional relationship among muscles that can be described by a mapping. In some respects, the mapping is not unlike the equation for a circle given earlier. An example is $(F = -s(l-l_0))$, which describes the spring-like behavior of the muscles governing forearm movement at the elbow under some conditions (Asatryan and Fel'dman, 1965; Fel'dman, 1966a, b). The mapping expresses what is context-free about acts. Importantly, the context-free properties are not realized as movement invariance, but as something closer to functional equivalence. The mapping also expresses the dimensions along which different instances are free to take on different values. In the spring system of the elbow, those dimensions are s and l_0. Thus, the values of these parameters are the distinctive features of the different movements allowed by the mapping, or they may be the dimensions along which the movement may adjust to the context.

Despite the lack of movement invariance (the elbow system governs both extension and flexion over various extents), the acts governed by the elbow system have invariant properites. In essence, these invariant properties are actualizations of the constraints on possible movements as described by the mapping. We suspect that the essential properties of linguistic segments will turn out to be relational properties of this sort. Shortly, we will provide a speculative example to illustrate this. Here our concern is only to show that the coordinative structure type of organization, as noted above, engenders various kinematic outcomes with properties that may be superficially dissimilar (context-adjusted), but have underlying dynamic invariance.

Given the abstractness or depth of the invariance on the action side, it may seem unlikely that any corresponding acoustic invariance can be found. Indeed, it is generally agreed that the perception of speech sounds is not based on acoustic invariants (but see Stevens, 1975). However, the kinds of invariants that have been sought are of a superficial nature (e.g. discrete and context-free representations of a linguistic segment with invariant properties that are visible on a spectrogram). These *evident* acoustic invariants may well be absent, but this in no way implies the absence of invariants of a less obvious sort. Perhaps, instead, we should expect to find acoustic invariants analogous to (or, better, complementary to) the abstract and relational invariants putatively underlying speech production.

We borrow from investigations of visual perception the insight that the invariants supporting perception are abstract. Investigators, in the visual domain, as in speech, have failed to discover simple correspondences between dimensions of the proximal stimulus for visual perception and those of the percept. For example, the perception of a rigid object's size and shape is invariant across any perspective that an observer chooses to adopt on the object, despite enormous variability in the received descriptors of the retinal image. Thus a shape, invariantly perceived, is not represented by an invariant shape on the retina. Nonetheless, under a different analysis that does not equate the description of the light at an eye with the traditional description of the retinal image (cf. Gibson, 1961), the light to an eye can be shown to contain invariant information about shape and other properties of an environment, and about the perceiver's relation to it (Gibson, 1973; Lee, 1974; Johansson, 1973; Shaw and Pittenger, 1977). Invariants prove to be difficult to find and to describe because they do not *resemble* the properties to which they correspond, but they are *specific* to them. The invariants that have been isolated are abstract and relational rather like those that we propose underlie action.

Indeed, in some cases, the invariants underlying activity and its perception seem very close even in the visual domain. Johansson (e.g. 1973) shows that perceivers readily recognize locomoting human forms based on films displaying only point lights of the figures' joints. A vector analysis of the movements of these points of light expresses their regularities. Presumably the regularities correspond to constraints on point-light movement. (That is, no given light can move any arbitrary distance from the others, along any arbitrary path, because in fact it is attached to a body.) Over time, the constraints evidently are detected and specify a locomoting human form to a perceiver. Yet these same constraints follow not only from fixed properties of a walker's form, but also from the particular organization of his body that engenders walking. In short, Johansson's vector analysis most probably expresses the invariants in the motion of the point lights that specify a walking human figure to a perceiver; but simultaneously they express the invariant organization of the actor's body that enables locomotion.

We believe that an analogous story will unfold in the speech domain. The regularities underlying articulation will be as abstract and relational as those underlying walking. These regularities nonetheless impose a patterning on an acoustic signal which specifies them to a hearer.

2. Can the separateness and serial ordering of segments be preserved in an utterance despite coarticulation?

As noted earlier, we replace the characterization "discrete" with "separate and serially ordered". Outside the speech domain, we are not always puzzled that two temporally overlapping events are perceived as separate. Consider, for example, a recording of a singer and his musical accompaniment. Perceivers do not find if difficult to hear the singer's voice as separate from the instrumental accompaniment, although the impressions of each source on the compression wave at the ear must be thoroughly intermixed. Evidently, what specifies their separateness is that they constitute different kinds of sound-generating devices and they generate different kinds of acoustic products.

Vowels and consonants are different kinds of articulatory and acoustic events. Vowels are relatively slow, global changes in vocal tract shape effected primarily by moving the tongue body about in the oral cavity. On the other hand, consonants are rapid local obstructions of the vocal tract. Each kind of gesture produces a different kind of acoustic product: vowel gestures produce a relatively slowly changing pattern of formant frequencies, and consonant gestures yield acoustic evidence for obstruction.

In short, coarticulated segments in an utterance are nonetheless separate (but not discrete along the time axis) by virtue of being different kinds of gestures, each producing a different kind of acoustic product. Conversely, the complex of articulations that together constitute a given segment (e.g. lip-rounding, and movements of the tongue body and jaw to produce /u/) are perceived to cohere because they are similar *kinds* of articulations contributing to a coherent kind of acoustic event.

Johansson's work in the visual domain has an analogue to this as well. The spot of light at a walker's wrist may pass very close to that at his hip at some point in each walking cycle, and may even obscure it periodically. However, a perceiver is not persuaded, thereby, to treat the two spots of light as cohering. The *movement* of the spot of light at the wrist closely follows those of the spots at the elbow and shoulder. The three spots move as a collective and specify a coherent entity, the swinging arm. The wrist-spot movement follows that of the spot at the hip much less closely. Hence, the two do not seem attached or part of a single body-segment.

Not only the separateness, but also the serial ordering of segments is preserved in a coarticulated utterance. Two sequential segments in an utterance are never entirely concurrent. For example, movement towards a consonant may begin during a preceding vowel, and it may end during a following vowel, but it does not happen that a consonant's initiation and termination both co-occur with the initiation and termination of a given vowel segment.

Based on the foregoing considerations, we believe it plausible to suggest that linguistic segments as perceived are compatible with uttered segments. A dynamic segment, as well as a static one, can have context-free properties: furthermore, despite coarticulation, a dynamic segment can be separate from, and serially ordered with respect to its neighbors, both articulatorily and *acoustically*.

B. A Speculative Example of a Muscle System Underlying the Production of Vowels

We conclude by describing a rough and speculative model of some aspects of vowel production. It is based on many of the principles of coordinated movement outlined above. However, it does not purport to represent a theory of vowel production; indeed it is a *metaphor* for vowel production rather than a model. Its worth lies in demonstrating that a system embodying a coordinative-structural style of control exhibits some essential properties of vowels, many of which elude expression in theories equating vowels with feature bundles or with spatial targets. We first specify the kinds of properties of vowels that we take to be essential; we then proceed to describe the model.

An adequate theory of speech production accounts for the following kinds of vowel properties:

(1) Vowels constitute a natural articulatory class as distinct from consonants and from all other classes of acts. As a natural class, its members share the defining properties of the class and a theory of speech production optimally specifies these properties and accounts for them.

(2) Similarly, a given vowel must have essential (context-free) properties that are preserved across its instantiations.

(3) The essential properties of either vowels as a class or of a particular vowel are not invariant movements. This is evident, for example, in the production of the vowel /ɛ/. If /ɛ/ is produced from a high tongue position, it involves a lowering of the tongue body. If it is produced from a low tongue position it may involve raising the tongue.

(4) Although their context-free properties cannot be invariant movements, vowels are essentially dynamic (cf. Shankweiler *et al.*, 1977). Thus, while it may be fair to say that movement in vowel production is always toward some particular shape of the vocal tract, it is undesirable to treat the target as if it were the vowel's canonical form. For one thing, targets are often not even attained in running speech. More importantly, perhaps, a spatial target is static, while speaking is only dynamic. If a static shape were a vowel's essential property, movement toward and away from the target would be only a byproduct of the fact that targets are being produced in a flesh and blood system. (That is, by virtue of a vocal tract being a physical system, in order to get from one shape to another, it is necessary to traverse all intervening shapes.) However, if movement is merely a byproduct of planned static targets, it is curious that only these byproducts of production manifest themselves consistently in speech and that the static targets do not.

As we suggested earlier, it is implausible to suppose that linguistic segments as they are known to a language-user are resistant to nondestructive realization in a vocal tract. Therefore, it is unlikely that targets are a vowel's canonical form, and is more likely that a vowel's essential properties are dynamic in nature.

We propose that the class of all vowels is an equivalence class of *gestures* which are equivalent in a broad sense. The members of the class of vowels are all gestures that aim toward some global shape and length of the vocal tract, although the particular shapes and lengths differ for different vowels. This property is not a trivial one, since it is not common to the consonants. Consonantal gestures do not aim toward asymptotic targets. Nor (insofar as it is accurate at all to describe consonants in terms of targets) are their targets *global* shapes of the vocal tract.

Along similar lines, a given vowel is an equivalence class of gestures that are equivalent because they all aim toward some particular limiting shape and length of the vocal tract. As we will argue, this view of vowels as gestures differs from a "targets" view more or less as a curve, say a hyperbola, differs from its asymptotes. We partition vowel production into three components, control of vocal tract length, of tongue shape and of global shape of the vocal tract. Our proposal deals only with that the last of these, but we briefly consider the first two.

Perkell (1969) suggests that the lengthening and shortening of the vocal tract are realized by two neuro-muscular systems that coordinate the lips, mandible, hyoid bone and larynx. One coordinative structure governs vocal tract lengthening, including lip rounding, and the other governs shortening for non-high vowels. With respect to tongue shape, Perkell (1969) suggests, as a first approximation, that it is invariant across the vowels and is characteristic of vowels as a class. Some more recent evidence of Lindblom and Sundberg (1971) suggests that Perkell's claim is a simplification; their data reveals *three* shapes of the tongue for 11 Swedish vowels. Tongue shape, therefore, as a responsibility of the intrinsic musculature of the tongue, may or may not be set invariantly across the class of vowels.

Of immediate concern here is control over global vocal tract shape as determined primarily by the position of the tongue in the vocal tract. Tongue position is governed by the extrinsic tongue muscles and, hence, our metaphor concerns the organization imposed on those muscles when vowels are produced.

To describe the production of vowels, we are looking for a system for positioning of the tongue which captures those properties of the class of vowels that are equivalent across its membership. An equation like that of a vibratory system, say $F = -s(l - l_0)$, with the parameter l_0 unspecified, would satify that criterion because it represents a system which establishes l_0 as a variable (tunable) dimension for the class of vowels. In addition, we are looking for a description of a particular vowel that enables us to describe as equivalent the different gestures that instantiate it in different contexts. (The reader is reminded that for /ɛ/, the tongue is lower following /i/, but raised following /a/.) Possibly l_0 will work to do that, if we describe it at an abstract level as the zero-state of the extrinsic tongue system. (At a less abstract level, each extrinsic muscle may have its own l_0.) l is the actual state of the tongue system (the actual position of the tongue).

Consider what happens to a spring system when F and s are unchanged, but l_0 is reduced in magnitude. To counteract the same $-F$, the system decreases l by the same amount as l_0 was decreased. Thus l alters *in the direction of the new* l_0. (For example, let $l_0 = 10$ in arbitrary units, $F = 50$, $s = 25$. Transforming the equation above, $l = l_0 - (F/s)$, $= 10 - 2 = 8$. If now l_0 is reset to 5, $l = 5 - 2 = 3$.) Again, suppose that l_0 corresponds to the zero-state of the extrinsic tongue system—to the position that the tongue would adopt if $-F = 0$, and l is the actual position of the tongue. If a talker is able to alter l_0 volitionally, as the subjects of Asatryan and Fel'dman (1965) could, then he can change the zero-state of the extrinsic musculature. Suppose that corresponding to a particular vowel is a particular value of l_0, initiated by changing the value of l_0. In consequence of this, and *regardless of its current* value, l, the actual position of the tongue in the mouth, alters its value in the direction of l_0. Hence, in the case of the vowel /ɛ/ its l_0 is less than that for the vowel /i/ and greater than that for /a/. When $l_{\emptyset\varepsilon}$ is substituted for $l_{\emptyset i}$, the tongue is lowered; when it is substituted for $l_{\emptyset a}$, the tongue is raised. Although the gesture is different for /ɛ/ in the different contexts, the parameter $l_{\emptyset\varepsilon}$ is the same.

This proposal is highly speculative, of course, and it is likely to be falsified in its *particulars* (e.g. in the proposal that the extrinsic muscles of the tongue are organized to work as a *linear* spring). What is critical to the proposal, however, is the general suggestion that the invariants for vowels are *organizations* of the musculature. The organizations do not yield invariant movements, nor do they yield static configurations of the vocal tract (nor, for that matter, do they yield simple acoustic correlates). Thus a vowel, /ɛ/ for example, is essentially the functioning of the coordinative structure encompassing the extrinsic tongue muscles (among other coordinative structures) when a tunable parameter of the system is given its /ɛ/-characteristic value. Thereby, /ɛ/ is canonically dynamic. Furthermore, it is context-free since, regardless of context, it is always produced when its invariant parameter value is assigned to the mapping governing vowel production.

It is perhaps worth emphasizing how this view is distinct from one equating a vowel with a spatial target or a feature bundle. The parameter l_0 itself may turn out to be indistinct from a spatial target or a feature bundle. However, l_0 is just a parameter *of* a system. As we argued earlier, a parameter is an *attribute* of something; it is not something in itself. Hence, it makes no sense to speak of the parameter apart from the mapping that it parameterizes.

Furthermore, an advantage of including the mapping in a vowel's specification—that is, of including the description of the muscle organization underlying vowel production—is that the specification captures the dynamic character of vowels. Movement can be considered inherent to vowel production. In contrast, to exclude the muscle organization is to make the implausible claim that, ideally, vowels are static. That is why we suggest that it is as incorrect to equate $l_{\emptyset\varepsilon}$ with /ɛ/ as it is to equate a curve with its asymptote. $l_{\emptyset\varepsilon}$ is just the limiting shape of the vocal tract towards which /ɛ/ invariably aims.

To summarize, we suggest that vowels, as they are known and produced are "organizational invariants" of the vocal tract. As such they are dynamic and context-free. Furthermore, they are *separate* from consonants (and hence their serial ordering with respect to consonants can be detected by a perceiver) because the organizational invariants for vowels perpetrate a different *kind* of articulatory and acoustic event than those for consonants.

Finally, we return to our earlier discussion of the degrees of freedom problem and its implicit solution in theories of speech production. As we reported, these theories suppose talkers to include in their articulatory plans only specifications for the vocal tract that require idiosyncratic moment-to-moment control. In particular, suprasegmental regularities are excluded from the plan. This proposal makes the degrees of freedom problem manageable, but does not explain how and why suprasegmental properties are governed, nor how they are coordinated with segments.

We have suggested that vowels as an articulatory class are characterized by an invariant, tunable organization of the musculature. Ohman (1966, 1967) and after him Perkell (1969), argue that, for the most part, different muscles are involved in vowel and consonant production. Thus, vowels and consonants can be, and are, coarticulated. In addition, Ohman suggests that vowels are continuously produced, at least in a vowel-consonant-vowel utterance, and his suggestion is given support by the recent work of Barry and Kuenzel (1975) and Butcher and Weiher (1976). All of this is compatible with the proposal that a talker establishes the invariant organization of his musculature for vowels at the beginning of his utterance and, insofar as possible, maintains it throughout. Thus, his articulatory plan need not repeatedly reestablish the vowel characteristic vocal-tract organization. From moment to moment it has only to provide the appropriate parameter values that select the particular vowels he wishes to produce. This invariant organization of the musculature, with a duration that is suprasegmental, may be responsible for the prosody of speech. Consonant with this proposal, prosody is typically considered to be "carried" by the vowels.

Thus, at least with respect to vowels, theories of speech production may be correct in treating something like the spatial target as a constituent of a plan for the *moment-to-moment* control of speech. However, these targets are assigned *to* a muscle organization that a talker also regulates, though at a slower pace. In short, the degrees of freedom problem may be solved by a talker regulating as much as possible at a slower rate, and as little as possible from moment to moment.

The work reported here was supported by the following grants to Haskins Laboratories: NIH grants HD01994 and NS13617, NSF grant BNS76-82023.

References

Abbs, J. H. (1973a). Some mechanical properties of lower lip movement during speech production. *Phonetica* **28**, 65–75.

Abbs, J. H. (1973b). The influence of the gamma motor system on jaw movements during speech: a theoretical framework and some preliminary observations. *Journal of Speech and Hearing Research* **16**, 175–200.

Abbs, J. H. and Eilenberg, G. R. (1976). Peripheral mechanisms of speech motor control. *In* "Contemporary Issues in Experimental Phonetics" (N. J. Lass, ed.), pp. 139–168. Academic Press, New York.

Abbs, J. H. and Netsell, R. (1973). A dynamic analysis of two-dimensional muscle force contributions to lower lip movement. *Journal of the Acoustical Society of America* **53**, 295.

Abbs, J. H., Folkins, J. W. and Sivarajan, M. (1976). Motor impairment following blockade of the infraorbital nerve: Implications for the use of anesthetization techniques in speech research. *Journal of Speech and Hearing Research* **19**, 19–35.

Adams, J. A. (1971). A closed-loop theory of motor learning. *Journal of Motor Behavior* **3**, 111–150.

Amerman, J. D. and Daniloff, R. G. (1971). Articulation patterns resulting from modification of oral cavity size. *ASHA* **13**, 559.

Arbib, M. A. (1972). "The Metaphorical Brain. An Introduction to Cybernetics as Artificial Intelligence and Brain Theory". J. Wiley & Sons, New York.

Arshavskzy, Yu. I., Kots, Ya. M., Orlovsky, G. N., Rodionov, I. M. and Shik, M. L. (1965). Investigation of the biomechanics of running by the dog. *Biophysics* **10**, 737–746.

Arutyunyan, G. A., Gurfinkel, V. S. and Mirskii, M. L. (1968). Investigation of aiming at a target. *Biophysics* **13**, 642–645.

Arutyunyan, G. A., Gurfinkel, V. S. and Mirskii, M. L. (1969). Organization of movements on execution by man of an exact postural task. *Biophysics* **14**, 1162–1167.

Asatryan, D. and Fel'dman, A. (1965). Functional tuning of the nervous system with control of movement or maintenance of a steady posture—I. Mechanographic analyses of the work of the joint on execution of a postural task. *Biophysics* **10**, 925–935.

Ashby, W. R. (1956). "An Introduction to Cybernetics". J. Wiley & Sons, New York.

Barry, W. and Kuenzel, H. (1975). Co-articulatory airflow characteristics of intervocalic voiceless plosives. *Journal of Phonetics* **3**, 263–282.

Bell-Berti, F. and Harris, K. (1979). Anticipatory coarticulation: Some implications from a study of lip rounding. *Journal of the Acoustical Society of America*, **65**, 1268–1270.

Bernstein, N. (1967). "The Coordination and Regulation of Movements". Pergamon Press, London.

Borden, G. J., Harris, K. S. and Oliver, W. (1973a). Oral feedback I. Variability of the effect of nerve-block anesthesia upon speech. *Journal of Phonetics* **1**, 289–295.

Borden, G. J., Harris, K. S. and Catena, L. (1973b). Oral feedback II. An electromyographic study of speech under nerve block anesthesia. *Journal of Phonetics* **1**, 297–308.

Boylls, C. C. (1975). A theory of cerebellar function with applications to locomotion. II. The relation of anterior lobe climbing fiber function to locomotor behavior in the cat. *COINS Technical Report* 76–1, Department of Computer and Information Science, University of Massachusetts.

Butcher, A. and Weiher, E. (1976). An electropalatographic investigation of coarticulation in VCV sequences. *Journal of Phonetics* **4**, 59–74.

Carpenter, M. B. (1972). "Core Text of Neuroanatomy". Williams and Wilkins, Baltimore.

Chomsky, N. (1965). "Aspects of the Theory of Syntax". MIT Press, Cambridge, Mass.

Daniloff, R. and Hammarberg, R. (1973). On defining coarticulation. *Journal of Phonetics* **1**, 239–248.

Donegan, P. and Stampe, D. (1977). Natural phonology. Paper presented at the Conference on the Differentiation of Current Phonological Theories. Indiana University, Bloomington, September 30.

Draper, M. H., Ladefoged, P. and Whitteridge, D. (1959). Respiratory muscles in speech. *Journal of Speech and Hearing Research* **2**, 16–27.

Easton, T. A. (1972). On the normal use of reflexes. *American Scientist* **60**, 591–599.

Eccles, J. C. (1969). The dynamic loop hypothesis of movement control. *In*

"Information Processing in the Nervous System" (K. N. Leibovic, ed.), pp. 245–269. Springer-Verlag, New York.

Evarts, E. V., Bizzi, E., Burke, R. E., DeLong, M. and Thach, W. T. (1971). Central control of movement. *Neurosciences Research Program Bulletin* **9**, No. 1.

Fel'dman, A. G. (1966a). Functional tuning of the nervous system with control of movement or maintenance of a steady posture—II. Controllabe parameters of the muscles. *Biophysics* **11**, 565–578.

Fel'dman, A. G. (1966b). Functional tuning of the nervous system during control of movement or maintenance of a steady posture—III. Mechanographic analysis of the execution by man of the simplest motor tasks. *Biophysics* **11**, 766–775.

Fitch, H. and Turvey, M. T. (1978). On the control of activity: Some remarks from an ecological point of view. *In* "Psychology of Motor Behavior and Sports" (R. W. Christina, ed.), Human Kinetics, Urbana, Illinois.

Folkins, J. W. and Abbs, J. H. (1975). Lip and motor control during speech: Responses to resistive loading of the jaw. *Journal of Speech and Hearing Research* **18**, 207–220.

Folkins, J. W. and Abbs, J. H. (1976). Additional observations on responses to resistive loading of the jaw. *Journal of Speech and Hearing Research* **19**, 820–821.

Fowler, C. A. (1977). Timing control in speech production. Indiana University Linguistics Club, Bloomington.

Fowler, C. A. and Turvey, M. T. (1978). Skill acquisition: An event approach with special reference to searching for the optimum of a function of several variables. To appear in "Information Processing in Motor Control and Learning" (G. Stelmach, ed.), Academic Press, New York.

Garner, W. R. (1974). "The processing of Information and Structure". Lawrence Erlbaum Associates, Potomac, Maryland.

Gay, T. and Ushijima, T. (1974). Effect of speaking rate on stop consonant-vowel articulation. *In* "Proceedings of the Speech Communication Seminar, Stockholm, 1974". Almqvist and Wiksell, Uppsala, pp. 205–209.

Gel'fand, I. M. and Tsetlin, M. L. (1962). Some methods of control for complex systems. *Russian Mathematical Surveys* **17**, 95–116.

Gel'fand, I. M. and Tsetlin, M. L. (1971). Mathematical modeling of mechanisms of the central nervous system. *In* "Models of the Structural-Functional Organization of Certain Biological Systems" (I. M. Gel'fand, V. S. Gurfinkel, S. V. Fomin and M. T. Tsetlin, eds), pp. 1–22. MIT Press, Cambridge, Mass.

Gibson, J. J. (1950). "The Perception of the Visual World". Houghton-Mifflin, Boston.

Gibson, J. J. (1961). Ecological optics. *Vision Research* **1**, 253–262.

Gibson, J. J. (1966). "The Senses Considered as a Perceptual System". Houghton-Mifflin, Boston.

Gottlieb, G. L. and Agarwarl, G. C. (1972). The role of the myotatic reflex in the vocabulary control of movements. *Brain Research* **40**, 139–143.

Gottlieb, G. L. and Agarwarl, G. C. (1973). Coordination of posture and movement. *In* "New Developments in Electromyography and Clinical Neurophysiology" (J. E. Desmedt, ed.), pp. 418–427. S. Karger, Basel.

Gottlieb, G. L., Agarwarl, G. C. and Stark, L. (1970). Interactions between voluntary and postural mechanisms of the human motor system. *Journal of Neurophysiology* **33**, 365–381.

Greene, P. H. (1972). Problems of organization of motor systems. *In* "Progress in Theoretical Biology, Vol. 2" (R. Rosen and F. Snell, eds), pp. 304–322. Academic Press, New York.

Grillner, S. (1975). Locomotion in vertebrates: central mechanisms and reflex interaction. *Physiological Reviews* **55**, 247–304.

Groesberg, S. W. (1968). "Advanced Mechanics". J. Wiley & Sons, New York.

Gurfinkel, V. S., Kots, Ya. M., Pal'tsev, E. I. and Fel'dman, A. G. (1971). The compensation of respiratory disturbances of the erect posture of man as an example of the organization of interarticular interaction. *In* "Models of the Structural-Functional Organization of Certain Biological Systems" (I. M. Gel'fand, V. S. Gurfinkel, S. V. Fomin and M. L. Tsetlin, eds), pp. 382–395. MIT Press, Cambridge, Mass.

Hamlet, S. L. and Stone, M. (1976). Compensatory vowel characteristics resulting from the presence of different types of experimental dental prostheses. *Journal of Phonetics* **4**, 199–218.

Hammarberg, R. (1976). The metaphysics of coarticulation. *Journal of Phonetics* **4**, 353–363.

Harris, K. S. (1976). The study of articulatory organization: Some negative progress. *In* "Dynamic Aspects of Speech Production" (M. Sawashima and F. S. Cooper, eds), pp. 71–82. University of Tokyo, Tokyo.

Hintikka, J. (1975). Information, causality and the logic of perception. *In* "The Intention of Intentionality and Other New Models for Modalities" (J. Hintikka, ed.), pp. 59–75. D. Reidel, Dordrecht, Holland, Boston.

Hockett, C. (1955). "A Manual of Phonology". International Journal of Linguistics. Waverly Press, Baltimore.

Hubbard, A. W. (1960). Homokinetics: Muscular function in human movement. *In* "Science and Medicine of Exercise and Sport" (W. R. Johnson, ed.), pp. 7–39. Harper, New York.

Ito, M. (1970). Neurophysiological aspects of the cerebellar motor control system. *International Journal of Neurology* **7**, 162–176.

Johansson, G. (1973). Visual perception of biological motion and a model for its analysis. *Perception & Psychophysics* **14**, 201–211.

Kaplan, H. M. (1971). "Anatomy and Physiology of Speech". Second edition. McGraw-Hill, New York.

Kent, R. D. (1976). Models of speech production. *In* "Contemporary Issues in Experimental Phonetics" (N. Lass, ed.), pp. 79–104. Academic Press, New York.

Kent, R. D. and Minifie, F. D. (1977). Coarticulation in recent speech production models. *Journal of Phonetics* **5**, 115–133.

Kent, R. D. and Moll, K. L. (1975). Articulatory timing in selected consonant sequences. *Brain and Language* **2**, 304–323.

Kent, R. D. and Netsell, R. (1971). Effects of stress contrasts on certain articulatory parameters. *Phonetica* **24**, 23–44.

Kent R. D., Carney, P. J. and Severeid, L. R. (1974). Velar movement and timing: Evaluation of a model for binary control. *Journal of Speech and Hearing Research* **17**, 470–488.

Klatt, D. (1976). Linguistic uses of segmental duration in English: Acoustic and perceptual evidence. *Journal of the Acoustical Society of America* **59**, 1208–1221.

Kulagin, A. S. and Shik, M. L. (1970). Interaction of symmetrical limbs during controlled locomotion. *Biophysics* **15**, 171–178.

Kuypers, H. G. J. M. (1958). Cortico-bulbar connexions to the pons and lower brain stem in man. *Brain* **81**, 364–388.

Ladefoged, P. (1968). Linguistic aspects of respiratory phenomena. *Annals of the New York Academy of Sciences* **155**, 141–151.

Lambertsen, C. J. (1974). Neurogenic factors in control of respiration. *In* "Medical

Physiology, Vol. 2" (V. B. Mountcastle, ed.), pp. 1423–1446. C. V. Mosby, St. Louis.

Lashley, K. S. (1951). The problem of serial order in behavior. *In* "Cerebral Mechanisms in Behavior: the Hixon Symposium" (L. A. Jeffress, ed.), pp. 112–136. J. Wiley & Sons, New York.

Lee, D. N. (1974). Visual information during locomotion. *In* "Perception: Essays in Honor of James J. Gibson" (R. B. MacLeod and H. L. Pick, Jr., eds), pp. 250–267. Cornell University Press, Ithaca, New York.

Lenneberg, E. H. (1967). "Biological Foundations of Language". J. Wiley & Sons, New York.

Liberman, A. M., Cooper, F. S., Shankweiler, D. P. and Studdert-Kennedy, M. (1967). Perception of the speech code. *Psychological Review* **74**, 431–461.

Liberman, A. M. and Studdert-Kennedy, M. (1978). Phonetic perception. *In* "Handbook of Sensory Physiology, Vol. VIII, 'Perception' " (R. Held, H. Leibowitz and H.-L. Teuber, eds). Springer-Verlag, Heidelberg.

Lieberman, P. (1967). "Intonation, Perception and Language", MIT Press, Cambridge, Mass.

Lindblom, B. and Sundberg, J. (1971). Acoustical consequences of lip, tongue, jaw and larynx movement. *Journal of the Acoustical Society of America* **50**, 1166–1179.

Lindblom, B. and Sundberg, J. (1973). Neurophysiological representation of speech sounds. Paper presented at the XV World Congress of Logopedics and Phoniatrics, Buenos Aires, Argentina.

Lindblom, B., Lubker, J. and Gay, T. (1979). Formant frequencies of some fixed-mandible vowels and a model of speech motor programming by predictive simulation *Journal of Phonetics.* **7**, 147–162.

Lisker, L. (1974). On time and timing in speech. *In* "Current Trends in Linguistics (Vol. 12)" (T. A. Sebeok, ed.), pp. 2387–2418. Mouton and Co., The Hague.

Lisker, L. (1976). Phonetic aspects of time and timing. Paper presented at the 100th meeting of the American Speech and Hearing Association, Washington, D.C., November, 1975. Also in *Haskins Laboratories Status Report on Speech Research* SR–47, 113–120.

Mace, W. (1977). James J. Gibson's strategy for perceiving: Ask not what's inside your head, but what your head's inside of. *In* "Perceiving, Acting, and Knowing: Toward an Ecological Psychology" (R. Shaw and J. Bransford, eds), pp. 43–65. Erlbaum, Hillsdale, New Jersey.

MacKay, D. G. (1969). Forward and backward masking in motor systems. *Kybernetik* **2**, 57–64.

MacKay, D. G. (1970). Spoonerisms: The structure of errors in the serial order of speech. *Neuropsychologia* **8**, 323–350.

MacNeilage, P. F. (1970). Motor control of serial ordering of speech. *Psychological Review* **77**, 182–196.

MacNeilage, P. and Ladefoged, P. (1976). The production of speech and language. *In* "Handbook of Perception, Volume VII" (E. C. Carterette and M. P. Friedman, eds), pp. 75–120. Academic Press, New York.

Moll, K. L., Zimmerman, G. N. and Smith, A. (1976). The study of speech production as a human neuromotor system. *In* "Dynamic Aspects of Speech Production" (M. Sawashima and F. S. Cooper, eds), pp. 107–127. University of Tokyo, Tokyo.

Netsell, R. and Abbs, J. H. (1975). Modulation of perioral reflex sensitivity during speech production. Paper presented to the *Acoustical Society of America*, San Francisco, California.

Ohman, S. E. G. (1966). Coarticulation in VCV utterances: Spectrographic measurements. *Journal of the Acoustical Society of America* **39**, 151–168.

Ohman, S. E. G. (1967). Numerical model of coarticulation. *Journal of the Acoustical Society of America* **41**, 310–320.

Pattee, H. (1973). The physical basis and origin of hierarchical control. *In* "Hierarchy Theory: The Challenge of Complex Systems" (H. Pattee, ed.), pp. 71–108. Braziller, New York.

Perkell, J. S. (1969). "Physiology of Speech Production: Results and Implications of a Quantitative Cineradiographic Study". MIT Press, Cambridge, Mass.

Pew, R. W. (1974). Human perceptual-motor performance. *In* "Human Information Processing. Tutorials in Performance and Cognition" (B. H. Kantowitz, ed.), Erlbaum, New York.

Pisoni, D. (1978). Speech perception. To appear in "Handbook of Learning and Cognitive Processes" (W. K. Estes, ed.), Erlbaum, Hillsdale, New Jersey.

Powers, W. T. (1973). "Behavior: The Control of Perception". Aldine, Chicago.

Putnam, A. H. B. and Ringel, R. L. (1976). A cineradiographic study of articulation in two talkers with temporarily induced oral sensory deprivation. *Journal of Speech and Hearing Research* **19**, 247–266.

Remez, R. E. and Rubin, P. E. (1975). Is speech like *anything* else people do, or is it like *everything* else people do? Unpublished manuscript, University of Connecticut.

Ringel, R. L. and Steer, M. D. (1963). Some effects of tactile and auditory alterations on speech output. *Journal of Speech and Hearing Research* **6**, 369–378.

Riordan, C. J. (1977). Control of vocal-tract length in speech. *Journal of the Acoustical Society of America* **62**, 998–1002.

Saltzman, E. (1977). On levels of sensorimotor representation. Unpublished manuscript, University of Minnesota.

Schmidt, R. A. (1975). A schema theory of discrete motor skill learning. *Psychological Review* **82**, 225–260.

Scott, C. M. and Ringel, R. L. (1971). Articulation without oral sensory control. *Journal of Speech and Hearing Research* **14**, 804–818.

Sears, T. A. and Newsom Davis, J. (1968). The control of respiratory muscles during voluntary breathing. *Annals of the New York Academy of Science* **55**, 183–190.

Shankweiler, D., Strange, W. and Verbrugge, R. (1977). Speech and the problem of perceptual constancy. *In* "Perceiving, Acting, and Knowing: Toward an Ecological Psychology" (R. Shaw and J. Bransford, eds), pp. 315–345. Erlbaum, Hillsdale, New Jersey.

Shaw, R. and Pittenger, J. (1977). Perceiving the face of change in changing faces: Implications for a theory of object perception. *In* "Perceiving, Acting, and Knowing: Toward an Ecological Psychology" (R. Shaw and J. Bransford, eds), pp. 103–132. Erlbaum, Hillsdale, New Jersey.

Shaw, R., McIntyre, M. and Mace, W. (1974). The role of symmetry in event perception. *In* "Perception: Essays in Honor of James J. Gibson" (R. B. MacLeod and H. L. Pick, Jr., eds), pp. 276–310. Cornell University Press, Ithaca, New York.

Shaw, R., Turvey, M. T. and Mace, W. (In press). Ecological psychology: The consequence of a commitment to realism. "Cognition and the Symbolic Processes, Vol. 2" (W. Weimer and D. S. Palermo, eds), Erlbaum, Hillsdale, New Jersey.

Shik, M. L. and Orlovsky, G. N. (1965). Coordination of the limbs during running of the dog. *Biophysics* **10**, 1148–1159.

Shik, M. L. and Orlovsky, G. N. (1976). Neurophysiology of locomotor automatism. *Physiological Reviews* **56**, 465–501.

Shik, M. L., Orlovsky, G. N. and Severin, F. V. (1966). Organization of locomotor synergism. *Biophysics* **11**, 1011–1019.

Stevens, K. N. (1975). The potential role of property detectors in the perception of consonants. *In* "Auditory Analysis and the Perception of Speech" (G. Fant and M. A. A. Tatham, eds), pp. 303–330. Academic Press, New York.

Studdert-Kennedy, M. (1978). Universals in phonetic structure and their role in linguistic communication. "The Recognition of Complex Acoustic Signals" (T. H. Bullock, ed.), Dahlem Konferenzen, Berlin.

Sussman, H. M., MacNeilage, P. F. and Hanson, R. J. (1973). Labial and mandibular dynamics during the production of bilabial consonants: Preliminary observations. *Journal of Speech and Hearing Research* **16**, 397–420.

Timoshenko, S. and Young, D. H. (1948). "Advanced Dynamics". McGraw-Hill, New York.

Turvey, M. T. (1977a). Preliminaries to a theory of action with reference to vision. *In* "Perceiving, Acting, and Knowing: Toward an Ecological Psychology" (R. Shaw and J. Bransford, eds), pp. 211–265. Erlbaum, Hillsdale, New Jersey.

Turvey, M. T. (1977b). Contrasting orientations to a theory of visual information processing. *Psychological Review* **84**, 67–88.

Turvey, M. T. and Shaw, R. (1979). The primacy of perceiving: An ecological reformulation of perception as a point of departure for understanding memory. "Perspectives on Memory Research: Essays in Honor of Uppsala University's 500th Anniversary" (L-G Nilsson, ed.). Erlbaum, New Jersey.

Turvey, M. T., Shaw, R. and Mace W. (1979). Issues in the theory of action: Degrees of freedom, coordinative structures and coalitions. *In* "Attention and Performance, VII" (J. Requin, ed.), Erlbaum, Hillsdale, New Jersey.

Ushijima, T. and Hirose, H. (1974). Electromyographic study of the velum during speech. *Journal of Phonetics* **2**, 315–326.

Warren, R. M. (1976). Auditory illusions and perceptual processes. *In* "Contemporary Issues in Experimental Phonetics" (N. Lass, ed.), pp. 389–417. Academic Press, New York.

Weiss, P. (1941). Self-differentiation of the basic pattern of coordination. *Comparative Psychology Monograph* **17**, 21–96.

Wyke, B. D. (1967). Recent advances in the neurology of phonation: phonatory reflex mechanisms in the larynx. *British Journal of Communication Disorders* **2**, 2–14.

Wyke, B. D. (1974). Laryngeal myotatic reflexes and phonation. *Folia Phoniatrica* **26**, 249–264.

Zemlin, W. R. (1968). "Speech and Hearing Science: Anatomy and Physiology". Prentice-Hall, Englewood Cliffs, New Jersey.

V
Summary

15
Some Constraints on Models of Language Production

B. Butterworth   *University of Cambridge*

I. Preamble

In this concluding chapter, I shall try to make good some of the claims that motivated this volume and were outlined in Chapter 1. The first claim was that we actually know quite a lot about language production, even though this knowledge has come from rather scattered sources. The second claim was that the methodology of production studies is "transparent" compared, say, to studies of comprehension, since we have the opportunity of analysing directly the naturally-occurring exercise of speaking abilities. Thirdly, I claimed that since the many aspects of production are revealed by studying naturally-occurring speech—or close approximations to it—the outcomes of these studies can be combined to provide a coherent set of constraints on possible models.

If you have read the preceding chapters, no further justification is needed for the first two claims. However, to get the third claim off the ground, I need to find a common theoretical vocabulary to collate the findings reported by the contributors. This is necessarily a psychological vocabulary since only psychological processes can mediate the social conditions on production and the concomitant mechanical activity of the vocal musculature. In the following sections, I outline a plausible vocabulary and then attempt to use it to collate theory and data in a systematic way.

II. What's in a Model?

Models of psychological processes, if they don't actually abound, at least exist in reasonable numbers. However, there is almost nothing in the literature characterizing the general properties of the kinds of entities and processes that might be postulated, nor, more importantly, the general conditions on models of different sorts (though see, Turvey *et al.*, 1978). To cut a long story short, there are at least three distinct and fundamental questions that need to be asked of a model:

(1) What kinds of information are represented?

(2) What control processes regulate the transfer and transformation of information?
(3) What are the constraints on the capacity to transfer and transform information?

A. Levels of Representation

There seems broad agreement about certain kinds of information that must be represented in the model. These can be roughly characterized using the levels of description employed by linguists. That is to say, the model will have to represent phonetic, phonological, morphological, syntactic and lexical information. But, as in linguistics, there will be areas of dispute—for example, do lexical representations include all words used and understood by the speaker, or just open-class items, and of these, only stems, or all derived forms as well? (i.e. does the lexicon contain *divine* and *divinity*, or just *divine*, or even something more abstract like /dɪviːn/ as proposed by Chomsky and Halle (1968)?)

A second area of dispute can be treated as an issue of representations *or* of control processes: how do representations link up? This can be thought of either as a question of the representation of invariant mapping relations among units at different representational levels, or as a question of how the control processes utilize information from different representational levels to carry out the relevant computations. Take one case discussed by **Gazdar**†
(Chapter 3, this volume)—pragmatic constraints on deletion (p. 57). It can be argued that syntactic processes are directly sensitive to these constraints—i.e. that there occurs in the system a mapping from, say, Deep Structure syntactic representations *and* a representation of the pragmatic conditions on the utterance, to a surface realization. Alternatively, the model could simply cycle through syntactic realizations until a pragmatically suitable realization comes up. This latter treatment leaves syntax autonomous, and locates pragmatic constraints in the control process—that is, a control device is postulated to check the output from the syntactic system, and will only let through structures (representations) which conform to the pragmatic constraints.‡ It is not clear how one would decide between these models, but a research strategy which advocates keeping representational systems simple and fixed in their operation but allowing flexibility in control would favour the latter.

There will be cases where control processes cannot easily account for relations among representations. **Cooper** (Chapter 12) demonstrates the influence of Deep syntactic boundaries on syllable timing; the most natural

---

†Bold lettering indicates a reference to a chapter in this volume.

‡This kind of account invariably encounters the criticism that it would be too slow, or too inefficient, since the number of alternatives generated would be very large. Arguments based on cortical efficiency generally must wait upon better evidence about the brain's actual, not hypothesised, efficiency criteria. And it is not clear that a large number of alternatives would indeed be generated. In Gazdar's example, there are only two: deleted and undeleted.

way to treat this is to locate Deep syntactic markers directly in the phonological or phonetic representation, such that the system responsible for organizing timing is sensitive to boundary phenomena. (One way of achieving this is suggested below on page 433.)

B. Control Processes

The general properties of the principal kinds of control structure have been well described by Turvey *et al.* (1978). They discuss the possible arrangements of "dominance" relations among the components in a system. Roughly, **A** dominates **B** if **A** can transfer control to **B**, but **B** cannot transfer control to **A**. (We will need to extend the notion of "dominance" below.)

In a simple *chain*, Like (4), where ⟶ ⅃ indicates the dominance relationship

(4)

A dominates **B**, and **B** dominates **C**. In the simple divergent *hierarchy*, (5), **A** dominates both **B** and **C**.

(5)

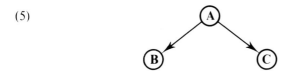

Heterarchies involve transfer of control from a node directly or indirectly dominated by a given node back to that given node. Thus, in the simple triadic heterarchy (6),

(6)

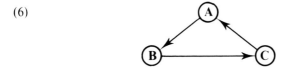

A dominates **B**, which dominates **C**, and **C** dominates **A**.

In addition, the effects of feedback loops can be characterized. For example, if feedback loops are added to (5), returning control to **A**, the hierarchically organized heterarchy (7), results.

(7)

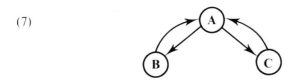

Here **A** transfers control to **B**, but **B**, in turn can transfer control to **A**.

Notice that these diagrams represent *control* structures: they define only dominance relations among nodes; they do not define the relations among the representations computed at nodes **A**, **B**, and **C**. Now it has been frequently pointed out that linguistic representations can be hierarchically related as in a standard phrase-structure tree. The general format is given in (8),

(8)

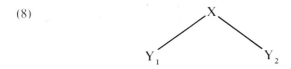

The structural similarity between (8) and (5) is obvious, but misleading. Representation (8) can be generated by any of the control structures mentioned above. (9) is an example of a chain structure producing this hierarchy.

(9)

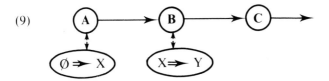

(9) states that the representational system controlled by **A** maps Øs (null symbols) into Xs, and representational system controlled by **B** maps the output of the **A** system, Xs, into Ys. There is nothing here to prevent any number of symbols at the Y-level being generated from a single X-level symbol; and, of course, the chain can be extended, via nodes **C**, **D**, etc., with their concomitant representational system, to generate trees of any desired depth.

Notice that I have surreptitiously introduced representational systems associated with control nodes—control structures have to control something. A control node is defined as having two functions with respect to their associated representational system: it regulates the flow of information into the representational system (i.e. **B** allows Xs, and only Xs, as input) and it initiates the transformation of input symbols into output symbols, in this case, Ys. It cannot, by definition, intervene in the transformation process. However, with the addition of a loop back from the representational system to the control node, it can carry out additional functions. Of most interest to us is a monitoring function, whereby the output from the representational system can be evaluated against a goal. In this way, for example, candidate syntactic structures can be evaluated for semantic or pragmatic appropriateness before control is transferred to the next control node.

Two further elaborations of control structure will need to be considered. First is what Turvey *et al.* (1978) call a "covergent" structure, as in (10)

(10)
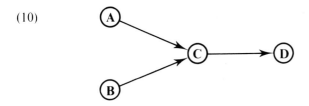

Convergent dominance can be realized in several ways: **C** can act as an AND-gate accepting transfer of control if control is passed by both **A** and **B**. **C** can act as an OR-gate, accepting control from either **A** or **B**. **C** can combine the outputs from the systems controlled by **A** and **B**. Or **C** can check the output of its own system against outputs from **A** or **B** or both, before transferring control to **D**. In the last case, for example, if **C** controls the syntactic system, it may only transfer control to **D** if the output structure is appropriate to the semantic information supplied by **A** and the pragmatic information supplied by **B**.

Second, there is the complementary "divergent" structure, in which a node transfers control to more than one other node (this is equivalent to (5), of course, but is repeated for convenience).

(11)
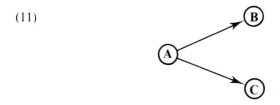

This will turn out to be useful if the output of a single representational system is transformed by two or more downstream systems. For example, if the data indicates that a given semantic output is independently transferred to the syntactic and lexical systems, this will be the appropriate control structure.

Naturally, the data may compel us to postulate complex control structures with convergent and divergent parts, perhaps with heterarchical components and feedback loops.

C. Autonomy and Interaction

A representational system, X, is defined as a system that takes one or more input codes and transforms them into a single output code, X. For example, the syntactic system takes as its input symbols in a semantic code, say, and transforms these into an output code consisting of, perhaps, a labelled bracketing with grammatical morphemes and some function words. The system will be autonomous if the transformational process makes reference only to the initial input symbols and to no other information. It will be interactive if, *in the course of the transformational process*, information is recruited from other systems.

A priori, the interaction between two representational systems can be achieved if their codes are common or overlap; a similar effect can be achieved if the control node of one system checks the output of its representational system against the output of another. (Computational models have been devised to work in this way, for example, see Reddy and Newell, 1979; Winograd, 1972; and see also Johnson-Laird, 1977, for an enlightening discussion of this issue.)

Let me take an example to illustrate the point. *Will*-deletion, a syntactic operation, is pragmatically conditioned, and can only occur if the speaker is committed to knowledge of the truth of his utterance. (See below, Section V.A, examples (47) and (48), for a fuller discussion: (47) b. The Yankees play tomorrow. (48) b. *The Yankees win tomorrow.)

If the syntactic system is interactive with respect to the pragmatic system, then the deletion transformation will be blocked directly in (48b), and will not occur. However, the same output can be realized if both the deleted and non-deleted forms are produced, but the deleted form may be rejected by the control node which can check system output against the output from the pragmatic system.

The deletion phenomena can thus be treated in two ways: in terms of the nature of the representational system, or in terms of the structure of control. Usually, the competing accounts will be too poorly specified to permit a decision between them. If both models can account for the pragmatic conditioning, further specification of the models is needed and additional data invoked. Processing time parameters could be hypothesized and compared with production delays, for instance.

Another kind of data that could be brought to bear are errors. Each system will have certain rules of operation. Its output may conform to these rules while violating the output of another system. The most striking examples are where speech is phonologically correct, but because of a spoonerism, deviates from the intended semantics ("hissed a mystery lesson") or contains a nonword ("heft lemisphere"). Such data yield very conveniently to an autonomy treatment. The lexical system supplies representations of the intended words, and a post-lexical system dealing with phonological structure misorders some of the phonological parts. Since this latter system will have rules of operation ensuring that its output conforms to the principles of

English phonology, errors will also conform to the principles. Internal error checking will weed out phonological errors, but checking lexical status will require returning via the control structure to recover the original lexical outputs, if still available, or to check its output against one of many items in the lexicon. Presumably, this checking routine is, to some extent discretionary, and also time-consuming, thus unintended sequences will get to articulation and may not be corrected. If the error results in a word, but the unintended word ("hissed the mystery lesson" instead of "missed the history lesson"), this may require two checks: one for lexical status (which will return a "Yes") and one for semantic appropriateness (which will return a "No"). The autonomy hypothesis, thus, explains these data and predicts fine-timing characteristics—in this case, phonological errors resulting in real words will take longer to correct than those not. Moreover it is not at all clear to me what an interactive treatment of this class of errors would be like. I shall, therefore, treat errors that conform to the rules of operation for some system X, but violate outputs from other systems, as *prima facie* evidence for the autonomy of X. That is to say, errors are a function of both the operation of representational systems and of the organization of control.

III. Defining Constraints on The Model

We can raise, therefore, three distinct general issues: constraints on representational systems, constraints on control processes, and constraints on capacity.

A. Representational Systems

Empirical and theoretical considerations indicated by the contributors (mainly) will help us to identify what representational systems need postulating, and to classify some aspects of their operation. By "theoretical considerations" I mean considerations of the conventions of language structure, interpretation and use, rather than considerations of how it is processed. For example, there are well-understood ways of representing the semantics of a sentence in terms of its truth-conditions; there are also ways of representing non-truth-conditional aspects of meaning. In fact, for some classes of sentence, truth-conditions can remain unaltered, while other aspects of meaning may vary (see Section IV.F). A sensible strategy would be to keep separate the representational systems responsible for these two sorts of meaning, even to look for additional processing evidence in support of the separation, unless, of course, other data compel us to amalgamate them into a single meaning-generating system.

B. Control Processes

The constraints to be defined here concern how information and control is transferred from system to system, so that at least the major phenomenon, that speech is coherent, appropriate and correct most of the time, is accounted for. In particular, we will be concerned with "dominance" relations among systems, and to what extent the operation of each system is autonomous.

C. Capacity

Representational systems will have limitations on how much they can do in a given amount of time, and what sized units they operate with. Capacity constraints mean defining the parameters of limitation on these individual systems, but also on the temporal relationship among the operations of the various systems. If, for instance, two systems converge in a third, but one takes longer to complete operations than the other, what will the third do? We will also consider how non-linguistic conversational behaviour coexists with linguistic behaviour; one does not converse by speech alone.

IV. Constraints on Representational Systems

A. Articulation

Conceptually, the problem of how to represent the articulatory component of the production system appears straightforward even though many details are still unclear. In essence, there must be a level at which a set of linguistic commands to the vocal musculature is represented—e.g. a string of phonemes or phonetic features. This much seems obvious. The difficult part, according to **Perkell**, is to find the transformation operations from the higher-level representations into the muscle commands in such a way that the linguistically relevant information is preserved in the vocal output. Notice that the higher level representation will consist of abstract featural descriptions of discrete entities, phonetic segments, with a complete ordering defined on them; whereas actual articulation cannot be broken down into discrete segments, and moreover articulatory movements do not correspond in one-to-one fashion to segments of features, or even in any discovered regular one-many or many-one correspondence. A given segment will be realized by different muscle movements according to the segmental context, the current state of the musculature, the degree of precision desired by the speaker, the temporal characteristics of the utterance, whether the segment occurs in a stressed or unstressed syllable, etc. Thus the mapping problem is exceedingly complex, since a given segment-to-muscle-command mapping must be sensitive to these features.

   Perkell attempts to solve this by invoking a number of intervening representational systems between featural descriptions and motor commands with a control structure including internal ("orosensory") and external (auditory) feedback loops to enable higher levels to be sensitive to the current state of the vocal tract. In this way the mapping problem gets broken down into more manageable components so that mapping relations between levels becomes simpler.

On the other hand, **Fowler, Remez, Rubin** and **Turvey** adopt a radically different approach. They argue that a translation programme that looks for the mappings between levels is fundamentally misconceived. They conclude that articulation, like other skilled actions, is the outcome of the activity of a "co-ordinative structure" organizing muscle groups. These structures couple muscular movements together in such a way that the degrees of freedom for each muscle are highly constrained by being in that structure; these constraints can be expressed in terms of an "equation of constraint" which defines the parameters of the structure and the relations among parameters in a relatively invariant way. The act of speaking sets values of parameters not already set by the current state of the system. Thus the volitional component in speaking—i.e. the component controlled by higher level representations— can be thought of as choosing the appropriate equation and setting the parameters left free in it. One handy feature of this kind of account is that "tuning" notions can be introduced very simply. Affective states conveyed through amplitude or frequency variation will be a consequence of embedding the co-ordinative structures for speech in other co-ordinative structures conditioning the behaviour of the whole person, where the embedding structure sets parameters in the embedded structure. Additionally, some of the pragmatic phenomena documented by **Gazdar** can be expressed straightforwardly as tunings of the system. For example, "ironic nasalization" in American English, or "dismissive labialization" in French, can be thought of as a setting of a single parameter contextually, and the higher level components, containing the phonetic information, set the remaining parameters in such a way as to preserve the invariant relationships among the parameters.

However, **Fowler** *et al.*, have only worked out an explanation for the vowel system, and this simply retrodicts the major phenomena—especially the consequences of parameters set by abnormal resistive loadings on the mandible: speakers can adapt so as to produce the correct vowel on the first pitch pulse though the vocal tract is distended. Although conceptually their account is very different from **Perkell's** it is not yet clear how to distinguish it empirically.

We have to say, then, that what appeared at first a straightforward problem, turns out to be controversial in principle.

Two things emerge clearly: *moment-to-moment* control of articulation requires information about the current state of the vocal tract musculature; but, ontogenetically, getting articulatory patterns to correspond to linguistic entities, and maintaining that correspondence requires auditory feedback. Whether we should talk about the establishment, exercise and maintenance of "orosensory goals" or "equations of constraint" will be the basis for future controversy.

There are also a range of problems to do with the timing of articulatory gestures, but these are not sufficiently well-documented to formulate clear constraints. First, there is the fine-grained timing of muscular movements to produce the intended syllables. Both **Perkell** and **Fowler** *et al.*, locate the timing mechanism in the motor system itself—**Perkell** postulates a matrix of "motor goal urgencies", **Fowler** *et al.*, imply that it will be a function of the co-ordinative structures themselves. Second, there is the coarser-grained timing involved in getting the syllables to come out sounding regularly-spaced. **Cutler and Isard** call this the "isochrony problem", and it is not clear where this effect should be located. The work of Morton *et al.* (1976) demonstrates that timing control at the syllable level depends, not on syllable onsets, offsets, or even amplitude maxima, but on the "perceptual centre" of the syllable and this is probably a complex function of the whole waveform envelope. Where such information should be represented is anyone's guess, but for a well-informed guess see Fowler (1977). Third, there are local variations in syllable timing conditioned by major syntactic boundaries. **Cooper** represents this constraint in the phonetic representation. In any event, timing parameters conditioned syntactically and by the need to preserve isochrony, must be made available to the articulatory system and must somehow form part of the information represented there.

B. The Phonetic System

The articulatory system must take as input a representation of the intended sound-sequence detailed enough for it to produce the appropriate phones in the correct order and with the appropriate intonation contour. Thus the model requires a representational system that can generate this representation as its output. Theoretical considerations indicate two levels of sound structure—the "systematic phonological level" ("Level 1") and the "systematic phonetic level" ("Level 2") (**Comrie**). Error data reinforce this distinction.

Widely reported in the error literature is the phenomenon of "phonetic accommodation" (**Garrett**, Fromkin (1971) etc). When an intended item, often a grammatical morpheme, shifts into an unintended position, its phonetic form accommodates to its new phonetic environment. Roughly, in an example like (12)

(12) . . . add ups ([ʌps]) to
       (Target: adds ([ædz]) up to)

the shifted grammatical morpheme /s/, which would have been pronounced /z/ in the target phrase is devoiced in the error environment where it follows an unvoiced obstruent. This suggests there is a level that has a representation like (13):

(13) a. Level 1: add + /s/ up to.

The error relocates the /s/ at this level, and the resultant representation (13b)

(13) b. Level 1: add up + /s/ to

is transferred to a system, which by its own rules of operation, transforms this representation into one where the sequence of phones conforms to the rules for English sequences: /æd + s/ would become [ædz], but /ʌp + s/ would become [ʌps]. In general, the rule is: /s/ is voiced only if the previous phoneme is voiced, unless the previous phoneme is a fricative or affricate when it becomes [əz] (e.g. mass + s → [mæsəz]). Thus (31b) becomes transformed into phonologically regular sequence (14)

(14)   Level 2: [æd ʌps tu].

Notice that the system that produces Level 2 representations, which I shall call the "Phonetic System", did not, for (14), check its output for lexical status. I therefore deduce that this system is autonomous with respect to the lexical system, though it may have the (discretionary) facility to cycle back, check and edit out erroneous sequences. Another example from Garrett illustrates this autonomy:

(15) I want to eated my beans first.

   (Target: I wanted to eat my beans first.)

Eated is not an English word. Fromkin (1971) reports an error where the transformation does appear to be lexically conditioned:

(16) Rosa always date shranks.

   (Target: Rosa always dated shrinks.)

She claims that the past tense morpheme /+əd/ has shifted from *date* to *shrink* giving the appropriate (irregular) form of the past tense, *shrank*. But this kind of case is very rare indeed. A check back for lexical status only will give a "Yes" for both *date* and *shrank* (assuming that the *s* had been stripped before the check). It would have given a "No" for *shrinked*.

It is convenient to propose that phonetic system operations include the specification of, at least, the regular allomorphic alternants. And there is some evidence that specification of allophonic alternants are handled by this system.

Cooper reports a number of phenomena that link syllable length to clausal location: generally, syllables are lengthened immediately before clause boundaries. In addition, a number of phonetic processes that link adjacent syllables are blocked by a "string" intervening boundary. The "Trochaic Shortening Rule" shortens a stressed syllable when it is followed by an unstressed syllable. If a clause boundary intervenes, this does not happen. "Inter-word palatalization", which turns *did you* into [dɪdʒu] is similarly blocked by a boundary between *did* and *you* (see also Cooper *et al.*, 1978). There is a straightforward account of these phenomena in terms of the model framework. The rules of operation of the phonetic system will include clause final lengthening, trochaic shortening and inter-word palatalization. Now suppose that clause boundaries are marked in the Level 1 representation, and suppose, moreover, that the phonetic system takes as input only one clause at a time, then it would be a simple matter to lengthen the last item in, and it would be impossible for rules applying to adjacent syllables to operate on syllables from different clauses. Notice that these phenomena are explained in terms of the organization of control as well as the nature of the representational systems.

Both **Cutler and Isard** and **Gazdar** note that, generally, intonational patterns are pragmatically conditioned. This comes out very clearly in the [sʌm sm̩] example (see Gazdar, p. 64).

(17)   a. [sʌ́m] graduate students were at the meeting.

       b. [sm̩] gráduate students were at the meeting.

(17a) and (17b) have the same truth conditions: they will be true just in case at least two graduate students were at the meeting; but in (17a) the speaker implies that some were *not*, whereas the speaker of (17b) remains neutral in that respect (see Butterworth and Gazdar, 1977, for a fuller discussion).

Gazdar observes that a whole range of phonetic phenomena are pragmatically conditioned. For instance, in Basque, consonants become palatalized when the speakers wish to show solidarity—but not otherwise, similarly with "Dismissive labialization" in French and "ironic nasalization" in American English.

Generally, there will be convergent dominance on the phonetic system from the Level 1 system and the pragmatic system. Other examples of this come from phonetic differences conditional on the social circumstances of the utterance: the degree of formality and the desired solidarity relations affect the phonetic character of the speech. Perhaps the best-known example is the occurrence of the post-vocalic /r/ in New York speech. This prestige feature is more likely to occur in formal speech than in casual speech (Labov, 1966). Comparible findings are reported by Trudgill (1974) for British speech except that the post-vocalic /r/ is a low-prestige feature (it sounds rather rural to us) and speakers who casually produce /r/ drop it in more formal speaking situations.

One simple way of locating these pragmatic effects in a production model, is to postulate a kind of parameter-setting device that conditions the operation of the phonetic system. Alternative solutions would include direct social conditioning of Level 1 (thus the post-vocalic /r/ will or will not occur in the appropriate morphological contexts, e.g. *pour*).

Speech error data provides important clues about the fine-structure of Levels 1 and 2. First, as Garrett (1975) has noted, phoneme movement errors (perseverations, anticipations, and transpositions) occur between syllables of similar stress—i.e. between two stressed syllables, and between two unstressed syllables, but only very, very rarely between a stressed and an unstressed syllable. Thus stress must be represented at the point of phoneme movement.

Secondly, the syllabic location of the phoneme conditions phoneme errors. Generally, the involved phonemes have to be in the same position in the syllable, usually the syllable-initial position, but medial and final position errors can be found. And thirdly, phonemes move into locations where the target phoneme was very similar to the intruder, typically the error and the target differ by only one distinctive feature (Shattuck, Hufnagel and Klatt, 1977).

Moreover, errors have been reported (for example, by Fromkin, 1973) that are best explained by the movement not of a phoneme but of a single phonetic feature.

(18)   Cedars of Lemadon
        (Target: Cedars of Lebanon)

Notice that neither /m/ nor /d/ exist in *Lebanon*; however, /b/ and /n/ can be represented as a feature matrix like (19a)

(19)   a.   /b/   /n/
            +consonant   +consonant
            +stop   −stop [= nasal]
            +bilabial   +alveolar
            +voiced   +voiced

and /m/ and /d/ can be represented by (19b)

(19)   b.   /m/   /d/
            +consonant   +consonant
            −stop [= nasal]   +stop
            +bilabial   +alveolar
            +voiced   +voiced

The difference between (19a) and (19b) is just the transposition of the *nasal* and *stop* features.

These observations jointly suggest that these errors are located at a stage in the production mechanism where stress, syllable structure, and distinctive features are all represented. In terms of the model suggested so far, Level 2 fits this bill nicely. The phoneme similarity data rule out Level 1, since it will be proposed that phonetic features are not represented at this level, only unitary phoneme symbols; however, Level 1 representations must contain enough information for the transduction process to produce a unique Level 2 representation, thus, these errors may not be a consequence of the instability of Level 2, but of the operation of the phonetic system.

One way of looking at this process has been suggested by Shaffer (1976). For speech (as well as a number of other output systems, like typing), he proposes a double buffer mechanism. The first buffer contains higher level symbols—in this case, phoneme symbols—and in the second, lower level symbols—here, feature matrices. A "pointer system" translates from one kind of symbol into the other—in this case, the translation is carried out by the phonetic system, and provides addresses for getting from one to the other. Misaddressing could lead to phoneme movement errors; mistranslating could lead to mixing up the phonetic features involved in the transduction. So, the features in (19) may occasionally get mixed up, particularly if a feature can find an appropriate slot in a neighbouring matrix. For example, [−stop] can move into the slot that should be occupied by [+stop]; but presumably, [+alveolar] could not. If it did, the matrix would be incoherent, containing contradictory place features, and the speaker would have to stop, temporarily.

C. Phonological Assembly

Since the phonetic system needs as input a Level 1 representation sufficient for a unique transformation into a phonetic sequence, the range of possible formats for Level 1 is highly constrained. Level 2 phonetic feature matrices must be mapped uniquely from more abstract Level 1 symbols; so Level 1 must contain a string of phonemes. Syntactic structure must be marked, as must intonation contour information (for reasons discussed in Section IV.B). And, or course, it must contain some kind of representation of the sound patterns of the words to be spoken. The system that assembles this syntactic, lexical and intonational information and transforms it into a sequence of phonemes that constitutes Level 1, I call the "phonological assembly system" (PAS).

Error data reveals additional features of the operation of this system. First of all, it looks as if the internal morphological structure of words is marked; indeed, grammatical morphemes can shift to the wrong stem, e.g. (20), and stems can transpose, picking up the "stranded" grammatical morpheme left in its intended location:

(20) It wait*s* to pay
      (Target: It pay*s* to wait). (Garrett, 1976)

If PAS is obtaining syntactic information (including grammatical morphemes) from a source distinct from the source of lexical stems, then it may simply mislocate them in the course of assembly. Provided it does not check back to the syntactic, lexical or other systems (see below, Sections IV.D and E) the Level 1 output will conform to its own criteria of successful operation, and will be transferred to the phonetic system. Of course, whole words may be exchanged, and again without checking, an output acceptable to PAS will be generated.

Garrett argues that whole word exchange errors and part word exchanges and shifts result from errors at different levels in the production system, because only the former observe form-class constraints. That is whole word Nouns only exchange with Nouns, whereas part word exchanges (e.g. (22) below, and (12)) more often involve words of a different form class. So, he argues, whole word exchanges occur at a level where form-class is marked, but part word errors occur where they are not. This view is not consistent with the model I am advocating here, since, as will become apparent, PAS is the locus at which lexical items are ordered, prior to this in the production process they are not ordered, and subsequent to this they keep the order assigned in Level 1.

In defence of my position, I would suggest that there may be an artefact in Garrett's data analysis. In nearly all the examples he cites in this volume and elsewhere the words invoked are nouns separated by a preposition: a *foot* of one *depth*; *room* to my *door*; etc. And in Fromkin's published corpus (1973: Appendix, Section P), 15 out of 35 whole word exchanges are of this type. These examples almost invariably involve singular nouns where there is no grammatical morpheme to strand. Now there may just be something funny about prepositional phrases which causes this class of errors. In fact, a closer analysis of Fromkin's corpus reveals an interesting fact. 12 out of her 35 examples involve words of a different form class, and 11 of these may not be genuine exchanges at all. Consider the following examples, underlined items were exchanged: a plus *segment nasal*; does *smoke Jack*; the way we can characterize the situation would *by be*; a *many good* years; as far as *page typing* one; etc. In each case, the result could be achieved if *one* word shifts position; preposition phrase exchanges cannot be achieved by shifting along or back a single word. So the tendency of whole word exchanges to obey form-class constraints is, first, not so pronounced in another corpus, and, second, may be in part accounted for by an, as yet unexplained, peculiarity of prepositional phrases.

In order to understand the operation of PAS more fully, we need to examine the outputs that converge on it: lexical, syntactic, and prosodic.

D. The Lexical System

In essence, a lexical system is a device which (in production) produces as output one of a finite number of pre-established phonological patterns. We can ask a number of specific questions about this device: (1) what kind of patterns are represented? In particular, are all words available to the speaker represented, or perhaps just stems or even more abstract items like Chomsky and Halle's "lexical formatives" where some or all of the morphological affixes will be added later? Also are all classes of items represnted or just open-class items? This question is related to questions about the arrangement—or addressing system—of the device. Notice that these questions refer, in part, to control processes associated with the lexical system: for example, a decision has to be made on the basis of the input as to what the output should be—and presumably, the decision-making procedure can be tuned to varying degrees of specificity.

1. *What kinds of pattern are represented?*
Garrett makes a case for treating lexical roots as distinct from grammatical morphemes and most closed class words (function words). He adduces support from the error data, and from studies of agrammatic aphasic speech, where lexical items are relatively well-preserved, but function words and grammatical morphemes are largely lost. A complementary study (Butterworth, 1979) analyses an aphasic patient for whom lexical items (especially infrequent ones) are lost, but function words and grammatical morphemes are preserved. This patient makes up words—neologises—but applies the appropriate morphology to them.

(21) a. She weexes (= [wiksəz]) a zen (= [zɛn])
      b. They are, sir, two mytreks (= [maitrɛks])

Notice that in (21a) the third person singular morpheme on the verb has the appropriate phonetic shape, and that the noun phrase matches the singular article with the appropriate (null) morpheme on the noun; and in (21b) the noun neologism is appropriately pluralized. Indeed, only 11 out of his 138 neologisms can be said to have inappropriate morphonological marking, and 10 of the 11 are arguably correct. This patient showed generally correct syntax; whereas the agrammatic patients typically had negligible syntax (see **Saffran** *et al.*) the double dissociation, good syntax with appropriate function words and correct morphology, versus poor syntax with no function words and no morphology, emphasises the close link between syntax and the function word-grammatical morpheme system. Generative phonologists, e.g. Chomsky and Halle (1968), have maintained this link on theoretical grounds. But it should be recalled that **Saffran** *et al.* have observed that not all function words and grammatical morphemes become impaired to the same degree, and report a patient who seems to have a "constructional" impairment without the morphological deficits typically found in "agrammatic" aphasics. Although their patient shows preservation of articles, pronouns, prepositions, etc. these are frequently used inappropriately (see their examples (30)–(43)). † I will discuss in more detail how this might come about in Section V on Control Processes; I will simply suggest here that it looks as if Level 1 is receiving degraded information from the syntactic system and has to make decisions on the basis of insufficient information.

With the provisos noted by **Saffran** *et al.*, function words can be selectively impaired by cerebral insult; complementarily, access to closed-class items can be selectively impaired, leaving function words intact. **Cutler and Isard** note that phrasal stress errors involve stress on function words; lexical item errors leave phrasal stress in its intended position, but on the wrong word. These data certainly support the idea of a device specific to open class items.

Recall also that the "morpheme stranding" errors observed by **Garrett** and others (e.g. Fromkin, 1973) indicates a level of representation where stem and at least grammatical affixes are separate (presumably our Level 1). This is prima facie evidence for the representation only of basic forms, rather than all conjugations of verbs and declensions of nouns.

Interestingly, in the jargon aphasic case (Butterworth, 1979) derivational as well as grammatical morphology is applied to neologisms, for example, adding -*ly* to make adverbs; sometimes -*ly* gets added to words that were already adverbs (*yetly*). In addition to control of these common morphological processes, the patient seemed to retain control of the more arcane principles governing English place-name morphology; he described, for instance, his sister as living in a place that was "nearest to Emchurch in Exshire".

These data support the claim that only stems (denuded of all affixes) are accessed from the lexicon and that *all* morphology is added and some additional support can be formed in the error data. In one error from the MIT corpus, not only do the exchanged stems leave behind grammatical affixes, but also the derivational affix -*er*:

† In English, word order indicates case relations, some other languages use case-endings. It would be interesting, therefore, to see whether there are patients speaking these languages who preserve case-endings but not other sorts of endings.

(22) McGovern favors pushing busters.
    (Target: McGovern favors busting pushers.)

Alas, this simple picture is all too simple. A large number of morphological forms are lexically-conditioned and cannot be handled by rules operating on the phonological form of the stem. In grammatical morphology, the past tense of *swim* is not *swimmed*, and, of course, cases of suppletion, as in *go* + past tense becoming the phonologically quite distinct from, *went*. **Comrie** lists a number of cases where the derivational morphology too is lexically conditioned. Many adjectives can be nominalized by adding *-ity* and shortening the long stressed syllable, e.g.

(23) a. divine [dɪ'vain] divinity [dɪ'vɪnɪti]
    b. profound [prə'faund] profundity [prə'fʌndɪti]
    c. obscene [ob'si:n] obscenity [ob'sɛnɪti]

However, apparently similar adjectives, which also add *-ity*, do not shorten the stressed syllable; *obese* [o'bi:s] does not become [o'besɪti] but [o'bi:sɪti].

How can these data be accommodated? Full forms of all derivations (but especially irregulars) could be represented in the lexicon and sent on to PAS. Alternatively, a basic form or a stem could be marked somehow to show what derivation applies, or what grammatical morpheme is to be added. This would require an extremely large number of special rules.

Since the relevant errors occur, productive word-forming rules do seem to be part of the speaker's capability. For example, I heard recently *fortuity* instead of *fortuitousness*, and *voluptitude* instead of *voluptuousness*. These examples, like Fromkin's (1973) case, *ambigual*, seem to indicate a stem, *ambig-*, *fortu-*, *volupt-*, rather than the basic adjective, undergoes derivation.

Comrie has pointed out that historical data creates difficulties for the Generative Phonologists' description of underlying abstract lexical stems. Lexical representations will have to be close to their realized phonological forms.

There is other evidence that *derived* forms, at least, are fully represented in the lexicon and involved in the production process. **Cutler and Isard's** analysis of lexical stress errors demonstrates that cognate derived forms are invariably implicated: a differently stressed form interfering with the intended form.

(24) Now the paradigm involves présenting . . . presénting.

Where cognate forms have the same stress pattern, or where there are no cognates, these errors do not occur. There are never errors like *administrative* or *window*.

There are three alternatives open. (1) As **Cutler and Isard** argue, all forms of a word are represented in the lexicon *and* are utilized in production. (2) All forms are represented, but only the basic form is *normally* utilized in production, derivations being added in PAS. In this case, errors will arise, just on those occasions when a dormant derived form is accessed instead of the basic form. (3) Only basic forms are used in production (though derived forms may be represented), and there are rules for assigning lexical stress according to syntactic function. Errors arise when PAS mistakes the syntactic function. Notice that only words with derivations fall into this category, since only these will be syntactically ambivalent. The examples they cite seem to be regular enough for this account: *present* (noun and verb) and *conflicts* (noun and verb)—stress on first syllable if noun, but on second if verb; *economi* (adjective and noun), and *psychologi* (adjective and noun)—stress on third syllable if adjective, on second if noun.

2. *The organization of the lexicon*

Contributors have reported two classes of error that are made by both normal speakers and aphasics—first, choosing a word similar in *meaning* to the target, but different in sound, e.g. (from Garrett)

(25)   a. He rode his bike to school *tomorrow*
          (Target: yesterday)
       b. You go *wash* your hair
          (Target: brush);

second, choosing a word similar in *sound*, but different in meaning, e.g. (from **Garrett**)

(26)   a. No—I'm *amphibian*
          (Target: ambidextrous)
       b. They haven't been *married* . . . uh, measured with the precision you're using.

This immediately suggests two forms of organization: by meaning and by sound. And this dual organization is plausible, particularly if the lexical system is to serve both production and comprehension purposes: in production the speaker needs to go from a meaning he wishes to express to the phonological form that expresses it; in comprehension, he needs to take phonological input and discover what it means. This dual organization can be represented in, at least, two ways: first by having two addressing representations, that is, each lexical item will have at least one semantic address, say S539, and at least one phonological address, P176. But, in this case, there should be confusion only between semantically similar items in production and only between phonologically similar items in comprehension. Second, it could also be represented by having two sets of *items*—one set could consist of abstract meaning items M_1, M_2, . . . M_n, the other set would consist of, say, phoneme strings P_1, P_2, . . . P_n, such that semantic or phonological similarity is a function of the similarity of the subscript numbers. In addition, a mapping relation between M_i and P_j needs to be represented so that the speaker can get from a meaning item to a phoneme string, and the listener from a phoneme string to a meaning item. The mapping relations can be thought of as addresses: thus associated with M_i would be, the address for P_j, (and perhaps P_k . . . P_m if these bear the same meaning), conversely, associated with P_j would be the address for M_i. In the event of partial degradation (transient or permanent) of the addressing information from M items to P items, the speakers would locate P_k instead of P_j, where P_j is similar in sound but not necessarily similar in meaning. Analogously, in trying to locate M_i from higher level representation, address information may be partially degraded leading to the location of M_j, which would be similar in meaning to

M_i. (This is perhaps no more that a reinterpretation of Pick's idea that there can be a failure of "differentiation"; at the various levels of representation between thought and speech. Here I argue for failure to differentiate M_i and M_j leading to meaning-related wrong words, and failure to differentiate P_i and P_j leading to phonologically-related wrong words. (1931 trans., 1973, especially Chapters 5 and 10. See also my Introduction to this volume).)

Phonological relatedness, at the lexical level, is, strangely problematic. Fay and Cutler (1977) have examined the dimensions along which sound-related errors seem to occur. They find errors of the sort exemplified in

(27)	Target	Error
	emulate	emanate
	trampolines	tambourines
	lucrative	ludicrous
	resort	result
	concern	confirm
	shed	shield
	experiment	experience

Typically, the error will have the same initial phoneme, the same number of syllables and the same stress pattern as the target. (Incidentally, these constraints do not apply to meaning related errors.) They argue, therefore, for an arranagement of phonological items such that each item is classified by initial phoneme, and number of syllables (stress pattern). The details of this arrangement are not yet clear. If there is a hierarchy, does initial phoneme take precedence over number of syllables, or stress pattern, or what? And what is the relative status of the second phoneme? etc.

Meaning relatedness has been extensively explored, and inquiring readers can do no better than consult Miller and Johnson-Laird (1976) for a thoroughgoing analysis. Nevertheless, they concentrate almost exclusively on what I have termed "semantics"—that is, aspects of meaning concerned with the truth-conditional properties of lexical items, but as **Gazdar** has pointed out, lexical selection will depend on non-truth-conditional, i.e. "pragmatic" aspects of the utterance. He cites instances where choice of lexical item is conditioned by the intended courteousness of the utterance; another pragmatic condition concerns the speaker's model of the current state of knowledge of the listener. This will determine how the speaker refers to some entity—e.g. *he, John, Smith, that man, the man (I was telling you about)* etc. etc. Thus access to M-items will be constrained by both semantic and pragmatic factors. Therefore the lexcial system must represent pragmatic as well as semantic aspects of meaning.

A further question is whether an M-item is mapped on to single items or on to phrases as well. **Gazdar** treats them as interchangeable, and aphasics with an anomic syndrome substitute circumlocutory phrases for lexical items they cannot find. However, tip-of-the-tongue experiences suggest that you can know that it is a word you want, not a phrase, even though you do not know what that word is. It is possible, of course, that M-items are marked M_{word} and M_{phrase} so that a phenomenological distinction can be made in advance of locating the appropriate P-item. To have phrases, or even sentences, in the P-system would blur the nice representational distinctions we have been able to achieve so far—the distinction between lexical items and function words, between lexical items and syntax (see below) etc.

Of course, we may need to postulate ready-made phrases (cf. Hughlings Jackson's distinction between "automatic" and "propositional" speech), where the components are stuck together by force of habit. This is not **Gazdar's** point: he does not distinguish candidate referring expressions on the basis of, say, frequency in the language.

Many other authors, however, have proposed frequency as a basic organizational feature of the lexical system (e.g. Morton, 1969); these studies, far too numerous to list here, have employed perceptual paradigms of one sort or another. Studies of spontaneous speech have typically employed an estimate of predictability in context, rather than frequency as such (e.g. Goldman-Eisler, 1958). Although these two variables may be correlated, in principle, they can be separated. Beattie and Butterworth (1979) note that in a sentence like (28)

(28)   Too many cooks spoil the broth.

broth is infrequent but highly predictable, but in (29)

(29)   Too many cooks spoil the soup.

soup is frequent but unpredictable. Insofar as it has been possible to partition out the effects of these two variables, predictability has an effect independent of frequency, but it is not at all clear that frequency has an effect independent of predictability. Moreover, words that are infrequent and unpredictable on the first occasion of their utterance and typically preceded by a lexical pause, become significantly more predictable but scarcely more frequent, in a neighbouring sentence. In cases like this, the second occurrence is rarely preceded by a pause (**Butterworth**; Good and Butterworth, 1979).

In any event, the accessibility of lexical items involves consideration not only of the organization of the lexicon, but also the control structures employed in searching it (see Section V).

3. *Grammatical representation in the lexical system*

Certain kinds of error reveal dramatic form-class effects indicating that at the error locus grammatical information is represented. **Garrett** has observed that word exchanges and word blends almost invariably involve words of the same form-class. Similarly, Ray and Cutler (1977) report that "malapropisms"— substituting a word of a similar sound to the target—again involve words of the same form-class. **Saffran** *et al.*'s account of aphasic syndromes reveals that language disturbances show specific form-class effects: agrammatics have nouns better preserved than verbs, whereas in anomics, verbs are better preserved than nouns.

It is not clear, however, exactly where in the lexical system this grammatical information is located. The items output from the system (i.e. P-items) do not seem to be grammatically marked.

For example, "Morpheme stranding" errors, where stems interchange, do not observe the form-class constraint to anything like the same extent. About 70% of these errors involve interacting elements that have a different form-class (**Garrett**). **Cutler and Isard** note that for lexical stress errors, cognate forms of a different form-class interact with the form of the target form-class.

Even if P-items are not marked for grammatical function, M-items might still be. But this seems to involve the (dubious) assumption that semantic and syntactic functions correspond, e.g. objects are realized as nouns, actions as verbs, etc. Another serious problem with any evaluation of data on the representation of grammatical information is that the studies have been carried out on English where many, if not most, lexical items are grammatically ambivalent. For instance, *close* can be a noun, adjective, adverb, or preposition, and, as [kloʻz], can also be a verb. Should we postulate four (or five) separate lexical representations?

E. The Syntactic System

1. *Output of the syntactic system*
The syntactic system has to produce a representation of the necessary grammatical information for the phonological system to do its work. We know it has to provide grammatical morphemes—number markers, tense markers, etc. These can be thought of as instructions to the phonetic system (the transformation from Level 1 to Level 2) to provide the appropriate phonetic shapes to mark plurality, tense, aspect, etc. It probably provides at least some function words, not only since these are closely associated with syntactic function in language pathologies, and errors, but also because many seem to serve a purely grammatical role—*to* in the infinitive, *for*, *that* as complementizers and so on. Presumably it provides instructions for the order of lexical items—what grammatical role each item is to have. **Garrett** has talked of "frames" and "inserts", that is the syntactic system provides a frame with function words and grammatical morphemes associated with slots in the frame, and into these slots lexical items are inserted. He takes the view that lexical items and frames are selected interdependently at, what he calls, the "Functional Level". **Cooper** adopts a somewhat similar position. That is to say, lexical information has to be utilized in syntactic processing, otherwise, for example, subcategorization errors would routinely arise: structure and lexical items are closely related; *expect* and *persuade* enter into different kinds of structure, as has been pointed out by many linguists, notably Chomsky (1965). What this would mean for output from the syntactic system is that frames would come complete with lexical formatives.

This idea that the syntactic frame for a sentence and all the lexical items for the slots in it, are selected simultaneously, though independently, is inconsistent with the data from hesitations. These show that sentence output can be delayed to search for an appropriate lexical item. What is at issue in this case are P-items, the phonological form of the filler words. It may still be reasonable to argue that all M-items are available concurrently with the syntactic frame, and it is these that get transposed in word exchanges.

Fay and Cutler (1977) on the other hand, require each lexical slot to have semantic features "attached as leaves to the phrase-structure tree". These feature sets guide lexical search. This model would accommodate the hesitation data: the filled slots and associated function words would be output, but this will be interrupted when an unfilled slot is encountered and the features on the slot employed to do the search for the P-item. However, if the system only searches for one P-item at a time (not clear on their account), or even if each lexical slot has a very specific semantic valency accepting only semantically appropriate items, there would be no way that whole or part word exchanges would occur.

Thus the construction of a syntactic frame and the choice of P-items must be independent and non-simultaneous, though roughly concurrent. Further evidence for this position comes from **Saffran** et al.'s analysis of agrammatic patients. When the syntactic system is impaired, lexical selection can still be carried out. **Cooper** provides direct evidence that the output from the syntactic system will have phrase bracketings marked on it (which determine syllable timing); if these bracketings are not available due to impairment, lexical ordering cannot be governed by syntactic principles, and **Saffran** et al. show that these patients indeed use non-syntactic principles to order items in output.

Notice that impairment to the syntactic system should also deprive the phonological system of adequate morphological instructions, and the Level 1–Level 2 transduction should produce either no morphology or erroneous morphology, and no function words or the wrong function words. This is what seems to happen in fact, with the cases they describe (see also Section V).

2. *The operation of the syntactic system*

One capacity characteristic is evident: the system does its work very quickly, and does not need more time to produce complex structure than simple structures (**Butterworth**). In terms of the model this is not surprising: if the syntactic system outputs frames, the frame is likely to have been used on innumerable previous occasions, and thus the process of producing it will be a highly practised activity.

What forms of representation does the syntactic system work on? In this volume, we have two opposing views, reflecting the debate in linguistics: on the one hand, **Cooper** argues for a distinct level of Deep Structure representation whose effects can be seen at the phonetic level; on the other hand, **Steedman and Johnson-Laird** argue for a single level of representation embodied in an Augmented Transition Network model. The latter has certain computational advantages, not least that it can easily accommodate interactions with semantics and pragmatics; however, there is no direct evidence that ATN-like processes are employed in the mental operation of the syntactic system. We must therefore leave open both possibilities.

We do know, however, that there are pragmatic constraints on syntactic structure. **Steedman** and **Johnson-Laird** present persuasive arguments that the speaker's model of the listener's state of knowledge, in the light of recent discourse, conditions structure—surface NPs will be ordered according to what has been given (or can be assumed to be known by the listener); pronominalization will be conditioned by past referential work in an interestingly systematic way; and choice of certain other function words, connectives like *and*, *but*, *although*, will reflect these pragmatic factors also, and notice that the choice of *although* will determine surface subordination. **Gazdar** lists other pragmatic constraints on syntactic operations— "movement" rules like *slifting*, *raising* and *locative preposing* can be blocked by well-defined pragmatic conditions. Deletion rules are similarly constrained by pragmatic factors involving the presumed state of knowledge of the co-conversationalists.

3. *Input to syntactic system*
It may therefore be seen that among the kinds of information that has to be available to the syntactic system, either directly represented in the system parameters, or via control processes sensitive to this information, are the pragmatic factors cited above.

Semantic input is also required—that is the syntactic system has to have a way of representing both semantic and pragmatic aspects of meaning in order to generate an appropriate output. **Goldman-Eisler** reports that simultaneous translators do not start to output in the target language until at least an NP + VP unit is heard. She proposes that such a unit is the minimal structure that can express a "proposition", and, following Hughlings Jackson, it is the propositional nature of speech that is characteristic of fully fledged human linguistic communication.

I do not think we can be much more specific about the nature of the input to the syntactic system at this time. A number of different suggestions can be found in the literature, notably in Clark and Clark (1977), in the writings of the late Richard Montague (1974), and in the work of "generative semanticists", but the psychological evidence is really too scanty to be convincing.

F. The Semantic System

Semantics, broadly, has to do with the relationship between utterance and the world. Enormous controversies have raged among philosophers and linguists as to how this relationship should be represented, and this is not the place to raise or to try to resolve them. Psychologists appear even more confused about the matter. What I have in mind for the representation of semantics in the production system is something like this: the semantic system generates (the mental equivalents of) formulae that are a first analysis and arrangement of the thoughts the speaker intends to express (see my Introduction, p. 9). Attempts to specify the character of these formulae can be found in Clark and

Clark (1977) and Fodor (1976). Roughly speaking, formulae contain functions and arguments. For Clark and Clark, verbs are realizations of functions, Noun Phrases of arguments. Thus: *Hit* (*John*, *Bill*) will be realized as *John hit Bill* or *Bill was hit by John*, etc. The terms in the formulae are not words, but "concepts" that are realized as verbs. For Clark and Clark, the relation between concept and word is very close, but more distant relations are possible. Thus concepts can consist of sets of features, (or "procedures" as in Miller and Johnson-Laird, 1976), and the whole formulae as ordered feature sets (cf. Fodor). Most authors take the view that pragmatic features (see below, Section IV.H) will not be represented, but pragmatic aspects will emerge as a function of the formula and the speech situation. So "Given-New" structure in the speech realization will constitute a principle for the final arrangement of words in the expression of the formula, and will require information about the speech situation in addition to the information contained in the formula (**Steedman and Johnson-Laird**). Formulae, themselves, will have to contain enough information to motivate the selection of (a small set of) appropriate lexical items and (a small set of) appropriate syntactic structures. The final choice of these will depend on pragmatic factors. It is unclear whether selection of intonation contours should be regarded as depending, at least partially, on semantics; **Cutler and Isard** demonstrate the roles of syntax and pragmatics in choice of contour, but the involvement of semantics rests on how speech acts are to be treated. That is, is. the illocutionary force of an utterance an aspect of its semantics (as proposed by Karttunen, 1977, for instance) or solely of its pragmatics? If the former, then, for example, question-intonation will be determined by the semantic formula. If not, pragmatic input would have to select this contour. Notice that the issue of how illocutionary force is to be represented, will affect how syntax is selected too.

G. The Prosodic System

This is really two systems: one that deals with the selection of intonation contours, including sentence stress placement, and one that deals with lexical stress. The latter is part of the lexical system and has been dealt with in that section. The salient data on the former has been neatly summarized in **Cutler and Isard's** chapter, and little purpose will be served by recapitulating the points here. The main implication of their account is that the selection of an intonation contour and its scope is not the automatic consequence of a choice in either the syntactic, semantic or pragmatic systems, but is linked to choices made in all of those systems. The intonational system appears to be autonomous in just the way that, say, the syntactic system is.

H. The Pragmatic System

The pragmatic system is concerned with the speaker's model of the context of utterance—that is, with the particulars and the general non-linguistic conventions of the situation in which his utterance occurs, and influences most of the other production systems. It will have to include among its resources apparatus for representing the referents of referring expressions (the domain of interpretation for the semantics of the utterances), apparatus for representing the principles needed to derive illocutionary force, implicature, presupposition and context dependent acceptability (Gazdar, 1979; also **Gazdar**, Chapter 3; **Steedman and Johnson-Laird**, Chapter 5). Notice that this treatment of "pragmatics", although vague, defines a set of problems for the linguist and the psycholinguist which have become relatively well-understood (see the above references), and it requires us to treat utterances as part of a wider arrangement of social means and purposes.

One crucial pragmatic factor, discussed by several authors, is where the utterance is located in the discourse. Steedman and Johnson-Laird note that the topical structure of an utterance will be affected by its conversational location. Thus, speakers will select (39b) but not (39a) after (38)

(38)   Did Mary meet John at 2 o'clock?

(39)   a. No, at 3 o'clock Mary met John.

      b. No, Mary met John at 3 o'clock.

Notice that sematnically (39a) and (39b) are identical (the truth conditions are the same). The pragmatic principle involved here is that "given" information should precede "new" information—and, of course, what is given may be determined by the previous turns in the conversation. The "given-new" distinction also effects the *kind* of accent and its *placement*, as **Cutler and Isard** point out—again the given information is located in the prior turn:

(40)   a. London's the capital of Scotland, isn't it?

      b. No. Èdinburgh's the capital of Scŏtland, Lŏndon's the capital of England.

The falling accent (ˋ) marks new information, *Edinburgh, England,* and the fall-rise (ˇ) the given information. Had the question been

(41)   Edinburgh's the capital of England, isn't it?

the *kinds* of accent would have been reversed, fall-rises instead of falls, and vice versa.

Gazdar cites a well-known example of G. Lakoff's, where accent location is a function of the speaker's assumptions:

(42)   a. John called Máry a virgin, and then shé insulted hím.

      b. John called Mary a virgin, and then she insúlted him.

The utterance (42a) assumes that being called a virgin is an insult, but (42b) does not.

Gazdar also notes that conversationally-determined topic conditions which of two clauses can be relativized. Both (44a) and (44b) are grammatical, and both are true under the same conditions, but only (44a) can be the next turn after (43):

(43)   None of your friends are alcoholic.

(44)   a. John who was at last night's party drinks a lot.

      b. John who drinks a lot, was at last night's party.

The pragmatic principle involved here concerns topic relevance. "Given two clauses S_0 and S_1, if S_0 is more relevant to the topic in hand than S_1, then S_1 may occur as a nonrestrictive relative in S_0, but not conversely."

Thus the pragmatic system has to represent the current topic. It is not clear how this is to be achieved, since it is not just a case of keeping track of lexical items—in example (44a), *drinks a lot* links back to *alcoholic*, and the speaker must therefore be keeping track of something more abstract.

However, it is evident that speakers can and do represent more concrete features of prior discourse, as well, in constructing their current utterance. Schenkein reports conversations in which turn-sequences recur, such that each turn-position recurrence will mirror in its speech act, and often in its lexical, syntactic, and prosodic character, its counterpart in a prior sequence. A particularly symmetrical example can be found on p. 34.

(I)   Aaron: . . . It was a *to*tal disaster for me.
(II)   Betty: And we'll *ne*ver buy another Chevy.
(III) Colin: I would have screamed bloody *mu*rder.
(IV)   Debra: And we would have been arrested for disturbing the *pea*ce.
       (pause)
(I)   Aaron: I used to think a new car was free of headaches for a whi(hh)le hheh
(II)   Betty: But we sure had our share with tha(hh)t one hh
(III) Colin: I never considered buying *any*thing but a used car.
(IV)   Debra: So we've never had *that* kind of tr-trouble.

                                                            (ARCD:8:6)

Analysis
(I)   A: "I" Statement
(II)   B: "we" (A and B) Continuation
(III) C: "I" Comment (on A's Statement)
(IV)   D: "We" (C and D) Continuation
       (pause)
(I)   A: "I" Statement
(II)   B: "We" (A and B) Continuation
(III) C: "I" Comment (on A's Statement)
(IV)   D: "We" (C and D) Continuation

Notice, first of all, that what may loosely be called "the speech act" of (I) parallels (III), and (II) parallels (IV), and that this whole structure is repeated, even though the semantics of the utterances change. But notice also how the accent in the first (I) and (II) is on a modifier and in (III) and (IV) is on the final noun. Moreover the accent pattern of the second (I) and (II) is neutral, but the marked accent of (III) shows up again in (IV).

The repeating sequences can be much longer (as in the example on p. 37ff), and a speaker need not take the same role in each recurrence of the structure, he must therefore be able to represent the relevant features of both his own and other conversationalists' utterances.

So, a speaker needs to keep track of what has happened during the conversation: he will have to update his representation of his co-conversationalist's current conversational purposes and update his model of the co-conversationalists's state of knowledge. That is, he will add to or subtract from the set of propositions he assumes, or infers, the other is committed to. This is essential if the speaker is to fulfil his obligations to the general principles that conversationalists operate with; these have been formulated by Grice (1973) in the form of four "Maxims".

1. Maxim of *Quantity*. (a) Make your contribution as informative as is required (for the current purposes of the exchange). (b) Do not make your contribution more informative than is required.

2. Maxim of *Quality*. Try to make you contribution one that is true.

3. Maxim of *Relation*. Be relevant.

4. Maxim of *Manner*. Be perspicuous.

In order to satisfy Maxim 3, the speaker has to know the recent history of the exchange; in order to satisfy Maxim 1, the speaker must have an up-to-date *model of the other*: a set of propositions that the other is presumed to be committed to. If the speaker utters P, where P is already part of that set, it may be interpreted as the violation of Maxim 1. **Steedman and Johnson-Laird** propose a few simple principles—which they call "demons"—to enable the speaker to construct a plausible set. Generally, assume the other knows what you know, unless you have specific reasons to believe otherwise—e.g. if he asks a question.

In addition to selecting from the range of true and relevant propositions, the speaker will have choices as to how to convey the proposition. A proposition can be directly asserted, or it can be conveyed using the Maxims to create presuppositions and implicatures. This can be made clear using Butterworth and **Gazdar's** example (Gazdar, p. 64). Suppose the domain in which propositions are to be interpreted consists of

a. A set of ten individuals present at a meeting.

b. A set of ten individuals who are graduate students.

c. Relations defined on joint membership of the two sets such that four graduate students were present at the meeting.

Now the speaker can truly assert any of the following in response to the question "who was at the meeting?"

(45) a. Four graduate students were at the meeting.

   b. Three graduate students were at the meeting.

   c. Some [sʌm] graduate students were at the meeting.

   d. Some [sm̩] gráduate students were at the meeting.

The utterer of (45a) and (45b) does not assert that exactly four and three graduate students, respectively, were at the meeting. Now if the speaker is making his contribution as informative as required (Maxim 1) and that is true, for which he has adequate evidence (Maxim 2), he is implying that that exact number was present, and that he has grounds for believing that that number was present. Thus (45b), though true, is misleading. (46) would simply be false.

(46) Only three graduate students were at the meeting.

In example (45c), where the emphasis is on *some*, Maxims 1 and 2 lead to the implicature that some graduate students were not present; but (45d), where the *some* is not emphasized, no such implicature arises. Notice that this pragmatic decision affects sentence stress, and this, in turn, affects the phonetic realization of *some*—[sʌm] or [sm̩].

V. Control Processes and Capacity Limitations

How are all these representations fitted together to produce coherent linguistic output? In my discussion of levels of representation I have partly prejudged the answer. For example, I have mentioned three kinds of information that get transduced into the phonological representation—syntactic, lexical and prosodic, and possibly pragmatic. This implication is that these inputs are separately generated and are assembled at this point: the evidence being that each can be separately interfered with in normal errors or in pathology, as was discussed above. Nevertheless, the control structure now needs to be considered as a whole.

A. The Structure of Control

A control structure has to specify the logical relations among the components of a system, namely, to which component X sends its output, and when a Y gets it input; and it has to specify the temporal relation among components: if Y and Z take the output of X, and W needs the output of both Y and Z, then W can only start to operate when both Y and Z have supplied their output. Thus W will only be able to start after Z has finished. To take one plausible example of this: where a word is sufficiently unpredictable in context, searching the lexicon for it will take longer than the organizing of the syntax of the sentence in which it is located, thus one commonly finds a pause *after* a function word defining the syntactic category of the next constituent (. . . because the feedback is to the [pause] ideal . . .; . . . it will enable them to go on [pause] uhm [pause] developing in an educational sense . . . (data from Butterworth, 1972)). Now, this scheme does not require that lexical selection should always take longer than the organization of syntax; if all lexical items are predictable enough, the pause will precede the unit currently being organized and not before any of the lexical items in it.

Generally, I assume that there is a strict sequence of processes. Once X has produced its representation and sent it onward, it no longer has a role in the further realization of that representation. One system may send its representation to several other systems. I will argue that this is the case for the semantic system; it also seems to be the case for the pragmatic system, which influences most, if not all, other processes (**Gazdar**). For example, a pragmatic decision to be ironic will result in a semantic decision to use a sentence of the opposite truth value to a sentence the speaker believes to be true. In American English, it also causes the phonetic system to nasalize its output.

I also assume that associated with each system is a buffer that can retain the current representation it has output. This enables discretionary checking of the output of the system against the output of prior systems. In the limit, the speaker can hold a complete phonological or phonetic representation and check it carefully before uttering a sound. A man on trial for his life would be well advised to make use of this facility.

It should also be remembered that the production system is embedded in other systems involved in conversational behaviour. Of these, Beattie has shown that gesturing and visual monitoring are linked to production processes. Gestures appear linked to individual words, more particularly to some specification of their semantics so that gestures can start before the word. Speakers adapt the pattern of visual monitoring so that they tend to look at the listener only when they are not carrying out some demanding production task—like semantic planning or difficult lexical selection. Occasionally, adaptation is imperfect, and the speaker will try to monitor and plan at the same time. In such cases, false starts—evidence of planning failure—increase dramatically.

The most obvious non-linguistic input into the production system is the thought that the speaker wishes to express, James's "intention of saying a thing" (1890, p. 253), Jonckheere's "cloud . . . with 'thinks' inside it" (1966, p. 89) or Wundt's "whole at the cognitive level" (1970, p. 21). We cannot say much about this, except to reiterate that non-linguistic thoughtful aspects of production can be experimentally dissociated from those involved in determining the linguistic expression of the thought. For example, familiarity with the non-linguistic content can be varied independently of the familiarity of the linguistic content (Good and Butterworth, 1979; O'Connell et al., 1969; discussed in Chapter 7; see also Section IV.E).

Our analysis of the representational systems indicates that the syntactic, lexical and prosodic systems operate independently of each other, and thus potentially in parallel over time. To account for typical speech, where the syntactic, lexical and prosodic characteristics match, one can postulate two kinds of structure. Either (a), all three systems are dominated by the same system such that the output from this dominant system is sufficiently specific to ensure coherence of the output of the dominated systems; or (b), the systems take input from each other to keep a running check on the compatibility of their outputs. **Garrett** and **Cooper** propose models where this cross-talk takes place between the lexical system and a "deep" (Cooper) or "functional" (Garrett) level of the syntactic system.

(a) Parallel control

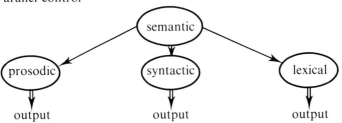

For the utterance "Some graduates attended the meeting", (a) might look something like this, where G, A(M) stand for the semantic specifications of the lexical items, and *some* for the existential quantifier.

(a')

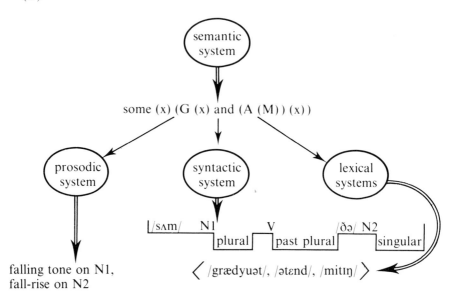

some (x) (G (x) and (A (M)) (x))

falling tone on N1,
fall-rise on N2

(b) Heterarchical cross-talk

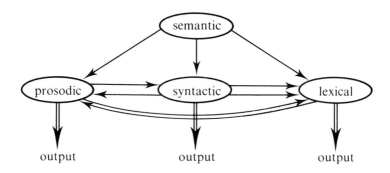

I have outlined my arguments against (b) above. However, there may turn out to be complications with the simple model, (a). It has been generally, but tacitly, assumed that there is a single fixed ordering of processes in production: one can find arguments as early as Pick's (see Chapter 1) about whether lexical selection precedes or follows syntactic decisions, or whether they are carried out in parallel, or whether, as with (a), they operate autonomously.

There is an alternative, namely, that the ordering is not fixed. Perhaps on some occasions the speaker selects a word or two,† then decides on a syntactic structure and an intonation that are appropriate to the initial decision; on other occasions, decides on the structure first, and on yet other occasions, chooses the intonation contour first. Somehow, the *leading decision* will set constraints on the operation of the other two systems. In this way coherence of decision making would usually be ensured. It's not clear how such an arrangement would work, and there is no direct evidence in its favour. **Schenkein's** data suggest the prosodic structure of a previous turn can be identified and re-employed; and it is more than likely that words can be culled from previous context and re-employed. But these are no more than hints.

In any event, the outputs from these three systems converge on the phonological assembly system: (PAS):

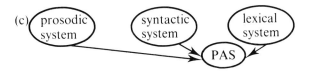

Here, the relevant information has to be combined so that the phonological forms of root morphemes find their correct syntactic slot, which will be marked with appropriate morphological instructions. Prosodic information is probably marked at this level as well. Thus, for an example, (c) might look something like this:

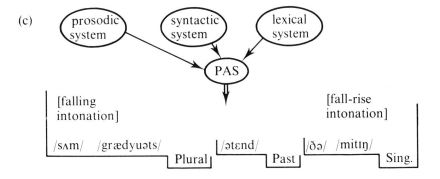

---

†Sacks (1973) offers data that throw an interesting side-light on this issue. He claims that puns are a conversational resource that get deployed at particular conversational locations, normally as topic or story termination, particularly where the word in a cliche is a homonym of another word. For example, to use a pun deliberately would mean re-ordering the normal sequence of processing: the availability of the word's sound must become available earlier in the process, before final syntactic and other lexical choices (at a semantic level) are made. Thus punning may be a special case of a leading decision.

From Level 1 via the phonetic system to articulation will broadly be a chain of control

(d)

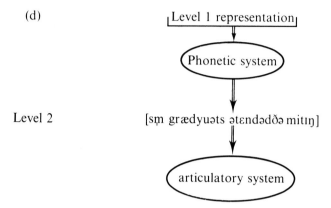

Level 2   [sm̩ grædyuəts ətɛndədðə mitɪŋ]

This simple picture needs to be complicated in two ways. First, the pragmatic system will exert convergent dominance on most other systems. Second, I have left out the distinction between the control node and its associated representational system. By reintroducing the distinction, not only can interactions between convergent systems be located, but checking routines via feedback loops proposed, as in (e), where the output from the syntactic system can be checked for compatibility with prior semantic and pragmatic decisions.

(e)

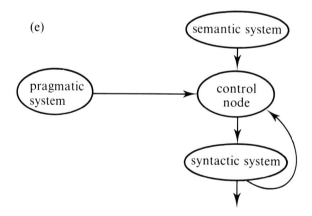

Notice that the transfer of information via the *control nodes* enables us to remain neutral about the autonomy of the controlled processes. Either, we could say that the syntactic system is sensitive in its operation to semantic and pragmatic factors: that is, refers back to these factors at stages *within* processing; or, we could say that it operates "in executive ignorance",—it takes an input and does its thing—but that candidate representations are filtered out by the control node which requires a match to all semantic and all pragmatic factors. The case diagrammed in (e) can be classified with the particular example of pragmatic constraints on syntactic deletion (**Gazdar**):

(47). a. The Yankees will play tomorrow.

b. The Yankees play tomorrow.

(48). a. The Yankees will win tomorrow.

b. The Yankees win tomorrow.

All these structures are grammatical, but (48b) would be unacceptable in most contexts, since *will*-deletion is acceptable only if the speaker knows (as far as is feasible) that the Yankees will win. Good guesses don't count. Now, either the deletion transformation (or equivalent) will check back to see if it is allowable in the current utterance—the "interaction" position; or, it will delete, *ad libitum*, but this representation will be rejected by the control node which has access to the relevant pragmatic information.

As I have argued, autonomous processes whose output is checked by a control node provide a natural treatment for many classes of errors—a system produces a representation which satisfies only its own criteria of acceptability, as in "phonetic accommodations" (**Garrett**), but not those of higher levels. In such cases, correction—i.e. check, rejection, generation of a new output—may follow after a delay; in which case we need only postulate that the feedback loop is activated later than usual.

For the lexical system, the postulation of a control node linking the meaning items with the phonological items, neatly accounts for hesitation data and certain aphasic syndromes. The control module takes as input a meaning item, M_i, and searches for a P_i appropriate to it. This enables us to define a temporal parameter on the search for the appropriate phonological item, explaining why there are lexically-conditioned delays in output. Presumably, the lexical system constitutes the "critical path" in the parallel part of the mode. Secondly, if the component of the control module that checks sound against meaning is incapacitated temporarily or permanently (as seems to be the case in jargon aphasia) then one would predict the output of wrong words, or even of neologisms, as indeed happens (Butterworth, 1979). The system will not be filtering out these errors; though, of course, the occurrence of the errors requires not only the postulation of a control malfunction, but also on information-transfer malfunction, such that the wrong mapping is made between M_i and P_i.

A similar kind of explanation can be given for the malfunctioning responsible for the agrammatic patients described by **Saffran** *et al.* The output of the syntactic system is presumed not to contain enough information for the phonological-phonetic system to find the appropriate function words and other grammatical morphemes; the phonological-phonetic system's control node nevertheless has to do the best it can with the information available and may not transfer control until some particle is found and thus in some cases will produce the wrong grammatical particles; in others, no particles at all, either because there is a phonological malfunction as well, or because the syntactic information is so degraded that control assumes no particle is needed. Notice again degraded information affects both mappings and checking functions.

C. Capacity Parameters

Having the kind of control structures here described, allows us to look at *when* control is passed from one control module to another, and it takes for the control node and its associated representational system to generate its output, and *what kinds of information* are necessary for its proper functioning. (This last has been largely dealt with above.)

Control appears to be transferred from the semantic system to the lexical, syntactic and prosodic systems, so that these latter can operate in parallel. When the speaker embarks on an extended utterance, say, more that 30 s, the hesitation data indicate need for a certain amount of silent time to formulate a semantic plan, or some part of one, before control gets transferred. Transfer of control seems to be fairly flexible: the speaker can be completely silent until a plan for several clauses has been formulated, or he can transfer control back and forth producing a bit of output, then formulating more of the plan. How much silence, and therefore how much planning, will constitute the "front-end-load", probably depends on how constrained the speaker is to keep on talking. This constraint can be manipulated by visual feedback from the listener (cf. Beattie and Bradbury, 1979), and generally, by the speaker's perception of his conversational task.

There are constraints on the overall proportion of silent time needed for planning. These are imposed by the novelty and complexity of the semantic planning (Chapter 7). These constraints are quite powerful, since an additional task during planning, like monitoring the listener, produces a startling increase in planning errors (**Beattie**). It is unclear how extensive a plan can be formulated at one time, but plans for up to about 12 clauses have been reported (**Butterworth, Beattie**). The minimum seems to be a single proposition, whatever that is, and certainly simultaneous translators need to hear enough to be able to formulate a NP + VP structure before they start to output in the target language (**Goldman-Eisler**).

The semantic plan, as has been mentioned, is fairly detailed. Enough information to locate M-items in the lexicon is represented. This is why the onset of iconic gestures precedes the onset of the word it is associated with (Chapters 4 and 7); the onset asynchrony can be as long as 2 s, and this is an indication of the lower bound of the time it takes to search the set of P-items given that particular M-item, since it is postulated that the M-item is responsible for the shape of the gesture as well as the output P-item. More typically the onset asynchrony is somewhat less that 1 s. In spite of much research it is unclear why some lexical P-item searches take longer than others. As was mentioned in Section IV.D, this does not seem to be a function of the frequency organization (if any) of the lexicon, but of unpredictability in context, and this concept, though operationally straightforward, is theoretically murky.

The syntactic system appears to operate one clause at a time. The data in support of a clause by clause functioning comes from the distribution of pauses *within* clauses. **Beattie** reports that there is a level of processing constrained by clausal structure and that this processing has a fine-structure "front-end-loading" requirement.

Finally it should be added that the operation of the whole structure is very flexible. Feedback loops, which keep higher level control modules in operation, may be activated at any time to check the output of lower-level systems. This would lead to the editing out of most errors. At the limit, the speaker can rehearse verbatim what he is to say before he puts vocal cords to work. At the other extreme, we find speakers who continually revise their vocal output, where presumably early checking occurs hardly at all. Each sub-system will have its own parameters that can be set according to the current conversational purposes. For example, the value of the search time parameter in the lexical system can be lengthened in order to generate exactly the right word, or shortened to trade-off silence for only a fair approximation of the intended meaning. Similarly the phonetic system can be set to accept a rather approximate articulatory rendering in casual conversation between intimates, or to accept only precise pronunciation in a lecture.

It may be that checking one's own speech uses the same systems as understanding someone else's speech, if so we have another research tool for investigating the production system. Another way might consist of examining other kinds of non-vocal production like writing or sign-language where possibly one or more parts the phonological-phonetic-articulatory systems have no role; or by examining the development in the child of the various systems. All these approaches will generate new constraints of the model, and may force revisions on the current ones; but these are issues for Volume 2.

References

Austin, J. L. (1962). "How to do Things with Words." Oxford University Press, Oxford.

Beattie, G. W. and Bradbury, R. (1979). An experimental investigation of the temporal structure of spontaneous speech. *Journal of Psycholinguistic Research.*

Beattie, G. W. and Butterworth, B. L. (1979). Contextual probability and word frequency as determinants of pauses and errors in spontaneous speech. *Language and Speech*, **22**, 201–211.

Broadbent, D. E. (1958). Perception and Communication. Pergammon Press, London.

Butterworth, B. L. (1972). Ph.D. Thesis, University of London.

Butterworth, B. L. (1979). Hesitation and the production of neologisms in jargon aphasia. *Brain and Language*, **8**.

Butterworth, B. L. and Gazdar, G. (1977). Quantifier Contraction. Paper presented to Linguistic Association of Great Britain.

Chomsky, N. (1965). "Aspects of the Theory of Syntax." M.I.T. Press, Cambridge, Mass.

Chomsky, N. and Halle, M. (1968). "The Sound Pattern of English." Harper and Row, New York.

Clark, H. H. and Clark, E. (1977). "Psychology of Language." Jovanovich, New York.

Cooper, W., Egido, C. and Paccia, J. (1978). Grammatical control of a phonological rule: palatalization. *Journal of Experimental Psychology: Human Perception and Performance,* **4**, 264–272.

Fay, D. and Cutler, A. (1977). Malapropisms and the structure of the mental lexicon. *Linguistic Inquiry,* **8**, 505–520.

Fodor, J. A. (1976). "The Language of Thought." The Harvester Press, Hassocks, Sussex.

Fowler, C. (1977). Ph.D. Thesis, University of Connecticut.

Fromkin, V. (1971). The nonanomalous nature of anomalous utterances. *Language,* **47**, 27–52.

Fromkin, V. (1973). "Speech Errors on Linguistic Evidence," Mouton, The Hague.

Garrett, M. (1975). The Analysis of Sentence Production. *In* "The Psychology of Learning and Motivation," Vol. 9. (G. Bower, ed.). Academic Press, New York.

Garrett, M. (1976). Syntactic processes in sentence production. *In* "New Approaches to Language Mechanisms" (R. Wales and E. Walker, eds). North Holland Press, The Netherlands.

Gazdar, G. (1979). "Pragmatics: Implicature, Presupposition and Logical Form. Academic Press, New York.

Goldman-Eisler, F. (1958). Speech production and the predictability of words in context. *Quarterly Journal of Experimental Psychology,* **10**, 96–106.

Good, D. and Butterworth, B. L. (1978). Hesitation as a conversational resource: Some methodological considerations. *In* "Temporal Variables in Speech" (H. Dechert, ed.). Mouton, The Hague.

Grice, H. P. (1973). Logic and Conversation. *In* "Syntax and Semantics" (P. Cole and J. L. Morgan, eds), Vol. 3. Academic Press, New York.

Jackson, J. Hughlings (1958). "Selected Writings", Vol II. Basic Books, New York.

James, W. (1890). "Principles of Psychology", Vol. I. Macmillan, London.

Johnson-Laird, P. (1977). Procedural semantics. *Cognition* **5**, 189–214.

Johnson-Laird, P. and Steedman, M. (1979). The psychology of syllogisms. *Cognitive Psychology* **10**, 64–99.

Jonckheere, A. (1966). Discussion in J. R. Lyons and R. J. Wales (eds), pp. 84–89. "Psycholinguistics Papers". University of Edinburgh Press, Edinburgh.

Karttunen, L. (1977). The syntax and semantics of questions. *Linguistics and Philosophy,* **1**, 3–44.

Labov, W. (1966). "The Social Stratification of English in New York City." Center for Applied Linguistics, Washington, D.C.

Miller, G. A. and Johnson-Laird, P. (1976). "Perception and Language." Cambridge University Press, Cambridge.

Montague, R. (1974). "Formal Philosophy" (R. Thompson, ed.). Yale University Press, New Haven, Conn.

Morton, J. (1969). Interaction of information in word recognition. *Psychological Review,* **76**, 165–178.

Morton, J. and Long, J. (1976). The effect of word transitional probability on phoneme identification. *Journal of Verbal Learning and Verbal Behavior,* **14**, 43–51.

Morton, J., Marcus, S. and Frankish, C. (1976). Perceptual centres (P-centres). *Psychological Review,* **83**, 405–408.

Morton, R. (1974). "Formal Philosophy: Selected Papers of Richard Montague" (R.H. Thomason, ed.). Yale University Press, New Haven.

O'Connell, D., Kowal, S. and Hörmann, H. (1969). Semantic determinants of pauses. *Psychologische Forschung,* **33**, 50–67.

Pick, A. (1973). "Aphasia." Translated by J. Brown. Thomas, Springfield, Ill.

Reddy, P. R. and Newell, A. (1975). Knowledge and its representation in a speech understanding system. *In* "Knowledge and Cognition" (L. W. Gregg, ed.). Lawrence Erlbaum, Potomac, Maryland.

Rumelhart, D. E., Lindsay, P. H. and Norman, D. A. (1972). A process model for long-term memory. *In* "Organisation of Memory" (E. Tulving and W. Donaldson, eds). Academic Press, New York.

Sacks, H. (1973). On some puns with some intimations. *In* "Report of the Twenty-Third Georgetown Round Table in Linguistics" (R. Shuy, ed.). Georgetown University Press, Washington D.C.

Savin, H. and Bever, T. G. (1970). The nonperceptual reality of the Phoneme. *Journal of Verbal Learning and Verbal Behavior,* **9**, 295–302.

Shaffer, L. M. (1976). Intention and performance. *Psychological Review,* **83**, 375–393.

Shattuck Huffnagel, S. and Klatt, D. (1978). Single phoneme error data rule out two models of error generation. Paper give to XII International Congress of Linguistics. Vienna.

Trudgill, P. (1974). "Social Differentiation of English in Norwich." Cambridge University Press, Cambridge.

Turvey, M. T., Shaw, R. and Mace, W. (1978). Issues in the theory of action: Degrees of freedom, co-ordinative structures and coalitions. *In* "Attention and Performance, VII" (J. Requin, ed.). Hillsdale, Erlbaum, Hillsdale, N.J.

Winograd, T. (1972). "Understanding Natural Language." University of Edinburgh Press, Edinburgh.

Wundt, W. (1970). *In* "Language and Psychology" (A. L. Blumenthal, ed.), pp. 20–33. John Wiley and Sons, New York.

Author Index

Page numbers in italics refer to reference lists

461

Subject Index